INSTANT WEB SCRIPTS
WITH CGI PERL

Selena Sol & Gunther Birznieks

M&T BOOKS

M&T Books
A Division of MIS:Press, Inc.
A Subsidiary of Henry Holt and Company, Inc.
115 West 18th Street
New York, New York 10011
http://www.mispress.com

ISBN 1-55851-490-2

10 9 8 7 6 5 4 3 2 1

Associate Publisher: *Paul Farrell*

Executive Editor: *Cary Sullivan*
Editor: *Michael Sprague*

Copy Edit Manager: *Shari Chappell*
Production Editor: *Stephanie Doyle*

CONTENTS

Contents

Chapter 6: Using DATE.PL 85

Chapter 7: E-Mailing with CGI 93

Chapter 8: Using HTTP-LIB.PL 109

Contents

Contents

Contents

PREFACE

SELENA SOL

In the Fall of 1995, I put my first CGI application on the web. It was a modest bulletin board script which I had hacked together from a number of other CGI applications which I found in various nooks and crannies in print and on the web; a form processing routine from Robert Mudry's *Serving the Web*, some array handling routines from Randall Schwartz's *Learning Perl*, some HTML management functions from Matt Wright ("Matt Wright's Script Archive"), and other routines from numerous sites.

Starting with such a complex project was probably not the best way to learn about CGI of course, but like so many CGI developers out there in the real world, I was assigned a project at work that needed to be completed regardless of how well I was prepared in theory.

The process of writing BBS 1.0 was frustrating to say the least. At that time, there were very few books on advanced CGI techniques. At best, there were small CGI chapters within larger HTML books. And these chapters were pretty fluffy for the most part. Most dealt in abstract theory and few provided useful, working examples.

Examples existed on the web of course. Freeware and shareware scripts were available, but most of them were difficult to find and even more difficult to understand, written as it were, for the wizard rather than the beginner. I spent many, many hours with *Learning Perl* by Randall Schwartz in one hand and a printout of some CGI application in another trying desperately to decrypt the routines.

One four AM morning, red-eyed and dizzy, I vowed that if ever I got a script to run, I would not only make the script freely available to others so they would not have to struggle like I did, but that I would attempt to document each design decision I made and every type of Perl trick I used so that I, months earlier, would have been able to pick it up, read it through, and have a pretty good idea how it worked. This was the conception of Selena Sol's Public Domain Script Archive.

Over the next nine months, I slowly populated the site with CGI script after CGI script, added a FAQ, an offsite resource section, a help found area, and various other services. The hope was to provide an area in which new and experienced CGI programmers could learn from how I wrote scripts by detailed examples and for them to share their own ideas with me as well.

The site was a fantastic success. Thousands of netizens stopped by and hundreds sent me notes explaining how the "learning by example method" was an effective way for HTML programmers to make the transition to CGI. Dozens of visitors took my scripts and ported them successfully to other systems all over the world.

Finally, I was contacted by Michael Sprague, the editor for this book, who asked me to create a print version of the web site for all of the people who wanted to study real-life CGI in one book.

Excited, I contacted Gunther Birznieks who had begun to take an active role in contributing knowledge to the Script Archive and who I knew to be a true Wizard. Together, we developed the book which you now hold. We hope that this book will be accessible to beginners and educational for the experienced. We also hope to save you time by providing you with an arsenal of scripts which you will actually be asked to produce at one time or another or which you will just want to produce for your own enjoyment.

Along the way, of course, many people have contributed directly and indirectly, knowingly and not, to this work. In particular, I would like to thank my mom, my grandfather, and all of my family who have spent so much time, money and energy making sure I did not become a serial killer or a drug addict. I'd also like to thank Barnaby Fell and all of my friends who have done their best to the contrary.

A further thanks to Rachada Yodvanich for putting up with my nineteen hour work days during the time I was writing my chapters, and thanks to Johnnie Pearson of R.O.W. Sciences and Ed Whitley of The National Center for Human Genome Research for providing me with such an educational and demanding work environment in which I was able to learn how to program CGI applications.

Finally, I would like to thank all the employees, volunteers and members of the Board of Directors at the Electronic Frontier Foundation for valiantly holding the front line in the war to keep cyberspace free for ourselves and our children.

All comments, questions, and error reports are welcomed. For the latest information regarding the scripts in this book and to contact us, go to Selena Sol's Script Page at

```
http://www.eff.org/Scripts/
```

Enjoy the book.

P.S.: I can't believe you actually read the Preface, how rare!

—Selena Sol

GUNTHER BIRZNIEKS

Many years ago, soon after I received my first computer, I got hold of a BBS program and a modem and hooked myself up to the old, small-time equivalent of Cyberspace. However, like the netizens of today, I experienced disappointment with the lack of source code and documentation for the program that I was attempting to use.

Out of my frustration, I started running a BBS system that had less features but came with source code. From there, I learned how to program for myself by carefully examining every nook and cranny of the program and discussing it with other people doing the same thing at the time. At first, I merely modified the program to suit my needs. Then my needs grew more and more sophisticated. Several years later I finally finished writing a full BBS system from scratch (C-BASE on the Commodore 64).

I have tried never to lose sight of the fact that two factors were invaluable to my growth as a programmer. First of all, examining working source code for a program is an extremely worthwhile endeavor. The "Learn By Example" approach really does work. Secondly, having people (especially authors of programs I was looking at) take the time to explain to me why they implemented a feature a particular way also taught me a great deal.

Then, I started distributing my BBS widely and gave out the source code with it. I wanted to promote the same learning experience with my programs that I had gotten previously from others. Soon after this, I found that the majority of people who ran the program appreciated my open willingness to provide the capability to allow them to do their own modifications and programming.

Although people may not use the Commodore 64 computer anymore that much (and therefore my program), it has been worthwhile knowing that I have affected the world in a positive way. Even now, I get letters and calls from people who tell me that they have been inspired to go into programming as a result of releasing the source code to my BBS and giving them the motivation to go in and make their own modifications. In addition, others have also told me that despite the already glutted market of BBSs for the PC, that they have wanted me to write one for this platform.

However, by the time I started programming on IBM PCs, I was already heavy into the Internet—reading newsgroups, searching with Gopher/Web, and using other Internet tools. I felt that someday the Internet would supersede lone PCs running BBSes for local people so I did not pursue this venue much further.

A couple of years later, when I first saw Selena Sol's Scripts page, I knew that this site had a noble cause. To provide programs such as keyword search engines, form processors, and more to the public along with source code was exactly the type of thing that would turn other people on to programming, just as giving out my BBS source code on an old 8-bit computer did for others. Soon, I started providing Selena Sol with my own programs such as a newly-written BBS to supplement this already vast library of code.

By contributing to the Web and people who need my help, I hope to help "pay forward" those numerous people who have helped me in the past. I also hope that this will produce an environment where the people that learn from our scripts "pay forward" in the future to other people who may need encouragement and guidance themselves.

Many people have contributed to this book both directly and indirectly. I would like to first thank my parents who have been very supportive of my efforts with this book and who provided me with an environment in which I was able to learn about computers while I was growing up.

In addition, Dino Macris of the American Red-Cross, whose vision of the World Wide Web being the future was right on the money, provided me with a challenging environment in which I was able to always stretch my skills to the limit and learn Web programming. Likewise, Bruce Vincent, Bill Lee, Jeff Shao, and Anand Modak were instrumental in my growth by providing me with many an occasion for technical debate.

Also, I would like to acknowledge Johnnie Pearson of R.O.W. Sciences and Ed Whitley of The National Center For Human Genome Research for supplying the same technically challenging environment to allow my Perl/CGI programming skills to grow even further. And last but not least, I would like to thank all the netizens who have provided us with suggestions and who have been invaluable in testing the scripts that were provided in this book.

—Gunther Birznieks

INTRODUCTION

In the last few years, the need for CGI/Perl programming on the Web has literally exploded. Unfortunately, many books written about CGI are beginner books. These tend to provide toy examples that you would never find useful in real-life or programs that are so esoteric that you would not want to use them on your web site. In contrast, the main purpose of this book is to provide a comprehensive source of CGI/Perl applications that are useful for the real world as well as a detailed explanation of how they are setup and how they were programmed.

In addition, because the scripts you see in this book are running on Web sites around the world, they have been tested and subjected to the scrutiny of a variety of netizens. The programs you see are as much written by us as they are by all the people who have ever submitted a bug report or idea to us.

WHO THIS BOOK IS FOR

This book was written primarily for the intermediate-level CGI developer who may be working for a company which is providing a Web site or who may be doing freelance work for companies on the Web. This type of developer is assumed to be fluent in HTML and will already be comfortable in the CGI/Perl environment.

However, the beginning CGI developer can also use this book. The chapters provide a straight-forward, example-based way to learn CGI. The scripts have been explained simply enough that we hope they will be accessible to all and we have taken great pains to isolate the basic installation and usage issues into their own section so that the non-programmer does not need to spend much time deciphering the code if all they want to do is run the scripts.

Additionally, this book is for advanced CGI developers who are looking for good, well-documented tools that they can add to an existing arsenal of routines. The scripts in this book have been chosen because they are all in high demand in the marketplace and are the types of programs that the advanced CGI developer should be able to install on-the-fly.

WHAT YOU NEED TO KNOW TO START

The book assumes at least a basic understanding of Perl 4. We have chosen this as the minimum standard for this book because many Web servers still have not upgraded to Perl 5. Perl 5, though it has good enhancements, is still widely unsupported. Thus, all the applications in this book have been made to be Perl 4 compatible.

The book also assumes a working knowledge of the HTTP and HTML protocols which drive CGI. Though we are careful to do our best to explain these protocols when necessary, this book is not meant to be an introductory resource on protocols or CGI. There are dozens of excellent books focusing on those basic issues available. In particular, we recommend *Introduction to CGI/Perl* by Steven Brenner and Edwin Aoki as a perfect complement to this work.

WHY PERL?

So why exactly did we choose to use the programming language Perl for the CGI applications in this book? Could a programmer use another language like C, C++, Apple Script, or Visual Basic instead?

This is a good question. In fact, CGI applications can be written in any programming language which is able to accept and process input and which is able to output the results of that processing. However, for this book and for most of the CGI applications we have designed, Perl has been far and above the best choice. Specifically, we have chosen to use Perl for two reasons: Perl is the right tool for the job and Perl is easy.

Perl is the Right Tool for the Job

Perl is a good general language whose original purpose was parsing different inputs and generating output based on incoming data. It turns out that this is a perfect match for what CGI applications have to do. CGI applications typically must parse incoming HTML form data from the Web and then process that data so that it can finally output formatted HTML code to the user's Web browser. The set of problems that Perl solves best happens to correlate well with the demands of CGI. Perl and CGI are simply a match made in heaven.

Common Gateway Interface (CGI), as its name implies, provides a "gateway" between a human browser with unexpected and complex needs, and Web server that must be told exactly what to do. As a gateway, CGI programs must perform two tasks very well.

CGI PROGRAMS AS TRANSLATORS

First, CGI programs must be good translators. All CGI applications must translate the needs of clients into server requests as well as translate server replies into meaningful and well-presented "answers." This can be quite a chore since computers and humans typically speak very different languages.

As such, CGI scripts must be adept at manipulating text whether it is the text that has been input by the client or that which has been received from the server. A CGI application must be able to take "strings" of data and translate them from one language to another consistently and quickly. As we will see throughout this book, Perl has a wide variety of tools with which to manipulate strings of data. It is, in fact, one of the best languages we know of for string manipulation.

CGI ACROSS PLATFORMS

Second, CGI programs must serve as a gateway for many types of clients and servers. It must be more than a bilingual translator, it must be multi-lingual—providing translation services between dozens of browser types, Web server types, and operating systems. Fortunately, Perl is highly portable. Due to the hard work and good intentions of many net hackers, Perl has been ported to just about every operating system you would want to run a Web server on. By pointing your web browser to:

```
http://www.shareware.com/
```

you can download a Perl interpreter for your local operating system with no difficulties. And better yet, the Perl you write for your UNIX server today will be portable later when you add an NT server to your network tomorrow.

Though compiled languages may boast ten times the power and speed and offer countless complex functions; the fact is that for the demands of most CGI applications, a compiled language is like bringing in the hydrogen bomb to kill an ant. Most CGI applications are ultimately at the mercy of bandwidth speed and limited enough in scope so as not to demand much gusto anyway. Perl is simply the right tool for the job. Other languages are typically an overkill for writing CGI applications.

Perl is Easy

Perl is also easy to understand. Because Perl is an interpreted language, for example, there are no compilers and therefore no machine-specific programs which look like a foreign language when you try to view them. With a Perl script, what you see is what you get. The code that is run by the Web server, is the code that you see in your text editor window.

Since Perl is simple in design, it is also easy to modify, maintain, and customize (this is really where most of the cost of software comes from anyway). In other words, because Perl source code is so legible, it is very easy for a programmer to pick up a script and quickly modify it to solve similar or new problems. Perl is a "cut and paste" language and its logic is easily transferred and manipulated between projects.

The benefit of this, of course, is that Perl is supported by a wide body of CGI freelance programmers. Unlike more cryptic or platform-specific languages like C++ or Visual Basic, Perl is accessible to anthropology majors and computer science majors alike. In fact, newsgroups like comp.lang.perl are often too prolific in their postings to read on a regular basis. The Perl community is thriving and, thanks to the Web, expanding rapidly.

Thus, since so many people can write and modify Perl, it is very easy for you to find someone to do it for you cheaply and to do it well. You need not kneel at the mercy of the few reclusive wizards of other arcane languages who confidently slide on the curves of supply and demand. There is an abundance of qualified, starving undergraduate and graduate students with enough skills to solve most of your programming needs for very cheap rates, especially if they are given a working program to modify (like the code in this book) rather than asked to write a program from scratch.

How This Book is Structured

This book is divided into six parts, each made up of several chapters, and a few supplementary appendices. Both the parts and the chapters are organized according to the "process" that we use when we are installing scripts on new servers. This process includes:

1. Getting scripts and integrating them with your server environment.
2. Understanding the logic of the scripts.
3. Customizing them according to local needs.

For example, most chapters are organized into three parts: an overview, a discussion of application-specific installation and usage, and a detailed description of the programming used to make the scripts run.

The Overview

The Overview attempts to outline the purpose of the script, the metaphors involved, and the problems we sought to solve. In this section, we have attempted to define the applications broadly and perhaps suggest various uses for them that we have come across while installing them for different clients.

Installation and Usage

The installation and usage section outlines the steps that you will need to take in order to port the scripts to your own server. Most often, this section will contain information on setting permissions, a discussion of defining server specific variables and options and instructions relating to the process of running the script from the Web. It is our hope that the intermediate-level developer will be able to install the distributed, generic versions of all the scripts in this book by reading only the installation and usage section.

The Design Discussion

The design discussion outlines line-by-line, the methods we used to make the scripts work. Inevitably, you will want to customize the generic scripts included here for your local needs. To this end, the design discussion is written to communicate the entire logic of the script so that you will easily be able to modify the code for your own applications. It also provides an excellent "learn-by-example" tool for learning how to write your own code.

Your Path Through the Parts

The organization of the six parts of this book follow the same logic. Though we have tried to modularize each Part well enough so that it can stand alone, it is probably a good idea for you to read Parts One and Two before you go about trying to install one of the CGI applications in the other Parts. Part One provides essential information about how to install scripts in general and Part Two provides detailed explanations of the shared libraries used repeatedly by applications throughout this book. Once you finish reading these two Parts, you should feel free to skip to any chapter in any of the other Parts you are interested in.

PART ONE: INSTALLING, USING, AND BUILDING SCRIPTS

Part One deals with obtaining and installing scripts since that is the first thing that you will be concerned with when trying to find scripts to suit your project needs. Chapter One outlines the steps that you will need to take in order to find CGI scripts on the web, download them to your local server, and install them so that you can use them there. It also overviews the methods you will need to know in order to set the correct permissions and find the system files necessary to actually run the scripts.

Chapter Two outlines various methods that you may need to utilize in order to troubleshoot scripts in case more significant customizations are required based on your particular Web server configuration.

Finally, Chapter Three discusses Intranet design issues, providing an analysis of how Internet CGI scripts can be utilized by an Intranet.

PART TWO: CGI LIBRARIES

Part Two deals with managing routines and libraries. These chapters are extremely vital because they represent the very foundation of most scripts. Understanding libraries is the first step towards understanding entire applications.

Chapter Four introduces the concept of using algorithms, subroutines, and libraries in preparation for the libraries discussed in the rest of the chapters in this part. This chapter includes a more theoretical discussion of web-based software design which may be very useful for the beginning developer.

Chapters Five through Ten outline the libraries that are used continually throughout this book such as valuable routines for reading form data, providing Web security, file locking, and emailing.

PART THREE: DATABASES

Part Three is dedicated to a discussion of web-based databases. The part begins with the most fundamental application: the Database Manager in Chapter Eleven. The Database Manager allows a database administrator to manipulate a server-based database files from the web. Chapter Twelve introduces a database search engine that is meant to accompany the Database Manager for users of the database.

Chapter Thirteen discusses the Groupware Calendar, which uses the previously discussed database management and searching functions along with added date routines to provide a shared calendar on the Web.

Chapter Fourteen involves a second example of a modified database management system, the Classified Ad Manager, to further exemplify the ways you might modify the search logic from the original script explained in Chapter Twelve.

Finally, Chapter Fifteen provides a look into heavy-duty SQL Database integration with a discussion of a SYBASE-based address book.

PART FOUR: WORKING WITH HTML

Part Four is dedicated to the discussion of working with HTML from within CGI applications. These applications are focused on the interactions between users and HTML files.

Chapter Sixteen introduces a keyword search engine that can be used by a web site administrator to provide keyword searching functionality to a web site. Using this application, visitors can search all the HTML documents in a web site.

Chapter Seventeen outlines a web-based HTML shopping cart system which is one of the more popular applications right now. Such an application affords clients the ability to browse a companies inventory via HTML pages and order items for purchase.

Chapter Eighteen provides a means for site administrators to keep track of the daily usage of their pages. By using the Page Tracking application, a site administrator can keep track of such vital statistics as who has visited which pages and how often.

Chapter Nineteen provides a CGI backend to feedback and comment HTML forms which can allow clients of your web pages the ability to send their valuable comments and criticisms to you while they are browsing your pages.

Finally, Chapter Twenty outlines the Web-based Guestbook which is a perennial favorite on the web.

PART FIVE: CGI-BASED GRAPHICS AND ANIMATION

Part Five takes a quick look at CGI-based animation using the non-parsed header method to generate server push animations.

Chapter Twenty-One discusses several methods which one could use to animate text and Chapter Twenty-Two outlines the graphics-based animations of random image banners.

PART SIX: MISCELLANEOUS APPLICATIONS

Part Six overviews several miscellaneous applications that you can use to greatly enhance the value of your web site.

Chapter Twenty-Three introduces the Fortune Cookie Script which generates random quotes to be displayed on a page.

Chapter Twenty-Four discusses the Advertising Tracker script which allows a Web site to collect statistics on how many people use a hypertext link to jump to an advertised company's site.

Chapter Twenty-Five provides a full-featured Bulletin Board System on the Web (WebBBS).

Chapter Twenty-Six tops off the book with a real-time chat script (WebChat).

APPENDICES

Finally, the Appendices includes discussions of Perl 4.0 and 5.0 which may be valuable for the reader who still has questions about basic Perl Syntax. In addition, Lincoln Stein's CGI.pm Perl 5 library is introduced with regard to the future of CGI/Perl programming. The appendices also contain a cursory discussion of how the accompanying CD-ROM is organized.

Some Closing Words

These Parts and Chapters are designed to walk you through obtaining, installing, understanding, and modifying scripts in the ways that we have found most efficient. Unlike most of the CGI books out there, this book is written for the real world programmer who may not be interested in theory right off the bat but may need to get a complex CGI application up and running in short order. In addition, we hope that our thorough documentation of the scripts in this book will give you a better understanding of how to customize the scripts should you find yourself needing to modify them to your Web site's specific needs.

Good luck and be a good netizen. We will all be living much of our lives on the net in the future. Support the free flow of information and be everyone's teacher and student. Information wants to be free. Support public domain software applications and their authors.

CHAPTER 1

Getting and Setting Up
Your Scripts

OVERVIEW

Obtaining CGI scripts and configuring them to work under your Web server software are the first steps in getting a CGI application up and running. For many Web servers, these tasks are easy, but other Web servers make it difficult. For example, some servers have been configured to make it difficult to run scripts for security reasons. This chapter covers the basics of obtaining CGI scripts as well as the secrets of making them work in almost any Web server environment that allows them to run.

This book comes with a great many CGI scripts that we have written, and there are also a variety of scripts and programs on the Internet that you may want to use to complement the array of applications provided here. The guidelines in this chapter are useful for configuring these third-party scripts as well.

In addition, we will explain the major techniques used to unpack the scripts from the variety of formats you'll find on the Internet. Once unpacked, the scripts may need slight modifications to run on your Web server. We'll discuss techniques for doing this in reference to a variety of Web server platforms such as NCSA, Apache, and Netscape servers.

FINDING CGI APPLICATIONS ON THE WEB

Much of what is called "CGI development" does not involve the creation of new Web applications. Rather, Webmasters tend to use prewritten CGI scripts, customizing them for their own needs. Certainly, there will be unique projects that require new algorithms. But for most projects, a good CGI developer can draw from a huge arsenal of routines and pre-designed applications that need only minor tweaking to use in a local Web server environment.

In the spirit of public domain, many authors have offered their work to the Web community so that developers need not continually reinvent the wheel and can move rapidly to bigger and better projects.

NOTE Each archive or reference has its own unique form of intellectual property protection, so you should be careful about how you use the scripts you find. For example, although many scripts are in the public domain, others may be considered shareware. This usually means that you can try the script for free but should eventually pay for it if you like it. It is almost always appropriate, however, to notify the author that you are using one of his or her scripts even if it is in the public domain.

The following list outlines of some of the sites that we have found most when trying to find applications that have already been written to handle projects we've been asked to complete. When the site contains noteable features, we have attempted to note them in the description.

> **Selena Sol's Public Domain CGI Script Archive**. This site contains all the scripts in this book in their most recent form. It also contains various other scripts and scripting information that didn't make it to press, but is worth your persisting.
>
> http://www.eff.org/~erict/Scripts

Web Masters. The ultimate reference page for CGI developers.

http://kufacts.cc.ukans.edu/info/forms/forms-intro.html

Netamorphix CGI Resource Page. A fantastic site for basic information on CGI scripting as well as detailed and encompassing lists (Unlike most CGI resource lists, Netamorphix provides well-described list elements—short abstracts of each and every script on a monthly rotation) of shareware and freeware CGI scripts.

http://www.netamorphix.com/cgi.html

Pure CGI Scripts. A very good list of links to freeware scripts recommended by Pure Web.

http://www.netlink.co.uk/users/PureAmiga/pcgi/index.html

The Zone Coasters Scripts. A small, but well-written script archive containing an excellent survey script, a guestbook, a BBS, a chat script, and a homepage maker that were particularly interesting to us.

http://www.ocii.com/~bsowa/scripts.html

Shareware.com. You can grab almost any shareware around for NT, Mac, or UNIX Web servers, including Perl, gzip, and tar. Each of these is a good addition to any CGI support library, because nearly all the CGI scripts on the archives listed here are either tarred or gzipped.

http://www.shareware.com/

CGI Scripts To Go. A good collection of various CGIs in one place. The maintainer has taken a good deal of time to describe each script and to compare it to similar ones on the same topic.

http://www.virtualville.com/library/scripts.html

Rod Ellis's Script Archive. An excellent archive with examples of form processing, search engine, message board, HTML-CGI interfaces for building HTML pages on the fly, shopping carts, and authentication.

http://www.microlink.net/~gentle/Demo/

Storm's Public Domain CGI Archive. Storm is a great programmer who is highly respected. His scripts include Guestbook, Feedback,

Random Image Gen, Addlink, Chat, Web Forum, and Random Link. He also continues to develop new programs.

http://www.he.net/~storm/html/scripts/index.html

Jon Weiderspan's CGI Applications Directory. An excellent launchpad! Jon has put together a fantastic list of links for almost any CGI application you want (both public domain listings and commercial listings).

http://www.comvista.com/net/www/cgi.html

Dale Bewley's Public Domain Tools Site. Contains a motley of excellent tools (especially graphics tools) for the Web administrator.

http://www.engr.iupui.edu/~dbewley/perl/

David Woolley's List of BBS Conferencing Systems. This is an excellent launch point for links to the various messaging systems on the Web.

http://freenet.msp.mn.us/people/drwool/webconf.html

New Breed's Software Page. Includes SSI, CGI libraries, index creator, **leave_link.cgi**, Guestbook, and Counter programs.

http://zippy.sonoma.edu/~kendrick/nbs/unix/www

Matt Wright's Script Archive. What can I say? Matt's Script Archive is one of the best out there and has been for a long time.

http://www.worldwidemart.com/scripts/

Nick Bicanic's Animation Page. This is an especially good site from which to learn animation. Nick is one of the original CGI animation pioneers and has continued to keep up with the latest methods and technologies.

http://bakmes.colorado.edu/~bicanic/altindex.html

Yahoo CGI Resources. No surprises here. Yahoo is one of the premier indexing sites on the Internet.

http://www.yahoo.com/Computers_and_Internet/Internet/
World_Wide_Web/CGI_Common_Gateway_Interface/

EIT Software Archive. Contains a bunch of cool Web administration tools.

http://www.eit.com/goodies/software/

The CGI Collection. A nice listing of various CGI resources, such as Mailform, W3OClock, Guestbook, PickMail, Logger, Access Counter, SWISH, and Register.

http://www.selah.net/cgi.html

Matt Johnson's CGI Page. This extensive CGI resource contains information about CGI scripts, Perl, and lots of sample code.

http://www.hamline.edu/personal/matjohns/webdev/cgi/

Web Developer's Virtual Library. A great many CGI links. It is an excellent resource for the C CGI programmer and even contains a couple of NT links.

http://www.stars.com/Vlib/Providers/CGI.html

Otis's CGI Library. A good collection of CGIs (multimailer, lottery, log analyzers, animation).

http://www.middlebury.edu/~otisg/Scripts/index.shtml

Chris Stephens's Shareware CGIs. A good collection, including the rare AppleScript CGIs and even VMS scripts.

http://www.cbil.vcu.edu:8080/cgi-bin/cgis.html

Grant Neufold's Random URL Shareware CGI. Random URL is a CGI application for WebSTAR or MacHTTP that randomly returns a URL to clients from a given text file. The program also works with any other Macintosh CGI sdoc–compatible Web server.

http://arpp1.carleton.ca/grant/mac/cgi/random.html

Christoffer "Toffe" Sundqvist's Web Developers' Bookmarks. A fairly good list of links. Not particularly well organized or presented, but it does list some resources not found elesewhere.

http://www.abo.fi/~csundqvi/cgi.htm

Mooncrow's CGI/PERL Source Page. A fantastic list of links that no CGIer should miss with topics ranging from magic cookies to supporting develper's applications to related programming resourdces (like sed resources).

http://www.seds.org/~smiley/cgiperl/cgi.htm

O'Reilly's WebSite Software Library. If you are an NT CGI programmer, this is a "must have" for your bookmarks. It is almost the best NT resource we have seen.

http://website.ora.com/software/

Dave Elis's CGI Page.

http://www.cyserv.com/pttong/cgi.html

INSTALLING A PREDESIGNED CGI APPLICATION

Once you locate a CGI application that meets your needs, you need to download it to your local CGI executable directory. Most of the time, scripts on the Internet are compacted into one file to make them easier and faster to download. Generally, all you need to do is to click on a hyperlink on the Web to download the file. You should also be aware that some sites do not archive applications in a neatly packed single file. You may need to download multiple files to get the entire CGI application. Figure 1.1 shows a listing for a mailing list manager program on Selena Sol's Archive (http://www.eff.org/~erict/Scripts/).

Notice the link for **mailing_list_tar.gz**. This is the type of file you will want to look for. The **.gz** extension lets us know that this file has been compressed by gnuzip. (Other extensions may include **.zip** [Windows] or **.sit** [Mac]). The **.tar** extension means that the file contains an archive of files archived using tar, a utility that compacts many files into one. So, in this example, all the files related to the mailing_list_.cgi CGI program are contained in the **mailing_list_tar.gz** file. To get the mailing list archive, you transfer one file to your local machine and then expand all the files locally into the predesignated directory structures.

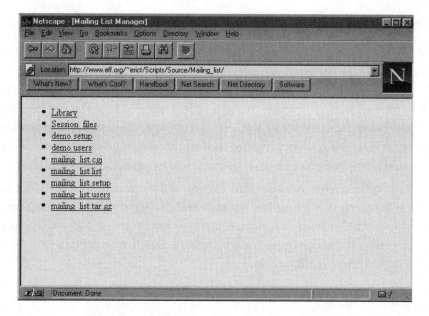

Figure 1.1 *Example of downloading an application.*

Archiving and Compressing Files

There is an important distinction between archive utilities and compression utilities. *Archiving* is a process that combines many files and directories into one file. *Compressing* makes a file (or files) smaller so that less time is needed to download it. Because tar, gzip, and compress are by far the most common archive and compression utilities used by CGI developers—and because they are generally the least understood—we will cover them here in greater detail.

NOTE

The following utilities are typically distributed with most flavors of Unix. If your Unix system does not have the following utilities or you are using another operating system such as Windows NT http://www.shareware.com is an excellent resource for downloading these utilities.

Gzip

According to the man pages for gzip, "Gzip reduces the size of the named file using Lempel-Ziv coding." Thus, gzip compresses a large file into a file that is much smaller. The benefit of compression is that when you're downloading the file to your local server, it will take less time because there is less data in the file to transfer. Once you download the **.gz** file to your local directory, the first thing you need to do is to decompress it. This process is easy and uses a sister program called gunzip.

Gunzip has many options and can be made to do complex things. If you are interested in complex management of gzip files, we recommend that you read the man pages on gunzip. However, for most CGI scripts that are downloaded in the gnuzip format, it will be enough to type the following on the command line:

```
gunzip filename.gz
```

In the case of our mailing list script, type the following:

```
gunzip mailing_list.tar.gz
```

Gunzip will decompress the program and remove the **.gz** extension. If you ran this step on the **mailing_list_tar.gz** file and pulled up a directory listing, you would see the file **mailing_list.tar** in its place. The library would be in the tar format, which we discuss next.

Tar

Tar is a UNIX command that allows you to create a single archive file containing many files. Such archiving allows you to maintain directory relationships and facilitates the transfer of complex programs that have many separate but integrated parts whose relationships must be preserved. Like gzip and gunzip, tar has a motley of options that allow you to do archiving and unarchiving in many ways. But for the purpose of untarring CGI files, the commands are fairly simple. At the command line, simply type

```
tar xvf filename.tar
```

Or, in the case of our mailing list file, type

```
tar xvf mailing_list.tar
```

Tar will go through the archive file and separate each individual directory and file, expanding them into their appropriate places underneath the current directory. Figure 1.2 shows the output of the above command. The "xvf" letters in the tar command are parameters that tell the program to extract the files and directories out ot the archive. Specifically, "x" tells tar extract; "w" tells tar to output information about the status of the extraction, and "f" informs tar to use the ".tar" filename as the source of the files to be extracted. Tar is actually short for [T]ape {AR}chive and by default archives to a tape drive.

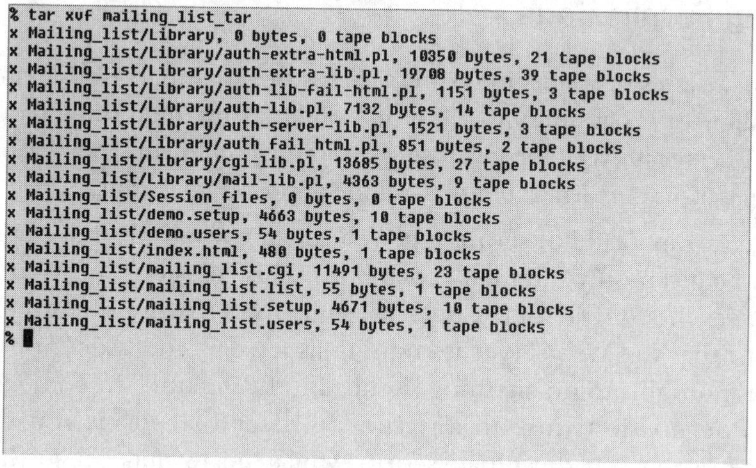

```
% tar xvf mailing_list_tar
x Mailing_list/Library, 0 bytes, 0 tape blocks
x Mailing_list/Library/auth-extra-html.pl, 10350 bytes, 21 tape blocks
x Mailing_list/Library/auth-extra-lib.pl, 19708 bytes, 39 tape blocks
x Mailing_list/Library/auth-lib-fail-html.pl, 1151 bytes, 3 tape blocks
x Mailing_list/Library/auth-lib.pl, 7132 bytes, 14 tape blocks
x Mailing_list/Library/auth-server-lib.pl, 1521 bytes, 3 tape blocks
x Mailing_list/Library/auth_Fail_html.pl, 851 bytes, 2 tape blocks
x Mailing_list/Library/cgi-lib.pl, 13685 bytes, 27 tape blocks
x Mailing_list/Library/mail-lib.pl, 4363 bytes, 9 tape blocks
x Mailing_list/Session_files, 0 bytes, 0 tape blocks
x Mailing_list/demo.setup, 4663 bytes, 10 tape blocks
x Mailing_list/demo.users, 54 bytes, 1 tape blocks
x Mailing_list/index.html, 480 bytes, 1 tape blocks
x Mailing_list/mailing_list.cgi, 11491 bytes, 23 tape blocks
x Mailing_list/mailing_list.list, 55 bytes, 1 tape blocks
x Mailing_list/mailing_list.setup, 4671 bytes, 10 tape blocks
x Mailing_list/mailing_list.users, 54 bytes, 1 tape blocks
%
```

*Figure 1.2 Untarring **mailing_list.tar**.*

WARNING

Sometimes programmers forget to untar an archive starting at the directory above where the files are located. This is a problem, because, when the tar file expands, all the individual files will end up in the current subdirectory. If you are in a subdirectory where you have other files, they can make your work area messy. It is always best to create a subdirectory and then untar the files in that subdirectory. Later, you can move the previously archived files when you know the directory and file structures.

Compress

On occasion, some files on the Internet will be compressed using the UNIX compress command. These files can be recognized easily by the **.Z** extension. To decompress these files, merely use the uncompress command:

```
uncompress compressedfile.Z
```

The file will now be uncompressed and ready for further processing.

Setting Permissions

Copying a series of scripts into directories is only one part of the equation of installing or programming CGI scripts and making them run. Frequently, the Web server needs to be given special permission to run your scripts and have the scripts perform their job with the appropriate "rights."

The cardinal rule of setting up Web server software is that the server should be given only minimal capabilities. This rules out the Web server running as the ROOT user (Super user on UNIX). More often than not, it means that the Web server is running as a user—the user "nobody"—and has no rights to do anything significant. By default, "nobody" usually has no permission to read any files in directories that you create. However, when you download scripts, you need to make it so that the scripts can be read and executed by the Web server software. In other words, "nobody" must be able to get to the files.

In UNIX, the magic command for performing this task is chmod. The directory structure of a message board CGI script is a good example of how you should use the chmod command. For this example, we will assume that you are sharing a server on an Internet service provider, which is typically the most restrictive situation in terms of your security options. For this example, all your CGI scripts are located in a directory called **Bbs**. The messages themselves need to be located in a directory called **Messages** under the **Bbs** directory. The example assumes we are in the directory above the one where the CGI scripts reside when we execute the chmod command.

Four different sets of permissions need to be granted for the user "nobody" to run this CGI script. First, the **Bbs** directory must be both readable and executable by the world. We need to read the entries in the directory, and it must be executable so that we can go into the directory and open the files in it:

```
chmod 755 Bbs
```

The 755 tells chmod to make the **Bbs** directory readable, writable, and executable by the owner of the file (you) while making it only readable and executable by the world and the group you are in.

How did we come up with the number? Files in UNIX have three types of permissions: user (the owner of the file), group (the security group you are in), and other (for the world to see). Each digit in the number corresponds to one of these categories. The first digit is user, the second digit is group, and the final digit is other. Thus, in the example, 7=USER, 5=GROUP, and 5=OTHER.

The value of the digit determines the permissions granted to that area. Permissions consist of three numbers: 4 for read, 2 for write, and 1 for execute access. By adding these numbers together, you form the permissions that make up one digit. For example, $4 + 2 + 1 = 7$, which grants read, write, and execute permissions. $4 + 1 = 5$, which grants only read and execute permissions. Thus, 755 grants 7 (read, write, execute) to the owner of the file, and 5 (read and execute) to the group the file is in, and 5 to the world.

The files within the **Bbs** directory need to be readable and executable, because the Web server will be running the CGI scripts in it.

```
chmod 755 Bbs/*
```

This command operates the same as the previous one except that it changes all the files (* pattern matches everything) inside the **Bbs** directory to be readable and executable by everyone. These scripts should not be writable! Nor should the **Bbs** directory be writable, because that would allow other users on the system to place scripts there. The **Messages** directory is another issue. Because it contains messages generated by the users, the **Messages** directory must be made writable so that the CGI script can write to the directory. In addition, the files generated in that directory should also be writable in case the **Bbs** script needs to access them. To change the directory so that it is also writable, use the following command:

```
chmod 777 Bbs/Messages
```

This command will change the **Messages** directory under the **Bbs** directory to be readable, writable, and executable by the world.

WARNING

You may be tempted to simply use chmod 777 on all the files and directories, because it ensures that the Web server can do anything with the files. However, it is strongly advised that you do not leave the files in this state. It is considered a significant security risk to leave your scripts open to changes by the Web server instead of being read-only. Anyone on the server could use a rogue CGI script to write over your scripts and make them do something different. There is still a risk involved in making the **Messages** directory writable, but if someone messes with your area, the intruder will destroy only a bit of data and not your main programs. It is OK to set the scripts to 777 if you are trouble-shooting a problem and want to rule out permissions entirely, but do not leave the scripts like this.

On another security note, if you are concerned with the security of your data such as running a shopping cart, please do not use a shared server where other people can write CGI scripts using the same Web server configuration. It is much better to use your own server software or purchase space on a *virtual server*, which can be shared but is set up so that each user's scripts are shielded from those of other users.

Server-Based CGI Execution Issues

Assuming your Web server is set up to run CGI scripts, you may find that there are various ways the server can be set up to recognize that a script is an executable program. There are two common ways that Web servers typically handle the recognition of CGI scripts; each has its benefits and drawbacks.

First, a specific directory or directories are earmarked as containing only executable programs. Any file in such a directory will be run as a program no matter what its extension. The second way a server can be set up to recognize CGI scripts is by file extension. In this case, you indicate CGI scripts by adding a **.cgi** extension to the end of the filename. Thus, if you called a script, **bbs_forum.pl**, you would rename it to **bbs_forum.cgi** to have it recognized as a runnable CGI script by the Web server.

Typically, the first method is an option only if you have your own Web server. Internet service providers find it time-consuming to set up a specific CGI binary executable (**cgi-bin**) directory for each user on the system. The advantage of this method is that it is relatively straightforward. HTML files belong in a documents directory area, and scripts belong in a scripts directory. Keep in mind, though, that the Web server cannot read HTML files inside a script directory. If a CGI script relies on an HTML file for something such as form input, you'll need to place that HTML file in a document directory.

When you belong to an Internet service provider, the likelihood is high that you are sharing the Web server with other people whom you do not know. ISPs try to be very careful about the sorts of permissions they allow a Web server to have on a machine. On the other hand, restricting the access of the Web server greatly reduces your file options: how to name files, where to put them, how to run them, and what they can do. The most common way around this problem is for an ISP to require users of a shared server to use the **.cgi** extension for all CGI scripts. One advantage of this technique is that HTML files that belong to the CGI application can reside in the same directory with the CGI files. This arrangement makes it easier to maintain the application, because you do not have to go to two different directories to maintain the files.

All the scripts in this book end in **.cgi** by default. This is the most flexible way to initially name your scripts, because if they are placed on a server that recognizes the **.cgi** suffix, they will run. As a bonus, if they are placed in a directory using the CGI-specified directory method, they will also run.

Some ISPs may not give their users access to run CGI scripts using the **.cgi** extension by default. For example, they may provide a directory such as **public_html** inside your home directory to hold HTML files; if you put a **.cgi** file there, it will not run. If this happens, there are a couple of tricks you may be able to pull to make your ISP's Web server run the scripts. If your ISP is using the NCSA or Apache Web server, there is a good possibility that it has been configured to allow a user to "override" Web server options by placing an **.htaccess** file in the directory where you wish to run CGI scripts. The "." before **htaccess** is not a typo. It is important to include. In the directory you wish to run CGI scripts in, create an **.htaccess** file containing the following line:

```
Options ExecCGI
```

This single line is all you need! Hopefully, it will get you up and running with CGI scripts. However, keep in mind that **.htaccess** is the default filename for overriding Web server configuration options. Your Web server may be set up differently.

You can spend a great deal of time going through these steps, but the easiest way to find out how your server is configured is to ask your Internet service provider.

Finding System Files

On UNIX, CGI scripts written in Perl usually contain a magic line that expects to find Perl in a particular directory. In addition, some CGI applications may expect external programs such as sendmail to be located in a certain location on the server. Most of the time, the references to these locations will be correct, because most servers are set up in a standard way. However, you may run across a situation in which the programs used by the scripts are not where they are supposed to be. One of the last steps in setting up scripts is to figure out the location of these files so that the scripts can be changed to reflect the new file locations.

The classic example of a reference to an absolute path in a CGI script is the first line of the Perl code:

```
#!/usr/local/bin/perl
```

This line instructs the server to run the ensuing script through the Perl interpreter and indicates where to find the Perl interpreter. The Perl interpreter is a program that reads your script and translates it into a form that your server can run. In the preceding example, the server will know that it can find the Perl interpreter in the directory **/usr/local/bin**. Although many servers may contain Perl in **/usr/local/bin**, others may have installed it in other areas, such as **/usr/bin** or **/opt/bin**.

If Perl is not in **/usr/local/bin**, your first bit of customizing is to find out where your local Perl is and change this line to reference the correct location. There are several ways of finding files on your system. Not all of them work on every server, so be prepared to experiment with the following techniques.

The first command to try is **which**. At the command prompt of your UNIX server, you type **which perl** and receive the following reply:

```
$ which perl
/bin/perl
```

In other words, Perl is located in **/bin** on this system. Thus, you will need to change the first line of your script to

```
#!/bin/perl
```

If that does not work, try the **whereis** command. This command could give you the following output:

```
$ whereis perl
perl: /usr/bin/perl /usr/local/bin/perl /usr/local/bin/perl4.036
/usr/local/bin/
perl5.002
```

This output tells us a little bit more information than we get with the **which** command. It gives us information about all the Perl interpreters contained in the system. In other words, there are several versions of Perl installed on this server, including 4.036 and 5.002! Because there are several versions, you could choose whichever one you wish to reference in the CGI script.

If those two commands fail, the next step is to try **whence**. This command is more specific to the Korn shell, so you should first change to the Korn shell if you can: Type **ksh** at the command line of your UNIX system. Now you should be free to use **whence** and get output that looks similar to the following:

```
$ ksh
$ whence perl
/usr/local/bin/perl
```

If all else fails, you might try the **find** command, but that is really pulling out all the stops when a simple E-mail to your system administrator might suffice. The syntax for **find** is as follows:

```
find / -name perl
```

In a few other cases you may need to find other programs on your system. Some CGI applications make calls to external system programs other than Perl. For example, many mail-enabled CGI scripts rely on the UNIX sendmail program to send E-mail. Usually, this application is located in **/usr/lib**. On some UNIX systems it may be located elsewhere. In such instances, you may have to define the directory paths for those programs in addition to Perl. All the commands we've discussed will help you find the location of other programs.

You may also run into a problem that is specific to some "virtual" Web servers on shared systems: What you see as your root directory when you log on may not be what the Web server sees. For example, your documents may be located in **/home/smithj/www/cgi-bin**, but a virtual Web server may see documents as being located in **/www/cgi-bin**. Some ISPs configure it that way, because it enhances security by making sure that the Web server you are using cannot touch the files created by any other Web server instance on a shared machine. CGI scripts on Virtual Web servers are more time-consuming to set up and are specific to each customer; if you are using such a server, make sure you are given instructions about how to access external programs such as Perl or sendmail.

CROSS-PLATFORM CONSIDERATIONS

A few years ago, UNIX was synonymous with the Internet. Almost anyone who wanted to get on the Internet did it by using a UNIX server. More recently, however, other types of operating systems have expanded their list of features to include Internet-based services. Shareware as well as commercial Web server products are available for Apple Macintosh, Windows 95, Windows NT, and a variety of other operating systems.

Unfortunately, Perl takes on slightly different forms depending on the operating system in use. Perl for UNIX has a number of features that are difficult or impossible to implement on other operating system architectures. This incompatibility can be a major problem, because Perl has become the de facto standard language for writing CGI scripts on the Internet.

Most of the scripts in this book have been written with cross-platform compatibility in mind. However, you may still need to make some changes to get the scripts to run. In addition, not all the scripts you download from the Internet are written to be so cross-platform–friendly. The guidelines that follow will help you to set up the scripts in this book and other Perl scripts downloaded from the Internet on your non-UNIX server. Many of these guidelines are programming-related and are meant to help you modify a Perl program if you find that it has not been written in a cross-platform–friendly manner.

We will focus on Windows NT versus UNIX for developing CGI scripts. Windows NT appears to be an up-and-coming contender for heavy network computing. In addition, it is also sufficiently different from UNIX that most of the guidelines will help you write scripts that should also work on other platforms such as Macintosh and Windows 95.

Batch File Encapsulation

Some Windows NT Web servers cannot recognize the **.cgi** or **.pl** file extensions. Nor do they look at the first line of the file (as UNIX does) to see which program should run the script using the magic `#!/usr/local/bin/perl` designation. The easiest way to get around this problem is to encapsulate the script in a batch file. Simply create an MS-DOS **.bat** file with roughly the same CGI script name and call the original CGI script with Perl. For example, the BBS script discussed later in this book has been designed to be compatible with NT Perl 5, but the script name is **bbs_forum.cgi**. To get this script to run on a server that cannot recognize **.cgi**, create a **bbs_forum.bat** file in the same directory as **bbs_forum.cgi** and place in it the following lines:

```
@echo off
perl bbs_forum.cgi
```

That's it! Now, whenever you refer to the script, use **bbs_forum.bat** file instead of **bbs_forum.cgi**. All that remains is to make sure that any references inside the program to **bbs_forum.cgi** are changed to **bbs_forum.bat**. For the BBS script, there is a variable in the **bbs.setup** file that allows you to specify the name to refer to the script by. In other programs, however, you may need to be careful to edit the scripts to reference the new batch filename.

WARNING

Encapsulating your scripts inside batch files can have security implications. To get a full appreciation of the problems that may arise, you should read the CGI programming security FAQ located at the following URL:
`http://www-genome.wi.mit.edu/WWW/faqs/www-security-faq.html`

Shell Commands

Don't use shell commands. This rule is easier said than done, though, and, in some cases, using shell commands may be unavoidable. There may be a UNIX command, such as the **sendmail** command, that has no equivalent in the other operating system. On the other hand, it is easy to fall into the trap of using easy UNIX commands to substitute for programming the same thing in Perl.

For example, the UNIX **date** command is called frequently from some CGI scripts. This practice is unnecessary. Perl has a good facility for returning the current date and time. Simply use the **localtime** command:

```
($sec, $min, $hour, $mday, $mon,
     $year, $wday, $yday, $isdst)
         = localtime(time);
$mon++;
$date = "$mon/$mday/$year";
```

instead of using the UNIX-specific command:

```
$date = `date`;
```

The UNIX-specific command is short and easy, but if your script is already 100 or more lines long, a few more lines to get today's date won't hurt you—and the script will be cross-platform–friendly. In addition, it's bad practice to call external commands; spawning extra programs and processes takes computing time on busy Web servers.

UNIX Function Calls

Some functions listed in the Perl manual pass their parameters to a low-level UNIX system call. Frequently, these commands do not translate well to other systems, because UNIX calls are not implemented in every operating system. Two especially problematic functions tend to be used often in CGI programs: `crypt` and `flock`.

Crypt takes a password and encrypts it the same way passwords are encrypted in the UNIX **/etc/passwd** or **/etc/shadow** file. Windows NT encrypts passwords using a proprietary algorithm. Thus, Windows NT does not support the crypt function call; as of this writing, Perl for NT does not support it, either. For scripts that use the crypt function, such as the authentication library discussed later in this book, it is considered a good practice to have a flag variable that can be set so that encryption is turned off for systems that do not support crypt.

Flock is a file-locking function call. Although Windows NT Perl has recently started supporting flock, it is important to minimize your use of this function, because not even all UNIX systems support it. The best thing to do, if you wish to use file locking in your CGI scripts, is to implement a simple file-locking mechanism of your own. **CGI-LIB.SOL**, discussed later in this book, implements such a routine.

NOTE It is better to use flock than a hand-rolled file-locking routine, especially if you have heavy server activity. But be aware of the trade-off of incompatibility with other servers and platforms.

Directory Referencing

UNIX separates directory names with a forward slash (/), such as **/usr/local/bin**. Windows NT separates directory names with a backslash (\), such as **\winnt351\system**. Because Perl for NT translates the UNIX convention into the Windows NT convention automatically, you should code your scripts on Windows NT to reference directories using a / slash instead of a \ slash to be compatible with UNIX.

E-Mail on NT

Windows NT before version 4.0 does not have the built-in capability to send Internet mail, which many Web applications use. For example, when someone submits an order to the shopping cart, frequently the order is E-mailed to the administrator of the shopping area to complete the order. The chapter on **MAIL-LIB.PL** includes a discussion of a Perl script that sends E-mail on Windows NT.

CONCLUSION

After reading this chapter, you should have a good idea of the general guidelines for downloading and running CGI scripts in a variety of environments. Merely downloading scripts is easy. Configuring them to run on a Web server can be more of a challenge, but by following the steps of dearchiving the applications, setting the appropriate permissions, and making sure the files are in a CGI executable directory or end with **.cgi**, you should be able to get the scripts up and running in no time. Similarly, you need to resolve cross-platform issues, such as running scripts for UNIX on a Windows NT Web server. By going through the steps outlined here, you should also be able to get a script running on a non-UNIX server.

CHAPTER 2

Troubleshooting CGI Scripts

OVERVIEW

Web servers and their CGI environment can be set up in a variety of ways. Chapter 1 covered the basics of the installation and configuration of scripts. However, you may encounter situations in which the scripts still do not work. After all, no two servers work the same way, because their system administrators have configured them differently. Thus, what works on one server may not necessarily work on another. The tips and tricks outlined here will help you to get past many of the problems you might encounter.

The first few sections of this chapter will focus on the most common problems that can arise in the course of using scripts. The later sections will discuss some complex but useful troubleshooting tools to add to your repertoire of CGI setup skills.

SERVER ERRORS

Whenever the Web server responds to a request from a browser for a document or CGI program, a status code is returned. This status code can tell you a great deal about the sort of problem you are encountering. Table 2.1 contains a list of the possible status codes a Web server might return. The codes serve as a road map to errors that may be occurring in an incorrect script installation. Each error-related code serves as a first step in figuring out what is going wrong with a script's execution.

Table 2.1 *The major HTTP response codes.*

CODE	STATUS	MEANING
2xx (Codes for a successful Processing)		
200	OK	Request was successful.
202	Accepted	Request is still processing but was successful.
204	No response	Request was processed, but there is no data to be sent to the client.
3xx (Codes for Redirection)		
301	Moved	Document was moved permanently to a new location.
302	Found	Document is at a different location on the server. Response typically includes a Location header to direct the browser to a new document.
304	Use Local Copy	Document was found but was not modified since last request.
4xx (Codes for Client Errors)		
400	Bad Request	Syntax of browser's request was not recognized.
401	Unauthorized	Server has restricted the document to be viewed. Typically, the document is protected by password or IP address and authentication has failed.
403	Forbidden	Request was forbidden, typically because of access rights.
404	Not Found	Server could not find the document.

Code	Status	Meaning
5xx (Codes for Server Errors)		
500	Internal Error	Server was not able to carry out the request but does not know the explicit reason. A catch-all error.
501	Not Implemented	Sender knows about the requested service but does not know how to handle it.
502	Service Is Overloaded	Server cannot process more requests than it is currently processing.

204 (No Response)

This typical response is given if the script has executed successfully but has failed or exited before it could return any HTML data other than the "Content-type: text/html" header. The techniques for troubleshooting this status code are basically the same as those used to figure out a 500 (Internal Error) code, described later. However, one item to check out here is the permissions that exist on a particular directory or file.

The script may not have permission to create, write, and read certain data files or subdirectories that it expects to work on. When this happens, the script may work up to the point that it prints the "Content-type: text/html\n\n" message output by all CGI programs. But because a file is not found or cannot be written, the rest of the program logic may not be able to generate the dynamic HTML based on the contents of the data files. As a result, a "Document Contains No Data" or "No Response" error message may pop up. Make sure that any subdirectories required by the script have been created and that it has the appropriate level of access to them. For example, if a Web application needs to write files in a subdirectory such as **Sessions**, you need to give the Web server write access to the subdirectory. This access is discussed more thoroughly in Chapter 1.

401 (Unauthorized)

This code means that the script was placed in a protected area of the Web server and the authentication failed. The script may be protected by allowing only certain IP addresses or Internet hosts to read the document, or it may be restricted by a username/password combination. The solution to this problem is to place the script in an unprotected area or figure out how to satisfy the security restrictions.

403 (Forbidden)

Typically, the 403 (Forbidden) error occurs when you try to access a script that the Web server does not have the permissions or rights to read and execute. This situation is easy to remedy. On UNIX, merely use the **chmod** command, as specified in Chapter 1, to make the script readable and executable to the Web server.

404 (Not Found)

404 (Not Found) is output when the Web server cannot find the document the browser has requested. This error is also easy to correct. Typically, it is caused by the user typing the URL incorrectly, or perhaps no mapping has been set up from the URL to the actual directory on the Web server. For example, on most Web servers the /**cgi-bin** URL is mapped to another directory structure on the server, such as /**usr/local/etc/httpd/cgi-bin**. If this mapping is not set up, the Web server may attempt to look for the script in a **cgi-bin** directory underneath the document root, which may be an incorrect location.

 Since URL directory mappings may be entirely different in nature to the real directory path on the Unix server, you should be very careful of this error. Many virtual servers are setup with a completely different URL structure than what you see when you are logged into the actual UNIX server.

500 (Internal Error)

500 errors can be difficult to solve, because it is a catch-all error message. Anything else that can go wrong with a script that is not caught by the

previous errors is typically sent as a 500 error. Basically, a 500 server error is caused because the Perl program did not print "Content-type: text/html\n\n" before anything else was printed. This "magic header" must always print before anything else in the Perl program. Frequently, the cause of this failure is that the Perl program was not able to run at all. The following are some possible ways to resolve this problem.

First, the script may have syntax errors or some other problem that causes it not to run. An easy way to check for this kind of error is to run the script from the command line using Perl's -c parameter to check syntax. If **foobar.cgi** contained an error, you could run `perl -c` on it:

```
$perl -c foobar.cgi
literal @whatnot now requires a backslash at foobar.cgi line 5, within
string
foobar.cgi had compilation errors.
```

The output shows an error in line 5. Specifically, the programmer has placed an @whatnot inside a string in Perl. Perl version 5.x must have the @ symbol escaped with a backslash (\ ) character.

NOTE

A common cause of @ symbols not being escaped is that an E-mail address has been entered into the Perl program without escaping the @ symbol. For example, "selena@eff.org" is wrong for Perl version 5. You must use "selena\@eff.org."

To fix this error, you could inform the original author or go into the script and fix it yourself, depending on your level of expertise. Even if you can fix it yourself, it's considered good etiquette to inform the original programmer that you are encountering a syntax error on your system. In that way, the programmer can fix the problem for other people who may not be as clever at solving Perl problems.

Another cause of 500 errors is that the libraries called by the script may have errors or may not be found in the path. Any libraries, such as **cgi-lib.pl**, that have been downloaded with the script should be run with `perl -c` to check for syntax errors. If that does not reveal the problem, run the script itself from the command line. The following example shows how you might run the script from the command line to see whether there is a problem with the `require` statement that loads libraries. For example, if **bbs_forum.cgi** is run from the command line and the required file **bbs.setup** is not present, you will see the following output. The error at the bottom tells you that **bbs_forum.cgi** tried to include **bbs.setup** but was not able to. The way to fix this error is to make sure that a file called **bbs.setup** is in the path where **bbs_forum.cgi** expects it.

```
$ bbs_forum.cgi
Content-type: text/html

Can't locate bbs.setup in @INC at bbs_forum.cgi line 99.
```

A similar problem is that the correct path to Perl is not set up in the first line of the script. For example, if the script has `#!/usr/local/bin/perl` in the first line of the file, perhaps Perl is not in the /**usr**/**local**/**bin** directory. Chapter 1 contains a section on finding out where Perl is located in your directory. Remember that this magic line must appear by itself on the first line of the script.

It is considered better to run the scripts through `perl -c` **before you run them using** `perl`. `perl -c` **checks for syntax;** `perl` **actually runs the program. Running the program by itself may display strangely, because it is not running in the environment of the Web server.**

N O T E

If the server is running in a different environment from that of the script, certain utilities and commands may not be available to the Web server. Some Web servers run in a `chroot` environment where they lack basic utilities such as `ls` and `pwd`. If a CGI script relies on calling external commands, it can also cause the script to fail. In this case, you could attempt to copy the binaries of the external commands into the `chroot` directories that the Web server can see, or you may need to contact your Web server administrator to make these utilities available. Note that it is considered bad practice to call external programs when Perl can do the job internally. You may also want to consider attempting to find a different script that does something similar but without relying on an external command.

WARNING

If you are in a `chroot` environment, do *not* copy the Perl interpreter itself to any CGI directories. Doing so would have serious security consequences, because any user of your Web site would be able to call Perl directly from Netscape and pass it new Perl commands, telling it to do all sorts of destructive things such as `rm -rf *` to remove all files in all subdirectories. Yikes!

A related problem may be that the script calls an external program whose output displays before the "Content-type: text/html" header has been output. How can this happen? Essentially, Perl buffers data internally before sending it to STDOUT (standard output) with print statements. This arrangement can cause a problem when a system call is generated that outputs data and then ends. The system call, because it is completed, will tend to flush its own STDOUT before Perl has a chance to flush the statements it has previously buffered internally. The trick to solving this problem is to start the Perl script with the following piece of code:

```
$| = 1;
```

This code sets the current default file handle in Perl (STDOUT) to not buffer the output. There is a slight performance loss, because buffering exists to send the data in large blocks at a time, a faster technique than many little requests. However, this method will frequently solve a problem that occurs when system() calls in Perl output data before the Perl script has a chance to.

Another problem that you may run across is mismatched ASCII types of files on your server. This mismatch can happen when you download an archived set of scripts to a local machine running a non-UNIX operating system such as DOS or Windows, edit the files there, and then use FTP to transfer the files to your server again. DOS editors typically save files with a CR-LF (carriage return/line feed) combination of two characters (\R\N, in

Perl terminology). However, UNIX reads ASCII files with only an LF and no CR. If you edit a file on a DOS machine and FTP the file to the UNIX server, always remember to transfer it using the ASCII mode of the FTP program. This mode will perform the CR-LF to LF translation automatically.

NOTE Many Perl scripts may not have a problem with the added CR on UNIX. Generally, a Perl script will be most affected by the CR-LF problem if it uses the "here" method of assigning multiple lines of character output to a string. Basically, with the "here" document method, you define a boundary at which point the lines of character output stop, much as a quotation mark delimits a string on a single line. Unfortunately, if the boundary marker appears on a single line by itself and has a CTRL-M (CR) after it, Perl will not recognize it as the boundary marker because of the extra character. The moral of the story is that just because some Perl scripts may work with the method of file transfer you were using, it's not a good idea to assume that all of them will.

Another useful diagnostic tool is the error log of your Web server. If you are sharing a server of an Internet service provider, you may not have access to the Web server's error log. However, if you run your own Web server or if you use one that lets you see and access the error log, it can be an invaluable source of information. Typically, whenever an error occurs in a Perl script, it gets output to a standard error channel (STDERR). Anything output to STDERR, including syntax errors and runtime errors, typically gets written to the error log. Examining the error log can save you a great deal of time by telling you immediately what the Web server found wrong with the CGI program.

OUTPUT ERRORS

The last problem that may occur when you're setting up scripts is that the output is valid but unexpected. In other words, the script works but the output is wrong. This problem is a complex one to solve, because it generally indicates a logic error in the programming rather than a problem with the way the script was set up.

However, there are a couple of tricks you can use to solve this. First, it is possible, as with the 500 error, that subdirectories and files do not exist that the script expects to see and have read or write access to; or the permissions may be set incorrectly. It cannot be emphasized enough that many of the problems that arise in setting up scripts boil down to access permission problems.

Beyond this solution, there are a few tricks to helping solve logic problems in scripts if you feel up to modifying someone else's Perl code. It is possible to "fool" a script, from the command line, into thinking it is running in the server's environment. To do this is, set up key environment variables before running the script. If the method that is being tested is a POST, then you must also have a file that contains the post information that can be redirected to the script as STDIN.

The trick just described is a more advanced technique that should be used by programmers who feel comfortable modifying Perl scripts. It is a good idea to back up the scripts to another directory in case you want to go back to the original version of one or more of your CGI scripts.

WARNING

For the following examples of fooling a script into thinking it is getting form data passed, the form variable name will be set to John Smith, and the form variable bdate will be set to 12/2/30. Because the form variables contain characters that a Web server has trouble recognizing, the variables must be converted to a urlencoded format. This means that the characters such as spaces must be converted to escape characters. The urlencoded form of the above variables is name=John%20Smith&bdate=12%2f2%2f30. If you are testing a script to use the GET method of passing form data, then the top of the Perl script must be modified to include the following environmental variable settings:

```
$ENV{"REQUEST_METHOD"} = "GET";
$ENV{"QUERY_STRING"} = "name=John%20Smith&bdate=12%2f2%2f30";
```

The script should now run and decode the data as form variables.

If you want to emulate the POST method of transferring form data, the process is slightly different. First, you create a file that contains the post data. For this example, we will assume that the value of the QUERY_STRING environmental variable set previously will be placed in a file called **test.in**. Next, we determine the CONTENT_LENGTH of the file in bytes. In UNIX, the easiest way to do this is to use the wc command:

```
$ wc -c test.in
35
```

The -c parameter returns the character count of the file. In this case, the file is 35 characters long.

The following environmental variables must be set at the top of the Perl script:

```
$ENV{"REQUEST_METHOD"} = "POST";
$ENV{"CONTENT_LENGTH"} = "35";
```

Then call the script from the command line and also pass the **test.in** file to the script (**foobar.cgi**):

```
$ foobar.cgi <test.in
```

On the other side of the coin, instead of forcing different form variables at the beginning of the Perl script, you may want to edit the script to print the value of the form variables that have been passed by the Web server. For scripts that use **CGI-LIB.PL** to parse form variables, this is easy. Simply use the &PrintVariables routine and pass it the array that you used to read form variables (%in, by default) by reference. You would add the following line:

```
print &PrintVariables(*in);
```

In addition, you might want to print environmental variables. This is also easily done with **CGI-LIB.PL**. Merely use this code:

```
print &PrintEnv;
```

The techniques we've described will allow you to test various types of form input to the CGI script. Although some of them may be a little advanced, they are valuable techniques to add to your CGI debugging toolbox.

CONCLUSION

With the myriad of different ways a Web server can be set up, it should come as no surprise that troubleshooting CGI problems is common when attempting to set up scripts for the first time. The methods described here from tracking down server errors through working out a program's HTML output problems provide a step-by-step prescription for detecting the source of the most common problems you may encounter when trying to use CGI scripts.

CHAPTER 3

Intranet Design

OVERVIEW

The explosion of the Web as a means of sharing information on the Internet has evolved into means for organizations to share documents and data internally. The buzzword that sums up this new direction is *intranet*. It is important to note that an intranet is not merely an internal Internet. Because internal company data is generally considered proprietary or confidential, security is an important concern within a company intranet.

Many applications that can be used on the Internet are ideal groupware applications for use within a company. Many of the applications discussed in this book are ideal additions to any company intranet.

A BULLETIN BOARD SYSTEM

Many companies already have an internal E-mail system, but most of them are not yet equipped to handle more public discussions. A Web-based BBS message board system can help by giving a public forum for talking about a variety of topics.

For example, many organizations have committees that discuss topics relevant to the company. Unfortunately, in a busy company, finding a time when five or ten people can meet to discuss the same topic is difficult. A BBS can facilitate this discussion by letting committee members post their ideas and comments at times that are convenient for each person. Because the messages stay around, the message board is a natural "secretary," keeping an archive of all discussions about a particular topic (see Figure 3.1).

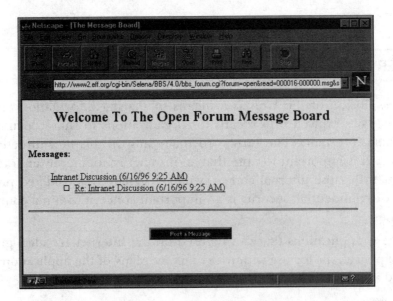

Figure 3.1 Example of a message board system.

Forums, too, can be set up to discuss a variety of topics. For example, employees can ask questions about company policies and procedures. Announcements can be made on a BBS system about forthcoming system downtimes and planned upgrades, and employees can also ask computer-related questions. Because the forums are public within the company, the employees can always search on previously posted messages to see whether their questions have already been asked and answered in a related discussion forum.

GROUPWARE CALENDAR

Another Web-based application that a company intranet can benefit from is a calendar. A calendar accessible to everyone can help display company events such as special speakers or presentations (see Figure 3.2).

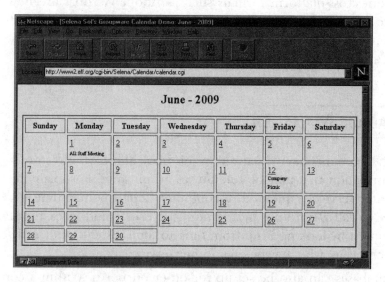

Figure 3.2 Example of a groupware calendar.

A calendar can be a great organizational device for scheduling common resources such as conference rooms. Instead of using a sign-up sheet for conference rooms and special equipment, a user could use the Web to sign up for a time slot. Using authorization techniques discussed in the authorization library chapter, resources can be controlled by an administrator while the rest of the company can view the changes. This arrangement is useful to stop employees from overwriting a previous reservation.

DOCUMENT SHARING

Probably the most common use of an intranet is the sharing of company documents. Policies and procedures manuals and other information can be disseminated using a company intranet. In fact, CGI scripting is not even needed. What is needed is a common means of storing and retrieving the information.

Typically, information on a Web server is stored in HTML form. Although manuals and documents within a company may be stored in another format, such as Word or WordPerfect documents, these word processors now have the capability of doing conversions to HTML. In addition, cross-platform formats such as Adobe Acrobat are now being used to store the information in a common format. Whatever the form of your internal company documents, an intranet can help distribute them to the appropriate people.

DATABASE MANAGER

The database manager discussed in this book allows you to store a variety of information that may be relevant to an intranet. For example, a user can enter service requests to a computer department online instead of having to call a hot line. In addition, the user could track the status of the request by looking it up from time to time instead of directly calling the technician, who may be on another service call.

Databases can also be set up for other purposes. Within a company, you may want to allow a user to query phone numbers and room locations of other employees. This can be done with a companywide address book. In addition, information regarding the status of projects can be posted and tracked inside a database, with milestone and status update information stored inside a workgroup database.

WEB CHAT

A Web chat program allows a number of people to discuss a variety of topics at the same time as if they were meeting in a conference room (see Figure 3.3). This "virtual" conference can help people meet without having to be in the same geographical location. As long as an employee has an Internet connection, he or she will be able to participate in the virtual conference.

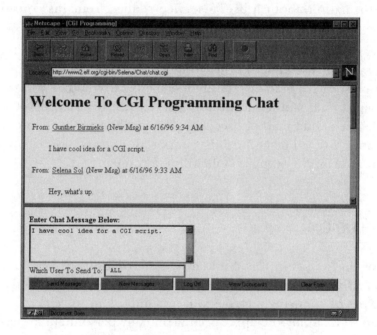

***Figure 3.3** Example of a Web chat session.*

SECURITY

Security is of paramount importance in the intranet. Instead of sharing information with the outside world, the intranet is used to share information within a company. However, an intranet allows so much discussion and transfer of information inside a company that strict guidelines must be maintained to make sure that proprietary information does not leak outside the company.

In addition, certain topics and types of database information should be viewable and changeable only by the appropriate employees. You would not want an intern, for example, to be able to change the CEO's salary online. As a more mundane example, you might want to make sure that information about a user's service request remains confidential between that user and the service department.

These types of security issues can be solved by using the authentication library discussed later in this book. In addition, many CGI programs have sophisticated, built-in security mechanisms. Whether you modify a CGI script to add authentication or get a script with user-level security built-in, you should map out security policies thoroughly before making an intranet "live" to make sure that important information is not leaked or controlled by the wrong people within a company.

CONCLUSION

Many of the scripts in this book are great additions to any company's intranet. However, because of the proprietary and confidential nature of some types of company information, it is important to remember to set them up so that only the appropriate company personnel have access to sensitive functions. Whatever the policies and procedures for your company, adding an intranet as a means of sharing information is bound to increase productivity and communication.

CHAPTER 4

Using Libraries

After digesting the previous chapters, you should be comfortable finding scripts, downloading them to your local CGI scripts directory, and configuring them to run on your intranet or Internet server. This is a great start, but there is only so much you can do with other people's scripts without being able to modify them.

Before you know it, your boss or clients will be clamoring for various customizations. Perhaps they will want different graphics, perhaps some new features, or maybe an entirely new look and feel for the graphical user interface (GUI). In other words, most likely the scripts you download will not be configured the way you want them to be set up. In fact, any well-designed script should be as generic (read "boring") as possible so that it can be ported to as many different environments as possible. It is up to the local programmer to add the bells and whistles that turn a generic Perl script into a dynamic Web application.

The next step in your evolution as a CGI programmer is to learn how to customize the scripts for your own needs. The first task is to understand how CGI programs are structured. Each of the scripting chapters in this book includes a design discussion, and many of our programs also use a common toolbox of routines—called *libraries*—that are included in every Web application. Although subsequent chapters will discuss each of the major libraries that we use in our Web programming, it is helpful to understand how libraries work.

Web applications are not ferocious. Certainly, in the beginning, a thousand lines of code can look daunting when seen as a whole—seething with what seems like endlessly intertwined loops and variables and arrays and subroutines. However, you should not let that stop you from studying the program. After a bit of delving into the lines of code, you'll often find that a well-written program can be tame. It's a good idea to view programs as a group of associated algorithms (or routines), all of which have small, well-defined functions. Algorithms are like ants in an ant colony, each doing one small job well. To decipher a program, you need only focus on understanding how these simple packets of code, called *subroutines*, interact. With practice, they will call out to you: "I add numbers," "I gather form input," "I parse that input," "I say hello world when asked." If you understand the program one routine at a time, the application's design will emerge and you will be more comfortable modifying and adding to the original program.

DESIGN DISCUSSION

There are three types of algorithms that you will be faced with in most Perl CGI applications: individual algorithms, application-specific subroutines, and interapplication libraries. Let's look at each of these types.

Individual Algorithms

Algorithms are merely pieces of code that perform an action in a specific way. An algorithm that adds two numbers can be expressed as x + y.

However, its usage is very specific. To add 31,289 and 23,990, you would use the following Perl code:

```
$sum = 31289 + 23990;
```

This is a simple routine, but it is also specific to just one case. Programs typically consist of many such routines put together. However, there comes a time when you will want to make the routine generic so that you can call it over and over again in other parts of the program without having to rewrite it. This is where application-specific subroutines come in.

Application-Specific Subroutines

Routines that are general enough that they are used several times in the same application should usually be placed in a subroutine. A subroutine encapsulates a routine so that other parts of the program can refer to it by its subroutine name. Consider the addition algorithm; what if we needed to add various numbers several times in our program but did not want to create a separate piece of code for each instance of addition? If the algorithm were four or five lines long, it would be annoying to type the similar lines over and over again. Even worse, if you ended up changing the logic of the algorithm you would have to hunt down every occurrence and change each one. Maintaining such a program could become a nightmare, because many errors could arise if you forgot to change one of the lines of code in any of the duplicate routines or changed one of them incorrectly.

When faced with such a circumstance, a programmer can create a subroutine that can be used again and again by other parts of the program. Figure 4.1 depicts how one subroutine could be used by several algorithms.

To create and use subroutines in Perl, we need three things: a subroutine reference, a subroutine identifier, and a parameter list of variables to pass to the subroutine. The & symbol precedes the name of the routine, telling Perl to look for the subroutine and call it. For example, &AddNumbers would direct Perl to execute the AddNumbers subroutine.

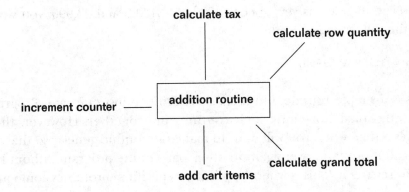

Figure 4.1 Using a subroutine.

We also need to be able to send the subroutine some information. Specifically, we need to send the subroutine parameters that it will use to customize its output. If we want to add 2 and 3, for example, we pass 2 and 3 to the subroutine using the following format:

```
&AddNumbers(2,3);
```

The & marker tells Perl to look for the subroutine in the program in order to call it. However, the *definition* of the subroutine is marked off in the program using a sub marker. The code belonging to the routine is delimited with curly brackets ({}). The following example shows what the AddNumber subroutine definition would look like:

```
sub AddNumbers
  {
    local($first_number, $second_number) = @_;
    print $first_number + $second_number;
  }
```

Note the third line above. We use the local keyword to make sure that the $first_number and $second_number variables will be considered local to only that subroutine. The subroutine will not affect any other variables that may be called $first_number or $second_number in other subroutines within the program. In Perl, the @_ is a list of parameters that have been passed to the function. $first_number is set equal to the first parameter, and $second_number is set equal to the second parameter in the @_ list of parameters. If the routine is called by &AddNumbers(2,3), 2 and 3 will be assigned to $first_number and $second_number, respectively.

It is important to use local variables within subroutines so that they do not overwrite variables used by the main script. In complex scripts that use dozens of variables, you may easily forget which variables you are using. Using local variables ensures that if you end up using the same name for a variable, you keep them separated.

N O T E

Whenever you want to add numbers, you can simply use the subroutine call &AddNumbers(x,y) instead of writing each addition individually. As a bonus, if you need to change the logic of the addition algorithm, you need only change it in the subroutine.

Interapplication Libraries

Good design does not stop with the use of subroutines. Often, several different scripts will be designed to incorporate the use of similar routines. In this case, it makes sense to remove the common routines from the programs and place them in a separate file of routines. This file can then be loaded as a library of subroutines into each program as needed. For example, in CGI, most applications will need a form gathering and parsing routine, a template for sending out the HTTP header, and perhaps one to generate template HTML code, such as the following:

```
<HTML><HEAD><TITLE>My Script Title</TITLE></HEAD><BODY>
```

In this case, we use library files and require them from the main script. A library file in Perl is simply a text file containing subroutines that are shared by several different Perl scripts. For these library files to be usable by the program, they must be readable by the script and must be in the Perl library path (or its location must be explicitly referenced). For example, if we wanted to load Steven Brenner's **cgi-lib.pl** library into our script, we would use the following:

```
require "cgi-lib.pl";
```

When this is done, every subroutine in **cgi-lib.pl** becomes accessible to the main script as if it were actually written into the script's code. We simply reference a subroutine contained in **cgi-lib.pl** as we would any other subroutine in the main program.

 Library files need to be readable by the script that requires them. If your server is running as "Nobody" (see Chapter 1 on setting up script permissions), you may need to make the library files readable by the world.

N O T E

CONCLUSION

As a preparation for the chapters to come, the concepts of subroutines and libraries are crucial to understanding the programs in this book. Many of our CGI scripts, both large and small, take strategic advantage of these libraries. The subsequent chapters in this section explain the internal workings of the Perl libraries we use and discuss how to use the routines in your own programs. The libraries discussed in this book are extremely useful in gaining an awareness of how our CGI scripts were built.

CHAPTER 5

Using CGI-LIB.PL

OVERVIEW

There are certain tasks that every CGI program must be capable of doing in order to perform Common Gateway Interface (CGI) functions. For example, form variables need to be read into the program, and specially formatted information must be communicated back to the server. Although there are several good libraries of CGI-related routines, all the scripts in this book use **CGI-LIB.PL**: It is small, efficient, Perl 4–compatible, and well supported throughout the CGI and Perl programming community.

CGI-LIB.PL was written by Steven Brenner and is the de facto standard library of CGI programming routines for Perl 4 and above. The library is short and simple, and it does 99 percent of what a CGI programmer needs to accomplish with regard to the Common Gateway Interface specification. An examination of this well-written library reveals many interesting Perl techniques.

The main thing that **CGI-LIB.PL** does is to read all the form variable input into an associative array for picking out the values. It also has the capability of printing standard HTML headers and footers along with the magic "Content-type: text/html\n\n" header. This header is absolutely necessary and printing it is generally the first thing every CGI programmer does in a script. CGI-LIB also has small routines to do general housekeeping, such as printing error messages as HTML output, printing associative arrays, and returning URLs and certain environmental variables related to CGI. Advanced features, such as the ability to support file uploads, have recently been added.

INSTALLATION AND USAGE

As with most of the libraries in this section, **CGI-LIB.PL** is easy to install. Merely insert a line to `require` **cgi-lib.pl,** such as the following:

```
require "cgi-lib.pl";
```

Reading and Parsing Form Variables

The `&ReadParse` function is used to read the form variables whether the form was called via a GET or by a POST method. If `&ReadParse` is called without a parameter, by default the form variables are read into an associative array called `%in`. You can use your own associative array if you pass it by reference to `&ReadParse`. For example, if you wanted to read the form variables into an associative array called `%form_data`, you would use this convention:

```
&ReadParse(*form_data);
```

N O T E   Normally, when a variable is passed to a subroutine in Perl, only a copy of its value is passed. By replacing the $, @, or % symbol with a * in front of normal scalar, array, and associative array variables respectively, you are telling it to copy the location in memory where the variable value exists. This way, when the variable is changed in the subroutine, that change is simultaneously done to the originally passed variable instead of a mere copy of the value of the variable.

NOTE While many CGI scripts use the default `%in` associative array to represent data, it is also common to see CGI programmers using a different associative array name. For example, many of the scripts discussed in this book use `%form_data` to hold form variable information. Both have their advantages. `%in` is a concise way of saying "input form variables" and is really quick to type. However, `%form_data` is more readable to some CGI authors especially when the script uses several associative arrays.

Uploading Files Using HTML

CGI-LIB.PL allows you to upload files using a new HTML input tag that specifies a filename to upload. Triggering the Web browser to upload a file takes several steps. First, the FORM METHOD must be POST. Second, a part in the FORM tag must say ENCTYPE=multipart/form-data. With this encoding type, whole files that are sent by the browser are broken apart using boundary information sent by the browser. Normally, by default, the encoding type is application/x-www-form-urlencoded, which means that the form variables are posted in roughly the same way as they would have been had they been part of the command line using the GET method. This common form of encoding is discussed in more detail in Chapter 2 where we discuss how to fool the CGI program into thinking that information has been posted to it. In addition, the new INPUT tag lets you specify TYPE=FILE to associate a filename with a particular INPUT FORM variable. When the file gets uploaded, **CGI-LIB.PL** has the capability of parsing the information automatically and downloading it. The following sample HTML code would let you perform a file upload:

```
<HTML><HEAD>
<TITLE>File Upload</TITLE>
</HEAD>
<BODY>
<FORM METHOD=POST ENCTYPE=multipart/form-data ACTION="upload.cgi">
<P>
<INPUT TYPE=FILE NAME="upload_file"><P>
<INPUT TYPE=SUBMIT VALUE="Do The Upload">
</FORM>
</BODY></HTML>
```

In addition to all the changes in the HTML form, you must make changes in the CGI program. Certain **CGI-LIB.PL** variables must be changed to allow the files to be uploaded. The following code snippet from **CGI-LIB.PL** lists the relevant variables that need to be changed:

```
$cgi_lib'maxdata    = 131072;
    # maximum bytes to accept via POST - 2^17
$cgi_lib'writefiles =       0;
    # directory to which to write files, or
    # 0 if files should not be written
$cgi_lib'filepre    = "cgi-lib";
    # Prefix of file names, in directory above
```

NOTE

Many variables in CGI-LIB.PL are prefixed with "cgi_lib" and an apostrophe. This tells Perl to distinguish these variables in their own package. Basically, the variables become global to the CGI-LIB.PL script, but are not seen or changed in the main CGI script unless you explicitly reference them with the "cgi_lib'" prefix. Because of this prefix, the likelihood that these variables will be mistakenly defined in another part of the CGI script, thus causing a naming conflict, becomes almost null.

`$cgi_lib'maxdata` should be set greater than 131072 bytes if you expect larger files to be uploaded. `$cgi_lib'writefiles` needs to be set to a subdirectory on your server where you can create and write to files. `$cgi_lib'-filepre` should be set to a standard prefix to append to filenames that get written in the CGI write files directory. The default is `cgi-lib`.

It should be noted that CGI-LIB creates a temporary name for each file upload instead of using the name specified by the user. One reason is that a filename from one operating system may not be compatible with your server's file system naming conventions. More important, there is a possibility that someone could maliciously overwrite an important file if he or she had full control over the naming space.

NOTE

CGI-LIB.PL creates a temporary name for each file upload instead of using the name specified by the user. There are several reasons CGI-LIB.PL uses a different, computer-generated name. First, the filename from one operating system may not be compatible with the way file-names are stored on your Web server. Secondly, there is a possibility that someone could maliciously overwrite a file that was important to you on your Web server if the user was allowed to truly specify the filename.

The chapter in this book regarding the Web Message Board System (BBS) provides a full example of using the file upload parameters. The BBS allows users to upload files as virtual "attachments" to their posted messages on the system.

WARNING

you are using an operating system other than UNIX, the Perl you are using may require you to use the command "binmode(STDIN);" before you call the ReadParse function to download the file and other form information. The reason for this is that some operating systems do "ascii" conversions when files are read in by default. For example, one dialect of Windows NT Perl actually takes the "\r\n" combinations that delimit a boundary and translates them to "\n". Unfortunately, this really messes up the CGI-LIB.PL parsing routine since it is explicitly looking for "\r\n" combinations. Setting the STDIN file handle to binary mode using Perl's binmode command solves this problem.

Printing HTML Information

&PrintHeader returns the standard "Content-type: text/html\n\n" header that every CGI program needs to print in order for the browser to recognize the type of information that is being printed. &HtmlTop prints the HTML head of a document and uses a passed parameter to determine how the `<TITLE>` and `<H1>` tags should be printed. `&HtmlBot` prints the HTML footer of a document. Both routines save time by printing standard HTML codes that normally are time-consuming to write over and over again for each document. Here is a sample usage of these three functions:

```
print &PrintHeader;
print &HtmlTop("The title of my page";
print &HtmlBot;
```

The above code, would result in the CGI program presenting the following output to the Web server. Note that by the time the Web browser displays this information, the `Content-type: text/html\n\n` message is stripped off so that the user only sees straight HTML code.

```
Content-type: text/html

<HTML>
<HEAD>
<TITLE>The title of my page</TITLE>
</HEAD>
<BODY>
<H1>The title of my page</H1>
</BODY>
</HTML>
```

Splitting Multiple-Valued Form Variables

If your form variable contains multiple values, an associative array will not help you, because only one value can be stored in an associative array for each key. Brenner gets around this problem by storing all the values for a key in one associative array entry, but he separates them with the `\0` character. Passing the value that you believe to contain multiple values to the `&SplitParam` routine splits the multiple-valued key and returns an array list of all the values. The following example would split the string "test\0test1\0test2" into an array list of "test," "test1," and "test2."

```
@split_values = &SplitParam("test\0test1\0test2");
```

Testing Which Form Method Was Used

&MethGet and &MethPost allow you to test which method was used when your CGI program was called. They return a true value if a particular method was used. If the following snippet of CGI code were called using the POST method, it would print "hello."

```
if (&MethPost) {
    print "Hello\n";
} # End of if &MethPost
```

Retrieving the Current URL

&MyBaseURL and &MyFullURL return the URL of the current script. &MyFullURL returns the complete URL, including form variables used in the GET method. &MyBaseURL returns just enough of the URL to include the basic script name. For example, if our script were called as http://mycompany.com/test.cgi?last_name=smith, then the script shown next would return the following pieces of information: http://mycompany.com/test.cgi and http://mycompany.com/test.cgi?last_name=smith.

```
print &MyBaseURL;
print &MyFullURL;
```

Printing CGI Errors

&CgiError and &CgiDie accept an error message as a parameter, convert the error message to HTML, and print it so that users can see the error on a Web browser. &CgiDie behaves exactly like &CgiError except that it exits the program with the DIE command.

Most Perl programs use the plain DIE command in case of a system failure. Using &CgiDie is much better in the case of CGI programs, because the DIE message frequently never gets sent to the browser, making problems difficult to troubleshoot. The following code gives an example of how you would use &CgiDie to trap an error if a file does not open correctly.

```
open(TESTFILE,"<test.file") ||
    &CgiDie("The File: test.file could not be opened.");
```

NOTE

For the code above, you could also have used `CgiError` to report the problem. However, opening a file is usually a crucial step in a program so you want the script to end cleanly instead of attempting to go on when the file could not be opened. I almost never use `CgiError`. I use `CgiDie` **instead.**

Printing Associative Arrays

Brenner includes a convenient routine to print the contents of an associative array. `&PrintVariables` accepts an associative array as input, goes through the keys one by one, and returns the value as HTML code for printing. The `&PrintEnv` subroutine calls the `&PrintVariables` subroutine to print the list of all the current environmental variables. In this example, `&PrintVariables` prints the `%in` associative array:

```
print &PrintVariables(*in);
```

DESIGN DISCUSSION

Brenner uses a variety of interesting Perl techniques to make his library small and efficient. Going through the inner workings of his routines goes a long way toward demonstrating how CGI and Perl work together.

We will review **CGI-LIB.PL** version 2.8, which is the latest version of CGI-LIB as of this writing. (Version 2.8 adds support for file uploads, increasing the size of the library. If you are not using file uploads in your CGI programs, you may want to use an older, more streamlined version of CGI-LIB.) For the purpose of being complete, we include Brenner's comments. Although the comments are very good, we have expanded on them. We rely so much on the library for our scripts that to customize them "like a pro," it helps to understand how CGI-LIB is doing its magic.

Main Script

The following piece of code descriptively sets the `$cgi_lib'version` variable to `$Revision: 2.8 $` for the purposes of reading the code. However, adding the `=~ s/[^.\d]//g` tells Perl to strip out the non-numeric information. Thus, `$cgi_lib'version` is actually equal to `2.8`. This allows a programmer to check for version information after requiring **cgi-lib.pl**. For example, if we knew we were enabling file upload, we might check to see that the version number was 2.8 or greater. Because all the CGI-LIB variables tend to be prefixed with `cgi-lib`, we will refer to the variables without the prefix.

```
($cgi_lib'version = '$Revision: 2.8 $') =~ s/[^.\d]//g;
```

`$maxdata`, `$writefiles`, and `$filepre` all affect file uploading in different ways. `$maxdata` is set to the maximum number of bytes that the CGI program will accept for a file upload. Note that this value is the total value that will be accepted for the entire POST process. If you are uploading multiple files, this value would have to be as large as all the files combined plus some minimal header information being sent by the browser. `$writefiles` should be set to a directory that you wish the uploaded files to go to. `$filepre` should be set to a file prefix to add to the program.

$bufsize is the maximum amount of data to handle in one pass. The ReadParse subroutine, discussed next, processes values in chunks of size `$bufsize`. Processing too large a string at one time can cause problems, especially if there is an error somewhere further down the stream of characters that are being interpreted. When you're processing MULTIPART data, each part is separated by an arbitrary boundary. The `$maxbound` variable is set to 100, which means that the divider can be only 100 characters long. `$headerout` is used by the CgiError reporting routines to see whether we have already output a "Content-type: text/html\n\n" header. Whenever the header is printed, `$headerout` is incremented by 1. Then the header will not print if the CgiError is called more than once to report a problem in the program.

```
# Parameters affecting cgi-lib behavior
# User-configurable parameters affecting file upload.
$cgi_lib'maxdata    = 131072;
    # maximum bytes to accept via POST - 2^17
$cgi_lib'writefiles =       0;
    # directory to which to write files, or
    # 0 if files should not be written
$cgi_lib'filepre    = "cgi-lib";
      # Prefix of file names, in directory above


# Do not change the following parameters unless you have special
# reasons
$cgi_lib'bufsize  =  8192;
# default buffer size when reading multipart
$cgi_lib'maxbound =   100;
# maximum boundary length to be encountered
$cgi_lib'headerout =     0;
# indicates whether the header has been printed
```

The about variables are used primarily in the ReadParse subroutine discussed below. Understanding how these variables can be configured is the first step to understanding how ReadParse works.

NOTE

ReadParse Subroutine

The following author's comment block explains how the ReadParse subroutine works. ReadParse is the heart of CGI-LIB. It takes all the form variables and reads them into an associative array. In addition, ReadParse processes file uploads. We will go over this routine in more detail below.

```
# ReadParse
# Reads in GET or POST data, converts it to
# unescaped text, and puts key/value pairs in %in,
# using "\0" to separate multiple selections
# Returns >0 if there was input,
# 0 if there was no input
# undef indicates some failure.


# Now that cgi scripts can be put
# in the normal file space, it is
# useful to combine both the form
```

```
# and the script in one place.  If no
# parameters are given (i.e., ReadParse
# returns FALSE), then a form could be
# output.


# If a reference to a hash is given,
# then the data will be stored in that
# hash, but the data from $in and @in
# will become inaccessible.
# If a variable-glob (e.g., *cgi_input)
# is the first parameter to
# ReadParse,
# information is stored there,
# rather than in $in, @in, and %in.
# Second, third, and fourth
# parameters fill associative arrays
# analogous to %in with data relevant to file uploads.


# If no method is given, the script
# will process both command-line arguments
# of the form: name=value and any text that is in
# $ENV{'QUERY_STRING'}
# This is intended to aid debugging
# and may be changed in future releases
```

By default, the ReadParse function generates four associative arrays. The first array, %in, contains a list of the form variables as keys in the associative array and their values. If another associative array is passed by reference, ReadParse will use this new array to store the form values. For example, many scripts in this book use %form_data instead of the default % in to store HTML form input.

The three other associative arrays that ReadParse uses as parameters have been added to deal with file upload. %incfn associates the client's filename with the form variable name. This value may not be provided by the browser. %inct is the content type of the file associated with the form variable name. This value also may not always be provided by the Web browser when uploading a file. It is important to note that because we are not guaranteed to get a filename from the browser, we must generate our own filename. This server-generated filename is stored in the %insfn associative array. Normal POST and GET mothods using the URL-encoding mechanism only assign form variables using the % in associate array.

```
sub ReadParse {
  local (*in) = shift if @_;      # CGI input
  local (*incfn,
          # Client's filename (may not be provided)
      *inct,
          # Client's content-type (may not be provided)
      *insfn) = @_;
          # Server's filename (for spooled files)
  local ($len, $type, $meth, $errflag, $cmdflag, $perlwarn);
```

Perl warnings are disabled in various places throughout the code, because environment variables are checked throughout the code. If we are using the Perl -w (warn) flag to execute the program at the command line, the environment variables will typically not be set to the values they would have when the program is run from the Web server. $^W is a special Perl variable that indicates the current warning level checker. $^W is set to 0 to clear it. The $perlwarn variable is used as a placeholder to set it back to $^W.

```
# Disable warnings as this code
# deliberately uses local and environment
# variables which are preset to
# undef (i.e., not explicitly initialized)
$perlwarn = $^W;
$^W = 0;
```

The following code takes some of the environment variables that we will be looking at and converts them to regular Perl variables:

```
# Get several useful env variables
$type = $ENV{'CONTENT_TYPE'};
$len  = $ENV{'CONTENT_LENGTH'};
$meth = $ENV{'REQUEST_METHOD'};
```

If we exceed the maximum amount of data that we are allowed to receive, then CGI-LIB will exit with an error printed to the Web browser as HTML code as well as to the STDERR error log.

```
if ($len > $cgi_lib'maxdata) { #'
    &CgiDie("cgi-lib.pl: Request to receive too much data: $len bytes\n");
}
```

If the method is GET, we know that the form variables are encoded as type `application/x-www-form-urlencoded`. Basically, this format is the same form that you see when you are calling a CGI script with variables on the URL line. For example, setting the form variable `test` equal to `test 1` and `testagain` to `test 2` would be encoded as `test=test+1&testagain=test+2`. If the method is POST, we do not necessarily know whether the POSTed data will be in the urlencoded format or the multipart/form-data format, so the last part of the following `if` statement checks whether the content type is equal to `application/x-www-form-urlencoded`.

```
if (!defined $meth || $meth eq '' || $meth eq 'GET' ||
   $type eq 'application/x-www-form-urlencoded') {
local ($key, $val, $i);
```

Because the content is in the `urlencoded` format, we read the form variables in the `urlencoded` format. If there is a QUERY_STRING environmental variable but no GET method, we can assume that the extra information in the URL is part of command-line parameters to the CGI program. Thus, `$cmdflag` is set to 1.

If the method is GET, the QUERY_STRING value is assumed to be the form variables themselves. If the method is POST, then STDIN is read into `$in` for the length of the CONTENT_LENGTH environmental variable. If none of these conditions is satisfied, CGI-LIB dies with an error.

```
# Read in text
if (!defined $meth || $meth eq '') {
  $in = $ENV{'QUERY_STRING'};
  $cmdflag = 1;  # also use command-line options
} elsif($meth eq 'GET' || $meth eq 'HEAD') {
  $in = $ENV{'QUERY_STRING'};
} elsif ($meth eq 'POST') {
    $errflag = (read(STDIN, $in, $len) != $len);
} else {
  &CgiDie("cgi-lib.pl: Unknown request method: $meth\n");
}
```

The following code splits the form variables in the urlencoded format by separating the fields on the basis of an `&` or `;` character:

```
@in = split(/[&;]/,$in);
push(@in, @ARGV) if $cmdflag;
          # add command-line parameters
```

Certain characters cannot be represented directly in the urlencoded format. Spaces are represented as either %20 or + symbols. The following routine first takes the +s and converts them to spaces. Then it splits the key and value pairs on the basis of the = character. The last parameter of the split statement ends the split after there are two distinct values. After all, it is possible that the value of a variable contains an = character.

```
foreach $i (0 .. $#in) {
  # Convert plus to space
  $in[$i] =~ s/\+/ /g;

  # Split into key and value.
  ($key, $val) = split(/=/,$in[$i],2);
      # splits on the first =.
```

The following code takes the %XX hexadecimal codes and converts them to ASCII. The regular expression %([A-Fa-f0-9]{2}) matches on anything that starts with % and is followed by a hexadecimal digit (0 through F). The {2} in the expression tells the expression to search for only two hexadecimal digits. The parentheses surrounding the hex digits make it so that the variable $1 in Perl will be automatically set equal to the found digits. The second part of the substitute expression takes the $1 variable and converts it to an ASCII character using the pack("c", hex($1)) command.

```
# Convert %XX from hex numbers to alphanumeric
$key =~ s/%([A-Fa-f0-9]{2})/pack("c",hex($1))/ge;
$val =~ s/%([A-Fa-f0-9]{2})/pack("c",hex($1))/ge;
```

Finally, if there is more than one value for the key, then the values become separated by the \0 character. Then the key is set equal to the whole value in the associative array.

```
# Associate key and value
$in{$key} .= "\0" if (defined($in{$key}));
```

```
            # \0 is the multiple separator
    $in{$key} .= $val;
  }
```

The following routine processes multipart/form-data if the encoding type was sent that way. Parsing multipart/form-data is much more complicated than parsing application/x-www-urlencoded data, because it involves parsing the input buffer for special boundary markers. When the encoding type is multipart, a boundary is specified that separates each part of the form input. An arbitrary boundary marker is selected and used throughout the document. The boundary variable is preceded by two dashes (–) before each boundary specifier. The final boundary marker is also followed by two dashes. Thus, if the boundary marker is TEST, then the following is an example of boundary code:

```
--TEST
(Some Form Data)
--TEST
(More Data)
--TEST
(The last piece of data)
--TEST--
```

The following routines also check to see whether the data being sent is a filename for uploading. If it is, then the file is parsed as multipart data and written to disk.

```
  } elsif ($ENV{'CONTENT_TYPE'} =~ m#^multipart/form-data#) {
    # for efficiency, compile
    # multipart code only if needed
$errflag = !(eval <<'END_MULTIPART');

    local ($buf, $boundary, $head, @heads, $cd, $ct, $fname, $ctype, $blen);
    local ($bpos, $lpos, $left, $amt, $fn, $ser);
    local ($bufsize, $maxbound, $writefiles) =
      ($cgi_lib'bufsize, $cgi_lib'maxbound, $cgi_lib'writefiles);

    # The following lines exist solely
    # to eliminate spurious warning messages
    $buf = '';
```

The following piece of code parses the multipart header to find out what the boundary is. The boundary is designated with a boundary=[boundary] message, where [boundary] is an arbitrary choice of the Web browser. If the boundary does not exist, the program dies.

```
($boundary) = $type =~ /boundary="([^"]+)"/; #";
        # find boundary
($boundary) = $type =~ /boundary=(\S+)/
  unless $boundary;
&CgiDie ("Boundary not provided") unless $boundary;
$boundary =  "--" . $boundary;
$blen = length ($boundary);
```

The request method must be POST in order for multipart data to be read.

```
if ($ENV{'REQUEST_METHOD'} ne 'POST') {
   &CgiDie("Invalid request method for  multipart/form-data:
$meth\n");
   }
```

$writefiles must be set to something for there to be a valid directory to write files to. If a valid directory exists, it is checked to see whether it is a directory, is readable, and is writable. If all these conditions are true, $writefiles prefixes the writefiles area with the filename prefix for the files that will be written to the Web server if any files are being uploaded.

```
if ($writefiles) {
  local($me);
  stat ($writefiles);
  $writefiles = "/tmp"
    unless  -d _ && -r _ && -w _;
  # ($me) = $0 =~ m#([^/]*)$#;
  $writefiles .= "/$cgi_lib'filepre";
}
```

The following huge block of code parses out the boundaries and the form variables in the boundary. For our purposes, this code will be called only if we are processing a form that uses the new file upload function. If there are form variables between the boundaries, the form variables get processed as usual. If there is a file, then the file gets processed block by block; the default size of each block is 8192 bytes. Most of the code is meant for processing out the filename as well as creating the new server filename in the $writefiles directory.

```
# read in the data and split into parts:
# put headers in @in and data in %in
# General algorithm:
#    There are two dividers:
#    the border and the '\r\n\r\n'
#    between header and body.
#    Iterate between searching for these
#    Retain a buffer of size(bufsize+maxbound);
#    the latter part is to ensure that dividers
#    don't get lost by wrapping between two bufs
#    Look for a divider in the current batch.
#    If not found, then save all of bufsize, move
#    the maxbound extra buffer to the front of
#    the buffer, and read in a new bufsize bytes.
#    If a divider is found, save everything up to
#    the divider.  Then empty the buffer of
#    everything up to the end of the divider.
#    Refill buffer to bufsize+maxbound
#    Note slightly odd organization.  Code before
#    BODY: really goes with code following HEAD:,
#    but is put first to 'pre-fill' buffers.  BODY:
#    is placed before HEAD: because we first need to
#    discard any 'preface,' which would be analogous
#    to a body without a preceding head.

    $left = $len;
   PART:
# find each part of the multi-part while reading data
   while (1) {
      last PART if $errflag;

      $amt = ($left > $bufsize+$maxbound-length($buf)
           ?  $bufsize+$maxbound-length($buf): $left);
      $errflag = (read(STDIN, $buf, $amt, length($buf)) != $amt);
      $left -= $amt;

      $in{$name} .= "\0" if defined $in{$name};
      $in{$name} .= $fn if $fn;
```

```
       $name=~/([-\w]+)/;
    # This allows $insfn{$name} to be untainted
       if (defined $1) {
          $insfn{$1} .= "\0" if defined $insfn{$1};
          $insfn{$1} .= $fn if $fn;
       }


    BODY:
     while (($bpos = index($buf, $boundary)) == -1) {
        if ($name) {
    # if no $name, then it's the prologue -- discard
          if ($fn) { print FILE substr($buf, 0, $bufsize); }
          else     { $in{$name} .= substr($buf, 0, $bufsize); }
        }
        $buf = substr($buf, $bufsize);
        $amt = ($left > $bufsize ? $bufsize : $left);
#$maxbound==length($buf);
        $errflag = (read(STDIN, $buf, $amt, $maxbound) != $amt);
        $left -= $amt;
     }
     if (defined $name) {
    # if no $name, then it's the prologue -- discard
        if ($fn) { print FILE substr($buf, 0, $bpos-2); }
        else { $in {$name} .= substr($buf, 0, $bpos-2); }
    # kill last \r\n
     }
     close (FILE);
     last PART
        if substr($buf, $bpos + $blen, 4) eq "--\r\n";
     substr($buf, 0, $bpos+$blen+2) = '';
     $amt = ($left > $bufsize+$maxbound-length($buf)
           ? $bufsize+$maxbound-length($buf) : $left);
     $errflag = (read(STDIN, $buf, $amt, length($buf)) != $amt);
     $left -= $amt;


     undef $head;  undef $fn;
    HEAD:
     while (($lpos = index($buf, "\r\n\r\n")) == -1) {
       $head .= substr($buf, 0, $bufsize);
       $buf = substr($buf, $bufsize);
       $amt = ($left > $bufsize ? $bufsize : $left);
#$maxbound==length($buf);
        $errflag = (read(STDIN, $buf, $amt, $maxbound) != $amt);
        $left -= $amt;
     }
     $head .= substr($buf, 0, $lpos+2);
     push (@in, $head);
     @heads = split("\r\n", $head);
```

```
      ($cd) = grep (/^\s*Content-Disposition:/i, @heads);
      ($ct) = grep (/^\s*Content-Type:/i, @heads);


      ($name) = $cd =~ /\bname="([^"]+)"/i; #";
      ($name) = $cd =~ /\bname=([^\s:;]+)/i unless defined $name;


      ($fname) = $cd =~ /\bfilename="([^"]*)"/i; #";
            # filename can be null-str
      ($fname) = $cd =~ /\bfilename=([^\s:;]+)/i unless defined
$fname;
      $incfn{$name} .= (defined $in{$name} ? "\0" : "") . $fname;


      ($ctype) = $ct =~ /^\s*Content-type:\s*"([^"]+)"/i;  #";
      ($ctype) = $ct =~ /^\s*Content-Type:\s*([^\s:;]+)/i unless
defined $ctype;
      $inct{$name} .= (defined $in{$name} ? "\0" : "") . $ctype;


      if ($writefiles && defined $fname) {
         $ser++;
      $fn = $writefiles . ".$$.$ser";
      open (FILE, ">$fn") || &CgiDie("Couldn't open $fn\n");
       }
      substr($buf, 0, $lpos+4) = '';
      undef $fname;
      undef $ctype;
    }


1;
END_MULTIPART
```

If none of the preceding conditions was satisfied, then the program dies
because there was a problem with figuring out the context in which this
CGI program was called.

```
  &CgiDie($@) if $errflag;
  } else {
    &CgiDie("cgi-lib.pl: Unknown Content-type:
$ENV{'CONTENT_TYPE'}\n");
  }
```

If everything was successful the lilbrary code ends up at the end of the
ReadParse routine. As part of the cleanup, the Perl $^W warn variable is set
to whatever value it was when this routine was entered. Finally, if every-

thing went OK, the number of elements in the `@in` array is returned. If everything was not OK, `undef` is returned.

```
$^W = $perlwarn;

return ($errflag ? undef :  scalar(@in));
}
```

PrintHeader Subroutine

The following code block is a simple routine that prints the "Content-type: text/html\n\n" header that all CGI programs must output before they start printing HTML code.

```
# PrintHeader
# Returns the magic line which tells WWW
# that we're an HTML document

sub PrintHeader {
   return "Content-type: text/html\n\n";
}
```

HtmlTop Subroutine

The `HtmlTop` subroutine is useful for quickly generating an HTML header and returning it in a scalar string variable for printing. The routine expects a string to be passed to it in order to generate the `<TITLE>` tags for the HTML header as well as the `<H1>` tags for the header. We typically do not use this routine—our `<H1>` tags tend to be different from our `<TITLE>` tags—but it is helpful for quickly generating an HTML header when we're testing and creating the CGI script initially. Note that the Perl HERE document method is used to block the HTML text between the END_OF_TEXT tags in the following code:

```
# HtmlTop
# Returns the <head> of a document
# and the beginning of the body
```

```
# with the title and a body <h1>
# header as specified by the parameter

sub HtmlTop
{
  local ($title) = @_;

  return <<END_OF_TEXT;
<html>
<head>
<title>$title</title>
</head>
<body>
<h1>$title</h1>
END_OF_TEXT
}
```

HtmlBot subroutine

HtmlBot returns the footer of the HTML document, which typically contains the closure for the <BODY> tag and the <HTML> tags.

```
# HtmlBot
# Returns the </body>, </html> codes
# for the bottom of every HTML page

sub HtmlBot
{
  return "</body>\n</html>\n";
}
```

SplitParam Subroutine

Some form variables can have multiple values returned for the same key name. When there are multiple values for a single key in the associative array returned by ReadParse, the values are separated by the \0 character. The SplitParam function takes the value and splits it, using the \0 character, into an array of all the values. This array is then returned as the value of the function. The wantarray function in Perl lets the function return an array if the function is called in the context of returning an array, or return just the first element of the array if the function is called in the context of returning a scalar. For example, $test = &SplitParam($test-values) would return the first element in $test2, and @test = &SplitParam($testvalues) would return the whole array of values.

```
# SplitParam
# Splits a multi-valued parameter
# into a list of the constituent parameters

sub SplitParam
{
  local ($param) = @_;
  local (@params) = split ("\0", $param);
  return (wantarray ? @params : $params[0]);
}
```

MethGet and MethPost Subroutines

The MethGet and MethPost subroutines return True or False depending on whether the CGI method currently being called by the browser is GET or POST. If the environment variable REQUEST_METHOD is GET, MethGet returns True and MethPost returns False. If the environment variable REQUEST_METHOD is POST, MethPost returns True and MethGet returns False. The environment variable is first checked to see whether it is defined. Because the && (AND) operator is used, if the defined function returns False, the rest of the statement after the && never gets processed and False is returned to the function for the whole statement. In Perl, the && can be thought of as a short-circuit operator. If the first value is False, the second value after the && doesn't matter, because the whole statement will evaluate to False anyway. Thus, if the first value is False, Perl will "short-circuit" the statement and avoid evaluating the second part, because it will make no difference to the outcome.

```
# MethGet
# Return true if this cgi call was
# using the GET request, false otherwise

sub MethGet {
  return (defined $ENV{'REQUEST_METHOD'} && $ENV{'REQUEST_METHOD'} eq
```

```
"GET");
}

# MethPost
# Return true if this cgi call was
# using the POST request, false otherwise

sub MethPost {
    return (defined $ENV{'REQUEST_METHOD'} && $ENV{'REQUEST_METHOD'} eq
"POST");
}
```

MyBaseUrl Subroutine

MyBaseUrl returns the URL that the browser used to call the script minus any command-line options such as PATH_INFO and QUERY_INFO variables. The Perl warning generator is turned off during the calculation.

```
# MyBaseUrl
# Returns the base URL to the script
# (i.e., no extra path or query string)
sub MyBaseUrl {
    local ($ret, $perlwarn);
    $perlwarn = $^W; $^W = 0;
    $ret = 'http://' . $ENV{'SERVER_NAME'} .
           ($ENV{'SERVER_PORT'} != 80 ? ":$ENV{'SERVER_PORT'}" : '') .
           $ENV{'SCRIPT_NAME'};
    $^W = $perlwarn;
    return $ret;
}
```

MyFullUrl Subroutine

MyFullUrl returns the same thing as MyBaseUrl except that it also returns the extra path information or query information if available. It also turns off Perl warnings for the duration of the calculation.

```
# MyFullUrl
# Returns the full URL to the script
# (i.e., with extra path or query string)
```

```
sub MyFullUrl {
  local ($ret, $perlwarn);
  $perlwarn = $^W; $^W = 0;
  $ret = 'http://' . $ENV{'SERVER_NAME'} .
      ($ENV{'SERVER_PORT'} != 80 ? ":$ENV{'SERVER_PORT'}" : '') .
      $ENV{'SCRIPT_NAME'} . $ENV{'PATH_INFO'} .
      (length ($ENV{'QUERY_STRING'}) ? "?$ENV{'QUERY_STRING'}" : '');
  $^W = $perlwarn;
  return $ret;
}
```

My URL Subroutine

It is recommended that you not use MyURL in your programs, because it is now superseded by the preceding two routines. You will notice that the MyURL function simply calls MyBaseUrl.

```
# MyURL
# Returns the base URL to the script
# (i.e., no extra path or query string)
# This is obsolete and will be
# removed in later versions
sub MyURL  {
  return &MyBaseUrl;
}
```

CgiError Subroutine

CgiError takes a list of error messages and prints a buffer of HTML code that would display the messages one after the other. If no message is given, an error message indicates that a problem occurred in the full URL. If $header_out is 0, then the "Content-type: text/html\n\n" header is printed. The first message in the list is printed as the title and header of the HTML code. All subsequent messages are printed as a list of messages below the header of the HTML code.

```
# CgiError
# Prints out an error message which
# contains appropriate headers,
# markup, et cetera.
```

```
# Parameters:
#  If no parameters, gives a generic error message
#  Otherwise, the first parameter will be the
#  title and the rest will be given as different
#  paragraphs of the body

sub CgiError {
  local (@msg) = @_;
  local ($i,$name);

  if (!@msg) {
    $name = &MyFullUrl;
    @msg = ("Error: script $name encountered fatal error\n");
  };

  if (!$cgi_lib'headerout) { #')
    print &PrintHeader;
    print "<html>\n<head>\n<title>$msg[0]</title>\n</head>\n<body>\n";
  }
  print "<h1>$msg[0]</h1>\n";
  foreach $i (1 .. $#msg) {
    print "<p>$msg[$i]</p>\n";
  }

  $cgi_lib'headerout++;
}
```

CgiDie Subroutine

CgiDie calls CgiError and then calls the Perl DIE routine so that the error can be printed to STDERR and the program exits.

```
# CgiDie
# Identical to CgiError, but also
# quits with the passed error message.

sub CgiDie {
  local (@msg) = @_;
  &CgiError (@msg);
  die @msg;
}
```

PrintVariables Subroutine

The `PrintVariables` subroutine takes an associative array and returns a buffer of nicely formatted HTML output. An interesting technique for passing parameters is used here. Normally, `@_` is the array or list of parameters. When `@_` is referred to in a numerical expression, its length is returned. If the length of the parameters is 1, we assume that a reference to the associative array was passed. If the length is greater than 1, we assume that the associative array was passed by value. Notice that the values are set differently in the following code for in if it is passed by reference or by value. Except for that, the program uses the standard Perl FOREACH statement to walk through the keys of the associative array and parse the value for each key.

```
# PrintVariables
# Nicely formats variables.  Three calling options:
# A non-null associative array - prints the
#   items in that array
# A type-glob - prints the items in the
#   associated assoc array
# nothing - defaults to use %in
# Typical use: &PrintVariables()

sub PrintVariables {
  local (*in) = @_ if @_ == 1;
  local (%in) = @_ if @_ > 1;
  local ($out, $key, $output);

  $output =  "\n<dl compact>\n";
  foreach $key (sort keys(%in)) {
    foreach (split("\0", $in{$key})) {
      ($out = $_) =~ s/\n/<br>\n/g;
      $output .=  "<dt><b>$key</b>\n <dd>:<i>$out</i>:<br>\n";
    }
  }
  $output .=  "</dl>\n";

  return $output;
}
```

PrintEnv Subroutine

`PrintEnv` calls the `PrintVariables` routine and passes the environment associative array by reference.

```
# PrintEnv
# Nicely formats all environment
# variables and returns HTML string
sub PrintEnv {
  &PrintVariables(*ENV);
}
```

End of the Main Script

The following code block sets a couple of variables equal to themselves in order to avoid a warning message about not using the variables. We know that these variables are used in the preceding subroutines, so we do not want a warning message to print if we run the program with the warn parameter turned on. Finally, as with all libraries, the last line is 1; in order to return a TRUE value to the REQUIRE subroutine.

```
# The following lines exist
# only to avoid warning messages
$cgi_lib'writefiles =  $cgi_lib'writefiles;
$cgi_lib'bufsize    =  $cgi_lib'bufsize ;
$cgi_lib'maxbound   =  $cgi_lib'maxbound;
$cgi_lib'version    =  $cgi_lib'version;

1; #return true
```

CHAPTER 6

Using DATE.PL

OVERVIEW

Although PERL has many built-in routines to do a fantastic job of parsing files and manipulating strings, it does not excel in the area of performing functions on dates. This chapter will add the **DATE.PL** library to our programming arsenal. **DATE.PL** was originally written by Gary Puckering.

DATE.PL works by converting dates to and from Julian dates. The Julian date system basically converts dates to a single whole integer. This is important because it allows us to easily calculate how many days exist between two calendar dates without worrying about such things as leap years and how many days are in each month; **DATE.PL** takes care of all that for you.

Chapter 13 uses this library to perform feats of date arithmetic without resorting to calling an operating system–specific function such as the date or cal command on UNIX. Although date and cal can return some useful information, a good CGI programmer should stay away from using operating system specific calls since it lessens the portability of the application to other platforms.

The **DATE.PL** library contains main functions to convert a Julian date to a month, day, year, and weekday and to do the reverse. In addition, DATE.PL has several functions that allow you to convert month names to month numbers, month numbers to month names, and weekday numbers to weekday names. Other functions get the Julian date for today, tomorrow, and yesterday.

INSTALLATION AND USAGE

Converting Julian Dates

The `jday` function takes a month, day, and year as parameters and returns a single integer that is a Julian date. Similarly, the `jdate` function returns the month, day, year, and weekday based on a Julian date passed to it as a parameter. Simple Perl code appears below, which uses these functions. The first line gets the Julian date of "12/1/95." The second line gets the correct date parameters (month, day, year, weekday) from the "1000" Julian date.

```
$juliandate=& jday (12,1,95)'
($month, $day, $yearn $weedat)=& jdate(1000);
```

Converting Month Numbers

The `monthname` function uses a month number parameter and returns a descriptive name of the month. The `monthnum` function takes three or more letters of the month name and returns the corresponding month number. For example, January is month number 1. The following code would print 1 : January. Note that the numbers passed to the monthname function do not have to be in any special format. You can pass "01," "1," or even "1.0" and monthname will return "January" for all of them.

```
print &monthnum("JAN") . ":" . &monthname(1);
```

Converting Weekday Numbers

The weekday function takes a weekday number, where 0 is Sunday, and returns an abbreviated weekday name. For example, if $number equals 2, the following code would produce Tue as the output: Just like month-name, the weekday routine accepts any whole integer as a parameter regardless of how it is formatted.

```
print &weekday($number);
```

Obtaining the Julian Date for Yesterday, Today, and Tomorrow

The today, yesterday, and tomorrow functions return the Julian dates for, respectively, today, yesterday, and tomorrow.

DESIGN DISCUSSION

Main Script

The first line of the **DATE.PL** library defines the whole file as part of a package called date. Normally, when a variable is declared outside a function, it is declared as global and so it affects all other functions in the currently running Perl program. Using a package allows declaration of variables that have a scope only within the package but yet are relevant outside the scope of the individual functions of the package. After this, a base Julian date number is assigned to $brit_jd for use in the following algorithms:

```
package date;

# The following defines the first
# day that the Gregorian calendar was used
# in the British Empire (Sep 14, 1752).
# The previous day was Sep 2, 1752
```

```
# by the Julian calendar.  The year began
# at March 25th before this date.

$brit_jd = 2361222;
```

jdate Subroutine

The `jdate` function takes a Julian date and converts it back to a normal
month, day, year, and weekday number. The WARN command, used in the
following code to warn of a problem in the date range, acts just like DIE
in that the message it is passed prints to STDERR, but it does not exit the
program. The rest of the function uses a standard algorithm for converting the Julian date back into our normal date format information.

```
sub main'jdate
# Usage:  ($month,$day,$year,$weekday) = &jdate($julian_day)
{
    local($jd) = @_;
    local($jdate_tmp);
    local($m,$d,$y,$wkday);

    warn("warning:  pre-dates British use of Gregorian calendar\n")
        if ($jd < $brit_jd);

    # calculate weekday (0=Sun,6=Sat)
    $wkday = ($jd + 1) % 7;
    $jdate_tmp = $jd - 1721119;
    $y = int((4 * $jdate_tmp - 1)/146097);
    $jdate_tmp = 4 * $jdate_tmp - 1 - 146097 * $y;
    $d = int($jdate_tmp/4);
    $jdate_tmp = int((4 * $d + 3)/1461);
    $d = 4 * $d + 3 - 1461 * $jdate_tmp;
    $d = int(($d + 4)/4);
    $m = int((5 * $d - 3)/153);
    $d = 5 * $d - 3 - 153 * $m;
    $d = int(($d + 5) / 5);
    $y = 100 * $y + $jdate_tmp;
    if($m < 10) {
        $m += 3;
    } else {
        $m -= 9;
        ++$y;
```

```
    }
    ($m, $d, $y, $wkday);
}
```

jday Subroutine

The jday function converts a normal date to a numerical Julian date. Note that the year must be a four-digit year. The divisions by 4 on the year in the following code are based on the fact that every four years is a leap year. The WARN function is used here to indicate a potential problem with the Julian date. The rest of the program is the actual mathematical algorithm for converting to a Julian day.

```
sub main'jday
# Usage:   $julian_day = &jday($month,$day,$year)
{
    local($m,$d,$y) = @_;
    local($ya,$c);

    $y = (localtime(time))[5] + 1900  if ($y eq '');

    if ($m > 2) {
        $m -= 3;
    } else {
        $m += 9;
        -$y;
    }
    $c = int($y/100);
    $ya = $y - (100 * $c);
    $jd =  int((146097 * $c) / 4) +
           int((1461 * $ya) / 4) +
           int((153 * $m + 2) / 5) +
           $d + 1721119;
    warn("warning:  pre-dates British use of Gregorian calendar\n")
        if ($jd < $brit_jd);
    $jd;
}
```

is_jday Subroutine

The is_jday function returns true if the value passed to it is within a reasonable date range of what would be considered a Julian date:

```
sub main'is_jday
{
# Usage:  if (&is_jday($number)) { print "yep - looks like a jday"; }
    local($is_jday) = 0;
    $is_jday = 1 if ($_[0] > 1721119);
}
```

monthname Subroutine

The monthname function takes the month number and returns the month name. It does this by taking the month number and using it as an index to an array of month names. If a second parameter is also passed to the monthname function, the month name that is returned will be truncated to the number of characters specified by the second parameter.

Note that in the code below, the month number that is passed as a parameter has 1 subtracted from it when the routine references the @names array. This is done because although the month numbers go from 1 through 12, arrays in Perl start being indexed at element number 0. Thus, the numbers that reference the month names in the @names array must go from 0 through 11 instead of 1 through 12.

Similar logic is used by Perl to truncate the month name if the $m parameter is specified. Basically, the substr command is called with the following parameters: string to extract, offset in the string to start extracting, and the length of the extraction. The similarity to how arrays are handled above is contained in the fact that the offset index into the character string starts at 0 for the first character. Thus, the command substr($names[$n-1], 0, $m) returns the month name starting from character 0 (first character) as a length of $m characters.

```
sub main'monthnum

sub main'monthname
# Usage:   $month_name = &monthname($month_no)
{
    local($n,$m) = @_;
    local(@names) =
('January','February','March','April','May','June',

'July','August','September','October','November',
```

```
                               'December');
       if ($m ne '') {
           substr($names[$n-1],0,$m);
       } else {
           $names[$n-1];
       }
   }
```

monthnum subroutine

The monthnum function takes the month name and converts it to a month number. It does this by taking the month name, stripping it to the first three characters, and making it uppercase. This conversion makes it compatible with an associative array that has the three-character month names as keys to the month number values. The appropriate element in the associative array is then returned in response to the month name.

```
# Usage:   $month_number = &monthnum($month_name)
{
    local($name) = @_;
    local(%names) = (
    'JAN',1,'FEB',2,'MAR',3,'APR',4,'MAY',5,'JUN',6,
        'JUL',7,'AUG',8,
        'SEP',9,'OCT',10,'NOV',11,'DEC',12);
    $name =~ tr/a-z/A-Z/;
    $name = substr($name,0,3);
    $names{$name};
}
```

weekday Subroutine

The weekday function takes a weekday number and converts it to a three-character weekday abbreviation. The function works by taking the value and using it as an index to an array of weekday names:

```
sub main'weekday
# Usage:   $weekday_name = &weekday($weekday_number)
{
    local($wd) = @_;
    ("Sun","Mon","Tue","Wed","Thu","Fri","Sat")[$wd];
}
```

today Subroutine

The today function returns today's Julian date. First, it calls the localtime(time) Perl function in which the elements of the current time and date are broken up as an array. The date, month, and year are extracted from this function as $d, $m, and $y. The month is incremented by 1, because the localtime function returns months on a scale from 0 to 11 instead of 1 to 12. The year is incremented by 1900 to provide a four-digit year. Then the jday function is called to convert this number to today's Julian date:

```
sub main'today
# Usage:  $today_julian_day = &today()
{
     local(@today) = localtime(time);
     local($d) = $today[3];
     local($m) = $today[4];
     local($y) = $today[5];
     $m += 1;
     $y += 1900;
     &main'jday($m,$d,$y);
}
```

yesterday and tomorrow subroutines

The following functions—yesterday and tomorrow—operate by calling the today function and, respectively, subtracting 1 from or adding 1 to the returned Julian date:

```
sub main'yesterday
# Usage:  $yesterday_julian_day = &yesterday()
{
     &main'today() - 1;
}

sub main'tomorrow
# Usage:  $tomorrow_julian_day = &tomorrow()
{
     &main'today() + 1;
}
```

CHAPTER 7

E-Mailing with CGI

OVERVIEW

One of the most important tasks of any CGI program is ultimately to let someone know that something has happened. The most convenient way for users is to have this done automatically using E-mail. In this chapter we will examine two mechanisms for sending E-mail.

The first method uses **SENDMAIL-LIB.PL**, a library that was written to allow a programmer to use the sendmail program on UNIX to send E-mail easily. This is the most reliable and safest way to send E-mail using a CGI script on UNIX.

Unfortunately, using the sendmail program is a UNIX-specificoption. If you want your scripts to run on Windows NT or another non-UNIX platform, you will have to use another option, such as the Windows NT–specific BLAT routines. Another alternative is the **SMTPMAIL-LIB.PL** library, which sends mail on either Windows NT or UNIX. This library uses TCP/IP sockets to communicate directly with simple mail transfer protocol (SMTP) servers to send mail. We will explain the concepts of sockets and the SMTP protocol later in this chapter.

NOTE Internet mail is notoriously insecure. Internet mail is sent as "cleartext" over the Internet. In other words, the packets that make up an Internet mail letter can be seen by anyone who has physical access to the network and the proper tools much like a person with the appropriate radio frequency scanner can listen in on cellular phone calls.

For example, with the shopping cart application, E-mail is not the best mechanism to use for sending information over the Internet especially when dealing with credit cart numbers submitted with an order.

A more secure way to send e-mail is to make sure that the CGI program is sending it to an account on the same machine or local network that the E-mail address is on. That way, the Internet mail never actually has to be transferred outside of the confines of your servers. If you need a secure way of sending E-mail to the outside world, you should look at programs such as PGP (Pretty Good Privacy) to encrypt your e-mail before using this library.

INSTALLATION AND USAGE

Both **SENDMAIL-LIB.PL** and **SMTPMAIL-LIB.PL** are designed to be used in exactly the same way. You can `require` one of them in a program; then, if you change your mind about the method of E-mailing, you simply use the other library. To use either one, you copy the library of choice over the filename **mail-lib.pl**. All of our CGI programs that rely on E-mail `require` **mail-lib.pl** as a standard mailing file. By copying over the appropriate library, you are making a choice as to which method to use (see Figure 7.1).

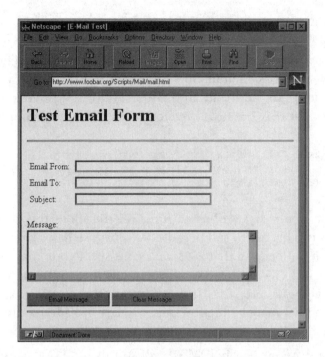

Figure 7.1 *Sample of using **MAIL-LIB.PL** in a CGI program.*

Sending Email

Both libraries have a `send_mail` function. Sending mail consists of passing the "From" E-mail address, the "To" E-mail address, the message subject, and the message body as parameters to the function. Here is an example of sending mail, with smith@zzz.org sending E-mail to jones@yyy.com:

```
&send_mail("smith\@zzz.org", "jones\@yyy.org",
  "Subject", "This is the message\nto send.\n\n");
```

Note that we escaped the @ symbol with a backslash. This arrangement is necessary for the code to operate correctly in Perl version 5, which requires that @ symbols be escaped.

Sending Email with More Options

There is also a `real_send_mail` function in each library. This function accepts the same basic parameters as `send_mail` except that it breaks up the "From" and "To" addresses into E-mail address, hostname pairs. Here is the equivalent `real_send_mail` version of the previous example:

```
&real_send_mail("smith\@zzz.org", "zzz.org",
  "jones\@yyy.org", "yyy.org", "Subject",
  "This is the message\nto send.\n\n");
```

It may seem weird that we have a function that does the same thing as `send_mail` but is harder to call because we must use more parameters. It is important to understand that `send_mail` consists of code that breaks apart the "From" and "To" addresses and separates them into parameters that it uses to call `real_send_mail`. In both libraries, the `real_send_mail` function is the actual mailer function. `Send_mail` is provided as an easier way to send the E-mail.

If you are using the SENDMAIL version of the library, you probably won't need to call `real_send_mail` directly. However, if you are using the SMTPMAIL version, you may need to use `real_send_mail`, because some servers use surrogate hosts to handle their E-mail. When you send mail to an address such as yyy.org, it is quite possible that yyy.org does not handle its own E-mail; instead it may use another host, such as mail.yyy.org to handle E-mail destined for yyy.org. The Internet tries to handle this by setting up MX (mail exchanger) records as part of the domain name resolution protocol. A host such as yyy.org would have an MX record set aside to tell the name lookup routine to return mail.yyy.org as the actual host to mail to. The UNIX sendmail program handles this problem automatically and resolves MX records transparently to the user. Unfortunately, because the SMTP version of the mail library communicates directly between SMTP mail hosts, it does not go through the MX record resolution.

When to Use the SMTP-MAIL.PL Library

Why would we want to use the SMTP library? It may sound as if the SMTP library is not very useful, but there are several cases in which you may still want to use it. For one thing, the SENDMAIL library operates only on UNIX. The SMTP library can be used on Windows NT and any other platform that supports sockets programming in Perl. Also, SENDMAIL cannot change the true From: address of the E-mail message. Because the SMTP library communicates using sockets, it can fool an SMTP server into thinking you are any user on that system; sometimes it is nice not to have mail being sent as wwwadmin or "nobody" to your users. Finally, we can get around the MX problem by calling the `real_send_mail` function, and, in place of the hostname to send mail to, we use the MX hostname if you happen to know it. Using the example where mail.yyy.org handles the E-mail for yyy.org, we could send mail using the following snippet of code:

```
&real_send_mail("smith\@zzz.org", "zzz.org",
"jones\@yyy.org", "mail.yyy.org", "Subject",
"This is the message\nto send.\n\n");
```

In addition, **SMTPMAIL-LIB.PL** has a global operating system variable called `$smtp_os`. By default, this variable is set to "UNIX." If you are using an NT server version of Perl that does not support the `SELECT()` command, you need to set this variable equal to "NT." In addition, if you are using a version of Perl that does not support the sockets package (**Socket.pm**), remove the line in the program that says `use Socket` and replace the `$AF_INET` and `$SOCK_STREAM` variable assignment values with 2 and 1, respectively. On some systems, these values may be different. For example, on Solaris UNIX, `$SOCK_STREAM` should be set to 2.

For the most part, you will probably want to use sendmail; it's reliable and well tested and handles many things, such as MX record resolution, transparently. However, if you need to do something that only the SMTP version of the library can handle, you always have the option of using it by copying it over the **mail-lib.pl** library program and calling the same routines you would if you had used the sendmail version.

DESIGN DISCUSSION

SENDMAIL-LIB.PL

SENDMAIL-LIB operates by using the sendmail program on UNIX to send the E-mail. Why do we use sendmail instead of some other UNIX program such as mail? The reason lies with security. Because a lot of mail that gets sent via a CGI script is sent to an address that was entered into an HTML form, it is at best precarious to pass user input as a command-line parameter to a program such as the UNIX mail program. However, the UNIX sendmail program allows us to pass the From:, To:, Subject:, and message body text as part of the STDIN input stream of the program when opened using the -t command-line parameter. In that way, no user form input actually gets passed as a command-line parameter to the UNIX-based Web server. In addition to using the -t flag, we call sendmail using the -n flag. This tells the sendmail program not to use the alias list of the server. Most servers consider the alias list to be somewhat protected information. The $mail_program variable is set to the path of the sendmail program plus the command-line parameters. If, for some reason, you wish the alias list to be used, you can take out the -n parameter.

```
$mail_program = "/usr/lib/sendmail -t -n";
```

REAL_SEND_MAIL SUBROUTINE

The real_send_mail performs the sending process. The send_mail subroutine described later in this chapter calls real_send_mail after parsing its own input parameters.

Real_send_mail accepts as parameters the "From" E-mail address and SMTP server hostname, the "To" address and SMTP server hostname, and the subject and message body. Some of these parameters may not be used within the `real_send_mail` function in this library, but we keep the parameters to maintain compatibility with the SMTP version.

```
sub real_send_mail {
    local($fromuser, $fromsmtp, $touser, $tosmtp,
        $subject, $messagebody) = @_;
```

First, we need to start the mail program and open a `pipe` to the program so that anything we print to the file handle, MAIL, gets output to the running program.

```
    open (MAIL, "|$mail_program") ||
    &web_error("Could Not Open Mail Program");
```

The rest of the function is relatively easy. Merely print the header information to the `$mail_program` that is currently running and then close the file handle to the program. Closing the file handle triggers the sendmail program on UNIX to send the mail. We use the HERE document method to print the message to the sendmail program between the __END_OF_MAIL__ tags.

```
print MAIL <<__END_OF_MAIL__;
To: $touser
From: $fromuser
Subject: $subject

$messagebody

__END_OF_MAIL__

    close (MAIL);

} #end of real_send_mail
```

SEND_MAIL SUBROUTINE

The `send_mail` function as parameters uses the "From" and "To" address as well as the subject and message body. It takes the "From" and "To" addresses and splits them up into E-mail address, hostname pairs, which are sent to `real_send_mail`, the routine that actually does the work of sending the E-mail.

```
sub send_mail {
    local($from, $to, $subject, $messagebody) = @_;
    local($fromuser, $fromsmtp, $touser, $tosmtp);
```

$fromuser and $touser are equal to the actual E-mail addresses that were passed before.

```
    $fromuser = $from;
    $touser = $to;
```

Split is used to break the address into user and hostname pairs. The hostname is the second element of the split array, so we reference the hostname with a 1 (arrays start at 0). We can do this because the output of the split command is an array; we reference the output of split as if it were elements of an array.

```
    $fromsmtp = (split(/\@/,$from))[1];
    $tosmtp = (split(/\@/,$to))[1];
```

Finally, we call the real_send_mail subroutine.

```
&real_send_mail($fromuser, $fromsmtp, $touser,
        $tosmtp, $subject, $messagebody);

} # End of send_mail
```

web_error Subroutine

web_error is a subroutine whose purpose is to print errors as HTML before exiting the program. Most Perl programs use the DIE subroutine to exit the program prematurely. Unfortunately, using DIE typically does not print any useful information to the user attempting to set up the script. Thus, we use web_error to print the message as HTML and then call DIE. The DIE subroutine in Perl is still useful for a Web server, because the message given by DIE is generally printed to the Web server's error log.

```
sub web_error {
    local ($error) = @_;
    $error = "Error Occured: $error";
```

```
    print "$error<p>\n";

# Die exits the program prematurely and
# prints an error to stderr

    die $error;

} # end of web_error
```

SMTPMAIL-LIB.PL

SMTPMAIL-LIB.PL works basically the same as **SENDMAIL-LIB.PL** except that the SMTP version communicates directly to mail servers to send mail from one person to another instead of using a prepackaged program such as the UNIX sendmail program. In this section, we will describe the socket-specific functions in detail and go over the other functions briefly, because they have same explanation as those in the **SENDMAIL-LIB.PL** library.

SMTPMAIL-LIB does all its work by using sockets programming. Basically, sockets can be thought of as synonymous with Telnet, except that instead of using Telnet to connect to a UNIX server and run programs, you are using Telnet to connect to a service such as an E-mail service (SMTP, POP) or an HTML service (HTTP). Whenever an E-mail package sends E-mail over the Internet, it ultimately connects to a mail server. In other words, it plugs itself into the mail server's "socket." SMTPMAIL-LIB operates by connecting to a mail server, sending the SMTP mail information, and then disconnecting from the mail server.

By default, we use the **Socket.pm** package in Perl 5. If you are not using Perl 5 or lack the **Socket.pm** file, you can delete this line and set the $AF_INET and $SOCK_STREAM variables manually in the Perl program according to the instructions in the usage section of this chapter. $http_os should be set to "NT" if you are using a Windows NT version of Perl. $http_os is set to "UNIX" by default.

REAL_SEND_MAIL SUBROUTINE

The real_send_mail function in SMTPMAIL-LIB has the same parameters as the real_send_mail in SENDMAIL-LIB. However, the real_send_mail function in SMTPMAIL-LIB operates by opening a socket connection to an SMTP server.

101

```
sub real_send_mail {
    local($fromuser, $fromsmtp, $touser, $tosmtp,
        $subject, $messagebody) = @_;
    local($ipaddress, $fullipaddress, $packconnectip);
    local($packthishostip);
    local($AF_INET, $SOCK_STREAM, $SOCK_ADDR);
    local($PROTOCOL, $SMTP_PORT);
    local($buf);
# We start off by making the message that will be sent
# By combining the subject with the message body text
#
    $messagebody = "Subject: $subject\n\n" . $messagebody;
```

The following variables are set using values defined in the **Socket.pm**
library. If your version of Perl does not have the sockets library, you can
substitute default values, such as 2 for AF_INIT and 1 for SOCK_STREAM. If 1
does not work for SOCK_STREAM, try using 2. $SOCK_ADDR is a special variable
that holds the IP address, port, and other relevant socket information.

```
    $AF_INET = AF_INET;
    $SOCK_STREAM = SOCK_STREAM;


    $SOCK_ADDR = "S n a4 x8";


# The following routines get the protocol information

    $PROTOCOL = (getprotobyname('tcp'))[2];
    $SMTP_PORT = (getservbyname('smtp','tcp'))[2];


    $SMTP_PORT = 25 unless ($SMTP_PORT =~ /^\d+$/);
    $PROTOCOL = 6 unless ($PROTOCOL =~ /^\d+$/);
```

We call the gethostbyname function to convert the hostname we are connecting to into a real IP address. $fullipaddress is the ASCII equivalent of
the IP address delimited with periods. We calculate this in case we want to
troubleshoot whether the hostname lookup actually worked. $packconnec-
tip is the host to connect to, given in the special $SOCK_ADDR format. $pack-
thishostip is also in the $SOCK_ADDR format and designates this local host.

```
    $ipaddress = (gethostbyname($tosmtp))[4];


    $fullipaddress
```

```
        = join (".", unpack("C4", $ipaddress));

    $packconnectip = pack($SOCK_ADDR, $AF_INET,
            $SMTP_PORT, $ipaddress);
    $packthishostip = pack($SOCK_ADDR,
            $AF_INET, 0, "\0\0\0\0");
```

The socket first needs to be created. Creating the socket is very much like opening a filename for writing except that it accepts information about the protocol it is using instead of a filename. In fact, "S" is actually a filehandle to and normal file operations can be performed on the socket.

Then, the program binds the socket to the local host ($packthishostip) using the bind command. This is a necessary extra housekeeping step just to let the socket know where to send the data back to. This may seem like a silly extra step, but keep in mind that a machine may have multiple network cards in it and have multiple IP addresses. Thus, it is generally good to explicitly bind the socket to one of those local addresses.

Finally, the script connects the bound socket using the connect statement to the address designated by $packconnectip. This is the part that actually connects the Web server's machine over the Internet to the mail SMTP server.

```
socket (S, $AF_INET, $SOCK_STREAM, $PROTOCOL) ||
    &web_error( "Can't make socket:$!\n");

bind (S,$packthishostip) ||
    &web_error( "Can't bind:$!\n");

connect(S, $packconnectip) ||
    &web_error( "Can't connect socket:$!\n");
```

We select the socket handle and then issue the $| = 1 command to turn off buffering. We want all commands that get transmitted to the socket to be sent right away. STDOUT is then selected as the current default output. The handle to the socket is returned to the routine that called OpenSocket so that other routines can use the socket.

```
    select(S);
    $| = 1;
    select (STDOUT);
```

Now the mail message is sent to the mail server. First, we read the connection line from the SMTP server we are connecting to. Then we send the SMTP mail commands one by one.

```
$buf = read_sock(S, 6);
```

The HELO command establishes a connection between the SMTP server we are on and the SMTP server from which we are supposed to be sending E-mail. We need not be connected to an E-mail server; it can refer to any SMTP server on the Internet. Because SMTP is an insecure protocol, you can send mail from any server to any server on the Internet and pretend you are someone else. Note that I do not recommend doing this for the purpose of deception. This library was created so that you can send E-mail without having the "Nobody" user ID show up as part of the E-mail message that the Web server sends.

```
print S "HELO $fromsmtp\n";

$buf = read_sock(S, 6);
```

The MAIL command sets up the "From: username" part of the E-mail.

```
print S "MAIL From:<$fromuser>\n";
$buf = read_sock(S, 6);
```

The RCPT sets up the "To: username" part.

```
print S "RCPT To:<$touser>\n";
$buf = read_sock(S, 6);
```

The DATA flags the SMTP server to start accepting the message as free-form input. This input is terminated by ending the line with a single period followed by a newline.

```
print S "DATA\n";
$buf = read_sock(S, 6);

print S $messagebody . "\n";
```

The period followed by a newline finishes the message and sends it. We send a QUIT statement to the server to log off, and we close the socket.

```
print S ".\n";
$buf = read_sock(S, 6);

print S "QUIT\n";

close S;
```

} #END OF REAL_SEND_MAIL

send_mail Subroutine

The send_mail routine in **SMTPMAIL-LIB.PL** operates exactly the same way as the same routine in **SENDMAIL-LIB.PL** described earlier.

```
sub send_mail
{
local($from, $to, $subject, $messagebody) = @_;

local($fromuser, $fromsmtp, $touser, $tosmtp);

$fromuser = $from;
$touser = $to;

$fromsmtp = (split(/\@/,$from))[1];
$tosmtp = (split(/\@/,$to))[1];

&real_send_mail($fromuser, $fromsmtp, $touser,
        $tosmtp, $subject, $messagebody);

} # End of send_mail
```

read_sock Subroutine

The read_sock command reads the next 1024 characters waiting to be read in the socket. It gets passed a handle to the socket to be read, along with a timeout value. The timeout value is listed in seconds. If there is no input on `read_sock` in that many seconds, `read_sock` returns with nothing in the read buffer.

```
sub read_sock {
    local($handle, $endtime) = @_;
    local($localbuf,$buf);
    local($rin,$rout,$nfound);
```

`$endtime` is the timeout. We set `$endtime` to `$endtime + time` and later keep looping until `time` is greater than `$endtime` + the original time that the read_sock was called. Additionally, we clear the buffer.

```
# Set endtime to be time + endtime.
    $endtime += time;

# Clear buffer
    $buf = "";
```

`$rin` is set to be a vector of the socket file handle. This Perl code sets up `$rin` as input to a special form of the `select()` function that checks whether input is waiting to be read from the file handle. Because the `read` command blocks the operating system from doing anything else if there is nothing to read, it makes sense that we want to check for this condition first.

Note that the Windows NT version of Perl does not support the `select` statement in this form, so we read the socket even if it happens to block us on Windows NT.

```
    $rin = '';
# Set $rin to be a vector of the socket file handle
    vec($rin, fileno($handle), 1) = 1;

# nfound is 0 since we have not read anything yet
    $nfound = 0;
```

The following code loops until there is something to read or we time out. If there is something to read, then `$nfound` is equal to the number of bytes waiting to be read.

```
read_socket:
while (($endtime > time) && ($nfound <= 0)) {
# Read 1024 bytes at a time
    $length = 1024;
# Preallocate buffer
    $localbuf = " " x 1025;
    # NT does not support select for polling to see if
    # There are characters to be received.
    # This is important Because we don't want to block
    # if there is nothing being received.
    $nfound = 1;
    if ($mail_os ne "NT") {
# The following polls to see if there is anything in
# the input buffer to read.  If there is, we will later
# call the sysread routine
    $nfound = select($rout=$rin, undef, undef,.2);
        }
}
```

If we have found characters waiting to be read as part of the $nfound command, we read the socket using the sysread command. Finally, the contents of the buffer are returned to the routine that called the read_sock function.

```
    if ($nfound > 0) {
    $length = sysread($handle, $localbuf, 1024);
    if ($length > 0) {
        $buf .= $localbuf;
        }
    }

$buf;
}
```

web_error Subroutine

There is nothing new here. This web_error subroutine is the same one you saw previously explained with sendmail-lib.pl.

```
sub web_error
{
local ($error) = @_;
```

```
$error = "Error Occured: $error";
print "$error<p>\n";

# Die exits the program prematurely
# and prints an error to stderr

die $error;

} # end of web_error
```

CHAPTER 8

Using HTTP-LIB.PL

OVERVIEW

Most people think that retrieving and displaying HTML documents over the Internet is the exclusive realm of Web browsers. But you might want a Perl program to go out on the Internet, grab HTML documents, and let you manipulate the information before displaying it. **HTTP-LIB.PL** is a set of routines that allows you to do that.

HTTP-LIB.PL allows you to perform two main functions. First, it can connect to a Web server on the Internet and retrieve any HTML document; by default, it strips out the header information that the Web server sends with the document. In addition, the HTTP library can submit form variables using either the POST or the GET method of CGI.

INSTALLATION AND USAGE

Using HTTP Lib

HTTP-LIB has two main functions that are designed to be called by other programs. HTTPGet and HTTPPost take the same four parameters and return a scalar variable that contains the HTML output by the server that they are connected to. The parameters are the URL, the server, the port number to connect to, and a reference to a scalar string that contains form data.

The string that contains the form data must be in the same format as a string that would be passed as form data if we were using the GET method: All the key and value pairs must be separated by &, and the key and value pairs must not have any illegal characters. Spaces are allowed only because there is a routine to automatically convert spaces to %20 codes within HTTP-LIB. The following code snippet would post data "test=test1" and "last_name=smith" to **http://www.eff.org/~eritct/Scripts/http.cgi**. $buf is returned with the output from the HTTPGet command.

```
$buf = &HTTPGet("/~erict/Scripts/http.cgi",
    "www.eff.org",80,"test=test1&last_name=smith");
```

As with the sockets-based E-mail program in Chapter 7, there is a global operating system variable called $http_os. By default, this variable is set to "UNIX." If you are using an NT server version of Perl that does not support the SELECT() command, you should set this variable to "NT." In addition, if you are using a version of Perl that does not support the sockets package (**Socket.pm**), remove the line that says use Socket and replace the $AF_INET and $SOCK_STREAM variable assignment values with 2 and 1, respectively. On some systems, these values may be different. For example, on Solaris, $SOCK_STREAM should be set to 2.

Example of HTTP-LIB.Pl in Action Using SAMPLE.CGI.

HTTP-LIB includes a set of CGI files that shows an example of how the library works. The files are **sample.html, sample.cgi, test1.cgi, and test2.cgi**.

110

SAMPLE.HTML

The following code listing, **SAMPLE.HTML**, contains a reference to **test1.cgi** and **test2.cgi**. Each CGI program uses a different method to connect to the server as a browser and send sample form data to **SAMPLE.CGI** (see Figure 8.1).

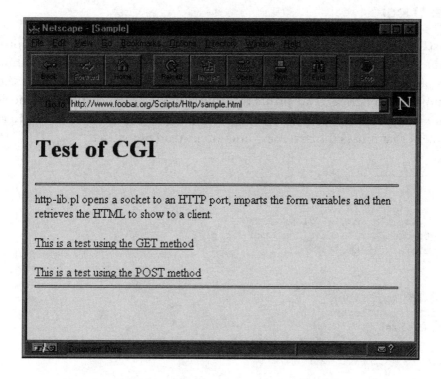

Figure 8.1 *HTML form testing **HTTP-LIB.PL**.*

```
<HTML><HEAD><TITLE>Sample</TITLE></HEAD>
<BODY>
<H1>Test of CGI</H1>
<HR>
http-lib.pl opens a socket to an HTTP port, imparts the
form variables, and then retrieves the HTML to show to
a client.
<p>
```

```
<A HREF=test1.cgi>This is a test using the GET
method</A><p>
<A HREF=test2.cgi>This is a test using the POST
method</A>
<HR>
</BODY></HTML>
```

test1.cgi

test1.cgi, shown next, follows the standard format of a simple CGI program except that it requires HTTP-LIB and uses the HTTPGet subroutine to pass the value what to the form variable whatever. Finally, it takes the output from HTTPGet and prints it to the user's browser. Figure 8.2 shows an example of this output. The **test2.cgi** program is identical to **test1.cgi** except that it uses the HTTPPost function instead of HTTPGet.

```
#!/usr/local/bin/perl


#
#  This is a sample cgi program
#  to demonstrate that the http-lib.pl
#  library works.
#

require "cgi-lib.pl";
print &PrintHeader;
&ReadParse;

require "http-lib.pl";

$in = "whatever=what";
$buf = &HTTPGet("/scripts/Http/sample.cgi",
     "www.eff.org",80,$in);

print $buf;
```

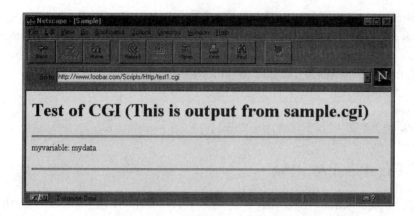

*Figure 8.2 Sample output from **test1.cgi** using **HTTP-LIB.PL**.*

DESIGN DISCUSSION

The magic behind HTTP-LIB is done using sockets programming. Basically, *sockets* is another word for Telnet except that, instead of using Telnet to connect to a UNIX server and run programs, you are using sockets to connect to a service such as an E-mail service (SMTP, POP) or an HTML service (HTTP). Whenever a Web browser connects to a Web server, it "plugs" itself into the Web server's "socket." HTTP-LIB operates by acting like a miniature Web browser: It connects itself to a Web server, retrieves the HTML data, and returns it to your CGI program. The CGI program then displays or otherwise deals with the HTML data.

Main Script

By default, we use the **Socket.pm** package in Perl 5. If you are not using Perl 5 or lack the **Socket.pm** file, you can delete the following line and set the AF_INET and $SOCK\_STREAM$ variables manually in the Perl program according to the instructions in the usage section of this chapter. $http\_os$ should be set to "NT" if you are using a Windows NT version of Perl. $http\_os$ is set to "UNIX" by default.

```
use Socket;
$http_os = "UNIX";
```

HTTPGet Subroutine

The HTTPGet function connects to the Web server using the GET method. This is the normal method that is used when a location is typed into a Web browser manually. The routine uses the URL, hostname, port, and a string containing the urlencoded form variables. If the string is blank, the HTTPGet function acts like a normal Web browser and retrieves the document specified by the URL path.

Before we delve into the this routine though, lets step back and look at an example of how a Web browser communicates with the Web server. If you went to the http://www.foobar.com/index.html URL, the Web browser is actually connecting to port 80 of www.foobar.com and attempting to retrieve index.html in the root directory. The Web browser translates this into the following request:

```
GET /index.html HTTP/1.0
Accept: text/html
Accept: text/plain
User-Agent: Mozilla/1.0
```

In response to this, the Web server would return a header followed by the HTML document. If the retrieval of the document is a success, the success code (200) is returned as part of the header. If an error occurs, a three digit error code will be sent instead of "200".

```
HTTP/1.0 200 Document follows
Date: Wed, 10 Jul 1996 01:59:51 GMT
Server: NCSA/1.4.1
```

```
Content-type: text/html
Last-modified: Wed, 10 Apr 1996 18:15:28 GMT
Content-length: 10

<HTML>
<HEAD>
<TITLE>FooBar Page</TITLE>
</HEAD><BODY>
Nothing To Say Really
</BODY></HTML>
```

HTTP-LIB.PL operates by sending the specific HTTP document request directly to the Web server. Then, when the document is returned with the header as shown above, HTTP-LIB.PL strips off the document information header and returns just the HTML code back to you.

```
sub HTTPGet {
    local($url, $hostname, $port, $in) = @_;
    local($form_vars, $x, $socket);
    local ($buf);
```

The first thing we need to do is to open the socket; here, we call a subroutine further down in the program. A socket consists of a hostname and a port number. Generally, the HTTP port number is 80.

```
    $socket = &OpenSocket($hostname, $port);
```

The form variables that are passed to this routine must be sent so that there are no illegal characters in the URL. Illegal characters are ones that might be mistaken for other things, such as a forward slash or a space. The &FormatFormVars converts spaces to a %20 code.

```
    $form_vars = &FormatFormVars($in);
# we need to add the ? to the front of the passed
# form variables
```

The $url is set equal to the URL plus the form variables separated with a "?":

```
    $url .= "?" . $form_vars;
```

Finally, we print the GET $url information to the Web server that we are connected to. After this information is sent, the Web server should send back the document with a success code (200) or an error code with the appropriate error message.

```
# The following sends the information
# to the HTTP Server.
    print $socket <<__END_OF_SOCKET__;
GET $url HTTP/1.0
Accept: text/html
Accept: text/plain
User-Agent: Mozilla/1.0

__END_OF_SOCKET__
```

&RetrieveHTTP returns the HTML code that the server outputs in response to the GET method. Finally, the $buf variable that contains the HTML code is returned to the program that called HTTPGet.

```
    # RetrieveHTTP retrieves the HTML code
    $buf = &RetrieveHTTP($socket);
    $buf;

} #end of HTTPGet
```

HTTPPost Subroutine

The HTTPPost function connects to the Web server using the POST method, the preferred method that CGI programs use to pass form variables. Instead of passing the variables as command-line parameters to the URL, HTTPPost passes the variables as part of the STDIN stream of the Web server. Thus, the Web server can read the variables as part of the normal STDIN input. The routine uses the URL, hostname, port, and a string containing the urlencoded form variables. If the string is blank, HTTPPost acts like a normal Web browser except that the content length of the POST is zero.

```
sub HTTPPost {
    local($url, $hostname, $port, $in) = @_;
```

```
local($form_vars, $x, $socket);
local ($buf, $form_var_length);
```

As with HTTPGet, we open the socket connection to the Web server specified by the $hostname and $port variables. HTML is usually served through port 80.

```
$socket = &OpenSocket($hostname, $port);
# The following sends the information to the HTTP Server.
```

Again, the form variables need to be formatted properly.

```
$form_vars = &FormatFormVars($in);
```

We need the length of the final form variables in order to pass the content-length information to the Web server for our POST information.

```
$form_var_length = length($form_vars);
```

The following code sends the POST command to the Web server along with the content-length; the POSTed variables are printed at the end as part of the normal output stream. The variables should be equal in size to content-length.

```
    print $socket <<__END_OF_SOCKET__;
POST $url HTTP/1.0
Accept: text/html
Accept: text/plain
User-Agent: Mozilla/1.0
Content-type: application/x-www-form-urlencoded
Content-length: $form_var_length

$form_vars
__END_OF_SOCKET__
```

Finally, the HTML code is retrieved into the $buf variable and the information is returned to the program that called HTTPPost.

```
$buf = &RetrieveHTTP($socket);
$buf;
```

```
} #end of HTTPPost
```

FormatFormVars Subroutine

The FormatFormVars function converts the spaces in the form variables to their special encoded form of %20. Spaces are not recognized as valid characters within variables in a URL.

```
sub FormatFormVars {
    local ($in) = @_;

    $in =~ s/ /%20/g;

    $in;
} # FormatFormVars
```

RetrieveHTTP Subroutine

RetrieveHTTP retrieves the HTTP output and returns it to the HTTPGet and HTTPPost functions.

```
sub RetrieveHTTP {
    local ($socket) = @_;
    local ($buf,$x, $split_length);
```

First, the read_sock function is called with a timeout value of 6 seconds to get the initial 1024 bytes of the HTML document. The returned buffer is tested to see whether it contains a 200. If it does, we figure that the success (200) status code has been sent, so we continue reading the rest of the socket as if it were a normal input file. The rest of the HTML document is appended to $buf.

```
    $buf = read_sock($socket, 6);

    if ($buf =~ /200/) {
        while(<$socket>) {
            $buf .= $_;
        }
    }
```

We strip off the HTTP header by looking for two newlines or two newlines preceded by carriage returns. Web servers do not always use the same standard header delimiters.

118

```
    $x = index($buf, "\r\n\r\n");
    $split_length = 4;

    if ($x == -1) {
        $x = index($buf, "\n\n");
        $split_length = 2;
    }
#
# The following actually splits the header off
    if ($x > -1) {
        $buf = substr($buf,$x + $split_length);
    }
```

Finally, the socket is closed and we return the buffer containing the HTML code to HTTPGet or HTTPPost.

```
    close $socket;

$buf;
} # End of RetrieveHTTP
```

OpenSocket Subroutine

The OpenSocket function opens the connection to the Web server.

```
sub OpenSocket {
    local($hostname, $port) = @_;

    local($ipaddress, $fullipaddress, $packconnectip);
    local($packthishostip);
    local($AF_INET, $SOCK_STREAM, $SOCK_ADDR);
    local($PROTOCOL, $HTTP_PORT);
```

The following variables are set using values defined in the **Socket.pm** library. If your version of Perl does not have the sockets library, you can substitute default values, such as 2 for AF_INIT and 1 for SOCK_STREAM. If 1 does not work for SOCK_STREAM, try using 2. $SOCK_ADDR is a special variable that holds the IP address, port, and other relevant socket information.

```
    $AF_INET = AF_INET;
    $SOCK_STREAM = SOCK_STREAM;
```

```
$SOCK_ADDR = "S n a4 x8";

$PROTOCOL = (getprotobyname('tcp'))[2];

$HTTP_PORT = $port;
$HTTP_PORT = 80 unless ($HTTP_PORT =~ /^\d+$/);
$PROTOCOL = 6 unless ($PROTOCOL =~ /^\d+$/);
```

We call the `gethostbyname` function to convert the hostname we are connecting to into a real IP address. `$fullipaddress` is the ASCII equivalent of the IP address delimited with periods. We calculate this in case we want to trouble-shoot whether the hostname lookup actually worked. `$packconnectip` is the host to connect to, given in the special `$SOCK_ADDR` format. `$packthishostip` is also in the `$SOCK_ADDR` format and designates this local host.

```
# Ip address is the Address of the
# host that we need to connect to
    $ipaddress = (gethostbyname($hostname))[4];

    $fullipaddress =
      join (".", unpack("C4", $ipaddress));

    $packconnectip = pack($SOCK_ADDR, $AF_INET,
            $HTTP_PORT, $ipaddress);
    $packthishostip = pack($SOCK_ADDR,
                $AF_INET, 0, "\0\0\0\0");
```

The socket first needs to be created. Then we bind the socket to the local host (`$packthishostip`) and connect the bound socket, using the connect statement, to the address designated by `$packconnectip`.

```
socket (S, $AF_INET, $SOCK_STREAM, $PROTOCOL) ||
    &web_error( "Can't make socket:$!\n");

bind (S,$packthishostip) ||
    &web_error( "Can't bind:$!\n");

connect(S, $packconnectip) ||
    &web_error( "Can't connect socket:$!\n");
```

We select the socket handle and issue the $| = 1 command to turn off buffering. Basically, we want all commands that get transmitted to the socket to be sent right away. STDOUT is then selected as the current default output. The handle to the socket is returned to the routine that called OpenSocket so that other routines can use the socket.

```
    select(S);
    $| = 1;
    select (STDOUT);

S;
} # End of OpenSocket
```

The read_sock command reads the next 1024 characters waiting to be read in the socket. It gets passed a handle to the socket to be read along with a timeout value in seconds. If there is no input on read_sock in that many seconds, read_sock returns with nothing in the read buffer.

```
sub read_sock {
    local($handle, $endtime) = @_;
    local($localbuf,$buf);
    local($rin,$rout,$nfound);
```

$endtime is the timeout. We set $endtime to $endtime + time and later keep looping until time is greater than $endtime + the original time that read_sock was called. Additionally, we clear the buffer.

```
# Set endtime to be time + endtime.
    $endtime += time;

# Clear buffer
    $buf = "";
```

$rin is set to be a vector of the socket file handle. Basically, this Perl code sets up $rin as input to a special form of the select() function that checks whether there is input waiting to be read from the file handle. Because the read command blocks the operating system from doing anything else if there is nothing to read, it makes sense that we want to check for this condition first.

Note that the Windows NT version of Perl does not support the `select` statement in this form, so we read the socket even if it happens to block us on Windows NT.

```
# Clear $rin (Read Input variable)
    $rin = '';
# Set $rin to be a vector of the socket file handle
    vec($rin, fileno($handle), 1) = 1;


# nfound is 0 since we have not read anything yet
    $nfound = 0;
```

The following code loops until there is something to read or we time out. If there is something read, `$nfound` equals the number of bytes waiting to be read.

```
read_socket:
while (($endtime > time) && ($nfound <= 0)) {
# Read 1024 bytes at a time
    $length = 1024;
# Preallocate buffer
    $localbuf = " " x 1025;
      # NT does not support select for polling to see if
      # There are characters to be received.
      # This is important because we don't want to block
      # if there is nothing being received.
    $nfound = 1;
    if ($http_os ne "NT") {
# The following polls to see if
# there is anything in the input
# buffer to read.  If there is, we
# will later call the sysread routine
    $nfound = select($rout=$rin, undef, undef,.2);
        }
}
```

If we have found characters waiting to be read as part of the `$nfound` command, we read the socket using the `sysread` command. Finally, the contents of the buffer are returned to the routine that called the `read_sock` function.

```
    if ($nfound > 0) {
    $length = sysread($handle, $localbuf, 1024);
```

```
   if ($length > 0) {
        $buf .= $localbuf;
        }
   }

$buf;
}
```

web_error Subroutine

web_error is a subroutine whose purpose is to print errors as HTML before exiting the program. Most Perl programs use the DIE subroutine to exit the program prematurely. Unfortunately, using DIE typically does not print any useful information to the user attempting to set up the script. Thus, we use web_error to print the message as HTML and then call DIE. The DIE subroutine in Perl is still useful for a Web server, because the message given by DIE is generally printed to the Web server's error log.

```
sub web_error
{
local ($error) = @_;
$error = "Error Occurred: $error";
print "$error<p>\n";

# Die exits the program prematurely
# and prints an error to stderr

die $error;

} # end of web_error
```

CHAPTER 9

Implementing Web Security Using auth-lib.pl

OVERVIEW

A natural extension of most applications is the capability to restrict or track access through the application. To do this, we need a system designed to authenticate users when they first start using the application. This is where **auth-lib.pl** comes in.

    auth-lib.pl is a Perl authentication library that provides the three core capabilities that any security library needs. First, it allows the administrator of a Web application to maintain a registration list or password file of users who are authorized to access the application (or who have recently registered, depending on the rules that the administrator sets up). Second, it allows users to log in to the application either through the Web server's built-in HTTP authentication or through a CGI form. Figure 9.1 shows an example of the CGI-based logon form. Once users are logged in, **auth-lib.pl** tracks them by using unique session files that are created when users complete a successful login. To support all these functions, the authentication library contains a great many configuration options, accommodating all sorts of security scenarios.

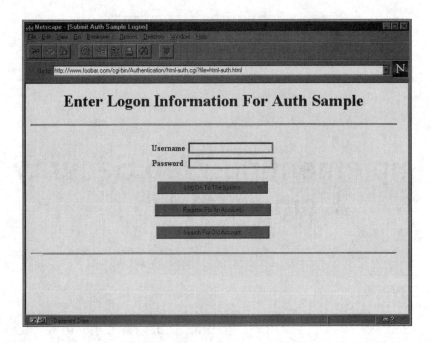

Figure 9.1 The CGI-based logon form.

Playing a major role in the flexibility of the authentication library is the ability to configure the fields of user information to store. By default, this library is configured with fields such as last name, first name, and E-mail address, and more fields can easily be added. Core fields include username, password, and the names of security groups a user belongs to. By using group names, a programmer can make a CGI script fully configurable. For example, you may want to allow only certain people to view a groupware calendar and other people to be able to post new events or change existing ones.

The authentication library can take advantage of CGI form-based login and authentication on its own, or it can integrate with Web server–based authentication. Web server–based authentication is useful if your company owns and maintains its own Web server and can configure it to log users in. CGI-based authentication, on the other hand, means that people log in using an HTML form that is processed by a CGI script. For people on the Internet who share a Web server on an Internet service provider, CGI-based authentication means that you need not lose authentication capability if you are not allowed to change the Web server configuration.

When a user logs in, all the configurable field information, such as username and last name, is stored in a session file. This file is associated with a uniquely generated *session code* that is passed from screen to screen of your Web application, providing the application with the user's information at all times. This is typically referred to as *maintaining state.*

Normally, Web servers have no concept of a continuous session. When a user goes from page to page, the Web server sends each page on an entirely new connection. The Web server has no knowledge of which pages have been previously viewed. The authentication library gets around this limitation by setting up a unique session code and assigning it to a hidden form variable. This session code is sent as a parameter to each CGI script access for the application. This technique allows the application to look at the session file to maintain the state of the application. The state of the application is always dependent on the user's most recent action, and this information is reflected in the session file.

INSTALLATION AND USAGE

When the authentication library is installed from the accompanying CD-ROM, your directories and files should be similar to Figure 9.2. This figure also shows the permissions needed on the files and directories. The additional **html-auth** files are a sample application for protecting HTML documents by using **auth-lib.pl**.

Figure 9.2 *Directory structure of the authentication library along with sample HTML filter scripts.*

Although the diagram shows the authentication library and **html-auth** CGI scripts in the same **Authentication** directory, the library files can be placed in any directory. By default, most of our applications that use this library store all their library files, including the authentication library, in a subdirectory called **Library** underneath the main scripts directory.

Authentication Library Files

auth-lib.pl is the core of the authentication library. You must `require` this library in your CGI scripts to enable authentication. This file needs to be readable by the Web server.

auth-extra-lib.pl is loaded by **auth-lib.pl** if any logon, registration, or searching functions need to be performed. This file must be readable.

auth-extra-html.pl is loaded by **auth-extra-lib.pl** and provides Perl code that prints the HTML related to logon, registration, and search functions in the authentication library. This file must be readable.

auth-lib-fail-html.pl is loaded by **auth-lib.pl** when a session is not valid. It outputs an HTML screen informing the user of the error. This file must be readable.

auth-server-lib.pl is loaded by **auth-extra-lib.pl** if Web server–based authentication is being used. This file must be readable.

auth.setup is a sample setup file for authentication. CGI scripts that use this library typically have their own setup file in which the authentication variables are specified.

mail-lib.pl is necessary so that the authentication library can send E-mail. **cgi-lib.pl** is necessary for any sample CGI applications that may be running in the same directory. These files should be readable.

The **Users** subdirectory is where the user file for CGI-based authentication is stored by default. This directory should be readable, writable, and executable.

The **Sessions** subdirectory is where sessions are created by the authentication library. This directory should be readable, writable, and executable.

html-auth Sample Authentication Application Files

html-auth.cgi is a sample application that uses authentication. Its purpose is to protect HTML files from being viewed by unauthorized visitors. This file must be readable and executable.

html-auth.setup is the setup file for **html-auth.cgi**. It includes all the setup variables that the authentication library needs. This file must be readable.

html-auth.html and **html-auth2.html** are simple HTML files that are used as example protected HTML files in this chapter.

Server-Specific Setup and Options

The authentication library assumes that certain setup variables are set before the main routine, GetSessionInfo, is called. These variables are usually set up in the CGI script that uses the authentication library. For example, the authentication variables for the bulletin board system script reside in the **bbs.setup** file.

$auth_lib contains a path to the directory where the authentication library is stored. Typically, libraries that are commonly used should be stored in a central directory. If you want to keep the authentication library in the same directory as the other CGI script that is using it, simply set $auth_lib to ".", which is shorthand notation for "the current directory I am in."

$auth_server is set to on if you are using server-based authentication. Web servers can be configured to ask the user for a username and password when certain pages are viewed or scripts are executed. If you set $auth_server to on, the authentication library reads the username from the Web server that has logged the user on. From there, the authentication library can be modified to look up other information about the user, such as first name, last name, E-mail address, and more, based on the username.

$auth_cgi is set to on if you are not using server-based authentication. CGI authentication is typically used in place of server-based authentication if you are on a shared server and do not have permissions to modify the Web server setup files to add access restrictions.

If you do not wish to use any authentication at all, you would set both $auth_cgi and $auth_server to off. You might use this option if you wish your application to be free of security checks. For example, the bulletin board script described later on in this book uses the authentication library to provide first name, last name, and E-mail information about the user when the user posts a message. However, if authentication is turned off, the BBS program makes users type that information when they post. Some sites prefer to have the BBS totally open to all users so that they do not have to type information unless they want to post a message.

You should not set both $auth_cgi and $auth_server to on at the same time. If both variables are set to on, the code that makes a session based on $auth_server being set to on will override the code that makes a session based on $auth_cgi set to on. We advise that you do not try this at home—or at least on your home page.

Many of the variables discussed here are CGI security–specific. When you're using CGI-based security, the authentication library must do much more work. The library must log users onto the system, allow them to register on the system if they are not yet there, and search for accounts if they forget their username. Variables related to these functions are specifically associated with the CGI-based security.

$auth_user_file is set to the directory and filename of the file that contains information about the users who are allowed to get into the system. This variable is used only when CGI authentication is on. When you use Web server–specific security, the user's password and username are stored in a Web server–specific file. This file is not needed if you are using Web server–specific security instead of CGI-based security. A sample of a user file is shown next:

```
gunther|mypassword|readaccess|Gunther|Birznieks
selena|selenapass|readaccess:writeaccess|Selena|Sol
```

$auth_alt_user_file is set to the directory and filename of the file that contains information about the users who have registered in the system. Normally, when users enter their information into the registration screen, their data is stored in $auth_user_file. Placing a value in $auth_alt_user_file, however, sends registrations to an alternative file instead of the original one. This arrangement allows you to check registrations before you decide to move them to the user file. This technique is also CGI security–specific.

$auth_allow_register is set to on if you wish to allow users to register at the logon screen using CGI-based security. Figure 9.3 shows an example of a registration screen.

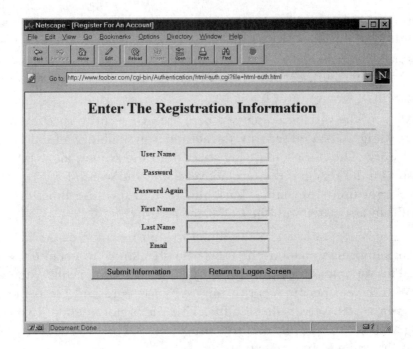

Figure 9.3 CGI-based HTML registration page.

$auth_allow_search is set to on to allow users to search for their username in case they forgot it at the CGI-based logon screen. Figure 9.4 shows an example of a search screen.

$auth_default_group is the security group assigned to users when they register for access using the CGI-based security mechanism. You can use this variable if you have a CGI that script calls the authentication library and you wish to distinguish whether a user has certain types of access, such as create, delete, or modification. The typical default is "normal." A user's groups determine the user's rights in the CGI script that is using the authentication library.

If $auth_generate_password is set to on, the CGI security mechanism generates user passwords when they register for the site instead of allowing them to choose their own password. The generated passwords are E-mailed to the users after they have submitted the registration. Figure 9.5 displays an example HTML registration form when this variable is set to on. Notice that users are no longer prompted to enter a password of their own choosing.

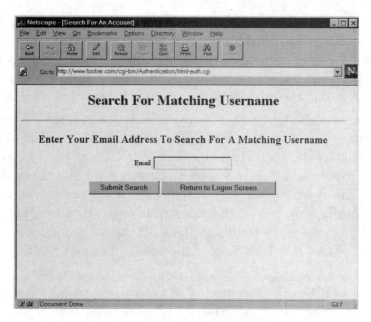

Figure 9.4 *CGI-based HTML search page.*

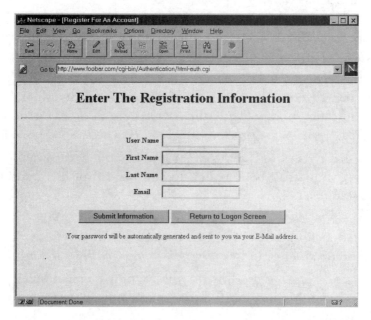

Figure 9.5 *CGI-based security HTML page for registration when*
auth-lib.pl generates the password.

$auth_use_cleartext is set to off in order to trigger the storage of passwords in the user file in encrypted form for CGI-based security. This arrangement is useful on a shared server where someone may be able to snoop in your user file and find out the passwords. If the passwords in the user file are encrypted, it will be more difficult for someone to break into your site.

Cleartext indicates that password information is sent as "clear text" that anyone can see. Thus, it is off when you do not want your passwords to be stored as clear text. It is administratively easier but less secure to keep the passwords unencrypted. When passwords are stored as plain text, you can look up a forgotten password quickly, or you can change the password manually. If the passwords are stored in encrypted form, it is difficult to change a password by editing the user file manually; you have to figure out what the new encrypted form of the password should be.

NOTE Using the crypt function in Perl to encrypt passwords may not work on some operating systems. If you are using another OS such as Windows NT, you may need to turn off password encryption to make this library work.

$auth_check_duplicates is set to on for CGI-based security when you wish to make sure that a person cannot register with the same username twice at the same site.

$auth_add_register is set to on for CGI-based security when you want the authentication library to add the user's registration to the designated user file ($auth_user_file or $auth_alt_user_file, described previously).

$auth_email_register is set to on for CGI-based security when you wish a user's registration to be E-mailed to you instead of or in addition to being written to a file.

$auth_admin_from_address is the source E-mail address that the authentication library uses for CGI-based security whenever it E-mails information to a user or to you.

$auth_admin_email_address is the destination E-mail address for you whenever the authentication library E-mails information about a CGI-based registration.

To send E-mail, the authentication library relies on the **mail-lib.pl** library discussed in Chapter 7. Remember to include this program in the directory that holds the authentication library files.

N O T E

$auth_session_length is the number of days that an authentication session is valid. Whenever a user logs in through the authentication library, a session file is created that is valid only for a short time. The authentication library then uses that session file to read the user's information based on a session ID code that is sent to the library after the initial logon. In that way, users need not type their username and password for every screen of the authenticated CGI application. Although this number represents the value in days, it is important to note that the value can be a fraction. If you want to have sessions last 1/24th of a day, you would set the value to "1 / 24" (one divided by 24). It is a good idea to keep this session file around for the maximum time the user will be using the application. Otherwise, the session file might be deleted before the user has finished using the Web program, and the user will get an error because the session is no longer valid.

It can be useful to set up a session to be an outrageous length, such as 8000 days. In this case, users can typically bookmark their sessions. If the session IDs become invalid after a mere day or so, users cannot bookmark the URLs related to the Web script. This is because when they try to go back, the session ID is not valid and they must log in again. Setting the session length to a huge number alleviates that problem.

N O T E

However, be aware that keeping the sessions and their files around lessens the security of the site, because a user can try different session IDs to break into your application instead of just a username and password. In addition, keeping the session files around for a long time clutters the directory with small session files and takes up disk space.

$auth_session_dir is the directory where the session files are stored. It is highly recommended that this be a separate subdirectory under the main scripts area so that the session files do not get mixed up with the main scripts. In addition, the directory that holds the session files must be writable by the Web server. You do not want the directory where your scripts reside to be writable.

`$auth_register_message` is set for CGI-based security to send users a brief message after they have registered to the system. You may need to change this variable depending on how the previous parameters are set. For example, if you have the authentication library set to generate passwords and send them via E-mail, the message should say something like, "Thanks, you will be E-mailed your password within the next few minutes."

`$auth_password_message` is set for CGI-based security to E-mail users a brief message related to their automatically generated password if you turn that option on.

The authentication library stores a set of core information for each user: username, password, and the groups the user belongs to. In addition to these fields, many CGI applications require additional fields of information about a user. For example, the bulletin board system requires first name, last name, and E-mail information. The information related to these extra fields is stored in a couple of arrays. One array (`@auth_extra_fields`) contains the field names, and the other array (`@auth_extra_desc`) contains the descriptions of the fields.

Field names should generally be lowercase alphabetic characters and contain no spaces. In addition, field names must start with `auth_`. The underscore ("_") character after `auth` is important. The authentication library uses the `auth_` prefix to figure out which form variables have been passed to it that belong to the authentication library. The descriptions can contain fancy formatting. For example, a field name for first name would be `auth_first_name`, whereas a field description would be `First Name`.

If you create extra field names, be sure to prefix them with `auth_`. **The authentication library relies on this designation to determine which form variables are related to the authentication process and which ones came from the previous Web application that happens to use this script.**

NOTE

NOTE

In addition, if you are collecting E-mail information about the users, always name the E-mail form variable `auth_email`. **The authentication library looks for the** `auth_email` **form variable when determining the address to send password information to. This happens when the library is configured to E-mail users a computer-generated password after they register.**

`$auth_logon_title` contains the title that is printed between the `<TITLE>` HTML tags in the CGI-based security logon screen. `$auth_logon_header` is the header that is printed between the `<H1>` HTML tags in the same page.

The following sample setup file illustrates the typical syntax:

```
$auth_lib = ".";
$auth_server =              "off";
$auth_cgi =                 "on";
$auth_user_file =           "Users/user.dat";
$auth_alt_user_file =       "";
$auth_allow_register =      "on";
$auth_allow_search =        "on";
$auth_default_group =       "normal";
$auth_generate_password =   "off";
$auth_check_duplicates =    "on";
$auth_add_register =        "on";
$auth_email_register =      "off";
$auth_admin_from_address =      "wwwadmin\@foobar.com";
$auth_admin_email_address =     "gunther\@foobar.com";
$auth_session_length = 2;
$auth_session_dir = "./Sessions";
$auth_register_message =
    "Thanks, you may now log on with your new username
        and password.";
$auth_password_message =
  "Thanks for applying to our site, your password is";
@auth_extra_fields = ("auth_first_name",
                      "auth_last_name",
                      "auth_email");
@auth_extra_desc = ("First Name",
                    "Last Name",
                    "Email");
$auth_logon_title = "Submit BBS Logon";
$auth_logon_header =
        "Enter Logon Information For The BBS";
```

Using the GetSessionInfo Function

GetSessionInfo is the only routine you need to call directly in order to use the authentication library. All the other subroutines support GetSessionInfo. Here is a sample usage of GetSessionInfo:

```
($session, $username, $group,
 $firstname, $lastname, $email) =
 &GetSessionInfo($session, "$bbs_script", *in);
```

The parameters to GetSessionInfo are the session ID, the name of the current script, and a reference to the associative array that contains all the form variables read via the ReadParse function in **cgi-lib.pl**.

The $session variable is typically read from a hidden form variable that has been previously set. If $session is not set, the GetSessionInfo function creates one based on the user's logon. When a session has been created, the main CGI script can then pass $session as a hidden variable so that the next time the script is activated, the session will be available.

The second parameter contains information related to the name of the script from which the authentication library is being called. Frequently, when you're using CGI-based security, the authentication library will have the user fill out HTML forms related to logging in and registration. When this happens, the authentication library needs the original script name to figure out where to post the form information for processing. Remember that the authentication library is only a library of routines; it is not, by itself, a CGI program. It must be called from another CGI script.

The third parameter is the associative array containing all the form variable entries from the previous form. %in is the default array used in **cgi-lib.pl**. However, if you read your form variables into a different associative array, such as %form_data, you use *form_data to call GetSessionInfo. The asterisk indicates that the array is passed as a reference to the location of its value in memory rather than making another copy of the values and passing them to the subroutine, a technique that would be inefficient.

GetSessionInfo returns an array of values. The first value is the current valid session ID. If there was no previous session ID, GetSessionInfo creates one. The subsequent values in the list of returned data relate to information about the user who has logged on, such as username, groups, first name, last name, and E-mail address.

Sample Application: HTML Filtering

This book contains a sample application that demonstrates the authentication library in the simplest possible setting. This application prevents a user from viewing certain HTML files without logging in through the authentication library. In addition, the HTML files have the word `session` filtered to include the current session ID so that further HTML files can be linked and protected using the current authentication session. Earlier, Figure 9.2 showed the directory structure of the authentication library, including the **html-auth.cgi** program.

The files **auth-lib.pl**, **auth-extra-lib.pl**, **auth-extra-html.pl**, **auth-lib-fail-html.pl**, and **auth-server-lib.pl** are part of the core authentication library. The **auth.setup** file is a sample setup file for authentication variables. The **Sessions** directory is where all the authenticated sessions are written to. The **Users** directory contains the user file for the CGI-based authentication. All the **html-auth** files—such as **html-auth.cgi**, **html-auth.setup**, **html-auth.html**, and **html-auth2.html**—belong to this sample HTML filtering and protection CGI script sample.

The setup file **html-auth.setup** is configured to use CGI-based authentication by default. Users are also allowed to register and gain immediate access to the HTML files by default. The users are stored in the **Users** directory, and the session files are stored in the **Sessions** directory.

Html-auth.cgi is the CGI program that calls the authentication library. It accepts the `file` form variable to determine which HTML file is to be read. To test this, you can call `html-auth.cgi?file=html-auth.html` as a URL in your Web browser. If this script were installed in the **cgi-bin** directory of www.foobar.com, we would refer to the script as follows:

```
http://www.foobar.com/cgi-bin/html-auth.cgi?file=html-auth.html
```

The logon screen would come up. After the user logged on, the **html-auth.html** file would be filtered and would be output to the Web browser. Figure 9.6 shows this process.

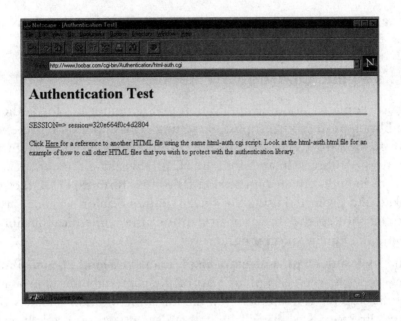

Figure 9.6 html-auth.html after it has been filtered by html-auth.cgi.

The URL reference inside **html-auth.html** has the session ID added to it so that **html-auth.cgi** need not ask for the logon username and password again when it attempts to use **html-auth.cgi** to access the second HTML file, **html-auth2.html**. Figure 9.7 displays an example of what happens when the link is pressed. Notice, from the URL location identifier in the figure, that **html-auth.cgi** is still used to filter the next HTML file. To understand how **html-auth.cgi** works, we need to look at the code for these HTML files.

HTML-AUTH.HTML

The code that appears next is the **html-auth.html** file. It contains the HTML code for a sample Web page that you might want to protect unauthorized viewers from seeing. To activate this protection, you reference this page using the **html-auth.cgi** program as `html-auth.cgi?file=html-auth.html`.

```
<HTML>
<HEAD>
<TITLE>
Authentication Test
</TITLE>
</HEAD>
<BODY>
<H1>Authentication Test</H1>
<HR>
SESSION=> session<P>
Click
<A HREF=html-auth.cgi?file=html-auth2.html&session>
 Here </A>
for a reference to another HTML file using
the same html-auth.cgi script. Look at the
html-auth.html file for an example of how to call
other html files that you wish to protect with the
authentication library.
<P>
</BODY>
</HTML>
```

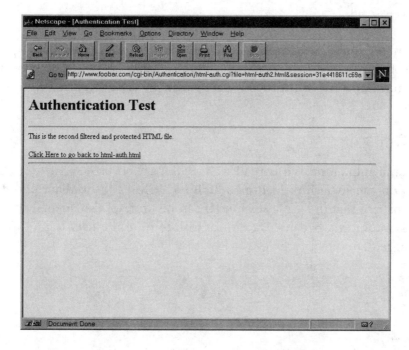

Figure 9.7 A second **html-auth.cgi** *filtered HTML file.*

NOTE For this protection of the HTML files to be effective, you should place them in a directory where the CGI script can read them but where a user cannot get to that HTML file by directly typing a URL to it.

When the user calls this HTML file using **html-auth.cgi**, a logon screen is displayed. When the user successfully enters a valid logon, the HTML file is read into the CGI script and is output to the user's Web browser. If the script sees a line that contains the word session, **html-auth.cgi** adds an equal symbol (=) to the end of session along with the session ID. Thus, if the session ID were 2000, the part of the HTML code that reads

```
<A HREF=html-auth.cgi?file=html-auth2.html
&session>
```

would be replaced with

```
<A HREF=html-auth.cgi?file=html-auth2.html
&session=2000>
```

The subsequent page, **html-auth2.html**, that the user may wish to read, would be protected by the same authentication library that protects the **html-auth.html** file without the user having to reauthenticate (log on again).

HTML-AUTH2.HTML

The **html-auth2.html** file is read by the user's Web browser if he or she clicks on the hyperlink in **html-auth.html**. It links to **html-auth.html** to demonstrate that the same session ID can be used to display many pages. This is important, because we do not wish to have the user log on to the site more than once.

```
<HTML>
<HEAD>
<TITLE>
Authentication Test
</TITLE>
</HEAD>
<BODY>
```

```
<H1>Authentication Test</H1>
<HR>
This is the second filtered and
protected HTML file.
<P>
<A HREF=html-auth.cgi?file=html-auth.html&session>
Click Here To Go Back to html-auth.html</A>
<HR>
</BODY>
</HTML>
```

A more detailed discussion of this sample application appears in the next section.

DESIGN DISCUSSION

The main function of the authentication library is to check to see whether a current session ID exists. If no session exists for the user, the authentication library needs to create a session. However, before a session can be created, the user needs to log in through an HTML form (for CGI-based authentication) or through the Web server's own authentication mechanism. The CGI-based authentication is more complex, because the authentication library has functionality to allow people to register as well as search for previously assigned usernames. Figure 9.8 shows the basic work flow options of this library.

auth-lib.pl

This short library file is the fulcrum of the authentication process. It contains code to see whether a session file exists and returns the information in the file if there is a valid session code. If there is no valid session file, **auth-lib.pl** reads another auxiliary library file, **auth-lib-extra.pl**, which contains all the other main functions of the authentication library. These functions are split into two Perl files for efficiency. The GetSessionInfo routine in **auth-lib.pl** is called every time CGI scripts execute that use authentication. However, the functions in **auth-extra-lib.pl** are called only when the initial session must be created and the user needs to log on or register for the CGI application.

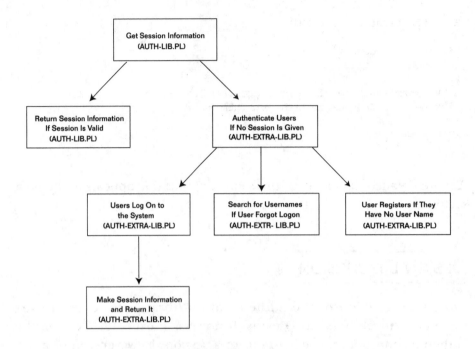

Figure 9.8 Basic flowchart for the authentication library.

THE GETSESSIONINFO SUBROUTINE

The GetSessionInfo function accepts as parameters a session number, a script name, and a reference to an associative array containing form variables. The session number tells GetSessionInfo whether there is a valid session file of information that it should look for. If there is no valid session number, GetSessionInfo logs the user on and creates a session file containing the user's information. The script name is needed for CGI-based authentication, because the logon and registration HTML forms that are displayed to the user need to post the information back to the original script. The original form variables are necessary, because the logon and registration processing used in CGI-based security needs to preserve them from screen to screen by embedding them as hidden variables in the HTML forms.

In addition to the authentication form variables, other form variables can be sent to the authentication library. For example, to activate the BBS, you send a `forum` form variable to the **bbs_forum.cgi** script. However, if the authentication library requires the user to log on via another HTML form, the `forum` form variable needs to be maintained. The authentication library does this by making sure that any form variable that does not begin with `auth_` is passed from form to form until the user logs on to the script. At that point, the original HTML form variables are sent to the script for processing.

`$session_file` is set up as a local variable to store the name of the session file. `@fields` is set up as an array of fields of user information that will be returned to the CGI script that calls `GetSessionInfo`. These fields include the session ID, username, groups, and more, depending on how the authentication library is configured.

```
sub GetSessionInfo {
local($session, $main_script, *in) = @_;
local($session_file, @fields);
```

If the session is not defined—that is, if it is equal to ""—the library does a `require` to load all the auxiliary routines for authentication and calls the `VerifyUser` routine to log the user into the system. `VerifyUser` also allows the user to register for the system as well as searches for prior used usernames depending on how security is configured for the library.

```
if ($session eq "") {
    require "$auth_lib/auth-extra-lib.pl";
    @fields = &VerifyUser($main_script, *in);
    } # End of if
```

If the session is defined, however, the program reads the session file and returns the information.

```
else {
```

`$session_file` is defined as the name of the session file. The session files consist of a session ID that is suffixed with a **.dat** extension. When the session file is opened, it is checked for success. If the open file operation is a failure, then **auth-lib-fail-html.pl** is called; it prints an error message, and the authentication library exits. This usually happens when the session ID passed to the script is not valid. In this case, "not valid" means that there is no longer a session file associated with the session ID, or perhaps someone was trying to fake a session ID.

```
$session_file = "$session.dat";
open (SESSIONFILE, "$auth_session_dir/$session_file") ||
     (require "$auth_lib/auth-lib-fail-html.pl" && exit);
```

If the session ID is valid, the session file is read. The session file should consist of one line of fields that are pipe-delimited (separated by the pipe (|) symbol). A chop removes the newline at the end of the last field. (A file read typically reads the whole line, including the newline character that separates lines in a file.) Finally, the session file is closed.

```
while (<SESSIONFILE>) {
        chop;
     @fields = split(/\|/);
     }
close (SESSIONFILE);
```

The session ID is placed at the beginning of the array of fields using the unshift operator. The final step in GetSessionInfo is to return the array of fields.

```
unshift(@fields, $session);
  } # End of else


# return the array of fields;
@fields;
} # End of GetSessionInfo
```

auth-lib-fail-html.pl

This file contains Perl code that prints a message stating that the session file had a problem trying to open. For efficiency, this message is placed in a separate file. Most of the time, the session file will be valid. So the error code is placed outside the normal required authentication library to make sure that only the Perl code needed to parse and compile will be interpreted. Figure 9.9 shows an example of the failure message.

```
print <<__FAILHTML__;
<HTML><HEAD>
<TITLE>Error Occurred</TITLE>
</HEAD>
<BODY>
<CENTER>
<H1>
Sorry, there appears to be a problem accessing a session file.
</H1>
</CENTER>
</BODY></HTML>
__FAILHTML__
```

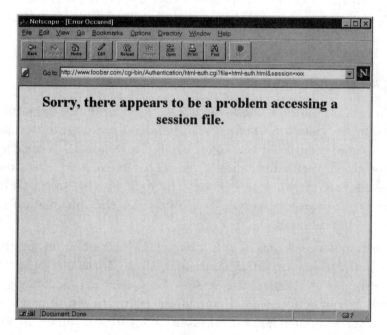

Figure 9.9 auth-lib-fail-html.pl's error message example.

auth-lib-extra.pl

auth-lib-extra.pl contains all the extra routines needed to perform CGI-based authentication as well as create sessions. Because these routines

147

are typically called only when the session is created and a user needs to log on, they have been placed in a separate file to make loading the original library file (**auth-lib.pl**) more efficient.

In addition, the HTML output in this library file has been separated into yet another file to make it easier for you to edit the look of the screens without altering the authentication routines. Thus, when the core authentication routines are updated, it will be less likely that you will need to redo your specific HTML changes. The following code loads this extra HTML code.

```
require "$auth_lib/auth-extra-html.pl";
```

When you're modifying the Perl code that prints the HTML, be careful to escape any special characters such as @ with a backslash.

N O T E

THE VERIFYUSER SUBROUTINE

The `VerifyUser` routine is the heart of the logon and user authentication process. It processes a CGI-based security logon and registration as well as server-based security. If the logon is valid, a session ID is created and the appropriate user information is passed to the `GetSessionInfo` routine discussed earlier. `VerifyUser` returns exactly the same fields as `GetSessionInfo` does, so `GetSessionInfo` can pass the information to the CGI script that called it.

As parameters, `VerifyUser` gets the main CGI script name and the reference to the associative array containing all the form variable information. Variables containing the session ID (`$session`), security groups (`$group`), username (`$username`), and all the other user information fields (`@extra_fields`) are declared in this routine for processing by the various security checking routines. In addition, `$bad_logon_message` is declared as a variable that is used to pass logon problems, such as using an invalid password, to the user as an HTML message.

```
sub VerifyUser {
    local ($main_script, *in) = @_;
    local ($session, $group, $username,
```

```
@extra_fields,
$bad_logon_message);
```

$bad_logon_message is initialized to contain no message. If the previous logon has failed, $bad_logon_message will contain a message to print to the user.

```
$bad_logon_message = "";
```

There are two ways of authenticating, or logging in, a user. CGI-based authentication uses this script's routines and HTML forms to log the user into the system. Server-based authentication uses the Web server's built-in authentication and relies on the environmental variable for the REMOTE_USER name containing a valid value set by the Web server itself.

When CGI-based authentication is used, the value of the submit buttons on the HTML forms—related to logging in, registration, searching for past usernames, and more—determine the type of processing that the authentication library should perform.

In the following code, if the form variable auth_logon_op has a value, the script knows that the user has pressed a button on an HTML form; the button's name was auth_logon_op. The only form with this button is the logon HTML form. In this case, the script calls the subroutine &CgiLogon to process the logon variables for username and password.

```
if ($auth_cgi eq "on") {

    if ($in{'auth_logon_op'} ne "") {
        ($bad_logon_message, $session,
         $username, $group, @extra_fields) =
         &CgiLogon($main_script, *in);
    } # End of auth_logon processing
```

Another case is auth_search_op. If this button is pressed, the subroutine is called to start searching for usernames. In addition, this routine is not called unless you have configured the script to allow searching using the $auth_allow_search variable. auth_search_screen_op is another form variable that is set when the HTML form should print using the PrintSearchPage routine for searching past usernames.

```
if ($in{'auth_search_op'} ne "" &&
    $auth_allow_search eq "on") {
    &SearchUsers($main_script, *in);
    exit;
}

if ($in{'auth_search_screen_op'} ne "" &&
    $auth_allow_search eq "on") {
    &PrintSearchPage($main_script, *in);
    exit;
}
```

When the `auth_register_op` submit button on the registration HTML form is clicked on and registration has been allowed by setting the `$auth_allow_reg-ister` variable to `on`, the `RegisterUser` function is called to register the user.

```
if ($in{'auth_register_op'} ne "" &&
    $auth_allow_register eq "on") {
    &RegisterUser($main_script, *in);
    exit;
} # End of register screen processing
```

Similarly, when the `auth_register_screen_op` submit button is pressed on the logon HTML form, `PrintRegisterPage` is called to print the HTML form for registering a user.

```
if ($in{'auth_register_screen_op'} ne "" &&
    $auth_allow_register eq "on") {
        &PrintRegisterPage;
    exit;
} # End of register screen
```

As a catch-all, the logon HTML form is printed using the `PrintLogonPage` function if the session ID has not yet been generated or if the user has pressed the `auth_logon_screen_op` submit button on one of the previous HTML forms. This ends the CGI-based security processing.

```
if ($in{'auth_logon_screen_op'} ne ""
    || ($session eq "")) {
    &PrintLogonPage($bad_logon_message,
      $main_script, *in);
    exit;
```

```
    } # End of Logon Screen

    } # End of Auth_CGI
```

The next section of the script processes Web server–based security if the
$auth_server variable has been set previously to on. The username is
retrieved using the REMOTE_USER environmental variable set by the Web
server. If there is a username, the **auth-server-lib.pl** library file is executed
to gather the rest of the user information.

```
    if ($auth_server eq "on") {
    $username = $ENV{'REMOTE_USER'};
    if ($username ne "") {
# The following calls a site-specific server based
# authentication routine
        require "auth-server-lib.pl";

    } # End of if username ne ""

    }  # End of if AUTH_SERVER is on
```

If neither CGI nor server-based security is used, the extra fields as well as
the username to return are set to a list of blank strings. The group name
is set to the default group so that a script that relies on security will be
able to use the default group for security even without the rest of the
user information. Finally, a session is created with this fake information
by a call to MakeSessionFile.

The final part of this routine returns a session ID and the user information to GetSessionInfo.

```
if ($auth_server ne "on" && $auth_cgi ne "on") {
    @extra_fields = ();
    $username = "";
    $group = $auth_default_group;
    foreach (@auth_extra_fields) {
        push (@extra_fields, "");
    }
    $session = &MakeSessionFile(@extra_fields);
    } # End of if neither server or cgi auth is on
```

```
($session, $username, $group, @extra_fields);

} # End of VerifyUser
```

THE CgiLogon SUBROUTINE

The next routine, CgiLogon, attempts to log the user in to the authentication library using CGI-based security. The form variables from the HTML logon screen are interpreted against the user file to see whether the user is valid. If the logon is invalid, an error message is generated as part of the $bad_logon_message variable. If the logon is successful, the session is created and the user information is passed to VerifyUser.

In addition, variables are set aside for the logon processing. $form_password is the password as it was entered into the form. $session is the session ID. @fields contains the fields of user information. $bad_logon_message contains an error message if the logon becomes unsuccessful for any reason. And finally, the $user_matched variable is set to true if the username was found in the file. Most of these variables are set to 0 or "" initially. $form_password is set to the form variable for the password that was entered on the HTML logon form.

```
sub CgiLogon {
    local ($main_script, *in) = @_;
    local($password, $username, $group, @extra_fields);
    local($form_password, $session, @fields);
    local($bad_logon_message);
    local($user_matched);

    $bad_logon_message = "";
    $session = "";
    @fields = ();
    $form_password = $in{"auth_password"};
```

Next, the file containing user information is opened to scan whether the logon information matches one of the records. The $user_matched flag is set to 0 initially to indicate that no match yet exists.

The while loop continually reads each line of the file. Each line is then split into individual user fields that are separated by the pipe symbol in the file. If the username that the user submitted is the same as a username in the file, the $user_matched variable is set to 1. Then the password that was entered is compared to the password in the user file. The password that was entered into the HTML logon form has been passed through the AuthEncryptWrap routine to encrypt the password in the same way that it appears in the file. If the password that the user entered has not been encrypted in this manner, it does not match the encrypted version that is already stored in the user file.

If the passwords match, the user fields are split into the @fields array. Because the password is the first element of the array and because we do not need to return its value, we strip it off the array by using the shift function. Finally, a session file is created with MakeSessionFile using this newly gathered user information.

```
open (USERFILE, "$auth_user_file");

$user_matched = 0;
while (<USERFILE>) {
 chop($_);
 ($password, $username, $group, $first_name,
  $last_name, $email) = split(/\|/, $_);
 if ($in{'auth_user_name'} eq $username) {
     $user_matched = 1;
 if (&AuthEncryptWrap($form_password, $password) eq
     $password) {
     @fields = split(/\|/, $_);
     shift(@fields); # Get rid of password field
     $session = &MakeSessionFile(@fields);
 } # End of if passwords match
 } # End of if username matches
} # End of While
close (USERFILE);
```

If no session was created but the username was found, the user probably did not have a matching password, so the program puts this information into the $bad_logon_message variable. If the username was not found, the user is notified and a different message is placed in $bad_logon_message. Finally, the $bad_logon_message, $session, and @fields user information is returned to VerifyUser for further processing.

```
   if ($user_matched == 1 && $session eq "") {
    $bad_logon_message =
        "<p><strong>Sorry, Your password did not";
    $bad_logon_message .=
        " match the username.</strong><p>";
   }
   if ($user_matched == 0) {
    $bad_logon_message =
        "<p><strong>Sorry, Your username was not";
    $bad_logon_message .=
        " found.</strong><p>";


   }
($bad_logon_message, $session, @fields);


} # End of CgiLogon
```

THE MAKESESSIONFILE SUBROUTINE

The MakeSessionFile routine creates the session file that stores the current user information. GetSessionInfo later uses this session file to retrieve information about the currently logged-on user every time the current session ID is sent to the routine. This routine starts by accepting a list of fields that make up the user information and then returns the newly acquired session ID that is associated with the session file.

```
sub MakeSessionFile
{
local(@fields) = @_;
local($session, $session_file);
```

The first thing MakeSessionFile does is to call a routine (RemoveOldSessions) to remove old session files that are no longer being used. Then a new session ID is generated. We do this by generating a random number. The random number is first seeded in the srand function by combining the value of the process ID and the current time variable using the or operator (|). Finally, this random number, the time, and the process ID are converted to a long hexadecimal number that serves as the new session ID. A hexadecimal number is made up of digits that include the numbers 0 through 9 and the letters A through F instead of the 0 through 9 digits found in the base 10 system. The session filename consists of the session ID plus a **.dat** extension.

```
&RemoveOldSessions;

# Seed the random generator
srand($$|time);
$session = int(rand(60000));
# pack the time, process id, and random $session into a
# hex number which will make up the session id.
$session = unpack("H*", pack("Nnn", time, $$, $session));

$session_file = "$session.dat";
```

Next, the session file is opened for creation in the directory specified by the `$auth_session_dir` variable, which is set in the script that uses this library. The user information fields are joined by the pipe symbol and are written to the file. Finally, the file is closed and the newly formed session code is returned from the subroutine.

```
open (SESSIONFILE,">$auth_session_dir/$session_file")
    || &CgiDie("Could Not Create Session File\n");
print SESSIONFILE join ("\|", @fields);
print SESSIONFILE "\n";

close (SESSIONFILE);

$session;

} # End of MakeSessionFile
```

THE REMOVEOLDSESSIONS SUBROUTINE

The `RemoveOldSessions` procedure goes into the `$auth_session_dir` directory and removes all files that are older than `$auth_session_length` days. These variables are set by the script that calls this library. The `@files` array contains all the filenames in the current directory. `$file` is a temporary variable that holds the filename of the current file the program is checking for age.

The directory is opened using the opendir command, and the files in the directory are read into an array using the readdir command. The output from readdir is passed to Perl's internal grep function to make sure that the special filenames "." and ".." escape the removal process.

```
sub RemoveOldSessions
{
local(@files, $file);
# Open up the session directory.
opendir(SESSIONDIR, "$auth_session_dir") ||
    &CgiDie("Session Directory Would Not Open\n");
# read all entries except "." and ".."
@files = grep(!/^\.\.?$/,readdir(SESSIONDIR));
closedir(SESSIONDIR);
```

Each file is then checked for age using the -M operator. This operator returns the age of the file in days. If this age is greater than $auth_ session_length, the unlink function is called to delete the file.

```
foreach $file (@files)
        {
# If it is older than auth_session_length, delete it
        if (-M "$auth_session_dir/$file" >
                $auth_session_length)
                {
                unlink("$auth_session_dir/$file");
                }


        }
} # End of RemoveOldSessions
```

THE SEARCHUSERS SUBROUTINE

SearchUsers searches for the users in the user file based on E-mail address and returns the username that matches the address. Sometimes users may forget their username, so this function provides a mechanism to allow them to find it again. SearchUsers accepts the main CGI script as a parameter so that it can print an HTML form that posts data to the original script. For the same reason, it also is passed the current form data in an associative array. The final output of this routine is an HTML form listing the found usernames if any were found.

$user_match keeps track of the currently matched usernames that are found later in the routine. $field_num is used to keep track of the element in the @auth_extra_fields array that contains the auth_email field. $user-name keeps track of the current username as the user file is searched. @extra_fields contains the fields that are read from the user file one line at a time. $auth_email is the form variable for the current E-mail address to search for. $user_list converts the usernames from the $user_match variable to an HTML list of names for later output to the user's Web browser. $form_tags contains a list of form variables passed by the previous CGI script that are not authentication-related. The library prints these as hidden variables on the forms it outputs so that the original CGI script form variables do not get lost during the CGI-based logon process.

```
sub SearchUsers {
    local($main_script, *in) = @_;
    local($user_match);
    local($field_num, $username, @extra_fields);
    local($auth_email);
    local($user_list);

    local($form_tags);

    $form_tags = &PrintCurrentFormVars(*in);
```

The first thing this function does is to open the user file for reading. The E-mail address being searched for is placed in the $auth_email variable, is changed to lowercase, and has spaces removed. This technique allows the search to be successful later even if the E-mail address is entered with a different case or with spaces embedded between characters. $user_match is set to nothing, because the program has not yet found any variables.

```
    open (USERFILE, "$auth_user_file") ||
        &CgiDie("Could Not Open User File\n");

    $auth_email = $in{'auth_email'};
    $auth_email =~ tr/A-Z/a-z/;
    $auth_email =~ s/ //g;
    $user_match = "";
```

The next part of this function iterates through the `@auth_extra_fields` array to find which element number in the list contains the `auth_email` field. Because the fields in `@extra_fields` are user-defined, you may have decided to use a different order of fields than is provided in the example. The index to the location in the array is stored in `$field_num`.

```
$field_num = 0;
foreach (@auth_extra_fields) {
  if ($_ eq "auth_email") {
      last;
  }
  $field_num++;
}
```

The file containing user information is parsed line by line until a match is found in the E-mail address. First, the extra newline is truncated from each line as it is read. Then any uppercase characters are converted to lowercase using the `tr` function. All the fields are `split` into an array using the pipe delimiter. The three fields are removed from the array, because they always consist of the password, username, and group information. They never contain the E-mail address. Finally, the E-mail address in the current user record is compared to the E-mail address that the user is searching for. If they match, the username is stored in the `$user_match` variable.

```
while (<USERFILE>) {
  chop($_);
  tr/A-Z/a-z/;
  @extra_fields = split(/\|/, $_);
  $username = $extra_fields[1];
  # Get rid of the first three fields
  shift(@extra_fields);
  shift(@extra_fields);
  shift(@extra_fields);
  if ($auth_email eq $extra_fields[$field_num]) {
      $user_match .= $username . "|";
  } # End of email match
} # End of While
close (USERFILE);
```

Next, the procedure checks to see whether there are any matches after the entire user file has been searched. If there are matches, they are converted to HTML code consisting of the list of usernames separated by the `<P>` HTML tag.

```
if ($user_match ne "") {
 $user_list = $user_match;
 $user_list =~ s/\|/<p>/g;
}
```

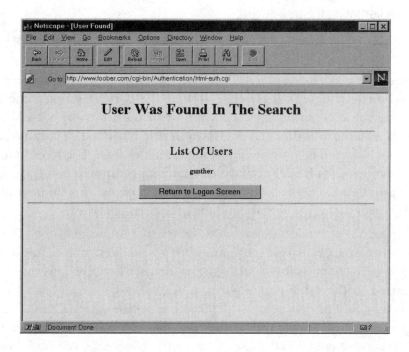

Figure 9.10 *Example of a successful search result.*

If no users were found, HTMLPrintNoSearchResults is called to print an HTML form that displays a message. If users were found, HTMLPrintSearchResults displays an HTML form with the newly found usernames. Figure 9.10 contains an example of the search results that are returned if a successful match is found.

```
if ($user_match eq "") {
 &HTMLPrintNoSearchResults($main_script,
                  $form_tags);
} else {
 &HTMLPrintSearchResults ($main_script,
```

```
                          $form_tags,
                          $user_list);

        } # End of no users matched


} # End of SearchUsers
```

THE REGISTERUSER SUBROUTINE

The RegisterUser function is one of the more complex procedures in the authentication library. Many different setup variables affect how RegisterUser processes a user's enrollment in the library. Like many of the other functions here, RegisterUser accepts the current script name and form variables as parameters. The output of the function is an HTML form indicating whether the registration was a success or a failure. In addition, depending on how the setup variables have been configured, this function sends E-mail notification that a registration has occurred, or, if the program has been configured to choose a password automatically, it sends E-mail to users telling them their generated password.

@form_vars keeps track of the form variables that are used in the registration process, such as the username, last name, first name, and other fields. $group contains the security group the user is given. This variable is initialized to the value contained in $auth_default_group. @f is an array that is used as a placeholder for fields in the routine. @write_fields is the array of items that is written to the user file upon a successful registration. $password contains the user's password. $form_tags is a placeholder for the HTML form variables that are passed to the original script. $user_matched is used as a flag to see whether the user already exists in the user file. $userfile is the name of the file that contains user data. $user_email is the E-mail address of the user. $real_password is the clear text version of the user's password. The $password variable is encrypted, so $real_password stores the nonencrypted version for further processing. $random is a randomly generated number from which a salt is generated for the encryption routine. A *salt* is basically a random two-character string added to the encryption routine. $salt contains the salt for the encryption routine. The encryption routine's behavior changes when different salts are added to it, providing extra security.

```
sub RegisterUser {
    local($main_script, *in) = @_;
    local($x, @form_vars, $group, @f);
    local(@write_fields, $password);
    local($form_tags, $user_matched);
    local($userfile,$user_email,$real_password);
    local($random,$salt);
    $form_tags = &PrintCurrentFormVars(*in);
    $group = $auth_default_group;
```

`@form_vars` contains a list of HTML form variables from the registration screen. If `$auth_generate_password` is `off`, the HTML registration screen prompts the user for a password and a confirmation of the password. These password variables are pushed into `@form_vars` in this case.

```
@form_vars = ('auth_user_name', @auth_extra_fields);

    if ($auth_generate_password ne "on") {
     push(@form_vars, "auth_password1");
     push(@form_vars, "auth_password2");
    }
```

The `%in` associative array contains all the form variables. In this case, all the variables in `@form_vars` are checked to see that they have a value and that the value contains no pipe symbols. Because pipe symbols delimit individual fields in the user file, problems would be caused if users were allowed to register using pipe symbols inside the fields. If there is a problem, the `HTMLPrintRegisterNoValidValues` routine is called to print the error message and the program exits. In addition, if there is an E-mail address designated with the `auth_email` form variable, that value is placed in the `$user_email` variable.

```
    foreach $x (@form_vars) {
     if ($in{"$x"} eq "" || $in{"$x"} =~ /\|/) {
         &HTMLPrintRegisterNoValidValues($main_script,
                            $form_tags);
         exit;
     } # End of if
     if ($x eq "auth_email") {
         $user_email = $in{"$x"};
     }
    } # End of Foreach form variable
```

If the password is not automatically generated, the passwords that are entered on the HTML registration form must match. Otherwise, an error HTML page is generated and the program exits.

```
if ($in{'auth_password1'} ne $in{'auth_password2'}) {
    &HTMLPrintRegisterNoPasswordMatch($main_script,
                        $form_tags);
    exit;
}
```

If $auth_check_duplicates is turned on, the user file is opened and scanned for duplicate usernames. In addition, this same routine is used again on the alternative user file ($auth_alt_user_file) if it is defined. $user_matched is set to 1 if any duplicates are found in the files. Setting $user_matched to 1 triggers the program to print an HTML error page and exit.

```
if ($auth_check_duplicates eq "on") {

    open (USERFILE, "$auth_user_file");
    $user_matched = 0;
    while (<USERFILE>) {
        chop($_);
        @f = split(/\|/, $_);
        if ($f[1] eq $in{'auth_user_name'}) {
         $user_matched = 1;
         last;
        }
    } # End of while userfile open
    close (USERFILE);

# Check for duplicates in the alternative
# file if it is defined.
    if ($auth_alt_user_file ne "") {
        open (USERFILE, "$auth_alt_user_file");

        while (<USERFILE>) {
         chop($_);
         @f = split(/\|/, $_);
         if ($f[1] eq $in{'auth_user_name'}) {
             $user_matched = 1;
             last;
         }
        } # End of while userfile open
```

```
        close (USERFILE);
    } # End of auth_alt_user_file

    if ($user_matched == 1) {
        &HTMLPrintRegisterFoundDuplicate($main_script,
                        $form_tags);
        exit;
    } # End of user matched (found duplicate)
} # End of if check duplicates on
```

Because the random number generator is used several times in this sub-routine, it is seeded in advance with the combined $$ (process ID) and current time variable. The random variable is a placeholder for a string that contains the list of characters from which we choose a password or encryption salt.

```
srand(time|$$);
$random = "abcdefghijklmnopqrstuvwxyz1234567890";
```

When $auth_generate_password is off, the $password variable is set to one of the form variables. Otherwise, $password is randomly generated based on a string consisting of six alphabetic characters or numbers. $real_password is then set to the value of $password, because $password will be encrypted.

```
    if ($auth_generate_password ne "on") {
     $password = $in{"auth_password1"};
    } else {
     $password = "";
     for (1..6) {
            $password .= substr($random,int(rand(36)),1);
        }
    }
    $real_password = $password;
```

The salt for the encryption function is a two-character string that changes the behavior of the encryption routine. The encrypted password appears differently, depending on which salt is used. The program calls the AuthEncryptWrap routine instead of Perl's crypt routine, because crypt is not supported in some operating systems. This makes it easy to turn off

or replace the encryption routine, because it is encapsulated in its own
subroutine.

```
    $salt = "";
for (1..2) {
    $salt .= substr($random,int(rand(36)),1);
    }
    $password = &AuthEncryptWrap ($password,
                    $salt);
    @write_fields = ($password, $in{'auth_user_name'},
                foreach (@auth_extra_fields) {
     push(@write_fields, $in{"$_"});
    }
```

If the $auth_add_register variable is set to on, the user information is added
to the user file. The information is instead added to the alternative user file
if $auth_alt_user_file is specified in the library configuration. Whenever
information is added to the user file, we use AuthGetLock to lock it first to
make sure no one else is writing to the file at the same time. The file is then
written to and the lock is removed using AuthReleaseFileLock. As with the
Perl crypt routine, the script uses encapsulated routines instead of Perl's
flock routine, because flock is not supported on some operating systems. In
fact, flock is not even supported on all flavors of UNIX.

```
if ($auth_add_register eq "on") {

# Lock the file to make sure no one else will write to
# it if anyone else registers at the same time
#
&AuthGetFileLock ("$auth_user_file.lock");
    $user_file = $auth_user_file;
    if ($auth_alt_user_file ne "") {
     $user_file = $auth_alt_user_file;
    }
open (USERFILE, ">>$user_file");

print USERFILE join("\|", @write_fields) . "\n";
close (USERFILE);
&AuthReleaseFileLock ("$auth_user_file.lock");

} # End of auth_add_register
```

If the `$auth_email_register` variable is on and if your E-mail address has been specified, the authentication library E-mails you with the fact that the user registered on your system. Note that this part of the code requires the **mail-lib.pl** library discussed in an earlier chapter to send the message.

```
if ($auth_email_register eq "on" &&
    $auth_admin_from_address ne "" &&
    $auth_admin_email_address ne "") {
    require "$auth_lib/mail-lib.pl";
local($subject, $message);
$subject = "Register User";

$message = join(",", @write_fields) . "\n";
&send_mail($auth_admin_from_address,
    $auth_admin_email_address,
    $subject, $message);
} # End of Email Register
```

If the password is generated by the authentication library and the registration has been successful so far, the program E-mails the user's new password using the **mail-lib.pl** library. Finally, an HTML form is output to the user's Web browser indicating that the registration was a success.

```
if ($auth_generate_password eq "on") {
    if ($auth_email_register ne "on") {
        require "$auth_lib/mail-lib.pl";
    }
    $subject = "Registered User Password";
    $message = $auth_password_message;
    $message .= " $real_password.\n\n\n";
    &send_mail($auth_admin_from_address,
                $user_email,
                $subject, $message);
    }
    &HTMLPrintRegisterSuccess ($main_script,
                    $form_tags);

} # End of RegisterUser
```

THE PRINTCURRENTFORMVARS SUBROUTINE

PrintCurrentFormVars takes all form variables not related to authentication and returns a string containing the HTML code for hidden input fields related to those form variables. The routine differentiates between the library form variables and regular CGI script variables because the authentication library variables always begin with `auth_`. The hidden input HTML tags are included with the forms that the library prints so that when the original CGI script is called again, the original form variables will still be intact.

```
sub PrintCurrentFormVars {
    local(*form_vars) = @_;
    local($x,$y,$form_tags);
    $form_tags = "";
    foreach $x (keys %form_vars) {
     if (!($x =~ /auth_/i)) {
         $y = $form_vars{"$x"};
         $form_tags .= qq!<input type=hidden name=$x
          value="$y">\n!;
     }
    }
    $form_tags;
} # PrintCurrentFormTags
```

THE AUTHGETFILELOCK SUBROUTINE

The `AuthGetFileLock` function first looks to see whether a lock file exists. If there is a lock file, the routine waits for it to be released and then creates its own. A lock file ensures that no instance of the same program is writing to the user file at the same time. In case the program that originally made the lock file has crashed or has been killed for some reason before it could release the file, `AuthGetFileLock` waits for the file to be released only 60 seconds. After that, it is assumed that the file can be removed. The reason a hand-rolled lock file routine is used instead of the Perl `flock` function is that `flock` is not supported by some operating system platforms. Comments are included indicating the function that might be used if you decided to implement the `flock` routine.

```
sub AuthGetFileLock {
    local ($lock_file) = @_;

    local ($endtime);
    $endtime = 60;
    $endtime = time + $endtime;
#    We set endtime to wait 60 seconds
```

```
# The $endtime is used for a timeout of how long we
# want to keep waiting for the lock if someone else
# already has it open.
    while (-e $lock_file && time < $endtime) {
        # Do Nothing
    }
    open(LOCK_FILE, ">$lock_file");
#     flock(LOCK_FILE, 2);
} # end of AuthGetFileLock
```

THE AuthReleaseFileLock SUBROUTINE

AuthReleaseFileLock is the opposite of the AuthGetFileLock routine. It removes the lock file using the unlink Perl function. If you decide to reprogram the routine to use flock instead, there are comments indicating the appropriate flock function to use.

```
sub AuthReleaseFileLock {
    local ($lock_file) = @_;

# 8 unlocks the file
#     flock(LOCK_FILE, 8);
    close(LOCK_FILE);
    unlink($lock_file);

} # end of ReleaseFileLock
```

THE AuthEncryptWrap SUBROUTINE

AuthEncryptWrap encrypts a string with the salt that is provided as a parameter and returns the newly encrypted string. If $auth_use_cleartext is on, the encryption does not occur. If your operating system does not support the Perl crypt function, you can write your own encryption routine inside this function or set the $auth_use_cleartext variable to on when you configure the authentication library.

```
sub AuthEncryptWrap {
    local ($field, $salt) = @_;

# If auth_use_cleartext is on, then we do not
# encrypt the password.
    if ($auth_use_cleartext ne "on") {
    $field = crypt ($field, $salt);
```

```
    }

    $field;

} # end of encrypt
```

auth-extra-html.pl

auth-extra-html.pl contains the routines that print the HTML forms for logon, registration, error messages, and other screens for the authentication library. By separating the HTML-related functions into their own file, you decrease the likelihood that this file will have to be replaced if there is an update to the logic in the main authentication routines that process the registration and logons. This is a benefit if you decide to make extensive cosmetic changes and do not wish to repeat the process whenever there is a minor bug fix or script update.

Typically, the routines here accept the current set of form variables and main CGI script name as parameters. This information is needed so that the HTML form can direct the user's Web browser to post the information to the original CGI script that uses the authentication library. In addition, the current CGI script form variables are passed from screen to screen to maintain the information that the user wanted to pass to the original CGI script. The variable $form_tags is generally used to store the HTML code related to hidden input fields that contain this previous CGI form information.

THE PRINTLOGONPAGE SUBROUTINE

PrintLogonPage prints the HTML form that logs the user in to the authentication library. $bad_logon_message is used as a parameter and contains an error message if the logon HTML page is being printed again as a result of a problem logging in. $register_tag is set up to contain the HTML code for the registration button if $auth_allow_register is set to on during configuration of CGI-based security. Similarly, $search_tag is used to store the HTML code for the search button if $auth_allow_search is set to on.

```
sub PrintLogonPage {
    local($bad_logon_message, $main_script, *in) = @_;
```

```
local($form_tags);
local($register_tag);
local($search_tag);
```

You can override the logon page title and header by setting the $auth_logon_title and $auth_logon_header variables as part of the authentication library setup. If these variables are not set, defaults are chosen for them.

```
if (length($auth_logon_title) < 1) {
    $auth_logon_title = "Submit Logon";
}


if (length($auth_logon_header) < 1) {
    $auth_logon_header = "Enter Your Logon Information";
}
```

The following piece of code sets up the $register_tag and $search_tag variables with HTML code for the register and search buttons if they are allowed in your setup using $auth_allow_register and $auth_allow_search.

```
$register_tag = "";
$search_tag = "";


if ($auth_allow_register eq "on") {
  $register_tag = <<__END_OF_REG_TAG__;
<input type=submit name=auth_register_screen_op
value="Register For An Account"><p>
__END_OF_REG_TAG__
}


if ($auth_allow_search eq "on") {
  $search_tag = <<__END_OF_SEARCH_TAG__;
<input type=submit name=auth_search_screen_op
value="Search For Old Account"><p>
__END_OF_SEARCH_TAG__
    }
```

$form_tags is set to the HTML code of hidden input fields that are set to the form variables passed to the original CGI script. Finally, the HTML code is printed with all the variables that have been set.

```
    $form_tags = &PrintCurrentFormVars(*in);


    print <<__END_OF_LOGON__;
<HTML><HEAD>
<TITLE>$auth_logon_title</TITLE>
</HEAD>
<BODY>
<CENTER>
<H1>$auth_logon_header</h1>
<hr>
$bad_logon_message
<FORM METHOD=POST ACTION=$main_script>
$form_tags
<TABLE>
<TR><TH>Username</TH>
<TD><INPUT TYPE=TEXT NAME=auth_user_name></td></tr>
<tr><th>Password</th>
<td><input type=password name=auth_password></td></tr>
</TABLE><p>
<input type=submit name=auth_logon_op
value="Log On To The System"><p>
$register_tag
$search_tag
<hr>
</center>
</form>
</body>
</HTML>
__END_OF_LOGON__


} # End of PrintLogonPage
```

THE PRINTSEARCHPAGE SUBROUTINE

PrintSearchPage prints the HTML form that asks users to enter the E-mail address to search for usernames on. This function sets up the hidden form tags for the original CGI script form variables and then prints the relevant HTML form.

```
sub PrintSearchPage {
local($main_script,*in) = @_;
    local($form_tags);
    $form_tags = &PrintCurrentFormVars(*in);
    print <<__END_OF_SEARCH__;
<HTML><HEAD>
<TITLE>Search For An Account</TITLE>
```

```
</HEAD>
<BODY>
<CENTER>
<H1>Search For Matching Username</h1>
<hr>
<h2>Enter Your Email Address To Search For A Matching Username</h2>
<FORM METHOD=POST ACTION=$main_script>
$form_tags
<TABLE>
<TR><TH>Email</TH>
<TD><INPUT TYPE=TEXT NAME=auth_email></td></tr>
</TABLE>
<p>
<input type=submit name=auth_search_op value="Submit Search">
<input type=submit name=auth_logon_screen_op value="Return to Logon
Screen">
<P>
</center>
</form>
</body>
</HTML>
__END_OF_SEARCH__


} # End of PrintSearchPage
```

THE HTMLPRINTSEARCHRESULTS SUBROUTINE

HTMLPrintSearchResults prints the HTML code related to a successful search for usernames. Again, this routine merely prints the HTML form that contains the variables related to the hidden HTML tags that correspond to the originally passed CGI script variables.

```
sub HTMLPrintSearchResults {
    local($main_script, $form_tags, $user_list) =
    @_;
    print <<__END_SEARCHRESULTS__;
<HTML><HEAD>
<TITLE>User Found</TITLE>
</HEAD>
<BODY>
<CENTER>
<H1>User Was Found In The Search</h1>
<hr>
<h2>List Of Users</h2>
<strong>$user_list</strong>
<FORM METHOD=POST ACTION=$main_script>
$form_tags
```

171

```
<input type=submit name=auth_logon_screen_op
value="Return to Logon Screen">
<hr>
</center>
</form>
</body>
</HTML>
__END_SEARCHRESULTS__

} # End of HTMLPrintSearchResults
```

THE HTMLPRINTNOSEARCHRESULTS SUBROUTINE

HTMLPrintNoSearchResults is just like HTMLPrintSearchResults except that it is called if no matching usernames were found.

```
sub HTMLPrintNoSearchResults {
    local($main_script, $form_tags) = @_;
     print <<__END_NOSEARCHRESULTS__;
<HTML><HEAD>
<TITLE>No Users Found</TITLE>
</HEAD>
<BODY>
<CENTER>
<H1>Sorry, No Users Found</h1>
<hr>
<h2>Sorry, No users were found that matched your email address</h2>
<FORM METHOD=POST ACTION=$main_script>
$form_tags
<input type=submit name=auth_logon_screen_op
value="Return to Logon Screen">
<hr>
</center>
</form>
</body>
</HTML>
__END_NOSEARCHRESULTS__

} # End HTMLPrintNoSearchResults
```

THE PRINTREGISTERPAGE SUBROUTINE

PrintRegisterPage prints the HTML form that lets the user enter and submit registration information. If the passwords are not automatically generated, the $password_input variable will contain HTML code for the password input fields. Similarly, if the password is being generated, the $password_message variable will contain a message that is sent to the user on the HTML form. The message tells users that the password will be sent via E-mail.

```
sub PrintRegisterPage {
local($main_script,*in) = @_;
local($form_tags);
local($more_form_input,$password_input, $x);
    $form_tags = &PrintCurrentFormVars(*in);
local ($password_message);

#
# We also check for the extra fields and output HTML
# asking for input on the extra fields.
#
$more_form_input = "";
for ($x = 0; $x <= @auth_extra_fields - 1; $x++) {
    $more_form_input .= <<__END_OF_EXTRA_FIELDS__;
<TR><TH>$auth_extra_desc[$x]</TH>
<TD><INPUT TYPE=TEXT NAME=$auth_extra_fields[$x]></td></tr>
__END_OF_EXTRA_FIELDS__
}
$password_input = "";
if ($auth_generate_password ne "on") {
    $password_input = <<__END_OF_PASSWORD_FIELDS__;
<tr><th>Password</th>
<td><input type=password name=auth_password1></td></tr>
<tr><th>Password Again</th>
<td><input type=password name=auth_password2></td></tr>
__END_OF_PASSWORD_FIELDS__
}
$password_message = "";
if ($auth_generate_password eq "on") {
$password_message = <<__PASSWORDMSG__;
Your password will be automatically generated and sent
to you via your E-mail address.
__PASSWORDMSG__
}
    print <<__END_OF_REGISTER__;
<HTML><HEAD>
<TITLE>Register For An Account</TITLE>
</HEAD>
<BODY>
<CENTER>
```

```
<H1>Enter The Registration Information</h1>
<hr>
<FORM METHOD=POST ACTION=$main_script>
$form_tags
<TABLE>
<tr><th>User Name</th>
<td><input type=Username name=auth_user_name></td></tr>
$password_input
$more_form_input
</TABLE>
<p>
<input type=submit name=auth_register_op value="Submit Information">
<input type=submit name=auth_logon_screen_op value="Return to Logon
Screen">
<P>
$password_message
</center>
</form>
</body>
</HTML>
__END_OF_REGISTER__


} # End of PrintRegisterPage
```

The HTMLPrintRegisterSuccess Subroutine

If the user's registration process is successful, a new HTML form reports the success using HTMLPrintRegisterSuccess. This simple form leads users back to the logon screen if they press the **Return To Logon Screen** button. Figure 9.11 is an example of this success screen.

```
sub HTMLPrintRegisterSuccess {
    local($main_script, $form_tags) =
     @_;
    print <<__END_OF_REGISTER_SUCCESS__;
<HTML><HEAD>
<TITLE>Registration Added</TITLE>
</HEAD>
<BODY>
<CENTER>
<H2>You have been added to the user database</h2>
</center>
<hr>
<FORM METHOD=POST ACTION=$main_script>
$form_tags
```

```
<BLOCKQUOTE>
    $auth_register_message
</Blockquote>
<center>
<input type=submit name=auth_logon_screen_op value="Return to Logon
Screen")
</center>
</form>
</body>
</HTML>
__END_OF_REGISTER_SUCCESS__


} # End of RegisterSuccess
```

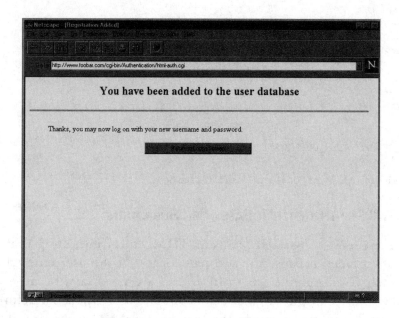

Figure 9.11 HTML form indicating a successful registration has occurred.

THE HTMLPRINTREGISTERFOUNDDUPLICATE SUBROUTINE

HTMLPrintRegisterFoundDuplicate prints an HTML form indicating that the user's registration was a failure because the username was already contained in the user file.

```
sub HTMLPrintRegisterFoundDuplicate {
    local($main_script, $form_tags) =
     @_;
print <<__END_OF_REGISTER_DUPLICATE__;
<HTML><HEAD>
<TITLE>Problem with Registration</TITLE>
</HEAD>
<BODY>
<CENTER>
<H1>Problem with Registration</h1>
</center>
<hr>
<FORM METHOD=POST ACTION=$main_script>
$form_tags
<BLOCKQUOTE>
Sorry, your username is already in the database
</Blockquote>
<center>
<input type=submit name=auth_logon_screen_op value="Return to Logon
Screen")
</center>
</form>
</body>
</HTML>
__END_OF_REGISTER_DUPLICATE__


} # End of HTMLPrintRegisterFoundDuplicate
```

THE HTMLPRINTREGISTERNOPASSWORD SUBROUTINE

HTMLPrintRegisterNoPassword prints an HTML form indicating that the
registration failed because the two passwords that the user entered did
not match. Two separate password entries are necessary, because this
field does not echo the original characters the user typed. Therefore, a
second field is used to confirm the first password and make sure that a
typo did not occur.

```
sub HTMLPrintRegisterNoPasswordMatch {
    local($main_script, $form_tags) =
     @_;

    print <<__END_OF_REGISTER_NOMATCH__;
<HTML><HEAD>
<TITLE>Problem with Registration</TITLE>
</HEAD>
```

```
<BODY>
<CENTER>
<H1>Problem with Registration</h1>
</center>
<hr>
<FORM METHOD=POST ACTION=$main_script>
$form_tags
<BLOCKQUOTE>
Sorry, the two passwords you typed in did not match.
</Blockquote>
<center>
<input type=submit name=auth_logon_screen_op value="Return to Logon
Screen")
</center>
</form>
</body>
</HTML>
__END_OF_REGISTER_NOMATCH__


} # End of HTMLPrintRegisterNoPasswordMatch
```

THE HTMLPRINTREGISTERNOVALIDVALUES SUBROUTINE

HTMLPrintRegisterNoValidValues prints yet another registration failure
HTML form. This one is printed if the user has left out any values in the
registration process.

```
sub HTMLPrintRegisterNoValidValues {
    local ($main_script, $form_tags) =
     @_;
    print <<__END_OF_REGISTER_NOVALUE__;
<HTML><HEAD>
<TITLE>Problem with Registration</TITLE>
</HEAD>
<BODY>
<CENTER>
<H1>Problem with Registration</h1>
</center>
<hr>
<FORM METHOD=POST ACTION=$main_script>
$form_tags
<BLOCKQUOTE>
Sorry, you need to enter a valid value for every field
</Blockquote>
<center>
<input type=submit name=auth_logon_screen_op value="Return to Logon
```

177

```
Screen")
</center>
</form>
</body>
</HTML>
__END_OF_REGISTER_NOVALUE__

} # End of HTMLPrintRegisterNoValidValues
```

auth-server-lib.pl

auth-server-lib.pl is called by the `VerifyUser` function in **auth-extra-lib.pl** if the method of security is Web server–based instead of CGI-based. This file has been broken out separately, because getting user information beyond the username in Web server–based security is usually quite server- and application-specific. For example, on a company intranet in which employees log into to the Web server itself, the rest of their information may need to be interfaced with an SQL database such as Sybase or Oracle from an employee database.

The following example code sets up a sample first name, last name, E-mail address, and security group that the user belongs to. If you were configuring your own server-based security, you would probably recode this routine to query a file or database of employee information. The final bit of the code calls the standard `MakeSessionFile` routine to create the session with the newly acquired user information. This call to `MakeSessionFile` must be included regardless of how you get the user information.

```
$firstname = "Gunther";
$lastname = "Birznieks";
$email = "gunther\@gunther.com";
$group = "$auth_default_group";

$session =
    &MakeSessionFile( ($username, $group, $firstname,
    $lastname,$email));
```

html-auth.cgi

html-auth.cgi is the sample CGI program included with the authentication library to demonstrate what **auth-lib.pl** is capable of. **html-auth.setup**

178

contains the sample authentication setup for this script. the purpose of **html-auth.cgi** is to protect certain HTML pages from being viewed unless the user logs in to the site.

Basically, you pass the name of the HTML file you wish to protect as a URL parameter to **html-auth.cgi**. For example, if you wished to protect **mypage.html**, you would call the program using the URL `html-auth.cgi?file=mypage.html`. If this program were in the **cgi-bin** of `www.foobar.com`, you would use the following URL:

```
http://www.foobar.com/cgi-bin/html-auth.cgi?file=mypage.html
```

If you have many pages that you wish to protect, you also need to reference the hyperlinks with this program and add the suffix `&session` to the URL parameter that is linked. This program filters the HTML page so that the tag `&session` is replaced, and the form variable is set equal to the current real session ID. The authentication library uses this session ID to make sure that the user has access to the page instead of asking the user to log in to read every page.

We append `&session` **instead of** `?session` **to the html-auth.cgi program URL because there is already a parameter (**`file`**) that html-auth.cgi expects to see. Thus, the natural continuation of the URL is with an** `&`**. A** `?` **is not used because the** `?` **has already separated the script name from the** `file` **URL variable.**

NOTE

If you are referencing a CGI script that uses the authentication library—such as the bulletin board script discussed in this book—then you would refer to it in a protected HTML page. For the BBS example, to access the "Open" forum you would use a URL such as `bbs_forum.cgi?forum=open&session` so that the session ID would also be passed to the **bbs_forum.cgi** script.

`$lib` is set to the path where you place your library files. Then Steven Brenner's **cgi-lib.pl** is used to read the form variables `file` and `session`. Before the authentication library is processed, **html-auth.setup** is loaded using the `require` command.

```
$lib = ".";
require "$lib/cgi-lib.pl";
```

```
#
# The following should be a setup file with your
# authorization variables.  In this case,
# we use test.setup for testing purposes.
#
require "html-auth.setup";
require "$auth_lib/auth-lib.pl";

print &PrintHeader;
&ReadParse;
```

The session is read from the form variable session first. Then GetSessionInfo is called. Note that the main script name is **html-auth.cgi** in this case. In addition, the current form variables are passed to the authentication library. Remember, the **html-auth.cgi** script requires the file form variable to be sent in order to know which file to parse and print to the user's Web browser. Thus, by passing the form variables, the authentication library makes sure that the file variable is passed from authentication screen to screen using hidden variables until this script is called into action again after the user successfully logs in.

```
$session = $in{"session"};

($session, @fields) =
    &GetSessionInfo($session, "html-auth.cgi", *in);
```

$htmlfile is set to the file form variable. If there is no form variable file, an HTML form is printed that lets the user know that a parameter is required. Otherwise, the file is opened. A while loop reads every line of the file into memory. If the line contains the word session, it is replaced with session=[THE REAL SESSION ID]. For example, if the session ID were 1234, the word session would be replaced with session=1234. This is done to preserve the current session between protected pages. Finally, the altered line is printed to the user's Web browser. This process continues until the end of the HTML file and then the program ends.

```
$htmlfile = $in{'file'};

if ($htmlfile ne "") {
    open(HTMLFILE, "$htmlfile") ||
```

```
            &CgiDie("Could not open $htmlfile");

        while (<HTMLFILE>) {
            if (/session/) {
             s/session/session=$session/;
            }
            print $_;
        }


        close (HTMLFILE);
} else {
```

The following code prints the HTML code that tells users how to use this program if they forgot to leave off the `file=` parameter on the URL that called this script.

```
print <<__END_OF_HTML__;
<HTML>
<HEAD>
<TITLE>
Authentication HTML Filter
</TITLE>
</HEAD>
<BODY>
<H1>Authentication HTML Filter</H1>
<HR>
<BLOCKQUOTE>
<STRONG>Error: </STRONG> You forgot to include
a "file=" parameter on the URL of this CGI script.
You need this parameter to tell the
html-auth.cgi program which HTML files
to protect from viewing as well as filter
session IDs in the file.
<P>
For example, you may want to use
a URL in the form of:
<P>
http://www.foobar.com/cgi-bin/html-auth.cgi?file=html-auth.html
</BLOCKQUOTE>
<HR>
</BODY>
</HTML>

__END_OF_HTML__
 } # End of if $htmlfile is there
```

CHAPTER 10

Using cgi-lib.sol

OVERVIEW

In writing the applications for this book, we found ourselves duplicating a number of routines in the scripts. To make our application more modular, we felt it would be a good idea to create a library of these routines. The result is **cgi-lib.sol**.

One function we added, `counter`, is used to create a unique ID number for every item in a database. Every added item must have a unique identification number if we are to search or modify the database, because the search or modification routines must have a way to identify each database row apart from all others. If a client says, "Delete item number 34 in the database," the script must be able to find item number 34 and delete it. If there were two item 34s or if the script had no way of knowing what item 34 meant, the script would not know which row to remove.

`open_error` returns a useful debugging note if a CGI script is having a problem opening a file. The script sends a note to the Web browser explaining the problem and specifying the problem file. Much as `CgiDie` in **cgi-lib.pl** does, `open_error` provides useful debugging information because it helps identify where the problem is occurring.

`header_tags` outputs the basic HTML header for every page:

```
<HTML><HEAD><TITLE>Insert your own title</TITLE></HEAD>
```

This routine does the same basic thing as `HtmlTop` in **cgi-lib.pl** except that `header_tags` isolates the header within the header tags; it outputs HTML only to `</HEAD>`. It does not force a `<BODY>` tag or a document header, which may need to differ from one library usage to another. By isolating the "true" document header, the function becomes more modular.

`table_header` is used to generate table headers using the `<TH>xxx</TH>` tags. Using a loop, this routine makes creating table headers much more elegant and generalizable to any table. `table_header` generates a series of table headers in HTML format when passed an array of headers.

`table_rows` is used like `table_header`, but it generates table rows instead (`<TD>Item1</TD>`).

`select_tag` is used to generate HTML `<SELECT>` tags for various input forms that are used in the scripts. The `select_options` routine is used to create the lists of select `<OPTION>` tags for each input field.

`build_input_form` takes information submitted by the main routine and creates an input form with multiple fields of multiple types. `make_form_row` is used by `build_input_form` to build the `<INPUT>` tags for an input form. If we give it information as to which tag we want and the desired name and value information, the subroutine can create an entire input form by itself with very little HTML programming on our part.

`get_database_rows` goes through a database file and gathers each line as a separate database row into an array. This array can then be manipulated in the main routine.

`GetFileLock` and `ReleaseFileLock` are used together to create and delete a lock file. Lock files are used to make sure that no more than one person modifies a datafile at any one time. A lock file is vital for the integrity of your data. Imagine what would happen if two or three people were using the same script to modify a shared database and each person accessed the shared database at the same moment. At best, the data entered by some of the users would be lost. Worse, the conflicting demands could possibly result in the corruption of the database file.

Thus, it is crucial to provide a way to monitor and control access to the database. This is the goal of the lock file routines. When a database modification script wants to access a shared database or other file protected by the lock file routines, it must first check for the existence of a lock file by using the file lock checks in GetFileLock. If GetFileLock determines that there is an existing lock file, it instructs the script that called it to wait until the lock file disappears. The script then waits and checks back with GetFileLock after some amount of time. If the lock file is still there, the script continues to wait.

If, on the other hand, the lock file has disappeared, the script asks GetFileLock to create a new lock file and then edits the database. When the script is finished editing the database, the lock file is erased using ReleaseFileLock.

INSTALLATION AND USAGE

Maintaining A Counter File

The counter routine is fairly simple. To use it, you need only call it from the main script as follows:

```
&counter("./Counter/counter.file");
```

Notice that the routine requires one parameter, the location of the counter file, which is created before the main script calls this subroutine. In this case, the counter routine is instructed to access a file called **counter.file** in the **Counter** subdirectory.

The counter routine keeps track of the current database ID number by maintaining a *counter file*, which is a file with the current unique number. By continually incrementing the number in the counter file by 1, the counter routine is able to keep generating new unique identification numbers.

The `counter` routine returns a variable named `$item_number`, which equals the value of the incremented counter. The script can use this number for any new database additions.

Handling Errors When Opening Files

Like `counter`, the `open_error` routine also takes one parameter, the name of the file the script is trying to open. Its usage follows this format:

```
open (DATABASE, ">>dat.file") || &open_error("dat.file");
```

In this example, if the script has trouble opening the file **dat.file**, it accesses the subroutine `open_error`, passing it the name **dat.file**. `open_error` then sends a useful error message to the Web browser.

Creating the HTML Header Tags

`header_tags` outputs the HTML header tags with any title submitted by the main program. For example, if you called the routine this way,

```
print &header_tags ("Selena Sol's Database Manager");
```

your script would output the following:

```
<HTML>
<HEAD>
<TITLE>Selena Sol's Database Manager</TITLE>
</HEAD>
```

Creating Multiple Table Headers:

`table_header` is used to create table header fields for HTML tables. For example, suppose you pass to the routine the following information:

```
print &table_header("Cell One", "Cell Two", "Cell Three");
```

You would receive the following table header:

```
<TH>Cell One</TH>
<TH>Cell Two</TH>
<TH>Cell Three</TH>
```

You can send `table_header` as many table headers as you want by adding elements to the list. This routine is particularly helpful if you are creating several tables throughout one script.

Building a Select Tag

`select_tag` is used to create a `<SELECT>` input tag. The routine is called with the following syntax:

```
&select_tag ("City", "3" ,"Multiple");
```

The three arguments reflect the values of the select arguments that you want included in the final tag. Hence, the `<SELECT>` tag generated from the preceding line would be

```
<SELECT NAME = "City" SIZE = "3" MULTIPLE>
```

We also need a routine to generate the `<SELECT>` tag options. We pass the `select_options` routine a list of options using this format:

```
print &select_options ("Los Angeles", "Burbank",
                       "Pasadena");
```

The routine returns the `<SELECT>` options as well as closes out the `<SELECT>` tag, returning to the main routine the following:

```
<OPTION>Los Angeles
<OPTION>Burbank
<OPTION>Pasadena
</SELECT>
```

Building an HTML Input Form

`build_input_form` automates the generation of form inputs even further. This function requires several variables to be set before it is called. Because we will

187

generate a form field, we need a list of form input titles, the variable names to be associated with those titles, and the type of form arguments used to gather the data for each title. In the end, we want a form input like the following:

```
<TH>Last Name:</TH>
<TD><INPUT TYPE = "text" NAME = "last_name" SIZE = "32"
          MAXLENGTH = "100"></TD>
```

To have the script generate these lines, we feed it the appropriate information. The following arrays provide that data.

```
@field_names = ("Last Name", "First Name", "Email");
%FIELD_ARRAY = ( 'Last Name', 'last_name',
                 'First Name', 'first_name',
                 'Email', 'email');
%FORM_COMPONENT_ARRAY = ( 'Last Name', 'text|SIZE =
                          "32" MAXLENGTH = "100"',
                          'First Name', 'text|SIZE =
                          "32" MAXLENGTH = "100"',
                          'Email', 'text|SIZE = "32"
                          MAXLENGTH = "100"');
```

@field_names defines the titles, %FIELD_ARRAY associates those titles with their variable names, and %FORM_COMPONENT_ARRAY associates them with the type of input boxes they are associated with.

%FORM_COMPONENT_ARRAY is complex enough to warrant more explanation. The previous example shows how you would generate a text input. The pipe-delimited list includes two fields: the name text and a listing of all the options as they would normally appear in your HTML.

<TEXTAREA> input boxes are generated in much the same way. Consider a line such as this one in the %FORM_COMPONENT_ARRAY associative array definition:

```
'Last Name', 'textarea|ROWS = "5" COLS = "40"'
```

That line would yield a TEXTAREA input box like the following:

```
<TH>Last Name:</TH>
<TD><TEXTAREA NAME = "last_name" ROWS = "5" COLS = "40">
</TEXTAREA></TD>
```

The <SELECT> tag is a bit more complex. Instead of using a pipe to delimit only two fields (type of input and arguments), the <SELECT> tag requires a third field: a list of options. Thus, a call such as

```
' Last Name', 'select|3|MULTIPLE|Flintstone|Rubble'
```

would produce a <SELECT> tag as follows:

```
<TH>Last Name</TH>
<TD><SELECT NAME = "last_name" SIZE = "3" MULTIPLE">
<OPTION>Flintstone
<OPTION>Rubble
</SELECT></TD>
```

To call the build_input_form from the main routine, you use syntax similar to the following:

```
print "<TABLE>";
```

A foreach loop is used to parse through the array:

```
foreach $field_name (@field_names)
  {
  print &build_input_form("$FIELD_ARRAY{$field_name}",
                "$FORM_COMPONENT_ARRAY{$field_name}",
                $field_name);
  }
print "<TABLE>";
```

Building a form automatically is somewhat complicated, and so is the subroutine call. In fact, build_input_form uses another routine, make_form_row.

make_form_row is a supplementary routine that builds each individual row assigned to build_input_form. The first thing it needs is a list of input field names. In the preceding example, the routine was asked to create a form with three input fields—last name, first name, and E-mail—which were stored in @field_names. However, to generate a full <INPUT> tag, the routine requires that a variable name be associated with each input field for the NAME attribute of the <INPUT> tag. To do this, the associative array %FIELD_ARRAY was defined to match the fields in @field_names with associated variable names.

Finally, we communicate the type of <INPUT> tag to be used on the form. Will it be a text box, a text area, or a select tag, for example? Furthermore, what options, if any, will modify those input tags? The final array, %FORM_COM-PONENT_ARRAY, defines such values.

When the subroutine is called, it processes each type of input field separately so that every input field created will have output a separate input description and input field. For every $field_name in our array, the routine goes through the process of creating the table row. The final output is a full-fledged input form embedded in a table:

```
<TABLE>
<TR>
<TH>Last Name</TH>
<TD><INPUT TYPE = "text" NAME = "last_name" SIZE = "32"
        MAXLENGTH = "100" ></TD>
</TR><TR>
<TH>First Name</TH>
<TD><INPUT TYPE = "text" NAME = "first_name" SIZE = "32"
        MAXLENGTH = "100" ></TD>
</TR><TR>
<TH>Email</TH>
<TD><INPUT TYPE = "text" NAME = "email" SIZE = "32"
        MAXLENGTH = "100" ></TD>
</TR><TR>
<TH>Email</TH>
<TD><INPUT TYPE = "text" NAME = "email" SIZE = "32"
        MAXLENGTH = "100" ></TD>
</TR><TR>
</TABLE>
```

make_form_row does most of the work for build_input_form by taking each input field and creating an input tag based on the parameters set in %FORM_COMPONENT_ARRAY. make_form_row is meant to be used from within the build_input_form subroutine but can be accessed from another program using this call:

```
&make_form_row ("$field_name",
                "$variable_name", "$form_type");
```

The make_form_row routine takes a name, a variable name, and a form input type (where type includes a pipe-delimited list of options) and translates them into an input field. Thus, `make_form_row` builds an `<INPUT>` tag as follows:

```
<INPUT TYPE = "text" NAME = "email" SIZE = "32"  MAXLENGTH = "100" >
```

At the time of this writing, only three types of input fields are supported by the routine: TEXT, SELECT, and TEXTAREA.

N O T E

Getting Rows from a Database

`get_database_rows` creates a list array of all the rows from a database. `get_database_rows` takes one argument, the name of the datafile it is using. An example call would look something like the following:

```
&get_database_rows ("data.file");
```

This code returns an array containing all the database rows in the ASCII text file **data.file**.

Outputting Multiple HTML Table Rows

`table_rows` does much the same thing as `table_header` except that it outputs table rows. Thus, the syntax:

```
&table_rows ("Bob", "Fred", "John");
```

generates the following output:

```
<TD>Bob</TD>
<TD>Fred</TD>
<TD>John</TD>
```

Manipulating Lock Files

Both `GetFileLock` and `ReleaseFileLock` take the name of the file in use and a parameter. Thus, you call the routines using

191

```
&GetFileLock ("lock.file");
```

and

```
&ReleaseFileLock("lock.file");
```

respectively. `GetFileLock` creates the **lock.file**, and `ReleaseFileLock` deletes it. It is not necessary for you to create the **lock.file** or delete it yourself. It is only necessary that you give the script the permissions to create and delete the file.

Design Discussion

The `counter` subroutine is used to create a unique ID number for every item in a database.

```
sub counter
  {
```

The subroutine first assigns to the local variable `$counter_file` the file-name that was passed to it from the main script.

```
local($counter_file) = @_;
```

Next, the subroutine opens the counter file. If the counter file cannot be opened, however, it accesses the `open_error` routine, passing it the filename.

```
open (COUNTER_FILE, "$counter_file") || &open_error($counter_file);
```

The, `counter` checks to see what number the counter is currently on and assigns that value to `$item_number`. `counter` is written to use the `while` method; if you want to, you can append to the counter file rather than write over it.

```
while (<COUNTER_FILE>)
  {
```

```
   $item_number = "$_";
   }
close (COUNTER_FILE);
```

Next, the subroutine adds one to the current counter number.

```
$item_number += 1;
```

Then it updates the counter file so that the file reflects the new number.

```
open (NOTE, ">$counter_file") || &open_error($counter_file);
print NOTE "$item_number\n";
close (NOTE);
```

Finally, the subroutine returns the number to the main script.

```
return $item_number;
}
```

The open_error Subroutine

open_error sends a note to the person debugging the script if it cannot open a file.

```
sub open_error
{
```

open_error begins by assigning to the local variable $filename the filename that was passed to it from the referencing routine.

```
local ($filename) = @_;
```

Next, the subroutine lets the client know that the script was unable to open the requested file and exits so that the routine does not continue.

```
print "I am really sorry, but for some reason I was
unable to open <P>$filename<P>Please make sure that the filename is
correctly defined, actually exists, and has the right permissions
relative to the Web browser. Thanks!";
```

```
exit;
}
```

The header_tags Subroutine

header_tags outputs the basic HTML header for every page.

```
sub header_tags
{
```

The subroutine first assigns to the local variable $title the value submitted by the main routine. Then it sends back the HTML header tags with the title inserted.

```
local ($title) = @_;
$header_tags = "<HTML>\n<HEAD>\n<TITLE>$title</TITLE>\n</HEAD>\n";
return $header_tags;
}
```

The table_header Subroutine

table_header is used to generate table headers.

```
sub table_header
  {
```

table_header assigns to the local array @headings the headings that were passed to it from the referencing routine. It also specifies that $table_header will be a variable local to this routine.

```
local (@headings) = @_;
local ($table_header);
```

Next, the subroutine dumps the HTML arguments into the $table_tag variable and returns $table_header to the main routine once it has been filled.

```
foreach $table_field (@headings)
  {
```

```
  $table_header .= "<TH>$table_field</TH>\n";
  }
$table_header .= "\n";
return $table_header;
}
```

The select_tag Subroutine

`select_tag` is used to generate HTML <SELECT> tags for input forms.

```
sub select_tag
 {
```

First, `select_tag` assigns to the local variables `$name`, `$size`, and `$multiple` the values that were passed to it from the referencing routine. It also defines `$select_tag`, `$select_argument`, `@select_arguments`, `@select_values`, and `%SELECT_ARGUMENTS` as local variables.

```
local ($name, $size, $multiple) = @_;
local ($select_tag, $select_argument);
local (@select_arguments, @select_values, %SELECT_ARGUMENTS);
```

Next, the associative array `%SELECT_ARGUMENTS` is created using the values supplied from the main routine, and then arrays are created for the keys and values.

```
%SELECT_ARGUMENTS = ("NAME", "$name",
                     "SIZE", "$size",
                     "MULTIPLE", "$multiple");
@select_arguments = keys %SELECT_ARGUMENTS;
@select_values = values %SELECT_ARGUMENTS;
```

Then `$select_tag`—which will be used to build and contain the entire select tag—and `$select_argument`—which will be used to keep track of the arguments—are initialized.

```
$select_tag = "";
$select_argument = "";
```

select_tag then creates the $select_tag variable, adding the <SELECT to the select tag.

```
$select_tag .= "<SELECT ";
```

Then the arguments are added to the select tag. If this is going to be a MULTIPLE select, the subroutine adds that argument. Otherwise, it adds each argument (size or name) and its value to the growing select tag.

```
foreach $select_argument (@select_arguments)
  {
  if ($select_argument eq "multiple")
    {
    $select_tag .= "MULTIPLE ";
    }
  elsif ($SELECT_ARGUMENTS{$select_argument} ne "")
    {
    $select_tag .= "$select_argument =
    \"$SELECT_ARGUMENTS{$select_argument}\" ";
    }
  }
```

Finally, the select tag is completed and returned to the main routine.

```
$select_tag .= ">\n";
return $select_tag;
}
```

The select_options Subroutine

select_options is used to create the lists of <OPTIONS> tags for each input field.

```
sub select_options
{
```

First, the options passed to this subroutine are assigned to the local array @select_options. Then $select_options, which will be used to keep track of the final options list, is initialized.

```
local (@select_options) = @_;
local ($select_options);
$select_options = "";
```

Next, the options that were put into the @select_options array are added to the growing variable $select_options.

```
foreach $option (@select_options)
  {
  $select_options .= "<OPTION>$option\n";
  }
```

Finally, the subroutine completes the HTML necessary for the select tag and returns the variable to be printed by the main routine.

```
$select_options .= "</SELECT>\n";
return $select_options;
}
```

The build_input_form Subroutine

build_import_form creates an input form.

```
sub build_input_form
{
```

build_input_form assigns to the local variables $variable_name, $form_type, and $field_name the values that were passed to it from the referencing routine. It also creates the local variable $input_form, which is used to create the entire form and which is initially set to "".

```
local ($variable_name, $form_type, $field_name) = @_;
local ($input_form);
$input_form = "";
```

Then the subroutine creates the input form within a table and adds the input fields. First, it uses the value of $field_name for the header cell and then uses the subroutine make_form_row to build the input form element for the input cell. It then passes the `make_form_row` subroutine the field name, the variable name, and the form type so that it will be able to build the input tag for that cell. Finally, the subroutine closes the table row and returns it to the main routine to print.

```
$input_form .= "<TR>\n";
$input_form .= &table_header ("$field_name");
$input_form .= "<TD>";
$input_form .= &make_form_row ("$field_name",
               "$variable_name", "$form_type");
$input_form .= "</TD></TR>\n";
return $input_form;
}
```

The make_form_row Subroutine

`make_form_row` is used to build the `<INPUT>` tags for an input form.

```
sub make_form_row
{
```

`make_form_row` assigns to the local variables `$name`, `$variable_name`, and `$type` the values that were passed to it from the referencing routine. Then it initializes the local array `@options_and_arguments`, which is used to temporarily store options and arguments to each input field, and the variable `$form_row`, which is used to store the growing form input tag.

```
local ($name, $variable_name, $type) = @_;
local (@options_and_arguments);
@options_and_arguments = ();
local ($form_row);
$form_row = "";
```

It then `splits` the `$type` variable into the type of input form to be created and the associated arguments that will modify it.

```
($type, @options_and_arguments) = split(/\|/, $type);
```

Next, it checks to see what type of input field the routine is being asked to generate and creates the appropriate tag.

```
if ($type eq "text")
  {
  $form_row .= "<INPUT TYPE = \"text\"
                      NAME = \"$variable_name\" ";
  foreach $argument (@options_and_arguments)
    {
    $form_row .= "$argument ";
    }
  $form_row .= ">";
  }


if ($type eq "textarea")
  {
  $form_row .= "<TEXTAREA NAME = \"$variable_name\" ";
  foreach $argument (@options_and_arguments)
    {
    $form_row .= "$argument ";
    }
  $form_row .= "></TEXTAREA>";
  }
```

In the case of a field that has been designated invisible, the subroutine outputs a note to the viewer of the input form that this is not modifiable data.

```
  if ($type eq "invisible")
     {
   $form_row .= "Not modifiable data";
   }
```

If the subroutine is being asked for a select input field, it references the select_tag and select_options routines to generate the <SELECT> tag and <OPTION> tag, respectively.

```
if ($type eq "select")
  {
  $number = shift (@options_and_arguments);
  $multiple = shift (@options_and_arguments);
  $form_row .= &select_tag("$variable_name", "$number");
```

```
    $form_row .= &select_options(@options_and_arguments);
    }
    return $form_row;
}
```

The get_database_rows Subroutine

get_database_rows gathers each line in a database into an array.

```
sub get_database_rows
{
```

First, get_database_rows assigns to the local variable $datafile the value that was passed to it from the referencing routine.

```
local ($datafile) = @_;
```

It then opens the datafile and gets every row that is not a comment line. (Comment lines are defined as having the word COMMENT: flush against the left margin.) Then it sends back the final array of all of the database rows.

```
 open (DATABASE, "$datafile");
 while (<DATABASE>)
    {
    unless ($_ =~ /^COMMENT:/)
     {
     push (@database_rows, $_);
     }
    }
@database_rows;
close (DATABASE);
}
```

The table_rows Subroutine

table_rows generates table rows.

```
sub table_rows
  {
```

`table_rows` assigns to the local array `@row` the row that was passed to it from the referencing routine. It also initializes the local variable `$table_cell`.

```
local (@row) = @_;
local ($table_cell);
```

Next, it dumps the HTML arguments into the `$table_tag` variable.

```
foreach $table_field (@row)
  {
  $table_field =~ s/~~/\|/g;
  $table_cell .= "<TD>$table_field</TD>\n";
  }
$table_cell .= "\n";
return $table_cell;
}
```

The GetFileLock Subroutine

The `GetFileLock` subroutine assigns to the local variable `$lock_file` the value passed to it from the main routine. It also initializes the local variable `$endtime` as 60 seconds. `$endtime` can be set to however long you want the routine to wait before it decides to create the lock file again. After 60 seconds, it is assumed that the original program instance that created the file either crashed or was killed before releasing the lock.

```
sub GetFileLock {
local ($lock_file) = @_;
local ($endtime);
$endtime = 60;
$endtime = time + $endtime;
```

As long as the lock file exists, and until the routine counts to 60 seconds, the routine does nothing. However, when all is clear, the routine creates the lock file.

```
while (-e $lock_file && time < $endtime) {
}
```

```
open(LOCK_FILE, ">$lock_file");
# flock(LOCK_FILE, 2); # 2 exclusively locks the file
} # End of get_file_lock
```

If you wish to use flock **(if your system has it), switch the comment sign from the open line to the** flock **line.**

NOTE

The ReleaseFileLock Subroutine

ReleaseFileLock works much the same as GetFileLock but deletes the lock file instead of creating it.

```
sub ReleaseFileLock
   {
   local ($lock_file) = @_;
   # 8 unlocks the file if you use flock
   # flock(LOCK_FILE, 8);
   close(LOCK_FILE);
   unlink($lock_file);
   } # end of ReleaseFileLock
```

CHAPTER 11

The Database Manager

OVERVIEW

The database manager script provides a Web interface with which to manipulate databases stored in ASCII text files (flatfiles). Such manipulations include the ability to add to, modify, and delete from multiple databases based on keyword recognition.

For example, suppose a company maintains a database of its employees' personal information (such as home phone number and address) and that employee John Doe moves to a new address and gets a new phone number. Using our script, the database administrator can hop on the Web, call up the script, choose the **modify** option, select **John Doe** as the search word, and modify the database row to reflect the new information. No great understanding of the operating system or the database formats is necessary, because the Web provides the interface. The database administrator, perhaps a secretary familiar with using the Web, simply points and clicks using a Web browser.

To protect the possibly sensitive information in the database, however, this script also implements the password authentication algorithms discussed in Chapter 9. Furthermore, the script supports multiple administrators by incorporating *lock file* routines so that no one can make changes to the datafile while someone else is modifying it.

INSTALLATION AND USAGE

This application takes advantage of multiple files and directories that must work together as a team. Thus, the first step in installing these scripts is to copy them into a CGI-executable directory on your Web server. When the scripts are unarchived, they expand into the default directory structure beginning with the root directory, **Database_manager**. Figure 11.1 outlines the expanded directory structure and the permissions needed for the search to operate.

The root **Database_manager** directory must have permissions that allow the Web server to read and execute and should contain three directories (**Databases**, **Library**, and **Session Files**) and one text file (**db_manager.cgi**).

db_manager.cgi is the meat of the application and contains most of the Perl code to make it run. This file, which should be readable andexecutable by the Web server, will be discussed in detail in the design discussion.

Databases is a subdirectory containing "pairs" of database files: a setup file and a datafile for every database that has the database manager as a front end. It also contains the user and counter files discussed later. The datafiles must be readable and writable by the Web server, and the setup files must be readable. The directory itself must be readable, writable, and executable.

db_manager.users contains the list of users who are allowed to use the application. This user file is formatted exactly the same as the default user file discussed in Chapter 9: a pipe-delimited database containing the encrypted password, username, group, last name, first name, and E-mail address. This file should be readable and, if you want users to be added via the Web interface (not necessarily recommended), should be writable by the Web server. It should also initially be empty.

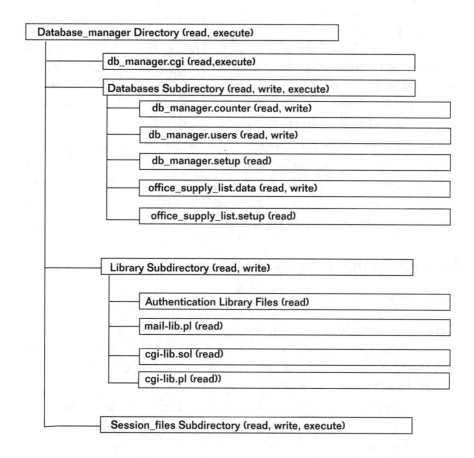

Figure 11.1 The directory layout for the database manager application.

db_manager.counter is a text file that is used to keep track of unique database ID numbers that have been assigned to database rows in the data file. Initially, this file should contain the number 1 on the first line and nothing else. As time goes by, **db_manager.cgi** will increment this number by 1 for every new database entry. Thus, the file should be readable and writable by the Web server.

The database manager can manipulate several databases at one time. To do this, however, it must have both a datafile and a setup file for every database.

NOTE

Library is a subdirectory containing the CGI libraries (discussed in Chapter 9) that **db_manager.cgi** uses. The following library files are used for this script: **auth-extra-html.pl**, **auth-extra-lib.pl**, **auth-lib-fail-html.pl**, **auth-lib.pl**, **auth-server-lib.pl**, **auth_fail_html.pl**, **cgi-lib.pl**, **cgi-lib.sol**, and **mail-lib.pl**. This subdirectory must be executable and readable by the Web server, and its files must be readable.

Session_files is the subdirectory used by the authentication libraries to store session files, as discussed in Chapter 9. Initially, the directory will be empty, but if it is set to be readable, writable, and executable, the Web server will continually fill up and prune the directory as part of its daily use of session files, lock files, and temporary files.

Server-Specific Setup and Options

THE SETUP FILE

There are three primary functions of the setup file: defining server-specific variables, determining the names of database fields and their relative display orders, and configuring authentication options. Each setup file sets the following variables.

`$counter_file` is the path of the counter file that is used to keep track of unique ID numbers. By default, this variable is set to `./Databases/db_manager.counter`, because on the accompanying disk, **db_manager.counter** is located in the subdirectory databases.

`$user_file` is the location of the file that contains the list of users who are authorized to use **db_manager.cgi**.

`$data_file` is the location of the default ASCII database file that is being managed.

`$temp_file` is a file that we'll use to temporarily store various data at various times. It's mainly used in modifying and deleting from the database, as explained later.

`$lock_file` is a file that we'll use to make sure that only one person can modify the database at any given time.

`$session_file_directory` is the location of the directory that will temporarily hold session files, the temporary file, and the lock file.

$database_manager_script is the local absolute path of **db_manager.cgi**.

$database_manager_script_url is the URL of **db_manager.cgi**.

%FIELD_ARRAY is an associative array that is used to define database fields and their associated variable names.

@field_names is a list of fields in our database. Because of the hash table functions for associative array handling, if we used

```perl
@field_names = (keys %FIELD_ARRAY);
```

the field names would not come up in the order that we chose to assign them in %FIELD_ARRAY. Thus, we must manually specify the keys in the order that we want them in the @field_names array and the @field_values array.

@field_values is an array that contains only the variable names associated with the database fields. Whereas the @field_names elements are descriptive and can include spaces and special characters (such as single quotation marks or exclamation marks), the @field_values elements are used to generate form variables and hence should be in a variable name format.

%FORM_COMPONENT_ARRAY is an associative array that matches database fields with the kind of input type and the kinds of input type arguments the fields are associated with. Arguments and options are pipe-delimited so that type is always the first in the list, usually followed by a second item that includes the input arguments. In the case of a <SELECT>, however, options—including multiple and size options—are also added and are separated by pipes. For more details, see the discussion of **cgi-lib.sol** in Chapter 10.

Authentication variables are explained in the discussion of authentication in Chapter 9.

As an example, here is the complete text of **db_manager.setup**, which we will use for the chapter example.

```perl
#!/usr/local/bin/perl
$counter_file = "./Databases/db_manager.counter";
$user_file = "./Databases/db_manager.users";
$data_file = "./Databases/db_manager.data";
$temp_file = "./Session_files/db_manager.temp";
$lock_file = "./Session_files/db_manager.lockfile";
$session_file_directory = "./Session_files";
```

```
$database_manager_script = "./db_manager.cgi";
$database_manager_script_url = "db_manager.cgi";

%FIELD_ARRAY = ( 'Last Name', 'last_name',
                 'First Name', 'first_name',
                 'Email', 'email',
                 'Phone Number', 'phone',
                 'Address', 'address');
@field_names = ("Last Name", "First Name", "Email",
                "Phone Number", "Address");
@field_values = ("last_name", "first_name", "email",
                 "phone", "address");


%FORM_COMPONENT_ARRAY = (
'Last Name', 'text|SIZE = "32" MAXLENGTH = "100"',
'First Name', 'text|SIZE = "32" MAXLENGTH = "100"',
'Email', 'text|SIZE = "32" MAXLENGTH = "100"',
'Phone Number', 'text|SIZE = "32" MAXLENGTH = "100"',
'Address', 'textarea|ROWS = "4" COLS = "30"');

$auth_lib = "$lib";
$auth_server = "off";
$auth_cgi = "on";


$auth_user_file = "./Databases/db_manager.users";
$auth_alt_user_file = "";
$auth_default_group = "view:add:modify:delete";
$auth_add_register = "on";
$auth_email_register = "off";
$auth_admin_from_address = "selena\@foobar.com";
$auth_admin_email_address = "selena\@foobar.com";
$auth_session_length = 2;
$auth_session_dir = "./Session_files";
$auth_register_message = "Thanks, you may now logon with
     your new username and password.";
$auth_allow_register = "on";
$auth_allow_search = "on";
$auth_generate_password = "off";
$auth_check_duplicates = "on";
$auth_password_message =
    "Thanks for applying to our site, your password is";
@auth_extra_fields = ("auth_first_name",
                      "auth_last_name",
                      "auth_email");
@auth_extra_desc = ("First Name",
                    "Last Name",
                    "Email");
```

The Datafile

Every datafile should be a pipe-delimited text file:

```
COMMENT: Item|Category|Description|Unique ID #
COMMENT:
100a|Bik Pen (Black)|10.00|1
100c|Mooky Stapler|12.00|3
100b|Bik Pen (Red)|11.00|2
```

Notice that the database manager scripts allow comment lines in the database. If you use comments, make sure that you follow the specific format for commenting. Any comment line must be flush against the left margin and must be preceded by COMMENT:.

Notice also that fields are delimited with the pipe symbol (|). Thus, you must not have any pipe symbols embedded in your data. The script has been configured by default to translate pipes into two tildes (~~), but if you make any manual additions, you must be careful to make the translation yourself. You are free to use a different delimiter by using search and replace to modify each occurrence of pipes in the scripts and datafiles, but we recommend the pipe symbol, because it is rarely found in user data.

You may have as many fields or rows as you want, but you must always allow the database manager to add a final field for the unique database ID number. To make sure that modifications and deletions affect only one database row, we need to make sure that every row is uniquely identifiable. Thus, the add routine in the database manager assigns a unique number as the last field of every row. If you wish to manually add data rows by editing the datafile directly, you must remember to insert ID numbers at the end of each of the rows as well as increment the counter file appropriately.

Running the Script

Once you have configured the setup file to the specifics of your server and databases, it is time to rev up the motor of the application, the **db_manager.cgi** script. If you have configured your setup file correctly and have set all the permissions for files and subdirectories properly, all you need to do is to create a hyperlink to the script. For example:

```
<A HREF = "http://www.foobar.com/cgi-
bin/Database_manager/db_manager.cgi">Database manager</A>
```

DESIGN DISCUSSION

When a user clicks on the link, the main script will run, taking advantage of your default setup configurations. Figure 11.2 documents the logic of this script as it manages the needs of the client with the abilities of the server.

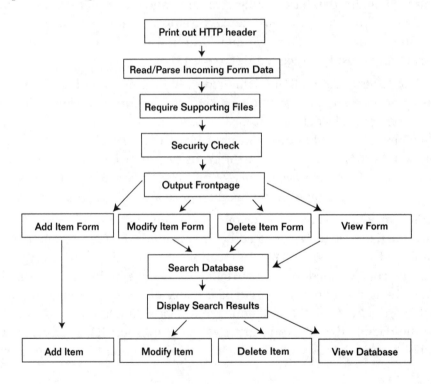

Figure 11.2 The script logic.

The script begins by starting the Perl interpreter and printing the HTTP header.

```
#!/usr/local/bin/perl
print "Content-type: text/html\n\n";
```

Loading the Libraries

Next, the **Library** subdirectory is added to the @INC array used by Perl to locate supporting libraries. By unshifting the subdirectory into the array, the script makes sure to add it to the beginning of the @INC array so that any duplicate subroutines in other libraries are not used. Notice that if you move the library files to a directory other than **Library**, you will need to change this hard-coded variable.

Once the **Library** directory has been included in the @INC array, the necessary supporting files are loaded using the CgiRequire subroutine at the end of this script. The CgiRequire subroutine returns a meaningful error message in case the script has a problem requiring one of the libraries.

```
$lib = "Library";
unshift (@INC, "$lib");
&CgiRequire("$lib/cgi-lib.pl", "$lib/cgi-lib.sol",
"$lib/auth-lib.pl");
```

Reading and Parsing the Incoming Form Data

Next, the script uses **cgi-lib.pl** to parse the incoming form data, passing the ReadParse subroutine the parameter *form_data so that the returned incoming form data associative array will be named %form_data instead of %in.

```
&ReadParse(*form_data);
```

In this script, we chose to name the associative array returned by cgi.lib.pl form_data rather than the default %in because it is easier to remember what the variable is when we have many associative arrays in one script.

N O T E

Loading the Setup File

Once the form data has been processed, the script checks to see whether the client has asked to see a database other than the default database.

Because **db_manager.cgi** can be used to manage several databases at once, we need a way of communicating to the script which database it should use and which setup file is associated with that database. Thus, when you're not accessing the default database, you must append some special information to the <A HREF> tag in the HTML that calls the script. You should use the following format:

```
<A HREF = "http://www.foobar.com/cgi-
bin/Db_manager/db_manager.cgi?database=office_supply_list.setup">Offic
e Supply Database</A>
```

The question mark signifies that you are passing parameters to **db_manager.cgi**. In the example, the variable database is set equal to office_supply_list.setup and passed to the script.

That the setup file is determined at this point is the reason we had to hard-code $lib. We still have not used the setup file, because we are not yet sure which setup file to use. Once we parse the data, if there was an incoming variable named database, we will know to use its value as the name of the database setup file to use. If no value came in, we can use (require) the default database's setup file.

Notice also the use of the hard-coded Databases. This could cause problems when you are customizing this script to your site if you are changing directory relationships. If you change the directory relationships, be aware that you will have to modify the require subroutine call to reflect the change.

```
if ($form_data{'database'} ne "")
   {
   $setup_file = $form_data{'database'};
   }
else
   {
   $setup_file = "db_manager.setup";
```

```
    }
&require("Databases/$setup_file");
```

Authenticating Users

After the script has gathered together all the supporting files, it must check to see whether the client is authorized to access or modify the datafile.

To do this, the script passes three parameters to the subroutine GetSessionInfo, which is contained in **auth-lib.pl**. $session_file will be null if a session file has not been set; otherwise, it will be the value associated with the session_file variable coming in from the form. As you'll see later, we will pass this value as a hidden variable once it has been assigned. GetSessionInfo also requires the name of this script so that it can provide links to this script. Finally, the script must pass to GetSessionInfo the associative array containing the form data returned from **cgi-lib.pl**.

In exchange, the routine returns to us several bits of authentication information; the main script passes this information as hidden form variables throughout the following routines to keep track of the user and his or her privileges with the database. If you are still unclear about this process, it is covered in greater detail in Chapter 9.

```
if ($form_data{'session_file'} ne "")
   {
   $session_file = $form_data{'session_file'};
   }
($session_file, $session_username, $session_group,
$session_first_name, $session_last_name, $session_email) =
&GetSessionInfo($session_file, $database_manager_script_url,
*form_data);
```

Next, the script splits the $session_group information so that it can keep track of what type of permission the user has. The session_group variable will look something like view:add:modify:delete (as defined in the setup file), so the script splits, based on the colons, to see what levels of security the user is cleared for.

```
@group_array = split (/:/, $session_group);
```

Displaying the Front Page

Next, the script checks to see whether the client is requesting the first page. The script knows that the client needs to see the first page if the client has just clicked on an input button named **return_to_frontpage** or has just made it through security and the `$session_file` is coming from the authentication routines rather than as hidden form input from other pages deeper in this script. The || means "or."

```
if ($form_data{'return_to_frontpage'} ne "" ||
    $form_data{'session_file'} eq "")
    {
```

If either condition is true, the script prints the database manager front page, which gives the client four choices of actions (add, modify, delete, and view).

```
print <<"    end_of_html";
<HTML>
<HEAD>
<TITLE>Database Manager Front Page</TITLE>
</HEAD>
<BODY>
<CENTER><H2>Database Manager Front Page</H2></CENTER>
<BLOCKQUOTE>
Thanks for checking out the Database Manager Scripts.  Feel free to
make any modifications that are necessary.
</BLOCKQUOTE>
<FORM METHOD = "post"
      ACTION = "$database_manager_script_url">
<CENTER>
<INPUT TYPE = "hidden" NAME = "database"
      VALUE = "$setup_file">
<INPUT TYPE = "hidden" NAME = "session_file"
      VALUE = "$session_file">
<INPUT TYPE = "submit" NAME = "add_form"
      VALUE = "Add an Item">
<INPUT TYPE = "submit" NAME = "search_form_delete"
      VALUE = "Delete an Item">
<INPUT TYPE = "submit" NAME = "search_form_modify"
      VALUE = "Modify an Item">
```

```
<INPUT TYPE = "submit" NAME = "search_form_view"
       VALUE = "View the Database">
end_of_html
exit;
}
```

In the routine, we chose to use the `end_of_html` **method for printing to make it easier for administrators to customize the look and feel of the HTML. However, be careful to escape Perl special characters such as** @ **within the HTML.**

NOTE

On the Web, the front page will look like Figure 11.3.

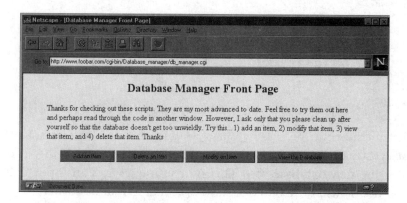

Figure 11.3 The database manager front page.

Displaying the Add Form

If the client asked for the form to add an entry to the database, the script prints that form instead.

```
if ($form_data{'add_form'} ne "")
  {
```

NOTE Notice that throughout these `if` tests, the standard `if submit but-` `ton ne ""` syntax is used. Thus, you can set the value of the submit buttons to whatever you want. An add button might be **Add New** `Employee Records` instead of **Add Item**. When the user clicks on the button, regardless of the value, this script will evaluate the `if` test as `true`. This is because if the submit button is pressed, its form value will not be null (`ne ""`).

The script prints the page header, body, document header, and form tags as it did for the front page–generating routine.

```
print <<"     end_of_html";
<HTML><HEAD>
<TITLE>Adding an Item to the Database</TITLE>
</HEAD><BODY>
<CENTER><H2>Adding an Item to the Database</H2></CENTER>
<FORM METHOD = "post"
      ACTION = "$database_manager_script_url">
<CENTER>
end_of_html
```

Using the subroutine `create_input_form` at the end of this script, the script creates an input form that the client uses to submit the information for the new database row. This subroutine creates an input field for each of the fields in the database and presents it in table format.

```
&create_input_form;
```

Finally, the script prints the page footers.

```
print <<"     end_of_html";
</TABLE><CENTER><P>
<INPUT TYPE = "hidden" NAME = "database"
      VALUE = "$setup_file">
<INPUT TYPE = "hidden" NAME = "session_file"
      VALUE = "$form_data{'session_file'}">
<INPUT TYPE = "hidden" NAME = "id"
      VALUE = "$item_number">
<INPUT TYPE = "submit" NAME = "submit_addition"
      VALUE = "Submit Addition">
```

```
<INPUT TYPE = "submit" NAME = "return_to_frontpage"
       VALUE = "Return to Front page">
</CENTER></FORM></BODY></HTML>
end_of_html
exit;
}
```

On the Web, the add form looks something like Figure 11.4.

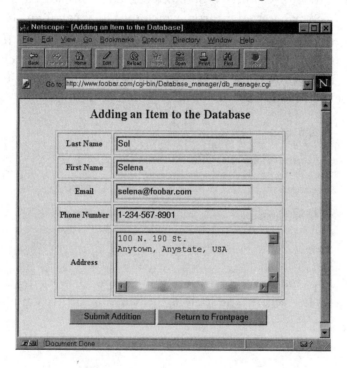

Figure 11.4 Database manager add form.

Displaying the Search Form for Deletion

On the other hand, perhaps the client wants to delete an item from the database. If so, the script outputs a form so that the client can specify which item to delete.

```
if ($form_data{'search_form_delete'} ne "")
  {
```

Before the script can begin deleting, it must find out which item to delete. To do that, the client must have a way of telling the script which item to delete and the script must tell the client which items are available to delete. However, the script cannot spew out all the items in the database, because the browser might run out of memory; also, you may not want the client to get all the information in the database. Instead, the client must be able to give the script one or more search terms so that it can put together a reasonably sized list from which the client can then choose.

This communication is created by using an HTML input form that includes an input field for every database field so that the client can search by keyword and field. The script begins by printing the HTML header for the HTML form.

```
print <<"    end_of_html";
<HTML><HEAD>
<TITLE>Query Database for Deletion</TITLE>
</HEAD><BODY>
<CENTER><H2>Query Database for Deletion</H2></CENTER>
<FORM METHOD = "post"
     ACTION = "$database_manager_script_url">
<CENTER>
end_of_html
```

Then the script outputs the form using the subroutine `create_input_form` at the end of this script. The logic is the same as for the equivalent call for add.

```
&create_input_form;
```

Next, the script adds a form input for "exact match" and the form, body, and HTML footers and tags. The exact match option lets users search by word boundary so that the script will return only rows with an exact hit.

```
print <<"    end_of_html";
<TH>Exact Match?</TH><TD>
<INPUT TYPE = "checkbox" NAME = "exact_match">
</TD></TR></TABLE><P>
<INPUT TYPE = "hidden" NAME = "database"
     VALUE = "$setup_file">
<INPUT TYPE = "hidden" NAME = "session_file"
```

```
        VALUE = "$form_data{'session_file'}">
<INPUT TYPE = "submit" NAME = "search_database_delete"
        VALUE = "Submit Search Term">
<P><BLOCKQUOTE>To get a full view of database, submit "no" keywords.
But beware, if there are too many items in your database, you will
exceed the memory of your browser.
</CENTER></FORM></BODY></HTML>
end_of_html
exit;
}
```

All searches are case-insensitive, but the exact match matches on word boundary so that it will not match gen'eric' if the search is for eric, whereas the nonexact search will find the item.

N O T E

On the Web, the previous routine will yield a page that looks exactly like Figure 11.4, except that the title will be specific to deletion and the exact match check box will appear on the page.

Searching the Database for Possible Items to Delete

The script also needs a routine to accept the client-defined search term(s) and search the database so that it can present a dynamically generated list of hits from which the client can choose items to delete.

```
if ($form_data{'search_database_delete'} ne "")
  {
```

The script conducts the search and prints the results using the following routines. First, the script prints the page header.

```
print <<"  end_of_html";
<HTML><HEAD>
<TITLE>Deleting an Item from the Database</TITLE>
</HEAD><BODY>
<CENTER>
<H2>Deleting an Item from the Database</H2>
</CENTER>
<FORM METHOD = "post"
      ACTION = "$database_manager_script_url">
<CENTER>
end_of_html
```

The script then begins searching the database by using the subroutine search_database, which can be found at the end of this script. The search_database subroutine is given one parameter, delete, so that it knows how to output the results of the search.

```
&search_database ("delete");
```

Finally, the script prints a list of hits in table format. $search_results, returned from &search_database, contains all the hits in the form of table rows. The client chooses which item to delete and deletes it with the if ($form_data{'submit_deletion'} ne "") routine.

```
print "<TABLE BORDER = \"1\" CELLPADDING = \"4\"
     CELLSPACING = \"4\">";
print &table_header ("Delete<BR>Item");
push (@field_names, "Id");
print &table_header (@field_names);
print "</TR>\n";
print "$search_results";
print <<" end_of_html";
</TABLE><P>
$search_notice<P>
<INPUT TYPE = "hidden" NAME = "database"
     VALUE = "$setup_file">
<INPUT TYPE = "hidden" NAME = "session_file"
     VALUE = "$form_data{'session_file'}">
<INPUT TYPE = "submit" NAME = "submit_deletion"
     VALUE = "Submit Deletion">
<INPUT TYPE = "submit" NAME = "return_to_frontpage"
     VALUE = "Return to Front page">
</CENTER></FORM></BODY></HTML>
end_of_html
exit;
}
```

On the Web, the delete form appears as shown in Figure 11.5.

Displaying the Search Form for Modification

Next, we repeat the same logic, adapting it for the modification operation.

```
if ($form_data{'search_form_modify'} ne "")
  {
```

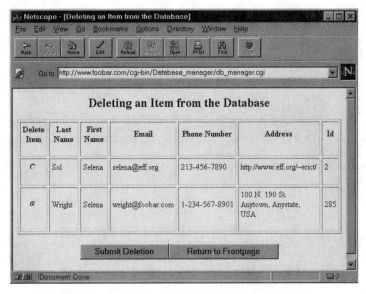

Figure 11.5 *Itemized delete form.*

The script begins by printing the familiar page header.

```
print <<"     end_of_html";
<HTML><HEAD>
<TITLE>Query Database for Modification</TITLE>
</HEAD><BODY>
<CENTER>
<H2>Query Database for Modification</H2>
</CENTER>
<FORM METHOD = "post"
     ACTION = "$database_manager_script_url">
<CENTER>
end_of_html
```

As it did in the delete routines, the script creates the input form using the subroutine `create_input_form`.

```
&create_input_form;
```

It then adds the footer.

```
print <<"     end_of_html";
<TH>Exact Match?</TH><TD>
```

```
<INPUT TYPE = "checkbox" NAME = "exact_match">
</TD></TR></TABLE><P>
<INPUT TYPE = "hidden" NAME = "database"
      VALUE = "$setup_file">
<INPUT TYPE = "hidden" NAME = "session_file"
      VALUE = "$form_data{'session_file'}">
<INPUT TYPE = "submit" NAME = "search_database_modify"
      VALUE = "Submit Search Term">
<P><BLOCKQUOTE>To get a full view of database, submit "no" keywords.
But beware, if there are too many items in your database, you will
exceed the memory of your browser.
</CENTER></FORM></BODY></HTML>
end_of_html
exit;
}
```

On the Web, the modification screen looks like Figure 11.4 except for
the new title and the addition of the exact match check box.

Searching the Database for Possible Rows to Modify

Just as it did for delete, the script prints the results of the query for modification.

```
if ($form_data{'search_database_modify'} ne "")
  {
```

The script prints the page header.

```
print <<" end_of_html";
<HTML><HEAD>
<TITLE>Modifying an Item in the Database</TITLE>
</HEAD><BODY>
<CENTER>
<H2>Modifying an Item in the Database</H2>
</CENTER>
<FORM METHOD = "post"
      ACTION = "$database_manager_script_url">
<CENTER>
end_of_html
```

Next, the script searches the database using the subroutine search_database.

```
&search_database ("modify");
```

Now the script prints a list of hits in table format. Recall that $search_ results, returned from &search_database, contains all the hits in the form of table rows.

```
print "<TABLE BORDER = \"1\" CELLPADDING = \"4\"
            CELLSPACING = \"4\">";
print "<TH>Modify<BR>Item</TH>";
push (@field_names, "Id");
print &table_header (@field_names);
print "</TR>\n";
print "$search_results";
print "</TABLE><P>";


print "$search_notice<P>";
```

The script uses the subroutine create_input_form to print the same form that was used for adding items. Now the client can specify an item in the created table and can type new information with which to update the database row.

```
&create_input_form;
```

Finally, the script prints the usual footer.

```
print <<"    end_of_html";
</TABLE><CENTER><P>
<INPUT TYPE = "hidden" NAME = "database"
      VALUE = "$setup_file">
<INPUT TYPE = "hidden" NAME = "session_file"
      VALUE = "$form_data{'session_file'}">
<INPUT TYPE = "submit" NAME = "submit_modification"
      VALUE = "Submit Modification">
<INPUT TYPE = "submit" NAME = "return_to_frontpage"
      VALUE = "Return to Front page">
</CENTER></FORM></BODY></HTML>
end_of_html
exit;
}
```

On the Web, the modification form and table look like Figure 11.6.

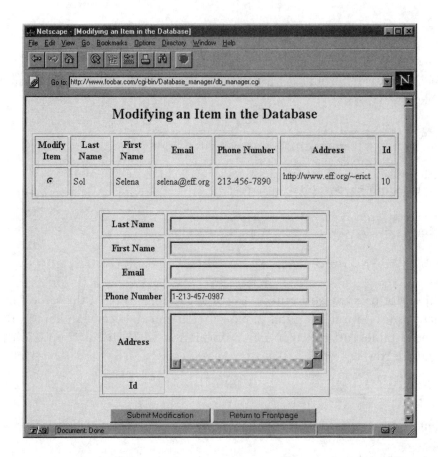

Figure 11.6 Itemized modification screen.

Displaying the Search Form for Viewing the Database

The script uses the same routines to produce a view of the database.

```
if ($form_data{'search_form_view'} ne "")
  {
```

The script begins by printing the usual header.

```
print <<"    end_of_html";
<HTML><HEAD>
```

224

```
<TITLE>Query Database for Viewing</TITLE>
</HEAD><BODY>
<CENTER><H2>Query Database for Viewing</H2></CENTER>
<FORM METHOD = "post"
      ACTION = "$database_manager_script_url">
<CENTER>
end_of_html
```

Then the script creates the input form using the subroutine create_input_
form at the end of this script, exactly as we've done before.

```
&create_input_form;
print <<"    end_of_html";
<TH>Exact Match?</TH><TD>
<INPUT TYPE = "checkbox" NAME = "exact_match">
</TD></TR></TABLE><P>
<INPUT TYPE = "hidden" NAME = "database"
       VALUE = "$setup_file">
<INPUT TYPE = "hidden" NAME = "session_file"
       VALUE = "$form_data{'session_file'}">
<INPUT TYPE = "submit" NAME = "search_database_view"
       VALUE = "Submit Search Term">
<P><BLOCKQUOTE>To get a full view of database, submit "no" keywords.
But beware, if there are too many items in your database, you will
exceed the memory of your browser.
</CENTER></FORM></BODY></HTML>
end_of_html
exit;
}
```

The previous routine produces the usual screen.

Searching the Database for Items to Display for Viewing

Now the script must search the database for the client to view. The
process is the same as we've done before.

```
if ($form_data{'search_database_view'} ne "")
  {
  print <<"    end_of_html";
  <HTML><HEAD><TITLE>Viewing the Database</TITLE></HEAD>
  <BODY>
  <CENTER><H2>Viewing the Database</H2></CENTER>
  <FORM METHOD = "post"
```

225

```
        ACTION = "$database_manager_script_url">
  <CENTER>
  end_of_html
```

This time, however, the script sends the subroutine a parameter of none, because we do not want any radio buttons in the resulting table. There will be no items to select, because all the client wants to do is to view the database.

```
&search_database ("none");
```

Finally, the script prints a list of hits in a table format.

```
print <<"  end_of_html";
<TABLE BORDER = "1" CELLPADDING = "4" CELLSPACING = "4">
end_of_html
push (@field_names, "Id");
print &table_header (@field_names);
print "</TR>\n";
print "$search_results";
print <<"  end_of_html";
</TABLE><CENTER><P>
$search_notice<P>
<INPUT TYPE = "hidden" NAME = "database"
       VALUE = "$setup_file">
<INPUT TYPE = "hidden" NAME = "session_file"
       VALUE = "$form_data{'session_file'}">
<INPUT TYPE = "submit" NAME = "add_form"
       VALUE = "Add an Item">
<INPUT TYPE = "submit" NAME = "search_form_delete"
       VALUE = "Delete an Item">
<INPUT TYPE = "submit" NAME = "search_form_modify"
       VALUE = "Modify an Item">
<INPUT TYPE = "submit" NAME = "return_to_frontpage"
       VALUE = "Return to Front page">
</CENTER></FORM></BODY></HTML>
end_of_html
exit;
}
```

On the Web, the search results page looks like Figure 11.7.

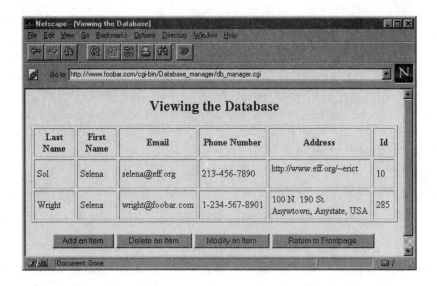

Figure 11.7 Search results page.

Adding an Item to the Database

Now that the user has the ability to use script-generated HTML forms to specify an addition, modification, or deletion, the script must be prepared to make those changes. The script begins by providing for a database addition.

```
if ($form_data{'submit_addition'} ne "")
  {
```

In the case of an addition, the script must assign the new database entry a unique database ID number. To do this, it accesses a counter file that keeps track of the last database ID number used. The counter subroutine, located in **cgi-lib.sol**, returns a new number (incremented by 1) and then adjusts the counter file appropriately. The unique ID number is essential for modifying the database; without it, the script would have no way of identifying unique rows. The counter routine takes one parameter, the location of the counter file.

Before the subroutine can begin editing the counter file, the script must make sure that no one else is incrementing the file at the same time. If that happened, we'd have two database rows with the same "unique" ID number, and that wouldn't do. The script uses the `GetFileLock` routine in **cgi-lib.sol** to create a lock file that prevents anyone else from accessing the counter file while it is being incremented. When the script is finished with the counter file, it uses the `ReleaseFileLock` subroutine to release the lock.

```
&GetFileLock ("$lock_file");
&counter($counter_file);
&ReleaseFileLock ("$lock_file");
```

The script then takes the incoming form data and formats it the way the database is set up to understand (delimited by | and ending with a new-line). In the process, the script also translates all hard returns into <BR> and paragraph breaks into <P> so that the database row will display correctly as HTML information. The script also changes all pipe characters (|) into two tildes (~~) so that input pipe data will not confuse the database manager later. Recall that the database manager stores database rows using the pipe character by default. If the user submitted a pipe character as part of the database information, the pipe character would confuse the database manager into thinking that there were too many database fields.

```
foreach $field (@field_names)
  {
  $value = "$FIELD_ARRAY{$field}";
  $form_data{$value} =~ s/\n/<BR>/g;
  $form_data{$value} =~ s/\r\r/<P>/g;
  $form_data{$value} =~ s/\|/~~/g;
```

Finally, if the user did not submit any data at all, the script changes the empty value into a centered "-" so that when the database row is displayed in table format, it will not look ugly.

```
  if ($form_data{$value} eq "")
    {
```

```
    $form_data{$value} = "<CENTER>-</CENTER>";
    }
```

For each $field, the script appends each formatted field to $new_row, taking off the last pipe when it is finished building the new database row.

```
  $new_row .= "$form_data{$value}|";
  }
$new_row .= "$item_number";
```

Next, the script creates a lock file while it edits the database file. Then it writes in the new row. Notice also that the script appends (>>) to the data file so that all the old data remains intact. Also, the script uses the subroutine open_error in **cgi-lib.sol** if there is a problem opening the datafile.

```
&GetFileLock ("$lock_file");
open (DATABASE, ">>$data_file") || &open_error($data_file);
print DATABASE "$new_row\n";
close (DATABASE);
```

When the script is finished adding the item, it deletes the lock file so that other instances of the script may access the datafile.

```
&ReleaseFileLock ("$lock_file");
```

Finally, the client is sent an HTML page letting her know that the item has been added and, once again, giving the basic administrative options.

```
print <<"    end_of_html";
<HTML><HEAD>
<TITLE>Item Added to the Database</TITLE>
</HEAD><BODY>
<CENTER><H2>Item Added to the Database</H2></CENTER>
<FORM METHOD = "post"
      ACTION = "$database_manager_script_url">
<CENTER>
<INPUT TYPE = "hidden" NAME = "database"
       VALUE = "$setup_file">
<INPUT TYPE = "hidden" NAME = "session_file"
       VALUE = "$form_data{'session_file'}">
<INPUT TYPE = "submit" NAME = "add_form"
```

```
        VALUE = "Add an Item">
<INPUT TYPE = "submit" NAME = "search_form_delete"
        VALUE = "Delete an Item">
<INPUT TYPE = "submit" NAME = "search_form_modify"
        VALUE = "Modify an Item">
<INPUT TYPE = "submit" NAME = "search_form_view"
        VALUE = "View the Database">
</CENTER></FORM></BODY></HTML>
end_of_html
exit;
}
```

On the Web, the response page takes the standard form depicted in Figure 11.8.

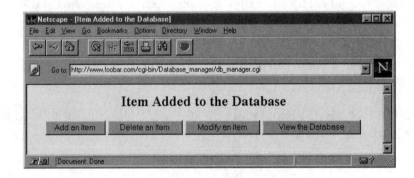

Figure 11.8 *Standard response after successful addition.*

Deleting an Item from the Database

If the client has asked to delete an item, the script uses the following routines to delete from the database:

```
if ($form_data{'submit_deletion'} ne "")
  {
```

The routine begins by opening the datafile using the open_error routine in **cgi-lib.sol** in case there is a problem.

```
open (DATABASE, "$data_file")
     || &open_error($data_file);
```

Then the script reads the datafile one line at a time.

```
while (<DATABASE>)
  {
```

If the line is a database comment line, the script adds it to a variable called $new_data. This variable will eventually contain every line in our datafile, because we continually append to it (.=). In this case, the script simply adds to $new_data all the comment lines before further processing.

```
if ($_ =~ /^COMMENT:/)
  {
  $new_data .= "$_";
  }
```

If the current line is not a comment line, the script splits the line into the @fields array using a pipe (|) as the element delimiter. The script then pops out the unique database ID number.

```
else
  {
  @fields = split (/\|/, $_);
  $item_id = pop(@fields);
```

NOTE Pop **is a Perl function that snips off the very last element in an array. In this case, in the setup file we defined the last element in every database row to be the unique database ID number gathered from the** counter **routine.**

Now the script compares the database ID number of the current row with the database ID number submitted by the client by way of the delete form. If the two numbers are not equal, the script adds the row to the growing $new_data variable. If they are equal, however, the script does not add the row.

Thus, by the end of the while loop, every row from the old database will have been added to $new_data except the line that the script was asked to delete.

```
unless ($item_id eq "$form_data{'delete'}")
  {
```

```
        $new_data .= "$_";
        }
    } # End of else
  } # End of  while (<DATABASE>)
close (DATABASE);
```

At this point, the script opens a temporary file and copies to it the old data-base rows contained in $new_data. Then it uses the rename command to copy the temporary file over the old database file to finalize the deletion.

```
&GetFileLock ("$lock_file");
open (TEMPFILE, ">$temp_file")
     || &open_error($temp_file);
print TEMPFILE "$new_data";
close (TEMPFILE);
rename ($temp_file, $data_file);
&ReleaseFileLock ("$lock_file");
```

Finally, the script prints the usual HTML response, which looks like Figure 11.8 except for the deletion-specific header.

```
print <<"    end_of_html";
<HTML><HEAD>
<TITLE>Your Item has been deleted</TITLE>
</HEAD><BODY>
<CENTER><H2>Your Item has been deleted</H2></CENTER>
<FORM METHOD = "post"
    ACTION = "$database_manager_script_url">
<CENTER>
<INPUT TYPE = "hidden" NAME = "database"
    VALUE = "$setup_file">
<INPUT TYPE = "hidden" NAME = "session_file"
    VALUE = "$form_data{'session_file'}">
<INPUT TYPE = "submit" NAME = "add_form"
    VALUE = "Add an Item">
<INPUT TYPE = "submit" NAME = "search_form_delete"
    VALUE = "Delete an Item">
<INPUT TYPE = "submit" NAME = "search_form_modify"
    VALUE = "Modify an Item">
<INPUT TYPE = "submit" NAME = "search_form_view"
    VALUE = "View the Database">
</CENTER></FORM></BODY></HTML>
end_of_html
exit;
}
```

Modifying an Item in the Database

Finally, the script checks to see whether the client is asking to make a modification.

```
if ($form_data{'submit_modification'} ne "")
  {
```

Before the script can make a modification, however, it must be sure that the client has submitted new information as well as a database row for modification. If the client has filled in the new information but has forgotten to select an item by using the radio buttons, the script must warn him or her to choose a database row.

```
if ($form_data{'modify'} eq "")
   {
   print <<"      end_of_html";
   <HTML><HEAD>
   <TITLE>Modifying an Item in the Database</TITLE>
   </HEAD>
   <BODY>
   <CENTER>
   <H2>Modifying an Item in the Database</H2>
   </CENTER>
   <BLOCKQUOTE>
   I'm sorry, I was not able to modify the database
   because none of the radio buttons on the table was
   selected and I was not sure which item to modify.
   Would you please make sure that you select an item
   "and" fill in the new information.  Please press the
   back button and try again.  Thanks.
   </BLOCKQUOTE>
   end_of_html
   exit;
   }
```

Once we're sure that the user has selected an item and has typed new information into the text input boxes, the script modifies the database. As usual, the script opens the datafile for reading.

```
open (DATABASE, "$data_file")
     || &open_error($data_file);
```

As it did for deletion, the script adds comment lines to $new_data.

```
while (<DATABASE>)
  {
  if ($_ =~ /^COMMENT:/)
    {
    $new_data .= "$_";
    }
```

The script also gets the item_id number from each database row. However, this time the script pushes the number back onto the end of the @fields array because we want that information to be stored with the rest of the database row for further processing.

```
else
  {
  @fields = split (/\|/, $_);
  $item_id = pop(@fields);
  push (@fields, $item_id);
```

This time, if the item ID is equal to the item number submitted by the client, the script renames the fields array to @old_fields.

```
if ($item_id eq "$form_data{'modify'}")
  {
  @old_fields = @fields;
  }
```

Once the row to be modified has been identified, the script dumps all the other rows into the $new_data array, as was done for delete.

```
else
  {
  $new_data .= "$_";
  }
} # End of else
} # End of while (<DATABASE>)
```

The script then initializes a couple of variables. $counter is used to keep track of the number of fields in the database row, and $new_line is used to build the new database row. Both variables will be discussed later.

```
$counter = 0;
$new_line = "";
```

Next, the script goes through the list of `field_values` as defined in the setup file. Recall that arrays begin at zero, so the first array element is `$arrayname[0]`. The script assigns the current element in our count of field values to `$value`, thus going through every field in the database.

```
until ($counter >= @field_values)
   {
   $value = "";
   $value = "$field_values[$counter]";
```

If the `form_data` variable associated with that field does not have a value, the script adds the "old" field value stored in `@old_fields` to the `$new_line` variable.

```
if ($form_data{$value} eq "")
   {
   $new_line .= "$old_fields[$counter]|";
   }
```

On the other hand, if the client submitted new information, the script formats the information as it did for the add routine and adds the resulting value to `$new_line`.

```
else
   {
   $form_data{$value} =~ s/\n/<BR>/g;
   $form_data{$value} =~ s/\r\r/<P>/g;
   $form_data{$value} =~ s/\|/~~/g;
   if ($form_data{$value} eq "")
      {
      $form_data{$value} = "<CENTER>-</CENTER>";
      }
   $new_line .= "$form_data{$value}|";
   }
   $new_line .= "$sold_fields[$counter]\n";
```

Next, the script increments the counter by 1 so that the loop goes through every field in a database row. Once it is finished with the loop, the script closes the database.

```
    $counter++;
    } # End of until ($counter >= @field_values)
close (DATABASE);
```

Finally, as before, the script locks the datafile and opens a temporary file. It then prints the $new_data variable (containing all the old, unmodified database rows) and $new_line (containing the modified row) to the temp file. Then the script copies over the old datafile with the temp file and removes the lock. This action finalizes the modification.

```
chop $new_line;
&GetFileLock ("$lock_file");
open (TEMPFILE, ">$temp_file")
    || &open_error($temp_file);
print TEMPFILE "$new_data";
print  TEMPFILE "$new_line";
close (TEMPFILE);
rename ($temp_file, $data_file);
&ReleaseFileLock ("$lock_file");
```

Finally, the script prints the usual HTML response, which looks like Figure 11.8 except for the modification-specific title.

```
print <<"    end_of_html";
<HTML><HEAD>
<TITLE>Your Item has been Modified</TITLE>
</HEAD><BODY>
<CENTER><H2>Your Item has been Modified</H2></CENTER>
<FORM METHOD = "post"
    ACTION = "$database_manager_script_url">
<CENTER>
<INPUT TYPE = "hidden" NAME = "database"
    VALUE = "$setup_file">
<INPUT TYPE = "hidden" NAME = "session_file"
    VALUE = "$form_data{'session_file'}">
<INPUT TYPE = "submit" NAME = "add_form"
    VALUE = "Add an Item">
<INPUT TYPE = "submit" NAME = "search_form_delete"
    VALUE = "Delete an Item">
<INPUT TYPE = "submit" NAME = "search_form_modify"
    VALUE = "Modify an Item">
<INPUT TYPE = "submit" NAME = "search_form_view"
    VALUE = "View the Database">
</CENTER></FORM></BODY></HTML>
```

```
end_of_html
exit;
}
```

The CgiRequire Subroutine

The first supporting subroutine, CgiRequire, checks to see whether the file that we are trying to exists and is readable by us. This subroutine provides developers with an informative error message when they're attempting to debug the scripts.

```
sub CgiRequire
   {
```

First, the @require_files array is defined as a local array and is filled with the filenames sent from the main routine.

```
local (@require_files) = @_;
```

The subroutine then checks to see whether the files exist and are readable. If they are, the files are loaded.

```
foreach $file (@require_files)
   {
   if (-e "$file" && -r "$file")
     {
     require "$file";
     }
```

If any of the files are not readable or do not exist, the subroutine sends back an error message that identifies the problem.

```
else
   {
   print "I'm sorry, I was not able to open
   $file.  Would you please check to make sure
   that you gave me a valid filename and that the
   permissions on $require_file are set to allow me
   access?";
   exit;
   }
```

```
} # End of foreach $file (@require_files)
} # End of sub CgiRequire
```

The create_input_form Subroutine

The `create_input_form` subroutine is used to create the input forms for the add, modify, and delete user interfaces so that the user can search by keyword and enter the needed data.

```
sub create_input_form
  {
```

First, the subroutine prints a table header.

```
print "<TABLE BORDER = \"1\" CELLPADDING = \"4\"
          CELLSPACING = \"4\">";
```

Next, `create_input_form` makes an HTML form so that administrators can add items to the database. This form has one input field for each field in the database except the database ID field, which is set by this script and not by the administrator. The subroutine gets the list of database fields from the `@field_names` array and, for every element in the array, creates an input field. The subroutine sends the `build_input_form` subroutine in **cgi-lib.sol** a few things: the name of the field, the variable to be associated with that name, and the type of input we are going to use (TEXTAREA, TEXT, or SELECT).

```
foreach $field_name (@field_names)
  {
  print &build_input_form("$FIELD_ARRAY{$field_name}",
       "$FORM_COMPONENT_ARRAY{$field_name}",
       $field_name);
  }
}
```

The search_database Subroutine

The `search_database` subroutine is used to search the database based on keyword input from the client. The `main` routine passes to this subroutine the type of search (modify, delete, or view) for which the results should be formatted.

Notice that the routine uses the keyword none **as the submit type for viewing the data. A view is not a submission as much as it is a simple request.**

N O T E

First, the subroutine assigns the submit type value to the local variable $submit_type.

```
sub search_database
   {
     local($submit_type) = @_;
```

Next, the subroutine opens the database file and begins checking each field in every row against the keywords submitted. It also initializes the $number_of_hits variable, which is used to keep track of how many hits come up in the search.

```
$number_of_hits = "0";
open (DATABASE, "$data_file");
while (<DATABASE>)
   {
   $database_row = $_;
```

Then $not_found_flag is defined as zero to make sure that it has not been initialized elsewhere. The $not_found_flag variable is used to keep track of whether a hit was made based on the client-submitted keyword. If a match was found, the variable will equal 1, but more on that in a bit.

```
$not_found_flag = "0";
```

The next line ensures that the search disregards any line that is a database comment line.

```
unless ($database_row =~ /^COMMENT:/)
   {
```

The subroutine then splits the database row into the @row array.

```
@row = split(/\|/,$database_row);
```

For each key in the %form_data associative array, the script sets $field_number equal to -1. That's because both the pesky "submit" and "exact match" key/value pairs may come in along with the rest of the form data. We do not want the script to search the database for those fields, because they don't exist! By setting $field_number equal to -1, we filter out such nonfield keys using the following routine:

```
foreach $form_data_key (keys %form_data)
  {
  $field_number = -1;
```

Then the subroutine goes through the fields in the database (@field_values), checking to see whether there is a corresponding value coming in from the form ($form_data_key). However, because arrays are counted from zero rather than from 1 and because @field_values gives us a count of the array starting at 1, the subroutine must offset the counter by 1. Thus, if the form "key" submitted is indeed a field in the database, $field_number ($y - 1) will be its actual location in the array.

```
for ($y = 1; $y <= @field_values; $y++)
  {
  if ($form_data_key eq @field_values[$y-1] &&
      $form_data{"$form_data_key"} ne "")
    {
    $field_number = $y - 1;
    last; # Exit out of the for loop because we have
          # verified field
    }
  } End of for loop
```

Next, the script checks the submitted value against the value in the database. It also makes sure that the value is not on or submit keyword. If $field_number is still equal to -1, it means that the form data key did not match an actual database field, so we should try the next key. Otherwise, the script knows that it has a valid database field to check against. Again, $field_number must be less than or equal to -1, because array starts from zero.

```
if ($field_number > -1)
   {
```

Now the subroutine performs the match, checking the database information against the submitted keyword for that field. If it is requested to do so, the script performs an exact match test. If $form_data{'exact_match'} is equal to nothing, then the exact match check box was not checked. The match is straightforward. If the keyword string ($form_data{"$form_data_key"}) matches (=~) a string in the field being searched (@row[$field_number]) with case insensitivity (/i), the script knows that it has found a hit!

```
if ($form_data{'exact_match'} eq "")
   {
   unless (@row[$field_number]
          =~/$form_data{"$form_data_key"}/i)
   {
```

If there was no match, the subroutine sets $not_found_flag equal to 1. In the end, if it gets through all the fields and still has not found a match, the script will be able to tell the client that no matches were found.

```
$not_found_flag = "1";
last; # Exit out of ForEach keys in FormData
} # end of unless
} # end of if ($form_data{'exact_match'} eq "")
```

On the other hand, the client may have clicked the exact match check box.

```
else
   {
```

This time, the subroutine proceeds with an exact match using the \b switch to define the word boundary of the keyword while still keeping the search case-insensitive (/i). The same $not_found_flag setting applies.

```
unless (@row[$field_number] =~/\b$form_data{"$form_data_key"}\b/i)
    {
```

```
   $not_found_flag = "1";
   last; # Exit out of ForEach keys in FormData
    } # end of unless
    } # end of else
  } # End of if ($field_number > -1)
} # End of ForEach keys in FormData
```

If a match was found ($not_found_flag still equals 0), the script checks for group privileges.

```
if ($not_found_flag eq "0")
  {
  $number_of_hits++;
  if ($number_of_hits > "25")
    {
    $search_notice .= "This search engine will only
                        return 25 hits, and, your
            search turned up more than that.
            Would you please refine your
        search?";
    last;
    }
  $hit_counter = "1";
  $db_id_number = pop (@row);
  push (@row, $db_id_number);
```

In the case of a deletion, the subroutine checks to see whether the client is authorized to make a deletion. Recall that the script defined this @group_array when it initially made the security check with GetSessionInfo. If the user is not allowed to delete, the element in group_array will not have a value and the subroutine will set the variable $permission equal to no.

```
if ($submit_type eq "delete")
    {
    $group_test = "$group_array[3]";
    if ($group_test eq "")
      {
    $permission = "no";
      }
    } # End of if ($submit_type eq "delete")
```

The subroutine then does the same for modification.

```
if ($submit_type eq "modify")
   {
   $group_test = "$group_array[2]";
   if ($group_test eq "")
      {
      $permission = "no";
      }
   }
```

If the subroutine has gone through those last three routines and at some point $permissions has been set to no, clients are told that they are not allowed to go forward.

```
if ($permission eq "no")
   {
   print <<"    end_of_html";
</CENTER><BLOCKQUOTE>
I am sorry, it appears that you do not have \
permission to $submit_type.  Please contact the
database administrator to find out how to gain
access.  Sorry about that!
</BLOCKQUOTE><CENTER>
<INPUT TYPE = "hidden" NAME = "database"
       VALUE = "$setup_file">
<INPUT TYPE = "hidden" NAME = "session_file"
       VALUE = "$session_file">
<INPUT TYPE = "submit" NAME = "add_form"
       VALUE = "Add an Item">
<INPUT TYPE = "submit" NAME = "search_form_delete"
       VALUE = "Delete an Item">
<INPUT TYPE = "submit" NAME = "search_form_modify"
       VALUE = "Modify an Item">
<INPUT TYPE = "submit" NAME = "search_form_view"
       VALUE = "View the Database">
end_of_html
exit;
   }
```

Otherwise, the subroutine creates database rows to display. First, the subroutine appends to $search_results an initial <TR>.

```
$search_results .= "<TR>";
```

Then, if the client has asked for a modify or delete form, the subroutine creates a radio input button so that the client can select a database row.

N O T E None **is the value used if there is no need to create a submit radio option. If the client wants only to view the database and does not need to select an item for further processing, we should return a table without a radio button.**

The radio button has a value equal to the database_id number so that each row can be identified when its corresponding radio button is clicked.

```
if ($submit_type ne "none")
    {
    $search_results .= "<TD ALIGN = \"center\">\n";
    $search_results .= "<INPUT TYPE = \"radio\"
                        NAME = \"$submit_type\"
                        VALUE = \"$db_id_number\">";
    $search_results .= "\n</TD>\n";
    }
```

Next, the subroutine adds to the $search_results variable the individual database fields for every row and adds a closing </TR> for every row.

```
foreach $field (@row)
    {
    $search_results .= "<TD>$field</TD>\n";
    }
   } # End of if ($not_found_flag eq "0")
 $search_results .= "</TR>\n";
 } # End of unless ($database_row =~ /^COMMENT:/)
} # End of while (<DATABASE>)
close (DATABASE);
```

Finally, the subroutine handles the possibility that a client-submitted keyword may turn up nothing in the search. At this point, if $hit_counter is not equal to 1, it means that the search did not turn up a hit. Thus, the subroutine must send a note to the client with a link to the search form.

Notice that we use a hyperlink rather than a submit button. We want the client to access this script without a CONTENT_LENGTH so that the form will pop up.

N O T E

If no hits were found, the subroutine exits. We do not want to print an empty table.

```
if ($hit_counter ne "1")
  {
  print "I'm sorry, I was unable to find a match for the
  keyword that you specified in the field that you
  specified.  Feel free to
  <A HREF = \"db_manager.cgi\">try again</A>";
  print "</CENTER></BODY></HTML>";
  exit;
  }
          }
```

CHAPTER 12

The Database Search Engine

OVERVIEW

Another useful database function you can provide through the Web is a
search engine that allows users to search a shared database by keyword
but doesn't give them the power of a larger database manager script.
Database administrators can provide a database management interface
for themselves and a corresponding database search interface for other
people in the company. Users are spared the confusion of having too
many options (most of which they're not allowed to use anyway), and the
sensitive database management functions are hidden behind yet another
level of security.

The database search engine provides a client with text input boxes
for each of the searchable fields in the database. The client types one or
more keywords in any of the input boxes, submits the information to the
CGI script, and receives from the script a list of database rows that match
the keywords.

INSTALLATION AND USAGE

Taking advantage of multiple files and directories, this application is best installed by expanding it into the default directory structure with the root **Database_search**. Figure 12.1 outlines the directory structure and the permissions needed for the search to operate.

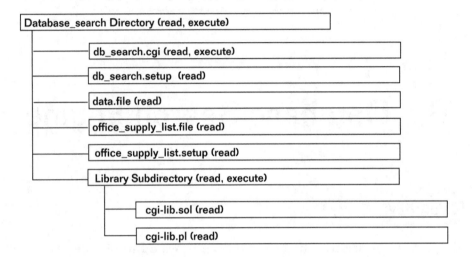

Figure 12.1 Directory layout for the database search application.

The root **Database_manager** directory must have permissions that allow the Web server to read and execute and should contain one directory (**Library**) and five text files (**data.file**, **db_search.cgi**, **db_search.setup**, **office_supply_list.file**, and **office_supply_list.setup**).

db_search.cgi is the application that searches the assigned databases. This file, which should be executable and readable, will be explained in detail in the design discussion.

data.file is the default database that is searched by **db_search.cgi**, and **office_supply_list.file** is an example "secondary" database file that can also be searched with the same **db_search.cgi**. These files must be readable by the Web server so that they can be searched.

db_search.setup and **office_supply_list.setup** are the setup files that communicate to **db_search.cgi** the specific properties of the related datafiles. These files must be readable by the Web server and are discussed in greater detail later.

Library is a subdirectory containing a couple of supporting library files. The library files used for this script are **cgi-lib.pl** and **cgi-lib.sol** (discussed in Part Two). Needless to say, this subdirectory must be executable and readable by the Web server, and its files must be readable.

Server-Specific Setup and Options

THE SETUP FILE

As with the setup file for **db_manager.cgi**, there are two functions performed by the setup file for **db_search.cgi**: defining server-specific variables and determining the names of database fields and their relative display orders. Each **setup** file sets the following variables.

$database_search_script is the location of **db_search.cgi** on your local system.

$database_search_script_url is the URL of **db_search.cgi**.

$data_file is the location of the default datafile. In some cases, this datafile will be located in a separate directory (such as the directory containing the databases for **db_manager.cgi**), but the accompanying disk contains a sample datafile for the purposes of explanation, and we have referenced this variable to that file. In the case of **office_supply_list.setup**, notice that $data_file points to the appropriate data file.

$max_hits specifies the number of hits that should be displayed at any one time. We set this variable to an amount that most browsers will have enough memory to handle.

%FIELD_ARRAY is an associative array that we use to define database fields and their associated variable names.

@field_names is a list of fields in our database. Because of the hash table functions for array handling, if we used the line

```
@field_names = (keys %FIELD_ARRAY);
```

the field names would not come up in the order that we chose to assign them in the database. Thus, we must manually assign the keys in the order that we want them in the @field_names array and the @field_values array.

@field_values is an array that contains only the variable names associated with our database fields.

%FORM_COMPONENT_ARRAY is an associative array that matches database fields with the kind of input type and the kinds of input type arguments the fields are associated with. Arguments and options are pipe-delimited so that type is always the first in the list, usually followed by a second item that includes the input arguments. In the case of a SELECT, however, options—including the size and multiple options—are also separated by pipes. The details can be found in Chapter 10.

As an example, here is the complete text of **db_search.setup**, the default setup file.

```
#!/usr/local/bin/perl
$database_search_script = "./db_search.cgi";
$database_search_script_url = "db_search.cgi";
$data_file = "./data.file";
$max_hits = "5";
%FIELD_ARRAY = ( 'Last Name', 'last_name',
                 'First Name', 'first_name',
                 'Email', 'email',
                 'Phone Number', 'phone',
                 'Address', 'address',
                 'Id', 'id');
@field_names = ("Last Name", "First Name", "Email",
          "Phone Number", "Address", "Id");
@field_values = ("last_name", "first_name", "email",
          "phone", "address", "id");
%FORM_COMPONENT_ARRAY = (
'Last Name', 'text|SIZE = "32" MAXLENGTH = "100"',
'First Name', 'text|SIZE = "32" MAXLENGTH = "100"',
'Email', 'text|SIZE = "32" MAXLENGTH = "100"',
'Phone Number', 'text|SIZE = "32" MAXLENGTH ="100"',
'Address', 'textarea|ROWS = "4" COLS = "30"',
'Id', 'invisible');
```

THE DATA FILE

Every datafile should be a pipe-delimited text database and should be readable by the Web server. The text of **office_supply_list.file** is as follows:

```
COMMENT: Item|Category|Description|Unique ID #
COMMENT:
100a|Bik Pen (Black)|10.00|1
100c|Mooky Stapler|12.00|3
100b|Bik Pen (Red)|11.00|2
```

As you can see, this datafile is formatted exactly the same as the datafiles used by the **db_manager.cgi** script discussed in Chapter 11. This is because both scripts are meant to work together. For more information about the datafile, see the design discussion in Chapter 11.

Running the Script

Once you have configured the setup file to the specifics of your server setup, you can test the search on the sample datafile. To access the script, create a hyperlink to the location of the main script as follows:

```
<A HREF = "http://www.foobar.com/cgi-
bin/Database_search/db_search.cgi">Database Search</A>
```

When you click on this link, you will run **db_search.cgi**, which will take advantage of the default setup file. Alternatively, you can use this same script to search another database on the system by using the following format:

```
http://www.foobar.com/cgi-
bin/Search/db_search.cgi?database=xxx
```

The xxx is the name of the alternative database to use, such as **office_supply_list**.

DESIGN DISCUSSION

Figure 12.2 summarizes the logic of the script as it responds to the demands of the client.

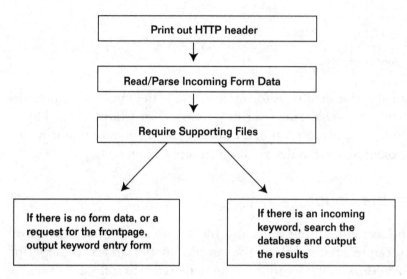

Figure 12.2 The script logic.

The script begins by starting the Perl interpreter and printing the HTTP header.

```
#!/usr/local/bin/perl
print "Content-type: text/html\n\n";
```

Loading the Library Files

Then the script gathers the necessary supporting library files. First, the script makes sure that the library is in the Web server's path and then it loads each library that it will use. To do so, the script adds the library to the array of directories (@INC) known to the Perl interpreter as valid libraries. It adds the directory to the beginning of the array using unshift; in case there is another library in another directory with the same name as ours, Perl will choose the one in **Library** first.

```
$library_path = "./Library";
unshift (@INC, "$library_path");
```

Next, the necessary library files are loaded using CgiRequire, the subroutine at the end of this script. If there is a problem with the require, a meaningful error message will be sent to the Web browser.

```
&CgiRequire("$library_path/cgi-lib.pl",
        "$library_path/cgi-lib.sol");
```

If there is an error, the most likely cause is a typo in the path location of the file to be required.

N O T E

Reading and Parsing Incoming Form Data

Now **cgi-lib.pl** is used to parse the incoming form data. The script passes *form_data to **cgi-lib.pl** so that the associative array returned will come out as %form_data instead of %in.

```
&ReadParse(*form_data);
```

Loading the Setup File

Once it has loaded the basic set of libraries, the script determines which database it should use. The determination depends on client-provided information coming in as url-encoded data. By default, the requested database is the main database:

```
http://www.foobar.com/cgi-bin/Search/db_search.cgi
```

Or the client may have asked to use this script to search a different database on the system:

```
http://www.foobar.com/cgi-
bin/Search/db_search.cgi?database=xxx
```

The following routine determines whether the requested database is other than the default one:

```
if ($form_data{'database'} ne "")
 {
 $database_to_use = "$form_data{'database'}";
 }
else
 {
 $database_to_use = "db_search"; # Default setup file
 }
```

Once the script determines which database to search, it loads the associated setup file.

```
 &CgiRequire("$database_to_use.setup");
```

Displaying the Database Search Form

Next, the script checks whether the client is asking for the form used to submit a keyword. There are two cases in which this test will return true: first, the client may have accessed this script for the first time, having "submitted" no information; content length should equal nothing. Second, the client may have pressed a **submit** button asking to return to the front page. The next line asks for either case 1 or (||) case 2.

```
if ($ENV{'CONTENT_LENGTH'} eq "" ||
$form_data{'return_to_frontpage'} ne "")
 {
```

If this if test returns true, the script knows that it is being asked to display the front page. First, the script outputs the HTML page header.

```
print <<"     end_of_html";
<HTML><HEAD>
<TITLE>Database Search Engine</TITLE>
</HEAD><BODY>
<CENTER>
<H2>Database Search Engine Front Page</H2>
</CENTER>
<FORM METHOD = "post"
```

```
      ACTION = "$database_search_script">
<CENTER>
<TABLE BORDER = "1" CELLSPACING = "4" CELLPADDING = "4">
end_of_html
```

Next, the script generates an HTML form so that the client can submit keywords. This HTML form has one input field for each field in the database except for the database ID field, which is an administrative field.

The script gets the list of database fields from the @field_names array and, for every element in the array, creates an input field. To create the HTML form, the script sends the build_input_form subroutine in **cgi-lib.sol** three things: the name of the field, the variable to be associated with that name, and the type of input we are going to use (TEXTAREA, TEXT, or SELECT).

```
foreach $field_name (@field_names)
  {
  print &build_input_form("$FIELD_ARRAY{$field_name}",
      "$FORM_COMPONENT_ARRAY{$field_name}",
       $field_name);
     }
```

At the end of the form, the script tacks on a form input for exact match and the page footer.

```
print <<"    end_of_html";
<TH>Exact Match?</TH>
<TD><INPUT TYPE = "checkbox" NAME = "exact_match"></TD>
</TR></TABLE><P>
<INPUT TYPE = "hidden" NAME = "database"
     VALUE = "$database_to_use">
<INPUT TYPE = "submit"  NAME = "search_database"
     VALUE = "Submit Search Term">
</CENTER></FORM></BODY></HTML>
end_of_html
exit;
} # End of if ($ENV{'CONTENT_LENGTH'} eq "" ......
```

All searches are case-insensitive, but the exact match matches on word boundary so that it will not match gen'eric' if the search is for eric, whereas the non-exact search will find the item.

NOTE

Figure 12.3 shows what the query form looks like on the Web.

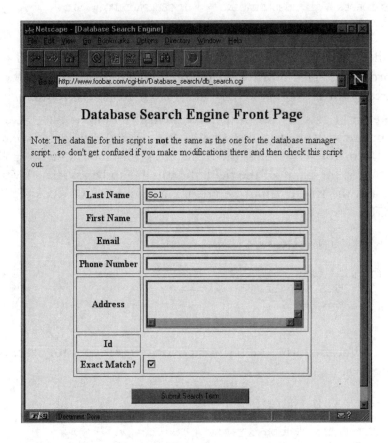

Figure 12.3 *The query form.*

Searching the Database for Client-Submitted Keywords

If the script gets past the previous if test, it means that the client has submitted a keyword. The script conducts the search and prints the results. As usual, the process begins by printing the page header.

```
print <<"     end_of_html";
<HTML><HEAD>
<TITLE>Database Search Engine Results</TITLE>
</HEAD><BODY>
```

```
<CENTER><H2>Database Search Engine Results</H2></CENTER>
<FORM METHOD = "post"
      ACTION = "$database_search_script">
<INPUT TYPE = "hidden" NAME = "database"
      VALUE = "$database_to_use">
<CENTER>
end_of_html
```

Next, the script searches the database. Searching begins by opening the database file and checking each field in every row against the keywords submitted.

The script also assigns to the variable $initial_hits the value of $number_of_hits, which may or may not be coming in as form data. The script uses this variable to keep track of how many screens' worth of search results the user has seen. So that we do not overwhelm the Web browser, this script has been built to display no more than a specific amount of hits at one time. In the distribution setup file, we have set this amount to 5.

```
$initial_hits = $form_data{'number_of_hits'};
open (DATABASE, "$data_file");
while (<DATABASE>)
  {
  $database_row = $_;
```

Then the script sets the variable $not_found_flag equal to zero to make sure that it has not been initialized elsewhere. The $not_found_flag variable is used to keep track of whether a hit was made based on the client-submitted keyword. If a match was found, the variable will equal 1. If, at the end of all the searching, $not_found_flag is still equal to zero, we tell the client the bad news.

```
$not_found_flag = "0";
```

The script must also disregard any line that is a database comment line. If you have not read Chapter 11 and don't understand this, it's a good idea to jump back and check out the description there.

```
unless ($database_row =~ /^COMMENT:/)
  {
```

Then the script `splits` the current database row into the `@row` array, assigning elements for every occurrence of a pipe character.

```
@row = split(/\|/,$database_row);
```

We escape the pipe character, because it has meaning other than as a delimiter for our database.

NOTE

Next, for each key in the `%form_data` associative array, the script sets `$field_number` equal to –1. That's because both the pesky "submit" and "exact match" key/value pairs may come in along with the rest of the form data. We do not want the script to search the database for those fields, because they don't exist! By setting `$field_number` equal to –1, we filter out such nonfield keys using the following routine:

```
foreach $form_data_key (keys %form_data)
  {
  $field_number = -1;
```

Now the script goes through the fields in the database (`@field_values`), checking to see whether there is a corresponding value coming in from the form (`$form_data_key`). However, because arrays are counted from zero rather than from 1 and because `@field_values` gives us a count of the array starting at 1, the script offsets its counter by 1. Thus, if the form "key" submitted is indeed a field in the database, `$field_number` (`$y - 1`) will be its actual location in the array.

```
for ($y = 1; $y <= @field_values; $y++)
  {
  if ($form_data_key eq @field_values[$y-1] &&
      $form_data{"$form_data_key"} ne "")
    {
    $field_number = $y - 1;
    last; # Exit out of the for loop because we have
          # verified field
    }
  } # End of for loop
```

Before we check the submitted value against the value in the database, we make sure that the value is not `on` or `submit` keyword. If `$field_number` is still equal to –1, the script knows that the form data key did not match an actual database field, so the script tries the next key. Otherwise, the script knows that it has a valid field to check against. Again, `$field_number` must be less than or equal to –1, because the array starts from zero.

```
if ($field_number > -1)
  {
```

Then the script performs the match, checking the database information against the submitted keyword for that field. It performs an exact match test if requested to do so. If `$form_data{'exact_match'}` is equal to nothing, it means that the exact match check box was not checked. The match is straightforward. If the keyword string (`$form_data{"$form_data_key"}`) matches (`=~`) a string in the field that we are searching (`@row[$field_number]`) case insensitively (`/i`), then the script knows that it has found a hit!

```
if ($form_data{'exact_match'} eq "")
  {
  unless (@row[$field_number] =~
          /$form_data{"$form_data_key"}/i)
    {
```

If there was no match, the script sets `$not_found_flag` equal to 1. In the end, if it gets through all the fields and has still not found a match, the script will be able to tell the client that no matches were found.

```
  $not_found_flag = "1";
  last; # Exit out of ForEach keys in FormData
  } # End of unless
} # End of if ($form_data{'exact_match'} eq "")
```

On the other hand, the client may have clicked the exact match check box.

```
else
  {
```

This time, the script proceeds with an exact match using the \b switch to delimit the keyword absolutely while still matching it with case sensitivity off (/i). The same $not_found_flag setting applies.

```
unless (@row[$field_number] =~
        /\b$form_data{"$form_data_key"}\b/i)
   {
   $not_found_flag = "1";
   last; # Exit out of ForEach keys in FormData
   } # End of unless
  } # End of else
 } # End of if ($field_number > -1)
} # End of ForEach keys in FormData
```

If the script finds a match ($not_found_flag still equals 0), it must create a table row for the output. The variable $search_results collects all the hits and formats them as table rows for the output. A hit adds each of the fields of the database row to a table row.

However, because the script may be working with a huge database having thousands of rows, we must make sure that the client-submitted keyword does not overwhelm the client's browser or our own server's memory. Thus, for every hit, the script increments $number_of_hits by 1. In addition, the script sets $adjusted_max_hits to $initial_hits plus $max_hits. That way, $adjusted_max_hits takes into account rows that have been seen by the client, who will have pressed the **submit** button to see the next group of hits. Then, provided it receives these values as incoming form data, the script can ignore all hits whose values are less than the number of hits already seen by the client. It can also ignore those greater than the number of $max_hits defined in the setup file plus the $initial_hits already seen by the client.

```
if ($not_found_flag eq "0")
   {
   $number_of_hits++;
   $adjusted_max_hits = $initial_hits + $max_hits;
   if ($number_of_hits > $initial_hits &&
       $number_of_hits <= $adjusted_max_hits)
      {
```

If the row is within the boundary, the script outputs the row to the Web-based table.

```
$search_results .= "<TR>";
$hit_counter = "1";
foreach $field (@row)
  {
  $search_results .= "<TD>$field</TD>";
  }
$search_results .= "</TR>";
}
```

If, on the other hand, the script finds too many hits, we stop the printing of table rows and let the user choose to see more if desired.

```
else
  {
  $search_notice .= "This search engine will only
        return $max_hits hits, and your
     search turned up more than that.
Would you please refine your
search?";
```

If it has displayed all the data, the script breaks out of the loop.

```
if ($number_of_hits eq "$adjusted_max_hits")
  {
  last;
  }
  }
} # End of unless ($database_row =~ /^COMMENT:/)
} # End of while (<DATABASE>), try the next row...
close (DATABASE);
```

But what if the client-submitted keyword turns up nothing in the search? At this point, if $not_found_flag is still equal to zero, it means that the search did not turn up a hit. Thus, the script must be prepared to send a note to the client with a link to the search form and exit.

```
if ($not_found_flag eq "0")
  {
```

```
print "I'm sorry, I was unable to find a match for the
     keyword that you specified in the field that you
     specified.  Feel free to
     <A HREF = \"db-search.cgi\">try again</A>";
print "</CENTER></BODY></HTML>";
exit;
}
```

NOTE Notice that we use a hyperlink rather than a **submit** button. We want the client to access this script without a CONTENT_LENGTH so that the front page form will pop up.

Otherwise, the script prints a list of hits in a table format. $search_results contains all the hits, in the form of table rows. table_header, a subroutine in **cgi-lib.sol** that separates table headers out of the @field_names array, is used to generate the header. The script also prints $search_notice in case its search results exceeded the maximum number of hits defined in $max_hits.

```
print "<TABLE BORDER = \"1\" CELLSPACING = \"4\"
          CELLPADDING = \"4\">";
print &table_header (@field_names);
print <<"  end_of_html";
</TR>
$search_results
</TABLE><P>$search_notice<P>
end_of_html
foreach $form_data_key (keys %form_data)
   {
   unless ($form_data_key eq "database" ||
          $form_data_key eq "number_of_hits")
      {
      print "<INPUT TYPE = \"hidden\"
            NAME = \"$form_data_key\"
            VALUE = \"$form_data{$form_data_key}\"\n";
      }
   }
print <<"  end_of_html";
<INPUT TYPE = "submit" NAME = "return_to_frontpage"
       VALUE = "Return to Frontpage">
</CENTER></FORM></BODY></HTML>
end_of_html
exit;
```

Figure 12.4 shows what a sample search results page might look like.

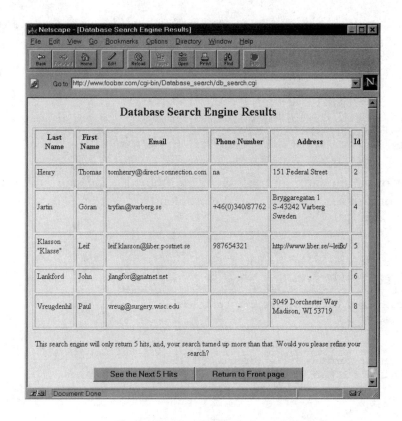

Figure 12.4 Database search results.

The CgiRequire Subroutine

CgiRequire checks to see whether the file that the script is trying to require exists and is readable by us. This subroutine provides developers with an informative error message when they're attempting to debug the scripts.

```
sub CgiRequire
  {
```

First, the @require_files array is defined as a local array and filled with the filenames sent from the main routine.

```
local (@require_files) = @_;
```

The subroutine then checks to see whether the files exist and are readable. If they are, the files are `required`.

```
foreach $file (@require_files)
   {
   if (-e "$file" && -r "$file")
     {
     require "$file";
     }
```

If any of the files are not readable or do not exist, the subroutine sends an error message that identifies the problem.

```
else
   {
   print "I'm sorry, I was not able to open
   $file.  Would you please check to make sure
   that you gave me a valid filename and that the
   permissions on $file are set to allow me
   access?";
   exit;
   }
 } # End of foreach $file (@require_files)
} # End of sub CgiRequire
```

CHAPTER 13

The Groupware Calendar

OVERVIEW

Many offices have a calendar tacked to the wall in a central location. Employees add items such as scheduled vacations, reservations of conference rooms, or notices about meeting, conferences, or seminars. By using a shared calendar, employees can more efficiently coordinate their work with that of others in the organization. The groupware calendar script provides a Web interface to a similar shared calendar. Every user can read what other people have added and, if the script is configured to do it, can modify the other entries. Calendar entries are stored in an ASCII database file.

The calendar has two primary views: the month view and the day view. In the month view, users can see calendar months for any year within a range specified at installation. Each day in the month displays the subjects of events scheduled for that day. In the day view, the events for a given day can be viewed in greater detail. Users can easily change the displayed month or year depending on their needs.

Varying levels of security are configurable. For example, the calendar can be made to be viewable by anyone or by authenticated users only. Items within the calendar database can be made to be modifiable or deletable only by the person who posts them or by everyone.

Installation and Usage

The application should be installed into the default directory, **Calendar**. Figure 13.1 outlines the expanded directory structure and the permissions of files and subdirectories.

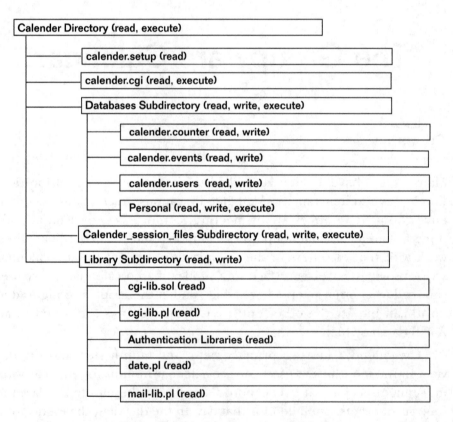

Figure 13.1 Directory layout for calendar.

This script should be placed in a directory that has permissions set to allow the Web server to read and execute and should expand to include three directories (**Calendar_session_files**, **Library**, and **Databases**) and two files (**calendar.cgi** and **calendar.setup**).

calendar.cgi is the application that provides most of the calendar processing. This file should be readable and executable by the Web server and will be discussed in greater detail in the design discussion.

calendar.setup is the file used to set the options and variables that pertain to your local setup. The file must be readable by the Web server and will be discussed in greater detail in the "Server-Specific Variables and Options" section.

Calendar_session_files is the subdirectory used by the authentication libraries to store session files, as discussed in Chapter 9. Initially the directory will be empty, but if it is set to be readable, writable and executable relative to the Web server, it will continually fill up and be pruned as a part of daily usage.

Library is a subdirectory containing the supporting CGI libraries, which are discussed in Part Two. The subdirectory should be readable and executable by the Web server and should contain the following libraries, which should be readable by the Web server: **auth-extra-html.pl**, **auth-extra-lib.pl**, **auth-lib-fail-html.pl**, **auth-lib.pl**, **auth-server-lib.pl**, **auth-fail_html.pl**, **cgi-lib.pl**, **cgi-lib.sol**, **date.pl**, and **mail-lib.pl**.

Databases is a subdirectory containing the counter, events, and user files as well as any other calendar database files for alternative calendars. Because **calendar.cgi** must be able to write to this directory, its permissions should be set to be readable, writable, and executable.

calendar.counter is a text file used to keep track of unique ID numbers that have been assigned to each event in the calendar database. Initially, this file should contain the number 1 on the first line and nothing else. As time goes by, **calendar.cgi** will increment this number for every new entry. The file must be readable and writable by the Web server.

calendar.events is the datafile used to store all the entered events. The format is exactly the same as for the databases we have discussed in previous chapters, including the protocol for comment lines and the use of pipe (|) as a field delimiter. If you have jumped right to this chapter and do not understand the database format, read the section on the datafile in Chapter 11.

The default fields for the events file are as follows: the day, month, year, username, first name, last name, E-mail address, subject, event time, event description, and ID number. The file must be readable and writable by the Web server.

calendar.users is a file containing the list of users who are allowed to modify the events database. This user file is formatted exactly the same as the default user file discussed in Chapter 9. This file should be readable and writable by the Web server and should initially be empty.

Personal is a sample subdirectory used to describe how to create separate calendar databases to be displayed by the same **calendar.cgi** script. The directory contains three files: **calendar.counter**, **calendar.events**, and **calendar.users**. These files define all the specific formats of each separate calendar.

Server-Specific Setup and Options

calendar.setup is the setup file used by **calendar.cgi** to define server-specific variables, configure authentication, and configure the events database. Defined variables are as follows:

$this_script_url is the location of **calendar.cgi**. Because we refer to it from here and because, theoretically, this file will be in the same directory, you need only state the name of the script. If that is the case and if you don't change the name of the file, don't bother changing this variable.

$the_current_year is pretty obvious. Set this to the current year.

$greatest_year is the highest-numbered year for which you want people to be able to submit calendar events on the Add Item form.

$database_file is the location of the file that contains the calendar database. Because this file can be defined by the user, we tag onto this variable the value of $calendar_type, which is given to us by the main script, **calendar.cgi**. In short, $calendar_type is a value set by the initial link via urlencoding

```
http://www.foobar.com/cgi-
bin/Calendar/calendar.cgi?calendar=Personal
```

Thus, the $calendar_type should be the directory name of each separate calendar.

NOTE We don't recommend that you change this variable. The only reason to change it is if you don't like our file-naming conventions or if you are working with DOS and can have only 8.3 filenames.

$counter_file is the path of the file that you are using to keep track of unique ID numbers. To make deletions and modifications, we must have a unique ID number so that the script can determine which database item to delete. These ID numbers should always be the last field in any database row. Again, because we need to isolate each of the calendars, we will reference the counter file including the $calendar_type variable.

$temp_file is a file that the script uses to temporarily store various data at various times. The file will be generated and deleted by the script.

$lock_file is a file that the script uses to make sure that only one person can modify the database at any given time.

Authentication variables are explained in Chapter 9.

@day_names is an array containing the names of the weekdays. A word of caution for all the arrays: the most common source of configuration errors is to forget to put a comma here or a quotation mark there, or even to forget to add one of the fields. So be very careful here; everything must be perfect!

@month_names is—yup, you got it—a list of month names.

%MONTH_ARRAY is an associative array that pairs month names with their numbers.

%TIME is an associative array that pairs time names with military time values.

@time_values is an ordered list of military time values.

%FIELD_ARRAY is an associative array that pairs database field names with their variable names.

@field_names is the list of database fields.

@field_values is the list of the variable names associated with the database fields in @field_names. By the way, the reason that we don't use key and value commands to define the arrays relative to all the associative arrays is that we want to predefine an order for them. If we used keys and values, we would lose our order in the hash table entry to the associative array.

$field_num_time is the element number in the array of the event_time field in the database. We need this value to sort the database by time so that when you click on a day view, the day events come up in order. When setting this variable, remember that arrays count from zero and not from 1.

As an example, the complete **calendar.setup** file is listed next:

```
$this_script_url = "calendar.cgi";
$the_current_year = "1996";
$greatest_year = "2011";
$database_file = "./Databases/$calendar_type/calendar.events";
$counter_file = "./Databases/$calendar_type/calendar.counter";
$temp_file =
"./Calendar_session_files/$calendar_type/calendar_temp.file";
$lock_file =
"./Calendar_session_files/$calendar_type/calendar_lock.file";
$auth_lib = "$lib";
$auth_server =  "off";
$auth_cgi =  "on";
$auth_user_file =  "./Databases/$calendar_type/calendar.users";
$auth_alt_user_file =  "";
$auth_default_group =  "user";
$auth_add_register =  "on";
$auth_email_register =  "off";
$auth_admin_from_address =  "selena\@foobar.com";
$auth_admin_email_address =  "selena\@foobar.com";
$auth_session_length = 2;
$auth_session_dir = "./Calendar_session_files";
$auth_register_message = "Thanks, you may now logon with
        your new username and password.";
$auth_allow_register =  "on";
$auth_allow_search =  "on";
$auth_generate_password =  "off";
$auth_check_duplicates =  "on";
$auth_password_message = "Thanks for applying to our
        site, your password is";
@auth_extra_fields = ("auth_first_name",
```

```
                         "auth_last_name",
                         "auth_email");
@auth_extra_desc = ("First Name",
                    "Last Name",
                    "Email");
@day_names = ("Sunday", "Monday", "Tuesday",
              "Wednesday", "Thursday", "Friday",
              "Saturday");
@month_names = ("January", "February", "March", "April",
                "May", "June", "July", "August",
                "September", "October", "November",
                "December");
%MONTH_ARRAY = ('January', '1',        'February', '2',
                'March', '3',          'April', '4',
                'May', '5',            'June', '6',
                'July', '7',           'August', '8',
                'September', '9',      'October', '10',
                'November', '11',      'December', '12');
%TIME = ('01:00', '1 AM', '02:00', '2 AM', '03:00',
         '3 AM', '04:00', '4 AM', '05:00', '5 AM',
         '06:00', '6 AM', '07:00', '7 AM', '08:00',
         '8 AM', '09:00', '9 AM', '10:00', '10 AM',
         '11:00', '11 AM', '12:00', '12 Noon', '13:00',
         '1 PM', '14:00', '2 PM', '15:00', '3 PM',
         '16:00', '4 PM', '17:00', '5 PM', '18:00',
         '6 PM', '19:00', '7 PM', '20:00', '8 PM',
         '21:00', '9 PM', '22:00', '10 PM', '23:00',
         '11 PM', '24:00', '12 Midnight');
@time_values = ("01:00", "02:00", "03:00", "04:00",
                "05:00", "06:00", "07:00", "08:00",
                "09:00", "10:00", "11:00", "12:00",
                "13:00", "14:00", "15:00", "16:00",
                "17:00", "18:00", "19:00", "20:00",
                "21:00", "22:00", "23:00", "24:00");
%FIELD_ARRAY = ('Day', 'day',
                'Month', 'month',
                'Year', 'year',
                'Username', 'username',
                'First Name', 'first_name',
                'Last Name', 'last_name',
                'Email Address', 'email',
                'Subject', 'subject',
                'Event Time', 'time',
                'Body', 'body',
                'Database Id Number',
                'databse_id_number');
@field_names = ("Day", "Month", "Year", "Username",
```

```
              "First Name", "Last Name",
              "Email Address", "Subject",
              "Event Time", "Body",
              "Database Id Number");
@field_values = ("day", "month", "year", "username",
              "first_name", "last_name", "email",
              "subject", "time", "body",
              "databse_id_number");
$field_num_time = "8";
```

Running the Script

Once you have configured the setup file to the specifics of your server and calendar datafile, it is time to try out your installation. To reference the script, use the following URL format.

```
<A HREF="http://www.foobar.com/cgi-
bin/Calendar/calendar.cgi">Calendar</A>
```

When clients click on this link, they should see the front page of your calendar with the default configurations. To reference separate calendar databases, the link to this script must have ?calendar=Some_subdirectory added at the end of the URL. For example,

```
http://www.foobar.com/cgi-
bin/Calendar/calendar.cgi?calendar=Personal
```

DESIGN DISCUSSION

Figure 13.2 outlines the logic of the script as it manages the needs of the client and the demands of the server.

The script begins by starting the Perl interpreter and printing the HTTP header.

```
#!/usr/local/bin/perl
print "Content-type: text/html\n\n";
```

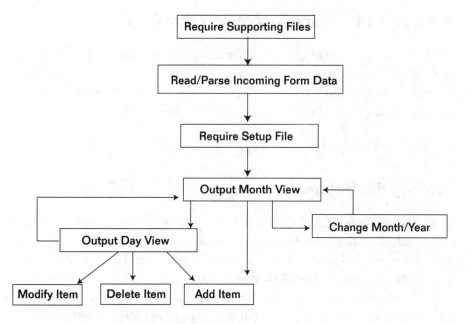

Figure 13.2 *The script logic.*

Loading the Supporting Libraries

Next, the script loads the necessary files using the subroutine `CgiRequire` at the end of this script. If there is a problem loading files, this subroutine returns a message that's valuable for debugging. `$lib` is the location of the **Library** directory, where these files are to be stored; because it is hard-coded in the main script, you must be careful to change it here if you move the library elsewhere. Keep `$lib` equal to `./Library` if you do not have a **Library** directory and are going to use the default directory included on the accompanying disk.

```
$lib = "./Library";
&CgiRequire("$lib/cgi-lib.pl", "$lib/cgi-lib.sol",
        "$lib/auth-lib.pl", "$lib/date.pl");
```

Reading and Parsing Incoming Form Data

cgi-lib.pl is used to parse the incoming form data. By passing it (`*form_data`), the subroutine returns an associative array that we reference as `$form_data{'key'}` instead of `$in{'$key'}`. In the end, the script will reference all the incoming form data as `$form_data{'variablename'}`.

```
&ReadParse(*form_data);
```

Loading the Setup File

Once the incoming form data has been processed, the script determines which calendar database to use. If the calendar administrator has set up more than one calendar, each calendar database will be in a subdirectory, such as the example **Personal Database** that is included in the accompanying disk. To reference these separate databases, the link to this script must have `?calendar=Somesubdirectory` added at the end of the URL. For example:

```
http://www.foobar.com/cgi-
bin/Calendar/calendar.cgi?calendar=Personal
```

If the client does not submit a new database to use, the script will simply assign the default database and calendar. The `$calendar_type` variable will be used within the **calendar.setup** file, as addressed earlier.

```
if ($form_data{'calendar'} ne "")
  {
  $calendar_type = "./$form_data{'calendar'}";
  }
else
  {
  $calendar_type = "./";
  }
```

Then the script defines all the calendar-specific variables by using the setup file, which you should have customized for your site.

```
&require("calendar.setup");
```

Defining Intrascreen Variables

Next, we make sure that the script "remembers" the $session_file so that it can continually check for authentication and keep track of the current client. However, if the client has already logged on, the script does not need to revalidate the client, because it will be getting the $session_file as form data (the same hidden field we are about to define). Thus, the script renames $form_data{'session_file'} to $session_file so that in both cases (the client's first time at this point or subsequent script access by a continuing client) it will have the session_id in the same variable name form.

```
if ($form_data{'session_file'} ne "")
  {
  $session_file = $form_data{'session_file'};
  }
```

The script also renames some other variables using the same principle. In doing so, the script uses a couple of routines in **date.pl**, as discussed in Chapter 6, to manipulate date information so that it can use the date information in a standardized way.

```
if ($form_data{'year'} ne "")
  {
  $current_year = "$form_data{'year'}";
  }
else
  {
  $current_year = "$the_current_year";
  }
if ($form_data{'month'} eq "")
  {
  @mymonth = &make_month_array(&today);
  $current_month_name = &monthname($currentmonth);
  }
else
  {
  @mymonth =
&make_month_array(&jday($form_data{'month'},1,$current_year));
  $current_month_name = &monthname($form_data{'month'});
  }
```

Printing the Calendar for the Current Month

The script prints the dynamically generated calendar in two cases. First, the calendar is printed if the client has just logged on and is asking for the first page ($form_data{'session_file'} ne ""). Second, the calendar is printed if the client has already been moving through various pages and has asked to view the calendar again ($form_data{'change_ month_year'} ne ""). The || means "or." If either case is true, the script may proceed.

```
if ($form_data{'change_month_year'} ne "" ||
    $ENV{'REQUEST_METHOD'} eq "GET" &&
    $form_data{'day'} eq "")
    {
```

Displaying the Calendar Header

The script begins outputting the calendar by first printing the HTML calendar header.

```
&header ("Selena Sol's Groupware Calendar Demo:
$current_month_name - $current_year");
print <<"    end_of_html";
<CENTER>
<H2>$current_month_name - $current_year</H2>
</CENTER>
<TABLE BORDER = "2" CELLPADDING = "4" CELLSPACING = "4">
<TR>
end_of_html
```

NOTE You can modify everything between the `print <<"` `end_of_html";` and the `end_of_html`, but be careful of illegal characters. For example, @ must be preceded by a backslash (selena\@foobar.com).

The script then prints the table header (Weekdays). Essentially, for every day (`foreach $day`) in our list of days (`@day_names`), the script prints the day as a table header.

```
foreach $day (@day_names)
    {
```

```
  print "<TH>$day</TH>\n";
  }
print "</TR>\n<TR>\n";
```

Next, the script creates the variable `$count_till_last_day`, which it uses to make sure that it does not add too many `<TR>`s. Also, the script clears out a new variable, `$weekday`, which it uses to keep track of the two-dimensional aspect of the calendar: the script breaks the calendar rows after every seventh cell to represent a week. We will talk more about this later.

```
$count_till_last_day = "0";
$weekday = 0;
```

Displaying Calendar Days as Table Cells

For every day in the `mymonth` array, the script creates a cell for the calendar. The array `@mymonth`, if you recall, is an array returned from the subroutine `make_month_array`.

```
foreach $day_number (@mymonth)
  {
```

The script begins by incrementing the two counter variables: `$count_till_last_day` and `$weekday`.

```
  $count_till_last_day++;
  $weekday++;
```

The script must also make sure that it adds a break for every week to make the calendar two-dimensional. Thus, when it has gone through sets of seven days in this `foreach` loop, it resets `$weekday` to zero. In the following code, the script uses these values to determine where it should place the `</TR><TR>`, making a new calendar row. When `$weekday` is greater than 6, the script knows that it needs a `</TR><TR>`, so by setting the `$weekday` flag to zero, we notify the script a few lines later to insert the row break.

```
$weekday = 0 if ($weekday > 6);
```

Next, the script prints a table cell for each day. Because we want to make each of the numbers in each of the cells clickable so that someone can click on the number to see a day view, the script must manage a great deal of information here.

First, the script builds a variable called $variable_list, which is used to create a long URL appendix to transfer information using urlencoding. As we will discuss more specifically later, the routine that generates the day views needs to have the day, year, and month values if it is to bring up a day view. It must also have the $session_file value (as all the routines in this script must), the name of the calendar database, and the special tag view_day=on. So the script gathers all that information and appends it to the $variable_list variable.

```
$variable_list = "";
$variable_list = "day=$day_number&year=$currentyear";
$variable_list .= "&month=$currentmonth";
$variable_list .= "&session_file=$session_file";
$variable_list .= "&calendar=$form_data{'calendar'}";
$variable_list .= "&view_day=on";
```

Then the script creates the calendar cell. Notice that the number in each cell is made clickable by using urlencoding to tag the URL with all the variables we want passed.

```
print "<TD VALIGN = \"top\" WIDTH = \"150\">\n";
print "<A
HREF=\"$this_script_url?$variable_list\">$day_number</A
>\n";
```

Adding Subject Listings to Calendar Cells

The cell is not yet complete. The script must also grab from the calendar database the subject listings for all the entries on that day. In doing so, the script makes sure that, if it cannot open the database file, it sends a useful message to us for debugging. It uses the open_error subroutine in **cgi-lib.sol**, passing the routine the location of the database file.

```
open (DATABASE, "$database_file") ||
     &open_error($database_file);
```

If it successfully opens the database file, the script goes through each line, splitting the fields into their associated variables.

```
while (<DATABASE>)
    {
    ($day, $month, $year, $username, $first_name,
    $last_name, $email, $subject, $time, $body,
    $database_id_number) = split (/\|/,$_);
```

For every row searched, the script determines whether the day, month, and year of each item on that row are equal to the day, month, and year of the cell it is currently building.

```
if ($day eq "$day_number" && $month eq "$currentmonth"
&& $year eq "$currentyear")
    {
```

If it was able to answer true to all the preceding conditions, the script knows that it has found a match and prints the subject in that cell.

```
 print "<BR><FONT SIZE = \"1\">$subject</FONT>\n";
   } # End of if ($day eq "$day_number" && $month eq ...
} # End of while (<DATABASE>)
```

Once the script has checked all the lines in the database, it closes that cell and moves to the next cell.

```
print "</TD>\n";
```

If, however, the script reached the end of a week row, it must begin a new table row for the next week. If $weekday is equal to zero, then the script knows that it is time to begin a new row. Otherwise, it continues with the row.

```
if ($weekday == 0)
  {
  print "</TR>\n";
```

NOTE

By the way, here we use == instead of =. If we used =, Perl would interpret the part inside the `if ()` **to be assigning the value of zero to** `$weekday`**, and it would evaluate the whole process as** `true`**. That would undercut the whole point of counting with** `$weekday`**.**

Before the script blindly prints another table row, it makes sure that it has not reached the end of the month. If `$count_till_last_day` equals `@mymonth`, it knows that there are no more days left and it should not begin a new row. Notice that when we reference `@mymonth` without quotation marks, we receive the numerical value of the number of elements in the array.

```
unless ($count_till_last_day == @mymonth)
  {
  print "<TR>";
  } # End of unless ($count_till_last_day == @mymonth)
 } # End of if ($weekday == 0)
} # End of foreach $day_number (@mymonth)
```

Displaying Footer Information for the Month View

Once the script has finished making all the cells for the calendar, it prints the HTML footer.

```
print <<"    end_of_html";
</TABLE>
</CENTER>
<BLOCKQUOTE>
For day-at-a-glance calendar, click on the day number on the
calendar above.
<BR>
Or, to see another month, choose one
end_of_html
```

To let the user select a different month to view, the script creates a select box using the subroutine `select_a_month` at the end of this script.

```
&select_a_month;
print "<P>Or, to see another year, select one\n";
```

Likewise, it creates a select box that allows the client to choose a new year to view using `select_a_year` at the end of this script.

```
&select_a_year;
```

Then the script outputs the usual footer.

```
print <<"     end_of_html";
<P>
* Note: This calendar is best viewed by opening your
browser window to its maximum size. And, you can only submit
a month if the year field is cleared!<P>
</BLOCKQUOTE>
<CENTER>
<INPUT TYPE = "submit" NAME = "change_month_year"
       VALUE = "Change Month/Year">
<INPUT TYPE = "reset" VALUE = "Clear this form">
<INPUT TYPE = "submit" NAME = "add_item_form"
        VALUE = "Add Item">
</FORM>
</CENTER>
</BODY>
</HTML>
end_of_html
exit;
} # End of if ($form_data{'change_month_year'} ne "" ||...
```

On the Web, the front page looks like Figure 13.3.

Displaying a Day View

In the preceding routine, the script made every number in every cell of the calendar clickable so that the client could view the detailed descriptions of the events scheduled for that day. In the urlencoded string it built, the script included a tag `view_day = on`. Here is where that tag comes in handy. The following `if` test checks to see whether the person has clicked on a number; if the person has, the test will evaluate to `true`. If the test evaluates to `true`, the script prints the page header.

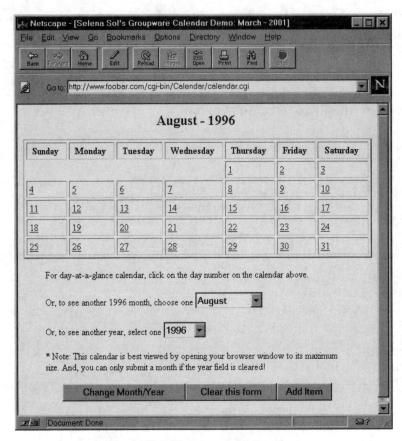

Figure 13.3 *The view month interface.*

```
if ($form_data{'view_day'} eq "on")
  {
  &header ("$current_month_name $form_data{'day'},
          $current_year");
  print <<"    end_of_html";
  <CENTER>
  <H2>$current_month_name $form_data{'day'},
      $current_year</H2>
  </CENTER>
  end_of_html
```

Next, the script opens the database again and looks for database rows
that match the requested day, month, and year.

```
open (DAYFILE, "$database_file") ||
&open_error($database_file);
while (<DAYFILE>)
    {
```

Just as it did in the routine for generating subject lines for day cells, the script pays attention only to database rows that match the client-defined day, month, and year.

```
($day, $month, $year, $username, $first_name,
 $last_name, $email, $subject, $time, $body,
 $database_id_number) = split (/\|/,$_);
if ($day eq "$form_data{'day'}" &&
    $month eq "$form_data{'month'}" &&
    $year eq "$current_year")
        {
```

Next, the script sets the `$item_found` flag so that it can keep track of whether it has found an item in the database.

```
$item_found = "yes";
```

The script then prints an <HR>-delimited, detailed list of events of the day, followed by a standard HTML footer.

```
  print <<"          end_of_html";
  <B>Time:</B> $TIME{$time}<BR>
  <B>Subject:</B> $subject<BR>
  <B>Poster:</B>
  <A HREF = "mailto:$email">$first_name
            $last_name</A><BR>
  <B>Body:</B><BLOCKQUOTE>$body</BLOCKQUOTE>
  <P><CENTER><HR WIDTH = "50%"></CENTER><P>
  end_of_html
  } # End of if ($day eq "$form_data{'day'}" &&........)
} # End of while (<DAYFILE>)
```

If the script was not able to find any items in the database, it must let the client know. So if `$item_found` was never set to `yes`, the script sends the client a note of explanation.

```
if ($item_found ne "yes")
  {
  print "<BLOCKQUOTE>It appears that there are no
         entries posted for this day.  Would you like to
         add one?</BLOCKQUOTE>";
  }
print <<"    end_of_html";
<CENTER>
<INPUT TYPE = "hidden" NAME = "day" VALUE = "$form_data{'day'}">
<INPUT TYPE = "hidden" NAME = "month"
             VALUE = "$form_data{'month'}">
<INPUT TYPE = "hidden" NAME = "year" VALUE = "$current_year">
<INPUT TYPE = "submit" NAME = "modify_item_form"
           VALUE = "Modify Item">
<INPUT TYPE = "submit" NAME = "delete_item_form"
           VALUE = "Delete Item">
<INPUT TYPE = "submit" NAME = "add_item_form"
           VALUE = "Add Item">
<INPUT TYPE = "submit" NAME = "change_month_year"
           VALUE = "View Month">
</FORM></CENTER></BODY></HTML>
end_of_html
exit;
}
```

Figure 13.4 shows the day view interface on the Web.

Authenticating the User

Allowing clients to view the calendar is one thing. Letting them modify the calendar database is another. The following routine checks to see whether the client is authorized to do anything in addition to viewing. The script passes GetSessionInfo, which is contained in **auth-lib.pl**, three parameters: the $session_file value (which will be nothing if one has not yet been set), the name of this script (so that it can provide links), and the associative array of form data we got from **cgi-lib.pl**.

```
($session_file, $session_username, $session_group,
 $session_first_name, $session_last_name,
 $session_email) =
 &GetSessionInfo($session_file, $this_script_url,
*form_data);
```

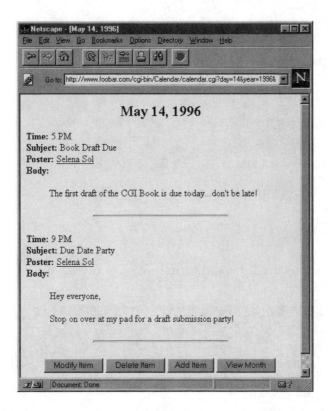

Figure 13.4 The day view.

Displaying the Add Event Form

Once the client has been authenticated, the script determines the desired action. This first routine checks to see whether the client wants to add an item. If so, the script presents a form that the client uses to submit information for each of the database fields.

```
if ($form_data{'add_item_form'} ne "")
   {
   &header ("Add an Item to Selena's Groupware Calendar Demo");
```

The subroutine submission_form at the end of this script is used to generate a form with input fields for every database item that can be manipulated by the client.

```
&submission_form;
```

The script then prints a standard HTML footer and quits.

```
print <<"    end_of_html";
<CENTER><P>
<INPUT TYPE = "submit" NAME = "add_item" VALUE = "Add
Item">
<INPUT TYPE = "reset" VALUE = "Clear This Form">
<INPUT TYPE = "submit" NAME = "change_month_year" VALUE
= "View Month">
</CENTER></BODY></HTML>
end_of_html
exit;
}
```

Figure 13.5 shows what the add form looks like on the Web.

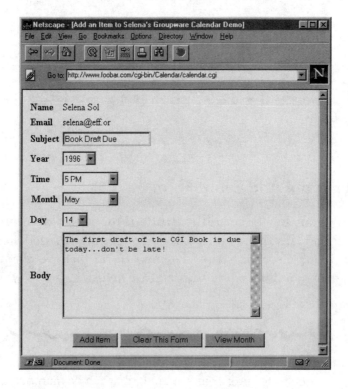

Figure 13.5 The calendar add form.

Adding an Event to the Database

Once the client submits a new event, the script must be prepared to add the item to the calendar database. The following routine does just that.

```
if ($form_data{'add_item'} ne "")
  {
```

The routine begins by printing the page header.

```
&header ("Adding an Item to the Calendar Database");
```

Next, the script makes sure that the client has filled out all the necessary fields in the submission form. The script gets a list of the variable names (keys) associated with the associative array %form_data given to us by **cgi-lib.pl**.

```
@form_data = keys (%form_data);
```

For every element in the list array @form_data, the script checks to see whether the associated value in %form_data has content. If it doesn't, the script sends an error message and quits.

```
foreach $variable_name (@form_data)
    {
    if ($form_data{$variable_name} eq "" &&
       $variable_name ne "calendar")
     {
   print <<"         end_of_html";
   <BLOCKQUOTE><FONT SIZE = "+3">
   I'm very sorry but you must enter something in
   the <B>$variable_name</B> input box.  Please press
   the back button and try again.
   </BLOCKQUOTE></BODY></HTML>
   end_of_html
   exit;
     }
    }
```

On the other hand, if the client entered data into all the fields, the script adds the new entry. First, it uses the subroutine GetFileLock in **cgi-lib.sol** to create a lock file to protect database integrity during modification.

287

The script passes as the sole parameter the location of the lock file used by this program. If the script makes it past the lock file routine, it means that the script is the sole owner of the database file and can safely make changes.

```
&GetFileLock ("$lock_file");
```

Before it can add a new entry, though, the script must acquire a unique number from the counter file by using the subroutine counter in **cgi-lib.sol**. counter receives as its one parameter the location of the counter file used by this program.

```
&counter($counter_file);
```

NOTE The unique counter number is essential, because every row must be uniquely identifiable for modifications and deletions. The numbers don't need to be in any order, and there can be gaping holes between numbers (as when items are deleted), but they must be unique.

Next, the script writes the contents of the new entry to the database file, appending (>>) the new data to the end of the existing list of items.

```
open (DATABASE, ">>$database_file") || &open_error($database_file);
```

Then it formats the incoming form data so that the new event will be confined to one database line. To do this, the script changes (=~ s/) all occurrences (/g) of newlines (\n) into <BR>, and all occurrences of two hard returns (\r\r) into <P>.

```
foreach $value (@field_values)
    {
    $form_data{$value} =~ s/\n/<BR>/g;
    $form_data{$value} =~ s/\r\r/<P>/g;
    $form_data{$value} =~ s/\|/:/g;
    }
```

Finally, the script simplifies some of the variables and generates the new database row.

```
if ($session_first_name eq "")
   {
   $session_first_name =  "$form_data{'first_name'}";
   $session_last_name =  "$form_data{'last_name'}";
   $session_email = "$form_data{'email'}";
   }
$subject = "$form_data{'subject'}";
$event_time = "$form_data{'time'}";
$month = "$form_data{'month'}";
$day = "$form_data{'day'}";
$year = "$form_data{'year'}";
$body = "$form_data{'body'}";
$new_row = "";
$new_row .= "$day\|$month\|$year\|$session_username\|";
$new_row .=
"$session_first_name\|$session_last_name\|$session_email\|";
$new_row .= "$subject\|$event_time\|$body\|$item_number";
```

The script now safely adds the new database row to the database file and deletes the lock file so that someone else may modify the database file.

```
print DATABASE "$new_row\n";
close (DATABASE);
&ReleaseFileLock ("$lock_file");
```

Don't forget the newline at the end of the database row so that the next item entered will be on its own line.

NOTE

Finally, the script prints the standard page footer.

```
print <<"    end_of_html";
<H2><CENTER>Your item has been added, thanks.</H2>
<INPUT TYPE = "hidden" NAME = "day" VALUE = "$form_data{'day'}">
<INPUT TYPE = "hidden" NAME = "month" VALUE = "$form_data{'month'}">
<INPUT TYPE = "hidden" NAME = "year" VALUE = "$current_year">
<INPUT TYPE = "submit" NAME = "change_month_year"
      VALUE = "Return to the Calendar">
</BODY></HTML>
end_of_html
```

Figure 13.6 shows the response on the Web.

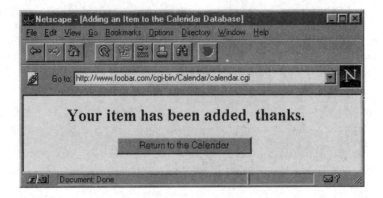

Figure 13.6 Web response.

Sorting the Calendar Database by Time

We are not finished with the add quite yet. The script must also sort the entries in the database file so that when clients choose day views, their entries come out ordered by time. Again, the script creates the lock file so that no one else can modify the database file while it is being modified.

```
&GetFileLock ("$lock_file");
open (DATABASE, "$database_file") || &open_error($database_file);
```

The script adds every row in the database file to an array called @data-base_fields.

```
while (<DATABASE>)
  {
  @database_fields = split (/\|/, $_);
```

Next, it creates a variable called $comment_row, which is used to hold comment lines in the database file. We do not want them sorted along with the rest of the items.

```
if ($_ =~ /^COMMENT:/)
    {
    $comment_row .= $_;
    }
```

If the database row is not a comment row, the script finds the field that has the time of the event and appends it to the front of the database row. (So it occurs twice: once at the beginning of the line and again in the middle somewhere.) The script also adds (pushes) the whole string ($sortable_row) into a growing array called @database_rows. (We'll explain why in the next paragraph.)

```
else
  {
  $sortable_row = "$database_fields[$field_num_time]~~";
  $sortable_row .= $_;
  push (@database_rows, $sortable_row);
  }
}
```

When all the "modified" rows have been added to the array @database_rows, the script sorts the array. This is why we appended the time to the beginning of each of the rows: the sort routine sorts all the database items by event time.

```
@sorted_temp_database = sort (@database_rows);
```

NOTE There is no need to sort on the date, because database rows are already displayed by date. We need only sort the items by time within a day.

Now the script goes through @sorted_temp_database and takes out the extra event_time string at the beginning of each database row, and we're back where we started except that the rows are sorted. The script splits the string at ~~ and then pushes the part of the string that corresponds to the original database row back into the array @final_sorted_database.

```
foreach $database_row (@sorted_temp_database)
  {
  ($extra_event_time, $true_database_row) = split (/~~/,
   $database_row);
  push (@final_sorted_database, $true_database_row);
  }
close (DATABASE);
```

Next, the script modifies the original database file so that it represents the sorted order. To do this, it creates a temporary file to which it reprints all the comment rows stored in the variable $comment_row.

```
open (TEMPFILE, ">$temp_file") || &open_error($temp_file);
print TEMPFILE "$comment_row";
```

Then, for each of the database rows stored in @final_sorted_database, the script prints to the temporary file.

```
foreach $row (@final_sorted_database)
   {
   print TEMPFILE "$row";
   }
close (TEMPFILE);
```

Finally, the script copies the temporary file over the original database file using the rename command so that the resulting file represents the sort. Then the lock file is deleted.

```
rename ($temp_file, $database_file);
&ReleaseFileLock ("$lock_file");
exit;
}
```

Displaying the Modification Form

Next, if asked to do so, the script prints the modify event form.

```
if ($form_data{'modify_item_form'} ne "")
{
&header ("Modify and Item");
```

First, it prints the basic header, including the hidden fields, which must be transferred to the modification routines so that they will have all the user information necessary to re-create database rows.

Because the modification routines will compare incoming form data to database row information, this information must come in with the rest of the form data.

```
print <<"    end_of_html";
<INPUT TYPE = "hidden" NAME = "username"
        VALUE = "$session_username">
<INPUT TYPE = "hidden" NAME = "first_name"
        VALUE = "$session_first_name">
<INPUT TYPE = "hidden" NAME = "last_name"
        VALUE = "$session_last_name">
<INPUT TYPE = "hidden" NAME = "email"
        VALUE = "$session_email">
<CENTER>
<H2>$current_month_name $form_data{'day'}, $current_year</H2>
</CENTER>
end_of_html
```

The script then begins a table that will display all the items posted by the client on the day of interest. But, for the time being, instead of printing the table immediately, it builds it in a variable called $table.

```
$table .= "<TABLE BORDER = \"1\" CELLSPACING = \"2\"
          CELLPADDING = \"2\" WIDTH = \"1100\">\n";
$table .= "<TR>\n";
$table .= "<TH>Modify Item</TH>\n";
```

Similarly, the script adds the header row to $table.

```
foreach $name (@field_names)
  {
  $table .= "<TH>$name</TH>\n";
  }
$table .= "</TR>\n";
```

Then the script opens the database and checks for items that correspond to the user as well as the requested day, month, and year.

```
open (DAYFILE, "$database_file") ||
      &open_error($database_file);
while (<DAYFILE>)
  {
  chop $_; # Make sure to take out the newline.
```

Next, it splits the database row as usual, but this time it also creates the list array @database_values, which will be discussed soon.

```
($day, $month, $year, $username, $first_name,
$last_name, $email, $subject, $time, $body, $database_id_number) =
split (/\|/,$_);
@database_values = split (/\|/,$_);
```

The script is directed to pay attention only to items specific to user, day, month, and year.

```
if ($day eq "$form_data{'day'}" &&
    $month eq "$form_data{'month'}" &&
    $year eq "$form_data{'year'}" &&
    $session_username eq "$username")
        {
```

The script also flags the fact that it found an item.

```
$item_found = "yes";
```

Then the script continues adding to `$table` by adding the table row corresponding to the database row that was matched. Also, it adds a radio button so that the client can select the table row to modify.

```
$table .= "<TR>\n";
$table .= "<TD ALIGN = \"center\">";
$table .= "<INPUT TYPE = \"radio\" NAME =\"item_to_modify\"";
$table .= "VALUE=\"$database_id_number\"></TD>\n";
foreach $value (@database_values)
    {
     $table .= "<TD>$value</TD>\n";
     }
     $table .= "</TR>\n";
   }
 }
$table .= "</TR></TABLE><P><CENTER>\n";
```

If `$item_found` is still not equal to `yes`, it means that we did not match any items and that the script should send the client a note of explanation.

```
if ($item_found ne "yes")
  {
  print <<"      end_of_html";
```

```
<BLOCKQUOTE>
I'm sorry, you have not posted any items for this day,
so there is nothing for me to modify.
</BLOCKQUOTE><CENTER>
<INPUT TYPE = "submit" NAME = "change_month_year"
        VALUE = "View Month"></BODY></HTML>
end_of_html
exit;
}
```

If, however, `$item_found` equals `yes`, the script prints `$table`.

```
print "$table";
```

In the case of modification, the client also needs a form similar to the add form so that he or she can make any desired modifications. We use the `submission_form` subroutine at the end of this script, passing it the parameter `modify` so that it will know to output that form.

```
&submission_form("modify");
```

Finally, the script prints a standard footer and quits.

```
print <<"    end_of_html";
<CENTER><P>
<BLOCKQUOTE><I>Note: Make sure to select an item to modify using the
radio buttons on the top table.  Then change any of the form inputs
you want changed, leaving the others as they are.  Feel free to cut
and paste from the top table to the bottom table if you only need to
change a small amount of
text</I></BLOCKQUOTE>
<INPUT TYPE = "submit" NAME = "modify_item"
        VALUE = "Modify Selected Item">
<INPUT TYPE = "reset" VALUE = "Clear This Form">
</CENTER></FORM></BODY></HTML>
end_of_html
exit;
}
```

On the Web, the modify form looks like Figure 13.7.

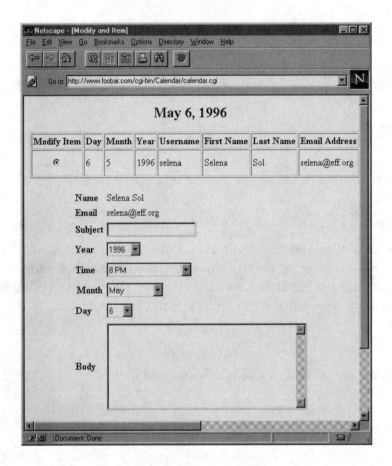

Figure 13.7 *Calendar modify form.*

Displaying the Delete Event Form

Next, the script prints a form for item deletion if requested by the client.

```
if ($form_data{'delete_item_form'} ne "")
  {
  &header ("Delete an Item");
  print "<CENTER>\n";
  print "<H2>$current_month_name $form_data{'day'},
          $current_year</H2>\n";
  print "</CENTER>\n";
```

Just as it did for the modify form, the script creates the `$table` variable and prints the delete form (or the error message if no items were found). First, the script outputs the header.

```
$table = "";
$table .= "<TABLE BORDER = \"1\" CELLSPACING = \"2\"
          CELLPADDING = \"2\" WIDTH = \"1100\">";
$table .= "\n<TR>\n";
$table .= "<TH>Delete Item</TH>";
foreach $name (@field_names)
  {
  $table .= "<TH>$name</TH>\n";
  }
$table .= "</TR>\n";
```

Then it creates the possible delete rows.

```
open (DAYFILE, "$database_file") || &open_error($database_file);
while (<DAYFILE>)
  {
  chop $_;
  ($day, $month, $year, $username, $first_name,
   $last_name, $email, $subject, $time, $body,
   $database_id_number) = split (/\|/,$_);

  @database_values = split (/\|/,$_);

  if ($day eq "$form_data{'day'}" &&
      $month eq "$form_data{'month'}" &&
      $year eq "$form_data{'year'}" &&
      $session_username eq "$username")
    {
    $item_found = "yes";
    $table .= "<TR>\n";
    $table .= "<TD ALIGN = \"center\">";
    $table .= "<INPUT TYPE = \"radio\"
                    NAME =\"item_to_delete\"";
    $table .= "VALUE=\"$database_id_number\"></TD>\n";

    foreach $value (@database_values)
      {
```

```
    $table .= "<TD>$value</TD>\n";
    }
    $table .= "</TR>\n";
  }
}
```

Next, if necessary, the script prints an error message.

```
if ($item_found ne "yes")
  {
  print <<"       end_of_html";
  <BLOCKQUOTE>
  I'm sorry, you have not posted any items for this day,
  so there is nothing for me to delete.
  </BLOCKQUOTE><CENTER>
  <INPUT TYPE = "submit" NAME = "change_month_year"
         VALUE = "View Month"></BODY></HTML>
  end_of_html
  exit;
  }

print <<"     end_of_html";
$table
</TR></TABLE><CENTER><P>
<INPUT TYPE = "hidden" NAME = "day"
       VALUE = "$form_data{'day'}">
<INPUT TYPE = "hidden" NAME = "month"
       VALUE = "$form_data{'month'}">
<INPUT TYPE = "hidden" NAME = "year" VALUE = "$current_year">
<INPUT TYPE = "submit" NAME = "delete_item"
       VALUE = "Delete Selected Item">
<INPUT TYPE = "submit" NAME = "change_month_year"
       VALUE = "Return to the Calendar">
</CENTER></FORM></BODY></HTML>
end_of_html
exit;
}
```

On the Web, the delete form looks like Figure 13.8.

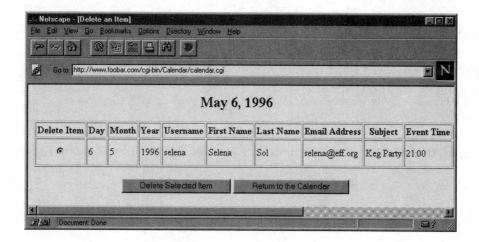

Figure 13.8 *The calendar delete form.*

Deleting an Event from the Database

If asked, the script deletes an item from the database.

```
if ($form_data{'delete_item'} ne "")
  {
```

The script must be sure that the client actually chose an item to delete with the radio buttons.

```
if ($form_data{'item_to_delete'} eq "")
  {
  &header ("Woopsy");
  print <<"      end_of_html";
  <CENTER><
  H2>Delete an Item in the Database Error</H2>
  </CENTER>
  <BLOCKQUOTE>
  I'm sorry, I was not able to modify the database
  because none of the radio buttons on the table was
```

```
selected so I was not sure which item to delete.
Would you please make sure that you select an item
\"and\" fill in the new information. Just press the
back button.  Thanks.
</BLOCKQUOTE>
end_of_html
exit;
}
```

First, the script locks the database file as it did for the add item routines.

```
&GetFileLock ("$lock_file");
```

Then it creates a temporary file as before.

```
open (TEMP, ">$temp_file") || &open_error($temp_file);
close (TEMP);
```

If there is data in the database file, the script checks to see which item matches the deletion.

```
open (DATA, "$database_file") || &open_error($database_file);
while (<DATA>)
  {
  @grepfields=split(/\|/,$_);
```

To do so, the script gets the unique database ID for each database row and chops off the newline.

```
$database_id = pop (@grepfields);
chop $database_id;
```

If the unique database ID of the row is not equal to the database ID number submitted by the client, the script knows not to delete that row. Instead, it prints it to the temporary file.

```
if ($database_id ne "$form_data{'item_to_delete'}")
  {
  open (TEMP, ">>$temp_file") ||
        &open_error($temp_file);
  print TEMP "$_";
  close (TEMP);
```

```
  }
} # End of while (<DATA>)
```

Once it has gone through all the items in the database, the script copies the temporary file over the database file; the deletion will have been made, because the row that matched the database ID number will not have been printed to the temporary file. Then the script closes the database file and deletes the lock file so that others can modify the database.

```
close (DATA);
rename ($temp_file, $database_file);
&ReleaseFileLock ("$lock_file");
```

Finally, the script prints a standard footer.

```
&header ("Deleting an Item from the Calendar");
print <<"    end_of_html";
<CENTER>\n<FONT SIZE = \"+3\">Your item has been deleted
</FONT>\n<P>
<INPUT TYPE = "hidden" NAME = "day"
        VALUE = "$form_data{'day'}">
<INPUT TYPE = "hidden" NAME = "month"
        VALUE = "$form_data{'month'}">
<INPUT TYPE = "hidden" NAME = "year" VALUE = "$current_year">
<INPUT TYPE = "submit" NAME = "change_month_year"
        VALUE = "Return to the Calendar">
</CENTER></BODY></HTML>
end_of_html
exit;
}
```

Modifying an Event in the Database

The script can also be used to modify an item.

```
if ($form_data{'modify_item'} ne "")
  {
```

First, the script must be sure that the client chose an item to modify.

```
&header("Modify an Item in the database");
if ($form_data{'item_to_modify'} eq "")
```

```
   {
   print <<"        end_of_html";
   <CENTER><H2>Modifying an Item in the Database Error</H2></CENTER>
   <BLOCKQUOTE>
   I'm sorry, I was not able to modify the database because none of the
   radio buttons on the table was selected so I was not sure which item
   to modify.  Would you please make sure that you select an item \"and\"
   fill in the new information. Just press the back button.   Thanks.
   </BLOCKQUOTE>
   end_of_html
   exit;
   }
```

As it did before, the script creates the lock file and the temporary file.

```
&GetFileLock ("$lock_file");
open (TEMPFILE, ">$temp_file") || &open_error($temp_file);
open (DATABASE, "$database_file") ||
      &open_error($database_file);
```

And as it did for deletion, the script gets the unique database ID number
for each row by popping it out of the @fields array. But this time, it makes
sure to add the database ID number into the array so that it will have a
whole array again (push (@fields, $item_id)). Finally, as usual, the script
chops off the newline.

```
while (<DATABASE>)
    {
    @fields = split (/\|/, $_);
    $item_id = pop(@fields);
    chop $item_id;
    push (@fields, $item_id);
```

If the item ID of the database row matches the one that the client submitted, the script renames the @fields array to @old_fields. Otherwise, it
adds the line to the growing list of database rows in $new_data.

```
if ($item_id eq "$form_data{'item_to_modify'}")
   {
   @old_fields = @fields;
   }
```

```
else
  {
  $new_data .= "$_";
  }
} # End of  while (<DATABASE>)
```

Once it gets through all the items in the database, the script should have found one that matched the item selected by the client, and the rest should have been stored in $new_data. Now the script prints the rows in $new_data to the temporary file.

```
print TEMPFILE "$new_data";
```

Then it prepares to substitute the new data submitted by the client for the old data that was in the database. First, the script initializes a couple of variables: $counter and $new_line. $counter will be used to keep track of the database fields that we have edited, and $new_line will be used to create the new database row.

```
$counter = 0;
$new_line = "";
```

Now the script begins going through the list of field_values as defined in the setup file.

```
until ($counter >= @field_values)
  {
  $value = "";
  $value = "$field_values[$counter]";
```

NOTE

Recall that arrays begin with a zero so that the first array element is $arrayname[0]. **In this case, the script assigns the current element in the count of field values to** $value, **thus going through every field in the database.**

If the form_data variable associated with that field does not have a value, the script adds the "old" field value stored in @old_fields to the $new_line variable.

```
if ($form_data{$value} eq "")
  {
  $new_line .= "$old_fields[$counter]|";
  }
```

On the other hand, if the client submitted new information, the script formats the information as it did for the add routine and adds the resulting value to $new_line.

```
else
  {
  $form_data{$value} =~ s/\n/<BR>/g;
  $form_data{$value} =~ s/\r\r/<P>/g;
  $form_data{$value} =~ s/\|/~:~/g;

  if ($form_data{$value} eq "")
    {
    $form_data{$value} = "<CENTER>-</CENTER>";
    }
  $new_line .= "$form_data{$value}|";
  } # End of else
```

Then it increments the counter by 1 so that the loop goes through for every field in a database row. Once the loop is finished, the script closes the database.

```
  $counter++;
} # End of until ($counter >= @field_values)
chop $new_line; # take off last |
```

Next, the script closes everything, copies the temporary file over the original, and releases the lock file.

```
print  TEMPFILE "$new_line\n";
close (TEMPFILE);
close (DATABASE);
rename ($temp_file, $database_file);
&ReleaseFileLock ("$lock_file");
```

Then it prints the usual footer.

```
print <<"    end_of_html";
<CENTER><H2>Your Item has been Modified</H2>
<INPUT TYPE = "hidden" NAME = "day"
       VALUE = "$form_data{'day'}">
<INPUT TYPE = "hidden" NAME = "month"
       VALUE = "$form_data{'month'}">
<INPUT TYPE = "hidden" NAME = "year" VALUE = "$current_year">
<INPUT TYPE = "submit" NAME = "change_month_year"
       VALUE = "Return to the Calendar">
</CENTER></BODY></HTML>
end_of_html
```

Again, it is time to sort the entries in the database file so that when people choose day views, their entries are ordered by time. The script creates the lock file so that no one else can modify the database file while we are modifying it.

```
&GetFileLock ("$lock_file");
open (DATABASE, "$database_file") || &open_error($database_file);
```

Then the script adds every row in our database file to the list array @database_fields and creates $comment_row as before.

```
while (<DATABASE>)
  {
  @database_fields = split (/\|/, $_);
  if ($_ =~ /^COMMENT:/)
    {
    $comment_row .= $_;
    }
```

If the database row is not a comment row (COMMENT:), the script finds the field that has the time of the event and appends it to the front of the database row. It also adds (pushes) the whole string ($sortable_row) into a growing array called @database_rows.

```
else
  {
  $sortable_row = "$database_fields[$field_num_time]~~";
  $sortable_row .= $_;
  push (@database_rows, $sortable_row);
```

```
   }
}
```

When it has added all the modified rows to the array `@database_rows`, the script sorts `@database_rows`.

```
@sorted_temp_database = sort (@database_rows);
```

Next, the script goes through `@sorted_temp_database` and takes out the extra `event_time` string at the beginning of each database row.

```
foreach $database_row (@sorted_temp_database)
   {
   ($extra_event_time, $true_database_row) =
        split (/:/, $database_row);
   push (@final_sorted_database, $true_database_row);
   }
close (DATABASE);
```

Then the script creates the temporary file for the modification as it did for the addition.

```
open (TEMPFILE, ">$temp_file") ||
        &open_error($temp_file);
print TEMPFILE "$comment_row";
```

Next, for each of the database rows stored in `@final_sorted_database`, the script prints to the temporary file.

```
foreach $row (@final_sorted_database)
   {
   print TEMPFILE "$row";
   }
close (TEMPFILE);
```

Finally, the script copies the temporary file over the original database file so that the resulting file will represent the sort. Then the lock file is removed.

```
rename ($temp_file, $database_file);
&ReleaseFileLock ("$lock_file");
exit;
}
```

Displaying the Default Error

The script adds a default in case clients got through everything without finding what they wanted (probably because they pressed **Return** when typing into a text box).

```
&header("Wooopsy");
print <<" end_of_html";
<BLOCKQUOTE>I'm sorry, you are not allowed to press the Return key
when typing in your subject.  Please press the back button and try
again.</BLOCKQUOTE><CENTER>
<INPUT TYPE = "submit" NAME = "change_month_year"
        VALUE = "Return to the Calendar">
</CENTER></BODY></HTML>
end_of_html
```

The make_month_array Subroutine

The `make_month_array` subroutine is used to generate the month arrays used by the main routine.

```
sub make_month_array
  {
```

First, the subroutine defines some variables that will be local to this sub-routine.

```
local($juldate)  = $_[0];
local($month,$day,$year,$weekday);
local($tempjdate,$firstweekday,$numdays,$lastweekday);
local(@myarray);
```

Next, the subroutine defines variables based upon the passed parameter.

```
($month, $day, $year, $weekday) = &jdate($juldate);
```

Then `make_month_array` makes a new date based on the first of the month.

```
$tempjdate = &jday($month, 1, $year);
```

make_month_array also gets the weekday of the first of the month and then builds @myarray to be passed to the main routine.

```
($month, $day, $year, $weekday) = &jdate($tempjdate);
$firstweekday = $weekday;
$currentmonth = "$month";
$currentyear = "$year";
$month++;
if ($month > 12)
  {
  $month = 1;
  $year++;
  }
$tempjdate = &jday($month,1,$year);
$tempjdate—;
($month, $day, $year, $weekday) = &jdate($tempjdate);
$numdays = $day;
$lastweekday = $weekday;

for ($x = 0;$x < $firstweekday; $x++)
  {
  $myarray[$x] = " ";
  } # End of for

for ($x = 1; $x <= $numdays; $x++ )
  {
  $myarray[$x + $firstweekday - 1] = $x;
  }

  for ($x = $lastweekday; $x < 6; $x++)
  {
  push(@myarray,"");
  }

return @myarray;
}
```

The CgiRequire Subroutine

This subroutine checks to see whether the file that we are trying to require exists and is readable by us. This subroutine provides developers with an informative error message when they're attempting to debug the scripts.

```
sub CgiRequire
  {
```

First, the `@require_files` array is defined as a local array and is filled with the filenames sent from the main routine.

```
local (@require_files) = @_;
```

The subroutine then checks to see whether the files exist and are readable. If they are, the files are loaded.

```
foreach $file (@require_files)
  {
  if (-e "$file" && -r "$file")
    {
    require "$file";
    }
```

If any of the files are not readable or do not exist, the subroutine sends an error message that identifies the problem.

```
else
  {
  print "I'm sorry, I was not able to open
  $file.  Would you please check to make sure
  that you gave me a valid filename and that the
  permissions on $file are set to allow me
  access?";
  exit;
  }
  } # End of foreach $file (@require_files)
} # End of sub CgiRequire
```

The select_a_month Subroutine

The `select_a_month` subroutine is used to generate a select list of months that the client can use to select months in the various forms throughout the script. It is a straightforward routine with no new syntax.

```
sub select_a_month
  {
```

```
print "<SELECT NAME=\"month\">\n";
foreach $month (@month_names)
  {
  if ($month ne "$current_month_name")
    {
    print "<OPTION VALUE =
          \"$MONTH_ARRAY{$month}\">$month\n";
    }
  else
    {
    print "<OPTION SELECTED VALUE =
        \"$MONTH_ARRAY{$month}\">$month\n";
    }
  }
print "</SELECT>\n";
}
```

The select_a_year Subroutine

As with select_a_month, the select_a_year subroutine generates a select
input tag and options for the client to select from a list of years. The only
thing of note in this subroutine is that $the_current_year is defined in the
setup file and must be changed annually.

```
sub select_a_year
  {
  print "<SELECT NAME = \"year\">\n";

  for ($i = $the_current_year; $i < $greatest_year; $i++)
    {
    if ($i eq "$currentyear")
      {
      print "<OPTION SELECTED VALUE = \"$i\">$i\n";
      }
    else
      {
      print "<OPTION VALUE = \"$i\">$i\n";
      }
    }
  print "</SELECT>\n";
  }
```

The submission_form Subroutine

The `submission_form` subroutine is used to generate a form that clients can use to submit new events to the database. As with the previous subroutines, the logic includes no new Perl tricks or syntax.

```
sub submission_form
  {
  local ($type_of_form) = @_;

  if ($session_first_name ne "")
    {
    print <<"       end_of_html";
    <TABLE BORDER = "0" CELLSPACING = "2"
          CELLPADDING = "2">
    <TR ALIGN = "LEFT">
    <TH>Name</TH>
    <TD>$session_first_name $session_last_name</TD>
    <TR ALIGN = "LEFT">
    <TH>Email</TH>
    <TD>$session_email</TD>
    </TR>
    end_of_html
    }
  else
    {
    print <<"       end_of_html";
    <TABLE BORDER = "0" CELLSPACING = "2"
          CELLPADDING = "2">
    <TR ALIGN = "LEFT">
    <TH>First Name</TH>
    <TD><INPUT TYPE = "text" NAME = "first_name"
              SIZE = "20" MAXLENGTH = "20"></TD>
    </TR>
    <TR ALIGN = "LEFT">
    <TH>Last Name</TH>
    <TD><INPUT TYPE = "text" NAME = "last_name"
              SIZE = "20" MAXLENGTH = "20"></TD>
    </TR>
    <TR ALIGN = "LEFT">
    <TH>Email</TH>
    <TD><INPUT TYPE = "text" NAME = "email" SIZE = "20"
              MAXLENGTH = "20"></TD>
    </TR>
```

```
   end_of_html
   }
print <<"   end_of_html";
<TR ALIGN = "LEFT">
<TH>Subject</TH>
<TD><INPUT TYPE = "text" NAME = "subject" SIZE = "20"
          MAXLENGTH = "20"></TD>
</TR>
<TR ALIGN = "LEFT">
<TH>Year</TH>
<TD>
end_of_html
&select_a_year;
print <<"   end_of_html";
</TD>
</TR>
<TR ALIGN = "LEFT">
<TH>Time</TH>
<TD>
<SELECT NAME = "time">
end_of_html
if ($type_of_form eq "modify")
   {
   print "<OPTION VALUE = \"\">Don't Change Time\n";
   }
foreach $time_value (@time_values)
   {
   if ($time_value ne "09:00")
      {
      print "<OPTION VALUE =
           \"$time_value\">$TIME{$time_value}\n";
      }
   else
      {
      if ($type_of_form ne "modify")
         {
         print "<OPTION SELECTED VALUE =
              \"$time_value\">$TIME{$time_value}\n";
         }
      }
   }

print "</SELECT></TD></TR>\n";

print "<TR>\n<TH>Month</TH>\n";
print "<TD>\n";
&select_a_month;
print "</TD>\n";
```

```perl
print "</TR>";

print "<TR ALIGN=LEFT>\n";
print "<TH>Day</TH>\n";
print "<TD><SELECT NAME=\"day\">\n";
for ($i = 1; $i < 32; $i++)
  {
  if ($i eq "$form_data{'day'}")
    {
    print "<OPTION SELECTED VALUE = \"$i\">$i\n";
    }
  else
    {
    print "<OPTION VALUE = \"$i\">$i\n";
    }
  }
print <<"    end_of_html";
</SELECT></TD>
</TR>
<TR ALIGN=LEFT>
<TH>Body</TH>
<TD><TEXTAREA WRAP = "virtual" NAME = "body" ROWS = "8"
            COLS = "40"></TEXTAREA></TD>
</TR>
</TABLE>
end_of_html
}
```

The Header Subroutine

The header subroutine is used by the main script to generate the HTML header common to every script-generated HTML page.

```perl
sub header
  {
  local ($title) = @_;
  if ($title eq "")
    {
    $title = "Selena Sol's Groupware Calendar Demo";
    }
  print <<"    end_of_html";
<HTML><HEAD><TITLE>$title</TITLE></HEAD>
<BODY>
<FORM METHOD = "post" ACTION = "$this_script_url">
```

```
<INPUT TYPE = "hidden" NAME = "session_file"
       VALUE = "$session_file">
<INPUT TYPE = "hidden" NAME = "calendar"
       VALUE = "$form_data{'calendar'}">
end_of_html
}
```

CHAPTER 14

The Classified Ad Manager

OVERVIEW

The classified ad manager simulates a classified ad newspaper section, allowing clients to browse a master database of classified ads using a simple Web-based user interface. Clients browse any one of several categories according to keyword or other search parameters such as a price range or a post date. For example, a client might run a search for Ampeg Bass Amps priced less than $1,000 and posted within the last week.

The classified ad manager also allows clients to post, modify, and delete their own ads. Omitting the classified ad intermediaries from the equation, this application allows clients to directly modify their ads at any hour and as often as they want. By using the authentication algorithms discussed in Chapter 9, this application protects the integrity of every client's data by refusing to allow anyone except the poster to modify or delete the ad.

Together, ad searching and ad management create an environment in which clients buy, sell, and trade their wares with efficiency, privacy, and ease. The classified ad manager is also a fine example of how you might reconfigure the database management and searching algorithms discussed in Chapters 11 and 12 to handle other creative projects.

INSTALLATION AND USAGE

This script should be expanded into a directory from which the Web server is allowed to execute CGI scripts. Once unarchived, it will expand into the root directory **Classified_ad**. Figure 14.1 shows the directory structure along with a description of how permissions should be set graphically.

Classified_ad, the root directory, must have its permissions set to be readable and executable by the Web server. It contains two files (**class_ad.cgi** and **class_ad.setup**) and four subdirectories (**Databases**, **Images**, **Library**, and **Session_files**).

class_ad.cgi is the main script for the classified ad manager and should have its permissions set to be readable and executable by the Web server. The specifics of the script will be discussed in the design discussion.

class_ad.setup is the setup file that **class_ad.cgi** uses to gather server-specific information and obtain authentication options. It must have its permissions set to be readable by the Web server. It is discussed in greater detail in the "Server-Specific Setup and Options" section.

Databases is a subdirectory containing each of the classified ad databases and their associated setup files as well as the counter and user files. The **Databases** subdirectory must be readable writable, and executable by the Web server. The datafiles, user files, and counter file must be readable and writable by the Web server, and the setup files must be readable by the Web server.

class_ad.counter is a text file used to store unique classified ad database ID numbers. Initially, this file should contain the number 1 on the first line and nothing else. As time goes by, **class_ad.cgi** will increment this number by 1 for every new classified ad posted.

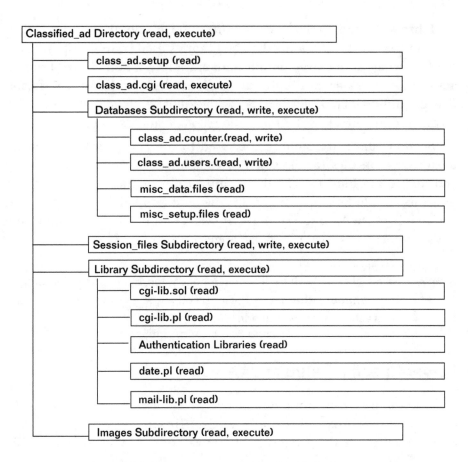

Figure 14.1 Directory structure of the classified ad manager.

class_ad.users is the list of users who have been authorized to manipulate ads in the database. Chapter 9 includes an in-depth discussion of the use of the user file and the authentication libraries, so they will not be discussed here.

The datafiles and their associated setup files are discussed in greater detail in the "Server-Specific Setup and Options" section.

Images is a subdirectory containing the image map used for the example on the accompanying CD-ROM. The directory must be executable by the Web server, and any graphics within it must be readable.

Library is a subdirectory containing the CGI libraries (discussed in Chapter 9) that this script needs. The libraries used by this script include the following: **auth-extra-html.pl**, **auth-extra-lib.pl**, **auth-lib-fail-html.pl**, **auth-lib.pl**, **auth-server-lib.pl**, **auth_fail_html.pl**, **cgi-lib.pl**, **cgi-lib.sol**, **date.pl**, and **mail-lib.pl**. Each of these files must be readable by the Web server, and the directory itself must be readable and executable.

Session_files is the subdirectory used by the authentication libraries to store session files (as discussed in Chapter 9) as well as the lock file and temporary files used by the script during operation. Initially, this directory should be empty, but if it is made to be readable, writable, and executable by the Web server, the script will continually add to and prune this subdirectory as part of its daily usage.

NOTE Never create the lock file or temporary file by yourself. As long as you configure the setup file correctly, the script will create and delete those files as it needs them.

Server-Specific Setup and Options

class_ad.setup is the setup file that **class_ad.cgi** uses to gather server-specific information and obtain authentication options. Within **class_ad.setup**, the following variables must be set to their server-specific values.

`$user_file` is the location of the file that contains the list of users who are authorized to use this script.

`$counter_file` is the path of the file that you are using to keep track of unique ID numbers. To make deletions and modifications, each item must have a unique ID number so that this script can determine which database item to delete. These ID numbers should always be the last field in any database row.

`$session_file_directory` is the location of the directory that temporarily holds session files. These session files are used to validate users and to keep track of their information should we need it.

$database_manager_script is the location of **class_ad.cgi**.

$database_manager_script_url is the URL of **class_ad.cgi**.

$data_file is the location of the flatfile ASCII text database that is being managed.

$temp_file is a file that **class_ad.cgi** uses to temporarily store various data at different times.

$lock_file is a file that **class_ad.cgi** uses to make sure that only one person can modify the database at any given time.

Authentication variables are defined and explained in Chapter 9, so they will not be discussed here.

The setup file included on the accompanying CD-ROM is shown next as an example of usage.

```
$counter_file = "./Databases/class_ad.counter";
$user_file = "./Databases/class_ad.users";
$temp_file = "./Session_files/class_ad.temp";
$lock_file = "./Session_files/class_ad.lockfile";
$session_file_directory = "./Session_files";
$database_manager_script = "./class_ad.cgi";
$database_manager_script_url = "class_ad.cgi";
$auth_lib = "$lib";
$auth_server = "off";
$auth_cgi = "on";
$auth_user_file = "./Databases/class_ad.users";
$auth_alt_user_file =  "";
$auth_default_group = "user";
$auth_add_register = "on";
$auth_email_register = "off";
$auth_admin_from_address = "selena\@foobar.com";
$auth_admin_email_address = "selena\@foobar.com";
$auth_session_length = 2;
$auth_session_dir = "./Session_files";
$auth_register_message = "Thanks, you may now log on with
                          your new username and
                          password.";
$auth_allow_register = "on";
$auth_allow_search = "on";
$auth_generate_password = "off";
$auth_check_duplicates = "on";
$auth_password_message = "Thanks for applying to our
```

```
                              site, your password is";
@auth_extra_fields = ("auth_first_name",
                      "auth_last_name",
                      "auth_email");
@auth_extra_desc = ("First Name",
                    "Last Name",
                    "Email");
```

Each datafile follows the format discussed in Chapters 11 through 13, so we will not repeat the discussion here. The accompanying CD-ROM includes the following examples, which can be explored separately: **employment.data**, **housing.data**, **misc.data**, **personals.data**, and **vehicles.data**.

Every datafile comes with an accompanying setup file that defines each database's specific features. This chapter's example of a setup file explains the server-specific options that must be included with every datafile. The first example is from **vehicles.setup**.

$data_file is the location of the datafile associated with each setup file.

$price communicates whether price is one of the possible search parameters when a client searches this classified database. If this variable is set to yes, an extra input box will appear on search forms. The script also requires that you define $price_field_num.

$price_field_num is the location of the database field that contains the price information. It is essential that you provide the script with this location, because if you change the fields in the database, the script will have no idea which field should be compared to the client-defined price range. When defining this variable, remember that arrays start counting from zero.

$date_field_num is the array location of the date field. We need to identify this field to compare and search on date. When defining this variable, remember that array counting starts at zero.

%FIELD_ARRAY communicates the makeup of the database and specifies which fields are associated with which header and variable names. @field_names and @field_values are the ordered keys and values arrays for %FIELD_ARRAY.

@field_names_user_defined defines which fields the clients can submit when adding a new entry, whereas @field_names_non_user_defined defines which fields are supplied by the script.

As always, %FORM_COMPONENT_ARRAY describes which database fields are associated with which types of form input fields so that when we create forms for adding and searching, each database field will get an appropriate form input type.

Following is the text of **vehicles.setup** as it appears on the accompanying CD-ROM:

```
$data_file = "Databases/vehicles.data";
$price = "yes";
$price_field_num = "6";
$date_field_num = "8";
%FIELD_ARRAY = ( 'Last Name', 'last_name',
                 'First Name', 'first_name',
                 'Email', 'email',
                 'Phone Number', 'phone',
                 'Category', 'category',
                 'Location', 'location',
                 'Price', 'price',
                 'Your Ad', 'ad',
                 'Time', 'time',
                 'Id', 'id');
@field_names = ("Last Name", "First Name", "Email",
                "Phone Number", "Category", "Location",
                "Price", "Your Ad", "Time", "Id");

@field_names_user_defined = ("Category", "Phone Number",
                             "Location","Price",
                             "Your Ad");

@field_names_non_user_defined = ("Last Name",
                                 "First Name", "Email",
                                 "Time", "Id");

@field_values = ("last_name", "first_name", "email",
                 "phone", "category", "location",
                 "price", "ad", "time", "id");
```

```
%FORM_COMPONENT_ARRAY = (
'Last Name', 'text|SIZE = "32" MAXLENGTH = "100"',
'First Name', 'text|SIZE = "32" MAXLENGTH = "100"',
'Email', 'text|SIZE = "32" MAXLENGTH = "100"',
'Phone Number', 'text|SIZE = "32" MAXLENGTH =
"100"',
'Category', 'select|||Automobiles|Auto Parts|T
rucks|Vans|Motorcycles|4X4s|RVs|Mopeds|Water Craft|Air Craft|Other',
'Location', 'text|SIZE = "32" MAXLENGTH = "100"',
'Price', 'text|SIZE = "32" MAXLENGTH = "100"',
'Your Ad', 'textarea|ROWS = "4" COLS = "30"',
'Time', 'invisible',
'Id', 'invisible');
```

Running the Script

Once you have configured the setup files, created your own databases, and set the permissions, you can access the classified ad manager with a hyperlink such as this one:

```
<A HREF = "http://www.foobar.com/cgi-
bin/Classified_ad/class_ad.cgi">Classified Ad Manager</A>
```

DESIGN DISCUSSION

The logic of the classified ad manager is depicted in Figure 14.2.

As always, this script begins by calling on the Perl interpreter to print the HTTP header.

```
#!/usr/local/bin/perl
 print "Content-type: text/html\n\n";
```

Loading the Supporting Libraries

Next, the $lib variable fixes the path of your current library.

```
$lib = "Library";
```

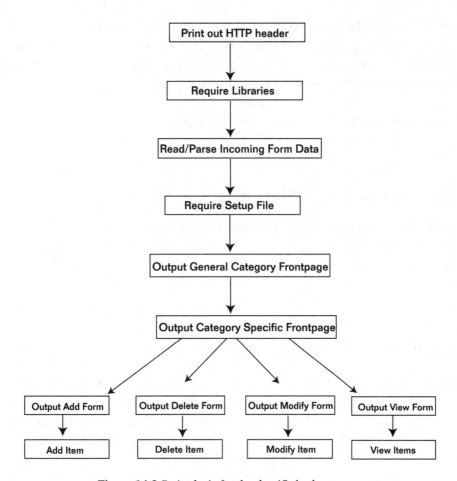

Figure 14.2 Script logic for the classified ad manager.

By default, all library files used by this script have been placed in the Library subdirectory. Eventually, however, the best thing to do is to put them in your "real" CGI library and reference that path here.

Then the script adds the libraries to the beginning of the @INC array so that they will be read before any other libraries that may have routines with the same name.

```
unshift (@INC, "$lib");
```

At this point, **class_ad.cgi** requires the necessary files using CgiRequire, the subroutine at the end of this script. This subroutine is used so that if there is a problem with the require, the script will be able to send the client a meaningful error message.

```
&CgiRequire("$lib/cgi-lib.pl", "$lib/cgi-lib.sol",
            "$lib/auth-lib.pl", "./class_ad.setup",
            "$lib/date.pl");
```

Reading and Parsing Incoming Form Data

Next, the script uses **cgi-lib.pl** to parse the incoming form data, passing the subroutine ReadParse (*form_data) so that the variable will come out as $form_data{'key'} instead of $in{'$key'}.

```
&ReadParse(*form_data);
```

Loading the Setup File

Once the form input has been parsed, the script determines which database the client is asking it to display. This script should have been called with the name of the datafile appended to the URL. For example, we may have linked to this script using the following hyperlink:

```
<A HREF = "class_ad.cgi?database=vehicles.setup">Vehicles Database</a>
```

In this example, the %form_data associative array contains the variable database with its associated value **vehicles.setup**. If there is such a value, the script assigns that to the variable $setup_file. If the value is empty and the person called this script without the parameter, the script assigns **basic.setup** to $setup_file instead.

```
if ($form_data{'database'} ne "")
  {
  $setup_file = $form_data{'database'};
  }
```

```
else
  {
  $setup_file = "basic.setup";
  }
```

Once the script has determined which setup file to use, it uses `CgiRequire` to `require` the setup file that it was asked for.

```
&CgiRequire("Databases/$setup_file");
```

Reformatting Variables

Next, the script reformats the name of the setup file so that it can display the name of the datafile in a user-friendly way on subsequent pages. If the user asked to see **vehicles.setup**, for example, the script should reformat the name to "Vehicles" so that it can later use the reformatted value to output something like, "Add an Item to the Vehicles Database" instead of "Add an Item to the vehicles.setup database."

So, if the script was given a database name, it first `splits` the name into a variable for the word *name* and a variable for the word *setup*. Thus, what was once **name.setup** becomes `name` and `setup`. Then the script assigns the first letter of the name to `$first_letter`, and the rest of the word to `$rest_of_the_word`. So `$first_letter` equals "n" and `$rest_of_the_word` equals "ame." Then the script turns the `$first_letter` into an uppercase letter using the translate (`tr`) function so that `$first_letter` now equals "N" instead of "n." Finally, the script splices the variables using (.). That's a lot of work for such a small change, but it makes the client GUI much nicer.

```
if ($form_data{'database'} ne "")
  {
  ($name, $junk) = split (/\./, $form_data{'database'});
  $first_letter = substr($name,0,1);
  $rest_of_the_word = substr($name,1);
  $first_letter =~ tr/a-z/A-Z/;
  $database = $first_letter . $rest_of_the_word;
  }
```

The script also defines the `$session_file` variable if one is coming in as form data. We will talk more about session file information later.

```
if ($form_data{'session_file'} ne "")
{
$session_file = $form_data{'session_file'};
}
```

Displaying the General Category Front Page

Now the script is ready to print the front page. This, however, will happen in only two cases. First, the script will output the front page if no database has been defined in the incoming form data (`$form_data{'database'} eq ""`) or (`||`) if the script is being asked specifically to return to the front page (`$form_data{'return_to_frontpage'} ne ""`). Second, the script outputs the front page if no values have yet been assigned to (`$ENV{'CONTENT_LENGTH'} eq ""`). If `CONTENT_LENGTH` is equal to zero, it means that this script is being accessed from an outside hyperlink rather from a script-generated HTML page.

```
if (($form_data{'database'} eq "" ||
     $form_data{'return_to_frontpage'} ne "")
     &&
    ($ENV{'CONTENT_LENGTH'} eq ""))||
($form.data{'return.to.frontpage'}ne""))
{
```

The routine shown next prints the basic front page. However, notice that the image map hyperlinks reference this script with

```
?database=xxx&session_file=$session_file.
```

It's important to always remember to pass this information so that the client does not get lost. As discussed in Chapter 9, the session file is used to maintain state. By passing the name of the session file from HTML page to HTML page, this script ensures that it will "remember" who the client is.

```
print <<"end_of_html";
<HTML>
```

```
<HEAD>
<TITLE>The Classified Ad Manager</TITLE>
</HEAD>
<BODY BGCOLOR = "FFFFFF" TEXT = "000000">
<CENTER>
<IMG SRC = "/Graphics/class_ad_title.gif">
<P>
<A HREF = "/cgi-bin/imagemap/Graphics/classified.gif">
<IMG SRC = "/ Graphics/classified.gif"
 ISMAP USEMAP = "#map" BORDER = "0"></A>
<MAP NAME = "map">
<AREA COORDS = "11,18 191,53" HREF = "$datab
ase_manager_script_url?database=employment.setup&session_file=$ses-
sion_file">
<AREA COORDS = "9,
71 192,107" HREF =
"$database_manager_script_url?database=housing.setup&session_file=$ses
sion_file">
<AREA COORDS = "11
,124 191,160" HREF =
"$database_manager_script_url?database=misc.setup&session_file=$ses-
sion_file">
<AREA COORDS = "28
2,18 463,54" HREF =
"$database_manager_script_url?database=personals.setup&session_file=$s
ession_file">
<AREA COORDS = "28
4,72 463,107" HREF =
"$database_manager_script_url?database=vehicles.setup&session_file=$se
ssion_file">
<AREA COORDS = "28
4,125 465,160" HREF = "mailto:selena\@eff.org">4,125 </MAP>
<P>
<A HREF = "$database_manager_script_url?database=employment.setup&ses-
sion_file=$session_file">Employment</A>
| <A HREF = "$database_manager_script_url?database=housing.setup&ses-
sion_file=$session_file">Housing</A>
| <A HREF = "$database_manager_script_url?database=misc.setup&ses-
sion_file=$session_file">Misc. For Sale</A>
| <A HREF =
"$database_manager_script_url?database=personals.setup&session_file=$s
ession_file">Personals</A>
| <A HREF = "$database_manager_script_url?database=vehicles.setup&ses-
sion_file=$session_file">Vehicles</A>
</CENTER></BODY></HTML>
end_of_html
exit;
}
```

On the Web, the general category front page looks like Figure 14.3.

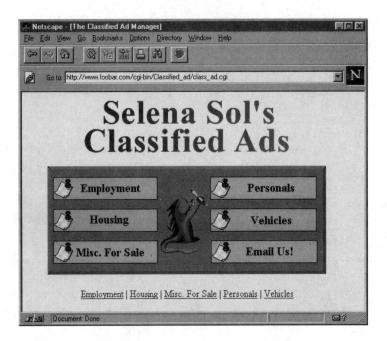

Figure 14.3 *General category front page.*

NOTE

We have included the cheesy little graphic as an example in the **Images** subdirectory on the accompanying CD-ROM.

Displaying the Specific Category Front Page

If the client has clicked on one of the links from the front page image map, the client has submitted a request via GET rather than POST (which is used for all the forms throughout the rest of this script). If the request method is GET, the script knows that the client must be asking for the database-specific front page.

```
if ($ENV{'REQUEST_METHOD'} eq "GET")
{
```

In response, the script prints the database-specific front page of the requested database, displaying several options.

```
print <<"end_of_html";
<HTML>
<HEAD>
<TITLE>The Classified Ad Manager - $database</TITLE>
</HEAD>
<BODY>
<CENTER>
<H2>The Classified Ad Manager - $database</H2>
</CENTER>
<BLOCKQUOTE>
Welcome to the Classified Ad Manager...Feel free to enter your ads
here and use the modification options if your information
changes...good luck.
</BLOCKQUOTE>
<FORM METHOD = "post" ACTION = "$database_manager_script_url">
<CENTER>
<INPUT TYPE = "hidden" NAME = "database"
       VALUE = "$form_data{'database'}">
<INPUT TYPE = "hidden" NAME = "session_file"
       VALUE = "$session_file">
<INPUT TYPE = "submit" NAME = "search_form_view"
       VALUE = "View $database Ads">
<INPUT TYPE = "submit" NAME = "add_form"
       VALUE = "Submit an Ad">
<INPUT TYPE = "submit" NAME = "search_form_delete"
       VALUE = "Delete Your Ad">
<INPUT TYPE = "submit" NAME = "search_form_modify"
       VALUE = "Modify Your Ad">
<INPUT TYPE = "submit" NAME = "return_to_frontpage"
       VALUE = "Return to Front page">
end_of_html
exit;
}
```

Here is where we use the $database **variable that we worked so hard to create. Also, notice that we are passing database and session IDs as hidden variables.**

NOTE

On the Web, the category-specific front page might look like Figure 14.4.

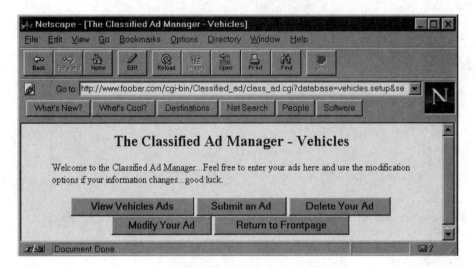

Figure 14.4 Category-specific front page.

Displaying the Classified Ad Add Form

Next, the script checks to see whether the client has asked for the form to add an entry to the database. If so, it logs the client in to be assigned a session ID number that the script can pass through the authentication routine if required. It is one thing to view the database; it is quite another to modify it!

```
if ($form_data{'add_form'} ne "")
{
```

To authenticate a client, the script passes the subroutine GetSessionInfo, which is contained in **auth-lib.pl**, three parameters: the $session_file value, which will be nothing if one has not yet been set, the name of this script so that it can provide links; and the associative array of form data we got from **cgi-lib.pl**. This process is discussed in greater depth in Chapter 9.

```
($session_file, $session_username, $session_group,
$session_first_name, $session_last_name, $session_email) =
&GetSessionInfo($session_file, $database_manager_script_url,
*form_data);
```

Because we also want to keep track of the date when new entries are made, the script also uses the get_date subroutine at the end of this script to get the current date.

```
&get_date;
```

Next, the script prints the header of the add form.

```
print <<"end_of_html";
<HTML><HEAD><TITLE>Add a Classified Ad - $database</TITLE></HEAD>
<BODY>
<CENTER><H2>Add a Classified Ad - $database</H2></CENTER>
<FORM METHOD = "post" ACTION = "$database_manager_script_url">
<CENTER>
end_of_html
```

It also creates an input form using the subroutine create_input_form at the end of this script. This subroutine creates an input field for each of the fields in the database and presents it in table format.

```
&create_input_form;
```

Finally, the script prints the page footers as it did for the front page.

```
print <<"end_of_html";
</TABLE><CENTER><P>
<INPUT TYPE = "hidden" NAME = "first_name"
        VALUE = "$session_first_name">
<INPUT TYPE = "hidden" NAME = "last_name"
        VALUE = "$session_last_name">
<INPUT TYPE = "hidden" NAME = "email"
        VALUE = "$session_email">
<INPUT TYPE = "hidden" NAME = "time" VALUE = "$date">
<INPUT TYPE = "hidden" NAME = "database"
        VALUE = "$form_data{'database'}">
<INPUT TYPE = "hidden" NAME = "session_file"
        VALUE = "$session_file">
<INPUT TYPE = "submit" NAME = "submit_addition"
        VALUE = "Submit Addition">
<INPUT TYPE = "submit" NAME = "return_to_frontpage"
        VALUE = "Return to Front page">
</CENTER></FORM></BODY></HTML>
end_of_html
```

```
exit;
}
```

Figure 14.5 shows the Add Form for the vehicles database that comes on the accompanying CD-ROM.

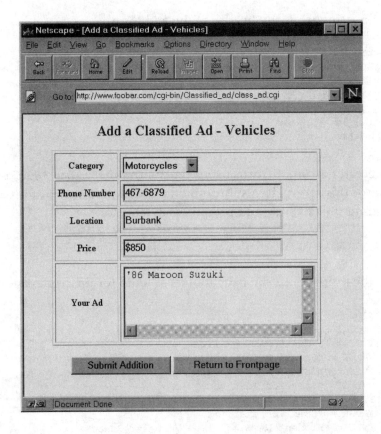

Figure 14.5 *The classified ads add form.*

Displaying the Classified Ad Delete Form

If the client wants to delete an ad, the script sends a form so that the client can specify which database item to delete.

```
if ($form_data{'search_form_delete'} ne "")
{
```

First, the script passes the client through the security check using the GetSessionInfo subroutine in **cgi-lib.sol**.

```
($session_file, $session_username, $session_group,
$session_first_name, $session_last_name, $session_email) =
&GetSessionInfo($session_file, $database_manager_script_url,
*form_data);
```

Before it can begin deleting, however, the script must find out which item to delete. To do that, the script needs some information from the client—specifically, which item to delete—so it must be able to tell the client which items are available to delete. However, the script cannot simply output all the items in the database; the Web browser might run out of memory. Instead, the client gives the script one or more search terms so that it can put together a reasonably sized list from which the client can choose.

```
print <<"end_of_html";
<HTML>
<HEAD>
<TITLE>Query Database for Deletion - $database</TITLE>
</HEAD>
<BODY>
<CENTER>
<H2>Query Database for Deletion - $database</H2>
</CENTER>
<FORM METHOD = "post"
      ACTION = "$database_manager_script_url">
<CENTER>
end_of_html
```

The script creates an input form using the subroutine create_input_form at the end of this script. The client uses this form to input keywords.

```
&create_input_form;
```

Then the script adds a form <input> tag for "exact match" and the page footer.

```
print <<"end_of_html";
<TR>
<TH>Exact Match?</TH><TD>
<INPUT TYPE = "checkbox" NAME = "exact_match" CHECKED>
</TD></TR></TABLE><P>
<INPUT TYPE = "hidden" NAME = "database"
      VALUE = "$form_data{'database'}">
<INPUT TYPE = "hidden" NAME = "session_file"
      VALUE = "$session_file">
<INPUT TYPE = "submit" NAME = "search_database_delete"
      VALUE = "Submit Search Term">
<P><BLOCKQUOTE>To get a full view of database, submit \"no\" keywords.
But beware, if there are too many items in your database, you will
exceed the memory of your browser.
</CENTER></FORM></BODY></HTML>
end_of_html
exit;
}
```

On the Web, the delete search form looks like the form shown in Figure 14.5 except for the delete-specific information.

Searching for Items to Delete

The script also needs a routine to accept the client-defined search term(s) and search the database, presenting a dynamically generated list of "hits."

```
if ($form_data{'search_database_delete'} ne "")
{
```

The process begins with a security check.

```
($session_file, $session_username, $session_group
 $session_first_name, $session_last_name, $session_email)
 = &GetSessionInfo($session_file,
 $database_manager_script_url, *form_data);
```

Next, the script prints the page header.

```
print <<"end_of_html";
<HTML>
<HEAD>
<TITLE>Deleting an Item from the Database -
$database</TITLE>
</HEAD>
<BODY>
<CENTER>
<H2>Deleting an Item from the Database - $database</H2>
</CENTER>
<FORM METHOD = "post"
      ACTION = "$database_manager_script_url">
<CENTER>
end_of_html
```

Then the script begins searching the database by using the subroutine search_database, which can be found at the end of this script. The script passes to search_database one parameter, delete, so that the subroutine will know how to output the results of the search.

```
&search_database ("delete");
```

Finally, the script prints a list of hits in a table format. $search_results, returned from the subroutine search_database, contains all the hits in the form of table rows. The client then chooses which item to delete and deletes it.

```
print "<TABLE BORDER = \"1\" CELLPADDING = \"4\"
            CELLSPACING = \"4\">";
print &table_header ("Delete<BR>Item");
print &table_header (@field_names);
print "</TR>\n";
print "$search_results";

print <<"end_of_html";
</TABLE><P>
<INPUT TYPE = "hidden" NAME = "database"
       VALUE = "$form_data{'database'}">
<INPUT TYPE = "hidden" NAME = "session_file"
       VALUE = "$session_file">
<INPUT TYPE = "submit" NAME = "submit_deletion"
       VALUE = "Submit Deletion">
<INPUT TYPE = "submit" NAME = "return_to_frontpage"
       VALUE = "Return to Front page">
```

```
</CENTER></FORM></BODY></HTML>
end_of_html
exit;
}
```

On the Web, the deletion screen looks similar to Figure 14.6.

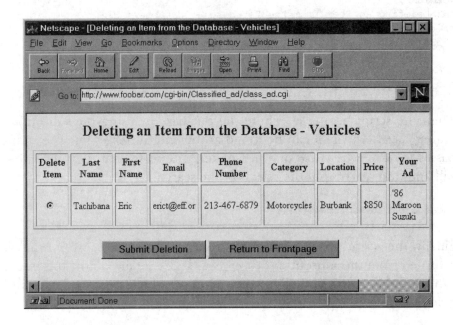

Figure 14.6 Deletion screen example.

Displaying the Modify Item Form

Next, the script repeats the same process, this time for modification.

```
if ($form_data{'search_form_modify'} ne "")
{
```

As usual, the client is authenticated first.

```
($session_file, $session_username, $session_group,
$session_first_name, $session_last_name, $session_email) =
```

```
&GetSessionInfo($session_file,
$database_manager_script_url, *form_data);
```

Then the usual header is printed.

```
print <<"end_of_html";
<HTML>
<HEAD>
<TITLE>Query Database for Modification -
$database</TITLE>
</HEAD>
<BODY>
<CENTER>
<H2>Query Database for Modification - $database</H2>
</CENTER>
<FORM METHOD = "post" ACTION = "$database_manager_script_url">
<CENTER>
end_of_html
```

Next, the script creates the input form using the subroutine create_input_form at the end of this script.

```
&create_input_form;
```

Finally, the script adds the HTML footer as it did for delete.

```
print <<"end_of_html";
<TH>Exact Match?</TH><TD>
<INPUT TYPE = "checkbox" NAME = "exact_match" CHECKED>
</TD></TR></TABLE><P>
<INPUT TYPE = "hidden" NAME = "database"
       VALUE = "$form_data{'database'}">
<INPUT TYPE = "hidden" NAME = "session_file"
       VALUE = "$session_file">
<INPUT TYPE = "submit" NAME = "search_database_modify"
       VALUE = "Submit Search Term">
<P><BLOCKQUOTE>To get a full view of database, submit \"no\" keywords.
But beware, if there are too many items in your database, you will
exceed the memory of your browser.
</CENTER></FORM></BODY></HTML>
end_of_html
exit;
}
```

On the Web, the modify search form looks exactly like Figure 14.5 except for the modification-specific information in the header.

Searching the Database for Items to Modify

As it did for delete, the script prints the results of the query for modification after a security check.

```
if ($form_data{'search_database_modify'} ne "")
{
($session_file, $session_username, $session_group,
$session_first_name, $session_last_name, $session_email)=
&GetSessionInfo($session_file, $database_manager_script_url,
*form_data);
```

First, the script prints the page header.

```
print <<"end_of_html";
<HTML>
<HEAD>
<TITLE>Modifying an Item in the Database -
$database</TITLE>
</HEAD>
<BODY>
<CENTER>
<H2>Modifying an Item in the Database - $database</H2>
</CENTER>
<FORM METHOD = "post"
      ACTION = "$database_manager_script_url">
<CENTER>
end_of_html
```

Then the script begins searching the database using the subroutine search_database at the end of the script as it did for delete.

```
&search_database ("modify");
```

Next, it prints a list of hits in a table format. You will recall that $search_results, returned from the subroutine search_database, contains all the hits in the form of table rows.

```
print "<TABLE BORDER = \"1\" CELLPADDING = \"4\"
            CELLSPACING = \"4\">";
print "<TH>Modify<BR>Item</TH>";
print &table_header (@field_names);
print "</TR>\n";
print "$search_results";
print "</TABLE><P>";
```

Furthermore, the script uses the subroutine &create_input_form to print the same form that was used for the "Add an Item" form. The client can now specify an item to modify in the table and then type new information to update the database fields.

```
&create_input_form;
```

Finally, the script prints the usual footer.

```
print <<"end_of_html";
</TABLE><CENTER><P>
<INPUT TYPE = "hidden" NAME = "database"
       VALUE = "$form_data{'database'}">
<INPUT TYPE = "hidden" NAME = "session_file"
       VALUE = "$session_file">
<INPUT TYPE = "submit" NAME = "submit_modification"
       VALUE = "Submit Modification">
<INPUT TYPE = "submit" NAME = "return_to_frontpage"
       VALUE = "Return to Front page">
</CENTER></FORM></BODY></HTML>
end_of_html
exit;
}
```

On the Web, the modification screen looks like Figure 14.7.

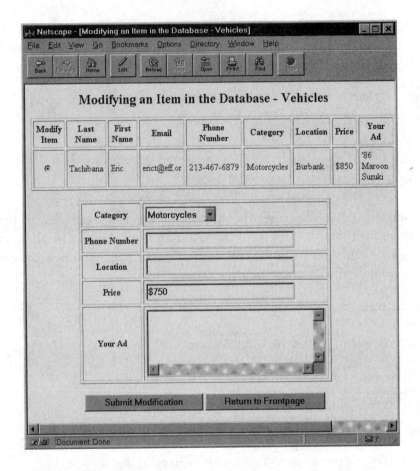

Figure 14.7 Modification screen example.

Displaying the View Form

The next routines, beginning with the printing of the page header, allow a client to view the database.

```
if ($form_data{'search_form_view'} ne "")
{
print <<"end_of_html";
<HTML>
<HEAD>
<TITLE>Classified Ad Search Engine - $database</TITLE>
</HEAD>
```

```
<BODY>
<CENTER>
<H2>Classified Ad Search Engine - $database</H2>
</CENTER>
<FORM METHOD = "post"
      ACTION = "$database_manager_script_url">
<CENTER>
<TABLE BORDER = "1" CELLSPACING = "4"
       CELLPADDING = "4">
end_of_html
```

Next, the script creates an HTML form so that the client can submit keywords with which to search. For each field in the database—except for database ID and time fields, which are set by this script and not by the administrator—the script generates an input field. It gets the list of database fields from the @field_names array defined in the setup file.

However, to build the form, the script must send a few things: the name of the field, the variable to be associated with that name, and the type of input we are going to use (TEXTAREA, TEXT, SELECT). We don't want to send it the price or time of submission, though, because we will create new input boxes for these items based on maximum and minimum acceptable prices and posting date. Thus, these two fields must be removed from the array before it is passed to the build_input_form subroutine.

```
$id = pop (@field_names);
$time = pop (@field_names);
```

Pay close attention to this if you are going to add other search features. Here is the first occurrence of a special customizing area.

NOTE

Then the script uses build_input_form in **cgi-lib.sol** to create a form input field for every client-defined database field.

```
foreach $field_name (@field_names)
  {
  if ($field_name ne "Price")
    {
    if ($field_name ne "Time of Submission")
```

341

```
       {
 print &build_input_form("$FIELD_ARRAY{$field_name}",
 "$FORM_COMPONENT_ARRAY{$field_name}",
 $field_name);
       }
   } # End of if ($field_name ne "Price")
 } # End of foreach $field_name (@field_names)
```

Next, it adds the special new search boxes. In the setup file for each data-base is a variable called $price. If this variable is set to yes, it means that you want the client to be able to search this type of database by price.

```
if ($price eq "yes")
{
print <<"end_of_html";
<TH>Highest Acceptable Price</TH>
<TD><INPUT TYPE = "text" NAME = "price.high"
          SIZE = "35" MAXLENGTH = "35">
</TD></TR><TR>
<TH>Lowest Acceptable Price</TH>
<TD><INPUT TYPE = "text" NAME = "price.low" SIZE = "35"
          MAXLENGTH = "35" VALUE = "0.00">
</TD></TR><TR>
end_of_html
}
```

Clients are also allowed to search by database row age. The script prints this second input field and finishes with a form input for exact match and the form, body, and ending HTML tags.

```
print <<"end_of_html";
<TH>Posted within how many days</TH>
<TD><INPUT TYPE = "text" NAME = "num_days_ago"
          SIZE = "35" MAXLENGTH = "35" VALUE = "30">
</TD></TR><TR>
<TH>Exact Match?</TH>
<TD><INPUT TYPE = "checkbox" NAME = "exact_match"
          CHECKED></TD>
</TR></TABLE><P>
<INPUT TYPE = "hidden" NAME = "database"
       VALUE = "$form_data{'database'}">
<INPUT TYPE = "hidden" NAME = "session_file"
       VALUE = "$session_file">
<INPUT TYPE = "submit" NAME = "search_database_view"
```

```
      VALUE = "Submit Search Parameters">
</CENTER></FORM></BODY></HTML>
end_of_html
exit;
}
```

On the Web, the view form looks like Figure 14.8.

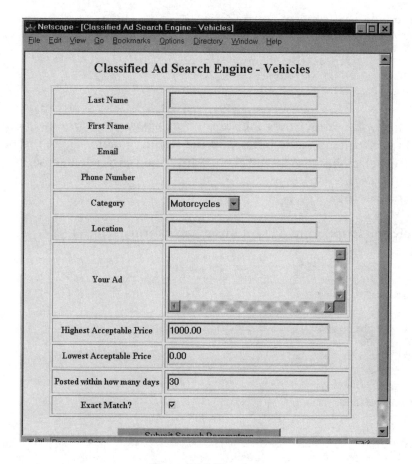

Figure 14.8 View form.

Searching the Classified Ad Database for Items to View

Next, the script searches the database for items to view. All this is exactly the same as we've done before.

```
if ($form_data{'search_database_view'} ne "")
{
print <<"end_of_html";
<HTML>
<HEAD>
<TITLE>Viewing the Database - $database</TITLE>
</HEAD>
<BODY>
<CENTER>
<H2>Viewing the Database - $database</H2>
</CENTER>
<FORM METHOD = "post"
      ACTION = "$database_manager_script_url">
<CENTER>
end_of_html
```

This time, the script sends the subroutine a parameter of none, because we do not want any radio buttons in the resulting table. There will be no items to select, because all the client wants is to view the database.

```
&search_database ("none");
```

Finally, the script prints a list of hits in table format.

```
print <<"end_of_html";
<TABLE BORDER = "1" CELLPADDING = "4" CELLSPACING = "4">
end_of_html

print &table_header (@field_names);
print "</TR>\n";
print "$search_results";

print <<"end_of_html";
</TABLE><CENTER><P>
<INPUT TYPE = "hidden" NAME = "database"
       VALUE = "$form_data{'database'}">
<INPUT TYPE = "hidden" NAME = "session_file"
       VALUE = "$session_file">
<INPUT TYPE = "submit" NAME = "search_form_view"
       VALUE = "View $database Ads">
<INPUT TYPE = "submit" NAME = "add_form"
       VALUE = "Submit an Ad">
<INPUT TYPE = "submit" NAME = "search_form_delete"
       VALUE = "Delete Your Ad">
<INPUT TYPE = "submit" NAME = "search_form_modify"
```

```
        VALUE = "Modify Your Ad">
<INPUT TYPE = "submit" NAME = "return_to_frontpage"
        VALUE = "Return to Front page">
</CENTER></FORM></BODY></HTML>
end_of_html
exit;
}
```

On the Web, the search results for a view might look like Figure 14.9.

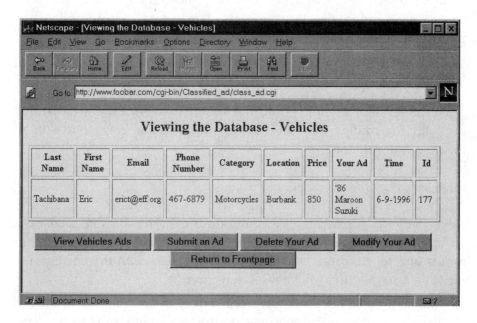

Figure 14.9 Viewing the database.

Adding an Item to the Classified Ad Database

The following routines direct the script when a client asks to add a new item to the database.

```
if ($form_data{'submit_addition'} ne "")
{
```

First, the client is passed through security.

```
($session_file, $session_username, $session_group,
$session_first_name, $session_last_name, $session_email) =
&GetSessionInfo($session_file, $database_manager_script_url,
*form_data);
```

In the case of an addition, the script assigns the new database entry a unique database ID number. It accesses the counter file, which keeps track of the last database ID number used. The counter subroutine, located in **cgi-lib.sol**, sends us a new number (incremented by 1) and then adjusts the counter file appropriately. The counter routine takes one parameter: the location of the counter file.

```
&counter($counter_file);
```

Then the ID value is slipped into the %form_data associative array so that the following routine will add it to the new database row along with all the other information.

```
$form_data{'id'} = "$item_number";
```

Next, the script formats the incoming form data the way the database is set up to understand (delimited by I and ending with a newline). It also makes sure to substitute new lines and line breaks with the corresponding HTML so that they will be displayed correctly.

The script also takes out any occurrences of I. If entered as part of the data, this pipe character would destroy our ability to read the database, because the script would interpret it as a field delimiter.

```
foreach $field (@field_names)
{
$value = "$FIELD_ARRAY{$field}";
$form_data{$value} =~ s/\n/<BR>/g;
$form_data{$value} =~ s/\r\r/<P>/g;
$form_data{$value} =~ s/\|/~~/g;
```

Also, the script formats the price entered by the client so that it can later be compared numerically. The script removes any dollar signs ($) or commas (,) as well as any words such as "or best offer" ([a-zA-Z]) or spaces (\s).

```
if ($field eq "Price" ||
    $field eq "Cost (per month for rentals)"
 {
$form_data{$value} =~ s/\$//g;
$form_data{$value} =~ s/[a-zA-Z]//g;
$form_data{$value} =~ s/,//g;
$form_data{$value} =~ s/\s//g;
 }
```

To improve the table presentation, the script changes any blank fields with <CENTER>-</CENTER> so that when the table is displayed, it won't have an ugly, empty-cell look.

```
if ($form_data{$value} eq "")
{
$form_data{$value} = "<CENTER>-</CENTER>";
}
```

Finally, the script creates and then appends $new_row with the value, thus creating a database row such as field1|field2|field3|. When all the fields have been spoken for, the script takes off the final pipe symbol and the database row is complete.

```
 $new_row .= "$form_data{$value}|";
} # End of foreach $field (@field_names)
chop $new_row; take out the last |
```

Next, the script creates a lock file so that it can edit the database file. If two people are trying to edit the locked datafile at one time, one person will not destroy the modifications made by the other person. The lock file is created using the subroutine GetFileLock in **cgi-lib.sol**, passing it one parameter: the location of the lock file used by this program.

```
&GetFileLock ("$lock_file");
```

Once the database is protected, the script opens it for appending (>>) and writes to it the value of $new_row.

```
open (DATABASE, ">>$data_file") ||
      &open_error($data_file);
```

```
print DATABASE "$new_row";
print DATABASE "\n";
```

Then, after the change has been made, the script closes the database and deletes the lock file so that others may access the datafile.

```
close (DATABASE);
&ReleaseFileLock ("$lock_file");
```

Finally, the script sends a note telling the client that the item was added to the database.

```
print <<"end_of_html";
<HTML>
<HEAD>
<TITLE>Item Added to the Database - $database</TITLE>
</HEAD>
<BODY>
<CENTER>
<H2>Item Added to the Database - $database</H2>
</CENTER>
<FORM METHOD = "post"
      ACTION = "$database_manager_script_url">
<CENTER>
<INPUT TYPE = "hidden" NAME = "database"
      VALUE = "$form_data{'database'}">
<INPUT TYPE = "hidden" NAME = "session_file"
      VALUE = "$session_file">
<INPUT TYPE = "submit" NAME = "search_form_view"
      VALUE = "View $database Ads">
<INPUT TYPE = "submit" NAME = "add_form"
      VALUE = "Submit an Ad">
<INPUT TYPE = "submit" NAME = "search_form_delete"
      VALUE = "Delete Your Ad">
<INPUT TYPE = "submit" NAME = "search_form_modify"
      VALUE = "Modify Your Ad">
<INPUT TYPE = "submit" NAME = "return_to_frontpage"
      VALUE = "Return to Front page">
</CENTER></FORM></BODY></HTML>
end_of_html
exit;
}
```

Figure 14.10 shows the client response on the Web.

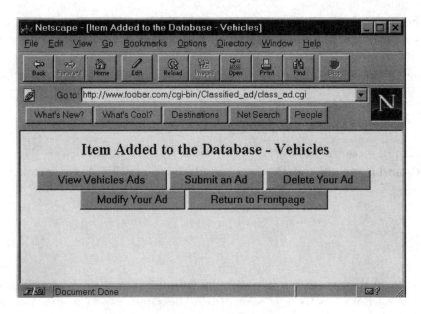

Figure 14.10 *Client response for an addition.*

Deleting an Item from the Classified Ad Database

Next, the script checks to see whether it is being called on to make a deletion.

```
if ($form_data{'submit_deletion'} ne "")
{
```

If it is, it passes the client through security.

```
($session_file, $session_username, $session_group,
$session_first_name, $session_last_name, $session_email) =
&GetSessionInfo($session_file, $database_manager_script_url,
*form_data);
```

Then it opens the database and reads it one line at a time.

```
open (DATABASE, "$data_file") ||
      &open_error($data_file);
while (<DATABASE>)
{
```

If the script finds a comment line, it adds it directly to $new_data, a variable used to store all the nondeleted database rows.

```
if ($_ =~ /^COMMENT:/)
   {
   $new_data .= "$_";
   }
```

If it is not a comment row, however, the script splits the row by database fields and pops the item ID, which should be the last field in the row.

```
else
   {
   @fields = split (/\|/, $_);
   $item_id = pop(@fields);
```

If the item ID does not match the one submitted by the client, the script adds the whole row to $new_data. If it is the same, however, the database row will not be added to $new_data and thus will be deleted by default.

```
 unless ($item_id eq "$form_data{'delete'}")
    {
    $new_data .= "$_";
    }
 } # End of else
} # End of while (<DATABASE>)
```

Next, the script closes the database, opens a lock file as it did for the add routine, and creates a temporary file that contains all the rows we dumped into $new_data.

```
close (DATABASE);
&GetFileLock ("$lock_file");
open (TEMPFILE, ">$temp_file") ||
      &open_error($temp_file);
print TEMPFILE "$new_data";
close (TEMPFILE);
```

It then copies the temporary file over the old database file, thereby deleting the entry, because it was not added to the temporary file. Then the script releases the lock file so that someone else can use it.

```
rename ($temp_file, $data_file);
&ReleaseFileLock ("$lock_file");
```

Finally, it prints the usual footer.

```
print <<"end_of_html";
<HTML>
<HEAD>
<TITLE>Your Item has been deleted - $database</TITLE>
</HEAD>
<BODY>
<CENTER>
<H2>Your Item has been deleted - $database</H2>
</CENTER>
<FORM METHOD = "post"
      ACTION = "$database_manager_script_url">
<CENTER>
<INPUT TYPE = "hidden" NAME = "database"
      VALUE = "$form_data{'database'}">
<INPUT TYPE = "hidden" NAME = "session_file"
      VALUE = "$session_file">
<INPUT TYPE = "submit" NAME = "search_form_view"
      VALUE = "View $database Ads">
<INPUT TYPE = "submit" NAME = "add_form"
      VALUE = "Submit an Ad">
<INPUT TYPE = "submit" NAME = "search_form_delete"
      VALUE = "Delete Your Ad">
<INPUT TYPE = "submit" NAME = "search_form_modify"
      VALUE = "Modify Your Ad">
<INPUT TYPE = "submit" NAME = "return_to_frontpage"
      VALUE = "Return to Front page">
</CENTER></FORM></BODY></HTML>
end_of_html
exit;
}
```

On the Web, the client response looks like Figure 14.10 except for the delete-specific header.

Modifying an Item in the Database

Last, but not least, the script takes care of any modifications asked of it.

```
if ($form_data{'submit_modification'} ne "")
{
```

As usual, the script begins with a security check.

```
($session_file, $session_username, $session_group,
$session_first_name, $session_last_name, $session_email) =
&GetSessionInfo($session_file, $database_manager_script_url,
*form_data);
```

Next, the script makes sure that the client clicked one of the radio buttons on the modification table; without that information, it would not be able to know which item to modify. `$form_data{'modify'}` will be equal to the database ID number of the item if one of the radio buttons has been selected.

```
if ($form_data{'modify'} eq "")
{
print <<"end_of_html";
<HTML>
<HEAD>
<TITLE>Modifying an Item in the Database -
$database</TITLE>
</HEAD>
<BODY>
<CENTER>
<H2>Modifying an Item in the Database - $database</H2>
</CENTER>
<BLOCKQUOTE>
I'm sorry, I was not able to modify the database because none of the
radio buttons on the table was selected so I was not sure which item
to modify. Would you please make sure that you select an item "and"
fill in the new information. Please press the back button and try
again. Thanks.
</BLOCKQUOTE>
end_of_html
exit;
}
```

Next, the script opens the database and reads through it one line at a time, adding the comment lines to `$new_data`.

```
open (DATABASE, "$data_file") ||
      &open_error($data_file);
while (<DATABASE>)
  {
```

```
if ($_ =~ /^COMMENT:/)
   {
   $new_data .= "$_";
   }
```

If the line is not a comment line, however, the script pops the item_id as it did for deletion. But this time, it also pushes the item_id back into the array after it has read it, because we still want to have the ID in the row when the routine is finished. We'll need the complete row for the final modified row.

```
else
   {
   @fields = split (/\|/, $_);
   $item_id = pop(@fields);
   push (@fields, $item_id);
```

If the item ID from the database equals the one submitted by the client, the script creates a new array, @old_fields, equal to the current fields in the row.

```
if ($item_id eq "$form_data{'modify'}")
   {
   @old_fields = @fields;
   }
```

If the two values are not equal, however, the script adds the row to $new_data. By the end, the script will have copied every line in the database to $new_data except for the item that the client wanted modified. Fortunately, the script saved that line in the @old_fields array.

```
else
   {
   $new_data .= "$_";
   }
   } # End of else
} # End of while (<DATABASE>)
close (DATABASE);
```

To add the modified line to the database, the script begins by initializing a few variables. $new_line will contain the modified database row, and $counter will be used to count database fields in the row.

```
$counter = 0;
$new_line = "";
```

Then the script goes through each of the fields in @field_values, which is a list containing each of the database fields as defined in the setup file.

```
until ($counter >= @field_values)
{
```

For each field, the script initializes the variable $value and sets it equal to an incremented field according to the current value of counter.

```
$value = "";
$value = "$field_values[$counter]";
```

If that field, as represented by the form input, is equal to zero (the client did not wish to modify that field), the script takes the old value (as stored in the @old_fields array) and adds it to $new_line, appending a pipe (|) at the end to denote the end of the field.

```
if ($form_data{$value} eq "")
{
$new_line .= "$old_fields[$counter]|";
}
```

On the other hand, if the user wanted to edit that field, the script formats the incoming data as it did for the add routine and adds the new data to $new_line.

```
else
  {
$form_data{$value} =~ s/\n/<BR>/g;
$form_data{$value} =~ s/\r\r/<P>/g;
$form_data{$value} =~ s/\|/~~/g;

  if ($field eq "Price" ||
      $field eq "Cost (per month for rentals)")
   {
   $form_data{$value} =~ s/\$//g;
   $form_data{$value} =~ s/[a-zA-Z]//g;
   $form_data{$value} =~ s/,//g;
```

```
  $form_data{$value} =~ s/\s//g;
  }

 if ($form_data{$value} eq "")
  {
  $form_data{$value} = "<CENTER>-</CENTER>";
  }

 $new_line .= "$form_data{$value}|";
 } # End of else
$counter++;
} # End of until ($counter >= @field_values)
chop $new_line; Take off the final |
```

Next, the script opens the temporary file and prints the $new_data lines as well as the modified database line contained in $new_line. Then it closes the temporary file, copies the temporary file over the old database file, and releases the lock.

```
&GetFileLock ("$lock_file");
open (TEMPFILE, ">$temp_file") || &open_error($temp_file);
print TEMPFILE "$new_data";
print TEMPFILE "$new_line";
close (TEMPFILE);
rename ($temp_file, $data_file);
&ReleaseFileLock ("$lock_file");
```

Finally, the script prints the usual footer.

```
print <<"end_of_html";
<HTML>
<HEAD>
<TITLE>Your Item has been Modified - $database</TITLE>
</HEAD>
<BODY>
<CENTER>
<H2>Your Item has been Modified - $database</H2>
</CENTER>
<FORM METHOD = "post"
      ACTION = "$database_manager_script_url">
<CENTER>
<INPUT TYPE = "hidden" NAME = "database"
       VALUE = "$form_data{'database'}">
<INPUT TYPE = "hidden" NAME = "session_file"
```

```
        VALUE = "$session_file">
<INPUT TYPE = "submit" NAME = "search_form_view"
        VALUE = "View $database Ads">
<INPUT TYPE = "submit" NAME = "add_form"
        VALUE = "Submit an Ad">
<INPUT TYPE = "submit" NAME = "search_form_delete"
        VALUE = "Delete Your Ad">
<INPUT TYPE = "submit" NAME = "search_form_modify"
        VALUE = "Modify Your Ad">
<INPUT TYPE = "submit" NAME = "return_to_frontpage"
        VALUE = "Return to Front page">
</CENTER></FORM></BODY></HTML>
end_of_html
exit;
} # End of if ($form_data{'submit_modification'} ne "")
```

On the Web, the client response looks like Figure 14.10 except for the modify-specific header.

The CgiRequire Subroutine

CgiRequire checks to see whether the file that the script is trying to require exists and is readable by it. This subroutine provides developers with an informative error message when they're attempting to debug the scripts.

```
sub CgiRequire
{
```

The @require_files array is first defined as a local array and is filled with the filenames sent from the main routine.

```
local (@require_files) = @_;
```

CgiRequire then checks to see whether the files exist and are readable by the script. If so, the files are required.

```
foreach $file (@require_files)
  {
  if (-e "$file" && -r "$file")
    {
    require "$file";
    }
```

If there is a problem, however, CgiRequire sends an error message that will help the developer isolate the problem.

```
else
   {
   print "I'm sorry, I was not able to open
   $file. Would you please check to make sure
   that you gave me a valid filename and that the
   permissions on $file are set to allow me
   access?";
   exit;
   }
 } # End of foreach $file (@require_files)
} # End of sub require
```

The create_input_form Subroutine

The create_input_form subroutine is used to generate the input forms that the client will use to input new data for an addition or keywords for a search.

```
sub create_input_form
{
```

First, the table header is printed.

```
print "<TABLE BORDER = \"1\" CELLPADDING = \"4\"
             CELLSPACING = \"4\">";
```

Then the subroutine is used to create an HTML form. In the end, we must have one input field for each field in the database (except the database ID field, which is set by this script and not by the client).

The subroutine gets the list of database fields from the @field_names array defined in the setup file and, for every element in the array, creates an input field. To do so, it sends the build_input_form subroutine in **cgi-lib.sol** a few parameters: the name of the field, the variable to be associated with that name, and the type of input we are going to use (TEXTAREA, TEXT, SELECT).

```
foreach $field_name (@field_names_user_defined)
  {
```

357

```
$variable_name = $FIELD_ARRAY{$field_name};
$form_type = $FORM_COMPONENT_ARRAY{$field_name};
local ($input_form);
$input_form = "";
$input_form .= "<TR>\n";
$input_form .= &table_header ("$field_name");
$input_form .= "<TD>";
$input_form .= &make_form_row ("$field_name",
                               "$variable_name",
                               "$form_type");
$input_form .= "</TD></TR>\n";
print"$input_form";
 }
} # End of sub create_input_form
```

The search_database Subroutine

The search_database subroutine is used to search the database for key-word matches.

```
sub search_database
{
```

First, the local variable $submit_type is set equal to the value sent to us from the main routine. This will be either modify, delete, or, in the case of a view search, none.

```
local($submit_type) = @_;
```

Next, the subroutine opens the database file and begins checking each field in every row against the keywords submitted, disregarding comment lines (COMMENT:).

```
open (DATABASE, "$data_file")||
      &open_error($data_file);
while (<DATABASE>)
 {
 $database_row = $_;
 unless ($database_row =~ /^COMMENT:/)
  {
```

`$did_we_find_a_match` is initially set equal to `no` to make sure that it has not been initialized elsewhere. The `$did_we_find_a_match` variable is used to keep track of whether a hit was made based on the client-submitted keyword. If a match was found, the variable will equal `yes`.

```
$did_we_find_a_match = "no";
```

Next, the subroutine `splits` the database row into the `@row` array and creates some variables based on values specified in the setup file.

```
@row = split(/\|/,$database_row);
$row_price = "$row[$price_field_num]";
$row_date = "$row[$date_field_num]";
$last_name_field_number = "0";
$row_last_name = "$row[$last_name_field_number]";
($month,$day,$year) =
    split (/-/, $row[$date_field_num]);
```

It then uses the **date.pl** library to convert the row date into a Julian date that it uses to compare to today's date and generate the number of days ago that the row was posted.

```
$julian_day = &jday($month,$day,$year);
($today_month,$today_day,$today_year) = split (/-/,
        &get_date);
$today = &jday($today_month,$today_day,$today_year);
$posted_days_ago = ($today - $julian_day);
```

Next, `search_database` checks to see whether the client asked us to weed out by price or age. By the way, the `if` tests will pass if the user did not submit any pruning value.

```
if (($row_price <= $form_data{'price.high'} ||
     $form_data{'price.high'} eq "")
&&
($row_price >= $form_data{'price.low'} ||
$form_data{'price.low'} eq "")
&&
($form_data{'num_days_ago'} >= $posted_days_ago ||
     $form_data{'num_days_ago'} eq ""))
{
```

Then, for each key in the `%form_data` associative array, the script sets `$field_number` equal to –1. We do this because both the pesky "submit" and "exact match" key/value pairs may come in along with the rest of the form data. We do not want the script to search the database for those fields, because they don't exist! By setting `$field_number` equal to –1, the script will be able to filter such non–field keys with the following routine:

```
foreach $form_data_key (keys %form_data)
  {
  $field_number = -1;
```

The subroutine first goes through the fields in the database (`@field_values`), checking to see whether there is a corresponding value coming in from the form (`$form_data_key`). However, because arrays are counted from zero rather than from 1 and because `@field_values` gives us a count of the array starting at 1, the script offsets the counter by 1.

Thus, if the form "key" submitted is indeed a field in the database, `$field_number` (`$y - 1`) will be its actual location in the array.

```
for ($y = 1; $y <= @field_values; $y++)
  {
  if ($form_data_key eq @field_values[$y-1] &&
      $form_data{"$form_data_key"} ne "")
    {
    $field_number = $y - 1;
    last; # Exit out of the for loop because we have
          # verified field
    }
  } # End of for ($y = 1; $y <= @field_values; $y++)
```

Then the script checks the submitted value against the value in the database. However, the script must make sure that the value is not on or submit keyword. If `$field_number` is still equal to –1, it means that the script did not match the form data key against an actual database field, so it should try the next key. Otherwise, it knows that it has a valid field to check against. Again, `$field_number` must be less than or equal to –1, because the array starts from zero.

```
if ($field_number > -1)
  {
```

360

Next, the script performs the match, checking the database information against the submitted keyword for that field. First, it performs an exact match test. If $form_data{'exact_match'} is not equal to on, it means that the exact match check box was not checked. The match is straightforward. If the keyword string ($form_data{"$form_data_key"}) matches (=~) a string in the field that the subroutine is searching ($row[$field_number]) with case insensitivity off (/i), then the script knows it got a hit.

```
if ($form_data{'exact_match'} ne "on")
{
if ($row[$field_number] =~
   /$form_data{$form_data_key}/i)
{
```

However, before we get too excited, the script must make sure either that the client is an administrator (and is allowed to see all rows) or that the row the client got a hit on is actually a row that the client initially entered; it also must make sure that this is not a general view request. The first two if tests are obvious. The reason for the last test is that if the client is asking to view, we don't care whether the client entered the row. We want him or her to see everything. Only in the case of modifying and deleting do we want the extra level of filtering.

```
if (($session_group eq "admin" ||
     $row_last_name eq "$session_last_name") &&
     $submit_type ne "none")
  {
  $did_we_find_a_match = "yes";
  last; # Exit out of ForEach keys in FormData
}
```

The subroutine also handles a general view request. It is basically the same routine, but it covers whatever was left by the previous if test.

```
 if ($submit_type eq "none")
  {
  $did_we_find_a_match = "yes";
  last; # Exit out of ForEach keys in FormData
  }
 } # End of if (@row[$field_number]....
} # End of if ($form_data{'exact_match'} eq "")
```

On the other hand, the client may have clicked the exact match check box. This time, the script proceeds with an exact match using the \b switch, keeping it case-insensitive (/i). The same $did_we_find_a_match setting and if tests apply as before.

```
elsif ($row[$field_number] =~
/\b$form_data{$form_data_key}\b/i)
   {
   if (($session_group eq "admin" ||
        $row_last_name eq "$session_last_name") &&
        $submit_type ne "none")
     {
     $did_we_find_a_match = "yes";
     last; # Exit out of ForEach keys in FormData
     }
   if ($submit_type eq "none")
     {
     $did_we_find_a_match = "yes";
     last; # Exit out of ForEach keys in FormData
     }
   } # End of elsif ($row[$field_number]....
 } # End of if ($field_number > -1)
} # End of foreach $form_data_key (keys %form_data)
```

If the script finds a match ($did_we_find_a_match equals yes), it needs to create a table row for the output. $search_results is used to collect all the hits formatted as table rows for the output. A hit adds each of the fields of the database row to a table row. The subroutine also creates a variable called $hit_counter to remind it that it got a hit. If $hit_counter is never set to 1, the script knows that it must tell the client that her keyword turned up nothing.

```
if ($did_we_find_a_match eq "yes")
{
$search_results .= "<TR>";
$hit_counter = "1";
```

Then the subroutine gathers the database ID row number so that it can use it and then puts it back into the @row array.

```
$db_id_number = pop (@row);
push (@row, $db_id_number);
```

The subroutine then begins creating the database rows created by the HTML. If this is not a view and if it is a row that satisfies security, the script creates a first column for the radio button that the client will use to select a database row to modify or delete.

```
if (($session_group eq "admin" ||
     $row_last_name eq "$session_last_name")
&&
($submit_type ne "none"))
 {
 $search_results .= "<TD ALIGN = \"center\">\n";
 $search_results .= "<INPUT TYPE = \"radio\"
                 NAME = \"$submit_type\"
                 VALUE = \"$db_id_number\">";
 $search_results .= "\n</TD>\n";
} # End of if ($session_group eq "admin" ||....
```

Then the subroutine fills in the HTML database table row. In the case of viewing, it adds every row, and in the case of modification and deletion, it gives them only the appropriate rows.

```
foreach $field (@row)
  {
  if ($submit_type eq "none")
    {
    $search_results .= "<TD>$field</TD>\n";
    }
    elsif ($row_last_name eq "$session_last_name" ||
           $session_group eq "admin")
    {
    $search_results .= "<TD>$field</TD>\n";
    }
    } # End of foreach $field (@row)...
  } # End of if ($did_we_find_a_match eq "yes")....
  } # End of if (($row_price <=....
 } # End of unless ($database_row =~ /^COMMENT:/)
} # End of while (<DATABASE>)
close (DATABASE);
```

Next, the subroutine provides an algorithm to handle the possibility that a client-submitted keyword may turn up nothing in the search. At this point, if $hit_counter is not equal to 1, it means that the search did not turn up a hit. Thus, the script sends a note to the client with a link to the search form.

NOTE We use a hyperlink rather than a **submit** button, because we want the client to access this script without a CONTENT_LENGTH so that the form will pop up.

Also, the script exits the routine here if no hits were found. We do not want it to print an empty table.

```perl
if ($hit_counter ne "1")
 {
 print "I'm sorry, I was unable to find a match for the
        keyword(s) that you specified in a database row
        that you are authorized to see. Feel free to
        <A HREF = \"class_ad.cgi\">try again</A>";
 print "</CENTER></BODY></HTML>";
 exit;
 }
} # End of sub search_database
```

The get_date Subroutine

The get_date subroutine is used to get the current date of each added classified ad database row.

```perl
sub get_date
 {

 @days = ('Sunday', 'Monday', 'Tuesday', 'Wednesday',
          'Thursday', 'Friday', 'Saturday');
 @months = ('January', 'February', 'March', 'April',
            'May', 'June', 'July', 'August',
            'September', 'October', 'November',
            'December');
```

The localtime command is used to get the current time, splitting it into variables.

```perl
($sec,$min,$hour,$mday,$mon,$year,$wday,$yday,$isdst) =
localtime(time);
```

Then the variables are formatted and assigned to the final $date variable.

```
if ($hour < 10) { $hour = "0$hour"; }
if ($min < 10) { $min = "0$min"; }
if ($sec < 10) { $sec = "0$sec"; }
$date = "$mon-$mday-19$year";
}
```

CHAPTER 15

SQL Database Address Book

OVERVIEW

So far, the chapters in this part of the book have explained how to interface various ASCII text file–based databases on the Web. This provides a useful service, because many companies cannot afford the high cost associated with commercial relational database management systems (RDBMS). However, for those people who have access to a robust RDBMS, this chapter gives an example of how to perform basic database operations on a commercial database using CGI.

An address book is a good application to demonstrate the major functions that have been discussed in the previous chapters. In this example, we will use Sybase as the database server. However, the scripts are applicable to other RDBMSs, such as Oracle and Informix, and require minimal work to be converted to those systems. Basically, the Perl scripts here use the command-line utilities of whatever major RDBMS you happen to be using. The Structured Query Language (SQL) code gets passed to the command-line utility using the Perl scripts. The example discussed here uses Sybase's

ISQL command-line utility to send and receive data to and from a Sybase database. Although database-specific libraries for Perl, such as Sybperl and Oraperl, do exist, we have avoided using them. They are too specific to each database to allow us to program a database-independent script.

INSTALLATION AND USAGE

The SQL address book consists of multiple script files that process the various database operations. The files can be split into two categories: query and maintenance. In addition, other files are used for setup. Figure 15.1 outlines the expanded directory structure and permissions needed for the files belonging to this application.

The root **Address** directory must have permissions that allow the Web server to read and execute and should contain a subdirectory for temporary files called **Temp**.

Address Query Files

addr_query.cgi outputs an HTML form that allows the user to query on the address book. All the scripts prefixed with **addr_query** should be readable and executable.

addr_query_result.cgi processes the form variables from the HTML form output by **addr_query.cgi**. It sends an SQL query to the database server and returns the results to the user.

Address Maintenance Files

addr_maint.cgi outputs the first HTML page for the maintenance side of the address book. It outputs a form with three buttons: **add**, **delete**, and **modify**. All the scripts prefixed with **addr_maint** must be readable and executable.

addr_maint_search.cgi processes the form variable output of **addr_maint.cgi**. It prints an HTML form appropriate to whatever action is being taken: addition, modification, or deletion of an address book entry.

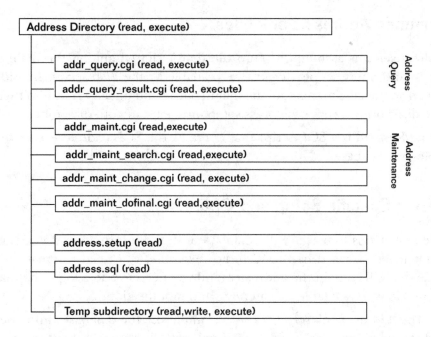

Figure 15.1 *Directory structure of the SQL address book.*

addr_maint_change.cgi processes the form output from **addr_maint_ search.cgi**. If the operation is an addition, it submits the new address information directly to the database server. If the operation is a modification or deletion, it submits the query information to the database server and returns a list of rows that the user can select from to perform the edit or removal.

addr_maint_dofinal.cgi is the final script in the maintenance process for modifications and deletions. It takes the form output of **addr_maint_ change.cgi** and submits SQL code to the database server to perform the operation.

NOTE The address book scripts as they exist here are Sybase-specific. Therefore, you will encounter some Sybase-specific terminology in this chapter. If you own another commercial RDBMS, you should talk to your database administrator about doing the equivalent operations. For example, ISQL is a Sybase command-line utility in which SQL code can be passed. There are similar utilities for other RDBMSes.

369

Common Address Book Files

address.setup is a common setup file that is shared among the maintenance and query scripts. It must be readable by the Web server. In addition, if you decide to separate the maintenance and query scripts into their own directories, a copy of **address.setup** must exist in both directories.

address.sql is a SQL script that contains the SQL code to create the table in a database.

Server-Specific Setup and Options

The first step is to prepare the database with the information it needs in order to be accessed by the Web. For example, you need to create the table that will contain the addresses, and you need to add a login that has permissions on the table for querying and modification.

The address book scripts in this example use the database "infobase" and the table "address" inside that database. All the scripts here must be able to find this information. If your database cannot be set up in this manner, you need to modify **address.setup** to reference a different area of your database server.

The **address.sql** file contains sample SQL code to create a simple address table inside the infobase database. Simply run this script using the ISQL command-line utility to create the table in the infobase database. The **address.sql** file is discussed in the design discussion later. Here is an example of running the command-line utility with a username of "user" and a password of "pass":

```
isql -Uuser -Ppass <address.sql
```

Next, you need a login ID and password that has rights to enter the infobase database and perform operations on the address table inside the database. Specifically, this login ID needs to be granted permissions to select, insert, update, and delete items in the address table. The query scripts need only permission to select. The maintenance scripts require the full set of permissions.

In addition, the scripts rely on Sybase having been installed in the default **/opt/sybase** directory on your UNIX server. Thus, the ISQL program should reside in **/opt/sybase/bin**. If Sybase is not installed here, you need to modify the **address.setup** file to change the path where Sybase is installed.

All the address query and maintenance scripts can reside in the same directory. This is the default placement of the files for the address book. However, you may want to separate the maintenance scripts into another directory and password-protect that directory using your Web server if you can. If you separate the scripts, make sure that **address.setup** exists in both areas. Both the maintenance scripts and the regular querying scripts require **address.setup** to work.

THE SETUP FILE

The **address.setup** file contains only a few configuration variables; they are related to the location of Sybase on your server and the way to access the address table within the Sybase RDBMS server.

$db_dir is the directory where Sybase is installed. The ISQL program is expected to be installed in a subdirectory under $db_dir called **bin**. The interfaces file that tells Sybase where to connect to the running RDBMS server should also be in this directory.

$db_server is the server name that ISQL uses to log on with. There can be multiple Sybase servers on a single machine. This name helps differentiate between them. The default server name is simply "sybase."

$db_name is the name of the database where the address table is stored. By default, the address table is stored in infobase.

NOTE If you use a database name other than infobase, you will want to modify the **address.sql** file so that the SQL code in it creates the address table in your database instead of a database called infobase.

$db_user is the name of the login ID that the Web server uses to log on to the Sybase database. Likewise, $db_password is the password associated with the login ID.

Here is an example of the **address.setup** file:

```
$db_dir = "/opt/sybase";
$db_server = "sybase";
$db_name = "infobase";
$db_user = "test";
$db_password = "test";
```

Running the Scripts

Using the address book query script is easy. Merely call the **addr_query.cgi** script through the Web browser. This action takes you to a screen that allows you to query on the various fields of the address book to get a list of employees and their information. Figure 15.2 shows an example of the address book query screen. Here is a sample URL for this script if it is installed in an **Address** subdirectory under a **cgi-bin** directory:

```
http://www.foobar.com/cgi-bin/Address/addr_query.cgi
```

To perform maintenance on the address table through the Web, use the **addr_maint.cgi** script. This action will take you to a screen that gives you a choice of operations: add, modify, or delete. Figure 15.3 shows an example of this screen. A sample URL for this script follows:

```
http://www.foobar.com/cgi-bin/Address/addr_maint.cgi
```

DESIGN DISCUSSION

The address book query and maintenance applications can be thought of as two separate applications, because neither CGI program interacts with the other. The programs that begin with **addr_maint** call only other scripts that begin with **addr_maint**. Similarly, the **addr_query.cgi** script calls only **addr_query_result.cgi**. Figures 15.4 and 15.5 show an example of the logic involved in both sets of programs.

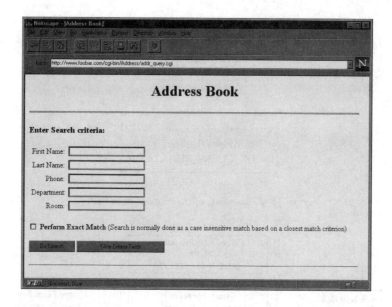

Figure 15.2 The SQL address book query screen.

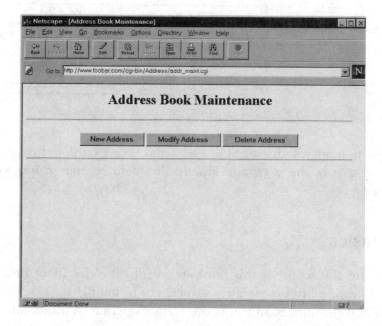

Figure 15.3 The SQL address book maintenance screen.

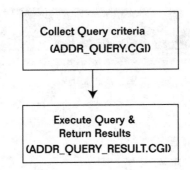

Figure 15.4 *Flowchart of the address book query.*

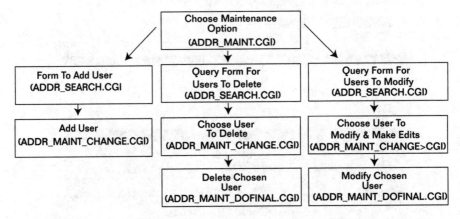

Figure 15.5 *Flowchart of the address book maintenance.*

In this section, we will discuss SQL basics and then examine the details of the query part of the program. Finally, the maintenance scripts will be explained.

SQL Basics

It is beyond the scope of this book to go into the details of how SQL works. Instead, a brief overview is given here to familiarize you with just enough SQL to understand how the scripts operate. Additionally, your RDBMS should have documentation related to the nature of the SQL code for your database. The specific SQL code in the address book scripts will also be commented later.

WARNING If you do not know SQL, this chapter may seem a bit daunting. Keep in mind that the generated queries are not very complex in the scripts. As you read this overview section, do not feel uncomfortable if you understand only some parts of the SQL language the first time around. The important thing is to get a general idea of SQL before moving on.

The databases that we have dealt with so far in this book have been ASCII text files. These files can be thought of as databases, because, although they are text files, they store information in a structured manner conducive to being searched and updated. Nonetheless, they are only files. To search or manipulate the files, Perl file operations must be used.

Commercial RDBMSes are different. You usually do not have any direct access to the data on the disk. You no longer have an option of opening a file and performing a query yourself by parsing all the lines in a Perl `while` loop. The only way to access tables in an RDBMS such as the one discussed here is to use SQL.

SQL is not a procedural language. Nothing in the SQL specification tells the server how to go about getting the data to you. SQL consists of commands that tell the database what you want the result to be; the database server figures out the "how" of getting it to you.

For example, suppose I wanted to obtain a list of all the employees who live in Texas. If I were dealing with a text file, I would open the file and read in all the lines one by one to see which lines happened to have an employee that lived in Texas. Then I would close the file. With SQL, I would simply send the appropriate SQL code saying, "I want the names of all employees who live in Texas," and the database server would return the whole result. With the SQL example, you only ask for the information you want instead of defining the procedure for getting that information.

Tables in a database are similar in concept to the ASCII text files discussed earlier. Instead of lines or records in a file corresponding to each employee, a database table is thought of as containing rows of data in which each row corresponds to an employee. Furthermore, whereas the text file has fields in each line that may be pipe- or comma-delimited, the table has columns that are logically defined. You need not be concerned about how the database server stores the fields (pipe-delimited or not). In addition, SQL does not care about the order of the rows or columns in a table. With a file, you must know the order of the fields, because the Perl script uses procedural code to read the fields in each line one by one.

QUERYING THE DATABASE WITH SQL

The workhorse of the SQL language is the select statement. select tells the database which field names you are interested in looking at. In addition, the from command added to the select statement lets the database know which table to get the fields from. Finally, if you do not want the whole table returned, you use the where command added to the select and from commands to tell the database the criteria to use in selecting the fields. The following example SQL statement asks for the first and last names of all employees whose first name is Bill.

```
select first_name, last_name
from address
where first_name = "Bill"
```

The select clause tells the database to return the first_name and last_name fields.

 The field names in a database normally follow standard variable-naming conventions and tend not to be "pretty." In our address book script, we generally output different headers for the field names.

N O T E

The from clause tells the database to return the field information from the address table. Finally, the where clause tells the database to restrict the rows returned to only those that contain the name Bill.

MODIFYING THE DATABASE WITH SQL

select statements are good for searching a table, but frequently we need to perform modification operations such as additions, deletions, and updates. These operations are done using the `insert`, `delete`, and `update` commands.

The syntax of an `insert` follows this format:

```
INSERT [TABLE_NAME]
([COLUMN_LIST])
VALUES
([VALUE_LIST])
```

Thus, to insert "John Doe" into the address table, we would use the following SQL statement:

```
insert address
(first_name, last_name)
values
("John", "Doe")
```

The syntax for the `delete` command follows this format:

```
DELETE [TABLE_NAME]
WHERE
[EXPRESSION_TO_SEARCH_FOR]
```

If the `where` clause is left out, all the rows in the table will be deleted by default. Thus, it is always important to include a `where` clause so that the database knows which records to remove. To delete "John Doe" from the address table, we would use the following statement:

```
delete address
where
first_name = "John" and last_name = "Doe"
```

The syntax for the `update` command follows this format:

```
UPDATE [TABLE_NAME]
SET [COLUMN_NAME = EXPRESSION]
WHERE [EXPRESSION_TO_SEARCH_FOR]
```

Again, the `where` clause is optional. Remember, though, that omitting it will result in the whole table being updated instead of just a few rows. To change the name of "John Doe" to "Joe Smith," we would use the following:

```
update address
set first_name = "Joe", last_name = "Smith"
where first_name = "John" and last_name = "Doe"
```

That's really all there is to it. SQL consists of a few operators that can do many things depending on how you combine them. The address book is a relatively simple application of SQL, so the SQL code that the scripts generate here is not very complex. SQL can do much more, but let's move on to discuss the address book, because it does not take advantage of the more advanced features of SQL.

address.sql

Address.sql contains the SQL code for creating the address table. Tables in SQL have variable types associated with them. For the purpose of this application, we stick to VARCHAR (variable-length character field) types of variables for every field. However, commercial databases typically support many datatypes, including date and time, integer, money, and more. The advantage of using these different datatypes is that the SQL language can make certain assumptions about a datatype. For example, with a datatype of money, you can use SQL to gather a sum of all the rows for that field without having to first convert a text string to a number. Because the address book is relatively simple, we use only text-based fields.

varchar is the Sybase keyword for indicating variable-length character data. The number in parentheses is the maximum length of each field. The go command is used to submit your SQL code. The use command at the beginning of the script tells the ISQL program to switch to the infobase database before the table is created. Note that the use command is Sybase-specific; you may need to use syntax appropriate for your own database. In addition, if you are using a database other than infobase to store your address table, you will need to change the reference from infobase to the name you are using for the database.

```
use infobase
go
```

```
create table address
(lname    varchar(15),
 fname    varchar(15),
 depart   varchar(35),
 phone    varchar(15),
 room     varchar(15))
go
```

addr_query.cgi

The **addr_query.cgi** script prints an HTML form with fields for searching the address table. Figure 15.2 showed an example of this form. In addition, a check box is included on the form so that the user can select an exact match search or a pattern match–based search. Both searches are performed without regard to upper- and lowercase, but the exact match search requires that all the characters in the search field exactly match the characters in the database column. A CGI script is used to print the HTML (instead of using an HTML file) because some CGI directories on Web servers are set up so that they cannot read HTML files there. In the interest of keeping all the address book files in one place, the HTML code is converted to a CGI script that outputs HTML.

The first thing the script does is to print the HTTP header "Content-type: text/html," which allows the rest of the CGI program to output HTML code. The remainder of the program prints this HTML code using the HERE DOCUMENT method of Perl. Figure 15.2 showed what the HTML looks like in a Web browser for this screen.

```
#!/usr/local/bin/perl
print "Content-type: text/html\n\n";

# The following is a PERL "Here" document,
# printed out as HTML
print <<__END_OF_HTML__;
<HTML>
<HEAD>
<TITLE>Address Book</TITLE>
</HEAD>
<BODY BGCOLOR = "FFFFFF" TEXT = "000000">
<CENTER>
<H1>Address Book</H1>
</CENTER>
```

```
<HR>
<FORM ACTION=addr_query_result.cgi METHOD=POST>
<H3><STRONG>Enter Search criteria: </STRONG></H3>
<TABLE>
<tr>
<td align=right>First Name:</td>
<td><input name=fname></td>
</tr>
<tr>
<td align=right>Last Name:</td>
<td><input name=lname></td>
</tr>
<tr>
<td align=right>Phone:</td>
<td><input name=phone></td>
</tr>
<tr>
<td align=right>Department:</td>
<td><input name=depart></td>
</tr>
<tr>
<td align=right>Room:</td>
<td><input name=room></td>
</tr>
</TABLE>
<P>
<INPUT TYPE=checkbox NAME=exactmatch><STRONG> Perform Exact
Match</STRONG>
(Search is normally done as a case insensitive match based on a clos-
est
match criterion) <P>
<INPUT TYPE=submit name=doquery value="Do Search">
<INPUT TYPE=reset value="Clear Criteria Fields">
</FORM>

<P><HR>

</BODY></HTML>
__END_OF_HTML__
```

addr_query_result.cgi

addr_query_result.cgi is called when the HTML form that is output by
addr_query.cgi is submitted to the Web server. It parses the query parameters
into SQL code. This SQL code is then sent to the database engine. Finally,

the SQL results are parsed and sent to the user in the form of HTML code. Figure 15.6 shows a sample query result.

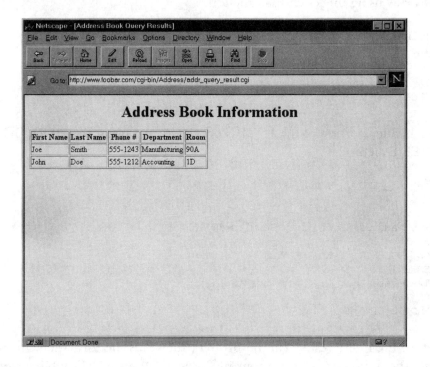

Figure 15.6 Sample address book query result.

The first step is to declare a path where libraries can be located. By default, the library files are located in the current directory. This is indicated by the "." that $lib is set to. Then **cgi-lib.pl** is loaded to process the incoming form data. The **address.setup** file is also loaded. It does not use the $lib path, because we expect **address.setup** always to be located in the same directory as these CGI scripts. Libraries, on the other hand, may be located in a directory shared by all scripts, or they may remain in the same directory as each of the CGI applications.

```
$lib = ".";
require "$lib/cgi-lib.pl";
require "address.setup";
```

The standard Web HTTP header is printed using the `PrintHeader` function from **cgi-lib.pl**. Then the form variables are read into the `%in` associative array using the `ReadParse` function.

```
# Print the magic HTTP header
print &PrintHeader;

# Parse the form variables into the %in associative array.
&ReadParse;
```

The header portion of the HTML code is printed using the HERE DOCUMENT method.

```
print <<__END_OF_HTML__;
<HTML>
<HEAD>
<TITLE>Address Book Query Results</TITLE>
</HEAD>
<BODY BGCOLOR = "FFFFFF" TEXT = "000000">
<CENTER>
<H1>Address Book Information</H1>
</CENTER>
__END_OF_HTML__
```

Before the query results can be printed, they must be formatted. In this case, the address results are sent in the form of an HTML table. `$header_format` contains the HTML code for printing the header. `$format_table` contains the HTML code for printing every row of the table. `$exactmatch` is set to `on` if the user chooses to do an exact match search on the previous HTML form.

```
$format_table = "<TR>";
$header_format = "<TR>";
$exactmatch = $in{"exactmatch"};
```

The `@field_names` array contains a list of the field names as they exist in the address table for performing the query.

NOTE The fields appear in the same order that they will be displayed to the user. The names of the fields must match the column names in Sybase as well as the <INPUT> tag names in the previous HTML form. If you are customizing this script to your own address book, you must take care to modify **addr_query.cgi** to update the <INPUT> tag names there.

Next, @field_desc contains the descriptive information about each field; the field names are not pretty enough to display to the user. The order of the field descriptions must be the same as in the @field_names array.

In addition, the @select_list array is set equal to the @field_names array for processing the list of fields to use in the select clause of the SQL code the program will generate.

```
@field_names = ("fname", "lname", "phone",
                "depart", "room");

@field_desc = ("First Name", "Last Name",
               "Phone #", "Department", "Room");

@select_list = @field_names;
```

NOTE If you customize this program, you may want to use a different select list from the field names. For example, you may want to retrieve fewer fields than are queried on with a where clause. Each employee record may include a note, which may be very long. In that case, you may want to query on that note but not display the note as part of the returned fields. The default is to display all the fields that we have the capability of querying on.

For each format variable, we need to make a field tag. The $header_format tag needs table header tags (<TH>) for each field, and the $format_table needs normal table column tags for each field (<TD>). The %s that is in the middle of each table column acts as a placeholder. Later, Perl's `printf` function will be used to map the column values to the list of `%s` symbols.

```
foreach (@field_desc)
{
$format_table .= "<TD>%s</TD>";
$header_format .= "<TH>%s</TH>";
}
```

After the `foreach` loop, the formats are ended with a table row closure (`</TR>`).

```
$format_table .= "</TR>";
$header_format .= "</TR>";
```

`@where_list` is an array that contains the expressions used by the `where` part of the SQL code as criteria to determine which address rows to return.

```
@where_list = ();
```

Each field in the `@field_names` array is cycled through, and the value is culled from the form variable corresponding to that field. The value is converted to lowercase, because the `where` clause compares it to the lowercased value of each field in each row.

```
foreach $field (@field_names)
{
    $value = $in{"$field"};
    $value =~ tr/A-Z/a-z/; # Force to lower case
    if ($value ne "")
    {
```

If `$exactmatch` is `on` and if a value exists for the field, a search expression is generated in the form of `lower(column_name) = 'value_to_search_for'`.

```
        if ($exactmatch eq "on") {
          push(@where_list,
              qq!lower($field) = ! .
              qq!"$value"!);
```

NOTE   The qq! is a Perl trick that allows us to change the double-quotation delimiter in a print statement. Normally, double quotations (") are used to delimit the characters in a print statement. However, by replacing the first quotation mark with two q's followed by another character, that final character becomes the new print statement delimiter. Thus, qq! tells Perl to use the ! character to delimit the string. This is explained in Appendix A.

If $exactmatch is not on, the expression takes the same form except that the value to search for has percent (%) symbols appended to the beginning and end of the value. The % symbol is roughly equivalent to asterisks (*) in normal UNIX regular expression matching. When the % symbol is used, the Sybase search will find instances of the value as part of a larger word; the matches found need not be exactly equal to the search value.

```
        } else {
                push(@where_list,
                qq!lower($field) like ! .
                qq!"%$value%"!);
        }
    }
}
```

Now that the program has the list of expressions to search on, the SQL code for the where statement is generated. To the word where, we append the list of expressions separated by and. Perl's join operator takes every expression in @where_list and makes it into one big string separated by the " and\n" string.

```
$where_clause = "";
if (@where_list) {
$where_clause =  "where\n" . join(" and\n",
    @where_list);
}
```

As an example, if exact match was not on and the user was querying for the address information of someone named John Doe, the $where clause would look like the following:

```
where
lower(fname) like "%john%" and
lower(lname) like "%doe%"
```

A `select` statement is generated using the same `join` operator to combine all the elements in the `@select_list` array. The `$sql` variable is used to generate the SQL statement sent to the database.

The `select` list is separated by pipe symbols in the resulting `select` statement. We do this because when ISQL outputs the results, it will be easier to pick individual field values when we know that pipes separate them.

```
$sql = "select\n" .
    join (qq! + "\|",\n"\|" +!,
        @select_list);
```

Next, the `from` clause (indicating the database name and table name we are selecting from) is appended to the `$sql` variable. The `$where_clause` is also appended to `$sql`. Finally, the `"order by 1,2"` in the `$sql` variable tells the database to return the results ordered by columns 1 and 2, which are first name and last name, respectively.

```
$sql .= "\nfrom $db_name..address\n";
$sql .= "\n$where_clause\n";
$sql .= "order by 1, 2";
```

In the search for John Doe, `$sql` would now contain the SQL statement shown next. Notice the pipe characters that we discussed. We use two periods between the database name and the table name in the `from` clause, the standard Sybase convention of referring to tables with an absolute database path.

```
select
fname + "|",
"|" +lname + "|",
"|" +phone + "|",
"|" +depart + "|",
"|" +room
from infobase..address
where
```

```
lower(fname) like lower("%john%") and
lower(lname) like lower("%doe%")
order by 1, 2
```

The initial table header is printed. The table header includes the $header_format command, which is printed using the @field_desc array to supply values to fill in the %s characters. The printf statement performs the magic of mapping each element of the @field_desc array to each %s character in the $header_format variable. printf basically performs a search on all %s characters in the string and then replaces them one by one with the elements in the @field_desc array.

```
# Print the header for the columns to be returned
    print "<TABLE BORDER>\n";
    printf $header_format . "\n", @field_desc;
```

A file is generated that contains the SQL code that will be processed by ISQL. $file is set to the current process ID plus an **.sql** extension. The first line of the file is the logon password. This is done because ISQL expects a password to be entered right away that matches the username entered as a command-line parameter. Finally, the $sql code variable and a go command to run the $sql are added to the file. Then the file is closed.

```
$file = "$$.sql";
open (QUERYFILE, ">$file");
print QUERYFILE "$db_password\n";
print QUERYFILE "$sql\n";
print QUERYFILE "go\n";
close (QUERYFILE);
```

Sybase expects the environmental variables of SYBASE and DSQUERY to be set to the directory path of Sybase and the server name respectively. These values are in the **address.setup** file. The command that is used for passing the query is the ISQL program located in the **bin** directory under the path specified by the $db_dir variable.

Next, the program stored in the $command variable is opened using the special pipe method. Normally, opening a filename in Perl actually opens the file. However, if we append a pipe symbol to the end of the filename,

Perl knows to execute the program instead. Then the output from the running program is sent back as file data to the ISQLPIPE file handle. In this case, the program expects the returned data to be the SQL results. ISQL uses the -U parameter to indicate the username of the user who is logging on, and the -w parameter to specify the width of each returned line (up to 255 characters). $file is provided as input to ISQL.

```
$ENV{"SYBASE"} = "$db_dir";
$ENV{"DSQUERY"} = "$db_server";
$command = "$db_dir/bin/isql";
open (ISQLPIPE,
      "$command -U$db_user -w255 <$file |");
```

The $rowcount is set to zero to start. Then the ISQLPIPE file handle is read line by line to get the results of the SQL query. For each line that contains pipes, $rowcount is incremented. Remember that the program has previously embedded pipe symbols as part of the select clause of the SQL code sent to the database server. Again, as with the search for John Doe, the sample output from ISQL appears as follows:

```
Password:


 ____     ____       _____      _____     __
 John|    |Doe|      |555-1212|    |Accounting|  |1D
```

In the sample output, the Password: line is a password prompt that ISQL expects before logging in to the database server. The rest of the lines consist of the SQL query result.

If the line contains a pipe symbol, further processing is done in the following code. In the example, only the line with John Doe's address information contains pipes.

```
$rowcount = 0;
 while (<ISQLPIPE>) {
    if ($_ =~ /\|/) {
```

The regular expressions before $rowcount is incremented serve to eliminate the spaces between the pipe symbols. That way, the values that are parsed out consist only of the values rather than values that are padded with spaces.

```
s/\| *\|/\|\|/g; # Clear away excessive spaces
                  # between pipes
    s/^ *//;     # Clear away space at the beginning
                 # of the select
```

`$rowcount` is incremented, because we have just read a line from the database.

```
$rowcount++;
```

We set `@field_values` to the resulting values by `split`ting the current line by its pipe symbols. Because each field begins and ends with a pipe symbol, fields are separated here using two consecutive pipe symbols. This is why the `split` command takes two pipe symbols instead of one. Also, the regular expressions and the `split` command are operating from the default Perl `$_` variable. This is why those commands do not explicitly state a variable name.

```
    @field_values = split(/\|\|/);
```

Finally, Perl's `printf` function is used to print the table rows. `Printf` takes all the elements in the `@field_values` list and maps them to the `%s` symbols previously defined in the `$format_table` string.

```
        printf($format_table, @field_values);
    } # End of IF
} # End of While
```

Now the program closes the pipe to the ISQL program and removes the file containing the generated SQL code using the `unlink` command. Then the closure for the table (`</TABLE>`) is printed.

```
close (ISQLPIPE);
unlink ("$file");

print "</TABLE><P>\n";
```

If $rowcount has not been incremented, the script returns a message telling the user that the query did not return any results.

```
if ($rowcount == 0) {
    print "<STRONG><P> No Records Found" .
          " That Matched Your Search" .
          " \nCriteria </STRONG>";
}
```

Finally, the program ends by printing the HTML footer using the HERE DOCUMENT method.

```
print <<__END_OF_FOOTER__;
</BODY>
</HTML>
__END_OF_FOOTER__
```

addr_maint.cgi

addr_maint.cgi outputs an HTML form that allows a user to choose which maintenance operation to perform. Figure 15.3 showed an example of this. No other libraries are called. Because extensive form processing is not needed, **cgi-lib.pl** is not required.

The script first prints the header that tells the Web server that this CGI program is printing HTML code.

```
#!/usr/local/bin/perl
print "Content-type: text/html\n\n";
```

Then the HERE DOCUMENT method is used to print the HTML page.

```
print <<__END_OF_HTML__;
<HTML><HEAD><TITLE>Address Book Maintenance
</TITLE></HEAD>

<BODY BGCOLOR="FFFFFF">
<CENTER>
<H1>Address Book Maintenance</H1>
<HR>
<P>
```

```
<FORM ACTION=addr_maint_search.cgi METHOD=POST>
<input type=submit
name=new_address_op value="New Address">
<input type=submit
name=mod_address_op value="Modify Address">
<input type=submit
name=del_address_op value="Delete Address">
</form>
</center>
<HR>
</BODY></HTML>
__END_OF_HTML__
```

The HTML code uses an interesting technique that will be used throughout our discussion of the address book maintenance scripts. Several different <INPUT TYPE=SUBMIT> HTML buttons make up the form. Each button has a different name and value. The submit buttons have different names so that when the user clicks on one of them, only the one that was clicked will have its value transferred to that form variable name for the subsequent CGI script to process. This technique allows us to provide a kind of menu to the user. Users can press any desired button, and the next CGI script will process the correct choice.

NOTE Another interesting trick is to place different forms in the same HTML page. If you ever use this technique, though, remember that information that is input into one form on an HTML page cannot be submitted with information on another form on that same page.

addr_maint_search.cgi

addr_maint_search.cgi is called from the HTML form that is output by **addr_maint.cgi**. It takes the input from the **addr_maint.cgi** form and sends a different HTML form based on whether the operation specified is an addition, deletion, or modification to the address book table.

The first step is to declare a path to the directory where libraries will be defined. By default, the library files are located in the current directory, as is indicated by the "." that $lib is set to. Then **cgi-lib.pl** is required for processing the previous form.

```
#!/usr/local/bin/perl

$lib = ".";
require "$lib/cgi-lib.pl";
```

The standard CGI HTTP header is printed using the PrintHeader function. Then the form variables are read into the %in associative array using ReadParse.

```
print &PrintHeader;
&ReadParse;
```

Next, the script determines which buttons were pressed. If a button is pressed, there will be a value for it. If the button was not pressed, the name of the button will not have a value.

```
$new_address_op = $in{'new_address_op'};
$mod_address_op = $in{'mod_address_op'};
$del_address_op = $in{'del_address_op'};
```

$address_op is set up as a header title based on the value of the button that was pressed. Because any one of the three buttons may have been pressed, all three variables are checked for a value to impart to $address_op.

```
$address_op = $new_address_op;
if ($address_op eq "") {
    $address_op = $mod_address_op;
}
if ($address_op eq "") {
    $address_op = $del_address_op;
}
```

The HTML header is then printed.

```
print <<__HTMLHEADER__;
<HTML><HEAD>
<TITLE>Address Book Maintenance</TITLE>
</HEAD>
<BODY BGCOLOR="FFFFFF">
<H1>$address_op</H1>
<HR>
<P>
```

```
<FORM ACTION=addr_maint_change.cgi METHOD=POST>
__HTMLHEADER__
```

Information is printed based on what was entered on the previous form. The script checks the $new_address_op, $mod_address_op, and $del_address_op variables for a value to determine which operation the client has requested. Appropriate instructions are given for the different operations.

The new address operation results in HTML that tells the user to enter a new address. Figure 15.7 shows an example of the add address book entry screen. The modify and delete operations result in HTML code that tells the user to enter criteria to search for a list of users to modify or delete. Figure 15.8 shows an example of a modification search screen.

```
if ($new_address_op ne "") {
print "Enter The New Information In The Form Below\n";
} elsif ($mod_address_op ne "") {
print "Enter Criteria To Query On In The Form Below.  You will then be
able to choose entries to modify from the resulting list.\n";
} else {
print "Enter Criteria To Query On In The Form Below.  You will then be
able to choose entries to delete from the resulting list.\n" }
```

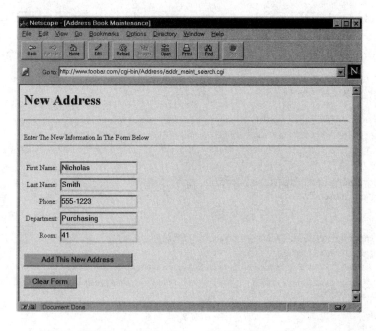

Figure 15.7 An example of the add address book entry screen.

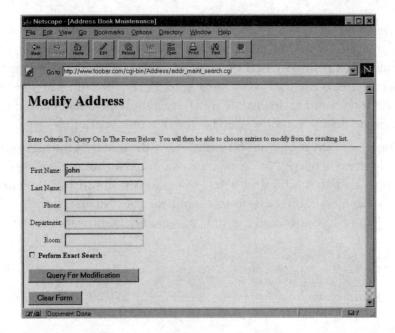

Figure 15.8 Example of a search screen for modifying the address book.

The __HTMLMIDDLE__ HERE DOCUMENT is used to print the HTML code related to a form where the user can enter search criteria or new address book information depending on the context this script is running in.

```
print <<__HTMLMIDDLE__;
<HR>
<P>

<TABLE>
<tr>
<td align=right>First Name:</td>
<td><input name=fname></td>
</tr>
<tr>
<td align=right>Last Name:</td>
<td><input name=lname></td>
</tr>
<tr>
<td align=right>Phone:</td>
<td><input name=phone></td>
</tr>
```

```
<tr>
<td align=right>Department:</td>
<td><input name=depart></td>
</tr>
<tr>
<td align=right>Room:</td>
<td><input name=room></td>
</tr>
</TABLE>


__HTMLMIDDLE__
```

Based on the operation being performed, different `<INPUT TYPE=SUBMIT>`
HTML buttons will be generated. Like the buttons printed on the previous HTML form, they have names that are appropriate to the operation
being performed. In addition, for the modify and delete search operations, an input variable for choosing an exact match search is output.

```
# Use different buttons for different operations
# just as before
if ($new_address_op ne "") {
    print "<p><input type=submit " .
        "name=new_address_op" .
    " value=\"Add This New Address\"><p>\n"; }
elsif ($mod_address_op ne "") {
    print "<INPUT TYPE=checkbox " .
        "NAME=exactsearch><STRONG>" .
    "Perform Exact Search</STRONG>";
    print "<p><input type=submit " .
        "name=mod_address_op" .
    " value=\"Query For Modification\"><p>\n"; }
else {
    print "<INPUT TYPE=checkbox " .
        "NAME=exactsearch><STRONG>" .
    "Perform Exact Search</STRONG>";
    print "<p><input type=submit " .
        "name=del_address_op" .
    " value=\"Query For List To Delete\"><p>\n"; }
```

The HTML footer is printed using the HERE DOCUMENT method, which ends
this script.

```
print <<__HTMLFOOTER__;
<input type=reset value="Clear Form">
</FORM>
```

```
</BODY></HTML>
__HTMLFOOTER__
```

addr_maint_change.cgi

addr_maint_change.cgi takes the client-defined input from the HTML form generated by **addr_maint_search.cgi** and performs operations based on it. If the operation from the previous screen was an addition, this script performs the insertion into the database, ending the maintenance process. If the operation is a deletion or modification, it prints a list of users that satisfies the previous screen's search criteria. Each returned row has a radio button to allow the user to choose the address book entry on which to perform the operation. The modify operation has additional data entry fields to allow the user to enter the new data. Figure 15.9 displays a sample modification screen. If the operation is not an addition, the HTML form is submitted to **addr_maint_dofinal** for the final change or deletion processing.

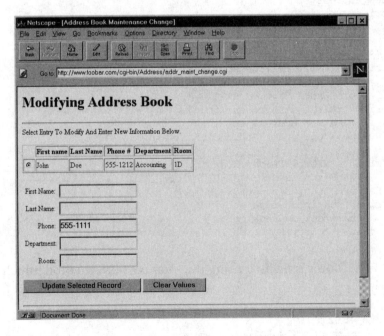

Figure 15.9 *An example of the address book modification screen.*

The first step is to declare a path to the directory where libraries will be defined. Then **cgi-lib.pl** is loaded for processing the incoming form data. The **address.setup** file is also loaded.

```
#!/usr/local/bin/perl
$lib = ".";
require "$lib/cgi-lib.pl";

require "address.setup";
```

The header to tell the Web server that HTML code is about to be printed is output using the `PrintHeader` function. Then the form variables are read into the `%in` associative array using `ReadParse`.

```
# Prints out the magic HTML Header
print &PrintHeader;

&ReadParse;
```

Next, the script determines which buttons were pressed. If a button is pressed, there will be a value for it. If the button was not pressed, the name of the button will not have a value. `$address_op` is set up as a header title based on the value of the button that was pressed. Because any one of the three buttons could have been pressed, all three variables are checked for a value to impart to `$address_op`.

```
$new_address_op = $in{'new_address_op'};
$mod_address_op = $in{'mod_address_op'};
$del_address_op = $in{'del_address_op'};

$address_op = $new_address_op;
if ($address_op eq "") {
    $address_op = $mod_address_op;
}
if ($address_op eq "") {
    $address_op = $del_address_op;
}
```

Now the HTML header is printed using the HERE DOCUMENT method.

```
print <<__HTMLHEADER__;
<HTML><HEAD>
<TITLE>Address Book Maintenance Change</TITLE>
</HEAD>
<BODY BGCOLOR="FFFFFF">
<FORM ACTION=addr_maint_dofinal.cgi METHOD=POST>
__HTMLHEADER__
```

Information is printed based on what was entered on the previous form. The script checks the $new_address_op, $mod_address_op, and $del_address_op variables for a value to determine which operation is being performed. $op is also set to be equal to a three-letter abbreviation of the current operation. Different instructions are given for the different operations.

The new address operation results in HTML telling the user that the address was inserted, and SQL code for inserting gets sent to the database. The modification and deletion operations result in SQL code sent to the server asking for a list of rows that satisfy the previously entered criteria. The modification operation also adds data entry fields for each address book field, allowing the user to enter the modified information. Recall that Figure 15.9 showed an example of this.

```
if ($new_address_op ne "") {
    $op = "new";
    $head = "Inserting New Address";
} elsif ($mod_address_op ne "") {
    $op = "mod";
    $head = "Modifying Address Book";
} else {
    $op = "del";
    $head = "Deleting From Address Book";
}

print "<H1>$head</H1>\n<HR>";
```

Just as in the other scripts, an array of field names is used to match the form variables to the database fields.

The @field_names array must have the field names spelled exactly as they are labeled in the address table and the previous HTML input form.

NOTE

```
@field_names = ("fname", "lname", "phone",
                "depart", "room");
```

The following section processes the addition operation, assuming that the `$op` variable was set to `new` as a result of addition being chosen on the previous HTML form. A few variables are set up in preparation for this processing. `$filledin` is set to 1. If any variables are left out, `$filledin` indicates this and refuses to enter the address. `$insertlist` and `$valuelist` contain the list of field names and values, respectively, to insert.

```
if ($op eq "new") {

$filledin = 1;

$insertlist = "";
$valuelist = "";
```

The array of field names is iterated. The `$insertlist` is generated from the field names, and the `$valuelist` is generated through the values that correspond to the form variables on the previous HTML form. If any value does not exist in the form variables, `$filledin` is set to zero.

```
foreach $n (@field_names)
{
$value= $in{$n};
     if ($value ne "")
     {
     $valuelist = $valuelist . ",\"$value\"";
     $insertlist = $insertlist . "," . $n ;
     }
     else
     {
     $filledin = 0;
     }
}
```

`$insertlist` and `$valuelist` are then surrounded by parentheses. Also, the first character of both variables is stripped off using the `substr` command, because the addition of the values separated the value and insert list with commas at the beginning of each item and the first comma needs to be removed. Strings and arrays in Perl begin counting at zero, so using an index of 1 with the `substr` command returns the string starting at the second character.

```
$insertlist = "(" . substr($insertlist,1) . ")";
$valuelist = "(" . substr($valuelist,1) . ")";
```

If the `$filledin` flag is equal to zero, an error message is displayed and the program exits.

```
if ($filledin == 0) {
print "<STRONG> Some Fields Were Not " .
    "Entered! Address" .
" Not Inserted. </STRONG>";
exit;
}
else
{
```

The `$sql` code variable is generated as an insert statement referencing the database name stored in `$db_name` and the address table in that database. The `$insertlist` of field names is appended to `$sql` along with the values in `$valuelist`.

```
$sql = "insert $db_name..address\n" .
    $insertlist .
        "\nvalues\n" . $valuelist;
```

If the address of John Doe was inserted and the location was Accounting with a phone number of 555-1222 in room 12B, then `$sql` would contain the following SQL code:

```
insert infobase..address
(fname,lname,phone,depart,room)
values
("John","Doe","555-1222","Accounting","12B")
```

A file is generated that contains the SQL code to be processed by the ISQL program. `$file` is set to the current process ID plus an **.sql** extension. The first line of the file is the logon password. ISQL expects a password to be entered right away that matches the username entered as a command-line parameter. Finally, the $sql code variable and a go command to run the $sql are added to the file. Then the file is closed.

```
$file = "$$.sql";
open (QUERYFILE, ">$file");
print QUERYFILE "$db_password\n";
print QUERYFILE "$sql\n";
print QUERYFILE "go\n";
close (QUERYFILE);
```

Sybase expects the environmental variables SYBASE and DSQUERY to be set to the directory path of Sybase and the server name, respectively. These values are in **address.setup**. The command that is used for passing the query is the ISQL program located in the **bin** directory under the path specified by the $db_dir variable.

Next, the program stored in the $command variable is opened using the special pipe method. Normally, opening a filename in Perl opens the file. However, if we append a pipe symbol to the end of the filename, Perl knows to execute the program instead. Then the output from the running program is sent back as file data to the ISQLPIPE file handle. In this case, the program expects the returned data to be the SQL results. ISQL uses the -U parameter to indicate the username of the user who is logging on, and the -w parameter to specify the width of each returned line (up to 255 characters). $file is provided as input to ISQL.

The script then takes the pipe and reads all the results into the @rows array. This array is defined for further trouble-shooting and is not actually used. If you wanted to see the output of the ISQL program, you could print the contents of the @rows array. Because the SQL code being passed to ISQL is insert code, we do not expect any query rows to be returned.

If the insertion is successful, @rows will contain the following information:

```
Password:
 (1 row affected)
```

Password: is the password prompt that ISQL is expecting. And (1 row affected) means that the insertion statement created one row.

Finally, the ISQLPIPE file handle is closed and the query file containing the SQL code is removed using the unlink command. A message is printed telling users that the address was inserted.

```
        $ENV{"SYBASE"} = "$db_dir";
        $ENV{"DSQUERY"} = "$db_server";
        $command = "$db_dir/bin/isql";
        open (ISQLPIPE,
           "$command -U$db_user -w255 <$file |");
        @rows = <ISQLPIPE>;
        close(ISQLPIPE);
    unlink($file);
        print "<STRONG> Address Was Inserted " .
          "Successfully! </STRONG>";
    }
```

The rest of the program is dedicated to the modification and deletion operations. For a modification, users are told to select an entry to modify from a generated list and then enter to the new information in data entry fields provided below the list. For a deletion, they are told to select a row to delete. Figure 15.10 is an example of the deletion screen.

```
} elsif ($op eq "mod") {
    print "Select Entry To Modify And Enter " .
    "New Information Below.\n";
} else {
print "Select Entry To Delete.\n" }

print "<P>";
```

If the operation is not an addition, the where clause needs to be generated. Then the SQL can be sent to the database server to get a list of addresses to choose from for modification or deletion.

$where_clause is a list of the expressions used by the where part of the SQL code as criteria to determine which address rows to return. Each field in the @field_names array is cycled through. The value is culled from the form variable corresponding to those fields.

```
if ($op ne "new") {
$where_clause = "";
$exactsearch = $in{"exactsearch"};
```

```
foreach $n (@field_names)
{
    $value = $in{"$n"};
    if ($value ne "")
    {
```

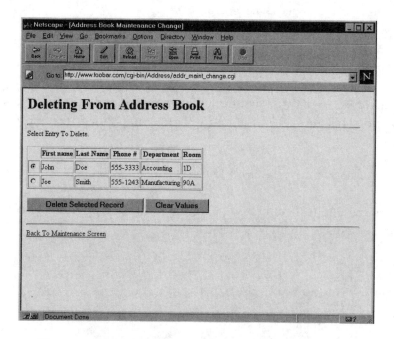

Figure 15.10 *An example of the delete address book entry screen.*

If $exactmatch is not on, the expression takes the same form except that percent (%) symbols are appended to the beginning and end of the search value. The % symbol is roughly equivalent to an asterisk (*) in normal UNIX regular expression matching. When the % symbol is used, the Sybase search will find instances of the value as part of a larger word; the matches found need not be exactly equal to the search value. The lowercase keyword is used to make sure that the SQL query search is case-insensitive.

```
    if ($exactsearch ne "on")
    {
$where_clause = qq!$where_clause and ! .
    qq!lower($n) like lower("%$value%")!;
    }
```

If $exactmatch is on and if a value exists for the field, a search expression is generated in the form of lower(column_name) = lower('value_to_search_for').

```
        else
        {
        $where_clause = qq!$where_clause and ! .
            qq!lower($n) = lower("$value")!;
        }
        }
}
```

The $where_clause has the first five characters stripped off using the substr command. This gets rid of the extra " and " appended in the preceding routine.

```
$where_clause = substr($where_clause,5);
```

A select statement is generated using the same join operator to combine all the elements in the @field_names array.

```
$sql = "select ";
$sql .= join(qq! + "\|","\|" + !,
        @field_names) . qq! + "\|","\|" +!;
$sql .= join(qq! + "\|","\|" + !,
        @field_names) . " \n";
```

Notice that the field names are appended twice. In the format variables used later, a duplicate set of values will be mapped to the %s symbols in the format variable. One set of values is used to display to the user, and the other set is used to compose the value of the radio button that the users click to select a row.

The select list is separated by pipe symbols in the resulting select statement. When ISQL outputs the results, it will be easier to pick individual field values when we know that pipes separate them.

Next, the from clause (indicating the database name and table name we are selecting from) is appended to the $sql variable. The $where_clause is also appended to $sql.

```
$sql .= "from $db_name..address \nwhere " .
    $where_clause;
```

The header for the table is printed in preparation for the returned rows that result from the SQL code (stored in the $sql variable) being sent to the server.

```
print "<TABLE BORDER>\n";
print <<__TABLEHEADER__;
<TABLE BORDER>
<TR><TH></TH>
<TH>First name</TH>
<TH>Last Name</TH>
<TH>Phone #</TH>
<TH>Department</TH>
<TH>Room</TH>
</TR>
__TABLEHEADER__
```

As with the **addr_query_result.cgi** program, format variables are set up with %s as a placeholder for field values. The $format variable consists of a definition of the radio button used to select an item plus the display of the fields inside <TD> HTML table field tags. Because there are only five fields, a for loop from 1 to 5 generates this list of values. The definition of $format ends with table row <TR> tags at its beginning and end.

```
$format = "<TR>\n";
$format .= qq!<TD><INPUT TYPE=radio NAME=rec !;
$format .= qq!VALUE="%s|%s|%s|%s|%s"></TD>\n!;
for (1..5) {
    $format .= "<TD>%s</TD>";
}
$format .= "\n";

$format = "<TR>" . $format . "</TR>\n";
```

A file is generated that contains the SQL code to be processed by ISQL. $file is set to the current process ID plus an **.sql** extension. The first line of the file is the logon password. ISQL expects a password to be entered right away that matches the username entered as a command-line parameter. Finally, the $sql code variable and a go command to run the $sql are added to the file. Then the file is closed.

```
$file = "Temp/$$.sql";
open (QUERYFILE, ">$file");
print QUERYFILE "$db_password\n";
```

405

```
print QUERYFILE "$sql\n";
print QUERYFILE "go\n";
close (QUERYFILE);
```

The next few lines of code, as before, set up the call to the database server command-line utility ISQL.

```
$ENV{"SYBASE"} = "$db_dir";
$ENV{"DSQUERY"} = "$db_server";
$command = "$db_dir/bin/isql";
open (ISQLPIPE,
      "$command -U$db_user -w255 <$file |");
```

The $rowcount is set to zero to start. Then the ISQLPIPE file handle is read line by line to get the results of the SQL query. For each line that contains pipes, $rowcount is incremented. Remember, previously the program embedded pipe symbols as part of the select clause of the SQL code being sent to the database server.

Before $rowcount is incremented, the regular expressions serve to eliminate the spaces between the pipe symbols. That way, the values that are parsed out will consist only of the values rather than values that are padded with spaces. We set @field_values to the resulting values by splitting the current line by its pipe symbols. Because each field begins and ends with a pipe symbol, fields are separated here using two pipe symbols. This is why the split command takes two pipe symbols instead of one. Also, the regular expressions and the split command are operating from the default Perl $_ variable. This is why those commands do not explicitly state a variable name.

```
$rowcount = 0;
while (<ISQLPIPE>) {
    if ($_ =~ /\|/) {
        s/\| *\|/\|\|/g;
        s/^ *//;
        $rowcount++;
        @field_values = split(/\|\|/);
```

Finally, Perl's printf function is used to print the table rows. Printf takes all the elements in the @field_values list and maps them to the %s symbols previously defined in the $format string.

```
   printf ($format, @field_values);
   } # End of if
} # End of while
```

Now the program closes the pipe to the ISQL program and removes the file containing the generated SQL code using the unlink command. Then the closure for the table (</TABLE>) is printed.

```
close (ISQLPIPE);
unlink ("$file");


print "</TABLE><P>\n";
} #End of IF OP is not insert a new record
```

If the operation is a modification, then a table of <INPUT> fields to modify is displayed. The user can then enter new information into any field related to the chosen row in the list of address book entries.

```
if ($op eq "mod")
{
print <<__ENDOFTABLE__;
<TABLE>
<tr>
<td align=right>First Name:</td>
<td><input name=fname></td>
</tr>
<tr>
<td align=right>Last Name:</td>
<td><input name=lname></td>
</tr>
<tr>
<td align=right>Phone:</td>
<td><input name=phone></td>
</tr>
<tr>
<td align=right>Department:</td>
<td><input name=depart></td>
</tr>
<tr>
<td align=right>Room:</td>
<td><input name=room></td>
</tr>
</TABLE>
__ENDOFTABLE__


} # End of IF op eq mod
```

Finally, the HTML footer is printed along with submit buttons appropriate to the operation being performed. If the operation is a modification, a submit button with the value **Update Selected Record** is displayed. If the operation is a deletion, a button that states **Delete Selected Record** is shown. No submit buttons are displayed for the addition operation; this script has already performed the addition, and there is no further CGI script to submit information to.

The modification and deletion operations have a **Clear Values** reset button. In addition, the footer contains a reference to the main address maintenance script.

```
if ($op eq "mod") {
    print "<p><input type=submit " .
        "name=mod_address_op" .
        " value=\"Update Selected Record\">\n";
} elsif ($op eq "del") {
    print "<p><input type=submit " .
        "name=del_address_op" .
        " value=\"Delete Selected Record\">\n";
}

if (($op eq "mod") || ($op eq "del")) {
    print qq!<input type=reset ! .
        qq!value="Clear Values"><p>!; }

# print the HTML footer.
print <<__HTMLFOOTER__;
<HR>
<A HREF=addr_maint.cgi>
Back To Maintenance Screen</A>
<P>
</FORM>
</BODY></HTML>
__HTMLFOOTER__
```

addr_maint_dofinal.cgi

addr_maint_dofinal.cgi is the final script that is called in the maintenance part of this application for modifications and deletions to the database. If the operation being performed is deletion, simple delete SQL code is generated. If the operation is modification, update SQL code is generated.

The following code declares the path to the shared library files for the application. **cgi-lib.pl** is loaded from the library area. By default, this is the current directory.

```
$lib = ".";
require "$lib/cgi-lib.pl";
```

Then the **address.setup** configuration parameters are read into the script. PrintHeader is called to tell the Web server that the CGI program is outputting HTML. ReadParse reads the incoming form variables, using the %in associative array to store the values.

```
require "address.setup";
print &PrintHeader;

&ReadParse;
```

If the user pressed the button on the HTML form corresponding to the <INPUT> field name mod_address_op, $mod_address_op contains a value. Similarly, $del_address_op will have a value if the user pressed the button corresponding to the deletion of the address book row.

```
$mod_address_op = $in{'mod_address_op'};
$del_address_op = $in{'del_address_op'};
```

The HTML header is printed using the HERE DOCUMENT method. It informs the user that an update to the database is about to occur.

```
print <<__HTMLHEADER__;
<HTML><HEAD>
<TITLE>Address Book Final Update</TITLE>
</HEAD>
<BODY BGCOLOR="FFFFFF">
__HTMLHEADER__
```

If $mod_address_op contains a value, then $op is set to mod for modification and the $head variable is set to a message indicating that we are updating an entry in the address book. Otherwise, the script assumes that the user is performing a deletion. In this case, $op is set to del and $head is set to a message stating that an entry is being deleted from the address book. The header is then printed as HTML code.

```
if ($mod_address_op ne "") {
    $op = "mod";
    $head = "Updating Entry In Address Book";
} else {
      $op = "del";
    $head = "Deleting From Address Book";
}

print "<H1>$head</H1>\n<HR>";
```

As in **addr_query_result.cgi**, the `@field_names` array contains a list of the field names for the address table as it exists on the database server. These field names must also match the field names in the various HTML forms that process the address book.

```
@field_names = ("fname", "lname", "phone",
                "depart", "room");
```

If the operation is a modification, the update query is generated. In preparation for this, two variables are set up. `$filledin` keeps track of whether any fields were entered for updating. `$updatelist` keeps track of the expression used to update the table.

The `@field_names` array is iterated. If a field has a value from the previous form, `$updatelist` is added to and the `$filledin` variable is set to 1, indicating that at least one field was entered. When the iteration is complete, `$updatelist` is chopped to get rid of the last comma in the values that are entered for `$updatelist`.

Next, if the `$filledin` variable is still zero, the program knows that none of the fields had a value entered into it for updating. In this case, the program prints an error and the `$erroroccurred` flag is set to 1, preventing the update query from being sent to ISQL later.

```
if ($op eq "mod") {

$filledin = 0;
$updatelist = "";
```

```
foreach $n (@field_names)
{
$value= $in{"$n"};
    if ($value ne "")
    {
    $updatelist .= qq!$n = "$value",!;
    $filledin = 1;
    }
}
# Get rid of the last comma from the
# appending of the values above
chop($updatelist);

    if ($filledin == 0) {
    print "<STRONG> No Fields Were Entered!" .
        " Address" .
    " Not Updated. </STRONG><p>";
    $erroroccured = 1;
    }

} # end of if operator is update
```

The value in the rec form variable contains the list of values that are used as criteria to determine which row to update or delete. Remember that the rec form variable is a radio button that the client uses to choose the row to delete or update. The value of the rec form variable is a pipe-delimited set of values for the various database fields that we filled in previously using printf with an extra set of %s symbols for the radio button definition.

The value list is then split via the pipes into an @value_list array. If the @value_list is not generated, an error message is sent and the $erroroccured flag is set to 1.

```
$value = $in{"rec"};

@value_list = split(/\|/,$value);

if (@value_list == 0)
{
print "<STRONG> No Record Was Selected! " .
    "</STRONG><p>";

$erroroccured = 1;
}
```

Next, the $where_clause is generated. In this program, there are five fields in the @field_names array. The script uses a for loop to process these fields from element number zero through 4. Remember that arrays start counting at zero. The where clause is generated by taking the field name values and matching them to the values in the rec form variable.

```
$where_clause = "";
# Make the where clause based on the number of fields
for (0..4)
{
    $value = $value_list[$_];
    $key = $field_names[$_];
    $where_clause =
        qq!$where_clause and $key = "$value"!;
}
```

At the end of the where clause generation, an extra " and " exists in the $where_clause variable. This is stripped off using the substr operator.

```
$where_clause = substr($where_clause,5);
```

If the operation is a mod for modification, the $sql code variable is set to an update clause referencing the database name in $db_name and the address table. The $updatelist is also appended to set the values in the update statement.

If the operation is not a mod, the script assumes that a deletion is occurring and makes $sql equal to a delete clause, referencing the database name in $db_name and the address table in that database.

To $sql, we append the where clause, restricting which row will be updated or deleted based on the radio button that the user selected on the previous HTML form.

```
if ($op eq "mod") {
$sql = "update $db_name..address\n set " .
        $updatelist . "\n ";
} else {
$sql = "delete $db_name..address ";
}

$sql .= "where $where_clause\n";
```

If no errors have occurred, the program will generate the SQL code file. The filename is specified as the current process ID with an **.sql** extension. This arrangement makes the file unique in case other instances of this script are running at the same time.

```
if ($erroroccured == 0) {
        $file = "Temp/$$.sql";
        open (QUERYFILE, ">$file");
```

The first line of the file is the logon password. ISQL expects a password to be entered right away that matches the username entered as a command-line parameter. Finally, the $sql code variable and a go command to run the $sql are added to the file. Then the file is closed.

```
        print QUERYFILE "$db_password\n";
        print QUERYFILE "$sql\n";
        print QUERYFILE "go\n";
        close (QUERYFILE);
```

The following block of code has been used before (in **addr_maint_ change.cgi**) to insert a new record. The discussion of that script explains in detail why the code is used.

```
        $ENV{"SYBASE"} = "$db_dir";
        $ENV{"DSQUERY"} = "$db_server";
        $command = "$db_dir/bin/isql";
        open (ISQLPIPE,
                @rows = <ISQLPIPE>;
        close(ISQLPIPE);
        unlink($file);
}
```

Finally, the script prints the HTML footer. A reference to the main address book maintenance script is printed as part of the footer.

```
print <<__HTMLFOOTER__;

<A HREF=addr_maint.cgi>
Back To Maintenance Screen</A>
<P>
</BODY></HTML>
__HTMLFOOTER__
```

CHAPTER 16

Keyword Searching

OVERVIEW

When a Web site starts to grow beyond a couple of pages, it can be time-consuming for visitors to find what they are looking for. As more Web pages are connected to one another via hypertext links, the resulting spaghetti-like relationship only exacerbates the complexity.

Although some Web sites allow a browser to find pages by keyword, these large search databases typically point you only to a particular page on a particular site rather than all the pages on the site that match the keyword. Furthermore, the big Internet search engines do not necessarily have up-to-date references to all the pages at your site.

Having a keyword search engine installed on your Web site solves these problems. First, it provides a quick way for people to find the pages they are looking for. Additionally, because the script is searching the actual pages on the Web site, the results of the search are always up-to-date.

The main interface to the keyword search engine allows you to search on any number of keywords. By default, the keywords are searched as parts of larger words, or you can use an exact match search for whole words. Figure 16.1 illustrates the keyword search engine.

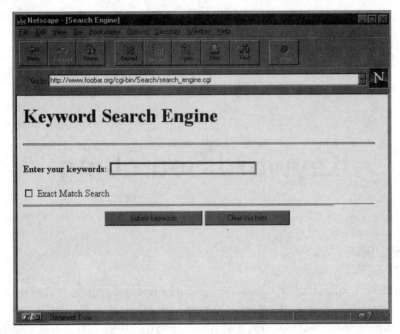

Figure 16.1 Keyword search query screen.

By default, the keyword search engine searches all files with **.HTM** or **.HTML** extensions in all directories below the document root. The search engine can also be configured to exclude certain classes of directories and files in case you want to protect certain areas of the Web server.

The results of a search include the title of a document as well as the HTML reference to that document. Figure 16.2 demonstrates the results of a search on the abbreviation "cda" as part of the Electronic Frontier Foundation (EFF) archive.

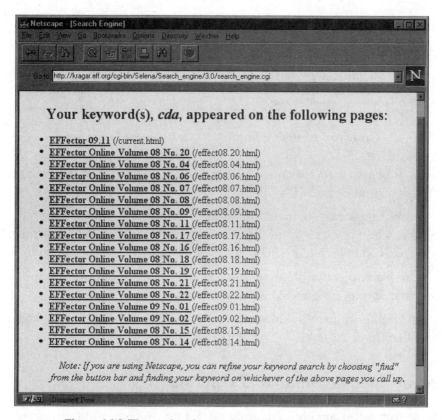

Figure 16.2 *The results of a search of "cda" in the EFF archive.*

INSTALLATION AND USAGE

The keyword search files should be installed in a directory called **Search**. Figure 16.3 shows an example of how the files should be structured and the permissions set so that they can be accessed by the Web server.

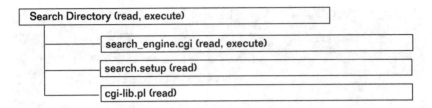

Figure 16.3 Directory structure of the search engine CGI scripts.

The root **Search** directory must have permissions that allow the Web server to read and execute files.

search_engine.cgi is the script that performs the keyword search. In addition, when it is called with no parameters, it prints an HTML form asking the user to enter a query. This file must be readable and executable.

search.setup is the file that contains all the setup options for the keyword search engine. This file must be readable.

cgi-lib.pl is an external library required by the keyword search engine. This file must be readable.

Server-Specific Setup and Options

The **search.setup** file contains the search engine configuration variables. The following is a list of these setup items.

$root_web_path is the directory path on the Web server at which you want to start your search. For example, /usr/local/etc/httpd/htdocs would make the search start in the **htdocs** directory under the **/usr/local/etc/httpd** directory. Using this configuration, the search would also continue searching all the files in the subdirectories underneath **htdocs**.

$server_url is the HTTP reference to the Web server that is serving the documents. When the searched files are found under the $root_web_path, they are appended with this server URL at the front of the path to the found file in order to provide a valid hypertext reference to search on. For example, if the $server_url were http://www.foobar.com/ and the file were found in **home/birzniek/index.html**, the full URL displayed to the user would become

```
http://www.foobar.com/home/birzniek/index.html
```

$search_results_title is the HTML title of the page that gets returned as the result of a successful keyword search.

$search_script is the name of the search engine CGI script program. This information is needed so that the HTML keyword search form printed by the script will post the keyword search information to the right script for processing. By default, the value of this parameter is search_engine.cgi.

@unwanted_files is a list of pattern-matched filenames that you wish to exclude from the search. These filenames can be pattern matches against the full local directory path, including the filename of each file being searched. Thus, you can pattern-match against directories as well as files you wish to be excluded from the search. The pattern matching is done according to normal UNIX pattern matching and regular expression rules. The example piece of code given next excludes a series of documents and a directory that you may typically not want to include. The directory (**Backup**) does not need a regular expression, because the pattern match implicitly matches zero or more characters at the beginning and end of each entry in the unwanted-files list. A regular expression is used for HTML files so that the beginning and end of the HTML filenames can be specified more explicitly while keeping the middle of the file open to any number of characters.

```
@unwanted_files = ("Error(.*)html",
            "error(.*)html",
            "Backup/",
            "feedback(.*)html");
```

The notation used in the @unwanted_files array is the standard UNIX regular expression format. The parentheses allow the results of the regular expression to be seen by the Perl script. The period (.) tells Perl to match against any one character. The asterisk (*) tells Perl to match any number of the previous characters. Because the previous character

N O T E

is a pattern-matched character that means any one character, the combination of ".*" matches zero or more of any characters. For example, if `error(.*)html` is an unwanted file, it will match any file beginning with "error" and ending with "html." This keyword would match files such as **errorlog.html** and **error_message.html**. The first two items on the sample list of unwanted files excludes any HTML file that has the word "Error" or "error" in the filename.

Typically, as a Web manager, you may have a series of common error files that tell the user that the document was not authorized or found. It does not make sense to return these documents as part of a search.

In addition, a feedback form is typically not part of the information that users are searching for. If they want to leave feedback, a hypertext link is usually available in the main home page area.

You could also use the `$unwanted_files` list to exclude directories that you may currently have protected against viewing by unauthorized people. If you regularly copy your HTML files into a **Backup** directory, you might want to exclude any HTML documents from being searched in that directory. The `Backup/` part of the example serves to do this.

WARNING

Even if your directories are restricted by a password or some other security mechanism, you should protect those directories from being searched via the **search_engine.cgi** script. Because the search engine is a CGI program, it has no idea what sort of Web server security may have been activated on the system. The search engine will search all directories indiscriminately as long as it can find new directories and files that do not match the unwanted files list.

Obviously, you do not want the results of a search to include specially protected documents. Although the user may not be able to click on the returned hypertext link, it can be a security breach for a user to know that an inaccessible document is on the server. It becomes a tempting goal for a hacker.

The following is an example usage of all the setup variables in the **search.setup** file:

```
$root_web_path = "/usr/local/etc/httpd/htdocs";
$server_url = "http://www.foobar.com";
$search_results_title = "The WWW Search Engine";
$search_script = "search_engine.cgi";
@unwanted_files = ("Error(.*)html",
                   "error(.*)html",
                   "Backup/",
                   "Images/",
                   "feedback(.*)html");
```

CUSTOMIZING THE HTML IN SEARCH.SETUP

The rest of the **search.setup** file contains subroutines that print HTML code that gives output depending on various actions of the keyword search engine. This HTML information is broken out from the main program to make it easier for you to customize the HTML to your site-specific graphics and HTML standards. If the keyword search engine gets updated, it is less likely that your GUI-specific customizations will have to be repeated, because most of the program logic resides in another file (**search_engine.cgi**).

The PrintHeaderHTML subroutine prints the HTML header for the keyword search when it is about to return results.

The code between the __HEADERHTML__ tags in the Perl script prints to the Web browser. The $search_results_title and $keywords variables print their values and are generated by **search_engine.cgi**, which uses this subroutine.

```
sub PrintHeaderHTML
{

print <<__HEADERHTML__;
<HTML><HEAD><TITLE>$search_results_title</TITLE></HEAD>
<BODY><CENTER>
<HR><P>
</CENTER>
<CENTER><H2>Your keyword(s), <I>$keywords</I>,
appeared on the following pages:</H2></CENTER><UL>
__HEADERHTML__
} # End of PrintHeaderHTML
```

421

`PrintFooterHTML` prints the HTML codes that correspond to the footer of the keyword results set. A sample of this code appears next. The actual HTML code prints between the __FOOTERHTML__ tags.

```
sub PrintFooterHTML
{
print <<__FOOTERHTML__;
<P><CENTER><I>Note: If you are using Netscape, you can
refine your keyword search by choosing "find" from the
button bar and finding your keyword on whichever of
the above pages you call up.
</I>
<P>
<CENTER>
<HR>
</CENTER> </BODY> </HTML>
__FOOTERHTML__


} # End of PrintFooterHTML
```

`PrintNoHitsBodyHTML` contains the HTML codes that print as the body between the keyword search header and footer if no matches were found.

```
sub PrintNoHitsBodyHTML
{
print <<__NOHITS__;
<P>
<CENTER>
<H2>Sorry, No Pages Were Found With Your Keyword(s).</H2>
</CENTER>
<P>
__NOHITS__


} # End of PrintNoHitsBodyHTML
```

`PrintBodyHTML` prints the HTML code related to each keyword search hit. Every time a file is found as a match to the keyword search, this routine prints another set of HTML statements related to the URL location and description of the file. When printed as HTML code, the variables $server_url, $filename, and $title are replaced with their values. The first line of the following subroutine gets information that is passed to it for that specific match. The HTML code exists between the __BODYHTML__ tags.

```
sub PrintBodyHTML
{
local($filename, $title) = @_;

print <<__BODYHTML__;
<LI>
<B>
<A HREF=
"$server_url/$filename">$title</A>
</B>
 (/$filename)<BR>
__BODYHTML__


} # End of PrintBodyHTML
```

PrintNoKeywordsHTML prints the form, asking the user to enter a keyword search term and to specify whether or not the search should be an exact match. In the following sample code, the HTML is printed between the __NOKEYHTML__ tags. If you modify the HTML code to omit the exact_match variable, the script will still work but will match the keyword on the basis of a pattern match by default; if the keyword exists as part of a larger word, the program will relay that as a positive match. The exact algorithm is discussed in the "Design Discussion" section. Basically, exact match turns on searching based on "whole word" matches only.

```
sub PrintNoKeywordHTML
{
    print <<__NOKEYHTML__;
<HTML><HEAD><TITLE>Search Engine</TITLE></HEAD>
<BODY BGCOLOR="#ffffff">
<H1>Keyword Search Engine</H1>
<HR>
<P>
<FORM METHOD="POST" ACTION="search_engine.cgi">
<B>Enter your keywords:</B>
<INPUT TYPE="text" SIZE="30" NAME="keywords"
MAXLENGTH="80">
```

```
<P>
<INPUT TYPE=checkbox NAME="exact_match"> Exact Match Search
<HR>
<CENTER>
<INPUT TYPE="SUBMIT" VALUE="Submit keywords">
<INPUT TYPE="RESET" VALUE="Clear this form">
</CENTER>
</FORM>
</BODY></HTML>


__NOKEYHTML__

} # End of PrintNoKeywordHTML
```

NOTE

The `<FORM>` tag refers to the original search engine script and accepts input for keywords as well as for the exact match checking. If you modify this form, you should make sure that the `<INPUT>` tag names `keywords` and `exact_match` have the same spelling and case as shown in the example code.

Running the Script

To use the **search_engine.cgi** program, refer to it as a hypertext reference on your site. When the search engine does not detect that it is being sent any form variables, it automatically prints a form to allow the user to enter search terms. Here is a sample URL for this script if it is installed in a **Search** subdirectory under a **cgi-bin** directory:

```
http://www.foobar.com/cgi-bin/Search/search_engine.cgi
```

DESIGN DISCUSSION

The basic algorithm of the keyword search involves first checking to see whether the script has been given a series of keyword form variables. If the script has not received the variables, the script prints an HTML form asking for keywords to search on. If there is a keyword variable, the script searches for documents down through the directory structure and returns those documents that satisfy the keyword search. A basic chart of this logic is shown in Figure 16.4.

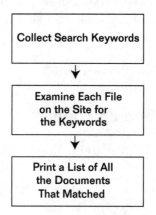

Figure 16.4 Basic flowchart for the search engine.

The first line of the following code sets up the location of the supporting files to the program. By default, `$lib` is set to the current subdirectory. Then the **cgi-lib.pl** library is loaded along with the **search.setup** variables.

```
$lib = ".";
require "$lib/cgi-lib.pl";
require "$lib/search.setup";
```

We first print the standard "Content-type: text/html\n\n" HTTP header using `PrintHeader` and then read the incoming form variables using `ReadParse`. This program uses the default associative array `%in` for storing the value of the form variables.

```
print &PrintHeader;
&ReadParse;
```

`$keywords` and `$exact_match` are set to be equal to the form variables for doing keyword search matching.

```
$keywords = $in{'keywords'};
$exact_match = $in{'exact_match'};
```

425

Once we have the `$keywords` variable, the script needs to `split` it apart so that each keyword can be searched separately within the files. We use the regular expression `/\s+/`. This expression matches on any white space (carriage returns, newlines, spaces, and so on) and `split`s the words accordingly.

```
@keyword_list = split(/\s+/,$keywords);
```

Printing the HTML Search Form

If there were no keywords to search, the HTML search form is output and the Perl program exits.

```
if ($keywords eq "") {
    &PrintNoKeywordHTML;
    exit;
} # End of if keywords
```

If there are keywords to search, the script prints the HTML header using the `PrintHeaderHTML` subroutine and moves to the heart of the keyword search engine code.

```
&PrintHeaderHTML;
```

Performing the Keyword Search

Before going further, let's step back and see how the script conducts a keyword search. The routine traverses the directory structure under `$root_web_path` and also parses the HTML files to see whether they contain the keywords we are searching for. If a match is found, the script determines the HTML titles and builds a list of successful "hits" for the client.

TRAVERSING THE DIRECTORY STRUCTURE OF YOUR WEB SITE

As the script goes down a directory looking for entries, one of those entries may be a directory. In that case, the directory is opened, and it becomes the new directory to traverse. To keep traveling down the directory tree, the script must keep track of where it has been. An array called @dirs keeps track of this by containing the names of the open directories that the script has not yet finished searching. As a directory gets opened for searching, it is appended as a new element to the end of the @dirs array.

The following code sets up the initial variables for the algorithm. The @dirs array of directories is used as a placeholder so that we can go back up the directory tree when we run out of files to read in a subdirectory. $cur_dir is the current directory number, a reference to the element in @dirs for the directory we are currently reading. The directory handles in this program are referred to as the string "DIR" followed by the current directory number indicated by "DIR$cur_dir." $number_of_hits is the current number of successful hits found in the files. The number of hits is equal to the number of files that will be returned as matches for the keyword terms.

```
$number_of_hits = 0;
$cur_dir = 0;
@dirs = ($root_web_path);
```

We initialize the process by opening the directory handle using the reference "DIR$cur_dir" and the path that has been passed to the @dirs array. When the $end_of_all_files flag is set to 1, it stops the searching routine, because it means that we have finished searching every file in every directory that we can search.

```
opendir("DIR$cur_dir", $dirs[$cur_dir]);
$end_of_all_files = 0;
```

The following while loop does not exit until the script is finished searching all the files. Within this loop is another one that goes on forever unless the last command is encountered inside. It is inside this second while loop that the directory tree for HTML documents is traversed.

```
while (!($end_of_all_files)) {
        while (1) {
```

First, the script gets from the $filename variable a reference to the next valid directory or filename. Next, $fullpath is set to the current path plus filename. Then, for the entry that was received, the routine goes through multiple cases and does different things on the basis of those cases. The five basic cases are discussed next.

```
$filename = &GetNextEntry("DIR$cur_dir",
            $dirs[$cur_dir]);
$fullpath = "$dirs[$cur_dir]/$filename";
```

Case 1: No More Files in Current Directory

In case 1, the file is NULL but there are still entries in the @dirs variable, so the program goes back up the directory tree and continues searching in a previous directory where it left off. Specifically, the program closes the current directory, subtracts 1 from the $cur_dir variable, and then issues a next command to force another iteration through the while(1) loop.

```
if (!($filename) && $cur_dir > 0) {
    closedir("DIR$cur_dir");
    $cur_dir--;
    next;
}
```

Case 2: The End of the Search

In case 2, there are no more filenames to search on but the script has been through all the previous entries in the @dirs array. Thus, the search needs to end. We close the current directory handle, set the $end_of_all_files to 1, and issue the last command to break completely out of the while(1) loop.

```
if (!($filename)) {
    closedir("DIR$cur_dir");
    $end_of_all_files = 1;
        last;
}
```

Case 3: The File Is a Directory

Case 3 discovers that the filename is actually a directory, so the script descends into the directory if it is both readable and executable. The program checks to see whether the file is a directory using the -d flag. It checks for readability and execute rights by using the -r and -x flags. Finally, the program goes down the directory tree if the filename is a directory: it increments the current directory counter, $cur_dir, by 1, pushes a new path onto the @dirs array, and opens a new directory handle. Finally, the next command is used to force the script to go back to the top of the while(1) loop.

```
if (-d $fullpath) {
    if (-r $fullpath && -x $fullpath) {
    $cur_dir++;
    $dirs[$cur_dir] = $fullpath;
    opendir("DIR$cur_dir", $dirs[$cur_dir]);
    next;
    } else {
    next;
    }
} # End of case 3 (File is a directory)
```

CASE 4: THE FILE IS "UNWANTED"

In case 4, the script checks to see whether the file about to be searched is unwanted. The program starts by setting the $unwanted_file flag to zero. Then the script performs a pattern match against each unwanted file in the @unwanted_files array to see whether the filename and path are unwanted. If they are unwanted, the $unwanted_file flag is set to 1. After all the @unwanted_files have been checked, if the $unwanted_file flag is equal to 1, the next command is issued to reiterate through the while(1) loop.

```
$unwanted_file = 0;
foreach (@unwanted_files) {
    if ($fullpath =~ /$_/) {
    $unwanted_file = 1;
    }
} # End of foreach unwanted files

if ($unwanted_file) {
    next;
} # End of Case 4 Unwanted File
```

Case 5: The File Needs to Be Searched

In the last case, the script finds that the file is a file that we want to search for keywords. The -r flag is used to check whether the file is readable; if it is, the `last` command is issued to force a break out of the `while(1)` loop. Breaking out of this loop allows the script to move on and search through the file.

```
if (-r $fullpath) {
    last;
} # Make sure the file is readable

} # End of While (1)
```

Searching the HTML File for Keywords

After the `while(1)` loop, we check again for the `$end_of_all_files` flag. If it is not equal to 1, the script can continue the file search.

```
if (!($end_of_all_files)) {
```

When we search a file, we initially set `@not_found_words` to the array of keywords we want to search. This corresponds to the idea that, initially, none of the words is found. As we later search the file and find keywords, they are deleted from the `@not_found_words` array. When this array has no elements left, we know that all the keywords were found in the file and that we have found a hit (a successful match).

```
@not_found_words = @keyword_list;
```

In addition to searching for the keyword, we attempt to parse out the name of the HTML file. The `$are_we_in_head` flag is set to zero initially. If it is zero, we know that we are still in the header of the HTML file. Upon reaching a </HEAD> or </TITLE> flag, the script knows that it is finished reading the header. The header is read into the `$headline` variable.

```
$are_we_in_head = 0;
open(SEARCHFILE, $fullpath);
$headline = "";
```

```
while(<SEARCHFILE>) {
    $line = $_;
    $headline .= $line if ($are_we_in_head == 0);
    $are_we_in_head = 1
     if (($line =~ m!</head>!i) ||
          ($line =~ m!</title>!i));
```

The &FindKeywords subroutine performs the search of the keywords in each line as it is read from the file. When &FindKeywords finds a match, it deletes the keyword from the @not_found_words array.

```
    &FindKeywords($exact_match, $line, *not_found_words);
} # End of SEARCHFILE
close (SEARCHFILE);
```

PRINTING A SUCCESSFUL KEYWORD MATCH

If the @not_found_words array is less than 1, the script knows that all the keywords were found, so it prints the matched files. Part of the routine that prints the match parses the title of the document out of the HTML code stored in $headline.

```
    if (@not_found_words < 1) {
```

The first thing the routine does is to replace all newlines with spaces in $headline. Then it sets up a match against the regular expression <title>(.*)</title>. This expression matches for zero or more characters between the <TITLE> HTML tags. In Perl, the successful match will make the variable $1 equal to the characters between the <TITLE> tags. The i at the end of the match expression indicates that the match is performed without regard to case. If the title turns out not to exist in this document, the $title variable is set to No Title Given.

```
$headline =~ s/\n/ /g;
$headline =~ m!<title>(.*)</title>!i;
$title = $1;

    if ($title eq "") {
        $title = "No Title Given";
    }
```

NOTE

We use a special form of the match operator. Most of the time we use forward slashes (/) to indicate the endpoints of a search. Here, we use the m (match) operator followed by a different character to use as the matching operator. In this case, we use the exclamation point (!) to delimit the search. We do this because we are including forward slashes inside the actual expression to search, and escaping them with the backslash (\) would look messy. The same technique can be used with the s (substitute) operator, which is used in the next code sample.

The program then strips out the $root_web_path, because it contains information we do not want to pass to the user about the internal directory structure of the Web server. Finally, the script prints the HTML code related to the hit and increments the hit counter.

```
$fullpath =~ s!$root_web_path/!!;
&PrintBodyHTML($fullpath, $title);
$number_of_hits++;
} # If there are no not_found_words
} # If Not The End of all Files
} # End of While Not At The End Of All Files
```

PRINTING DIFFERENT HTML IN CASE NO KEYWORDS WERE FOUND

If no keywords were found, the HTML for "getting no hits" is printed.

```
if ($number_of_hits == 0) {
&PrintNoHitsBodyHTML;
}
```

END OF THE MAIN PROGRAM

When the program is finished, the footer is printed.

```
&PrintFooterHTML;
```

The rest of the program consists of subroutines that were called in the main program.

The FindKeywords Subroutine

The FindKeywords subroutine is the core routine of the entire search engine. It accepts a line of a file and the keywords to search for in that line. If a keyword is found, the routine deletes it from the keyword array (@not_found_words). Thus, when the @not_found_words array no longer has any elements, the script knows that all the keywords in the file have been found.

```
sub FindKeywords
{
```

There are three parameters. The first one, $exact_match, is equal to on if the pattern match is based on an exact one-to-one match of each letter in the keyword to each letter in a word contained in the HTML document. The second parameter, $line, is a line in the HTML file that is currently being searched for the keywords. The final parameter, *not_found_words, is a reference to the array @not_found_words, which contains a list of all the keywords not found so far. As keywords get found in the searched file, words are removed from this array. When the array is empty, we know that the file contained all the keywords. In other words, there are no "not found words" if the search is successful.

```
    local($exact_match, $line, *not_found_words) = @_;
    local($x, $match_word);
```

If the exact match is on, the program matches all the words in the array by surrounding the keywords with \b. This means that the keyword must be surrounded by word boundaries to be a valid match. Thus, the keyword "the" would not match a word such as "there," because the characters are only part of a larger word.

```
if ($exact_match eq "on") {
    for ($x = @not_found_words; $x > 0; $x--) {
        $match_word = $not_found_words[$x - 1];
        if ($line =~ /\b$match_word\b/i) {
```

The splice routine can be used to cut out the words if they are satisfied by the search. The splice command is a Perl routine that accepts the original array, the element in the array to splice, the number of elements to splice, and a list or array to splice into the original array. Because we are omitting the fourth parameter of the splice, the routine by default splices "nothing" into the array as the element number. This technique deletes the element in one convenient little routine.

```
        splice(@not_found_words,$x - 1, 1);
      } # End of If
  } # End of For Loop
```

If the exact match is not on, the program will report a match if the letters in the keyword exist anywhere on the line, whether or not the keyword is part of a larger word. All the searches are case-insensitive, as indicated by the i following the slashes that define the search term.

```
} else {
    for ($x = @not_found_words; $x > 0; $x--) {
        $match_word = $not_found_words[$x - 1];
        if ($line =~ /$match_word/i) {
          splice(@not_found_words,$x - 1, 1);
        } # End of If
    } # End of For Loop
  } # End of ELSE

} # End of FindKeywords
```

The GetNextEntry Subroutine

The GetNextEntry subroutine reads the directory handle for the next entry in the directory. The routine accepts as parameters the current directory handle and the current directory path.

```
sub GetNextEntry {
    local($dirhandle, $directory) = @_;
```

If the next entry is a file, the program checks to see whether the file has an **.htm** or **.html** extension. This is accomplished by using the regular expression "/htm.?/i." The ".?" matches any character once after the htm. The i after the search terms tells the program to treat uppercase and lowercase characters equally.

```
while ($filename = readdir($dirhandle)) {
 if (($filename =~ /htm.?/i) ||
```

If the next entry is a directory, the routine returns the directory name if it is not a directory that is "." or "..".

```
(!($filename =~ /^\.\.?$/) &&
 -d "$directory/$filename")) {
```

If the program satisfies one of these two conditions, the `while` loop that reads subsequent directory entries is exited using the `last` command, and the found filename or directory name is returned from the subroutine.

```
   last;
 } # End of IF Filename is a document or directory
 } # End of while still stuff to read

 $filename;
} # End of GetNextEntry
```

CHAPTER 17

The Shopping Cart

OVERVIEW

The shopping cart applications are one of the more popular CGI applications available. They allow a company to put its inventories online, where clients can browse the items using a simple Web-based interface.

A shopping cart is one of the more demanding CGI applications to manage, because it integrates many CGI routines into one system. For example, in order for each client to maintain a unique set of shopping cart items, the application must keep track of each client and the cart that corresponds to him or her. *Maintaining state*, as this is called, is difficult because HTTP is a "connectionless" protocol: every time a Web browser requests the attention of your server, it is considered a new request, unrelated to any other requests fulfilled by the server. Because each request is considered independently of others, the server has no way to keep track of what clients have been doing in the past. If you want to keep track of a client's activities from page to page (perhaps keeping a list of items that the client has ordered), your CGI application must find a way to "remember" these transactions, because the server cannot.

Furthermore, the cart itself is a database file that is built and modified on the fly based on the client's needs. The client must be able to add and delete items as well as change the quantities of items ordered. The maintenance of the cart demands a full-fledged database manager.

Yet the script must do more than just display and modify shopping cart items that are contained in the datafile. It must also manipulate the database fields to perform price calculations, such as subtotaling and generating grand totals from subtotals.

Finally, the application must enable the client to browse throughout the store. They must have easy access to the inventory, and the script must provide the means of guiding them through.

In this version of the shopping cart script, we use an HTML-based method of storing information about items for sale. Product pages are built by the store administrator using plain HTML coding. A database version of this script is available at the following URL:

```
http://www.eff.org/~erict/Scripts/
```

INSTALLATION AND USAGE

The script should expand into a predesignated directory structure beginning with the root directory **Html_web_store**. Figure 17.1 shows the directory structure and the correct permissions for files and directories.

Html_web_store, the root directory, contains two files (**html_web_store. cgi** and **html_web_store.setup**) and three subdirectories (**Html**, **Library**, and **User_carts**). It must be readable and executable by the Web server.

html_web_store.cgi, the main script for the application, should be readable and executable by the Web server. It will be discussed in greater detail in the "Design Discussion" section.

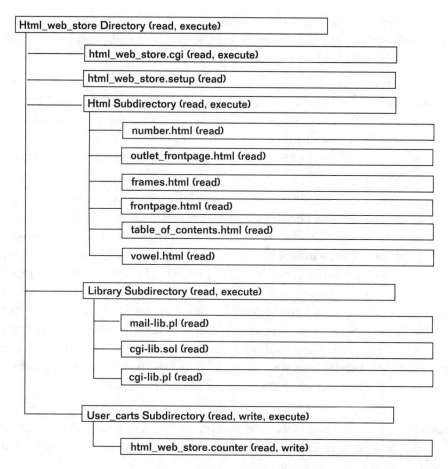

Html_web_store Directory (read, execute)
- html_web_store.cgi (read, execute)
- html_web_store.setup (read)
- Html Subdirectory (read, execute)
  - number.html (read)
  - outlet_frontpage.html (read)
  - frames.html (read)
  - frontpage.html (read)
  - table_of_contents.html (read)
  - vowel.html (read)
- Library Subdirectory (read, execute)
  - mail-lib.pl (read)
  - cgi-lib.sol (read)
  - cgi-lib.pl (read)
- User_carts Subdirectory (read, write, execute)
  - html_web_store.counter (read, write)

Figure 17.1 *HTML Web store directory structure.*

html_web_store.setup is the file you use to set all the server-specific variables and options. This file should be readable by the Web server and is discussed in greater detail in the "Setting Server-Specific Setup and Options" section.

Html contains all the miscellaneous HTML files used by the script. In the accompanying CD-ROM, this directory initially contains seven files: **number.html**, **outlet_frontpage.html**, **outlet_order_form.html**, **vowel.html**, **frames.html**, **frontpage.html**, and **table_of_contents.html**. These seven files are examples of how to maintain the HTML aspects of the shopping cart and will be discussed individually in the "Server-Specific Setup and Options" section. The subdirectory itself must be readable and executable by the Web server, and all files in it must be readable.

The **Library** subdirectory contains the supporting library files. This application uses **cgi-lib.pl** to read and parse form data, **cgi-lib.sol** for the lock file and counter routines, and **mail-lib.pl** for mailing orders. Each of these libraries is discussed in Part Two and should be readable by the Web server. The **Library** subdirectory must be executable and readable by the Web server.

User_carts is the subdirectory that **html_web_store.cgi** uses to hold the shopping carts used by clients as well as a counter file and a few temporary files used to manipulate the carts. This directory should initially contain only **html_web_store.counter**, which is used by **html_web_store.cgi** to keep track of unique shopping cart item ID numbers; when clients wish to modify their carts, the script uses these ID numbers to identify unique items in their carts. The counter file should be readable and writable by the Web server. The script also uses this subdirectory to store the shopping cart files for each client. When the subdirectory is set to be readable, writable, and executable by the Web server, the script fills it with user carts and temporary files and prunes it when it no longer needs them.

NOTE As you will see in the next section, the store administrator can define how long to keep old shopping carts and how often pruning takes place.

Server-Specific Setup and Options

THE SET-UP FILE

The setup file is used to configure the generic script for your own needs. It defines the following variables.

$counter_file is the location of the counter file used to assign unique numbers to every item added to the shopping cart.

$main_script is the local path of **html_web_store.cgi**.

$main_script_url is the URL of **html_web_store.cgi**.

$order_form is the location of the HTML order form that clients use to place their orders.

$admin_email is the E-mail address of the person who should receive the submitted orders.

$email_subject is the subject of the E-mail regarding an order.

$cart_directory is the location of the subdirectory where all the clients' shopping carts are stored.

$html_directory is the full path to the root directory where your HTML documents start. As archived on the accompanying CD-ROM, all HTML files are contained in the subdirectory where **html_web_store.cgi** is located, but it does not matter where your HTML files are as long as you include the entire path relative to the Web server's environment.

$cgi_lib_pl is the location of **cgi-lib.pl**.

$cgi_lib_sol is the location of **cgi-lib.sol**.

$mail-lib.pl is the location of **mail-lib.pl**.

$frontpage_file is the location of the very first HTML page that you want displayed when a new client enters the store.

@display_fields is the array containing all the shopping cart database fields that you want displayed when the user presses the view or modify button.

@display_numbers contains the corresponding array indexes to the elements specified in @display_fields. Thus, if price is the second element in @display_fields but you want it to be displayed first to the client, @display_numbers should have its first element set to 1. Remember that array counting starts at zero and not at 1.

$price_number is the array index of the price element within @display_fields. To make price calculation, the script must be able to identify this index.

@email_numbers are the indexes to the elements in the @display_fields array that are sent as part of the E-mail to the store administrator so that he or she knows which items have been ordered.

`%order_form_array` is the associative array that contains the variable names and their associated display names. Note that the preceding numbers (01-, 02-, 03-) are used to "force" an order. Because associative arrays use hash tables, the orders cannot be determined unless you sort them with numbers as shown here. This is not mandatory, but appropriate naming of variables will make the screen display more intelligible to users.

The following is the setup file for you to examine:

```
$counter_file = "./User_carts/html_web_store.counter";
$main_script = "./html_web_store.cgi";
$main_script_url = "html_web_store.cgi";
$order_form = "outlet_order_form.html";
$admin_email = "selena\@foobar.com";
$email_subject = "Html Web Form Order";
$cart_directory = "./User_carts";
$html_directory = "./Html";
$cgi_lib_pl = "./Library/cgi-lib.pl";
$cgi_lib_sol = "./Library/cgi-lib.sol";
$mail_lib_pl = "./Library/mail-lib.pl";
$frontpage_file = "./Html/outlet_frontpage.html";
@display_fields = ("Catalog Number", "Price After
      Options", "Description", "Options");
@display_numbers = ("0", "4", "2", "3");
$price_number = "4";
@email_numbers = ("0", "4", "2", "3");
%order_form_array = ( '01-name', 'Name',
      '02-b_street_address', 'Billing Address Street',
      '03-b_city', 'Billing Address City',
      '04-b_state', 'Billing Address State',
      '05-b_zip', 'Billing Address ZIP',
      '06-b_country', 'Billing Address Country',
      '07-m_street_adress', 'Mailing Address Street',
      '08-m_city', 'Mailing Address City',
      '09-m_state', 'Mailing Address State',
      '10-m_zip', 'Mailing Address ZIP',
      '11-m_country', 'Mailing Address Country',
      '12-phone', 'Phone Number',
      '13-fax', 'Fax Number',
      '14-e-mail', 'Email',
      '15-URL', 'URL',
      '16-link', 'Link',
      '17-type_of_card', 'Type of Card',
      '19-cardname', 'Name Appearing on Card',
      '20-card_number', 'Card Number',
      '21-ex_date', 'Card Expiration');
```

THE FRONT PAGE: OUTLET_FRONTPAGE.HTML

Next is an example of the sample front page HTML file included on the accompanying CD-ROM.

```
<HTML>
<HEAD>
<TITLE>Selena Sol's Electronic Outlet</TITLE>
</HEAD>
<BODY BGCOLOR = "FFFFFF" TEXT = "000000">
<B>Welcome to....</B>
<H2>Selena Sol's Electronic Outlet</H2>
where you will find the most up-to-date letters and numbers available.
All of our products are guaranteed for your lifetime, and our prices
are always competitive.
```

So far, all this is standard HTML. However, what follows is not. For the script to process your HTML pages, you need to follow a few standards. You should feel free to create any type of GUI you want for your store, but be sure to follow these standards in your HTML code. Specifically, any link that you create to another page must use the following format:

```
<A HREF = "html_web_store.cgi?page=xxx.html&cart_id=">XXX</A>
```

The shopper never sees a page directly. Instead, the shopper asks **html_web_store.cgi** to display a requested HTML document (in this case, **xxx.html**). This is why we do not have a link such as the following:

```
<A HREF="xxx.html">XXX</A>
```

The CGI script is actually a filter. It displays whatever HTML document that the page variable is set equal to.

The main reason we use this technique is that the script must "remember" a great deal of information, such as the name of the client using the script. Because the Web is connectionless, the Web protocols have no way to give the server or script the ability to remember information about a client. As far as the Web server is concerned, each new request is unrelated to any other request. Without these filtered variables, the script would not be able to remember whose cart was whose.

The trick is to pass such information as hidden form variables when a form is appropriate, or tagged on to the end of URL strings when a hyperlink is appropriate. In this case, we use a hyperlink that calls **html_web_store.cgi** and passes it the variable page. This page is set to the name of the HTML page that you want displayed.

The name that you set page **equal to must include the location relative to the variable** $html_directory. **Thus, if you had a subdirectory of your root HTML directory called Parts, with a file called carb.html, you would set** page **to** Parts/carb.html.

N O T E

The script finds the requested HTML document and displays it for the client. The accompanying CD-ROM includes two examples—**vowels.html** and **numbers.html**—which you should read thoroughly.

In the example hyperlink tag, what is cart_id? It appears to be equal to nothing! Actually, this is a special tag that **html_web_store.cgi** will recognize. When it sees that tag, it automatically inserts the value of the user's cart ID number.

That is the real reason we run all HTML pages through **html_web_store.cgi** as a filter. The page variable tells the script which page to filter, and the cart_id variable is what is actually filtered. Because the Web is connectionless, the only way to remember information such as unique shopping cart ID numbers is to append them to the URL string.

But the HTML is not smart enough to do it on its own. The HTML is predesigned and static. How can it know in advance what the cart_ids will be? Thus, the script serves as a liaison between the static HTML document and the interactive client. The rest of the front page appears as follows:

```
<UL>
<LI><A HREF = "html_web_store.cgi?page=vowel.html&cart_id="">Vowels</A>
<LI><A HREF =
"html_web_store.cgi?page=number.html&cart_id="">Numbers</A>
```

The following hyperlink references a "frames" version of the Web store, which is included in the accompanying CD-ROM. We'll discuss how the frames version works in the section titled "An Alternative Approach: Using Frames." For now, focus on the first two lines.

```
<LI><A HREF = "html_web_store.cgi?page=frames.html&cart_id="">Frames
    Version</A>
</UL>
</BODY></HTML>
```

On the Web, the front page will look like the one in Figure 17.2.

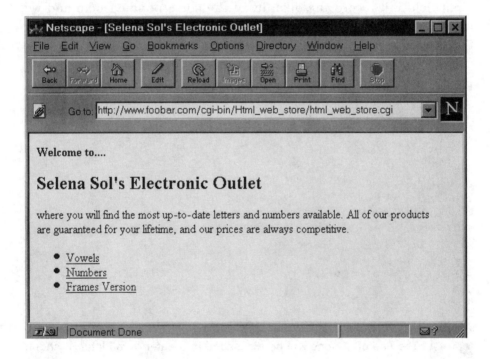

Figure 17.2 *The Web store front page.*

THE PRODUCT PAGE: VOWEL.HTML

Next is an example of a product page. Each product page begins with a standard header. You can change this header to reflect the specifics of your own site, but be absolutely sure that the form call in every page points to **html_web_store.cgi**.

```
<HTML>
<HEAD>
<TITLE>Vowel Page</TITLE>
</HEAD>
<BODY BGCOLOR = "FFFFFF" TEXT = "000000">
<FORM METHOD = "post" ACTION = "html_web_store.cgi">
```

The body of the product page appears below the header. You can customize this display in any way you would like. However, each item for sale must have an `<INPUT TYPE = "text">` field accompanying it. This text input field will record the quantity of the corresponding item and will have a NAME argument that contains all the item-specific information so that the script can identify the items in the client's cart.

Along similar lines, each item may also have user-configured options. For example, the shopper could choose a variety of colors or sizes.

```
<H2><CENTER>Vowel Mart!</CENTER></H2>
<TABLE>

<TR>
<TH>Quantity</TH>
<TH></TH>
<TH>Description</TH>
</TR>

<TR>
<TD COLSPAN = "3"><HR></TD>
</TR>
<TR>
```

The use of options will be discussed in greater detail later. It should be noted that in adding options you must be very careful not to make typos.

NOTE

DEFINING AN ITEM

Now comes the heart of the product page—the first occurrence of an item for sale. Notice first that it has a TEXT input field associated with it. This text field is three characters long and provides a maximum of four characters. This field corresponds to the quantity that the user wants to order and is set to a maximum of 9999. You can change this limit if you want to.

Second, notice that the NAME argument of the INPUT field is 0001|15.98| The letter A. This is where you define the information that gets added to the user's shopping cart. It is crucial that this list correspond to the list defined in line 199 of **html_web_store.cgi**:

```
($item_quantity, $item_id_number, $item_price, $item_description) =
split (/\|/, $item_ordered_with_options);
```

Notice that $item_id_number equals 0001, $item_price equals 15.98, and $item_description equals The letter A. $item_quantity will be defined by the user, so you need not worry much about that one. However, the others must correspond exactly. If you customize this script to your own inventory, take care to modify **html_web_store.cgi** as well as the setup file.

This information is also hard-coded into the arrays @display_fields, @display_numbers, @email_numbers, and the variable $price_number in the **html_web_store.setup** file.

The moral of this explanation is that if you want to add your own fields, you need to make sure that everything matches. You must change your HTML to reflect a new field as well as change line 199 and the lines in the setup file. Be very careful about doing this, because everything must be perfect for it to work!

```
<TD>
<INPUT TYPE = "text" NAME = "0001|15.98|The letter A"
       SIZE = "3" MAXLENGTH = "4"></TD>
<TD><IMG SRC = "http://www.eff.org/~erict/Graphics/Scripts/a.jpg"
ALIGN = "left"></TD>
<TD>You got it, the world-renowned letter "A" for the
low base price of $15.98<BR>
```

USE OF OPTIONS

Now let's look at the use of options. We need a way to communicate to the script what an option is, which item it belongs to, and the value set by the user.

The first step is to make sure that we associate options with items for sale. We do this by using the NAME argument. Following is an example of using a select menu for options. In this case, the name syntax breaks down as follows:

- An option tag, which tells the script that the incoming data is an option and not an item.

- A unique sequence number for the option. Each item for sale may have several options associated with it. It is essential that each one gets its own number. If all the options for item #0001 were called option|0001, it would be impossible to parse them separately. So we will name each option uniquely, such as option|1|0001, option|2|0001, and option|3|0001.

- The ID of the item that the option is associated with. Notice that this ID is the same as the one that was used in the NAME argument for the quantity text box. This is deliberate and essential. Options must be associated with the items they modify.

```
<P><B>Available Options<B><P>
Font: <SELECT NAME = "option|1|0001">
<OPTION VALUE = "Times New Roman|0.00">Times New Roman (No
charge)
<OPTION VALUE = "Arial|1.50">Arial (+ $1.50)
<OPTION VALUE = "Chicago|2.00">Chicago (+ $2.00)
</SELECT>
<P>
```

The following is an example of using a radio button to create an option. It uses the same naming conventions as the <SELECT> tag.

```
Color: <BR>
<INPUT TYPE = "radio" NAME = "option|2|0001"
    VALUE = "Red|0.00" CHECKED>Red<BR>
<INPUT TYPE = "radio" NAME = "option|2|0001"
    VALUE = "Blue|.50">Blue (+ $1.00)
</TD>
</TR>
<TR>
<TD COLSPAN = "3"><HR></TD>
```

```
</TR>
<TR>
<TD>
<INPUT TYPE = "text" NAME = "0002|12.98|The letter E"
      SIZE = "3" MAXLENGTH = "4"></TD>
<TD><IMG SRC = "http://www.eff.org/~erict/Graphics/Scripts/e.jpg"
ALIGN = "left"></TD>
<TD>You got it, the world-renowned letter "E" for the low base price
of $12.98<BR>
<P><B>Available Options<B><P>
Font: <SELECT NAME = "option|1|0002">
<OPTION VALUE = "Times New Roman|0.00">Times New Roman (No charge)
<OPTION VALUE = "Arial|1.50">Arial (+ $1.50)
<OPTION VALUE = "Chicago|2.00">Chicago (+ $2.00)
</SELECT>
<P>
Color: <BR>
<INPUT TYPE = "radio" NAME = "option|2|0002"
      VALUE = "Red|0.00" CHECKED>Red<BR>
<INPUT TYPE = "radio" NAME = "option|2|0002"
      VALUE = "Blue|.50">Blue (+ $1.00)
</TD>
</TR>
<TR>
<TD COLSPAN = "3"><HR></TD>
</TR>
```

SIMPLE ITEM DEFINITION

Finally, we have provided an example of an item with no options. This
example is much simpler, because all you need to worry about is the one
NAME argument of each item for sale.

```
<TR>
<TD>
<INPUT TYPE = "text" NAME = "0004|18.98|The letter I"
      SIZE = "3" MAXLENGTH = "4"></TD>
<TD><FONT SIZE = "+9"><B>I</B></FONT></TD>
<TD>Yep, this is the letter I am selling for the low price of $18.98.
No options are available on this model.</TD>
</TR>
<TR>
<TD COLSPAN = "3"><HR></TD>
</TR>
</TABLE>
```

Next, we see the standard page footer that must appear on every HTML page. The first two hidden input tags are specially marked with the double percent (%%) sign so that the script can identify the tags and substitute them for the actual values associated with the client. You should make sure to have these tags on every page.

```
<P>
<CENTER>
<INPUT TYPE = "hidden" NAME = "cart_id"
       VALUE = "%%cart_id%%">
<INPUT TYPE = "hidden" NAME = "page"
       VALUE = "%%page%%">
```

The remaining input tags, which are used by the client to select the operation to be performed, can have their VALUE argument modified but not their NAME argument.

```
<INPUT TYPE = "submit" NAME = "add_to_cart"
       VALUE = "I'd like to buy a vowel">
       VALUE = "View/Modify Cart">
<INPUT TYPE = "submit" NAME = "return_to_frontpage"
       VALUE = "Return to Front page">
<INPUT TYPE = "submit" NAME = "order_form"
       VALUE = "Checkout Stand">
,/FORM></BODY></HTML>
```

On the Web, the vowel page looks like Figure 17.3.

ALTERNATIVE APPROACH: USING FRAMES

It is also possible to use frames as a navigational tool throughout your store. To demonstrate this, we have included three extra HTML files that use frames: **frames.html**, **frontpage.html**, and **table_of_contents.html**.

If you recall from the discussion of **outlet_frontpage.html**, we noted that the following line references a frames version of the Web store:

```
<LI><A HREF = "html_web_store.cgi?page=frames.html&cart_id=">Frames
Version</A>
```

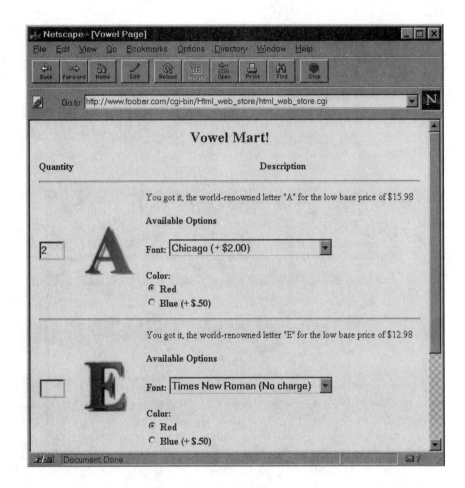

Figure 17.3 The vowel order page.

You can easily run the Web store with a frames interface by using this example. **frames.html** is the file that defines the windows. Here is the example of **frames.html** as it exists on the CD-ROM:

```
<HTML>
<HEAD>
<TITLE>Selena Sol's Public Domain CGI Script Archive and Resource
Library: Shopping Cart Frames Example</TITLE>
```

```
</HEAD>
<FRAMESET COLS = "111, 80%">
<FRAME SRC = "html_web_store.cgi?page=table_of_contents.html"
SCROLLING = "auto">
<FRAME NAME = "main" SRC = "html_web_store.cgi?page=frontpage.html">
</FRAMESET></BODY></HTML>
```

As you can see, in this case we used two windows. Figure 17.4 depicts the frames interface.

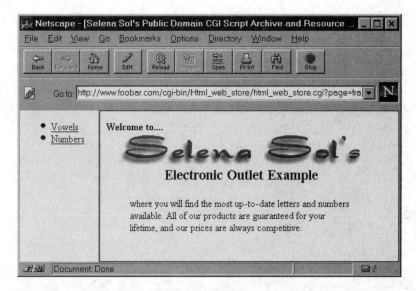

Figure 17.4 The frames interface.

The first window, **table_of_contents.html**, lists the different product pages that the client may wish to browse. This page is similar to the front page in the nonframes version and includes the urlencoded information that **html_web_store.cgi** must filter.

```
<HTML>
<HEAD>
<TITLE>Selena Sol's Electronic Outlet</TITLE>
</HEAD>
<BODY BGCOLOR = "FFFFFF" TEXT = "000000">
<UL>
<LI><A HREF="html_web_store.cgi?page=vowel.html&cart_id=" TARGET =
```

```
"main">Vowels</A>
<LI><A HREF="html_web_store.cgi?page=number.html&cart_id=" TARGET =
"main">Numbers</A> </UL>
</BODY></HTML>
```

The second window, **frontpage.html**, is used to generate a front page store banner. We have chosen to include no navigational links in this window, because the **table_of_contents.html** window is used for navigation. **frontpage.html** is simply a front banner for the store. Until the client begins shopping and the frame is used to display products, it serves the simple purpose of filling the main frame. Here is the text of **frontpage.html**:

```
<HTML>
<HEAD>
<TITLE>Selena Sol's Electronic Outlet</TITLE>
</HEAD>
<BODY BGCOLOR = "FFFFFF" TEXT = "000000">
<B>Welcome to....</B><BR>
<CENTER>
<IMG SRC =
"http://www.eff.org/~erict/Graphics/Scripts/web_store_frontpage.gif">
</CENTER>
<BLOCKQUOTE>
where you will find the most up-to-date letters and numbers available.
All of our products are guaranteed for your lifetime, and our prices
are always competitive.
</BLOCKQUOTE></BODY></HTML>
```

The window with **frontpage.html** is the "main" window, in which the various pages defined in the **table_of_contents.html** window are displayed. Because both pages are initially loaded through **frames.html**, if you wished to include navigational links in the **frontpage.html** window, they would also be filtered by **html_web_store.cgi**.

Because the pages are filtered through **html_web_store.cgi**, they are filtered as any other page and hence are able to maintain state.

THE ORDER FORM: OUTLET_ORDER_FORM.HTML

The accompanying CD-ROM also includes an example of an order form. There is no magic to this form; it is just a standard HTML form. It references **html_web_store.cgi**, which is used to process the order, and all variable names are prefixed with a number and a hyphen (-). The numbers represent the order in which you want the variables displayed. The numbers begin at 01- and count upward.

```
<HTML>
<HEAD>
<TITLE>Outlet Order Form!!</TITLE>
</HEAD>
<BODY BGCOLOR="#FFFFFF">
<FORM ACTION = "html_web_store.cgi" METHOD = "post">
<CENTER>
<TABLE WIDTH = "90%" BORDER="3" CELLPADDING="2">
<TR><TD COLSPAN=2><FONT SIZE=+1>Personal Information:</FONT></TD></TR>

<TR><TD>Name(First &amp; Last)</TD>
<TD><INPUT TYPE = "text" NAME = "01-name" SIZE = "30"
         MAXLENGTH = "30"></TD></TR>

<TR>
<TD COLSPAN = "2"><FONT SIZE = "+1">Billing Address:</FONT></TD>
</TR>

<TR><TD>Street:</TD>
<TD><INPUT TYPE="text" NAME="02-b_street_address" SIZE="30"></TD></TR>

<TR><TD COLSPAN=2>City:
<INPUT TYPE="text" NAME="03-b_city" SIZE="10">
State: <INPUT TYPE="text" NAME="04-b_state" SIZE="2" MAXLENGTH="8">
ZIP: <INPUT TYPE="text" NAME="05-b_zip" SIZE="5" MAXLENGTH="5">
Country: <INPUT TYPE="text" NAME="06-b_country" SIZE="10"
MAXLENGTH="20">
</TD></TR>

<TR><TD COLSPAN=2><FONT SIZE=+1>Mailing Address (If
Different):</FONT></TD></TR>

<TR><TD>Street:</TD>
<TD><INPUT TYPE="text" NAME="07-m_street_adress" SIZE="30"></TD></TR>

<TR>
<TD COLSPAN=2>City:
```

```
<INPUT TYPE="text" NAME="08-m_city" SIZE="10"> State:
<INPUT TYPE="text" NAME="09-m_state" SIZE="2" MAXLENGTH="8">ZIP:
<INPUT TYPE="text" NAME="10-m_zip" SIZE="5" MAXLENGTH="5">Country:
<INPUT TYPE="text" NAME="11-m_country" SIZE="10" MAXLENGTH="20">
</TD></TR>


<TR><TD>
Phone: <INPUT TYPE="text" NAME="12-phone" SIZE="10"
MAXLENGTH="12"></TD><TD> Fax: <INPUT TYPE="text" NAME="13-fax"
SIZE="10" MAXLENGTH="12">
</TD></TR>


<TR><TD>E-Mail:</TD><TD>
<INPUT TYPE="text" NAME="14-e-mail" MAXLENGTH="30">
</TD></TR>


<TR><TD>URL:</TD><TD>
<INPUT TYPE="text" NAME="15-URL" MAXLENGTH="30"> Request Link: <INPUT
TYPE="checkbox" NAME="16-link" VALUE="on">
</TD></TR>


<TR><TD COLSPAN=2><FONT SIZE=+1>Credit Card
Information:</FONT></TD></TR>


<TR><TD COLSPAN=2>
<INPUT TYPE="radio" NAME="17-type_of_card" VALUE="visa">Visa <INPUT
TYPE="radio" NAME="17-type_of_card" VALUE="mastercard">Mastercard
<INPUT TYPE="radio" NAME="17-type_of_card"
VALUE="discover">Discover</TD></TR>


<TR><TD>Name on Card:</TD><TD>
<INPUT TYPE="text" NAME="19-cardname" SIZE="30"
MAXLENGTH="30"></TD></TR>


<TR><TD>Number:</TD><TD><INPUT TYPE="text" NAME="20-card_number"
MAXLENGTH="20"></TD></TR>


<TR><TD>Exp. Date:</TD><TD>
<INPUT TYPE="text" NAME="21-ex_date" SIZE="10"
MAXLENGTH="10"></TD></TR>


</TABLE>
<P>
```

```
Allow 3-4 weeks for delivery.  Shipping prices and delivery times
may vary when shipping to cities outside the continental U.S.
<P>
<INPUT TYPE=reset>
<INPUT TYPE=submit NAME = "send_in_order"
       VALUE = "Submit Secure Order"><BR>
</CENTER>
</FORM>
</BODY></HTML>
```

On the Web, the order form looks like Figure 17.5.

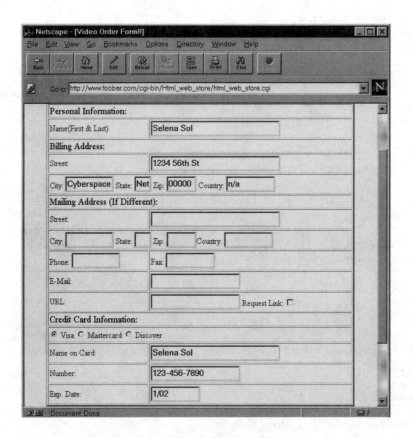

Figure 17.5 *The Web store order form.*

Running the Script

Once you have configured the setup file to the specifics of your local server setup, you can take a trip to the store. To access the script, create a hyperlink to the location of the main script as follows:

```
<A HREF = "http://www.foobar.com/cgi-
bin/Html_web_store/html_web_store.cgi">Html Web Store</A>
```

Because the front page HTML file is specified in the setup, you need not pass the script any extra information initially.

DESIGN DISCUSSION

The logic of the application is depicted in Figure 17.6.

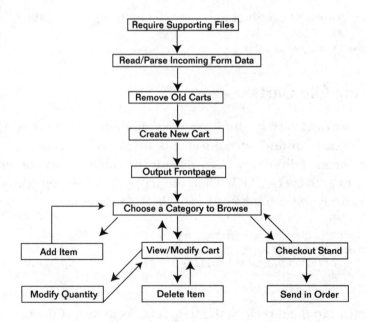

Figure 17.6 Script logic.

html_web_store.cgi begins by starting the Perl interpreter and printing the http header.

```
#!/usr/local/bin/perl
print "Content-type: text/html\n\n";
```

Loading the Libraries

Next, the script loads the supporting files.

```
require "./html_web_store.setup";
require "$cgi_lib_pl";
require "$cgi_lib_sol";
require "$mail_lib_pl";
```

Reading and Parsing Form Data

Next, the script uses **cgi-lib.pl** to parse the incoming form data.

```
&ReadParse(*form_data);
```

Removing Old Carts

Then the script cleans up the **User_carts** subdirectory; there is no need to keep old carts around once the clients are gone. The script first opens the **User_carts** subdirectory. Then it reads the subdirectory contents and uses grep to grab every CART. Then the script closes the directory. Thus, the @carts array will contain every cart file as an element.

```
opendir (USER_CARTS, "$cart_directory") ||
&open_error($cart_directory);
@carts = grep(/.cart$/,readdir(USER_CARTS));
closedir (USER_CARTS);
```

For every cart in the directory, the script checks its age. If the cart is older than half a day, it is deleted.

```
foreach $cart (@carts)
  {
```

```
if (-M "$cart_directory/$cart" > .5)
  {
  unlink("$cart_directory/$cart");
  }
}
```

Generating a New Shopping Cart

Next, the script creates a new cart for the new client. It first determines whether it has received a shopping cart ID number as form data. If it has not, the script knows that the client has not yet received a unique shopping cart. So it assigns the client a unique shopping cart file that is used while the client browses the store.

To generate a unique cart ID, the script first generates a random (rand) eight-digit (10000000) integer (int) and then adds to that the current process ID ($$). It then appends the process ID to the end of the integer. srand, which must be called before the rand command is used, is seeded with the process ID and the time, a technique that provides a better randomizing algorithm.

```
if ($form_data{'cart_id'} eq "")
  {
  srand (time|$$);
  $cart_id = int(rand(10000000));
  $cart_id .= ".$$";
```

Once the unique number has been generated, the script creates a new cart for the shopper using the value of $cart_id as the name of the file.

```
open (CART, ">$cart_directory/$cart_id.cart") ||
&open_error("$cart_directory/$cart_id.cart");
  }
```

If there was a shopping cart ID number coming in as form data, on the other hand, the script simply reads the form_variable into the $cart_id Perl variable.

```
else
  {
```

```
$cart_id = "$form_data{'cart_id'}";
}
```

Once the client has received a cart, that cart number must be passed from screen to screen as url-encoded information or as a hidden form variable so that the client does not lose the cart.

N O T E

Displaying the Front Page

Now that the client has received a cart, it is time to display the first page of the store. We will assume that the site administrator has created a front page and has set that location to $frontpage_file in the store-specific setup file.

There are two cases in which the script should display the front page: first, if the user has specifically asked to return to the front page and, second, if no product page has been assigned. The main purpose of the front page is to query the client for the product page the client is interested in browsing. The front page presents all the options and creates hyperlinks that specify the product pages for the script. (Recall the page variable in our HTML documents.)

```
if ($form_data{'page'} eq "" ||
$form_data{'return_to_frontpage'} ne "")
{
```

If it has been asked for the front page, the script opens it and displays it line by line.

```
open (FRONTPAGE, "$frontpage_file") ||
&open_error("$frontpage_file");
while (<FRONTPAGE>)
{
```

However, the script must do a couple of things to the front page before it is displayed. First, it must make sure that the client's unique cart ID gets passed from the front page to any successive pages. We do this by urlencoding. We have the user click on a link that says

```
<A HREF ="web_store.cgi?page=foo.html&cart_id=yyy">.
```

Notice two things in that line. First, we define a page in those links. Second, we add the other half to the previously half-completed variable userid. As discussed in the "Installation and Usage" section, this tag, userid=, is a tag that this script is looking for. Any time (/g) it sees the tag, the script substitutes (s/) occurrences of cart_id= with cart_id= the actual cart id of the user. Because we do not know the cart ID ahead of time, we cannot hard-code it into the HTML. Thus, we create the cart_id= tag so that this script can finish the job on the fly:

```
s/cart_id=/cart_id=$cart_id/g;
print "$_";
}
```

Then the script closes the front page file and quits.

```
  close (FRONTPAGE);
  exit;
} # End of if ($form_data{'page_to_view'} eq "")
```

An example of the front page was shown in Figure 17.2.

Adding an Item to the Client's Cart

Once the client has decided to purchase an item from one of the product pages, he or she adds a quantity to the text box and presses **submit**. The resulting displayed page is printed using routines we'll explain later. First, the script adds a new item to the cart.

```
if ($form_data{'add_to_cart'} ne "")
{
```

The script begins by using the %form_data array passed to it by **cgi-lib.pl**. All the keys of the %form_data associative array are dropped into the @incoming_data array. A key is like a variable name, whereas a value is the value associated with that variable name. Each of the text fields where the client can enter quantities is associated with the item IDs of the items (as defined in the displayed category view at the end of this script), so the HTML should read <INPUT TYPE = "text" NAME = "1234"...> for the item with database ID 1234, and <INPUT TYPE = "text" NAME = "5678"...> for item 5678. If the client orders two of 1234 and nine of 5678, then @incoming_data will be a list of 1234 and 5678 such that 1234 is "associated" with the value of 2 in %form_data and 5678 is associated with the value of 9.

```
@items_ordered = keys (%form_data);
```

Next, the script begins going through the list of incoming items one by one.

```
foreach $item (@items_ordered)
{
```

However, there are some incoming items—cart_id, page, and add_to_cart— that the script will not care about. These are administrative values set internally by this script and are not part of the client's order. These values come in as form data, and the script will need them for other things, but they're not used to fill the user's cart. Similarly, it will not need to worry about any items that have empty values. If the shopper did not enter a quantity for a product, then the script should not add it to the cart.

```
if ($item ne "cart_id" && $item ne "page" &&
    $item ne "add_to_cart" && $form_data{$item} ne "")
{
```

Next, the script separates the ordered items from the options that modify those items. If $item begins with the word option, which we set specifically in the HTML file, the script adds (pushes) that item to the array called @options.

```
if ($item =~ /^option/i)
  {
  push (@options, $item);
  }
```

On the other hand, if $item is not an option, the script adds it to the array @items_ordered_with_options, but it adds both the item and its value. The value will be a quantity, and the item will be something like 0001|12.98|The letter A, as defined in the HTML file.

```
else
  {
  push (@items_ordered_with_options,
          "$form_data{$item}\|$item\|");
  }
} # End of if ($item ne "cart_id"....
} # End of foreach $item (@items_ordered)
```

Then the script goes through the array @items_ordered_with_options one item at a time.

```
foreach $item_ordered_with_options
       (@items_ordered_with_options)
{
```

Next, the script initializes a few variables that it will use for each item. $options is used to keep track of all the options selected for any given item. $option_subtotal is used to determine the total cost of each option. $option_grand_total is used to calculate the total cost of all ordered options. $item_grand_total is used to calculate the total cost of the item ordered.

```
$options = "";
$option_subtotal = "";
$option_grand_total = "";
$item_grand_total = "";
```

Next, the script splits the $item_ordered_with_options into its fields.

```
($item_quantity, $item_id_number, $item_price,
 $item_description) =
 split (/\|/, $item_ordered_with_options);
```

For every option in @options, the script splits each option into its fields.

```
foreach $option (@options)
{
```

```
($option_marker, $option_number,
 $option_item_number) = split
     (/\|/, $option);
```

Then the script compares the name of the item with the name associated with the option. If they are the same, the script knows that this is an option that was meant to modify this item.

```
if ($option_item_number eq "$item_id_number")
     {
```

Because the script must apply this option to the item, it splits out the value associated with the option and appends it to $options. Once it appends all the options, using ".=," the script will have one big string containing all the options so that we can print them.

```
($option_name, $option_price) =
split (/\|/,$form_data{$option});
$options .= "$option_name $option_price,";
```

The script also calculates the cost with options:

```
$unformatted_option_grand_total = $option_grand_total +
                                  $option_price;
$option_grand_total = sprintf ("%.2f\n",
                  $unformatted_option_grand_total);


}
```

NOTE

We use the `sprintf` function to format the price only to two decimal places. The `sprintf` function returns a string formatted by the `printf` conventions. The string to be formatted contains an embedded field specifier (%) into which the formatted conversion (.2f) of a string ($unformatted_option_grand_total) is placed. The .2f option tells `sprintf` to format the string to only two decimal places. The `sprintf` function is also covered in depth in the UNIX man pages.

It also removes the last comma in $options. If you scan up a few lines, you will see that a comma is added to the end of each option. The last option does not need that last comma, so we strip it off.

```
chop $options;
```

Next, the script adds a space after each comma so that the display looks nicer.

```
$options =~ s/,/, /g;
```

Then it uses the subroutine counter in **cgi-lib.sol**, sending it the location of the counter file defined in the setup file. This routine returns one variable, $item_number, that we use to identify a shopping cart item absolutely. In this way, when we modify and delete items we know exactly which items to affect. The counter file is protected by using the lock file routines in **cgi-lib.sol**.

```
&GetFileLock("$counter_file.lock");
&counter ($counter_file);
&ReleaseFileLock("$counter_file.lock");
```

Finally, the script performs the last price calculations and appends every ordered item to $cart_row.

```
$unformatted_item_grand_total = $item_price +
                                $option_grand_total;
$item_grand_total = sprintf ("%.2f\n",
                    $unformatted_item_grand_total);
chop $item_grand_total;
$cart_row .=
"$item_quantity\|$item_id_number\|$item_price\|$item_description\|$opt
ions\|$item_grand_total\|$item_number\n";
}
```

When it has finished appending all the items to $cart_row, the script opens the user's shopping cart and adds the new items.

```
open (CART,
">>$cart_directory/$form_data{'cart_id'}.cart")
|| &open_error ("$cart_directory/$form_data{'cart_id'}.cart");
print CART "$cart_row";
close (CART);
```

It then sends the client back to the product page using the `display_items_for_sale` subroutine at the end of the script.

```
&display_items_for_sale;
exit;
}
```

Displaying the View/Modify Cart Screen

A client may decide to reduce the quantities of some of the chosen items or even to delete them from the cart. Or perhaps the client just wants to see what has been placed in the cart so far.

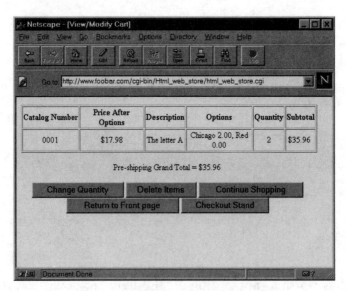

Figure 17.7 Cart modification interface.

The script's first step in such circumstances is to send an HTML form that includes a display of the client's current cart. We use the subroutine display_cart_contents at the end of this script.

```
if ($form_data{'modify_cart'} ne "")
{
&display_cart_contents
}
```

Figure 17.7 shows the cart interface on the Web.

Generating a Change Quantity Form

If the client asks to make a quantity modification, the script displays a form where the changes can be specified.

```
if ($form_data{'change_quantity'} ne "")
{
```

The script first outputs the header as it did before.

```
&page_header("Change Quantity");
print <<"end_of_html";
<CENTER>
<TABLE BORDER = "1">
<TR>
<TH>New Quantity</TH>
end_of_html
```

It then builds the table headers.

```
foreach $field (@display_fields)
  {
  print "<TH>$field</TH>\n";
  }
print "<TH>Quantity</TH>\n<TH>Subtotal</TH>\n</TR>\n";
```

Next, the client's cart is opened and the script begins going through it line by line.

```
open (CART, "$cart_directory/$form_data{'cart_id'}.cart")
|| &open_error("$cart_directory/$form_data{'cart_id'}.cart");
while (<CART>)
{
@cart_fields = split (/\|/, $_);
```

This time, however, the script pops out both the cart-specific item ID number and the store-specific item ID number and then pushes them back onto the array once it has assigned the values to some variables. Using the shift operator, the script also grabs the quantity, but it does not unshift it back into the array; we will not need it in the array, because we have assigned it to the variable $quantity. Finally, the script chops off the newline character for $cart_row_number.

```
$cart_row_number = pop(@cart_fields);
$db_number = pop(@cart_fields);
push (@cart_fields, $db_number);
push (@cart_fields, $cart_row_number);
$quantity = shift(@cart_fields);
chop $cart_row_number;
```

Then the script begins creating a table-based form for quantity changes. First, it creates an input text field where users can enter a new quantity. In this case, the script assigns the $cart_row_number to the name in the input field so that it will later remember which item was associated with the quantity change.

```
print "<TD ALIGN = \"center\">\n";
print "<INPUT TYPE = \"text\"
            NAME = \"$cart_row_number\"
            SIZE =\"3\">\n";
```

The script then creates the table rows and page footer as it did before.

```
foreach $display_number (@display_numbers)
  {
  if ($cart_fields[$display_number] eq "")
    {
    $cart_fields[$display_number] = "<CENTER>-
                                    </CENTER>";
    }
  print "<TD ALIGN =
  \"center\">$cart_fields[$display_number]</TD>\n";
  } # End of foreach $display_number (@display_numbers)

print "<TD ALIGN = \"center\">$quantity</TD>\n";
$unformatted_subtotal = ($quantity *
                           $cart_fields[$price_number]);
$subtotal = sprintf ("%.2f\n", $unformatted_subtotal);
$unformatted_grand_total = $grand_total + $subtotal;
$grand_total = sprintf ("%.2f\n",
               $unformatted_grand_total);
print "<TD ALIGN = \"center\">\$$subtotal</TD>\n";
print "</TR>\n";
} # End of while (<CART>)
close (CART);

print <<"end_of_html";
</TABLE>
<P>
Grand Total = \$$grand_total
<P>
<INPUT TYPE = "submit" NAME = "submit_change_quantity"
       VALUE = "Submit Quantity Changes">
<INPUT TYPE = "submit" NAME = "continue_shopping"
       VALUE = "Continue Shopping">
<INPUT TYPE = "submit" NAME = "return_to_frontpage"
       VALUE = "Return to Front page">
<INPUT TYPE = "submit" NAME = "order_form"
       VALUE = "Checkout Stand">
</CENTER></FORM></BODY></HTML>
end_of_html
exit;
}
```

On the Web, the change quantity screen looks like Figure 17.8.

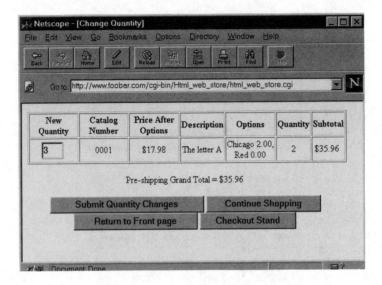

Figure 17.8 *Change quantity interface.*

Changing the Quantity of an Item in the Client's Cart

Once the client has typed some quantity changes and has submitted the information using the form generated in the previous section, the script makes the modifications to the database.

```
if ($form_data{'submit_change_quantity'} ne "")
{
```

First, it gathers the keys as it did for the front page generation earlier, checking to make sure the user entered a positive integer.

```
@incoming_data = keys (%form_data);
foreach $key (@incoming_data)
  {
  if ($key =~ /[\d]/ && $form_data{$key} =~ /[\D]/)
    {
    &bad_order_note;
    }
  }
```

As it did earlier, the script creates an array (@modify_items) of valid keys.

```
unless ($key =~ /[\D]/ && $form_data{$key} =~ /[\D]/)
  {
  if ($form_data{$key} ne "")
    {
    push (@modify_items, $key);
    }
  } # End of unless ($key =~ /[\D]/...
} # End of foreach $key (@incoming_data)
```

Next, it opens the client's cart and goes through it as usual.

```
open (CART,
"$cart_directory/$form_data{'cart_id'}.cart")
  || &open_error ("$cart_directory/$form_data{'cart_id'}.cart");
while (<CART>)
  {
  @database_row = split (/\|/, $_);
  $cart_row_number = pop (@database_row);
  push (@database_row, $cart_row_number);
  $old_quantity = shift (@database_row);
  chop $cart_row_number;
```

Then the script checks to see whether the item number submitted as form data is equal to the number of the current database row.

```
foreach $item (@modify_items)
  {
  if ($item eq $cart_row_number)
    {
```

If it is, the script creates the $shopper_row variable and begins creating the modified row. The script replaces the old quantity with the quantity submitted by the client ($form_data{$item}). Recall that $old_quantity has already been shifted off the array.

```
$shopper_row .= "$form_data{$item}\|";
```

Now the script adds the rest of the database row to $shopper_row and sets two flag variables. $quantity_modified is used to notify the script that the current row has had a quantity modification. $invalid_submission does basically the same thing but is used to make sure that the client submitted a valid quantity change.

```
foreach $field (@database_row)
  {
  $quantity_modified = "yes";
  $invalid_submission = "no";
  $shopper_row .= "$field\|";
  }
 chop $shopper_row; Get rid of last |
 } # End of if ($item eq $cart_row_number)
} # End of foreach $item (@modify_items)
```

If the script gets here and if $quantity_modified has not been set to yes, the script knows that the preceding routine was skipped, because the item number submitted from the form was not equal to the current database ID number. The script now knows that no quantity in the current row is being changed and the row can be added to $shopper_row as is. Remember, we want to add the old rows as well as the new, modified ones.

```
if ($quantity_modified ne "yes")
  {
  $shopper_row .= $_;
  }
 $quantity_modified = "";
} # End of while (<CART>)
close (CART);
```

Next, the script checks to make sure that somewhere along the line the client made a valid submission. If the submission was not made, the script executes the bad_order_note subroutine.

```
if ($invalid_submission ne "no")
  {
  &bad_order_note
  }
```

If the client made a valid submission, on the other hand, the script over-writes the old cart with the new information and sends the client back to the previous category page.

```
open (CART, ">
$cart_directory/$form_data{'cart_id'}.cart")
    || &open_error
```

```
("$cart_directory/$form_data{'cart_id'}.cart");
print CART "$shopper_row";
close (CART);
&display_cart_contents;
exit;
}
```

Generating the Delete Item Form

Now suppose that the client asked to delete an item rather than modify the quantity.

```
if ($form_data{'delete_item'} ne "")
{
```

In this case, the script prints the usual page and table headers.

```
&page_header("Delete Item");
print <<"end_of_html";
<CENTER>
<TABLE BORDER = "1">
<TR>
<TH>Delete Item</TH>
end_of_html
foreach $field (@display_fields)
  {
  print "<TH>$field</TH>\n";
  }
print "<TH>Quantity</TH>\n<TH>Subtotal</TH>\n</TR>\n";
```

It then opens the cart and this time adds a check box instead of an input text field so that the client can specify multiple items to delete. As it did in the routines used for modification, the script assigns the NAME equal to the cart_row_number.

```
open (CART,
"$cart_directory/$form_data{'cart_id'}.cart")
      || &open_error ("$cart_directory/$form_data{'cart_id'}.cart");
while (<CART>)
  {
  @cart_fields = split (/\|/, $_);
```

```
$cart_row_number = pop(@cart_fields);
$db_number = pop(@cart_fields);
push (@cart_fields, $db_number);
push (@cart_fields, $cart_row_number);
chop $cart_row_number;
$quantity = shift(@cart_fields);
print "<TD ALIGN = \"center\">\n";
print "<INPUT TYPE = \"checkbox\"
            NAME = \"$cart_row_number\">\n";
```

Next, the script displays the table rows as before.

```
foreach $display_number (@display_numbers)
  {
  if ($cart_fields[$display_number] eq "")
    {
    $cart_fields[$display_number] = "<CENTER>-</CENTER>";
    }
 print "<TD ALIGN =
\"center\">$cart_fields[$display_number]</TD>\n";
 } # End of foreach $display_number (@display_numbers)

 print "<TD ALIGN = \"center\">$quantity</TD>\n";
 $unformatted_subtotal = ($quantity *
                        $cart_fields[$price_number]);
 $subtotal = sprintf ("%.2f\n", $unformatted_subtotal);
 $unformatted_grand_total = $grand_total + $subtotal;
 $grand_total = sprintf ("%.2f\n",
                $unformatted_grand_total);
print "<TD ALIGN = \"center\">\$$subtotal</TD>\n";
print "</TR>\n";
} # End of while (<CART>)
close (CART);
```

The script also outputs the footer.

```
print <<"end_of_html";
</TABLE>
<P>
Grand Total = \$$grand_total
<P>
<INPUT TYPE = "submit" NAME = "submit_deletion"
    VALUE = "Submit Deletion">
<INPUT TYPE = "submit" NAME = "continue_shopping"
    VALUE = "Continue Shopping">
<INPUT TYPE = "submit" NAME = "return_to_frontpage"
```

```
        VALUE = "Return to Front page">
<INPUT TYPE = "submit" NAME = "order_form"
        VALUE = "Checkout Stand">
</CENTER></FORM></BODY></HTML>
end_of_html
exit;
}
```

On the Web, the delete interface looks like Figure 17.9.

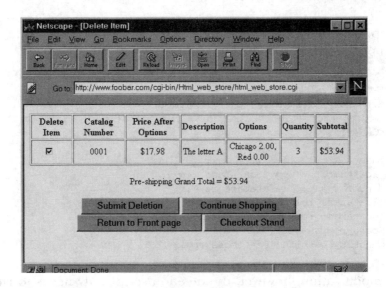

Figure 17.9 *Delete interface.*

Deleting an Item from the Client's Cart

If the client submits items for deletion, the script processes the following routines.

```
if ($form_data{'submit_deletion'} ne "")
{
```

Again, the script checks for valid entries. This time, though, it needs to make sure only that we filter out the extra form keys. It need not make sure that we have a positive integer value.

```
@incoming_data = keys (%form_data);
foreach $key (@incoming_data)
  {
  unless ($key =~ /[\D]/)
    {
    if ($form_data{$key} ne "")
      {
      push (@delete_items, $key);
      }
    } # End of unless ($key =~ /[\D]/...
  } # End of foreach $key (@incoming_data)
```

The script then opens the cart and gets the $cart_row_number, $db_id_number, and $old_quantity as it did for modification.

```
open (CART,
"$cart_directory/$form_data{'cart_id'}.cart")
    || &open_error ("$cart_directory/$form_data{'cart_id'}.cart");
while (<CART>)
{
  @database_row = split (/\|/, $_);
  $cart_row_number = pop (@database_row);
  $db_id_number = pop (@database_row);
  push (@database_row, $db_id_number);
  push (@database_row, $cart_row_number);
  chop $cart_row_number;
  $old_quantity = shift (@database_row);
```

Unlike modification, however, the deletion script only needs to check whether the current database row matches a submitted item for deletion. If it does not match, the script adds it to $shopper_row. Otherwise, the row is not added. Thus, all the rows are added except the ones that should be deleted.

```
$delete_item = "";
foreach $item (@delete_items)
  {
  if ($item eq $cart_row_number)
    {
    $delete_item = "yes";
    } # End of if ($item eq $cart_row_number)
  } # End of foreach $item (@add_items)
if ($delete_item ne "yes")
  {
```

```
    $shopper_row .= $_;
    }
} # End of while (<CART>)
close (CART);
```

Then the script overwrites the old cart with the new information and sends the client back to the category page.

```
open (CART, ">
$cart_directory/$form_data{'cart_id'}.cart")
        || &open_error ("$cart_directory/$form_data{'cart_id'}.cart");
print CART "$shopper_row";
close (CART);
&display_cart_contents;
exit;
}
```

Displaying the Order Form

Our hope is that the client fills the cart and heads to the cash register. Online, the cash register is analogous to the online order form.

```
if ($form_data{'order_form'} ne "")
{
```

The script prints an order form by reading the prepared form in the **Html** subdirectory.

```
open (ORDER_FORM, "$html_directory/$order_form")
        || &open_error("$html_directory/$order_form");
while (<ORDER_FORM>)
{
if ($_ =~ /<FORM/)
{
print <<"end_of_html";
<FORM METHOD = "post" ACTION = "$main_script_url">
<INPUT TYPE = "hidden" NAME = "page"
        VALUE = "$form_data{'page'}">
<INPUT TYPE = "hidden" NAME = "cart_id"
        VALUE = "$form_data{'cart_id'}">
<TABLE BORDER = "1"><TR>
end_of_html
```

NOTE To make this easier, we have created a subdirectory that contains the order form and front page HTML files. This way, it will be easier to modify them to your own needs. The preceding routine outputs your predesignated order form, but, as we did for the front page, we will insert our hidden variables.

Then the script prints the current cart contents using the previous routines.

```perl
foreach $field (@display_fields)
  {
  print "<TH>$field</TH>\n";
  }
print "<TH>Quantity</TH><TH>Subtotal</TH></TR>";

open (CART, "$cart_directory/$form_data{'cart_id'}.cart")
      || &open_error("$cart_directory/$form_data{'cart_id'}.cart");
while (<CART>)
  {
  @cart_fields = split (/\|/, $_);
  $quantity = shift(@cart_fields);
  foreach $display_number (@display_numbers)
    {
    if ($cart_fields[$display_number] eq "")
      {
      $cart_fields[$display_number] = "<CENTER>-</CENTER>";
      }
    print "<TD ALIGN
=\"center\">$cart_fields[$display_number]</TD>\n";
    }
  print "<TD ALIGN = \"center\">$quantity</TD>";
  $unformatted_subtotal =
     ($quantity*$cart_fields[$price_number]);
  $subtotal = sprintf ("%.2f\n", $unformatted_subtotal);
  $unformatted_grand_total = $grand_total + $subtotal;
  $grand_total = sprintf ("%.2f\n",
     $unformatted_grand_total);
  print "<TD ALIGN = \"center\">\$$subtotal</TD>";
  print "</TR>";
  } # End of while (<CART>)
 print <<"end_of_html";
</TABLE>
<P><CENTER>
```

```
Grand Total = \$$grand_total
<P></CENTER>
end_of_html
close (CART);
} # End of if ($_ =~ /<FORM/)
```

Once it has output the cart contents, the script continues outputting the predesignated order form.

```
  print "$_";
  } # End of while (<ORDER_FORM>)
close (ORDER_FORM);
exit;
}
```

Finalizing the Order

Finally, the script sends the order to whomever handles the order requests and sends the client a note thanking them for the order.

```
if ($form_data{'send_in_order'} ne "")
{
```

The script begins by sending the header and sorting the incoming form variables. We do this because the Perl keys function will not give us the form variables in any specific order due to hash routines. By encoding each form variable in your HTML document with a preceding number, such as 01-name or 05-city, you give yourself the ability to sort them in the order you want them to appear.

Take a look at the HTML in the accompanying CD-ROM. You will see that all the NAME values are ordered this way. The number corresponds to its order when all the variables are printed. The sort function takes all the unsorted variables in @variable_names, sorts them by this number, and then adds them to @sorted_variable_names.

```
&page_header("Your Order Has Been Sent");
@variable_names = keys (%form_data);
@sorted_variable_names = sort (@variable_names);
```

Once the variables are sorted, the script displays information the client entered on the order form and uses $email_body to begin creating the body of the E-mail message that it will send to the store administrator.

```
print "<H2><CENTER>
You submitted the following information</CENTER></H2>";
$email_body .= "Personal Information\n\n";
print "<TABLE>";
```

Then it prints the form variable and its associated value for every form field the client submitted. The script does not print administrative hidden variables used by this script, because the client does not care about them.

If you add other hidden variables, be sure to escape them here.

NOTE

The script also adds the list to the $email_body variable.

```
foreach $variable (@sorted_variable_names)
  {
  if ($form_data{$variable} ne "" &&
      $variable ne "cart_id" &&
      $variable ne "page" &&
      $variable ne "send_in_order")
    {
    print "<TR><TH ALIGN =
    \"left\">$order_form_array{$variable}</TH>\n";
    print "<TD>$form_data{$variable}</TD></TR>\n";
    $email_body .= "$order_form_array{$variable} =
                    $form_data{$variable}\n";
    }
  } # End of foreach $variable (@sorted_variable_names)
print "</TABLE>";
```

Then the current cart contents as ordered are displayed.

```
print "<H2><CENTER>
You ordered the following items</CENTER></H2>";
print "<TABLE BORDER = \"1\"><TR>";
```

```
foreach $field (@display_fields)
   {
   print "<TH>$field</TH>\n";
   }
print "<TH>Quantity</TH><TH>Subtotal</TH></TR>";
```

This time, however, the script does something a little bit different when it comes to mailing the store administrator. First, the script opens the cart again and reads it line by line.

```
$email_body .= "\nOrder Information\n\n";
open (CART,  "$cart_directory/$form_data{'cart_id'}.cart")
       || &open_error ("$cart_directory/$form_data{'cart_id'}.cart");
while (<CART>)
   {
   @cart_fields = split (/\|/, $_);
   $quantity = shift(@cart_fields);
   $cart_quantity = $cart_quantity + $quantity;
```

Because the store administrator does not need to have every single database row included with orders, the script includes only certain essential fields. First, the script notes the quantity of every item.

```
$email_body .= "$quantity";
```

Then, for every item that we have set to display in our setup file with the @display_numbers array, the script prints the whole row for the client on the Web.

```
foreach $display_number (@display_numbers)
   {
if ($cart_fields[$display_number] eq "")
   {
   $cart_fields[$display_number] = "<CENTER>-</CENTER>";
   }
print "<TD ALIGN=\"center\">$cart_fields[$display_number]</TD>";
```

But the store administrator receives a different list, which is defined in the setup file (@email_numbers). The administrator gets the values corresponding to the elements of @email_numbers, a sublist of @display_numbers that includes only those fields that the store administrator needs to see. For example, whereas the client may want to see the description, name, price, item number, size, and picture, the administrator may want to see only the item number, name, and quantity. Thus, the script sends the store administrator only those fields configured in the setup file.

```
foreach $display_field (@email_numbers)
  {
  if ($display_number eq $display_field)
    {
    $email_body .= "    $cart_fields[$display_number]";
    }
  }
} # End of foreach $display_number (@display_numbers)
```

The four spaces before `$cart_fields[$display_number]` **are just for formatting, as you will see when you get the E-mail.**

NOTE

The script adds a newline for every cart item.

```
$email_body .= "\n";
```

It then includes the footer information for the client on the Web and calculates costs.

```
print "<TD ALIGN = \"center\">$quantity</TD>";
$unformatted_subtotal =
    ($quantity*$cart_fields[$price_number]);
$subtotal = sprintf ("%.2f\n", $unformatted_subtotal);
$unformatted_grand_total = $grand_total + $subtotal;
$grand_total = sprintf ("%.2f\n",
    $unformatted_grand_total);
print "<TD ALIGN = \"center\">\$$subtotal</TD>";
print "</TR>";
} # End of while (<CART>)
```

The following routines are cost calculations for the example order form. They demonstrate how shipping costs might be figured.

```
if ($cart_quantity eq "1")
  {
  $shipping_cost = 2.50;
  }
if ($cart_quantity eq "2")
  {
  $shipping_cost = 3.50;
  }
if ($cart_quantity ne "2")
  {
  $cart_quantity = $cart_quantity - 2;
  $unformatted_shipping_cost = "3.50 + $cart_quantity";
  $shipping_cost = sprintf ("%.2f\n",
                  $unformatted_shipping_cost);
  }
  $unformatted_final_total = $grand_total +
                                $shipping_cost;
  $final_total = sprintf ("%.2f\n",
                $unformatted_final_total);
```

Next, the script prints the footer for both the client and the store administrator, including total price.

```
print <<"end_of_html";
</TABLE>
<P><CENTER>
Item Total = \$$grand_total
<P>
Shipping and Handling: \$$shipping_cost
<P>
Grand Total: \$$final_total
<P>
</CENTER>
end_of_html
close (CART);
$email_body .= "\nGrand Total = \$$final_total\n";
print "$_";
close (ORDER_FORM);
```

Finally, the script uses the send_mail routine in **mail-lib.pl** to send E-mail to the store administrator with the client's ordering information.

```
&send_mail("$admin_email","$admin_email",
    "$email_subject", "$email_body");
 exit;
}
```

On the Web, the client receives a page like that shown in Figure 17.10.

Displaying the Products for Sale

If it has advanced through all the preceding `if` tests, the script knows that the client simply wanted to see a page display. So it displays the current items within the page selected by the client.

It uses the `display_items_for_sale` subroutine:

```
else
  {
  &display_items_for_sale;
  exit;
  }
```

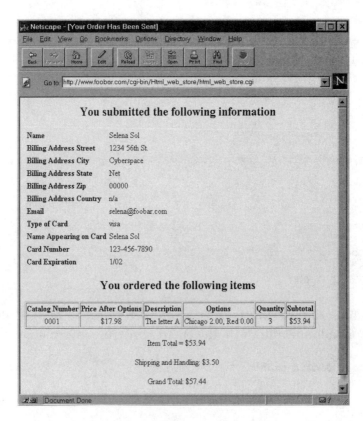

Figure 17.10 A successful order.

The display_items_for_sale Subroutine

This subroutine outputs the client-selected product page that has been prepared by the store administrator. Using the same filtering method used to output the front page, this routine loads the selected page, formats it with cart_id and page information, and outputs it to the client on the Web.

```
sub display_items_for_sale
  {
  open (HTML_FILE, "$html_directory/$form_data{'page'}")
     ||
  &open_error("$html_directory/$form_data{'page'}");
  while (<HTML_FILE>)
    {
    s/cart_id =/cart_id = $cart_id/g;
    s/%%cart_id%%/$form_data{'cart_id'}/g;
    s/%%page%%/$form_data{'page'}/g;
    print "$_";
    } # End of while (<HTML_FILE>)
  close (HTML_FILE);
  }
```

The bad_order_note Subroutine

The bad_order_note subroutine is used in case the client has typed an invalid character in one of the input fields. After all, we do not want to allow the client to enter a negative quantity and perhaps sneakily affect the grand total!

```
sub bad_order_note
{
&page_header("Wooopsy");
print <<"end_of_html";
<CENTER><H2>Wooopsy</H2></CENTER>
<BLOCKQUOTE>
I'm sorry, it appears that you did not enter a valid numeric quantity
(whole numbers greater than zero) for one or more of the items you
ordered and I am not allowed to modify your cart unless you do so.
Would you try again?  Thanks<P>
<CENTER><INPUT TYPE = "submit" NAME = "try_again"
            VALUE = "Try Again">
</CENTER></BLOCKQUOTE></BODY></HTML>
end_of_html
exit;
}
```

The page_header Subroutine

page_header prints the HTML page header. We pass the routine one argument, which differentiates pages that use this routine when it prints the HTML header.

```
sub page_header
  {
  local($type_of_page) = @_;
  print <<"end_of_html";
<HTML>
<HEAD>
<TITLE>$type_of_page</TITLE>
</HEAD>
<BODY>
<FORM METHOD = "post" ACTION = "$main_script_url">
<INPUT TYPE = "hidden" NAME = "page"
       VALUE = "$form_data{'page'}">
<INPUT TYPE = "hidden" NAME = "cart_id"
       VALUE = "$form_data{'cart_id'}">
end_of_html
  }
```

The display_cart_contents Subroutine

The display_cart_contents subroutine is used by the script to display the current items in the client's cart.

```
sub display_cart_contents
{
```

The subroutine first uses the page_header subroutine to output an HTML header, passing it one parameter relating to how the page title should be modified.

```
&page_header("View/Modify Cart");
```

Next, it begins to create a table to display the current cart contents.

```
print <<"end_of_html";
<CENTER>
```

```
<TABLE BORDER = "1">
<TR>
end_of_html
```

The script then creates the table headers. For every item in our special list of database items to be displayed, the script creates a header cell.

```
foreach $field (@display_fields)
  {
  print "<TH>$field</TH>\n";
  }
```

Now the script adds one cell for quantity and one for subtotal, because the client's cart has those "extra" fields.

```
print "<TH>Quantity</TH>\n<TH>Subtotal</TH>\n</TR>\n";
```

Next, it opens the client's cart again and goes through it one line at a time.

```
open (CART,  "$cart_directory/$form_data{'cart_id'}.cart")
|| &open_error ("$cart_directory/$form_data{'cart_id'}.cart");
while (<CART>)
  {
  @cart_fields = split (/\|/, $_);
  $cart_id_number = pop (@cart_fields);
  $quantity = shift(@cart_fields);
```

@display_numbers, defined in the database-specific setup file, gives the script the array numbers associated with the fields to be displayed on this table. @display_numbers gets the value associated with the field from the @cart_fields array.

```
foreach $display_number (@display_numbers)
{
if ($cart_fields[$display_number] eq "")
    {
    $cart_fields[$display_number] = "<CENTER>-</CENTER>";
    }
print "<TD ALIGN = \"center\">$cart_fields[$display_number]</TD>";
} # End of foreach $display_number (@display_numbers)
```

Using the quantity value it shifted earlier, the script fills the next table cell. After using the $price_number variable defined in the setup file, the script calculates the subtotal for that database row and fills the final cell. Next, it closes the table row and, once it has gone all the way through the cart file, also closes it.

```
print "<TD ALIGN = \"center\">$quantity</TD>";
$unformatted_subtotal = ($quantity*$cart_fields[$price_number]);
$subtotal = sprintf ("%.2f\n", $unformatted_subtotal);
$unformatted_grand_total = $grand_total + $subtotal;
$grand_total = sprintf ("%.2f\n", $unformatted_grand_total);
print "<TD ALIGN = \"center\">\$$subtotal</TD>";
print "</TR>";
} # End of while (<CART>)
close (CART);
```

Finally, the script prints the footer.

```
print <<"end_of_html";
</TABLE>
<P>
Grand Total = \$$grand_total
<P>
<INPUT TYPE = "submit" NAME = "change_quantity"
      VALUE = "Change Quantity">
<INPUT TYPE = "submit" NAME = "delete_item" VALUE = "Delete Items">
<INPUT TYPE = "submit" NAME = "continue_shopping"
 VALUE = "Continue Shopping">
<INPUT TYPE = "submit" NAME = "return_to_frontpage"
 VALUE = "Return to Front page">
<INPUT TYPE = "submit" NAME = "order_form" VALUE = "Checkout Stand">
</CENTER></FORM></BODY></HTML>
end_of_html
exit;
}
```

The open_error Subroutine

The open_error subroutine is used by this script to provide useful debugging information for the script administrator.

```
sub open_error
{
```

The subroutine begins by assigning the `filename` variable that was sent from the main routine to the local variable, $filename.

```
local ($filename) = @_;
```

It then sends back an error message and exits.

```
print "I am really sorry, but for some reason I was unable to open
<P>$filename<P>Please make sure that the filename is correctly defined
in your setup, actually exists, and has the right permissions relative
to the Web browser. Thanks!";
exit;
}
```

CHAPTER 18

Page Tracking Script

OVERVIEW

The page tracking script follows a user from page to page on a particular site. In addition to tracking which pages a user views, the script records the major "category" of the pages.

By collecting these kinds of statistics, an information provider can determine which pages are accessed more often and by whom. For example, an online store having different categories of items may want to keep track of visitors who often view the electronics section the most so that it can E-mail them selectively with sale information. Similarly, an information provider may want to keep track of a user's favorite categories so that the provider can program another CGI script to dynamically display content related to the user's individual interests.

The page tracking script uses the authentication library discussed in Chapter 9 to have the user log in to the system. Once the user logs in, each page can be tracked based on its category.

INSTALLATION AND USAGE

The page tracking files should be installed in a directory called **Page_track**.
The files and subdirectories associated with this application, along with
their required permissions, are shown in Figure 18.1.

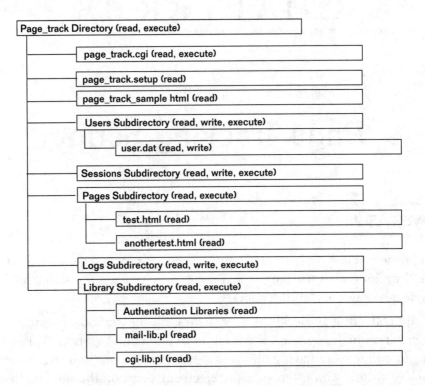

Figure 18.1 *Page tracking script directory structure and permissions.*

Page_track is the root application directory. It must be readable and executable by the Web server. In addition to the application files, the **Logs**,
Pages, **Library**, **Users**, and **Sessions** subdirectories reside here.

    page_track.cgi is the CGI script that filters the HTML and records the
user accesses to each file. This file must be readable and executable.

page_track.setup is the setup file for the **page_track.cgi** script. This file must be readable.

page_track_sample.html is a sample usage of the page tracking script. If your server is configured so that HTML files cannot be viewed from a CGI directory, you will need to move this file and update the reference to **page_track.cgi** to point to the new location. This file must be readable.

The **Library** subdirectory stores all the external libraries the script needs to access. This directory should be readable and executable. All the files within **Library** should be readable. These files include **cgi-lib.pl** (used for processing HTML forms), **mail-lib.pl** (used for sending E-mail), and the authentication library files (for logging a user into the page tracking script so that it knows which user it is tracking).

The **Users** subdirectory is used by the authentication library to store the user list. This directory needs to be readable, writable, and executable. The script creates a **user.dat** file in this directory the first time a user registers at the site. This file must be readable and writable.

The **Sessions** subdirectory is used by the authentication library to store the files related to each user's session after he or she first logs on to the site. This directory must be readable, writable, and executable.

The **Pages** subdirectory stores the sample HTML pages included on the accompanying CD-ROM. They contain special tags to tell the page tracker script how to handle the HTML. This directory must be readable and executable. In addition, it must contain page files that are readable.

The **Logs** subdirectory stores the logs related to the tracking of the Web pages. This directory must be readable, executable, and writable. Log files will be created by the **page_track.cgi** program and should be readable and writable by the Web server.

Server-Specific Setup and Options

The **page_track.setup** file contains the page tracker configuration variables. The following is a list of these setup items.

$page_track_log_file is the location and name of the file where HTML page accesses are stored. This variable needs to be set relative to the location of the **page_track.cgi** script.

$page_track_directory is the directory path where the HTML pages to be filtered are stored. This variable needs to be set relative to the location of the **page_track.cgi** script.

The rest of the variables set up the authentication library. These variables are discussed in great detail in Chapter 9. All the authentication variables start with the auth_ prefix. By default, the page tracker in this book turns CGI-based authentication on, registration is allowed, and the user gains access to the script right away so that it can begin tracking new users.

The following is an example of all the setup variables in the **page_track.setup** file.

```
$page_track_log_file =   "./Logs/pages.log";
$page_track_directory = "./Pages";
$auth_lib =              "./Library";
$auth_server =              "off";
$auth_cgi =                   "on";
$auth_user_file =        "Users/user.dat";
$auth_alt_user_file =       "";
$auth_allow_register =      "on";
$auth_allow_search =        "on";
$auth_default_group =        "normal";
$auth_generate_password =     "off";
$auth_check_duplicates =      "on";
$auth_add_register =           "on";
$auth_email_register =          "on";
$auth_admin_from_address =     "wwwadmin\@foobar.com";
$auth_admin_email_address =     "gunther\@foobar.com";
$auth_session_length = 2;
$auth_session_dir = "./Sessions";
$auth_register_message =
    "Thanks, you may now log on with your new username
    and password.";
$auth_password_message =
        "Thanks for applying to our site,
        your password is";
@auth_extra_fields = ("auth_first_name",
                    "auth_last_name",
```

```
                         "auth_email",
                         "auth_phone");
@auth_extra_desc = ("First Name",
                    "Last Name",
                    "Email",
                    "Phone Number");
```

Running the Script

To use the **page_track.cgi** program, you need to refer to it along with two URL variables: page and sessionid. page is set to the HTML page you want tracked and filtered. Initially, sessionid is blank; it is later generated by the authentication library after the user logs in. When an HTML file gets filtered by **page_track.cgi**, the sessionid variable is replaced with an exact sessionid value assignment so that the user's session is tracked throughout the site. The following is a sample URL for this script if it is installed in a **Page_track** subdirectory under a **cgi-bin** directory:

```
http://www.foobar.com/cgi-bin/Page_track/page_track.cgi?file=test.html
```

A sample HTML file that also has a sample version of this link appears in the next section. It also includes a reference to the log file that is generated by the default page tracking application setup that comes with this book. Figure 18.2 shows an example of what it looks like when displayed on a Web browser.

PAGE_TRACK_SAMPLE.HTML

```
<HTML>
<HEAD>
<TITLE>This Is A Test Filter</TITLE>
</HEAD>
<BODY>
<H1>Test Of Filter</H1>
<HR>
<A HREF="page_track.cgi?page=test.html">
Click Here For A Test Of The Filtering
</A>
<P>
<A HREF="Logs/pages.log">
```

```
See The Log Generated So Far By The Test
</A>
<HR>
</BODY>
</HTML>
```

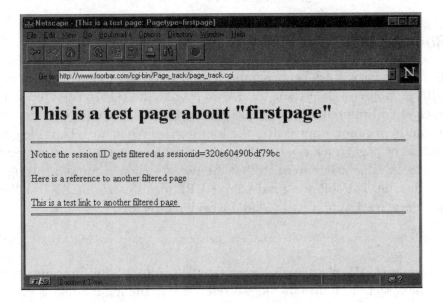

Figure 18.2 page_track_sample.html.

Notice that the hypertext reference in the preceding HTML page to the **page_track.cgi** script will filter **test.html** when selected. You may be wondering what will happen when this page is viewed. To examine this, let's look at the structure of **test.html**.

TEST.HTML

The first line of **test.html** contains an HTML comment field indicated by the <!– and --> tags. This comment is special to **page_track.cgi**. It tells the script what the page type of the HTML document is. Whenever **page_track.cgi** sees an HTML comment at the top of a file with the keyword pagetype: flush to the left of the comment, two things happen. First, the script reads the rest of the comment line to see what the page type is, and then the script writes the user and page type information to a log file.

```
<!--pagetype:The First Page-->
<HTML>
<HEAD>
<TITLE>This is a test page </TITLE>
</HEAD>
<BODY>
<H1>This is a test page about "firstpage"</H1>
<HR>
Notice the session ID gets filtered as sessionid
<P>
Here is a reference to another filtered page
<P>
<A HREF=page_track.cgi?page=anothertest.html&sessionid>
This is a test link to another filtered page
</A>
<HR>
</BODY>
</HTML>
```

In addition to this page tracking operation, the **page_track.cgi** script looks for any occurrence of sessionid and replaces it with sessionid=[the real current session id]. This technique lets the script track the user's current session from page to page without the user having to log on again. When the authentication library receives a valid session ID, it does not have to keep figuring out who the user is. Instead, it can read the information from its previously written session file. This process of storing session information is covered in Chapter 9 in the discussion about the authentication library.

ANOTHERTEST.HTML

The **test.html** file has a reference to another HTML file, **anothertest.html**. This file demonstrates that the **page_track.cgi** script can keep tracking a user through travels in multiple files.

The following HTML file uses the pagetype: comment tag to demonstrate yet another page type reference.

```
<!--pagetype:Another Page Type-->
<HTML>
<HEAD>
<TITLE>This is a another test page</TITLE>
</HEAD>
<BODY>
```

```
<H1>This is a test page about "Another Page Type"</H1>
<HR>
</BODY>
</HTML>
```

PAGES.LOG

As a user goes through the previous HTML pages using **page_track.cgi**, a log file is created and appended to with subsequent accesses. A sample of this log file follows. "John Doe" has first visited "The First Page" page type and subsequently has accessed the "Another Page Type" page type.

```
Page Type:The First Page: jdoe,John,Doe,join@foobar.com,555-1234
Page Type:Another Page Type: jdoe,John,Doe,join@foobar.com,555-1234
```

DESIGN DISCUSSION

The purpose of **page_track.cgi** is to track a user's accesses to HTML pages. This aim differs from that of the **html-auth.cgi** application that was used to demonstrate the authentication library in Chapter 9; **html-auth.cgi** protects documents from being viewed, whereas **page_track.cgi** goes one step further, making notes on the types of pages a user likes to go to. Figure 18.3 shows a diagram of the page tracking logic.

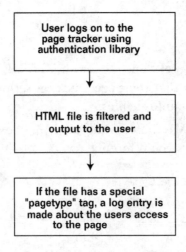

Figure 18.3 Basic flowchart for page tracking.

The first line of the following code sets up the location of the program's supporting files. By default, $lib is set to the **Library** subdirectory under the current directory. **cgi-lib.pl** is loaded along with the **page_track.setup** file.

```
$lib = "./Library";
require "$lib/cgi-lib.pl";
require "./page_track.setup";
```

$auth_lib is defined in **page_track.setup**. By default, it is set to the same location as $lib. The authentication library, discussed in Chapter 9, is then loaded from the directory specified by $auth_lib.

```
require "$auth_lib/auth-lib.pl";
```

First, the standard "Content-type: text/html\n\n" HTTP header is printed using the PrintHeader command from **cgi-lib.pl**. In addition, the incoming form variables are processed into the %in associative array by ReadParse.

```
print &PrintHeader;
&ReadParse;
```

The $sessionid variable is read from the incoming form variable session-id. The first time this script is called, $sessionid is blank, because the authentication library must first log the user in. This is done when the script calls the GetSessionInfo routine.

The conventions for calling GetSessionInfo are discussed thoroughly in Chapter 9. For our purposes here, it is enough to know that GetSessionInfo gathers the user's username, group, first name, last name, E-mail address, and phone number.

```
$sessionid = $in{"sessionid"};

($sessionid, $username, $group, $first_name,
 $last_name, $email,$phone) =
 &GetSessionInfo($sessionid, "page_track.cgi",*in);
```

Next, $page is assigned the value of the incoming form variable page. This variable is used to determine which page the script needs to process and display to the user.

```
$page = $in{"page"};
```

The DoFilter function is called with the user information. This routine does the work of filtering and displaying the HTML file. Then the program exits.

```
&DoFilter($page, $sessionid, $username,
        $first_name, $last_name,
        $email, $phone);
exit;
```

The DoFilter Subroutine

This routine filters the HTML page. It accepts as parameters the page, the session ID, and the user information fields. The page is stored in $page, and the session ID is stored in $session. The user information fields are stored in the @fields array. Each of these fields is defined as a variable that is local to the subroutine.

```
sub DoFilter {
    local($page,$session, @fields) = @_;
```

$page_type, $field_list, and $line are declared as local variables. $page_type is used to find out the current page type, and $field_list is used to store the user information fields in one long string. $line is used to keep track of each line as it is read from the HTML file.

```
    local($page_type,$field_list,$line);
```

First, the file itself is opened. If there is a problem with the file, CgiDie is called to print an error message and then stop the program.

```
    open (FILTERPAGE,"<$page_track_directory/$page") ||
      &CgiDie("$page could not be opened\n");
```

$field_list is set up as a string containing all the user information fields in a comma-delimited format. This is done using the join operator.

```
    $field_list = join(",", @fields);
```

The while loop goes through every line of the HTML file. The program finds a line that contains sessionid. It replaces the line with one that assigns the real session ID value to the $session variable.

```
while (<FILTERPAGE>) {
 s/sessionid/sessionid=$session/;
```

To keep track of the current line, we stuff it into the $line variable.

```
$line = $_;
```

If the line has a pagetype: comment, the $page_type is set to the characters that follow pagetype: within the HTML comment block. The parentheses that surround the .* in the regular expression tell Perl to stuff $1 with the results of the pattern match.

```
if ($line =~ /^<!--pagetype:(.*)-->$/) {
    $page_type = $1;
```

Then the log file is opened, and the previously collected information is written to it.

```
open(LOGFILE, ">>$page_track_log_file") ||
              &CgiDie("Could not open log file\n");
print LOGFILE
              "Page Type:$page_type: $field_list\n";
close (LOGFILE);
  }
```

Finally, the line is printed.

```
    print $line;
}
```

When the file is finished, the current HTML page is closed and the subroutine ends.

```
    close (FILTERPAGE);
} #End of DoFilter
```

CHAPTER 19

The Form Processor

OVERVIEW

Our form processing application allows a site administrator to process the results of Web-based forms in a number of ways. The script can be used to generate dynamic E-mail or to create and build a log file or database to track usage of HTML-based forms.

For example, a site administrator could use this script to help process customer feedback. The administrator would first create an HTML form–based questionnaire or other feedback form using standard HTML. Clients would fill out and submit feedback to the form processing script. The script would then send the feedback results to the administrator via E-mail as well as add it to a growing log of all feedback results, which could then be imported to a database application for further processing.

The processing of forms is configured by taking advantage of various hidden form tags included in the HTML form created by the administrator, so very little coding knowledge is needed to use this script. Furthermore, because the workings of the script are defined in the HTML form rather than in the Perl script, the HTML form author can use this one script to process all of the forms, no matter how different they are. The administrator need only modify the hidden variables that define how the script should act. Thus, we need not write separate CGI form processors for each of our forms. Instead, we can provide one centralized solution for all the forms on our system.

INSTALLATION AND USAGE

Once unarchived, the application should expand into the root directory **Form_processing**. Figure 19.1 shows the directory structure, including a summary of the correct permissions for files and directories.

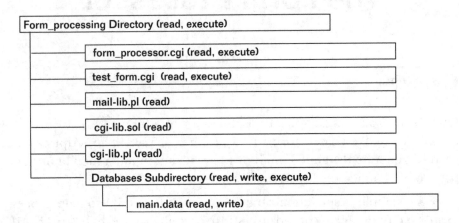

Figure 19.1 Form processor directory structure.

Form_processing, the root directory, contains five files (**form_processor.cgi**, **cgi-lib.pl**, **cgi-lib.sol**, **mail-lib.pl**, **test_form.cgi**) and one subdirectory (**Databases**), which contains one file (**main.data**). **Form_processing** must be executable and readable by the Web server.

form_processor.cgi is the main application and must be readable and executable by the Web server. This is the script that processes incoming data.

cgi-lib.pl, cgi-lib.sol, and mail-lib.pl are all discussed in Part Two. form_processor.cgi uses cgi-lib.pl to gather form data, cgi-lib.sol to create a lock file, and **mail-lib.pl** to E-mail on request. Each of these files must be readable by the Web server.

test_form.cgi is not necessary for the working of the program, but it is included on the accompanying CD-ROM as an example of a form interface to the script. It must be readable and executable by the Web server.

NOTE It is not necessary to have the HTML form generated by a CGI script. However, to keep everything in one directory structure for the example, we have made a script to generate a form instead of using basic HTML. Recall that Web browsers may not read HTML files in some **cgi-bin** directories.

Finally, **Databases** is the subdirectory in which **form_processor.cgi** will write when it is asked to append to database files that log the usage of the forms. Its permissions should allow the Web server to read, write, and execute. The directory can contain as many database files as you have HTML forms that write to them.

main.data is a sample database that we have included as an example of a datafile that logs usage of the script. It should be readable and writable by the Web server.

Server-Specific Setup and Options

THE HTML FORM

Before you run this script, you must prepare your HTML forms to send enough information so that the script can be most efficient. Specifically, you must send the information as hidden variables along with the client-defined information. The script uses these hidden variables to answer internal questions about how it should process the data it is receiving.

This script takes 17 hidden variables, which must be included in any HTML form (or, in the case of our example, **test_form.cgi**) that uses the script. The hidden variables are as follows.

`mailto` is the E-mail address of the person who should receive the results of form submission. This field is required.

`html_response` is the text of the HTML response that you want the client to receive after submitting information. This response is not required, but it's a good idea because it makes your site more user-friendly.

`email_subject` is the subject that you want to appear on the E-mail sent to the person who receives the results of form submission. This is not required but is also a good touch.

`variable_order` is the order in which you want all the variables to appear on the E-mail sent to the person who receives the results of form submission. The format of this tag is a pipe-delimited list, and every input field in your form must be represented in the list (see the following example). This is a required field.

`required_variables` is a list of variables that are required. If clients do not fill out information for these input fields, they get an error message requesting that they go back and fill out all the form fields. This field is not required.

`url_of_this_form` is the URL of the form that is being used to submit information; if clients do not submit all the required fields, they can link back to the form to try again. This variable is not required unless you have set a value for `required_variables`.

`background`, `bgcolor`, `text_color`, `link_color`, `vlink_color`, and `alink_color` relate to the body tag for all the HTML responses. None of them is required, but what is the good of having a fancy Web-based GUI without cool colors and stuff?

`response_title` is the title that you want to appear on the HTML response for successes. This title is not required, but it is suggested because it is good HTML style.

`return_link_url` is the URL of the page that defines the hyperlink that people click from the HTML response page after they have submitted their information. Again, this is not required, but it's recommended because it is best to provide the client with a simple way out of the form routine and back into your Web site.

`return_link_name` is the text of the clickable link related to `return_link_url`. This text is required only if you set `return_link_url` equal to something.

`database_name` is the path (relative to this script) of the datafile being used to store information submitted by this form.

`database_delimiter` is the delimiter your database uses to divide fields. Common ones are comma (,), colon (:), or pipe (|). We recommend the pipe symbol because it is rarely used in client-submitted data.

These hidden variables define how this script should perform, to whom it should send E-mail, how to sort the variables in the E-mail message, how to respond to the client, and so on. Following is an example of the short form, contained in the file **test_form.cgi**, that is displayed by pointing to a URL such as the following:

```
http://www.foobar.com/cgi-bin/Form_processing/test_form.cgi
```

You can use this form as a base example from which to create others.

```
#!/usr/local/bin/perl
print "Content-type: text/html\n\n";
print <<" end_of_html";
<HTML><HEAD><TITLE>Test Form</TITLE></HEAD><BODY>
<FORM ACTION = "http://www.foobar.com/cgi-bin/form_processor.cgi"
METHOD = "POST">
<INPUT TYPE = "hidden" NAME = "mailto"
       VALUE = "selena@foobar.com">
<INPUT TYPE = "hidden" NAME = "html_response"
       VALUE = "Thank you for submitting your personal
                information.">
<INPUT TYPE = "hidden" NAME = "email_subject"
       VALUE = "Form Test (From Scripts Page)">
<INPUT TYPE = "hidden" NAME = "variable_order"
       VALUE = "name|email|sign|purpose">
<INPUT TYPE = "hidden" NAME = "required_variables"
       VALUE = "name|email">
<INPUT TYPE = "hidden" NAME = "url_of_this_form"
       VALUE = "/cgi-
       bin/Selena/Form_processing/test_form.cgi">
<INPUT TYPE = "hidden" NAME = "background" VALUE = "">
<INPUT TYPE = "hidden" NAME = "bgcolor"
       VALUE = "FFFFFF">
<INPUT TYPE = "hidden" NAME = "text_color"
       VALUE = "000000">
<INPUT TYPE = "hidden" NAME = "link_color" VALUE = "">
<INPUT TYPE = "hidden" NAME = "vlink_color" VALUE = "">
```

```
<INPUT TYPE = "hidden" NAME = "alink_color" VALUE = "">
<INPUT TYPE = "hidden" NAME = "response_title"
       VALUE = "Thank You">
<INPUT TYPE = "hidden" NAME = "return_link_name"
       VALUE = "Selena Sol's Script Archive">
<INPUT TYPE = "hidden" NAME = "return_link_url"
       VALUE = "http://www.eff.org/~erict/Scripts/">
<INPUT TYPE = "hidden" NAME = "database_name"
       VALUE = "Databases/main.data">
<INPUT TYPE = "hidden" NAME = "database_delimiter"
       VALUE = ",">
<P><B>Name (Required):</B><BR>
<INPUT TYPE = "text" NAME = "name" SIZE = "35"
       MAXLENGTH = "35">
<P><B>Email (Required):</B><BR>
<INPUT TYPE = "text" NAME = "client_email" SIZE = "35" MAXLENGTH =
"35">

<P><B>Astrological Sign:</B><BR>
<INPUT TYPE = "text" NAME = "sign" SIZE = "35"
       MAXLENGTH = "35">

<P><B>Purpose in Life: </B><BR>
<INPUT TYPE="text" NAME="purpose" SIZE="35" MAXLENGTH="35">

<P><CENTER>
<INPUT TYPE = "submit" VALUE = "Tell me about yourself!">
</CENTER>
</FORM></BODY></HTML>
end_of_html
```

On the Web, the previous HTML form code looks like Figure 19.2.

In this example, the script E-mails selena@foobar.com when someone submits form data. It uses "Form Test (From Scripts Page)" as the subject of the E-mail and returns the client a little blurb with a pointer back to Selena Sol's Script Archive. Finally, the script appends the database **main.data** with a comma-delimited database row representing the four fields created here.

The body of the E-mail message contains the variables and their client-defined values in a specific order: name, E-mail address, sign, and purpose of life. I'll explain later how the script determines the order, but

I want to draw your attention to the way the order is predefined in the HTML form. It is pipe-delimited, and all variables must appear in the order you want them to be processed.

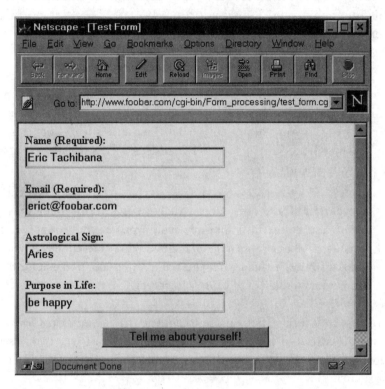

Figure 19.2 HTML form interface to form_processor.cgi.

THE SETUP VARIABLES

Just as the HTML form must be coded to send specific bits of information, the main script, **form_processor.cgi**, must be prepared to process those bits. Specifically, you must define certain variables within the main script. For ease, these variables are gathered near the top of the script.

$email_of_sender is the E-mail address of the account from which mail should be sent to the form processing administrator. This variable is

509

not necessarily required, because the script is set to understand the variable name client_email, which can be included in the HTML form. If client_email is defined, the script will send the mail as if it were coming from the client-submitted E-mail. (You may want to remind the client that this must be a valid E-mail address.) If client_email is not defined, however, you should define email_of_sender here so that sendmail will be able to function.

$your_server_name is the name of your Web server. We use this value to make sure that the form using this script is actually on your server. After all, we wouldn't want everyone in the universe using your server for form processing. If you are not sure what this value should be, it is probably the "www.foobar.com" in your URL address. This variable is required only if you want the greater security.

 Be careful if you are using a virtual server. The name may be an alias, and the script might not even process your forms! If you are unsure of what all this means, the best idea is to check with your site administrator, explain what you are trying to do, and ask for the valid server name relative to your Web server.

NOTE

$restricted_use is a flag that we use to activate the security just described. If you set this variable to no, it means that this script will process forms from any Web server on the net. This variable is required only if you want greater security.

$location_of_cgi_lib, $location_of_cgi_sol, and $location_of_mail_lib are the locations of the library files that should accompany this script.

$should_i_mail and $should_I_append_a_database are flags that you set depending on how you want the results of the form processing to be gathered. If you set $should_i_mail to yes, the form data will be sent to the administrator you have defined in the hidden form variables.

Similarly, if you set $should_i_append_a_database to yes, the form information will be saved in a database style that you can import to whatever database application you use. The name of the database is defined with hidden variables, as is the database delimiter.

Running the Script

Once you have configured the setup file to the specifics of your server setup and have prepared a form to be processed, you can try out the scripts by creating a hyperlink to the location of the form you are using (in this case, we reference the form-generating script):

```
<A HREF = "http://www.foobar.com/cgi-
bin/Form_processing/test_form.cgi">Sample Feedback form</A>
```

DESIGN DISCUSSION

Once the client has typed the information into the form fields you created in your HTML form, the client will press the **submit** button and **form_processor.cgi** will be responsible for handling the input as you have instructed it with the hidden variables. The logic of the script is depicted in Figure 19.3.

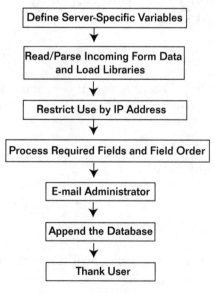

Figure 19.3 Script logic.

The script begins by starting the Perl interpreter and printing the HTTP header.

```
#!/usr/local/bin/perl
print "Content-type: text/html\n\n";
```

Defining Server-Specific Variables

Next, the script defines the server-specific variables discussed in the "Installation and Usage" section.

```
$email_of_sender = "admin\@foobar.com";
$your_server_name = "www.foobar.com";
$restricted_use = "no";
$location_of_cgi_lib = "./cgi-lib.pl";
$location_of_cgi_sol = "./cgi-lib.sol";
$location_of_mail_lib = "./mail-lib.pl";
$should_i_mail = "yes";
$should_I_append_a_database = "yes";
```

Loading Supporting Files and Reading and Parsing Form Data

Next, the script loads the supporting files and uses **cgi-lib.pl** to read the incoming form data. The script sends `*form_data` as a parameter to the subroutine `ReadParse` in **cgi-lib.pl** so that the associative array of form keys and values comes back with a descriptive name rather than `%in`.

```
require "$location_of_cgi_lib";
require "$location_of_cgi_sol";
require "$location_of_mail_lib";
&ReadParse(*form_data);
```

Restricting Use by IP Address

Next, the script determines the location of the form that is requesting its attention. It does this by accessing the environment variable `$ENV{'HTTP_REFERER'}`, which is equal to the URL of the form in question (http://www.foobar.com/Feedback/feedback.html). The script then `splits` that value into separate variables for every occurrence of "/" to isolate "www.foo-bar.com," which it compares to the value of $your_server_name. Thus, $referring_server is the only variable in the split that we give a hoot about. If $referring_server and $your_server_name are not the same, the script knows that it is being accessed by a form on another server.

```
($http, $empty, $referring_server, @path) = split (/\//,
$ENV{'HTTP_REFERER'});
```

If the $restricted_use has been set to yes, and if the $referring_server is not the same as $your_server_name, it means that we have had an illegal attempted access and the script should stop processing the form.

```
if ($restricted_use eq "yes")
  {
  if ($referring_server ne "$your_server_name")
    {
    &html_header("Form Error - Wrong Server");
    print "I'm sorry, you are not allowed to use this
           form processing script from a server other
           than $your_server_name<P>";
    print "As far as I can tell, you are coming from:
           $referring_server";
    print "<P>$restricted_use = restricted use<BR>";
    print "</BODY></HTML>";
    exit;
    }
  }
```

Processing Required Fields and Field Order

Once the script is sure that the form is within the security wall, the script breaks up the $variable_order variable that was sent from the form. $variable_order should look something like this:

name|email|sign|purpose|

This variable has been defined by the person who wrote the form that calls this script. The script then splits the variable into array elements every time it sees a pipe (|) so that @form_variables might look like this:

("name", "email", "sign", "purpose").

The script `splits` the variable using the following code:

```
@form_variables = split (/\|/, $form_data{'variable_order'});
```

It then repeats the same thing it did for `variable_order`, but this time for `required_variables`.

```
@required_variables = split (/\|/, $form_data{'required_variables'});
```

Once it has the list of required variables, the script checks to make sure that the client has submitted values for each of those variables. If any values are missing, the script produces a note explaining the problem along with a list of required variables. The script also adds a pointer back to the form.

```
foreach $variable (@required_variables)
  {
  if ($form_data{$variable} eq "")
    {
    &html_header("Form Error - Missing Data");
    print "Woops, I'm sorry, the following fields are
          required: ";
    print "<BLOCKQUOTE>";
    foreach $variable (@required_variables)
      {
      print "$variable<BR>";
      } # End of foreach $variable (@required_variables)
    print "</BLOCKQUOTE>";
    print "Please <A HREF =
        \"$form_data{'url_of_this_form'}\">go back to
        the form</A> and make sure you fill out all
        the required information.";
    print "</BODY></HTML>";
    exit;
    } # End of if ($form_data{$variable} eq "")
  } # End of foreach $variable (@required_variables)
```

NOTE

If you edit this note, make sure to escape any occurrences of @ or " with a backslash:

```
print "<A HREF = \"mailto:admin\@foobar.com\">admin\@foobar.com</A>";
```

E-Mailing Form Results to the Administrator

If the client submitted information for all the required fields, the script begins processing the data. It first checks to see whether it is supposed to generate E-mail.

```
if ($should_i_mail = "yes")
  {
```

If $should_i_mail has been set to yes in the define variables area, the script sends the results of the form to the administrator defined in the HTML hidden form data.

```
if ($form_data{'mailto'} ne "")
  {
  $email_to = "$form_data{'mailto'}";
  }
$email_subject = "$form_data{'email_subject'}";
```

Then the script begins building the body of the E-mail message. $email_body is used to store the information that the script will mail. First, the script notes the time using a little routine written by Matt Wright.

```
$email_body = "This data was submitted on: ";
$email_body .= &get_date;
$email_body .="\n\n";
```

NOTE The use of ".=" tells the script to append the new information to the end of the old. Thus, $email_body **keeps getting longer and longer as new information is tagged to the end of the old.**

Next, for every form variable, the script adds to $email_body the variable name and its values in the order specified by $form_data{'variable_order'}.

```
foreach $variable (@form_variables)
  {
  $email_body .= "$variable = $form_data{$variable}\n";
  }
```

Also, if the author of the HTML form has used the special form variable name client_email as one of the hidden input field names, the script changes $email_of_sender to the client-submitted E-mail address.

```
if ($form_data{'client_email'} ne "")
  {
  $email_of_sender = "$form_data{'client_email'}";
  }
```

NOTE

This change is not necessary, but from experience we've learned that it is nice to have the E-mail sent "from" the client submitting the information so that reply E-mail goes straight to the client rather than the form administrator.

Now the script uses the send_mail routine in **mail-lib.pl** to send the data.

```
&send_mail("$email_of_sender", "$email_to",
           "$email_subject", "$email_body");
} # End of  if ($should_i_mail = "yes")
```

The administrator will receive an E-mail message as shown in Figure 19.4.

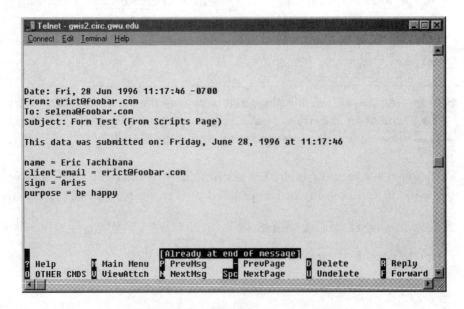

Figure 19.4 *Administrative E-mail.*

516

Appending to the Form Results Database

If the $should_I_append_a_database has been set to yes, the script also needs to append, to the database specified in the hidden field, the database_name specified in the form.

```
if ($should_I_append_a_database = "yes")
   {
```

The script first checks to see whether the database exists.

```
$database = "$form_data{'database_name'}";
if (-e $database)
  {
```

If the database exists, the script sets the $counter variable to zero. $counter is used to keep track of the number of fields sent from the form so that the script will know when the database row ends.

```
$counter = "0";
```

Then, for every field sent from the form, the script increments counter by 1.

```
foreach $variable (@form_variables)
   {
$counter++;
```

Next, the script appends the value of the variable to the growing $database_row variable.

```
$database_row .= "$form_data{$variable}";
```

If this is not the last item in the row, the script also divides each field with the database delimiter. When counter equals the number of elements in @form_variables, the script knows that it is at the end of the row and need not append another delimiter.

```
if ($counter <= @form_variables)
  {
  $database_row .= "$form_data{'database_delimiter'}";
```

```
    }
} # End of foreach $variable (@form_variables)
```

Finally, the script appends the new row, ending it with a newline character. To do so, it first creates a lock file using GetFileLock in **cgi-lib.sol**. It
then opens the database for appending (>>), prints to the database, and
closes it. Then the script releases the lock file.

```
&GetFileLock ("$database.lock");
open (DATABASE, ">>$database");
print DATABASE "$database_row\n";
close (DATABASE);
&ReleaseFileLock ("$database.lock");
} # End of if (-e $database)
```

If the database file did not exist, however, the script sends an error message to the user. Most likely, the hidden form variable is not correct (the
path is wrong), the permissions of the file are not set to be readable and
writable by the Web server, or its directory is not to be readable, writable,
and executable by the Web server.

```
else
  {
  &html_header("Form Error - Database Does Not Exist");
  print "I'm sorry, I am having trouble finding the
        database that this information should be sent
        to.  Please contact <A HREF =
\"mailto:$form_data{'mailto'}\">$form_data{'mailto'}</A>
        and let them know that there has been a
        problem.  Thank you very much.";
  print "</BODY></HTML>";
  exit;
  }
} # End of if ($should_I_append_a_database = "yes")
```

Thanking the User

Then the script prints a response to the client.

```
&html_header($form_data{'response_title'});
print "$form_data{'html_response'}";
print "<P>You sent us the following data:<P>";
foreach $variable (@form_variables)
```

518

```
    {
    print "$variable = $form_data{$variable}<BR>";
    }
print "<P>Please return to ";
print "<A HREF =
\"$form_data{'return_link_url'}\">$form_data{'return_link_name'}</A>";
print "</BLOCKQUOTE>";
print "</BODY></HTML>";
exit;
```

On the Web, the client will get something like the message shown in Figure 19.5.

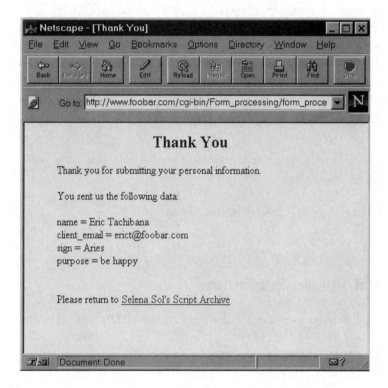

Figure 19.5 Response to client.

The get_date Subroutine

The get_date subroutine, written by Matt Wright, is used to find the current date.

```
sub get_date
  {
  @days = ('Sunday', 'Monday', 'Tuesday', 'Wednesday',
           'Thursday', 'Friday', 'Saturday');
  @months = ('January', 'February', 'March', 'April',
             'May', 'June', 'July', 'August',
             'September', 'October', 'November',
             'December');
```

The subroutine uses the `localtime` command to get the current time, splitting it into variables.

```
($sec,$min,$hour,$mday,$mon,$year,$wday,$yday,$isdst) =
localtime(time);
```

It then formats the variables and assigns them to the final `$date` variable.

```
if ($hour < 10) { $hour = "0$hour"; }
if ($min < 10) { $min = "0$min"; }
if ($sec < 10) { $sec = "0$sec"; }
```

The months and days arrays are used to format the date into a more human-readable form.

```
$date = "$days[$wday], $months[$mon] $mday, 19$year at
$hour\:$min\:$sec";
}
```

The html_header Subroutine

`html_header` is used to generate the header for all the HTML outputs.

```
sub html_header
  {
```

The subroutine begins by assigning to the local variable `$title` the `title` variable coming in from the subroutine call.

```
local($title) = @_;
```

It then prints the header.

```
print "<HTML><HEAD><TITLE>$title</TITLE></HEAD>";
print "<BODY";
```

Next, it creates the <BODY> tag according to the instructions defined in the hidden form variables.

```
if ($form_data{'background'} ne "")
    {
    print " BACKGROUND = \"$form_data{'background'}\"";
    }
if ($form_data{'bgcolor'} ne "")
    {
    print " BGCOLOR = \"$form_data{'bgcolor'}\"";
    }
if ($form_data{'text_color'} ne "")
    {
    print " TEXT = \"$form_data{'text_color'}\"";
    }
if ($form_data{'link_color'} ne "")
    {
    print " LINK = \"$form_data{'link_color'}\"";
    }
if ($form_data{'vlink_color'} ne "")
    {
    print " VLINK = \"$form_data{'vlink_color'}'}\"";
    }
if ($form_data{'alink_color'} ne "")
    {
    print " ALINK = \"$form_data{'alink_color'}\"";
    }
 print "><H2><CENTER>$title</CENTER></H2><BLOCKQUOTE>";
 }
```

NOTE

Notice in the last line that we include the end of the <BODY> tag as the first character printed.

CHAPTER 20

The Guestbook

OVERVIEW

Our guestbook script, based on the freeware guestbook written by Matt Wright called **guestbook.pl**, allows users to dynamically manipulate a guestbook HTML file by adding their own entries to the document. Thus, you can create a virtual guestbook that visitors can sign, leaving their contact information and perhaps comments about your pages.

The guestbook is configurable so that you can specify what your guestbook file looks like and how the script-generated responses are displayed. Most of the configuration takes little more than a knowledge of HTML, so it is fairly easy to use.

If configured to do so, the guestbook application will mail the guestbook administrator the text of new entries as well as add them to the guestbook. The script will also respond to new entrants with a configurable "Thank you" message. Thus, there is no need to continually monitor the page.

Finally, the script comes with the capability of "four letter word" filtering for a child-safe guestbook. You can censor words by adding them to a list of "bad words." If a guest attempts to use one of the excluded words in a guestbook entry, the word will be censored.

INSTALLATION AND USAGE

The application should expand into your local CGI-executable directory in the root directory **Guestbook**, as diagrammed in Figure 20.1.

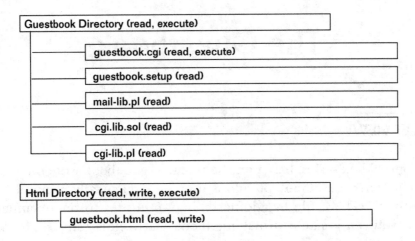

Figure 20.1 Guestbook directory structure.

Guestbook is the application's root directory and must be readable and executable by the Web server. It contains five files: **cgi-lib.pl**, **guestbook.cgi**, **guestbook.setup**, **guestbook.html**, and **mail-lib.pl**.

guestbook.cgi is the main body of the application and must be readable and executable by the Web server. We will discuss this file more thoroughly in the "Design Discussion" section.

guestbook.setup is the file that contains the configurable option variables and the variables that must be set to the specifics of your system. This file must be readable by the Web server and will be discussed in the "Server-Specific Setup and Options" section.

cgi-lib.pl, **cgi-lib.sol**, and **mail-lib.pl** are library files described in Part Two. **cgi-lib.pl** is used to parse form data, **mail-lib.pl** is used to send notifications by E-mail, and **cgi-lib.sol** is used for its lock file routines. Each library file must be readable by the Web server.

guestbook.html is the HTML guestbook file, which clients can read and add to if they desire. In Figure 20.1, **guestbook.html** is contained in a directory called **Html**.

Html, however, is not included on the accompanying CD-ROM. It represents a generic HTML directory on your system. We diagram it here because you will need to move the distribution copy of **guestbook.html** (which we will discuss soon) to an HTML directory elsewhere on your system; most servers are configured to disallow HTML in the **cgi-bin** directory. **guestbook.html** must be readable and writable by the Web server and will be discussed in greater depth in the "Server-Specific Setup and Options" section. The directory containing **guestbook.html** must be readable, writable, and executable by the Web server. You cannot use the **Guestbook** directory, which must remain read and execute only, for this purpose.

Server-Specific Setup and Options

THE SETUP FILE

The primary functions of the setup file are to define server-specific variables and to define options. The setup file contains the following variables.

$guestbookurl is the URL of **guestbook.html**.

$guestbookreal is the location and name of **guestbook.html** on your server.

$cgiurl is the URL of this script.

$cgi_lib_location, $cgi_sol_location, and $mail_lib_location are the locations on the server of the three library files that accompany this script.

@bad_words is a list of words that you want to censor from your guestbook. Any word in this list will be removed before the guestbook is modified. If you do not want to censor anyone, set @bad_words to nothing as follows:

```
@bad_words = ();
```

$mail determines whether to E-mail the guestbook administrator when a new entry has been made. If $mail is set to 1, the guestbook administrator will be notified; if it is set to zero, no E-mail will be sent.

$recipient is the E-mail address of the guestbook administrator who should receive the E-mail notification, and $email_subject is the subject of that message.

$linkmail determines whether you want E-mail addresses in your guestbook to be clickable. If you want them to be, set this equal to 1; otherwise, set it to zero.

$remote_mail determines whether a thank you note is sent to the guest who signed the guestbook. If you set this equal to 1, the guest will receive a thank you note. Set it to zero and the note will not be sent.

$allow_html is set to allow or disallow the use of HTML tags in guestbook entries. If you set this to 1, guests will be able to use HTML. If you set it to zero, they will not be able to use HTML.

@required_fields is the list of fields that the guest MUST submit to add the guestbook entry.

As an example, the complete text of **guestbook.setup** is shown next:

```
$guestbookurl = "http://www.foobar.com/Guestbook/guestbook.html";
$guestbookreal = "/Guestbook/guestbook.html";
$cgiurl = "guestbook.cgi";
$cgi_lib_location = "./cgi-lib.pl";
$cgi_sol_location = "./cgi-lib.sol";
$mail_lib_location = "./mail-lib.pl";
@bad_words = ("darn", "fudge", "frack", "poopoo", "Bob Dole");
$mail = 1;
$recipient = 'selena@foobar.com';
$email_subject = "Entry to Guestbook";
$linkmail = 1;
$remote_mail = 1;
$allow_html = 1;
@required_fields = ("realname", "comments");
```

THE GUESTBOOK FILE

Because it must be read as an HTML file, **guestbook.html** must be placed in a directory from which the Web server is allowed to read HTML files.

Thus, if your **cgi-bin** directory is configured to disallow HTML files, you must move **guestbook.html** to an HTML-friendly directory. If your server displays HTML files from the directory containing the CGI executables, you must take care to put the HTML file in a subdirectory that is writable and not in the root **Guestbook** directory.

As time goes by, this file will expand with guestbook entries. At first, however, the file will look like the following HTML page with a hyperlink reference to **guestbook.cgi** for additions:

```
<HTML>
<HEAD>
<TITLE>Selena Sol's Guestbook</TITLE>
</HEAD>
<BODY BGCOLOR = "FFFFFF" TEXT = "000000">
<CENTER><H1>Selena Sol's Guestbook</H1>
</CENTER>
Thank you for visiting my homepage.  Feel free to
<A HREF =
"http://www.foobar.com/cgi-bin/Guestbook/guestbook.cgi">Add</a>
to my guestbook! <HR WIDTH = "75%">
<!—begin—>


</BODY>
</HTML>
```

NOTE You also must change the hyperlink reference to **guestbook.cgi** to reflect your local directory structure. When clients click on the hyperlink to **Add an Entry**, they should be taken to the script that will handle things from there.

The initial guestbook is a simple, expected HTML file except for the following line:

```
<!—begin—>
```

This tag line tells the script where to add entries. We will discuss this later. For now, you should know what will happen when someone submits a guestbook entry, so the following listing shows one guestbook entry. Notice that each new entry is inserted after the `<!—begin—>` line.

```
<!—begin—>
<B>Name:</B><A HREF = "http://www.foobar.com/~erict">Selena
Sol</A><BR>
<B>Email:</B><A HREF =
"mailto:selena@foobar.com">selena@foobar.com</A><BR>
<B>Location:</B> Arlington, VA 22201<BR>
<B>Date:</B> Saturday, June 8, 1996 at 09:10:07<BR>
<b>Comments:</B><BLOCKQUOTE>This is a test</BLOCKQUOTE>
</BODY>
</HTML>
```

Figure 20.2 shows the **guestbook.html** interface on the Web.

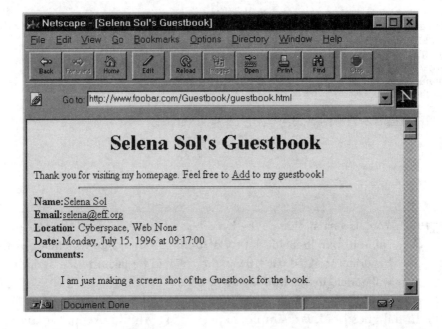

Figure 20.2 The guestbook.html interface.

RUNNING THE SCRIPT

Once you have configured the setup file, set all the appropriate permissions, and prepared your **guestbook.html** file, you can create a link to the guestbook so that clients can begin signing. The initial link should point to **guestbook.html** as follows:

```
<A HREF = "http://www.foobar.com/Guestbook/guestbook.html">The
Guestbook</A>
```

Clients can then read through guestbook entries. If they choose, they can click on the **Add an entry** link, which accesses the main script.

DESIGN DISCUSSION

Once you have configured the setup file, your guestbook is ready to go. The logic of the script is depicted in Figure 20.3.

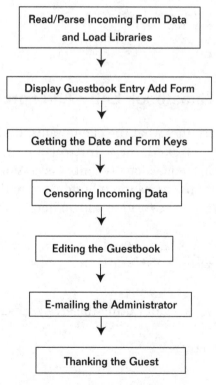

Figure 20.3 Script logic.

The script begins by starting the Perl interpreter and printing the HTTP header.

```
#!/usr/local/bin/perl
print "Content-type: text/html\n\n";
```

Loading Supporting Files and Reading Incoming Form Data

Next, the script loads the supporting files and uses **cgi-lib.pl** to read the incoming form data. It sends *form_data as a parameter to the subroutine ReadParse in **cgi-lib.pl** so that the associative array of form keys and values comes back with a descriptive name rather than %in.

```
require "./guestbook.setup";
require "./$cgi_sol_location";
require "$cgi_lib_location";
require "$mail_lib_location";
&ReadParse(*form_data);
```

Displaying the Guestbook Entry Add Form

Next, the script determines what the client wants. If $form_data{'action'} equals add (client clicked on a button somewhere) or if (||) $ENV{'REQUEST_METHOD'} equals GET (client is accessing this script for the first time as a link and not as a submit button), then the script knows that the client is asking to see the form to add an item to the guestbook.

```
if ($form_data{'action'} eq "add" ||
    $ENV{'REQUEST_METHOD'} eq "GET")
  {
```

First, it prints the form's header using the HERE DOCUMENT method.

```
print <<"    end_of_html";
<HTML>
```

```
<HEAD>
<TITLE>Selena Sol's Guestbook (Add Form)</TITLE>
</HEAD>
<BODY>
<CENTER>
<H2>Add to my Guestbook</H2>
</CENTER>
Please fill in the blanks below to add to my guestbook.  The only
blanks that you have to fill in are the comments and name section.
Thanks!
<P><HR>
end_of_html
```

Next, the script uses the subroutine `output_add_form` at the end of this form to print the form. It then quits and lets the client submit data.

```
&output_add_form;
exit;
}
```

Figure 20.4 shows the add form on the Web.

Getting Date and Form Keys

If the script gets to this point, it means that the client has filled out the add form and is submitting a new guestbook entry. The script uses the `get_date` subroutine at the end of this script to get the current date and time so that it can use it in the output.

```
$date = &get_date;
```

Then it creates an array of form variables by accessing the `keys` of the associative array `%form_data` given to it by **cgi-lib.pl**.

```
@form_variables = keys (%form_data);
```

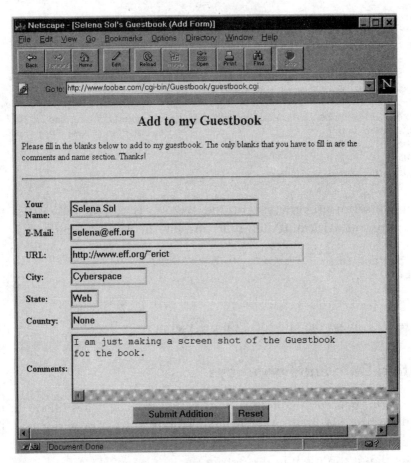

Figure 20.4 Guestbook add form.

Censoring Incoming Form Data

Next, the script checks to see whether it was asked to censor any particular words. For every variable sent to it from the form and for each word in the list of bad words, the script replaces (=~ s/), with case insensitivity off (/gi), every occurrence of the bad word ($word) with the word "censored." $form_data{$variable} should be equal to what the client filled in using the input boxes.

```
foreach $variable (@form_variables)
 {
 foreach $word (@bad_words)
   {
   $form_data{$variable} =~ s/\b$word\b/censored/gi;
   }
```

If the guestbook administrator has set `$allow_html` to zero (`!= 1`), it means that the administrator does not want the users to be able to use HTML tags. So the script deletes them.

```
 if ($allow_html != 1)
   {
   $form_data{$variable} =~ s/<([^>]|\n)*>//g;
   }
 }
```

Checking Required Fields

For every field that was defined in the list of required fields, the script then checks the form data to see whether that variable has an empty value. If it is empty, the script jumps to the subroutine `missing_required_field_data` at the end of this script, passing as a parameter the name of the field that was not filled out.

```
foreach $field (@required_fields)
   {
   if ($form_data{$field} eq "" )
     {
     &missing_required_field_data($field);
     }
   }
```

Editing the Guestbook

Now the script opens the guestbook HTML file and reads each of the lines into an array called @LINES. Thus, @LINES will contain every line of the guestbook file so that each array element will correspond to a line in the file. Then the script closes the guestbook file. Finally, it sets the variable $SIZE to the number of elements in the array, which is the same number of lines in the guestbook file.

```
open (FILE,"$guestbookreal") ||
die "Can't Open $guestbookreal: $!\n";
@LINES=<FILE>;
close(FILE);
$SIZE=@LINES;
```

The script opens the guestbook file again, but this time it opens the file for writing. In fact, it overwrites the existing guestbook file with new data using >. It also uses the GetFileLock subroutine in **cgi-lib.sol** to make sure that no one else writes to the guestbook at the same time.

```
&GetFileLock ("$guestbookreal.lock");
open (GUEST,">$guestbookreal") || &CgiDie ("Can't Open $guestbookreal");
```

Then the script goes through the @LINES array adding lines "back" to the guestbook file one by one and inserting the new entry along the way. For every line in the guestbook file (remember that $SIZE equals the number of lines), the script assigns the value of the line ($LINES[$i]) to the variable $_. It begins with the first line in the array ($i=0) and ends when it has gone through all the lines ($i<=$SIZE), counting by 1 all along ($i++). Then the script references the array in the standard form $arrayname[$element_number].

```
for ($i=0;$i<=$SIZE;$i++)
  {
  $_=$LINES[$i];
```

If the line happens to include the <!—begin—> tag, the script knows that it must add a new entry. This is why it is essential that your **guestbook.html** have that line all on its own somewhere in the body when you initialize the guestbook. If the line is not there, the new entry will not be added; if there is other information on the same line, that information will be deleted.

```
if (/<!--begin-->/)
  {
```

The script then adds the entry. It first prints the line <!–begin–> so that it will be able to find the top of the guestbook again next time.

```
print GUEST "<!--begin-->\n";
```

Then it begins adding the guest's information. First, it prints the name of the guest. If the guest submitted a URL, it makes the name clickable to the URL. If the guest did not submit a URL, however, it just prints the name.

```
if ($form_data{'url'})
  {
  print GUEST "<B>Name:</B>";
  print GUEST "<A HREF = \"$form_data{'url'}\">$form_data{'real-
name'}</A>";
  print GUEST "<BR>\n";
  }
else
  {
  print GUEST "<B>Name:</B>
              $form_data{'realname'}<BR>\n";
  }
```

Next, the script prints the E-mail address of the guest, and, if you have set $linkmail to 1 in the setup file, it makes the E-mail link clickable.

```
if ( $form_data{'email'} )
  {
  if ($linkmail eq '1')
    {
    print GUEST "<B>Email:</B>";
    print GUEST "<A HREF = \"mailto:$form_data{'email'}\">";
    print GUEST "$form_data{'email'}</A><BR>\n";
    }
  else
    {
    print GUEST " $form_data{'email'}<BR>\n";
    }
  }
```

The script then prints the guest's address if he or she submitted the values.

```
if ( $form_data{'city'} )
  {
  print GUEST "<B>Location:</B> $form_data{'city'},";
  }
if ( $form_data{'state'} )
  {
  print GUEST " $form_data{'state'}";
  }
if ( $form_data{'country'} )
  {
  print GUEST " $form_data{'country'}<BR>\n";
  }
```

Finally, the script prints the date and the guest's comments.

```
print GUEST "<B>Date:</B> $date<BR>\n";
print GUEST "<b>Comments:</B>

<BLOCKQUOTE>$form_data{'comments'}";

print GUEST "</BLOCKQUOTE><HR>\n\n";

}
```

If the line was not <!--begin-->, however, the script makes sure to print the line so that it retains all of the HTML that was in the guestbook before a new entry was added. Thus, the long for loop goes through each line, prints the header, and gets all the way down through whatever HTML you've written until it gets to the guestbook entries, which begin with the <!--begin--" tag. Then the script prints the new entry as well as all the old entries. When the script gets to the end of the file (@LINES), it's over.

```
else
  {
  print GUEST $_;
  }
}
```

The script closes the guestbook and releases the lock file so that others can access the guestbook.

536

```
close (GUEST);
&ReleaseFileLock ("$guestbookreal.lock");
```

E-Mailing to the Guestbook Administrator

Now the script prepares to E-mail a note to the guestbook administrator. First, it renames $form_data{'email'} to $email_of_sender.

```
$email_of_guest = "$form_data{'email'}";
```

If the guestbook administrator has set $mail to 1 (guestbook administrator wants to be notified when someone enters a guestbook entry), the script begins creating the body of the E-mail. It stores the body in the variable $email_body and continually appends this variable by using ".=".

```
if ($mail eq '1')
   {
   $email_body .= "You have a new entry in your guestbook:\n\n";
   $email_body .= "---------------------------\n";
   $email_body .= "Name: $form_data{'realname'}\n";
```

If the guest submitted values, the script adds them, too.

```
if ($form_data{'email'} ne "")
   {
   $email_body .="Email: <$form_data{'email'}>\n";
   }

if ($form_data{'url'} ne "")
   {
   $email_body .="URL: <$form_data{'url'}>\n";
   }

if ($form_data{'city'} ne "")
   {
   $email_body .= "Location: $form_data{'city'},";
   }

if ($form_data{'state'} ne "")
   {
   $email_body .= " $form_data{'state'}";
   }
```

```
if ($form_data{'country'} ne "")
  {
  $email_body .= " $form_data{'country'}\n";
  }
```

Next, the script finishes the message body.

```
$email_body .= "Time: $date\n\n";
$email_body .= "Comments: $form_data{'comments'}\n";
$email_body .= "------------------------\n";
```

Finally, the script uses the send_mail subroutine in the **mail-lib.pl** library file to send the E-mail to the guestbook administrator.

```
&send_mail("$email_of_guest", "$recipient",
          "$email_subject", "$email_body");
}
```

The guestbook administrator will receive the following E-mail summarizing the guestbook entry:

```
Date: Sat, 8 Jun 1996 13:33:41 -0700
From: selena@foobar.com
To: selena@foobar.com
Subject: Entry to Guestbook


You have a new entry in your guestbook:


------------------------------------
Name: Selena Sol
Email: <selena@foobar.com>
URL: <http://www.foobar.com/~erict>
Location: Arlington, VA USA
Time: Saturday, June 8, 1996 at 13:33:40


Comments: Testing
------------------------------------
```

Thanking the Guest through E-Mail

If the guestbook administrator has set $remote_mail to 1 and (&&) if the guest has submitted an E-mail, the script sends a "Thank you" E-mail to the guest. The process is identical to the previous one for generating and sending E-mail.

```
if ($remote_mail eq '1' &&
$form_data{'email'} ne "")
  {
  $email_body = "";
  $email_body .= <<"    end_of_message_to_guest";
  Thanks very much for stopping by my site, and a
  double thanks to you for taking the time to sign my
  guestbook. I hope you found something useful, and
  please let other netizens know of the existence of my
  little corner of the net.
  end_of_message_to_guest
  $email_body .= "\n";
  $email_body .= "    By the way, you wrote...\n\n";
  $email_body .= "    Name: $form_data{'realname'}\n";
  if ($form_data{'email'} ne "")
    {
    $email_body .="    Email: <$form_data{'email'}>\n";
    }

  if ($form_data{'url'} ne "")
    {
    $email_body .="    URL: <$form_data{'url'}>\n";
    }

  if ($form_data{'city'} ne "")
    {
    $email_body .= "    Location: $form_data{'city'},";
    }

 if ($form_data{'state'} ne "")
    {
    $email_body .= " $form_data{'state'}";
    }

 if ($form_data{'country'} ne "")
    {
    $email_body .= " $form_data{'country'}\n";
    }

  $email_body .= "    Time: $date\n\n";
  $email_body .= "    Comments:
                     $form_data{'comments'}\n";
  &send_mail("$recipient", "$email_of_guest",
          "$email_subject", "$email_body");
  }
```

The client who filled out the guestbook form will get an E-mail message something like the following:

```
Date: Sat, 8 Jun 1996 13:33:41 -0700
From: selena@foobar.com
To: gunther@foobar.com
Subject: Entry to Guestbook


Thanks very much for stopping by my site and a
double thanks to you for taking the time to sign my guestbook. I hope
you found something useful, and please let other netizens know of the
existence of my little corner of the net.


By the way, you wrote...


Name: Gunther Birznieks
Email: <gunther@foobar.com>
URL: <http://www.foobar.com/~gunther>
Location: Anytown, Anycity USA
Time: Saturday, June 8, 1996 at 13:33:40
Comments: Testing
```

Displaying HTML-Based Thank You

Then the script sends guests a thank you note on the Web and provides them with a way to get back to where they were before.

```
print <<" end_of_html";
<HTML><HEAD><TITLE>Thank You</TITLE></HEAD>
<BODY>
<CENTER>
<IMG SRC = "http://www.foobar.com/Images/thankyou.gif">
<P>
Thank you for signing the Guestbook, $form_data{'realname'}
</CENTER>
<P>
Your entry has now been added to the guestbook as follows...<BLOCK-
QUOTE>
end_of_html
```

As a check for the client, the script prints a copy of the submissions.

```
if ($form_data{'url'} ne "")
  {
  print "<B>Name:</B>";
  print "<A HREF =
\"$form_data{'url'}\">$form_data{'realname'}</A><BR>";
  }
else
  {
  print "<B>Name:</B> $form_data{'realname'}<BR>";
  }
if ( $form_data{'email'} )
  {
  if ($linkmail eq '1')
    {
    print "<B>Email:</B>
            (<a href=\"mailto:$form_data{'email'}\">";
    print "$form_data{'email'}</a>)<BR>";
    }
  else
    {
    print "<B>Email:</B> ($form_data{'email'})<BR>";
    }
  }

  print "<B>Location:</B> ";

  if ( $form_data{'city'} )
    {
    print "$form_data{'city'},";
    }

  if ( $form_data{'state'} )
    {
    print " $form_data{'state'}";
    }

  if ( $form_data{'country'} ){
    print " $form_data{'country'}";
  }

  print "<BR><B>Time:</B> $date<P>";
  print "<B>Comments:</B> $form_data{'comments'}<BR>\n";
  print "</BLOCKQUOTE>";
  print "<a href=\"$guestbookurl\">Back to the
```

```
        Guestbook</a>\n";
print "- You may need to reload it when you get there
        to see your\n";
print "entry.\n";
print "</body></html>\n";
exit;
```

The client's response will look something like Figure 20.5.

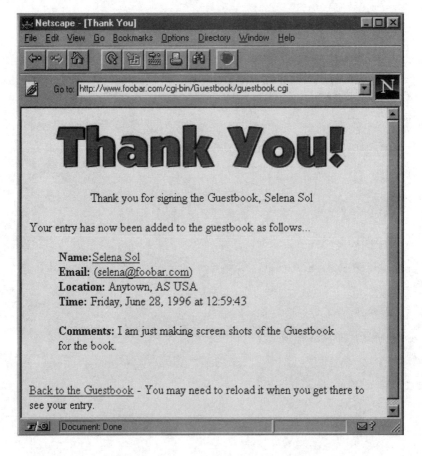

Figure 20.5 *Guestbook thank you response.*

The missing_required_field_data Subroutine

`missing_required_field_data` is used to warn clients that they failed to submit values for any or all of the required fields.

```
sub missing_required_field_data
  {
```

First, the passed parameter is set to the local variable `$field`.

```
local($field) = @_;
```

Then the script sends the client an informative error message.

```
print <<"     end_of_html";
<HTML><HEAD><TITLE>Data Entry Error</TITLE></HEAD>
<BODY>
<BLOCKQUOTE>Woopsy, You forgot to fill out $field and I am not allowed
to add your guestbook entry without it.  Would you please type some-
thing in below...</BLOCKQUOTE>
end_of_html
```

The script then reprints the add form using the subroutine `output_add_form` at the end of this script and exits.

```
 &output_add_form;
 exit;
}
```

The output_add_form Subroutine

`output_add_form` prints the form that clients use to add their entries.

```
sub output_add_form
  {
```

This subroutine is straightforward printing using the HERE DOCUMENT method.

```
print <<"    end_of_html";
<FORM METHOD = "POST" ACTION = "guestbook.cgi">
<TABLE>
<TR>
<TH ALIGN = "left">Your Name:</TH>
<TD><INPUT TYPE = "text" NAME = "realname" SIZE = "40"
            VALUE = "$form_data{'realname'}"></TD>
</TR><TR>
<TH ALIGN = "left">E-Mail:</TH>
<TD><INPUT TYPE = "text" NAME = "email" SIZE = "40"
            VALUE = "$form_data{'email'}"></TD>
</TR><TR>
<TH ALIGN = "left">URL:</TH>
<TD><INPUT TYPE = "text" NAME = "url" SIZE = "50"
            VALUE = "$form_data{'url'}"></TD>
</TR><TR>
<TH ALIGN = "left">City:</TH>
<TD><INPUT TYPE = "text" NAME = "city" SIZE = "15"
            VALUE = "$form_data{'city'}"></TD>
</TR><TR>
<TH ALIGN = "left">State:</TH>
<TD><INPUT TYPE = "text" NAME = "state" SIZE = "4"
            VALUE = "$form_data{'state'}"></TD>
</TR><TR>
<TH ALIGN = "left">Country:</TH>
<TD><INPUT TYPE = "text" NAME = "country" SIZE = "15"
            VALUE = "$form_data{'country'}"></TD>
</TR><TR>
<TH ALIGN = "left">Comments:</TH>
<TD><TEXTAREA NAME = "comments" COLS = "60" ROWS = "4">
$form_data{'comments'}
</TEXTAREA></TD>
</TR></TABLE>
<CENTER>
<INPUT TYPE = "submit" VALUE = "Submit Addition">
<INPUT TYPE = "reset">
</FORM>
<P>
<A HREF = "$guestbookurl">Back to the Guestbook Entries</A><BR>
</CENTER>
</BODY>
</HTML>
end_of_html
}
```

The get_date Subroutine

get_date is a subroutine written by Matt Wright that is used to get the current date to add to guestbook entries.

```
sub get_date
  {
  @days = ('Sunday', 'Monday', 'Tuesday', 'Wednesday',
           'Thursday', 'Friday', 'Saturday');
  @months = ('January', 'February', 'March', 'April',
             'May', 'June', 'July', 'August',
             'September', 'October', 'November',
             'December');
```

get_date uses the localtime command to get the current time. It also splits it into variables.

```
($sec,$min,$hour,$mday,$mon,$year,$wday,$yday,$isdst) =
localtime(time);
```

It then formats the variables and assigns them to the final $date variable.

```
if ($hour < 10) { $hour = "0$hour"; }
if ($min < 10) { $min = "0$min"; }
if ($sec < 10) { $sec = "0$sec"; }
$date = "$days[$wday], $months[$mon] $mday, 19$year at
$hour\:$min\:$sec";
}
```

CHAPTER 21

Animating Text

OVERVIEW

In this chapter, we will outline several ways to animate text using the non-parsed header (NPH) method of controlling the interaction between the server and the browser. Surely, newer technologies, such as Java, or plug-ins, such as Shockwave, are better suited for complex animation. However, the ability to use NPH scripts in creative ways is an important part of any CGI programmer's box of tools. NPH scripts add another dimension to multimedia and can make your site more diverse. They can also be used when the big guns of Java or Shockwave are not appropriate. Because they use Perl, NPH scripts are more accessible to the majority of Web administrators, who are not necessarily advanced programmers.

Non-parsed header scripts are used when we want to bypass the server. Usually, when we use the line

```
print "Content-type: text/plain\n\n";
```

we count on the fact that the server that executes the script will fill in the rest of the HTTP protocol lines, such as the "200 OK" status codes, the date and time, and other information defined in the protocol. With NPH scripts, we must generate those HTTP protocol messages internally, bypassing server parsing. In other words, we output directly to the browser without Web server intervention.

Most of the information that you might pass to the browser is optional. However, you should at least return the MIME content type of the data, the HTTP protocol revision, the status of the program, and the server name and version.

By bypassing the server, you can communicate directly with the browser. As long as the browser listens, you can continue to feed it more information. In this way, you can use cell animation to create an animated series of text or images.

However, the use of NPH scripts requires that all scripts begin with the characters nph-. This is the convention used by servers to recognize an NPH script. If you rename the script, the server will not know to treat it as an NPH script and instead will run it as a normal script.

NOTE

Because you are bypassing the server, you need to be careful that your NPH scripts do not run forever, because they will run to completion whether or not the browser has already moved to another page. If the script loops infinitely, it may never know to stop and may eat up your server resources.

Because all these animation scripts are fairly short, we have decided to group them in this chapter and discuss them one at a time. The following scripts are meant to build upon one another, exploring NPH-based animation from the simplest examples to the more complicated ones.

The first script, **nph-countdown1.0.cgi**, uses an NPH script to produce an animated countdown from 10 to 0. The client sees this countdown in real time in the browser window. Figure 21.1 shows the beginning, middle, and end frames of a sample session for **nph-countdown1.0.cgi**.

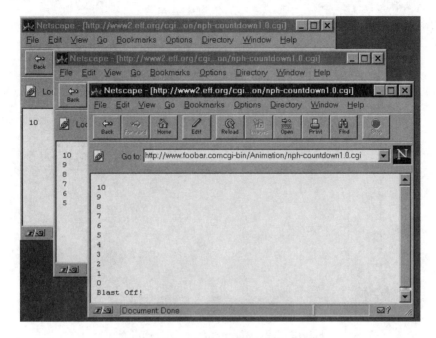

Figure 21.1 nph-countdown 1.0 example.

nph-countdown2.0.cgi takes the countdown to a new level. It counts up from 1 to 5, and instead of displaying the countdown as a chain of numbers, it erases the previous number and writes the new number where the old one used to be. Figure 21.2 shows the beginning, middle, and end frames of a sample session for **nph-countdown2.0.cgi**.

Similarly, **nph-text_animator_1.0.cgi** uses the NPH method combined with array manipulation to produce an animated series of words. Figure 21.3 shows the beginning, middle, and end frames of a sample session for **nph-text_animator_1.0.cgi**.

As **nph-countdown2.0.cgi** did for **nph-countdown1.0.cgi**, so **nph-text_animator_2.0.cgi** does for **nph-text_animator_1.0.cgi**. This little script animates the words by replacing each word with the next one so that a visible list does not develop. Figure 21.4 shows the beginning, middle, and end frames of a sample session for **nph-text_animator_2.0.cgi**.

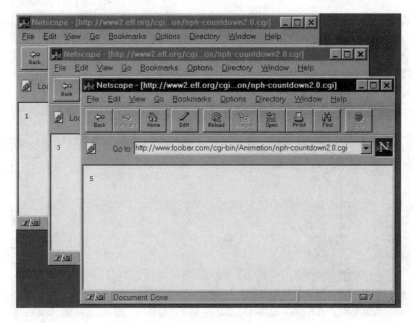

Figure 21.2 nph-countdown 2.0 example.

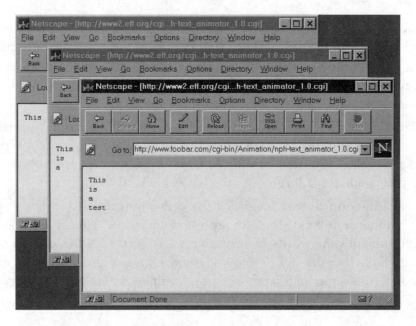

Figure 21.3 nph-text_animator 1.0 example.

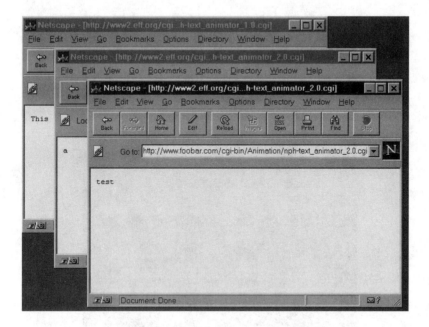

Figure 21.4 *nph-text_animator 2.0 example.*

nph-text_animator_3.0.cgi takes the animation one step further by integrating HTML output. Thus, we use HTML to affect the display of the animated words instead of simply outputting them as plain text. Figure 21.5 shows the beginning, middle, and end frames of a sample session for **nph-text_animator_3.0.cgi**.

In **nph-text_animator_4.0.cgi** we use the HTML <PRE> tag to introduce horizontal movement into the animation.

The <PRE> tag may not be supported by all browsers, but it is included here to show the method. You also can generate horizontal space by using transparent images that are invisible when displayed.

NOTE

Figure 21.6 shows the beginning, middle, and end frames of a sample session for **nph-text_animator_4.0.cgi**.

Figure 21.5 *nph-text_animator 3.0 example.*

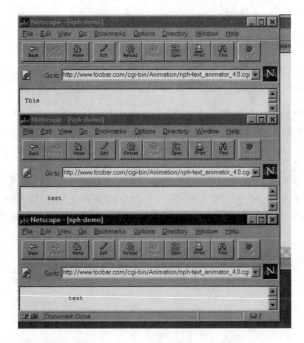

Figure 21.6 *nph-text_animator 4.0 example.*

Finally, in **nph-text_animator_5.0.cgi** we use the srand function to produce an HTML animation that uses random colors, size, and horizontal and vertical spacing. Figure 21.7 shows the beginning, middle, and end frames of a sample session for **nph-text_animator_5.0.cgi**.

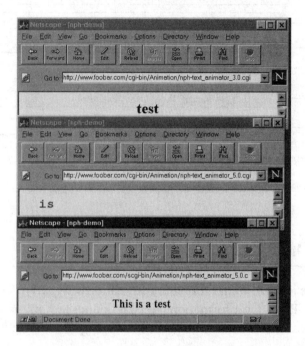

Figure 21.7 nph-text_animator 5.0 example.

INSTALLATION AND USAGE

Each of these scripts should be placed in a directory from which the Web server is allowed to read and execute CGI scripts. Each script should be readable and executable by the Web server. Figure 21.8 depicts the directory structure with the correct permissions for each of the scripts.

Then simply point your Web browser to the script, sit back, and watch. The scripts are referenced like any other script, using the following example syntax:

`http://www.foobar.com/cgi-bin/Animation/nph-countdown1.0.cgi`

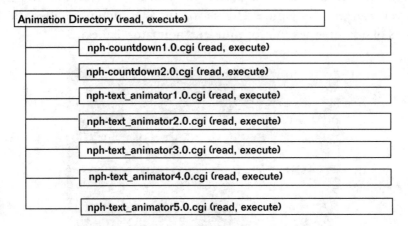

Figure 21.8 *Directory structure and permissions.*

DESIGN DISCUSSION

The logic is fairly similar for all the animation scripts. The script first outputs the HTTP header information. Next, it defines any animation variables, and then it creates the cell animation by looping. This logic is depicted in Figure 21.9.

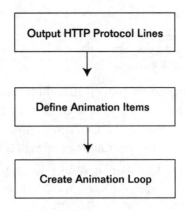

Figure 21.9 *Animation logic.*

nph-countdown1.0.cgi

nph-countdown1.0.cgi begins by starting the Perl interpreter and printing a complete HTTP header so that it can bypass the server and talk directly to the client.

```
!/usr/local/bin/perl
print "$ENV{'SERVER_PROTOCOL'} 200 OK\n";
print "Server: $ENV{'SERVER_SOFTWARE'}\n";
print "Content-type: text/plain\n\n";
```

Next, it tells the Perl interpreter to forgo buffering. We want to print straight to output so that the animation will be as smooth as possible. If we set $| to zero, the Perl interpreter would buffer the output. If we set it to 1, the script will "flush" the buffer continuously.

```
$| = 1;
```

Then the script creates the logic of the cell animation. First, it sets $loop = 10. Then it begins counting down ($loop–) one number at a time until it reaches zero ($loop >= 0). For each number, it prints the value to the browser and pauses (sleeps) for one second. The client sees a real-time countdown in the browser window.

```
for ($loop = 10; $loop >= 0; $loop–)
{
print "$loop\n";
sleep (1);
}
```

Finally, the script prints "Blast Off!" and exits.

```
print "Blast Off!\n";
exit (0);
```

nph-countdown2.0.cgi

As before, the Perl interpreter is started and the script outputs the standard HTTP header while bypassing the Perl buffer.

```
#!/usr/local/bin/perl
$| = 1;
print "$ENV{'SERVER_PROTOCOL'} 200 OK\n";
print "Server: $ENV{'SERVER_SOFTWARE'}\n";
```

However, this time the script tells the Web browser that it should not keep adding the numbers to a displayed list. Instead, the browser should continually replace the displayed number. Thus, instead of simply outputting a mime type of plain text or HTML, the script lets the browser know that it will be replacing each character and that every time the browser comes across —ARandomString\n\n, it knows that it is time to replace an old character with a new one.

```
print "Content-type: multipart/x-mixed-
replace;boundary=ARandomString\n\n";
```

The script begins sending characters by sending the flag string.

```
print "--ARandomString\n";
```

It then sets $loop to 1 and begins counting upward one number at a time ($loop++) until it hits five ($loop <= 5).

```
for ($loop = 1; $loop <= 5; $loop++)
  {
```

Meanwhile, the script prints the value of $loop in plain text, pauses for a second, and then tells the browser to overwrite the old value of $loop with the new value by sending the new character flag.

```
print "Content-type: text/plain\n\n";
print "$loop\n";
sleep (1);
print "\n--ARandomString\n";
}
```

When the script is finished counting, it quits.

```
exit (0);
```

nph-text_animator_1.0.cgi

As before, the script starts the Perl interpreter, tells it to bypass the buffer, and prints a complete HTTP header so that it can bypass the server's buffer.

```
#!/usr/local/bin/perl
$| = 1;
print "$ENV{'SERVER_PROTOCOL'} 200 OK\n";
print "Server: $ENV{'SERVER_SOFTWARE'}\n";
print "Content-type: text/plain\n\n";
```

Next, a list of words to be animated is defined and set equal to @words.

```
@words = ("This", "is", "a", "test");
```

Then the script sets $loop to zero (because all arrays start with zero as their first value) and begins incrementing $loop by 1 ($loop++) until $loop is equivalent to the number of words in @words ($loop <= @words;).

```
for ($loop = 0; $loop <= @words; $loop++)
  {
```

For every value of $loop, the script prints the value in @words that corresponds to the value of $loop. So when $loop equals zero, the script prints the first word in the @words array; when $loop equals 1, it prints the second word, and so on. Then the script pauses a second and prints another word until it is finished with all the words.

```
print "$words[$loop]\n";
sleep (1);
}
exit (0);
```

nph-text_animator_2.0.cgi

The script uses the Perl interpreter, bypassing the Perl buffer, and, as before, prints a complete HTTP header. However, as it did in **nph-counter2.0.cgi**, the script lets the browser know that it will be replacing each character and that every time the browser comes across the tag `--ARandomString\n\n`, it will know that it is time to replace an old word with a new one.

```perl
#!/usr/local/bin/perl
$| = 1;
print "$ENV{'SERVER_PROTOCOL'} 200 OK\n";
print "Server: $ENV{'SERVER_SOFTWARE'}\n";
print "Content-type: multipart/x-mixed-
replace;boundary=ARandomString\n\n";
```

The script then alerts the browser by sending the boundary flag.

```perl
print "--ARandomString\n";
```

Next, `@words` is filled with the list of words to be animated.

```perl
@words = ("This", "is", "a", "test");
```

Then `$loop` is set to zero and the script begins incrementing `$loop` by 1 until `$loop` is equivalent to the number of words in `@words`.

```perl
for ($loop = 0; $loop <= @words; $loop++)
{
```

For every value of `$loop`, the script prints the value in `@words` that corresponds to the value of `$loop`. It then pauses a second and prints the flag that notifies the browser to replace the next word with the current one until all the words have been displayed and the script exits.

```perl
print "Content-type: text/plain\n\n";
print "$words[$loop]\n";
sleep (1);
print "\n--ARandomString\n";
}
exit (0);
```

nph-text_animator_3.0.cgi

nph-text_animator_3.0.cgi begins as all the others have begun in this chapter.

558

```
#!/usr/local/bin/perl
$| = 1;
print "$ENV{'SERVER_PROTOCOL'} 200 OK\n";
print "Server: $ENV{'SERVER_SOFTWARE'}\n";
print "Content-type: multipart/x-mixed-
replace;boundary=ARandomString\n\n";
print "--ARandomString\n";
```

As before, @words is filled with the list of words to be animated. However, the is and test elements are modified with HTML <CENTER> tags; when displayed as HTML, they reflect the HTML formatting.

```
@words = ("This", "<CENTER>is</CENTER>", "a",
          "<CENTER>test</CENTER>");
```

Then the script sets $loop to zero and begins incrementing $loop by 1 until it is equivalent to the number of words in @words.

```
for ($loop = 0; $loop <= @words; $loop++)
{
```

Finally, the script displays the words as usual. The standard HTML header and footer are included, because we are now displaying an HTML document rather than just a text document.

```
print "Content-type: text/html\n\n";
print "<HTML><HEAD><TITLE>nph-demo</TITLE></HEAD><BODY>";
print "<H1>";
print "$words[$loop]\n";
print "</H1>";
print "</BODY></HTML>";
sleep (2);
print "\n--ARandomString\n";
}
exit (0);
```

nph-text_animator_4.0.cgi

Again, the script begins as usual.

```
#!/usr/local/bin/perl
```

```
$| = 1;
print "$ENV{'SERVER_PROTOCOL'} 200 OK\n";
print "Server: $ENV{'SERVER_SOFTWARE'}\n";
print "Content-type: multipart/x-mixed-
replace;boundary=ARandomString\n\n";
print "--ARandomString\n";
```

This time, each word in @words is offset by blank spaces so that we achieve the appearance of movement.

```
@words = ("This",
         "   is",
         "      a",
         "         test",
         "            of",
         "               animated",
         "                  text");
```

As before, the script loops the array and prints each horizontally affected word until all the words have been displayed.

```
for ($loop = 0; $loop <= @words; $loop++)
{
print "Content-type: text/html\n\n";
print "<HTML><HEAD><TITLE>nph-demo</TITLE></HEAD><BODY>";
print "<PRE>";
print "$words[$loop]\n";
print "</PRE>";
print "</BODY></HTML>";
sleep (1);
print "\n--ARandomString\n";
}
exit (0);
```

nph-text_animator_5.0.cgi

nph-text_animator_5.0.cgi prints the standard script header that we have seen throughout this chapter.

```
#!/usr/local/bin/perl
$| = 1;
print "$ENV{'SERVER_PROTOCOL'} 200 OK\n";
```

```
print "Server: $ENV{'SERVER_SOFTWARE'}\n";
print "Content-type: multipart/x-mixed-
replace;boundary=ARandomString\n\n";
print "--ARandomString\n";
```

Next, the script revs up the Perl randomizer so that it can generate some random numbers.

```
srand;
```

@words is defined with the list of words to be animated.

```
@words = ("This", "is", "a", "test");
```

@spaces is also defined so that the script can randomly offset the words horizontally when displayed.

```
@spaces = ("", " ", "   ", "     ", "        ", "
         ");
```

Similarly, @font_sizes is defined with tags that the script uses to randomly size words for non-Netscape browsers.

```
@font_sizes = ("H1", "H2", "H3", "H4", "H5", "H6");
```

Next, @font_colors is defined to generate random text colors.

```
@font_colors = ("FFFFFF", "000000", "00CCCC", "CC1523",
                "B916CC", "1F0DCC", "11CCC1", "07CC24",
                "C1CC10", "#D98719", "#D9D919",
                "#5C3317", "#2F4F2F", "#FF2400");
```

Then vertical_spacings is defined to randomly place displayed words vertically.

```
@vertical_spacings = (
"",
"<FONT COLOR = \"C9C3CC\">.<P></FONT>",
"<FONT COLOR = \"C9C3CC\">.<P>.<P></FONT>",
"<FONT COLOR = \"C9C3CC\">.<P>.<P>.<P></FONT>",
```

```
"<FONT COLOR = \"C9C3CC\">.<P>.<P>.<P>.<P></FONT>",
"<FONT COLOR = \"C9C3CC\">.<P>.<P>.<P>.<P>.<P></FONT>",
"<FONT COLOR = \"C9C3CC\">.<P>.<P>.<P>.<P>.<P>.<P>.<P></FONT>",
"<FONT COLOR = \"C9C3CC\">.<P>.<P>.<P>.<P>.<P>.<P>.<P>.<P></FONT>",
"<FONT COLOR =
\"C9C3CC\">.<P>.<P>.<P>.<P>.<P>.<P>.<P>.<P>.<P></FONT>",
"<FONT COLOR
=\"C9C3CC\">.<P>.<P>.<P>.<P>.<P>.<P>.<P>.<P>.<P>.<P></FONT>",
"<FONT COLOR = \"C9C3CC\">.<P>.<P>.<P>.<P>.<P>.<P></FONT>");
```

NOTE

The font color C9C3CC corresponds to the basic gray background of a browser. Thus, the periods will not be visible (as long as your browser isn't defaulted to a color other than gray) and will functionally offset the vertical placement. Alternatively, you could create invisible (transparent) images.

Finally, `@netscape_font_sizes` is defined to generate random font sizes for Netscape browsers.

```
@netscape_font_sizes = ("1", "2", "3", "4", "5", "6",
                        "7", "8", "9", "10");
```

Then the script sets `$loop` to zero and increments `$loop` by 1 until `$loop` is equivalent to the number of words in `@words`.

```
for ($loop = 0; $loop <= 20; $loop++)
{
```

As before, the script prints the words. But this time, it randomly affects each word in a number of ways. The script generates a random value for the word, its vertical and horizontal spaces, its size, and its color.

The script first chooses a random (`rand`) integer (`int`) between zero and the number of elements in each array and then sets the variable to the returned value. This value is used to reference the array again. If `$font_color` is set to 3, the random font color will be referenced by plugging 3 into the array, returning the value of "00CCCC," according to the array definition.

```
$word = int(rand(@words));
$space = int(rand(@spaces));
$font_size = int(rand(@font_sizes));
$netscape_font_size = int(rand(@netscape_font_sizes));
$font_color = int(rand(@font_colors));
$vertical_spacing = int(rand(@vertical_spacings));
print "Content-type: text/html\n\n";
print "<HTML><HEAD><TITLE>nph-demo</TITLE></HEAD>";
print "<BODY TEXT = \"$font_colors[$font_color]\">";
print "<PRE><B>";
print "$vertical_spacings[$vertical_spacing]";
```

In the special case of font size, the script determines whether the browser
understands <FONT SIZE> tags. If it does, the script displays the text as
<FONT SIZE>. Otherwise, it displays it with <H*> settings.

$ENV{'HTTP_USER_AGENT'} is the environment variable that keeps track
of the kind of browser accessing the CGI script. =~ /^Mozilla/ means that
if the value is something (=~) that begins with Mozilla, the script should
use the <FONT SIZE> tag.

```
if ($ENV{'HTTP_USER_AGENT'} =~ /^Mozilla/)
  {
  print "<FONT SIZE =
      \"$netscape_font_sizes[$netscape_font_size]\">";
  }
else
  {
  print "<$font_sizes[$font_size]>\n";
  }
print "$spaces[$space]$words[$word]\n";
```

The script then adds the closing font tags.

```
if ($ENV{'HTTP_USER_AGENT'} =~ /^Mozilla/)
  {
  print "</FONT>";
  }
else
  {
  print "</$font_sizes[$font_size]>\n";
  }
print "</B></PRE>";
print "</BODY></HTML>";
```

Next, it prints the flag that notifies the browser to replace the next word with the current one.

```
sleep (0);
print "\n--ARandomString\n";
}
```

Finally, the script prints a final version of the sentence so that if viewers are confused by the randomness they can see the whole sentence.

```
print "\n--ARandomString\n";
print "Content-type: text/html\n\n";
print "<HTML><HEAD><TITLE>nph-demo</TITLE></HEAD>";
print "<BODY>";
print "<CENTER><H2><BLINK>";
```

For every word in the list of words, the script prints the word.

```
foreach $word (@words)
{
print "$word\n";
}
print "</BLINK></H2></CENTER></BODY></HTML>";
exit (0);
```

CHAPTER 22

The Random Banner
Generator

OVERVIEW

One of the basic advertising tools developed for the Web is the random banner advertisement. This chapter discusses the random banner generator application, which is used to display a random advertisement within an HTML document to provide a link to the advertiser. In combination with the advertising tracker discussed in Chapter 24, this application allows site administrators to sell advertising space on their Web pages and track the usage for their advertising partners.

The random banner generator application is a "filter" that reads an HTML page, inserts a randomly generated banner in place of a special tag that you define in your HTML document, and then displays it to a client.

INSTALLATION AND USAGE

The random banner generator application should be placed in a CGI-executable directory and expanded into the root directory **Random_banner**. Figure 22.1 outlines the directory structure and the permissions needed for the application to operate.

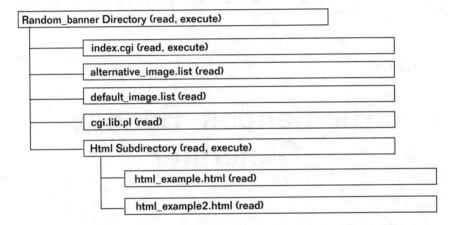

Figure 22.1 Directory layout for the random banner generator.

The root **Random_banner** directory must have permissions that allow the Web server to read and execute. It should contain one directory (**Html**) and four text files (**alternative_image.list**, **cgi-lib.pl**, **default_image.list**, and **index.cgi**).

 index.cgi is the main application used to output HTML files containing the advertisement banner. The file is called **index.cgi** because Web servers are often designed to automatically execute a file called **index.cgi** if none other has been specified. Also, because this script filters your HTML files, you do not want clients to reference a script such as **random_banner.cgi**. More likely, you want them simply to type in a URL:

```
http://www.foobar.com/
```

Then they are sent directly to the HTML page filtered by the script. Thus, the name **index.cgi** is used to make life simpler and more user-friendly. It would be fine for you to rename the file, but it must remain readable and executable by the Web server.

alternative_image.list and **default_image.list** are lists of banners and the hyperlink references associated with them. These files are simple text databases with two fields—image location and hyperlink reference—separated by a pipe symbol (|). The text of **alternative_image.list** is shown next:

```
eff_gry_lg.gif|http://www.eff.org/
Icons/ying_yang_icon.gif|http://www.eff.org/~erict/
Icons/yahoo_award_icon.gif|http://www.yahoo.com/
Icons/alerts_bar.gif|http://www.eff.org/pub/Alerts/
```

You can create as many image list datafiles as you want as long as they follow this basic format. These files should be readable by the Web server.

cgi-lib.pl is the library file used to read and parse form data. This file should be readable by the Web server.

Html is a subdirectory that has been included in the accompanying CD-ROM only as an example of a directory for HTML files that use this script. It contains two files—**html_example.html** and **html_example2.html**—which should be readable by the Web server. The directory itself should be readable and executable.

html_example.html is an example of an HTML file that displays a random banner. It should be readable by the Web server. It will be discussed in the "Server-Specific Setup and Options" section.

html_example2.html is another example HTML page.

Server-Specific Setup and Options

There are four variables that are initially defined in the first few lines of **index.cgi**.

`$html_directory_path` is the path of the directory that holds the HTML files to be filtered by this script.

`$default_html_file` is the name of the HTML file to be loaded by default. Usually, you want only one page to display a random advertisement. However, because you may want to have several pages display ads, you must set the default and later override it. Overriding the default is discussed in the "Preparing the HTML File" section.

$image_url is the URL of the subdirectory containing the images to be displayed within the HTML page.

$default_image_list is the name of the image list that the script uses by default to find images to display if the HTML that calls the script does not include some other list.

$location_of_cgi_lib is the location of **cgi-lib.pl**.

PREPARING THE HTML FILE

Each HTML file that calls upon **index.cgi** to filter in a random banner must be specially prepared so that **index.cgi** knows where to place the banner. The HTML is tagged with a special line that **index.cgi** will recognize:

```
<!--IMG GOES HERE-->
```

This line should be placed in the location where you want the random banner displayed. The script looks for this exact line, so it must be typed correctly. When the script finds this line, it replaces it with the <IMG SRC> and <A HREF> tags necessary to create a clickable banner. As an example, the text of **html_example.html** follows:

```
<HTML>
<HEAD>
<TITLE>Random Banner Example</TITLE>
</HEAD>
<BODY BGCOLOR = "FFFFFF" TEXT = "000000">

<CENTER>
<H2>Random Banner Example</H2>
</CENTER>

<BLOCKQUOTE>
This is just a very simple example of how you would reference a random
banner from a basic HTML file.  You will use a normal &LTIMG SRC&GT tag,
which will point to the index.cgi file instead of to an actual graphics
image.  The script will then send back an image that the browser will
put in the appropriate place.REload the screen to get another banner.
```

```
<P>
Below is an example banner:
<P>
<!--IMG GOES HERE-->
<P>
Check out the other
```

Notice also the following link. In this example, we call the second example HTML file using a url-encoded link, which is explained in greater detail in the "Running the Script" section.

```
<A
HREF="index.cgi?image_list=alternative_image.list&html_file=html_exam-
ple2.html">example</A>
</BODY>
</HTML>
```

On the Web, the example HTML file will look like Figure 22.2.

Figure 22.2 The HTML file with a randomly generated banner.

Running the Script

Once you have configured the setup variables and the HTML file to the specifics of your server setup, you can try out the random banner generator. To access the script, reference the location of the main script as follows:

```
http://www.foobar.com/cgi-bin/index.cgi
```

This code will run **index.cgi**, which will take advantage of the default image file and default front page. Alternatively, you can use this same script with a different image list and HTML file as follows:

```
http://www.foobar.com/cgi-bin/index.cgi?image_list=xxx&html_file=yyy
```

The xxx is the name of the alternative image list, such as **alternative_ image.list**, and the yyy is the name of the HTML file in which you want the random banner displayed. These two variables are separated with the ampersand (&) symbol, and the entire encoded part of the URL is defined after the question mark (?) symbol.

DESIGN DISCUSSION

Figure 22.3 summarizes the logic of the script as it responds to the demands of the client.

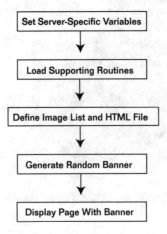

Figure 22.3 The script logic.

The script begins by starting the Perl interpreter and printing the HTTP header.

```
#!/usr/local/bin/perl
print "Content-type: text/html\n\n";
```

Defining Server-Specific Variables

Next, a few server-specific variables are defined as discussed in the "Installation and Usage" section.

```
$html_directory_path = "./Html";
$default_html_file =
    "$html_directory_path/html_example.html";
$image_url = "http://www.foobar.com/Images";
$default_image_list = "default_image.list";
$location_of_cgi_lib = "./cgi-lib.pl";
```

Loading the Supporting Routines

Perl's randomizer is then accessed using the `srand` command, which is seeded with the process ID and the time.

```
srand (time|$$);
```

Then **cgi-lib.pl** is loaded and the routine `ReadParse` is used to read and parse any incoming url-encoded data.

```
require "$location_of_cgi_lib ";
&ReadParse(*form_data);
```

Defining the Image List and HTML File

The url-encoded data coming in as form data may include the name of the image file that this script should use to find the locations of the images as well as the hyperlinks associated with them.

If an image file was specified in the URL, the script assigns that value to the variable `$image_database`. Otherwise, the script uses the value of `$default_image_list` as was defined previously.

```
if ($form_data{'image_list'} ne "")
  {
  $image_database = $form_data{'image_list'};
  }
else
  {
  $image_database = "$default_image_list";
  }
```

Similarly, the script determine which HTML file to display with the randomly generated ad. By default, it loads the HTML file defined in `$default_html_file`. However, if the client has specified an alternative file to load in the URL string, the script loads that file instead.

```
 if ($form_data{'html_file'} ne "")
    {
    $html_file = "$html_directory_path/$form_data{'html_file'}";
    }
  else
    {
    $html_file = "$default_html_file";
    }
```

Generating the Random Banner and Associated URL

Next, the script opens the image file, defaulting to `CgiDie` if there is a problem.

```
open (IMAGE_DATABASE, "$image_database") || &CgiDie ("Can't open $image_database");
```

It then goes through the image list file one line at a time. For every line, it gathers the image and the associated hyperlink by `split`ting the line on the pipe (|) symbol. Then it `push`es the location of the image to the list array `@imagelist`, and the URL associated with the image to `@url_list`. Finally, it closes the image list file.

```
while (<IMAGE_DATABASE>)
  {
  ($image, $url) = split (/\|/, $_);
  push (@imagelist, $image);
  push (@url_list, $url);
  }
close (IMAGE_DATABASE);
```

Now that the script has a list of all the images in the image file, it uses Perl's randomizer function to choose one of them at random. Because @imagelist is interpreted by Perl as the number of values in the array, $random_number is set to be a random (rand) integer value (int) from zero to the number of images in the @imagelist array.

```
$random_number = int(rand(@imagelist));
```

Then the script takes the number assigned to $random_number and accesses the array element in @imagelist that is associated with the number. $random_image then becomes the name of one of the images in @imagelist.

```
$random_image = $imagelist[$random_number];
```

Similarly, $random_url is set to the hyperlink associated with the image.

```
$random_url = $url_list[$random_number];
```

Displaying the HTML Page with Banner Inserted

Next, the script opens the HTML file that the client has requested, using CgiDie if it cannot be opened for some reason.

```
open (HTML_FILE, "$html_file") || &CgiDie ("Can't open $html_file");
```

The script then reads through the HTML file one line at a time.

```
while (<HTML_FILE>)
{
```

If it comes upon a line that looks like the following,

```
<!—IMG GOES HERE—>
```

the script knows that it is supposed to replace the line with the randomly generated image and the associated hyperlink. So, using the HERE DOCU-MENT method of printing, it replaces the line with the HTML code.

```
if (/\<!—IMG GOES HERE—\>/)
{
print <<"end_of_html";
<A HREF = "$random_url">
<IMG SRC = "$image_url/$random_image"></A>
end_of_html
}
```

NOTE Remember that because the greater than (>) and less than (<) symbols are Perl special characters, they must be escaped with a backslash (\) if they are to be treated as patterns to match for.

If the line is not the special tag, the script simply prints the line. Thus, every line in the HTML file is sent to the Web browser except for the special tag line, which is replaced with the <IMG> and <A HREF> tags.

```
 else
  {
  print "$_";
  }
} # End of while (<HTML_FILE>)
```

Finally, the HTML file is closed and the script exits.

```
close (HTML_FILE);
```

CHAPTER 23

The Fortune Cookie

OVERVIEW

The fortune cookie script goes through a datafile of "fortunes," chooses one of them at random, and then displays it on the Web. The script can also be configured to loop so that new fortunes are redisplayed automatically at a predefined interval. In this way, the client need not use the browser's reload option.

This script is a fun addition to any site, because it allows the site administrator to develop a database of short statements to be reloaded every time a client accesses the site. If you have funny or interesting fortunes, it may give the client an extra reason to visit your site a second and third time.

The fortunes can be displayed in either of two ways. You can use Netscape frames to display the messages in one automatically reloading frame along with an HTML page in another frame. Or you can display one fortune at a time on its own page or embedded in another document. The script can also be configured to choose from a variety of datafiles so that you can choose from multiple genres of fortunes for different types of pages.

INSTALLATION AND USAGE

The fortune cookie application expands into the root directory **Fortune_cookie**, which is depicted in Figure 23.1.

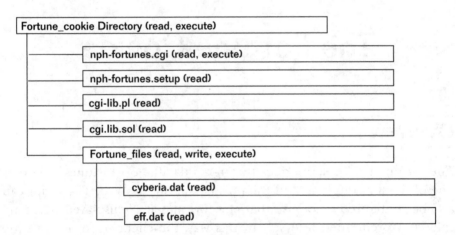

Figure 23.1 Directory structure for the fortune cookie.

Fortune_cookie is the root directory for the application. It contains three files (**nph-fortunes.cgi**, **cgi-lib.pl**, and **nph-fortunes.setup**) and one subdirectory (**Fortune_files**) and must be readable and executable by the Web server.

nph-fortunes.cgi, the main body of the program, randomly generates fortunes from the fortunes files. The Web server must have read and execute privileges for this file.

nph-fortunes.setup is the file you use to set up the script for your local installation. The file must be readable by the Web server and will be discussed in the "Server-Specific Setup and Options" section.

cgi-lib.pl is a supporting library file used to parse incoming form data. It must be readable by the Web server.

Fortune_files is a subdirectory that contains the fortune data files from which the script generates random fortunes. Both **eff.dat** and **cyberia.dat** are example fortune files in the accompanying CD-ROM. These files must be readable by the Web server. The subdirectory itself must be readable and executable by the Web server.

Server-Specific Setup and Options

THE SETUP FILE

nph-fortunes.cgi requires that you set a few variables in the setup file. These variables configure **nph-fortunes.cgi** to run on your server with your own predefined options.

`$number_of_fortunes_to_display` is the number of fortunes to display before stopping. If this variable is set to 3, for example, the script will generate three fortunes and display them one after another like a slide show. Although you can set this number as high as you want, you may want to limit the slide show to a specific number of fortunes. The **eff.dat** file is huge, with hundreds of fortunes, and you probably don't want the fortunes to be generated forever.

`$default_data_file` is the name of the datafile that **nph-fortunes.cgi** should grab fortunes from if the user does not specify a different one.

`$number_seconds_to_display` should be set to the number of seconds that the script should wait for the user to read the fortune before it loads another one.

`$fortune_file_directory` is the location of the directory that contains your fortune files.

The text of **nph-fortunes.setup** is shown next:

```
$number_of_fortunes_to_display = "10";
$default_data_file = "eff";
$fortune_file_directory = "./Fortune_files";
$number_seconds_to_display = "8";
```

THE FORTUNE FILE

The accompanying CD-ROM includes both **eff.dat** and **cyberia.dat**, and you can also create your own datafiles from which the fortunes are generated. These files are in a specific format that must be followed exactly.

Each fortune must be separated by two percent (`%%`) signs, and this same marker must be the last line of the file. Here is an example fortune file:

```
Hello
%%
Goodbye
%%
```

Based on this example, the script would randomly choose either "Hello" or "Goodbye."

Furthermore, every fortune file must end in the extension **.dat**. This is essential, because **nph-fortunes.cgi** receives the name of the file from client-defined input. Theoretically, if clients had free reign to load any file, they might choose to bypass your fortune files and load "/etc/passwd" instead! We have hard-coded the **.dat** extension to prevent this.

Running the Script

Using the default datafile, the script can be called by this standard hypertext reference:

```
http://www.foobar.com/nph-fortunes.cgi
```

Or it can be called to access a user-defined datafile as follows:

```
http://www.foobar.com/nph-fortunes.cgi?fortune_file=cyberia
```

Notice that we use url-encoding to pass to the script the name of the alternative datafile. This syntax assumes that you place any subsequent fortune files in the **Fortune_files** subdirectory, that they end in the **.dat** extension, and that they are made readable by the Web server.

DESIGN DISCUSSION

The logic of **nph-fortunes.cgi** is depicted in Figure 23.2.

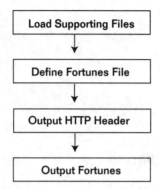

Figure 23.2 Script logic.

First, the script starts the Perl interpreter. Also, srand is seeded with the process ID and the time so that it will generate random numbers. The script also tells the Perl interpreter to skip buffering so that fortunes will be seamlessly animated.

```
#!/usr/local/bin/perl
srand(time|$$);
$| = 1;
```

Then the script loads the setup file and **cgi-lib.pl** and uses the ReadParse subroutine to parse the incoming data.

```
require "cgi-lib.pl";
require "nph-fortunes.setup";
&ReadParse(*form_data);
```

Loading the Fortunes File

Next, the script assigns the incoming client-defined fortune_file (if there is one) to the $fortune_file variable. If there is no incoming fortune file, the script uses the default value specified in the setup file. Notice that we hard-coded the extension **.dat** for the reasons explained in the "Server-Specific Setup and Options" section.

```
if ($form_data{fortune_file} eq "")
  {
  $fortune_file =
  "$fortune_file_directory/$default_data_file.dat";
  }
else
  {
  $fortune_file =
"$fortune_file_directory/$form_data{'fortune_file'}.dat;
  }
```

Sending the NPH Header

Then the script prints the HTTP header, letting the browser know that it will send multiple documents and that new documents should replace old ones. (The use of NPH headers is covered in greater depth in Chapter 21.) The browser knows that the CGI script is sending a new document when the script sends it the flag –ARandomString\n.

```
print "$ENV{'SERVER_PROTOCOL'} 200 OK\n";
print "Server: $ENV{'SERVER_SOFTWARE'}\n";
print "Content-type: multipart/x-mixed-
replace;boundary=ARandomString\n\n";
print "--ARandomString\n";
```

The fortunes are then printed. The following `for` loop counts from zero to the number that the fortune administrator has set for `$number_of_fortunes_to_display`. Thus, for every number from zero to `$number_of_fortunes_to_display`, the script prints the following HTML code as well as the randomly generated fortune (as discussed in the next section).

```
for ($loop = 1;
     $loop <= $number_of_fortunes_to_display;
     $loop++)
  {
  print "Content-type: text/html\n\n";
  print "<HTML><HEAD><TITLE></TITLE></HEAD>
        <BODY BGCOLOR = \"FFFFFF\">";
  print "<BLOCKQUOTE>";
```

Getting a Random Fortune

The script first grabs a randomly generated fortune using the subroutine `get_fortune` at the end of this script. The script sends the name of the fortune file to the subroutine as a parameter so that the subroutine will know which fortune file to grab the fortune from.

```
print &get_fortune($fortune_file);
```

Finally, the script prints the HTML footer using the HERE DOCUMENT method. In the accompanying CD-ROM, we have created hyperlinks to the sample fortune files.

```
 print <<" end_of_html";
</BLOCKQUOTE>
<CENTER>
<A HREF = "nph-fortunes.cgi?fortune_file=cyberia">Cyberia
Quotes</A> \|
<A HREF = "nph-fortunes.cgi?fortune_file=eff">EFF
Quotes</A>
</CENTER></BODY></HTML>
 end_of_html
```

Figure 23.3 shows a fortune displayed on the Web.

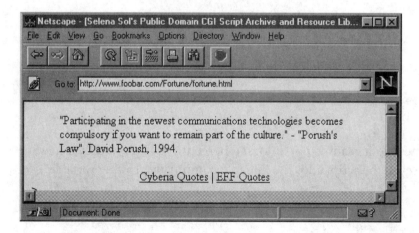

Figure 23.3 A sample fortune.

The script then pauses while the client reads the fortune. Using the `sleep` function, it waits for as many seconds as the administrator has set for `$number_seconds_to_display`. Then the browser is told that it is about to be sent a new fortune to display, and the script goes on to the next fortune (the `for` loop is incremented).

```
sleep ($number_seconds_to_display);
print "\n—ARandomString\n";
}
```

The get_fortune Subroutine

`get_fortune` is used to gather a random fortune from the fortune file.

```
sub get_fortune
  {
```

The routine begins by assigning to the local variable `$fortune_file` the filename sent from the main routine.

```
local ($fortune_file) = @_;
```

Then it opens that file for reading, defaulting to `CgiDie` if there is a problem.

```
open (FORTUNE_FILE, "$fortune_file")  ||
    &CgiDie ("Can't open $fortune_file");
```

Next, it reads the file one line at a time.

```
while (<FORTUNE_FILE>)
   {
```

If the line it reads is not a double percent (`%%`) followed by a newline (`\n`), however, the script adds the line to a continually growing variable, `$fortune`.

```
if ($_ ne "%%\n")
  {
  $fortune .= "$_";
  }
```

" .=" means to add to the end of the variable rather than resetting the variable. "$_" is another name for the current line we are reading.

N O T E

If the line is %% followed by a newline (\n), the script adds the current value of $fortune to the array @fortunes and then resets $fortune. This process creates a huge array in which each element is a separate fortune. The double percent (%%) defines the beginning and end of fortunes.

```
else
  {
  push (@fortunes, $fortune);
  $fortune = "";
  }
}
```

Can you see why you must have a double percent (%%) as the last line of the datafile? Otherwise, we would lose the last fortune, because it would never get pushed into the array.

N O T E

Once the script goes through all the lines in the fortune file, it is closed.

```
close (FORTUNE_FILE);
```

Then the script returns a randomly selected fortune to the main routine from the array @fortunes.

```
splice(@fortunes,int(rand(@fortunes)),1)."\n";
}
```

In this code, the script figures out how many elements are in @fortunes. Fortunately, the scalar @fortunes equals the number of elements in the fortunes array; if there are 10 fortunes in the array @fortunes, the scalar value of @fortunes will equal 10.

Then the script picks a random number from 0 to the number of fortunes in the @fortunes array (perhaps 0 to 10), using the function rand(@fortunes).

Because of the way Perl chooses random numbers, the result generated by the `rand` function will be funky such as 5.43245231. So the script rounds off that number to an integer using the `int` function. We can then reference the original `@fortunes` array and pull out a fortune.

Once the script has a random integer from zero to the number of elements in `@fortunes`, it figures out which number in the array `@fortunes` corresponds to the random number and returns that element to the calling routine for printing.

CHAPTER 24

The Advertising Tracker

OVERVIEW

The advertising tracker script allows a Web site to collect statistics on how many people use a hypertext link to jump to an advertised company's site. Just as television and radio stations, as purveyors of information, have seen the profit in selling advertising to companies whose products are displayed along with information people wish to see, so the Web has exploded with sites that offer advertising space on their Web pages. These sites are visited by enough people that companies want to pay to have their logo displayed there.

As Web sites compete for advertising dollars, they must increasingly gather statistics about the people who use the Web site as a point from which they jump to an advertised company's URL. Two statistics come to mind. The first is how many people view the ad. This statistic is easy to collect, because counter programs are relatively common and can be placed alongside an ad to count the number of times the page is displayed. A second statistic that an advertiser usually wants collected is how many people clicked on the ad to jump to the advertised site. This statistic—harder to collect—will be explained in this chapter.

Generally, ads on the Web consist of a clickable image that is referenced to another URL on the Internet. The user clicks on the image and is taken to the Web site that the image advertises. Unfortunately, this arrangement leaves you without a record of where the user went except via a server log. Even then, you may not have access to the server log if you are on a shared server set up by an Internet service provider.

The alternative solution is to have the clickable image send users to an ad tracker CGI script before sending them to the site. This script records the "hit" to the ad image and then sends a redirection signal to the user's Web browser to tell it to automatically go to the advertiser's Web site.

INSTALLATION AND USAGE

The ad tracking files should install into a directory called **Ad_track**. The files and subdirectories associated with this application, along with their required permissions, are shown in Figure 24.1.

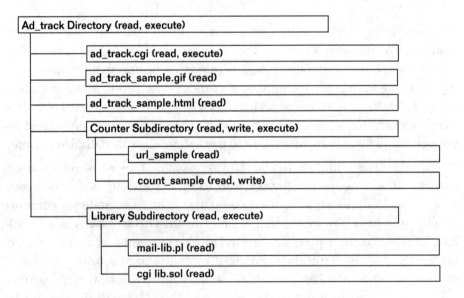

Figure 24.1 *Ad tracking script directory structure and permissions.*

Ad_track is the root application directory. It must be readable and executable by the Web server. In addition to the application files, the **Counter** and **Library** subdirectories are also located here.

ad_track.cgi is the CGI script that increments the counter information and redirects the user to a new URL. This file must be readable and executable.

ad_track_sample.html is a sample usage of the ad tracking script. If your server is configured so that HTML files cannot be viewed from a CGI directory, you need to move this file and update the reference to **ad_track.cgi** to address it from the new location. This file must be readable.

ad_track_sample.gif is an image file that is referenced by the **ad_track_sample.html** file. This file should be placed in the same directory as **ad_track_sample.html** and should be readable by the Web server.

The **Library** subdirectory stores all the external libraries the script needs to access. This subdirectory should be readable and executable. All the files in it should be readable. These files include **cgi-lib.pl** (used for processing HTML forms) and **cgi-lib.sol** (used for the counter and lock file routines).

The **Counter** subdirectory is used by the ad tracker to keep the URL setup and counter files. This directory must be readable, writable, and executable.

The **url_[page name]** file is located in the **Counter** subdirectory. This file contains the URL where the user is sent when **ad_track.cgi** is given the [page_name] as a variable on the URL calling the script. This file must be readable by the Web server.

The **count_[page_name]** file is located in the **Counter** subdirectory. This file contains the current count of clients who have been sent to [page_name] by **ad_track.cgi**. This file is created by the **ad_track.cgi** program and by default is readable and writable.

Server-Specific Setup and Options

Only one file needs to be set up for each ad you wish to track. You associate a word or "page" with the advertisement and then create a file in the **Counter** subdirectory called **url_[page_name]**, where **[page_name]** is your code word for the ad. For example, if a car is being advertised on your site, you would create a file called **url_car** in the **Counter** subdirectory.

This file contains only one line. The line contains the URL that the user's Web browser will be directed to load after incrementing the count file. Here is an example of **url_car**:

```
http://www.foobarcar.com/year2000car.html
```

Running the Script

To use the **ad_track.cgi** program, you need to refer to the script along with one URL variable: page. page needs to be set to the suffix of the **url_** file in the **Counter** subdirectory that contains the URL the user will be directed to. Here is a sample using the car example if it is installed in an **Ad_track** subdirectory under a **cgi-bin** directory:

```
http://www.foorbar.com/cgi-bin/Ad_track/ad_track.cgi?page=car
```

When this URL is called for the first time, a counter file is created in the **Counter** directory called **count_car** with the number 1 in it. This number is incremented every time someone accesses the **ad_track.cgi** with the page=car tag.

In addition to the car example, the script comes with a sample HTML file that contains a reference to the **ad_track.cgi** file using the **url_sample** file that comes on the accompanying CD-ROM. Clicking on the reference to the **ad_track.cgi** script in this HTML document takes you to Selena Sol's script page and increments the counter in the **count_sample** file. Figure 24.2 shows an example of what the HTML output looks like for the **ad_track_sample.html** file. The HTML for **ad_track_sample.html** follows:

```
<HTML>
<HEAD>
<TITLE>
Sample For Hit Counter
</TITLE>
</HEAD>
<BODY>
```

```
<A HREF=ad_track.cgi?page=sample>
<IMG SRC=ad_track_sample.gif></A>
</BODY>
</HTML>
```

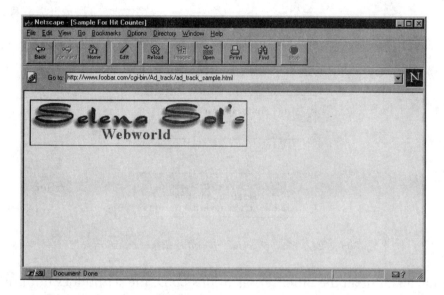

Figure 24.2 *ad_track_sample.html.*

DESIGN DISCUSSION

The purpose of **ad_track.cgi** is to track a user's clicks on an advertising banner displayed at a site. The script increments a counter for the advertised page being accessed and then sends the user to that page. Figure 24.3 shows a basic diagram of this logic.

First, the script starts Perl in the **/usr/local/bin** directory. The location of the supporting files is defined. The default is to store the libraries in the **Library** subdirectory under the current directory where the main script is located. **cgi-lib.pl** is loaded along with **cgi-lib.sol**. **cgi-lib.pl** is used to parse the form variables, and **cgi-lib.sol** supplies the lock file and counter routines.

```
#!/usr/local/bin/perl
$lib = "./Library";
require "$lib/cgi-lib.pl";
require "$lib/cgi-lib.sol";
```

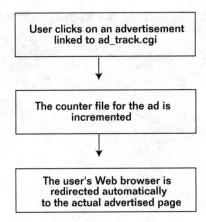

Figure 24.3 Basic flowchart for advertisement tracking.

Unlike almost all the other scripts in this book, the script does not print the standard "Content-type: text/html\n\n" HTTP header at the beginning. This is because the script does not output an HTML file. Instead, it outputs a special redirection signal telling the user's Web browser to go to a different URL to obtain an HTML document. The ReadParse function processes the incoming form variables into the %in associative array.

```
&ReadParse;
```

$countfile is set to the location and filename of the file that maintains the count of hits for the page being accessed by the user. The count file begins with count_ and ends with the contents of whatever the page form variable is set to. The counter file is located in the **Counter** subdirectory underneath the current directory.

```
$countfile = qq!Counter/count_$in{"page"}!;
```

NOTE We use a Perl technique to delimit strings using the **!** symbol instead of double quotes. This method lets us use double quotes within a string without having to escape them. The code looks more readable, because we need not escape the double quotes when referencing the form variables inside the associative array. This technique is documented in Appendix A.

$urlfile contains the location and filename of the file that contains the URL of the page the user is sent to after the counter file is updated. Like the counter file, the URL file is located underneath the **Counter** subdirectory. The name of the file is **url_** plus the value of the page form variable.

```
$urlfile = qq!Counter/url_$in{"page"}!;
```

First, the file containing the URL for the page is opened. Then a while loop is used to read the file. Any line that has a length greater than 1 becomes the new URL to which the user is redirected.

```
open (URLFILE, "$urlfile") ||
    &CgiDie("$urlfile won't open");
while (<URLFILE>)
     {
     chop;
     if (length($_) > 1)
          {
          $url = $_;
          }
     }
close URLFILE;
```

The counter routine in **cgi-lib.sol** is called to increase the counter for the page. The lock file routines in **cgi-lib.sol** are also used to protect the counter file so that no other instance of this script can change the counter file while the current instance is manipulating it. Remember, more than one person may be running the same script at the same time on the Web.

```
&GetFileLock("$countfile.lock");
&counter($countfile);
&ReleaseFileLock("$countfile.lock");
```

Finally, the special HTTP header "Location:" is printed to the Web server. This action causes a redirection signal to be sent to the user's Web browser. In this case, the $url is sent to the user's Web browser to tell it to move to the new site right away. The program then ends.

```
print "Location: $url\n\n";
```

NOTE Image maps work in the same basic way. When you click on an image map, a CGI program can be executed that accepts the coordinates as form variables and then translates them to a URL. This URL is sent to the user's Web browser, which redirects the user elsewhere.

CHAPTER 25

The Web-Based Bulletin Board System

OVERVIEW

There are many uses for a bulletin board system on the Web. A BBS can be used to make information continually available that would normally be shared only during infrequent meetings. Within a BBS, users can discuss topics, reading the responses to their ideas at their leisure.

On the Internet, vendors can use a BBS to discuss their products or offer technical support. For example, people can search a BBS for solutions to a problem that may have been brought up by another customer. Additionally, users on the Internet can set up a BBS spontaneously to discuss things that interest them or just for fun. For all these reasons and more, a Web-based bulletin board system (WebBBS) is an ideal asset in almost any Web site.

The ability of people to post messages to each other in a public BBS is a natural evolution in the information sharing of the Internet. Since the beginning of the Internet, electronic mail has allowed people to exchange information by sending private messages. List servers allow people to subscribe to a sort of "mailing list" where everyone who subscribes gets a copy of every E-mail message sent to the list. Unfortunately, because electronic mail was not designed for large-scale discussion groups, list servers have not proven to be the ideal solution for message sharing. In response to these shortcomings, Internet *newsgroups* were formed. They let people post messages that can then be reviewed by other people at their own pace.

However, not everyone on the Internet has the capability to access Internet newsgroups. In addition, the content of newsgroups tends to be replicated and transferred to sites all over the world. The information generated in some types of discussion groups is not appropriate for worldwide dissemination. For example, a technical support discussion about a small vendor's product may be of use only to 100–200 people in the world— hardly a good case for taking up valuable Internet newsfeed space. Also, with the exception of the "ALT" (Alternative) newsgroups, setting up a newsgroup on the Internet takes a great deal of time and effort.

A discussion board that is local to a particular Web site solves these problems. For one thing, because the discussion board is local to your Web site, you have complete control over the information stored in it. This is an important point, especially for vendors who want to avoid unofficial product information getting out on the Internet. Additionally, a local WebBBS does not have to go through a voting process to get approved; you just set it up. Finally, anyone who has a Web browser can view the WebBBS. There is no need to get an account with an Internet service provider that supplies newsgroup access.

The Web-based discussion board, also known as WebBBS, that accompanies this book has a variety of features that compare favorably with many of the core capabilities found in popular Internet newsgroup readers and servers. The main feature of any discussion forum, including WebBBS, is that the BBS allows a user to post messages as well as post replies to existing messages. The BBS keeps track of which messages are posts and which ones are replies and displays them in a hierarchical tree-like fashion. Posts that start new topics are at the top of each tree, and the replies are shown indented beneath the original posts. Figure 25.1 shows an example of how posts and their replies are displayed on WebBBS.

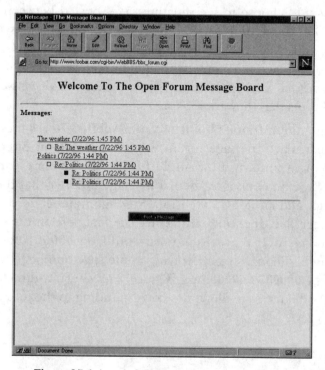

Figure 25.1 *A sample listing of posts using WebBBS.*

WebBBS is fully integrated with the user authentication library discussed in Chapter 9. If you opt to turn on user authentication, the user's last name, first name, and E-mail address are automatically placed into the message headers when the user logs in to the message forum. In addition, because authentication allows you to keep track of individual users, WebBBS allows users to view only messages they have not read instead of subjecting them to the full list of messages each time they log in.

Even when authentication is turned off, there are still other options to restrict the volume of messages viewed by the user. WebBBS allows a user to restrict the number of messages through a variety of query mechanisms. The user can conduct a keyword search and display only those messages that satisfy the search. In addition, the search can be specified as a pattern match or an exact match search. The user can also select a range of dates within which the viewed messages were posted. For example, a user could choose to see only messages posted between "6/1/96" and "6/10/96." In addition, the user can select a range of posts based on age in days, and choose to see, for example, only those messages posted between two days ago and four days ago. These powerful query mechanisms allow a great deal of flexibility so that users can view just the information and posts that they are looking for.

From an administrator's point of view, WebBBS stores messages in a simple format. Each message forum is stored in its own directory, with each post corresponding to a single file. Each filename consists of a unique message number, a hyphen, a message number that the message is replying to, and an **.MSG** extension. Message number zero is referred to as a message that does not exist. Thus, the first post on the system that is not replying to any previous post would be **000001-000000.msg**. Message number 5 on a system replying to message number 3 would have a filename of **000005-000003.msg**. Figure 25.2 shows a directory listing that contains the message filenames corresponding to the messages listed in Figure 25.1.

```
% ls -l
total 12
-rw-rw-rw-  1 wwwadmin wwwadmin   77 Jul 22 13:44 000001-000000.msg
-rw-rw-rw-  1 wwwadmin wwwadmin  139 Jul 22 13:44 000002-000001.msg
-rw-rw-rw-  1 wwwadmin wwwadmin  213 Jul 22 13:44 000003-000002.msg
-rw-rw-rw-  1 wwwadmin wwwadmin  213 Jul 22 13:44 000004-000002.msg
-rw-rw-rw-  1 wwwadmin wwwadmin  101 Jul 22 13:45 000005-000000.msg
-rw-rw-rw-  1 wwwadmin wwwadmin  199 Jul 22 13:45 000006-000005.msg

%
```

Figure 25.2 Listing of filenames corresponding to messages displayed in Figure 25.1.

The posts are stored in this format to allow WebBBS to look at the messages for a given forum and automatically know which messages were the most recently posted (the ones with the highest message numbers) and which messages replied to which other messages. In this way, WebBBS develops a hierarchical view of the messages. Because this view is generated dynamically, posts can easily be removed without the need to update any other files. Thus, a WebBBS administrator can turn on features such as automatic message deletion when a post reaches a certain age or when the number of posts in a directory exceeds a certain number. In addition, a WebBBS administrator can manually delete a message if it has been posted inappropriately to the WebBBS forum.

Another useful feature of WebBBS is the ability to define forums on the fly. The administrator need only create a new directory for each forum and then add the forum to a list of other forums in the setup file.

If a user is using a Web browser, such as Netscape version 2.0, that is compatible with the new <INPUT TYPE=FILE> HTML form tag, the administrator can allow attachments to be uploaded along with the contents of a post. This feature can be useful, because it allows people to transfer files to one another. For example, product updates and patches can be posted directly on a technical support BBS and be available for users to download.

INSTALLATION AND USAGE

The WebBBS files on the accompanying CD-ROM install into a directory called **WebBBS**. The files and subdirectories associated with this application along with their required permissions are shown in Figure 25.3.

WebBBS is the root application directory. It must be readable and executable by the Web server. In addition to the application files, the **Msg_open**, **Library**, **Msg_CGI**, **Attach**, **Images**, **Users**, and **Sessions** subdirectories are located here.

bbs_forum.cgi is the main CGI script that performs all the BBS functions, including reading and posting new messages. This file must be readable and executable.

bbs.setup is a setup file for the BBS. This file must be readable.

bbs_html_error.pl contains Perl code that outputs an error message to the user if anything goes wrong. This file must be readable. Figure 25.4 shows an example of this page on a Web browser.

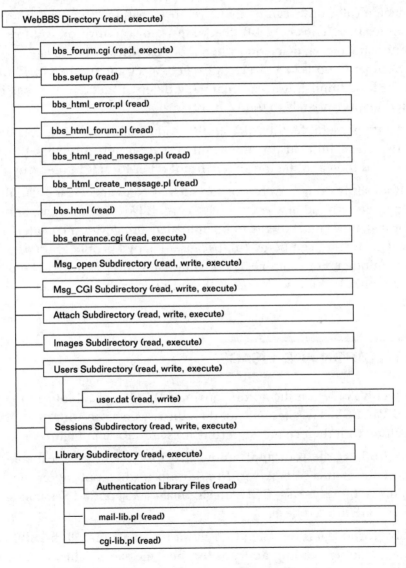

Figure 25.3 BBS script directory structure and permissions.

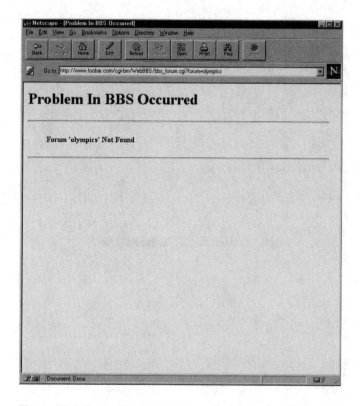

Figure 25.4 bbs_html_error.pl output displayed on a Web browser.

bbs_html_forum.pl contains Perl code that outputs the list of messages in a particular forum. This file must be readable. Figure 25.1 shows an example of the output from this file.

bbs_html_read_message.pl contains Perl code that outputs an HTML version of a message that has been previously posted on the BBS. This file must be readable. Figure 25.5 shows an example of the HTML output when a message is read.

bbs_html_create_message.pl contains Perl code that outputs an HTML form for creating a message on the BBS. This file must be readable. Figure 25.6 shows the output of the HTML for posting a message to a BBS.

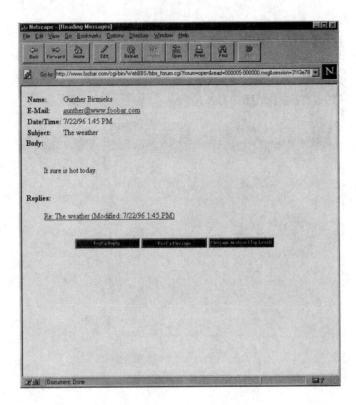

Figure 25.5 bbs_html_read_message.pl output displayed on a Web browser.

bbs.html is a sample HTML file showing how to access a forum from an HTML file. This file should be placed in a directory where your Web server is allowed to read HTML files. In addition, the file should be readable. It is discussed further in the "Running the Script" section.

bbs_entrance.cgi is a sample script that outputs an HTML form where the user chooses various options. These options are then posted to **bbs_forum.cgi** when the user presses a submit button. This file should be readable and executable. In the "Running the Script" section, **bbs_entrance.cgi** is discussed further.

The **Library** subdirectory stores all the external libraries the script must access. This directory should be readable and executable, and all the files in it should be readable. These files include all the files associated with the authentication library discussed in Chapter 9 (for logging a user on to the BBS), **cgi-lib.pl** (for processing HTML forms), and **mail-lib.pl** (for sending E-mail).

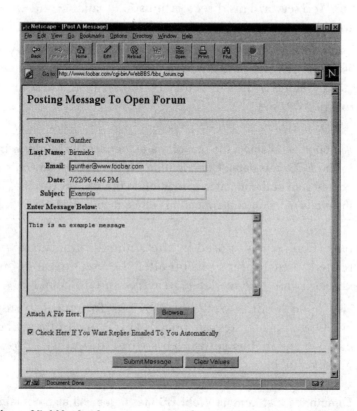

Figure 25.6 bbs_html_create_message.pl *output displayed on a Web browser.*

The **Attach** subdirectory is used to store the attachments that are uploaded by users of the WebBBS. If your Web server is set up in a way that disallows nonexecutable files in CGI directories, you may need to place this directory where the user's Web browser can download files directly. In addition, you may want to place this directory in a non-CGI area so that no one will be able to upload a file to a CGI directory and then run the program using a Web browser. This directory should be readable and executable by the Web server.

The **Images** subdirectory holds the images of the buttons used by the WebBBS. You may need to place this directory where HTML files can read images if image files are not allowed to be mixed with CGI executables on your Web server. This directory must be readable and executable. The files within it must be readable.

The **Users** subdirectory is used by the authentication library to store the user list. This directory must be readable, writable, and executable. A **user.dat** file is created in this directory by the script the first time a user registers for the Web site.

NOTE Although we discuss the use of the authentication library with regard to the BBS, the default distribution on the accompanying CD-ROM comes with authentication turned off in the **bbs.setup** file. The ramifications of using authentication will be discussed later.

The **Sessions** subdirectory is used by the authentication library to store the files related to each user's session after the user first logs on to the site. This directory must be readable, writable, and executable.

The **Msg_open** subdirectory is used by **bbs_forum.cgi** to store messages for the Open Forum message board. This is one of the default message forums set up in **bbs.setup**. This directory must be readable, writable, and executable.

NOTE Directories that contain WebBBS messages will also contain **[user-name].dat** files if authentication is enabled in the setup file. These files keep track of each user's last read message number.

The **Msg_CGI** subdirectory is used by **bbs_forum.cgi** to store messages for the CGI talk message board, just as **Msg_open** does for the Open Forum. This directory must be readable, writable, and executable.

Server-Specific Setup and Options

The **bbs.setup** file contains the configuration variables for **bbs_forum.cgi**. The following is a list of these setup items.

@forums is a list of forum names. These names are descriptive names of the forums that are available on the BBS. For example, if you had one forum for discussing open topics and another for discussing CGI programming, this variable would be set to ("Open Forum", "CGI Programming Forum").

@forum_directories is a list of the directory paths that correspond to the list of forums in @forums. Each of these directories stores the messages related to its own forum. An example list of values for @forum_directories that matches the preceding example would be ("Msg_open", "Msg_CGI").

@forum_variable is a list of forum variable names related to each BBS forum. Whenever **bbs_forum.cgi** is called, it must have the variable forum sent to it. This variable is equal to the name in the @forum_variable array. Each element of the array corresponds to the forums listed in the @forums array. Because the values here are variable names, you should use lower-case text, underscores instead of spaces, and no special characters. For example, @forum_variables could be set to ("open", "cgi"), which corresponds to the "Open Forum" and "CGI Programming Forum" values of @forums.

$bbs_script is the **bbs_forum.cgi** script name. Most systems keep this variable set to bbs_forum.cgi, but in some systems the script must be renamed. For example, some Windows NT Web servers require that the script name have a **.bat** extension. The $bbs_script variable is used by **bbs_forum.cgi** to make references to itself from URLs it generates.

$allow_user_attachments is set to on if you are allowing people to upload to the BBS.

$maximum_attachment_size is the size in bytes of the maximum amount of data you want sent to the WebBBS script from the user's Web browser when a file is uploaded.

$attach_dir is the path to the directory where attachments are uploaded. This should be set to a directory that allows users to download the files directly with their Web browser. On some Web servers, directories that can run CGI scripts cannot view HTML files. Generally, the same rules apply to the downloading of files.

$attach_url is the URL that is used to prefix attached files. In the event that the attached files are uploaded to a directory where HTML files can be read as opposed to being able to execute CGI scripts, this URL must point a user's Web browser to the new directory.

`$display_only_new_messages` is on if you want to keep track of the last new message that each user has read.

NOTE **There are several requirements for this to take place. First, you must use authentication to record the user name when the user enters the forum. Second, the form variable** `use_last_read=on` **must be in the first URL call to bbs_forum.cgi. The user may want to see all the new messages, so leaving off the** `use_last_read` **form variable allows the user to see everything even if the last read message has been recorded.**

`$display_thread_depth` is the number of descending nodes to be displayed in the message listing. For example, with a thread depth of 2, the user sees only the original posts and the replies indented beneath the message. With a thread depth of 3, the replies to the replies are seen, with further indentations. If you recall, Figure 25.1 shows an example of several message threads that are indented with respect to one another.

`$prune_how_many_days` is the number of days after which a message is considered too old to leave on the system. These messages are deleted. If this variable is set to zero, messages are not removed on the basis of age.

`$prune_how_many_sequences` is the maximum number of messages you want to leave on the system before the oldest ones are deleted. For example, if you specify this number to be 10, then only 10 messages will be allowed per forum. In this case, after the 11th message is posted, message number 1 would be deleted. Setting this value to zero means that you do not want any messages deleted on the basis of a maximum number of messages to keep on the system.

`$bbs_buttons` is the URL prefix for the directory that contains the BBS button images. By default, these images are located in the **Images** subdirectory underneath the directory in which the BBS script is installed. You may need to move these images to another directory if only CGI- executables are allowed inside this directory.

`$no_html` is set to on if you want to filter HTML from a user's post. It is a good idea to prevent users from posting HTML within their messages, because it can do nasty things. For example, users might leave off a closure tag in the subject, such as </H1> if they are including a header. This omission would make all the other messages inherit the header attribute.

$no_html_images is set to on if you want to prevent people from referencing images in their messages. Setting $no_html to on also filters out image-related HTML tags, so setting this variable, $no_html_images, to on is for administrators who want to continue to allow HTML posting but not images. In other words, $no_html being set to on includes filtering out all image tags, so $no_html_images need not be set if $no_html is already on.

$use_list_element is set to on if you wish the message threads to be displayed with HTML-style bullets. Displaying with bullets looks nicer but takes up more space on the screen.

$allow_reply_email is set to on if you want to allow users to choose whether to get E-mail notifications of replies to their posts.

$force_reply_email is on if you want to force users to get E-mail notifications of replies to their posts. In this case, users are not given a choice. They will always get the notifications.

$send_reply_email needs to be on for either of the preceding two variables to work. If $send_reply_email is off, then E-mail will not be sent even if the message specifies that an E-mail reply should be sent. This variable allows the administrator to turn off the E-mail reply feature even after people have posted messages asking for E-mail–based replies.

If authentication is being used, the user's first name, last name, and E-mail are specified at login. If this is the case, setting $force_first_name, $force_last_name, and $force_email to on forces those fields be to remain the same whenever a user posts on the BBS. Normally, a user can enter his or her name and E-mail address information when posting a message, but setting these variables on disallows that.

$require_subject , $require_first_name, $require_last_name, and $require_email are set to on if you want to make sure that the user enters something into these fields instead of leaving them blank. In other words, setting these variables to on makes them required fields; a post will not be created without them.

If replies are to be E-mailed, then `$from_email` must be set to an E-mail address from which you want the replies generated. Usually, you set this variable to the E-mail address of the Web server or your own E-mail address on the system.

The remaining variables are authentication library settings. By default, `$auth_cgi` and `$auth_server` are set to off. However, enabling one of these types of authentication enables the user's first name, last name, and E-mail information to automatically be entered when the user posts a message. Authentication also enables the BBS to track the last read message through the acquired username. Chapter 9 discusses the various authentication variables in detail.

The following is an example of all the setup variables in the **bbs.setup** file.

```
@forums = ("Open Forum", "CGI Programming");
@forum_directories = ("Msg_Open", "Msg_CGI");
@forum_variable = ("open", "cgi");

$bbs_script = "bbs_forum.cgi";
$allow_user_attachments = "on";
$maximum_attachment_size = 500000;
$attach_dir = "Attach";
$attach_url = "Attach";

$display_only_new_messages =        "on";
$display_thread_depth =        8;
$prune_how_many_days =          5;
$prune_how_many_sequences =     100;
$bbs_buttons = "Images";

$no_html = "off";
$no_html_images = "on";

$use_list_element = "on";
$allow_reply_email = "on";
$force_reply_email = "off";
$send_reply_email = "on";

$force_first_name = "on";
$force_last_name = "on";
$force_email = "off";
```

```
$require_subject = "off";
$require_first_name = "on";
$require_last_name = "on";
$require_email = "on";

$from_email = "gunther@foobar.com";

$auth_lib = ".";
$auth_server =                  "off";
$auth_cgi =                     "on";
$auth_user_file =               "Users/user.dat";
$auth_alt_user_file =           "";
$auth_allow_register =          "on";
$auth_allow_search =            "on";
$auth_default_group =           "normal";
$auth_generate_password =       "off";
$auth_check_duplicates =        "on";
$auth_add_register =            "on";
$auth_email_register =          "off";
$auth_admin_from_address = "wwwadmin\@fooobar.com";
$auth_admin_email_address = "gunther\@foobar.com";
$auth_session_length = 2;
$auth_session_dir = "./Sessions";
$auth_register_message =
        "Thanks, you may now logon with your new
        username and password.";
$auth_password_message =
        "Thanks for applying to our site,
         your password is";
@auth_extra_fields = ("auth_first_name",
                      "auth_last_name",
                      "auth_email");
@auth_extra_desc = ("First Name",
                    "Last Name",
                    "Email");
$auth_logon_title = "Submit BBS Logon";
$auth_logon_header = "Enter BBS Logon Information";
```

USING OTHER SETUP FILES

The BBS script has the ability to reference another setup file in case the default **bbs.setup** file does not meet the needs of every forum. For example, although **bbs.setup** accommodates multiple forums, you may want to assign a different automatic removal of messages policy for each one. On the Open Forum, you may want to delete messages older than 10 days, but on a CGI Programming forum, you may not want to delete any messages.

You can do this by using another setup file that is loaded with the same variables defined by **bbs.setup**. **bbs.setup** is always read into the **bbs_forum.cgi** script. However, if you set the setup variable on the URL link to the script as a form variable, **bbs_forum.cgi** will read a setup file on the basis of that variable. For example, if you specified the call to **bbs_forum.cgi** as

```
http://www.foobar.com/cgi-
bin/WebBBS/bbs_forum.cgi?forum=open&setup=test
```

then the **test.setup** file would be loaded by the BBS after the **bbs.setup** file is loaded.

NOTE
bbs.setup is always necessary. This means that if you choose to override **bbs.setup** using the setup form variable, you need only specify the variables you want changed in the new setup file instead of all the variables originally residing in **bbs.setup**.

The only variables you cannot override with the second setup file are the file upload variables. To read the second setup file, **cgi-lib.pl** must read the form variables first. Unfortunately, the files are uploaded inside the ReadParse routine in **cgi-lib.pl**. Thus, the files are already uploaded by the time the setup form variable has been read by ReadParse.

MODIFYING THE HTML

The HTML scripts for the core WebBBS script are stored in files that are prefixed with **bbs_html**. These Perl scripts output the HTML forms for posting and reading messages as well as other BBS operations. To modify the cosmetics of the BBS, you need only edit these files. They are discussed in more detail in the "Design Discussion" section.

Running the Script

To use the **bbs_forum.cgi** program, you refer to it along with urlencoded information. The only mandatory URL variable is forum. However, several others can be set up. Here is a sample URL for this script if it is installed in the **WebBBS** subdirectory underneath the **cgi-bin** directory:

```
http://www.foobar.com/cgi-bin/WebBBS/bbs_forum.cgi?forum=open
```

A sample HTML file that also has this link is shown next. The link also has a setup variable defined. Figure 25.7 shows what **bbs.html** looks like on a Web browser.

```
<HTML>
<HEAD>
<TITLE>BBS Forum List</TITLE>
</HEAD>
<BODY>
<H1>BBS Forum List</H1>
<HR>
<A HREF=
"bbs_forum.cgi?forum=open&setup=test ">
Enter The Open Forum</A>
<HR>
</BODY>
</HTML>
```

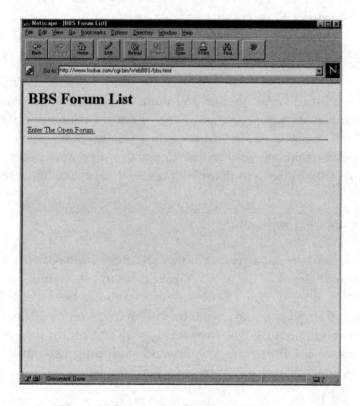

Figure 25.7 *bbs.html displayed in a Web browser.*

609

Optional URL Variables

There are several optional form variables that **bbs_forum.cgi** recognizes. These include `setup`, `use_last_read`, `keywords`, `exact_match`, `first_date`, `last_date`, `first_days_old`, and `last_days_old`.

`setup` is the form variable for specifying a new setup file for the BBS. It is set equal to the name of the setup file you wish to read minus the **.setup** extension. Thus, if you wish to use **test.setup** to override **bbs.setup**, you would set this variable equal to `test`. Here is an example URL:

```
http://www.foobar.com/cgi-
bin/WebBBS/bbs_forum.cgi?forum=open&setup=test
```

`use_last_read` must be set to `on` if you wish users to see only messages that they have not already seen. For this to work, the BBS must be configured to track last read messages for users, and authentication must be turned on. The following URL turns this variable on:

```
http://www.foobar.com/cgi-
bin/WebBBS/bbs_forum.cgi?forum=open&use_last_read=on
```

`keywords` is a list of keywords that you want the messages to contain. For example, if you set `keywords=hockey`, only messages containing the string "hockey" will be displayed. In addition, the `exact_match` variable can be set to `on` if you want the keyword search to match whole words only. Here is an example URL for searching for "hockey" with an exact match search:

```
http://www.foobar.com/cgi-bin/WebBBS/bbs_forum.cgi?forum=open&key-
words=hockey&exact_match=on
```

`first_date` and `last_date` are the range of dates within which a message can be viewed. For example, if `first_date` is set to 1/1/95 and `last_date` is set to 1/15/95, only messages between those dates will be seen by the user. A URL for doing this is shown next. Note that `%2F` replaces the forward slash (/) symbol, because Web browsers recognize forward slashes only as separations for subdirectories; the forward slash must be translated into its hexadecimal ASCII-code equivalent (`%2F`).

```
http://www.foobar.com/cgi-
bin/WebBBS/bbs_forum.cgi?forum=open&first_date=1%2F1%2F95&last_date=1%
2F15%2F95
```

`first_days_old` and `last_days_old` operate similarly to the date-related variables. This is also a date range on which to view posts, but it is based on the age of a post in days. If `first_days_old` is set to 30 and `last_days_old` is set to 15, messages between the ages of 30 and 15 days old will be seen by the user. The following example URL illustrates this:

```
http://www.foobar.com/cgi-
bin/WebBBS/bbs_forum.cgi?forum=open&first_days_old=30&last_days_old=15
```

The **bbs_entrance.cgi** program shown next prints a form allowing users to see and set the different options for restricting the view of their messages. Figure 25.8 shows an example of this form.

```
#!/usr/local/bin/perl
print "Content-type: text/html\n\n";
print <<__END_OF_HTML__;
<HTML>
<HEAD>
<TITLE>BBS Version 4.0 Sample Entrance</TITLE>
</HEAD>
<BODY BGCOLOR = "FFFFFF" TEXT = "000000">
<CENTER>
<H1>BBS Sample Entrance</H1>
<HR>
</CENTER>
<FORM ACTION="bbs_forum.cgi" METHOD=POST>
<TABLE BORDER = "1">
<TR>
<TH ALIGN = "left">Forum</TH>
<TD><SELECT NAME = "forum">
<OPTION VALUE = "open">Open Forum
<OPTION VALUE = "cgi">CGI Programming
</SELECT>
</TD>
</TR>
<TR>
<TH ALIGN = "left">
Display messages with what keywords?
</TH>
```

```
<TD>
<INPUT TYPE = "text" NAME = "keywords">
</TD>
</TR>
<TR>
<TH ALIGN = "left">
Exact Match for keyword search?
</TH>
<TD>
<INPUT TYPE = "checkbox" NAME = "exact_match">
</TD>
</TR>
<TR>
<TH ALIGN = "left">
Range of Dates Posted (First date in range to view
messages, e.g., 12/03/98)
</TH>
<TD>
<INPUT TYPE = "text" NAME = "first_date">
</TD>
</TR>
<TR>
<TH ALIGN = "left">
Range of Dates Posted (Last date in range to view
messages, e.g., 12/03/98)
</TH>
<TD>
<INPUT TYPE = "text" NAME = "last_date">
</TD>
</TR>
<TR>
<TH ALIGN = "left">
Range of Age of posts (earliest number of days old to
view msgs)
</TH>
<TD>
<INPUT TYPE = "text" NAME = "first_days_old">
</TD>
</TR>
<TR>
<TH ALIGN = "left">
```

Range of Age of posts (latest number of days old to
view msgs)
</TH>
<TD>
<INPUT TYPE = "text" NAME = "last_days_old">
</TD>
</TR>
</TABLE>
<P>
<CENTER>
<INPUT TYPE = "submit"
VALUE = "Enter the BBS with these parameters">
</CENTER>
<BLOCKQUOTE>
<STRONG>Instructions:</STRONG> All the fields that
appear above are optional except for the forum field.
The forum is needed in order to determine which
messages to view. Normally all messages in a forum
are displayed. However, entering values into the above
fields will narrow down the messages that are displayed.
<P>
Entering a keyword will display only messages with that
keyword. The keyword search can also be specified as an
exact match search.
<P>
You can also specify a range of dates to view the
posts. In other words, you can specify to view only
the posts that were created between a certain range
of days.
<P>
In addition to the above date range search, you
can choose to narrow down the age of posts as
a factor of days instead of an actual date range.
For example, if you wanted to view only posts 2 days
old and newer, then you would enter the number 2 into the
"earliest number of days to view messages" field.
</BLOCKQUOTE>
</BODY>
</HTML>
__END_OF_HTML__

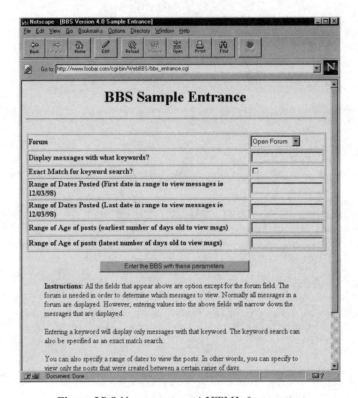

Figure 25.8 bbs_entrance.cgi HTML form output.

BBS MAINTENANCE

After you have been running the WebBBS for a little while, you may find yourself doing occasional maintenance on it. The two most common operations are the deletion of messages and the editing of messages.

Deleting messages is easy. Because the messages are stored in a directory you specify, finding the message to delete is a matter of looking at the directory and removing the file that corresponds to the message.

On UNIX, the **rm** command removes a file.

NOTE

Each message is stored as two six-digit numbers separated by a hyphen with an **.msg** extension. If an attachment is associated with the message, it has the same filename except that the extension is **.attach** instead of **.msg**. The first six-digit number is the message number. The second six-digit number is the message number that it is a reply to. If the second six-digit number is 000000, the message is an original post and is not a reply to anything previously posted. Here is an example list of message files:

```
000001-000000.msg
000002-000000.msg
000003-000001.msg
000004-000003.msg
000005-000002.msg
```

The preceding list shows message numbers 1 through 5. The leading zeros are necessary for the BBS programming to sort the messages. (This is discussed later in the "Design Discussion" section). We can see that messages 1 and 2 are original posts, because they have "000000" as the reply-to message number. Message 3 is a reply to message 1, message 4 is a reply to message 3, and message 5 is a reply to message 2.

If you want to delete message 2, simply delete the message. On UNIX, you can use the **rm** command to remove it by typing the following command while you are in the directory containing the messages:

```
rm 000002-000000.msg
```

Remember, if an **.attach** file exists with the same message number, you need to delete it also. Before you delete the **.attach** file, you should look at the contents. It contains a single line that tells you which directory and filename the attachment is stored in so that you can remove the uploaded file as well.

A neat feature of WebBBS is that you do not have to worry about deleting a message that other messages may be replying to. If a message is missing in the hierarchy of replies, WebBBS automatically readjusts the hierarchy in the message list display so that a reply to a post that is deleted becomes a top-level post. For example, if message 3 was deleted, message 4 would be seen by the BBS as an original post, because the reply-to message "000003" no longer exists. Thus, the BBS gracefully takes care of reordering the messages if you decide to delete some of them.

NOTE **To find out the message number of the message you want to delete, you can view the message in the BBS using your Web browser. When you are reading a message, the URL in the location box of your Web browser shows you a** message= **variable that is set to the message number currently being read. Figure 25.5 has a location box that illustrates this.**

If you want to edit a message, load the message in any text editor. Be careful to keep the message structure the same. Do not delete a line that contains any header fields, such as first name, last name, E-mail address, date and time of the post, subject, and options. Here is an example of a message in its "raw" form:

```
Gunther
Birznieks
gunther@foobar.com
7/1/96 8:14 AM
test subject
options:email:gunther@foobar.com

This is the message.
```

The first line of the file contains the first name of the poster. The next line contains the last name of the poster. The E-mail address appears on the third line, and the date and time stamp of the message is stored on the fourth line. The subject is on the fifth line of the message.

The sixth line may seem weird because of the options: tag. This line is needed because it contains information about the options the user intends for this message. Currently, only one option is implemented: email. When the options: tag has email associated with it, an E-mail will be generated whenever someone replies to the message.

The subsequent lines contain the body of the post. There is nothing unusual about the body of the post. It can contain multiple lines and continues to the end of the message file. The body of the preceding post consists of a couple of carriage returns for extra spacing plus the text "This is the message."

DESIGN DISCUSSION

WebBBS performs all its functions using the **bbs_forum.cgi** script. These operations include the listing of messages in a forum as well as the creation of those messages. Depending on the value of incoming form variables, **bbs_forum.cgi** determines which procedure to perform. A flowchart of the BBS features is shown in Figure 25.9.

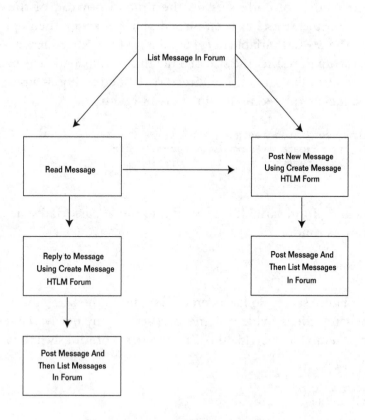

Figure 25.9 Basic flowchart for the BBS.

bbs_forum.cgi

The first line of the following code sets up the location of the supporting files of the program. By default, $lib is set to the current directory. The core setup variables are loaded from **bbs.setup**. Then **cgi-lib.pl** is loaded.

```
$lib = ".";
require "./bbs.setup";
require "$lib/cgi-lib.pl";
```

The standard "Content-type: text/html\n\n" HTTP header is printed.

```
print &PrintHeader;
```

The next section of code sets up the upload portion of the BBS. If $allow_user_attachments has been turned on in **bbs.setup**, then uploads are enabled. The maxdata variable in **cgi-lib.pl** is set to $maximum_attachment_size from **bbs.setup** to restrict the size of a file that is uploaded. The writefiles variable is set to the $attach_dir directory defined in **bbs.setup** so that all uploaded files are placed in this directory by **cgi-lib.pl**.

```
if ($allow_user_attachments eq "on") {
    $cgi_lib'maxdata = $maximum_attachment_size;
    $cgi_lib'writefiles = "$attach_dir";
}
```

The incoming form variables are read into the %in associative array using the ReadParse routine.

```
&ReadParse;
```

If an alternative setup file has been defined using the setup form variable, this new setup file is loaded by the BBS script. Any new variables in the alternative setup file override those that were set previously in **bbs.setup**.

```
$setup_file = $in{"setup"};
if ($setup_file ne  "") {
    require "$setup_file.setup";
}
```

Then the authentication library is read. The BBS uses the session information generated by the authentication library throughout this script.

```
require "$auth_lib/auth-lib.pl";
```

READING THE FORM VARIABLES

The next part of the script reads and sets up nearly all the form variables. $forum, the variable name of the current discussion forum, is read first. It corresponds to a name in the @forum_variables array from which other forum information is gathered. The GetForumInfo subroutine then translates the abbreviated forum name ($forum) to a more descriptive forum name ($forum_name) and the directory ($forum_dir) that the forum messages will be found in.

```
$forum = $in{"forum"};
($forum_name, $forum_dir) = &GetForumInfo($forum);
```

The current session is read from the session form variable. If session is blank, the BBS sets $is_this_a_new_session to yes as a reminder that this is the first time that the BBS script has been called. The form variable, session, will be carried throughout the rest of the user's interaction with the BBS. Next, GetSessionInfo is called in the authentication library to retrieve information about the user if it exists. The details of this function are discussed in Chapter 9.

```
$session = $in{"session"};
$is_this_a_new_session = "yes" if ($session eq "");

($session, $username, $group,
 $firstname, $lastname, $email) =
&GetSessionInfo($session, "$bbs_script", *in);
```

Whenever a button is pressed on an HTML form on the BBS, its name becomes associated with the value of the caption on the button. In addition, the BBS allows the user to specify the submit buttons as either images or normal buttons. For example, $reply_op will have a value assigned to it if a `reply_op` button was pressed on a form or if a `reply_op` image button was pressed on an HTML form.

When an image tag is used in a form to simulate a button, the value of x and y coordinates for the variable are set instead of the variable name by itself. For example, if `reply_op` is the name of the image button and it is pressed, then the form variables `reply_op.x` and `reply_op.y` will have values assigned to them instead of the name `reply_op` by itself. These x and y coordinates correspond to the location of the mouse on the button when it was clicked. We know that the image button was pressed if either coordinate has a value associated with it.

`$reply_op` is assigned a value if the current operation is a reply to a currently read message. `$post_op` is assigned a value if the current operation being performed by the user is an original post to the BBS.

```
$reply_op = $in{"reply_op"};
$reply_op = "on" if ($in{"reply_op.x"} ne "");
$post_op = $in{"post_op"};
$post_op = "on" if ($in{"post_op.x"} ne "");
```

`$create_message_op` contains a value if the user has just submitted a message for posting.

```
$create_message_op = $in{"create_message_op"};
```

`$read` contains a value if the user is reading a message. The value of `$read` is the message file to read.

```
$read = $in{"read"};
```

`$first_date`, `$last_date`, `$keywords`, `$exact_match`, `$first_days_old`, and `$last_days_old` are form variables that the user can use to narrow the scope of the messages to be listed on the main forum page.

If `$keywords` are specified, all the messages displayed must contain those keywords in order to be seen. If `$exact_match` is `on`, the keywords must match whole words within the messages. For example, if a user searches for "ram" within a message, messages with words such as "ram," "cram," and others with "ram" inside them will return a positive match. However, with exact_match equal to on, only messages that contain the whole word "ram" will return a positive match.

$first_date and $last_date is a date range within which posting dates of the messages must fall if they are to be displayed to the user. $first_days_old and $last_days_old are similar to the previous two variables except that the age range of the posts is defined by "number of days old" rather than the explicit dates on which they were posted. These variables are discussed in more detail in the "Installation and Usage" section.

```
$first_date = $in{"first_date"};
$last_date = $in{"last_date"};
$keywords = $in{"keywords"};
$exact_match = $in{"exact_match"};
$first_days_old = $in{"first_days_old"};
$last_days_old = $in{"last_days_old"};
```

$create_message_error is a message that prints when the message list in a forum is printed if the previous attempt to create a message by a user has failed. One of the most common reasons for a failure is that the user left off a field that was specified as required in **bbs.setup**. For example, if the first name field is required and the user did not enter a first name, the post will fail. The message list in the forum is printed again, along with the error message detailing what happened in $create_msg_error.

```
$create_msg_error = "";
```

$use_last_read and $last_read are used if authentication is turned on and if the user wishes to see only new messages displayed in the forum list. $use_last_read is on if the user wants to use the "view only new messages" feature. $last_read is the sequence number of the user's last read message, which is compared against the sequence numbers of the current message list. If a sequence number of a message is higher than $last_read, we know that the message is "new."

```
$use_last_read = $in{"use_last_read"};
$last_read = $in{"last_read"};
```

PERFORM THE BBS OPERATIONS

If $reply_op or $post_op has a value associated with it, it means that the user is either replying to a message or posting a new one, respectively. The PrintPostOrReplyPage function is called to print the HTML form for creating a message.

```
if (($reply_op ne "") || ($post_op ne ""))
{
    &PrintPostOrReplyPage;
}
```

If $create_message_op has a value, it means that a post or reply has been submitted to the BBS script for posting. In this case, the CreatePosting subroutine is called.

```
elsif ($create_message_op ne "")
{
    &CreatePosting;
}
```

If $read has a value associated with it, the BBS calls the ReadMessage subroutine to display the message. $read is a form variable—part of the URL hypertext link to each individual message in the message listing that is displayed to users when they first go into a discussion forum. For each hypertext link, $read corresponds to the message number to be read.

```
elsif ($read ne "")
{
    &ReadMessage($read);
}
```

Finally, as a catch-all, when $forum has a forum name associated with it, the list of messages is listed by the PrintForumPage procedure.

```
elsif ($forum ne "")
{
    &PrintForumPage;
}
```

THE READMESSAGE SUBROUTINE

The ReadMessage subroutine takes a message filename as a parameter and displays it to the user as an HTML page.

```
sub ReadMessage
{
    local($message) = @_;
```

$poster_firstname, $poster_lastname, $poster_email, $post_date_time, $post_subject, and $post_options in the message header are declared local and are retrieved from the message file using the GetMessageHeader routine.

```
    local($poster_firstname, $poster_lastname,
          $poster_email,$post_date_time,
          $post_subject, $post_options) =
          &GetMessageHeader("$forum_dir/$message");
```

Then the body of the message is assigned to the $post_message variable. Because the message header has already been read, the first six lines of the file are skipped with a quick for loop.

```
    open (MESSAGEFILE, "$forum_dir/$message") ||
     &CgiDie("Could Not Open Message File\n");
    for (1 .. 6) { <MESSAGEFILE>; } # Throwaway header
    $post_message = "";
    while (<MESSAGEFILE>)
    {
     $post_message .= $_;
    }
    close (MESSAGEFILE);
```

It may seem inefficient that we open the message file twice—once to read the header and again to read the body—instead of doing it in one subroutine. However, message headers are read several times in the WebBBS script, so encapsulating that part of the script in a subroutine allows the code to be more modular. A common modification to the WebBBS script is to add your own header fields or subtract ones you do not need. Encapsulating the header information into a subroutine makes it easier for another programmer to make changes to the message structure.

If $no_html_images is on, image-related HTML is filtered out of the message body and subject so that the HTML code, rather than the image, is displayed to the user.

```
if ($no_html_images eq "on")
{
    $post_message =~ s/<(IMG\s*SRC.*)>/&LT;$1&GT;/ig;
    $post_subject =~ s/<(IMG\s*SRC.*)>/&LT;$1&GT;/ig;
} # End of parsing out no images
```

If $no_html is on, all the HTML code in the subject and message is filtered. Figure 25.10 shows an example of a message when its HTML code is filtered so that it will not affect the Web browser.

```
if ($no_html eq "on")
{
    $post_message =~ s/<([^>]+)>/\&LT;$1&GT;/ig;
    $post_subject =~ s/<([^>]+)>/\&LT;$1&GT;/ig;
} # End of No html
```

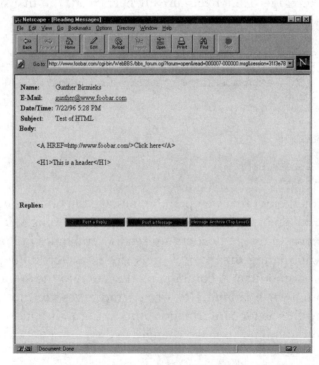

Figure 25.10 WebBBS messages with HTML tags filtered.

If there are multiple newlines (with a separating carriage return) in the BBS message, we assume that they indicate the start of a new paragraph and HTMLize them by replacing them with a <P> HTML tag. If one newline remains after the previous replacement, we assume it marks a simple line break, which is implemented using the
 HTML tag.

```
$post_message =~ s/\n\r\n/<p>/g;
$post_message =~ s/\n/<br>/g;
```

The following part of the routine opens the forum directory and attempts to read all the reply filenames to the @files array. Remember from the "Installation and Usage" section that message filenames follow the format **[message number] – [message number replied to].msg**. The grep command is used to read only those filenames whose "message number replied to" is the current message number being read. This information is used to generate a list of replies to the currently read message.

```
opendir(FORUMDIR, "$forum_dir") ||
    &CgiDie("Could not open $forum_dir directory\n");
$message_number = substr($message,0,6);
@files = sort(grep(/.......$message_number\.msg$/,
        readdir(FORUMDIR)));
closedir(FORUMDIR);
```

ReadMessageFields is called to create a URL listing of all the variables that must be passed from screen to screen on the BBS. This listing is placed into $message_url.

```
$message_url = &ReadMessageFields;
```

Next, the $post_replies HTML code is generated. First , $post_replies is cleared. Then, for every reply file in the @files array, the message header is read using the GetMessageHeader function, and a hypertext reference is generated and placed in $post_replies. At the end of the foreach loop, $post_replies will have all the message replies listed in HTML format.

```
$post_replies = "";
foreach (@files) {
    ($reply_firstname, $reply_lastname, $reply_email,
     $reply_date_time, $reply_subject,
```

```
    $reply_options) =
    &GetMessageHeader("$forum_dir/$_");
  $post_replies .=
    qq!<A HREF="$bbs_script?forum=$forum!;
  $post_replies .=
    qq!&read=$_&$message_url">!;
  $post_replies .=
  " $reply_subject " .
    "(Modified: $reply_date_time)</A><BR>\n";
}
```

The `$attach_file` filename is calculated by taking the message name minus the **.msg** extension and adding a new **.attach** extension. `$post_attach_html` is cleared and eventually is used to store the hypertext reference to an attached file if one exists.

```
$attach_file = substr($message,0,13) . ".attach";
$post_attach_html = "";
```

The -e operator is used to test whether the `$attach_file` exists. If it does, this file is opened and parsed to find out the name of the true attached file. The **[message name].attach** file contains only a descriptive reference to the uploaded file.

```
if (-e "$forum_dir/$attach_file") {
    open(ATTACHFILE, "$forum_dir/$attach_file") ||
     &CgiDie("Could Not Open $forum_dir/$attach_file\n");
    chop($attach_info = <ATTACHFILE>);

    ($post_attachment, $post_attachment_filename) =
     split(/\|/, $attach_info);
```

When the attached file has been found, a hypertext reference is generated to it in the `$post_attach_html` variable.

```
    $post_attach_html =
     qq!<BR><B>Attached File:</B> ! .
        qq!<A HREF="$attach_url/$post_attachment">
         $post_attachment_filename</A><BR>!;
    close (ATTACHFILE);
}
```

Finally, the **bbs_html_read_message.pl** library is called to print the full HTML related to the reading of a message. Figure 25.11 shows an example of a message that is displayed with replies and an attachment.

```
require "bbs_html_read_message.pl";

} # End of ReadMessage
```

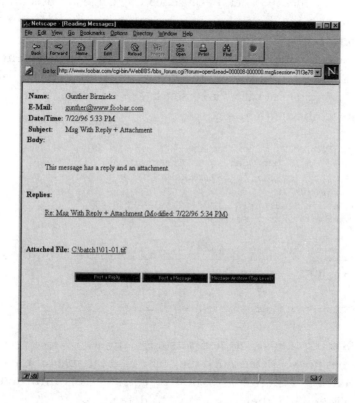

Figure 25.11 *WebBBS message with replies and an attachment.*

THE PRINTFORUMPAGE SUBROUTINE

The PrintForumPage subroutine displays the list of messages for the current forum in a hierarchical, threaded manner. There are no parameters to this routine other than the global form and setup variables that have been set previously. $x is set as a local variable and is used only to store temporary values.

```
sub PrintForumPage
{
    local($x);
```

The first step in displaying the messages is to read all the message files in the **$forum_dir** directory. The grep command is used to make sure that only files that end in **.msg** are listed. In addition, the sort command is used to sort the files in order. Because leading zeros are used to pad the six-digit message numbers, the messages are naturally sorted in ascending nu0meric order. The highest message number ($high_number) is set to the sequence number (the first six digits) of the last element of the @files array. $low_number is set to the first six digits of the first element of the @files array. These values are used later to determine how the messages relate to one another.

```
opendir(FORUMDIR, "$forum_dir") ||
 &CgiDie("Could Not Open Forum Directory\n");
@files = sort(grep(/.*msg$/,readdir(FORUMDIR)));
closedir(FORUMDIR);
$high_number = substr($files[@files - 1],0,6);
$low_number = substr($files[0],0,6);
```

PruneOldMessages is called to delete old messages based on the parameters set in the BBS setup file.

```
&PruneOldMessages($forum_dir, *files);
```

If the BBS setup file has defined $display_only_new_message as on and if the script has not yet determined the $last_read variable for the user, the GetUserLastRead function is called to retrieve this information. If $last_read is nothing, then it is set to 0 by default.

```
if ($display_only_new_messages eq "on"
 && $last_read eq ""
 && $use_last_read eq "on") {
 $last_read =
     &GetUserLastRead($forum_dir,
                  $username, $session,
                  $high_number);
}
```

```
$last_read = 0 if ($last_read eq "");
```

The `PruneFileList` function is called to take the files in `@files` and delete all the messages that do not satisfy the filtering criteria that the user has set up previously.

```
&PruneFileList(*files, $last_read, $first_date,
               $last_date, $first_days_old,
               $last_days_old, $keywords,
               $exact_match, $forum_dir);
```

Now the heart of this subroutine processes the messages into HTML hypertext links along with brief descriptions and titles. Initially, `$message_html` and the `@threads` array are cleared.

```
$message_html = "";
@threads = ();
```

The `MakeThreadList` routine is called once for each thread in the `@files` message list. Each time `MakeThreadList` is called, all the message numbers that correspond to a message thread are deleted from the `@files` array and are moved into the `@threads` array in a way that is structured to make the threads easy to print as a hierarchical tree. By "tree," we mean that original posts are at the top level, replies to posts are at the second level, replies to replies are at the third level, and so on.

```
while (@files > 0)
    {
    push(@threads,&MakeThreadList(*files));
    }
```

After the list of threaded messages has been processed, the HTML must be generated. `$ul_count` is initialized to zero and is used to keep track of how deep the HTML indentations have gone. `$prev_level` is set to −1 initially and is used to determine which level of the thread we are currently on. Whenever we go up a level, a `<UL>` tag is printed for indenting, and whenever we go back down a level, the `</UL>` closure tag is printed to reverse the indentation.

```
$ul_count = 0;
$prev_level = -1;
```

The `foreach` loop goes through each of the messages stored in the `@threads` array.

```
foreach $x (@threads) {
```

The current level of the thread, the message filename, and the date of the newest message in the thread are `split` into the `$level`, `$messagefile`, and `$thread_date` variables.

```
($level,$messagefile, $thread_date) =
    split(/\|/,$x);
```

If `$level` is greater than the previous level and if `$level` is greater than `$display_thread_depth`, then `$level` is set back to `$prev_level`. This is because you set `$display_thread_depth` in the BBS setup file to indicate the deepest level of indentation you want the messages to be listed in. By setting the level to what it was previously whenever it goes beyond the `$display_thread_depth`, the script avoids indenting any further.

```
if ($level > $prev_level &&
  $level > $display_thread_depth) {
  $level = $prev_level;
}
```

If `$level` is greater than `$prev_level`, the `$ul_count` is incremented and an indentation tag (`<UL>`) is added to `$message_html`. If `$level` is less than `$prev_level`, then `$ul_count` is decremented and a `</UL>` closure tag is generated for every level of difference. Although messages tend to increase in level gradually, messages may decrease in level abruptly if the next message after a deeply nested thread is actually an original post and is not replying to anything previously posted.

```
if ($level > $prev_level) {
  $ul_count++;
  $message_html .= "<UL>\n";
```

```
  } elsif ($level < $prev_level) {
   for (1 .. ($prev_level - $level)) {
       $ul_count—;
       $message_html .= "</UL>\n";
     }
 }
```

If $level is simply equal to the previous level, then a line break HTML code
(<BR>) is generated. If $use_list_element is on, a list button is generated
using the HTML <LI> tag. $use_list_element is defined in the BBS setup
file.

```
if ($level == $prev_level) {
 if ($use_list_element ne "on"
     || $level == 1) {
     $message_html .= "<br>";
 }
 $message_html .= "\n";
}
if ($level > 1 && $use_list_element eq "on") {
 $message_html .= "<LI>";
}
```

The header of the post is read using GetMessageHeader.

```
($poster_firstname, $poster_lastname, $poster_email,
 $post_date, $post_subject, $post_options) =
    &GetMessageHeader("$forum_dir/$messagefile");
```

The form variables that need to passed using hypertext links to the BBS
script are generated using ReadMessageFields.

```
$message_url = &ReadMessageFields;
```

For each message, $message_html has a hypertext link generated that con-
tains a call to **bbs_forum.cgi**. The parameters are set so that the particular message number is displayed if the user clicks the resulting hyperlink.

```
$message_html .=
  qq!<A HREF="$bbs_script?forum=$forum!;
$message_html .=
```

```
     qq!&read=$messagefile&$message_url">\n!;
$message_html .=
  " $post_subject ($post_date)";
```

Here is an example of a generated hyperlink from the previous code:

```
<A HREF="bbs_forum.cgi?forum=open&read=000001-000000.msg">
```

If we are at the top level of a thread and the date of the message is different from the date of the newest message in the thread ($thread_date), then an additional note lets the user know the most recent date that the thread was modified.

```
if ($level == 1 && $thread_date ne $post_date)
{
    $message_html .=
      " (Thread Modified:$thread_date)";
}
```

Then the end of the HTML hypertext reference is generated.

```
$message_html .= "</A>";
```

Before the script loops back to the next element of the @threads array, $prev_level is set to the current $level value.

```
    $prev_level = $level;
} # End of foreach thread
```

If all the messages have been processed and not enough </UL> tags have been generated, the rest are added to the $message_html variable.

```
$message_html .= "\n";
for (1..$ul_count) {
    $message_html .= "</UL>\n";
}
```

Finally, the script calls the **bbs_html_forum.pl** library to print the full HTML form listing all the messages in the forum. Figure 25.1 shows an example of the output from **bbs_html_forum.pl**.

```
require "bbs_html_forum.pl";

} # end of PrintForumPage
```

THE PRINTPOSTORREPLYPAGE SUBROUTINE

`PrintPostOrReplyPage` prints the HTML code for the screen where a user can enter a new message. It gets its information from global variables that have already been set on the basis of the incoming form variables and the BBS setup file.

The most important form variables that this subroutine looks at are `$reply_to_message`, `$email_reply`, and `$post_subject`. These variables are relevant only if the HTML form is printing a reply type of message input for the user. The `$reply_to_message` is the number of the message the user is replying to. This message number is needed in order to allow users to "quote" the previous message in their post. `$email_reply` is the E-mail address of the user who posted the message in case he or she has chosen to receive automatic E-mail replies. `$post_subject` is the previous post subject so that "RE:" can be appended to it as the new default subject in the case of a reply. An example of a "reply" HTML page is shown in Figure 25.12.

```
sub PrintPostOrReplyPage
{
```

Several variables are defined as local to the subroutine and will be used at various points. `$options` is used to figure out whether the message being replied to has an E-mail option embedded in the header. `$reply_to_message`, `$email_reply`, and `$post_subject` were discussed in the previous paragraph. `$title` and `$header` are used as variables containing HTML code for the title and header of the HTML form.

```
    local($options, $post_subject);
    local($reply_to_message, $email_reply);
    local($title, $header);
    local($email_tag, $reply_to_email);
    $reply_to_message = "";
    $email_reply = "";
    $title = "Post A Message";
    $header = "Posting Message To $forum_name";
```

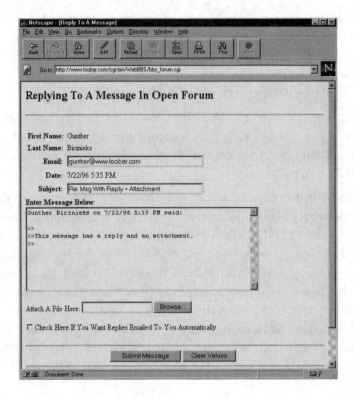

Figure 25.12 *Example of a reply screen.*

If the operation being performed by the user is a reply to a previously posted message, then the following code sets up the HTML posting form with the previous message's information.

```
if ($reply_op ne "")
{
```

$reply_to_message and $email_reply are initialized with their values from the form. In addition, the $title and $header of the HTML form are reassigned so that the user will be told that this is a reply rather than an original post HTML form.

```
$reply_to_message = $in{"reply_to_message"};
$email_reply = $in{"email_reply"};
```

```
$title = "Reply To A Message";
$header =
 "Replying To A Message In $forum_name";
```

Initially, $post\_message$ is cleared. Then the file for the message being replied to is opened and read to memory. The various fields—such as first name, last name, date and time of the post, and options—are read to variables that will be used later to generate the header of a quoted message.

```
$post_message = "";
open (REPLYFILE,
    "$forum_dir/$reply_to_message") ||
    &CgiDie("Could not open reply message");
chop($post_first_name = <REPLYFILE>);
chop($post_last_name = <REPLYFILE>);
<REPLYFILE>;
chop($post_date = <REPLYFILE>);
<REPLYFILE>;
chop($options = <REPLYFILE>);
if ($options =~ /^options:/) {
 $options = substr($options,8);
 ($email_tag,$reply_to_email) =
     split(/:/,$options);
}
```

The body of the message is read to the $post\_message$ variable.

```
while (<REPLYFILE>) {
 $post_message .= $_;
}
```

When the message is read, the beginning of the $post\_message$ buffer (^) is preceded with two greater-than symbols (>>). In addition, each newline or carriage return combination in the $post\_message$ buffer has the double greater-than symbols (>>) added to it. This is done so that the quoted text appears different from the user's own comments by default. The convention of preceding reply lines with ">>" is an Internet custom followed by many programs.

```
$post_message =~ s/^/>>/g;
$post_message =~ s/\r/\r>>/g;
$post_message =~ s/\n/\n>>/g;
```

In addition, the poster's information is added to the beginning of the $post_message variable as a header giving credit to the original author of the quoted post by default.

```
$post_message =
 "$post_first_name $post_last_name" .
    " on $post_date said:\n\n"
    . $post_message;
close (REPLYFILE);
```

$post_subject is read from the form variable, and "Re: " (short for "regarding") is added to the beginning of it if the subject does not already begin with this prefix.

```
$post_subject = $in{"post_subject"};
$post_subject = "Re: $post_subject"
 if !($post_subject =~ /^Re:/i);
}
```

$post_date_time is set equal to a formatted date and time generated by the GetDateAndTime subroutine.

```
$post_date_time = &GetDateAndTime;
```

The <INPUT> fields are generated based on the user information that was given previously.

```
$post_first_name_field = qq!<INPUT TYPE=text
 NAME=form_firstname VALUE="$firstname"
 SIZE=40 MAXLENGTH=50>!;
$post_last_name_field = qq!<INPUT TYPE=text
 NAME=form_lastname VALUE="$lastname"
    SIZE=40 MAXLENGTH=50>!;
$post_email_field = qq!<INPUT TYPE=text
 NAME=form_email VALUE="$email"
    SIZE=40 MAXLENGTH=50>!;
```

In the BBS setup file, you can define certain header fields to be forced values. If the values are forced, then instead of giving the user an <INPUT TYPE=TEXT> field, an <INPUT TYPE=HIDDEN> field is generated and the user sees only a display of header information and cannot change it. This is done for $force_first_name, $force_last_name, and $force_email. This feature works only if authentication is turned on in the BBS setup file in addition to these forced variables.

```
if ($force_first_name eq "on"
 && $firstname ne "") {
$post_first_name_field =
qq!<INPUT TYPE=hidden
NAME=form_firstname VALUE="$firstname">!;
$post_first_name_field .= "$firstname";
}


if ($force_last_name eq "on"
 && $lastname ne "") {
$post_last_name_field =
qq!<INPUT TYPE=hidden
NAME=form_lastname VALUE="$lastname">!;
$post_last_name_field .= "$lastname";
}

if ($force_email eq "on"
 && $email ne "") {
$post_email_field =
    qq!<INPUT TYPE=hidden
NAME=form_email VALUE="$email">!;
$post_email_field .= "$email";
}
```

If the $allow_reply_email variable is set to on in the BBS setup file, $post_want_email contains HTML code for a check box in which users can choose to have replies E-mailed to them.

```
$post_want_email = "";
if ($allow_reply_email eq "on") {
$post_want_email =
    "<BR><INPUT TYPE=CHECKBOX" .
    " NAME=post_want_email>" .
      "Check Here If You Want Replies " .
    "Emailed To You Automatically<BR>";
}
```

If $allow_user_attachments is set to on in the BBS setup file, $post_attachment contains HTML code for the file upload input box.

```
    $post_attachment = "";
    if ($allow_user_attachments eq "on") {
     $post_attachment =
        "<P>Attach A File Here:
<INPUT TYPE=FILE NAME=post_attachment><BR>";
    }
```

Finally, **bbs_html_create_message.pl** is loaded to print the HTML for the Create Message screen.

```
    require "bbs_html_create_message.pl";
```

```
} # End of PostOrReplyPage
```

THE CREATEPOSTING SUBROUTINE

The CreatePosting subroutine takes the information that a user has entered on a Post Message HTML form and posts it as a message file in the forum directory. After the message is posted, this function calls the subroutine that prints the message list. The form variables form_firstname, form_lastname, form_email, form_subject, form_message, reply_to_message, reply_to_email, and post_want_email make up the contents of the post information that is written to the message file.

```
sub CreatePosting
{
```

$create_error is declared as local. If there is any problem in posting the message to a file, $create_error will contain a positive numeric value. This triggers an error message that is sent to the routine that prints the forum's message list so that the user is notified of the problem.

```
    local ($create_error);
```

All the form variables related to the header of the message are read to variables.

```
    $form_firstname = $in{"form_firstname"};
    $form_lastname = $in{"form_lastname"};
```

```
$form_email = $in{"form_email"};
$form_subject = $in{"form_subject"};
```

Then newlines are stripped out as a precaution against multiline values. The header values should consist only of single lines.

```
$form_firstname =~ s/\n//g;
$form_lastname =~ s/\n//g;
$form_email =~ s/\n//g;
$form_subject =~ s/\n//g;
```

$form_message is set to the body of the message that was posted.

```
$form_message = $in{"form_message"};
```

$reply_to_message is the message number that is being replied to if the user is posting a reply. The message reply number is needed because when a message filename is generated, the second six-digit number is the message number that is being replied to. If the message number is less than 1, the message to reply to is set to six zeros, indicating that the message is not a reply to anything.

```
$reply_to_message = $in{"reply_to_message"};
if ($reply_to_message < 1)
{
    $reply_to_message = "000000";
} else {
    $reply_to_message =
     substr($reply_to_message,0,6);
}
```

$reply_to_email is the E-mail address of the person who posted the message that is being replied to if the message being created is a reply rather than an original post. $post_date_time is set to the current date and time returned by the GetDateAndTime function.

```
$reply_to_email = $in{"reply_to_email"};
$post_date_time = &GetDateAndTime;
```

$form_options consists of the options that the user has chosen for the post that is being created. The only option currently implemented is the automatic E-mail replies option. If $post_want_email is on or if $force_reply_email is set to on in the setup file, then the user's E-mail address is added to the options tag to indicate that the user wants automatic E-mail replies.

```
$form_options = "";
$post_want_email = $in{"post_want_email"};
if ($post_want_email eq "on"
 || $force_reply_email eq "on") {
 $form_options = "email:$form_email";
 }
```

$create_error is initialized to zero. This indicates that no error has occurred yet.

```
$create_error = 0;
```

If any of the required fields has not been entered by the user, $create_error is set to 1 and $create_msg_error is filled with the appropriate error message. The required fields are determined in **bbs.setup** by the $require_subject, $require_first_name, $require_last_name, and $require_email variables.

```
if ($require_subject eq "on" &&
    $form_subject eq "") {
    $create_error = 1;
    $create_msg_error .=
      "You Did Not Enter A Subject.</H2>";
}
if ($require_first_name eq "on" &&
    $form_firstname eq "") {
    $create_error = 1;
    $create_msg_error .=
      "You Did Not Enter Your First Name.</H2>";
}
if ($require_last_name eq "on" &&
    $form_lastname eq "") {
    $create_error = 1;
    $create_msg_error .=
      "You Did Not Enter Your Last Name.</H2>";
}
if ($require_email eq "on" &&
    $form_email eq "") {
    $create_error = 1;
    $create_msg_error .=
```

```
        "You Did Not Enter An Email Address.</H2>";
}
```

If $create_error is 1, then a header indicating an error posting to the BBS is appended to the beginning of $create_msg_error.

```
if ($create_error == 1) {
$create_msg_error = "<HR><H2>Error Posting To BBS. " .
  $create_msg_error;
}
```

If $create_error is not equal to 1, then the posting of the message can proceed.

```
if ($create_error != 1) {
```

$whole_msg is set equal to all the header fields plus the body of the message stored in $form_message.

```
        $whole_msg = "";
        $whole_msg .= "$form_firstname\n";
        $whole_msg .= "$form_lastname\n";
        $whole_msg .= "$form_email\n";
        $whole_msg .= "$post_date_time\n";
        $whole_msg .= "$form_subject\n";
        $whole_msg .= "options:$form_options\n";
        $whole_msg .= "$form_message\n";
```

The message files in the forum directories are read to the @files array. As before, the grep command is used to retrieve only the filenames corresponding to messages, and the sort command makes sure that the @files array is in numerically ascending order.

```
opendir(FORUMDIR, "$forum_dir") ||
    &CgiDie("Couldn't Open $forum_dir");
@files = sort(grep(/.*msg$/,readdir(FORUMDIR)));
closedir(FORUMDIR);
```

$high_number is set to the highest message number value in the @files array. Because the array is sorted, this is the last element of the array. @files minus 1 is the highest element number in the @files array, because arrays count from zero to the number of elements in the array minus 1. Once the high message number has been retrieved, the @files array is cleared. Then $high_number is incremented by 1. This determines the sequence number for the message filename that will be created later in the routine.

```
$high_number = substr($files[@files - 1],0,6);
@files = ();
$high_number++;
```

The $high_number is formatted to a length of six using the sprintf function (%6d). Then the leading spaces are converted to zeros using the tr function. If there is no $high_number (equal to 000000), then $high_number is set to "000001". Finally, the $message_name filename is generated by joining the high number and the $reply_to_message variable with a hyphen (-).

```
$high_number = sprintf("%6d",$high_number);
$high_number =~ tr/ /0/;
    $high_number = "000001"
      if ($high_number eq "000000");
$message_name = "$high_number-$reply_to_message";
```

The file is created with an **.msg** extension. $whole_msg is written to the file, and then it is closed.

```
open(WRITEMSG, ">$forum_dir/$message_name.msg") ||
    &CgiDie("Couldn't open $message_name.msg");
print WRITEMSG $whole_msg;
close (WRITEMSG);
```

$post_attachment is set equal to the post_attachment form variable that contains the name randomly assigned by **cgi-lib.pl** to the file that was uploaded. $post_attachment_filename is set to the value that **cgi-lib.pl** retrieved from the Web browser as the real filename of the uploaded file. The real filenames are stored by **cgi-lib.pl** in the %incfn associated array apart from the %in associative array for normal form variables. This is explained in more detail in Chapter 5.

```
$post_attachment = $in{"post_attachment"};
$post_attachment_filename =
    $incfn{"post_attachment"};
```

Any hexadecimal values in the filename are parsed into characters using a regular expression. Basically, the regular expression filters on any two-digit hexadecimal digits (A-Fa-f0-9). The result of the filter is placed inside the $1 variable by Perl, and the pack command is used to convert the two-digit number to an ASCII character.

```
$post_attachment_filename =~
    s/%([A-Fa-f0-9]{2})/pack("c",hex($1))/ge;
```

If a $post_attachment_filename exists, the uploaded file is renamed to a filename that represents the message that it belongs to except that it has a **.bin** extension instead of an **.msg** extension. The **.bin** extension is used because, by default, most Web browsers are configured to download **.bin** files—and not to display their contents—when they are selected by a hypertext link.

```
if ($post_attachment_filename ne "") {
 rename($post_attachment,
        "$attach_dir/$forum-$message_name.bin");
```

A descriptive message file with an **.attach** extension is created to keep track of the filename of the originally uploaded file and the new file-name assigned to it by the BBS.

```
open(WRITEATTACH,
        ">$forum_dir/$message_name.attach") ||
          &CgiDie("Could Not Open Attachment\n");
print WRITEATTACH
     "$forum-$message_name.bin" .
     "|$post_attachment_filename\n";
close(WRITEATTACH);
```

If there is no postattachment filename, the attachment is removed.

```
} else {
 unlink("$post_attachment");
}
```

If the message being posted is a reply to a previous message and if an automatic reply must be generated in E-mail, then **mail-lib.pl** is loaded to send the mail. The reply subject is set to a description telling the user that a post was made on the BBS, and the body of the message is sent as part of the body of the E-mail.

```
$reply_to_email = $in{"reply_to_email"};
    if ($reply_to_email ne "" &&
    $send_reply_email eq "on") {
    require "$lib/mail-lib.pl";
    $reply_subject =
        "Reply to your $forum_name message.";
    &send_mail($from_email, $reply_to_email,
            $reply_subject,
            "The Message:\n\n" . $form_message);
    } # End of reply_to_email
} # end of if $create_error == 1
```

Finally, the message list of the forum is displayed using the PrintForumPage function.

```
&PrintForumPage;
} # End of CreatePosting
```

THE PRUNEFILELIST SUBROUTINE

PruneFileList takes the message filenames in a forum directory as an array and removes any files that do not match certain user-defined criteria. The variables related to these criteria are $last_read, $first_date, $last_date, $first_days_old, $last_days_old, $keywords, and $exact_match. These variables correspond to the equivalent form variables that are used to filter the message list in the **bbs_entrance.cgi** script. These variables were discussed previously in the "Installation and Usage" and "Design Discussion" sections. $forum_dir is also passed to the routine so that the script knows which directory to search for files.

```
sub PruneFileList
{
    local(*files, $last_read, $first_date, $last_date,
        $first_days_old, $last_days_old, $keywords,
        $exact_match, $forum_dir) = @_;
```

$x, $filename, $month, $day, $year, $comp_date, and $file_date, which will be used in the filtering process later, are declared local.

```
local($x, $filename);
local($month, $day, $year, $comp_date);
local($file_date);
```

If a keyword search is being performed, the keywords are split into separate words into an array called @keyword_list. The regular expression \s matches on whitespace characters that might separate the keywords in the $keywords variable.

```
@keyword_list = split(/\s+/,$keywords);
```

Each file in the @files message filename is processed using the for loop. There are four different reasons that a filename would be removed from the list of messages displayed to the user: the user has already read the message, the age of the message does not fit the specified range of days, the date on which the message was posted does not fit the specified range of dates, and the message does not contain the specified keywords. If the message does not satisfy all the requirements, it is removed from the @files array and is not displayed to the user.

```
for ($x = @files; $x > 0; $x-)
{
```

In case 1, the message was already read. If the $last_read message number variable is greater than zero, if the current message number is less than $last_read, and if $display_only_new_messages has been set to on in the BBS setup file, then the filename is removed from the list of messages to display.

```
if ($last_read > 0
        && substr($files[$x-1],0,6) <= $last_read
        && $display_only_new_messages eq "on")
    {
    &RemoveElement(*files,$x-1);
    next;
    }
```

Remember that arrays start counting at zero. Thus, the elements of the @files array are referenced by $x minus 1, because $x counts from 1 to the number of elements in the array.

NOTE

In case 2, the message does not fit the days-old age range. Before we process the age of the messages, the full path and filename are placed in the $filename variable. We do this so that the BBS script can check the age of the post by looking at the individual message file.

```
$filename = "$forum_dir/$files[$x - 1]";
```

If the age of the filename (determined with the -M operator) is greater than $first_days_old, the filename is removed from the list of messages to display.

```
if (($first_days_old ne "")
 && ((-M $filename) > $first_days_old)) {
 &RemoveElement(*files,$x-1);
 next;
 }
```

Although -M technically checks the modification date of the file, for the purpose of the bbs_forum.cgi script, the value returned by -M effectively represents the age of the file.

N O T E

If the age of the filename (-M) is less than $last_days_old, the filename is removed from the list of messages to display.

```
if (($last_days_old ne "")
 && ((-M $filename) < $last_days_old)) {
 &RemoveElement(*files, $x-1);
 next;
 }
```

In case 3, the message does not fit the date range. To compare the dates of the files, the script rearranges the date range to make it more conducive to comparison. Normally, dates are stored in an MM/DD/YY format. However, it is impossible to compare such a date numerically with another date to see which one is greater. Instead, the dates are rearranged into a number in which the year is the first part, the month is the second part, and the day is last: a YYMMDD format. These newly formatted dates can be compared using normal numerical comparison methods.

Let's look at some example dates: 12/01/95, 01/01/96, and 11/15/96. If the slashes were removed, these dates would form the following numbers: 120195, 010196, and 111596. Although 01/01/96 is a greater date than 12/01/95, the number 120195 is greater than 010196. Thus, doing a numerical comparison does not work when the dates are formatted conventionally.

Reformatting these dates into a YYMMDD format makes them into 951201, 960101, and 961115. Clearly, a numerical comparison now yields the correct answer when the dates are compared. For example, 960101 is greater than 951201, which yields the correct answer that 01/01/96 is a greater date than 12/01/95. The BBS script converts dates to the YYMMDD numerical format for this reason. The following pieces of code perform this conversion.

```
if ($first_date ne ""
   || $last_date ne "") {
```

$month, $day, and $year are split from the date in $first_date.

```
($month, $day, $year) =
    split(/\//, $first_date);
```

If $month and $day are not two digits long, they are padded with a leading zero.

```
$month = "0" . $month
    if (length($month) < 2);
$day = "0" . $day
    if (length($day) < 2);
```

If the $year is a two-digit one, it is converted to a four-digit number so that when we reach the year 2000, 00 will not seem smaller than 99 after they are converted to 2000 and 1999, respectively. If a year is less than 95, it is basically converted to a 21st-century year (20xx) by adding 2000 to it. Otherwise, the year is considered a 20th-century year (19xx).

```
if ($year > 95 && $year < 1900) {
    $year += 1900;
```

```
    }
    if ($year < 1900) {
        $year += 2000;
    }
```

Finally, the date is rearranged into the YYMMDD format and is assigned to $comp_first_date.

```
    $comp_first_date = $year . $month . $day;
```

The same process is applied to $last_date. The YYMMDD format is placed in the $comp_last_date variable.

```
    ($month, $day, $year) =
        split(/\//, $last_date);
    $month = "0" . $month
        if (length($month) < 2);
    $day = "0" . $day if (length($day) < 2);
    if ($year > 50 && $year < 1900) {
        $year += 1900;
    }
    if ($year < 1900) {
        $year += 2000;
    }
    $comp_last_date = $year . $month . $day;
```

The actual date of the file is retrieved by using Perl's stat command, which returns an array of elements corresponding to different pieces of information about the file. The 10th piece of information is the modification date and time of the file. This means that the script references element number 9, because arrays start counting from zero.

```
    $file_date = (stat($filename))[9];
```

The localtime function is used to pull out the day, month, and year for the $file_date. Then the same process is applied to this date that was performed on $first_date and $last_date. $file_date ends up in the YYMMDD format of $comp_first_date and $comp_last_date.

```
    ($day, $month, $year) =
        (localtime($file_date))[3,4,5];
```

```
$month++;
$month = "0" . $month
    if (length($month) < 2);
$day = "0" . $day if (length($day) < 2);
if ($year > 50 && $year < 1900) {
    $year += 1900;
}
if ($year < 1900) {
    $year += 2000;
}
$file_date = $year . $month . $day;
```

The next two pieces of code compare $file_date against $comp_first_date and $comp_last_date. If $file_date is not in this range of dates, the filename is removed from the @files array.

```
if ($first_date ne "") {
    if ($file_date < $comp_first_date) {
        &RemoveElement(*files, $x-1);
        next;
    }
} # End of first date

if ($last_date ne "") {
    if ($file_date > $comp_last_date) {
        &RemoveElement(*files, $x-1);
        next;
    }
} # End of last date

} # End of First or Last Date
```

In case 4, the message does not contain the keywords. If $keywords exist, the message file is opened and searched for keywords. @not_found_words is initialized to the list of keywords. For each line of the file, @not_found_words is checked to see whether any of the words exist on the line using the FindKeywords function. If a keyword is found, it is removed from the @not_found_words array.

```
    if ($keywords ne "") {
@not_found_words = @keyword_list;
open(SEARCHFILE, $filename);
while(<SEARCHFILE>) {
```

```
        $line = $_;
        &FindKeywords($exact_match, $line,
                *not_found_words);
    } # End of SEARCHFILE
    close (SEARCHFILE);
```

This keyword searching algorithm is basically the same one used in Chapter 16 about the keyword search engine.

N O T E

If any words are still in the @not_found_words array, the file failed the keyword search and is removed from the @files array.

```
    if (@not_found_words > 0) {
        &RemoveElement(*files, $x - 1);
        next;
    }
      } # End of keywords
    } # End of for loop

} # End of PruneFileList
```

THE FINDKEYWORDS SUBROUTINE

The FindKeywords subroutine is the search routine that is called by the PruneFileList function. It accepts a line of a message file and the keywords to search for in that line. If a keyword is found, the routine removes it from the keyword array (@not_found_words). Thus, when the @not_found_words array no longer contains any elements, the script knows that all the keywords have been found in the message file.

```
sub FindKeywords
{
```

There are three parameters. The first, $exact_match, is equal to on if the type of pattern match we are doing is based on an exact one-to-one match of each letter in the keyword to each letter in a word contained in

650

the message. The second parameter, $line, is the line in the message that is currently being searched. The third parameter, *not_found_words, is a reference to the array @not_found_words, which contains a list of all the keywords not found so far. As keywords are found in the searched file, this array has its words removed. Thus, when the array is empty, we know that the message file contained all the keywords. In other words, there are no "not found words" if the search is successful.

```
local($exact_match, $line, *not_found_words) = @_;
local($x, $match_word);
```

If the exact match is on, the program matches all the words in the array by surrounding the keywords with \b. This means that the keyword must be surrounded by word boundaries to be a valid match. Thus, the keyword "the" would not match a word such as "there," because it is only part of a larger word.

```
if ($exact_match eq "on") {
  for ($x = @not_found_words; $x > 0; $x—) {
     $match_word = $not_found_words[$x - 1];
     if ($line =~ /\b$match_word\b/i) {
```

The splice routine cuts out the words if they are found in the search. The splice command is a Perl routine that accepts the original array, the element in the array to splice, the number of elements to splice, and a list or array to splice into the original array. Because we are leaving off the fourth parameter of the splice, the routine by default splices "nothing" into the array at the element number. This action deletes the element in one convenient little routine.

```
     splice(@not_found_words,$x - 1, 1);
   } # End of If
} # End of For Loop
```

If the exact match is not on, the program finds a match if the letters in the keyword exist anywhere on the line, whether or not the keyword is part of a larger word. All the searches are case-insensitive, as indicated by the i after the slashes defining the search term.

```
    } else {
    for ($x = @not_found_words; $x > 0; $x—) {
        $match_word = $not_found_words[$x - 1];
        if ($line =~ /$match_word/i) {
         splice(@not_found_words,$x - 1, 1);
         } # End of If
    } # End of For Loop
    } # End of ELSE

} # End of FindKeywords
```

THE GETUSERLASTREAD SUBROUTINE

The GetUserLastRead subroutine gets the user's last read message number. In addition, if this is the first time the session has been created, the user's last read message number is updated with the current high message number.

```
sub GetUserLastRead
{
```

$forum_dir (forum directory), $username (username of the user), $session (session ID), and $high_number (highest message number) are passed as local parameters to the routine. The $last_read and $old_session variables are declared local to GetUserLastRead.

```
    local($forum_dir, $username,
        $session, $high_number) = @_;
    local($last_read, $old_session);
```

[username].dat is used in each forum directory to keep track of the last read message of a user between sessions. If the user logs on to the BBS and if the BBS has been configured to allow users to read only new messages, the user's name, followed by a **.dat** extension, is created in each forum he or she reads. If the **[username].dat** file does not exist in the forum directory, then the last read message number is set to zero.

```
unless (-e "$forum_dir/$username.dat")
    {
    $last_read = 0;
    }
```

Otherwise, **[username].dat** is opened and the **$last_read** variable is read. In addition, the last session that was active when the file was created is read to the $old_session variable.

```
else
{
open (USERFILE, "$forum_dir/$username.dat") ||
    &CgiDie("Error Opening Userfile $username\n");
$last_read = <USERFILE>;
$old_session = <USERFILE>;
chop ($last_read);
chop($old_session);
close (USERFILE);
}
```

If the current session ($session) is not equal to the session ID that was used when **[username].dat** was created, the script knows that this is a new session; the file is rewritten with the new high message number and the current session ID. The current high message number then becomes the new last read message number the next time the user goes into the BBS script with a new session.

In other words, the first time a user logs in to a BBS discussion forum, the current last read message is retrieved from the user file and then the user file is updated with the highest message number. All subsequent accesses to the script within the same session will simply retrieve the last read message number from a form variable instead of accessing this file. Then, when the user logs in to the BBS again with a new session, the last read message is read again from the user file.

The reason the user file is updated immediately with the highest message number is that there is no guarantee that the user will return to the discussion forum after reading a message. Because the Web is connectionless, there is nothing to stop the user from going to another site on the Web. Thus, the user file is updated immediately with the high message number after the last read message number is read.

```
if ($session ne $old_session) {
 open (USERFILE, ">$forum_dir/$username.dat") ||
    &CgiDie("Error Opening Userfile $username\n");
 print USERFILE "$high_number\n";
```

```
    print USERFILE "$session\n";
    close (USERFILE);
  }
```

Finally, the `$last_read` message number is returned to the calling procedure.

```
$last_read;
```

```
} #End of GetUserLastRead
```

THE GETDATEANDTIME SUBROUTINE

`GetDateAndTime` returns a formatted string with the current date and time. The parts of the date and time returned from the `localtime` function are declared as local to the subroutine.

```
sub GetDateAndTime
{
    local ($sec, $min, $hour, $mday, $mon);
    local($year, $wday, $yday, $isdst);
    local ($ampm);
```

The `localtime(time)` function is called in Perl to get the current date and time values.

```
($sec, $min, $hour, $mday, $mon,
 $year, $wday, $yday, $isdst) =
    localtime(time);
```

Because months in the `localtime` function are numbered from zero to 11, we increment it by 1.

```
$mon++;
```

Next, the script determines whether we are in "AM" or "PM."

```
$ampm = "AM";
$ampm = "PM" if ($hour > 11);
$hour = $hour - 12 if ($hour > 12);
```

If the $min variable is only one digit, the script pads it with a leading zero.

```
if (length($min) == 1)
{
    $min = "0" . $min;
}
```

Finally, the formatted date is returned by the subroutine.

```
"$mon/$mday/$year $hour:$min $ampm";


} # End of GetDateAndTime
```

THE GETMESSAGEHEADER SUBROUTINE

GetMessageHeader takes a filename as a parameter and returns an array containing the values for all the header fields in the message file.

```
sub GetMessageHeader
{
    local($filename) = @_;
```

$poster_firstname, $poster_lastname, $poster_email, $post_date, $post_subject, and $post_options are declared local. Each variable corresponds to a field in the message header.

```
    local($poster_firstname, $poster_lastname,
        $poster_email, $post_date,
        $post_subject, $post_options);
```

The file is opened. If the open file routine is unsuccessful, CgiDie is called to output an error message to the user's Web browser and then exit.

```
    open (MESSAGEFILE, "$filename") ||
        &CgiDie("Could Not Open $filename hdr\n");
```

Each variable is read from the message file using the <MESSAGEFILE> command. By surrounding the file handle with brackets, Perl returns the next line of the file. In addition, the resulting variables are chopped to get rid of the superfluous newline character that is read with every line in the message header.

```
chop($poster_firstname = <MESSAGEFILE>);
chop($poster_lastname = <MESSAGEFILE>);
chop($poster_email = <MESSAGEFILE>);
chop($post_date = <MESSAGEFILE>);
chop($post_subject = <MESSAGEFILE>);
chop($post_options = <MESSAGEFILE>);
```

The options: portion of the post options line in the header is stripped off using the following code. This is because the word "options" is superfluous. If there is an E-mail option, it will be evident from the rest of the options line. substr($post_options, 8 returns everything except the first eight characters of $post_options. The message file is closed when all the header fields are read.

```
if ($post_options =~ /^options:/) {
 $post_options = substr($post_options,8);
}
close(MESSAGEFILE);
```

Finally, each of the header fields is returned as a separate element in an array.

```
($poster_firstname, $poster_lastname, $poster_email,
 $post_date, $post_subject, $post_options);
    } # End of GetMessageHeader
```

THE MAKETHREADLIST SUBROUTINE

The MakeThreadList subroutine takes the sorted list of messages stored in @file_list and returns an entire thread of messages that has been pulled out of the @file_list.

Why? Because @file_list merely stores messages in the order that they were posted. It does not show the relationship of the replies. It does not show that message number 3 may have been a reply to message number 1 and that message number 2 may be a post all by itself and not a reply to any other post.

Lets look at a simple example. A *thread* is a list of messages that are related by replies and have one post as the starting point. Let's start by taking a look at 10 sample message filenames (without the **.msg** extension). Remember, the fact that a message is a reply is shown in the second six-digit number.

```
000001-000000 (Message 1 Is An Original Message)
000002-000001 (Message 2 Replies To Message 1)
000003-000000 (Message 3 Is An Original Message)
000004-000002 (Message 4 Replies To Message 2)
000005-000001 (Message 5 Replies To Message 1)
000006-000000 (Message 6 Is An Original Message)
000007-000003 (Message 7 Replies To Message 3)
000008-000005 (Message 8 Replies To Message 5)
000009-000008 (Message 9 Replies To Message 8)
000010-000007 (Message 10 Replies To Message 7)
```

In this example, the messages appear in the order in which they were posted, but figuring out which messages are related to each other in separate groupings is difficult. MakeThreadList takes care of this task.

The best way to describe how MakeThreadList works is to discuss the basic algorithm. Imagine that MakeThreadList is given an array of the 10 filenames we were shown previously. The routine starts by looking at the highest message number (000010-000007). If it is a reply to a previous message, that message is examined (000007-000003); basically, any time a message has a reply, the routine goes to the replied message. In this case, message 3 is examined (000003-000000). Because the reply to message number 7 is all zeros, we know that message 3 is a top-level post. The routine stops going backward through the message list.

A neat side effect of the script starting to look for threads at the highest message number is that when the threads are retrieved, the threads naturally sort themselves so that the thread with the newest message appears first in the list.

Then 3 three is removed from the array and is placed into a threads list with a level number of 1 indicating that it is a top-level post. At this point, the message list looks like this:

```
000001-000000
000002-000001
000004-000002
000005-000001
000006-000000
000007-000003
000008-000005
000009-000008
000010-000007
```

And thread list consists of the following:

```
000003-000000 At Level 1
```

Then the script looks at all the replies to message 3. When it searches the file list, it finds 000007-000003 and places that in the thread list with a level of 2 (because it is a reply to an original post). The message list now looks like the following:

```
000001-000000
000002-000001
000004-000002
000005-000001
000006-000000
000008-000005
000009-000008
000010-000007
```

The thread list looks like this:

```
000003-000000 At Level 1
000007-000003 At Level 2
```

Because message 7 has been pulled out, the script looks at the file list for replies to message 7. At this point, message 10 is a reply and so is added to the thread list at level 3 (it is a reply to a reply). The message list now looks like this:

```
000001-000000
000002-000001
```

```
000004-000002
000005-000001
000006-000000
000008-000005
000009-000008
```

The thread list looks like this:

```
000003-000000 At Level 1
000007-000003 At Level 2
000010-000007 At Level 3
```

Now the script looks at the file list for replies to message 10. There are none, so the script goes back up one level (back to level 2) and looks for more replies to message 7. There are none, so the script goes back up one level (to level 1) and looks for more replies to message 3. There are none, and there are also no higher levels, so the thread is complete. The MakeThreadList routine ends and returns a complete thread to the BBS. The final ordered thread list remains the same:

```
000003-000000 At Level 1
000007-000003 At Level 2
000010-000007 At Level 3
```

The first example was a relatively simple hierarchy with only one reply branch. This next example is more complex. When MakeThreadList is called a second time with the previous pared-down file list, the routine looks at the highest message number (message 9) and sees that it is a reply to another message (message 8). Message 8 is seen as a reply to message 5, and message 5 is a reply to message 1 which has no successor. At this point, the routine places message 1 in the thread list. The message list now looks like this:

```
000002-000001
000004-000002
000005-000001
000006-000000
000008-000005
000009-000008
```

The thread list that we are starting again has just one message at level 1.

```
000001-000000 At Level 1
```

The routine then looks at the next reply to message number 1. The first reply is message 2. It is pulled into the thread list and is placed at level 2 because it is a reply to the original post (message 1). The message list now looks like this:

```
000004-000002
000005-000001
000006-000000
000008-000005
000009-000008
```

The thread list looks like this:

```
000001-000000 At Level 1
000002-000001 At Level 2
```

The routine then looks for replies to message 2. Message 4 fits this criterion. Thus, message 4 is placed in the thread list at level 3 (a reply to a reply). The message list now looks like this:

```
000005-000001
000006-000000
000008-000005
000009-000008
```

The thread list looks like this:

```
000001-000000 At Level 1
000002-000001 At Level 2
000004-000002 At Level 3
```

There are no replies to message 4, so the routine goes back to level 2 and checks for more replies to message 2. There are no more replies to message 2, so the routine goes back to level 1 and checks for more replies to message 1. Message number 5 is a match and is pulled from the message list and placed in the thread list at level 2 (because it is a reply to the original post). The message list now looks like this:

```
000006-000000
000008-000005
000009-000008
```

The thread list looks like this:

```
000001-000000 At Level 1
000002-000001 At Level 2
000004-000002 At Level 3
000005-000001 At Level 2
```

Next, the BBS looks for replies to message 5. Message 8 qualifies, so it is placed in the thread list at level 3. Next, replies to message 8 are searched for, and message 9 yields a match. Thus, message 9 is placed on the thread list at level 4 (a reply to a reply to a reply... Whew!). The message list now looks like this:

```
000006-000000
```

The thread list looks like this:

```
000001-000000 At Level 1
000002-000001 At Level 2
000004-000002 At Level 3
000005-000001 At Level 2
000008-000005 At Level 3
000009-000008 At Level 4
```

The routine then goes back one level and looks for more replies to message 8. There are none, so the routine goes back yet another level and looks for replies to message 5. There are none. Again, the routine goes back and looks for replies to message 1. There are no more replies to message 1, and there are no more levels to travel back to, so the routine stops. The thread has been determined.

At this point, a subsequent call to MakeThreadList would yield another thread with message 6 all by itself at level 1. If we were to take the threads from all three of these MakeThreadList calls and make one big list of messages, this would be the result:

```
000003-000000 At Level 1 (First MakeThreadList)
000007-000003 At Level 2 (First MakeThreadList)
000010-000007 At Level 3 (First MakeThreadList)
000001-000000 At Level 1 (Second MakeThreadList)
000002-000001 At Level 2 (Second MakeThreadList)
000004-000002 At Level 3 (Second MakeThreadList)
000005-000001 At Level 2 (Second MakeThreadList)
000008-000005 At Level 3 (Second MakeThreadList)
000009-000008 At Level 4 (Second MakeThreadList)
000006-000000 At Level 1 (Third MakeThreadList)
```

Notice that the messages within a thread are naturally sorted with the oldest, original message at the top. However, at the top level of display, the threads with the newest posts (the highest message numbers) appear at the top of all threads. This arrangement is useful because users typically want to see the newest posts first in a list, but they also want to see the relationship of the post as it exists within a thread or topic. If this list were displayed on the BBS, the messages would be indented according to the level they occupy:

```
000003-000000 At Level 1
  000007-000003 At Level 2
    000010-000007 At Level 3
 000001-000000 At Level 1
   000002-000001 At Level 2
     000004-000002 At Level 3
 000005-000001 At Level 2
   000008-000005 At Level 3
     000009-000008 At Level 4
000006-000000 At Level 1
```

As explained previously, the MakeThreadList routine starts with an array of all the message filenames in a file list array passed by reference (@file_list).

```
sub MakeThreadList
{
local(*file_list) = @_;
```

@threads is used as an array to hold the thread that is currently being built. $seq_ptr is the number of the element in the file list array that is currently being looked at. In addition, $sequence and $previous are used for housekeeping during the processing of the message list.

```
local(@threads,$seq_ptr);
local($sequence,$previous);
```

Initially, the script looks at the highest message number in the file list. If the highest message number exists (the @file_list array has elements in it), the routine processes the thread.

```
$seq_ptr = @file_list - 1;
if ($seq_ptr > -1)
{
```

First, the header information from the highest message number filename is read to retrieve the date that the message was posted. When the thread is processed, the $post_date is used to display the date of the newest message along with the date of the original post.

```
($poster_firstname, $poster_lastname, $poster_email,
 $post_date, $post_subject, $post_options) =
  &GetMessageHeader("$forum_dir/@file_list[$seq_ptr]");
```

The while loop backtracks through all the replies until it reaches the original post in the thread we are examining. When the loop exits, $sequence is the message number of the original post and $seq_ptr points to the element in the @file_list array that corresponds to this message. GetPointer is used to constantly get the updated number of the element in the array that the script is pointing to.

```
while(1)
    {
        @file_list[$seq_ptr] .= "|$post_date";
        $sequence = @file_list[$seq_ptr];
        $previous = substr($sequence,7,6);
        $previous_pointer =
         &GetPointer(*file_list, $previous);
    if (($previous eq "000000") ||
        ($previous_pointer == -1))
        {
```

```
        last;
        }
    $seq_ptr = $previous_pointer;
    } #End of while loop
```

@seq_stack is set to the current sequence pointer so that the routine always knows where to begin searching for messages in the @file_list array. $cur_stack_size is set to 1, which corresponds to the level in the thread that we had discussed earlier. Next, the @threads array is initialized and the original message is set to level 1. The level and the message number ($sequence) are pipe-delimited inside the @threads array.

```
@seq_stack = ($seq_ptr);
$cur_stack_size = 1;
push(@threads, "$cur_stack_size|$sequence");
```

Now that the routine has found the original post of the latest thread in the @file_list, the routine goes through the entire @file_list array to determine the thread order.

```
while(@file_list > 0)
{
```

$next_seq is set to the current message number. This message number is used to find the reply to this message by calling the GetNextThread function. $next_ptr is equal to the number of the element in the @file_list array that corresponds to the first reply to the current message number.

```
$next_seq = substr($sequence,0,6);
$next_ptr =
    &GetNextThread(*file_list, $next_seq, $seq_ptr);
```

If there is a reply ($next_ptr > -1), then $cur_stack_size is incremented (the level is increased), and this message is placed in the @threads array as the next message in the thread.

```
if ($next_ptr > -1)
    {
    $cur_stack_size++;
```

664

```
push(@seq_stack, $next_ptr);
$sequence = $file_list[$next_ptr];
$seq_ptr = $next_ptr;
push(@threads, "$cur_stack_size|$sequence");
}
```

Otherwise, if there is no reply, the last message is removed from the @file_list array, and we start looking for replies one level back.

```
else
    {
    @file_list =
        &RemoveElement(*file_list, $seq_ptr);
    $cur_stack_size—;
    pop(@seq_stack);
```

@seq_stack is greater than zero if there are more levels of replies to examine.

```
    if (@seq_stack > 0)
        {
        $seq_ptr =
            $seq_stack[@seq_stack - 1];
        $sequence = $file_list[$seq_ptr];
        }
```

If there are no more levels (because we are back to finding more replies to the original post), the while loop exits with the last command and the thread is complete.

```
    else
        {
        last;
        }
    }
} # End of While Loop
```

Finally, when the @threads list is fully generated, it is returned to the procedure that called this function.

```
@threads;

} # End of if seq_ptr > 0
```

If there are no sequence numbers in the array, an empty list is returned for the thread.

```
else {
  ();
} # End of IF Seq_ptr > 0

} # end of MakeThreadList
```

THE GETPOINTER SUBROUTINE

`GetPointer` returns a numerical pointer into an array of files where the sequence number appears as the message number. Remember, message filenames appear as **[message number]=[reply to message number].msg**, where the message number and reply-to number are a fixed six digits.

```
sub GetPointer
{
```

A reference to the `@file_list` array is passed along with the sequence number (`$seq`) to search for.

```
local(*file_list, $seq) = @_;
```

`$x` and `$pointer` are declared local to the subroutine. `$pointer` contains the number of the element in the array that `$seq` corresponds to, and `$x` is used as a temporary variable. Initially, `$pointer` is set to –1. Because arrays count from zero, if `$pointer` is –1, we will that the sequence number has not been found in the file list.

```
local($pointer,$x);
$pointer = -1;
```

The main part of the routine is a `for` loop that iterates through the filenames. If the first six digits of the filename match the sequence number, then `$pointer` is set to `$x` (the current element number) and the `for` loop exits with the `last` command.

```
for ($x = 0;$x < @file_list; $x++)
    {
    if (substr($file_list[$x],0,6) eq $seq)
        {
        $pointer = $x;
        last;
        }
    }
```

Finally, the $pointer is returned.

```
$pointer;
} # End of GetPointer
```

THE GETNEXTTHEAD SUBROUTINE

GetNextThread retrieves the next reply to a particular message number in
the sorted filenames list. The file list is passed by reference as the
@file_list array. The sequence number of the message ($seq) to find
replies for is also passed, as is the number of the element in the
@file_list to start looking for replies ($start).

```
sub GetNextThread
{
local(*file_list, $seq, $start) = @_;
```

$pointer and $x are declared local to the subroutine. $pointer will be
returned as a pointer to the next reply to the $seq message number in
the array. $pointer is initialized to –1. Remember that arrays start count-
ing at zero, and we want to differentiate between a number that points to
the array and one that does not. If $pointer was not initialized, it would
have a default value of zero which would be a valid pointer into the array.
Instead, when $pointer is returned as –1, the script knows that there are
no more replies to be found for the message number ($seq).

```
local($pointer, $x);
$pointer = -1;
```

The array is searched from $start to its end using a for loop.

```
for ($x = $start; $x < @file_list; $x++)
    {
```

If the second six-digit number in the filename (the reply to message number) is equal to the message number ($seq), then $pointer is set equal to $x as the current element number of the array, and the for loop is exited using the last command.

```
    if (substr($file_list[$x],7,6) eq $seq)
        {
        $pointer = $x;
        last;
        }
    }
```

The routine ends by returning the $pointer.

```
$pointer;

} # End of GetNextThread
```

THE REMOVEELEMENT SUBROUTINE

The RemoveElement subroutine is simple. It takes a reference to an array plus the number of the element to delete from the array and uses Perl's splice function to remove the element. Finally, the routine returns the resulting array.

```
sub RemoveElement
{
local(*file_list, $number) = @_;

if ($number > @file_list)
    {
    die "Number was higher than " .
        "number of elements in file list";
    }
splice(@file_list,$number,1);
@file_list;
} # End of RemoveElement
```

The GetForumInfo Subroutine

GetForumInfo takes the forum variable name ($forum) and returns the full descriptive name of the BBS forum as well as the directory where the BBS forum messages are stored.

```
sub GetForumInfo
{
    local($forum) = @_;
```

$forum_name, $forum_dir, $x, and $forum_number are defined as local variables that are used later in the subroutine.

```
    local($forum_name, $forum_dir, $x);
    local($forum_number);
```

Initially, $forum_number is set to −1. At the end of the routine, the script knows that the name was not found in the list of BBS forum names if $forum_number is still −1. If $forum has been found, $forum_number is set to the number of the element in the @forum_variable array in which the name of the forum is defined.

```
$forum_number = -1;
```

The body of the GetForumInfo routine uses a for loop to step through each element in the @forum_variable array.

```
for ($x = 1; $x <= @forum_variable; $x++)
    {
```

If the current element is equal to the contents of $forum, then $forum_number is set to the number of the current element in the array and the for loop exits when it encounters the last command.

```
    if ($forum_variable[$x - 1] eq $forum)
        {
        $forum_number = $x - 1;
        last;
        }
    } # End of FOR forum_variables
```

Now that the array has been processed, $forum_number should no longer be –1. If it is not –1, then $forum_name and $forum_dir are assigned their respective values based on the corresponding elements in the @forums and @forum_directories arrays.

```
if ($forum_number > -1)
{
    $forum_name = @forums[$forum_number];
    $forum_dir = @forum_directories[$forum_number];
```

If $forum_number is still –1, then $forum_name and $forum_dir are cleared. To generate a better error message, $forum is set to "None Given" if $forum is an empty string. $error is set to a message that tells the user that the $forum was not available. Then **bbs_html_error.pl** is loaded to print the error message to the user and the program exits with the die command.

```
} else
{
    $forum_name="";
    $forum_dir = "";
    if ($forum eq "") {
        $forum = "Forum Not Entered";
    }
    $error =
     "<strong>Forum '$forum' Not Found</strong>";
    require "bbs_html_error.pl";
    die;
}
```

If the routine successfully found the BBS forum information, it returns it as an array of two elements: $forum_name and $forum_dir.

```
($forum_name, $forum_dir);

} # end of GetForumInfo
```

THE PRUNEOLDMESSAGES SUBROUTINE

The PruneOldMessages subroutine is responsible for removing old messages in a BBS forum directory.

```
sub PruneOldMessages {
```

$forum_dir and a reference to the @files array are sent as parameters to PruneOldMessages. Both variables are declared local to this subroutine. However, the global variables $prune_how_many_days and $prune_how_many_sequences, which are defined in the **bbs.setup**, affect how this routine deletes messages. $x, $prunefile, $attachfile, and $attachfile2 are declared as local variables that will be used at various points during this subroutine.

```
local($forum_dir, *files) = @_;
local($x);
local($prunefile, $attachfile, $attachfile2);
```

The main body of this routine goes through each of the files in the @files array.

```
for ($x = @files; $x >= 1; $x—) {
```

$prunefile is set to the full path and filename of the file that is currently being checked for age.

```
$prunefile = "$forum_dir/$files[$x - 1]";
```

In addition, $attachfile and $attachfile2 are defined as filenames of attachments that may be associated with the $prunefile message if the user has uploaded a file with the message. $attachfile is the attachment description file in the forum directory, and $attachfile2 is the binary file that was uploaded and is referenced by the attachment description file.

```
$attachfile = "$forum_dir/" .
    substr($files[$x - 1],0,14) .
    "attach";
$attachfile2 = "$attach_dir/" .
    "$forum-" .
    substr($files[$x - 1],0,14) .
    "bin";
```

The -M parameter is used to check the last modification date in days. If it is greater than $prune_how_many_days and if $prune_how_many_days is greater than zero, then the file is deleted and the name is removed from the @files array. In addition, the attachments are removed if they exist.

```
    if ((-M "$prunefile" > $prune_how_many_days) &&
        ($prune_how_many_days > 0)) {
        unlink("$prunefile");
        unlink($attachfile);
            unlink($attachfile2);
        &RemoveElement(*files, $x - 1);
        next;
    }
```

$x is the current number of the element that we are processing in the @files array. If $x is less than or equal to the total number of elements in the array minus the maximum number of sequences to keep around ($prune_how_many_sequences) and $prune_how_many_sequences is not zero, then the file is deleted and the corresponding element is removed from the @files array. Also, the attachments are removed if they exist.

```
    if (($x <= (@files - $prune_how_many_sequences))
        && ($prune_how_many_sequences != 0)) {
        unlink("$prunefile");
        unlink($attachfile);
            unlink($attachfile2);
        &RemoveElement(*files, $x - 1);
        next;
    }
    } # End of for all files
} # End of PruneOldMessages
```

THE HIDDENFIELDS SUBROUTINE

The HiddenFields routine generates a string containing the HTML code for hidden <INPUT> tags containing variables that must be passed from screen to screen in WebBBS.

Basically, Web servers see each request to run the WebBBS script as a separate, individual use of WebBBS. The Web server has no idea that you have previously performed actions such as posting a message. To maintain continuity for the user, a series of hidden form fields is placed in each HTML form so that when the user submits an operation to the BBS script, it knows who the user is and can maintain the session the user is in.

$buf and $h are declared local. $buf serves as a continually growing string of hidden input fields. $h serves as shorthand for the "<INPUT

`TYPE=HIDDEN NAME"` part of the hidden field tag, because it must be assigned to $buf over and over again in the subroutine.

```
sub HiddenFields {
    local ($buf);
    local ($h);

    $h = "<INPUT TYPE=HIDDEN NAME";
```

The first variable passed is the session ID. It is used by the authentication library to retrieve the user information, such as first and last name, every time the BBS script is called. Chapter 9 discusses the need to pass the session variable from form to form.

```
$buf = qq!$h=session VALUE="$session">\n!;
if ($first_date ne "") {
 $buf .=
     qq!$h=first_date VALUE="$first_date">\n!;
}
```

The next group of hidden variables has to do with filtering of messages. If you will recall, there are certain form variables such as `keywords` and `last_date` that let a user choose to filter the list of messages to be displayed. Because the user may interrupt viewing by reading or posting a message, these variables are passed from the Create Message screen back to the list of messages when the forum is printed again.

```
if ($last_date ne "") {
 $buf .=
     qq!$h=last_date VALUE="$last_date">\n!;
}
if ($first_days_old ne "") {
 $buf .=
     qq!$h=first_days_old
      VALUE="$first_days_old">\n!;
}
if ($last_days_old ne "") {
 $buf .=
     qq!$h=last_days_old
      VALUE="$last_days_old">\n!;
}
```

```
if ($keywords ne "") {
 $buf .=
    qq!$h=keywords VALUE="$keywords">\n!;
}
if ($exact_match ne "") {
 $buf .=
    qq!$h=exact_match VALUE="$exact_match">\n!;
}
```

$use_last_read and $last_read also result in the filtering of messages and are passed from screen to screen for the same reason. These variables trigger the viewing of only new messages by the user.

```
if ($use_last_read = "on") {
 $buf .=
    qq!$h=use_last_read
      VALUE="$use_last_read">\n!;
}
if ($last_read ne "") {
 $buf .=
    qq!$h=last_read VALUE="$last_read">\n!;
}
```

If the setup file being used is an alternative one, the setup information must always be passed from screen to screen in the BBS. The setup form variable must be defined so that the alternative setup information can be read by each subsequent call to the BBS script.

```
if ($setup_file ne "") {
 $buf .=
    qq!$h=setup VALUE="$setup_file">\n!;
}
```

Finally, $buf is returned with all the appropriate hidden fields.

```
    $buf;
} # End of Hidden Fields
```

THE READMESSAGEFIELDS SUBROUTINE

ReadMessageFields sets up a list of URL variables that need to be passed from screen to screen in the BBS script. Basically, to read a message, the user must click on a URL link to that message. However, when you click on a URL link instead of doing a form submission, not all the normal <INPUT> tag form variables are passed. Thus, the URL for each message must include certain common form variables. These are the same basic variables that are generated as hidden <INPUT> tags in the HiddenFields routine.

$buf is declared local. $buf contains the extra variables that belong in the URL.

```
sub ReadMessageFields {
    local ($buf);
```

As in the HiddenFields subroutine, here $buf is set to a number of variables. In this case, the variables need to show up on a URL line and are generated as variable=value pairs instead of as hidden <INPUT> tags.

```
$buf = qq!session=$session&!;
if ($first_date ne "") {
 $buf .=
     qq!first_date="$first_date"&!;
}
if ($last_date ne "") {
 $buf .=
     qq!last_date=$last_date&!;
}
if ($first_days_old ne "") {
 $buf .=
     qq!first_days_old=$first_days_old&!;
}
if ($last_days_old ne "") {
 $buf .=
     qq!$last_days_old=$last_days_old&!;
}
if ($keywords ne "") {
 $buf .=
     qq!keywords=$keywords&!;
}
if ($exact_match ne "") {
 $buf .=
     qq!exact_match=$exact_match&!;
}
if ($use_last_read = "on") {
 $buf .=
     qq!use_last_read=$use_last_read&!;
}
```

```
if ($last_read ne "") {
 $buf .=
     qq!last_read=$last_read&!;
}
if ($setup_file ne "") {
 $buf .=
     qq!setup=$setup_file&!;
}
```

Because `$buf` will be placed on a URL, certain variables need to be filtered from the URL. Spaces and forward slash (/) characters are among the most common ones encountered, so we filter them. Spaces are replaced with `%20`, and forward slashes are replaced with `%2F`.

```
$buf =~ s/ /%20/;
$buf =~ s/\//%2F/;
```

Finally, because all the fields were appended with an ampersand (`&`) character, the very last ampersand is `chop`ped off and the resulting buffer is returned.

```
chop($buf);
$buf;
} # End of ReadMessageFields
```

Bbs_html_error.pl

Bbs_html_error.pl is a Perl library that contains code to print an HTML screen to the user's Web browser informing the user that an error has occurred. Figure 25.4 shows an example of the output from **Bbs_html_error.pl**.

The error message is defined in `$error`, which is printed between the HTML `<Blockquote>` tags.

```
print <<__ENDOFERROR__;
<HTML>
<HEAD>
<TITLE>Problem In BBS Occurred</TITLE>
</HEAD>
```

```
<BODY>
<h1>Problem In BBS Occurred</h1>
<HR>
<blockquote>
$error
</blockquote>
<HR>
</BODY>
</HTML>
__ENDOFERROR__
```

Bbs_html_forum.pl

Bbs_html_forum.pl is a library that prints the HTML screen for the list of messages in a given forum. The program relies on several variables having been defined previously: `$message_html`, `$forum_name`, `$print_hidden_fields`, `$create_message_error`, `$bbs_buttons`, and `$bbs_script`. The output of this routine can be seen in Figure 25.1.

The HTML related to all the individual messages is contained in the `$message_html` variable. `$forum_name` is the descriptive name of the current forum. `$print_hidden_fields` are set up as hidden input form fields that pass certain variables, such as session ID, from screen to screen in the BBS script. The forum name is treated as a separate hidden field, because the `$print_hidden_fields` string may be used in situations in which the forum name is not appropriate. For example, a screen might be added by a programmer who wants to allow the user to change forums dynamically without going back to the front page. `$create_message_error` is a message that tells the user that a previous post was unsuccessful. `$bbs_buttons` is set up in the **bbs.setup** file as the URL directory that contains the images for the BBS buttons. `$bbs_script`, also defined in **bbs.setup**, is the filename of the main BBS script (**bbs_forum.cgi**).

```
$print_hidden_fields = &HiddenFields;
print <<__END_OF_HTML__;
<HTML><HEAD>
<TITLE>The Message Board</TITLE>
</HEAD>
<BODY BGCOLOR = "FFFFFF" TEXT = "000000">
<CENTER>
```

```
<H2>Welcome To The $forum_name Message Board</H2>
</CENTER>
$create_msg_error
<HR>
<B>Messages:</B>
<BR>
$message_html
<CENTER>
<P>
<FORM ACTION=$bbs_script METHOD=POST>
<INPUT TYPE=HIDDEN NAME=forum VALUE=$forum>
$print_hidden_fields
<HR>
<P>
<INPUT TYPE=IMAGE NAME=post_op SRC="$bbs_buttons/post.gif" BORDER=0>
</CENTER>
</FORM>
</BODY>
</HTML>
__END_OF_HTML__
```

Bbs_html_read_message.pl

Bbs_html_read_messsage.pl is a Perl library that prints the HTML code for reading an individual message on the BBS. The main BBS CGI script defines many variables before calling this routine.

The $poster_firstname, $poster_lastname, $poster_email, $post_date-time, $post_subject, and $post_message variables are filled with the various header fields and body of the main message. $post_replies is a list of URLs that correspond to the replies to this message. $post_attach_html is a list of URLs that correspond to any attachments that the user may have uploaded. Figure 25.5 shows an example of the output from **Bbs_html_read_message.pl**.

As in **Bbs_html_forum.pl**, $print_hidden_fields is used to pass certain variables, such as session id, from BBS screen to screen. Additional hidden fields that are not universal to all WebBBS screens are also included in the following HTML code. $bbs_buttons is the URL directory containing the images for the BBS buttons. $bbs_script is the main CGI script name (**bbs_forum.cgi**). $forum is the current forum name. And finally, $message is the current message number. This information is passed to the

BBS script when this HTML form is submitted in order to keep track of which message the user is replying to if the user presses the reply button.

```
$print_hidden_fields = &HiddenFields;

print <<__ENDOFHTML__;
<HTML>
<HEAD>
<TITLE>Reading Messages</TITLE>
</HEAD>
<BODY BGCOLOR = "FFFFFF" TEXT = "000000">

<TABLE BORDER=0>
<TR>
<TH align=left>Name:</TH>
<TD>$poster_firstname $poster_lastname</TD>
</TR>
<TR>
<TH align=left>E-Mail:</TH>
<TD><A HREF="mailto:$poster_email">$poster_email</A></TD>
</TR>
<TR>
<TH align=left>Date/Time:</TH>
<TD>$post_date_time</TD>
</TR>
<TR>
<TH align=left>Subject:</TH>
<TD>$post_subject</TD>
</TR>
</TABLE>
<B>Body:</B>
<BLOCKQUOTE>
$post_message
</BLOCKQUOTE>
<FORM METHOD=POST ACTION="$bbs_script">
<B>Replies:</B>
$print_hidden_fields
<INPUT TYPE=HIDDEN NAME=post_subject VALUE="$post_subject">
<INPUT TYPE=HIDDEN NAME=forum VALUE="$forum">
<INPUT TYPE=HIDDEN NAME=reply_to_message VALUE="$message">
<BLOCKQUOTE>
$post_replies
</BLOCKQUOTE>
$post_attach_html
<CENTER><P>
<INPUT TYPE=IMAGE NAME=reply_op SRC="$bbs_buttons/post_a_reply.gif"
```

```
BORDER="0">
<INPUT TYPE=IMAGE NAME=post_op SRC="$bbs_buttons/post.gif"
BORDER="0">
<INPUT TYPE=IMAGE NAME=toplevel_op
SRC="$bbs_buttons/message_archive_top.gif"
BORDER="0">
</CENTER>
</FORM>
</BODY>
</HTML>
__ENDOFHTML__
```

Bbs_html_create_message.pl

Bbs_html_create_message.pl is called by **bbs_forum.cgi** to print an HTML form for creating a message. The Create Messsage HTML form serves the needs of both posting and replying to posts. The only difference is that the reply has additional fields that carry information from the post being replied to. An example of the output from **Bbs_html_create_message.pl** is shown in Figures 25.6 (an original post) and 25.12 (a reply to a post).

Most of the input fields are blank by default. However, depending on the logic that the main BBS script encounters, it may place default values into the various <INPUT> fields in this HTML form. $post_first_name_field, $post_last_name_field, $post_email_field, $post_date_time, $post_subject, and $post_message are all possible fillers for the corresponding fields on the HTML form. For example, if this message is a reply to another one, the contents of $post_message will be filled with the previous message so that users can quote the person they are replying to.

If attachments are turned on, $post_attachment will contain the text for the HTML of the new <INPUT TYPE=FILE> HTML tag. If $post_attachment has this value, the form header ($form_hdr) is assigned a string that contains the multipart encoding type tag in it. If, however, $post_attachment is empty, the default encoding type for the form is used. If you recall from the chapter on **Cgi-lib.pl**, an encoding type of multipart is necessary for processing file uploads.

$post_want_email contains the HTML code for an <INPUT> check box where users can choose to receive e-mailed replies automatically. This variable will be blank if you have configured the BBS not to allow the user to choose E-mail replies.

$title is set to the title of the Create Message screen. $forum is the forum name. $reply_to_email is the user's E-mail address; if the post generates automatic E-mail replies, this address will be stored along with the message when it is posted.

The default hidden fields are included with the $print_hidden_fields string. Additionally, the hidden fields related to forum and reply information are present in the HTML code.

As usual, after all the variables have been set up, the HTML code is printed using the HERE DOCUMENT method.

```
$print_hidden_fields = &HiddenFields;

$form_hdr =
  qq!<FORM METHOD=POST ACTION="$bbs_script" !;
$form_hdr .= qq!ENCTYPE="multipart/form-data">!;

if ($post_attachment eq "") {
$form_hdr = qq!<FORM METHOD=POST
            ACTION="$bbs_script">!;
}
print <<__ENDHTML__;
<HTML>
<HEAD>
<TITLE>$title</TITLE>
</HEAD>
<BODY BGCOLOR = "FFFFFF" TEXT = "000000">
<H2>$header</H2>
<HR>
$form_hdr
<INPUT TYPE=HIDDEN NAME=reply_to_message VALUE="$reply_to_message">
<INPUT TYPE=HIDDEN NAME=forum VALUE="$forum">
$print_hidden_fields
<INPUT TYPE=HIDDEN NAME=reply_to_email VALUE="$reply_to_email">
<TABLE>
<TR>
<TH align=right>First Name:</TH>
<TD>$post_first_name_field</TD>
```

```
</TR><TR>
<TH align=right>Last Name:</TH>
<TD>$post_last_name_field</TD>
</TR>
<TR>
<TH align=right>Email:</TH>
<TD>$post_email_field</TD>
</TR>
<TR>
<TH align=right>Date:</TH>
<TD>$post_date_time</TD>
</TR>
<TR>
<TH align=right>Subject:</TH>
<TD><INPUT TYPE=text NAME=form_subject VALUE="$post_subject"
SIZE=40 MAXLENGTH=50></TD>
</TR>
</TABLE>
<STRONG>Enter Message Below:</STRONG><BR>
<TEXTAREA NAME=form_message ROWS=10 COLS=60
WRAP=physical>
$post_message
</TEXTAREA>
$post_attachment
$post_want_email
<CENTER>
<HR>
<INPUT TYPE=SUBMIT NAME=create_message_op
VALUE="Submit Message">
<INPUT TYPE=RESET VALUE="Clear Values">
<HR>
<P>
<INPUT TYPE=IMAGE NAME=toplevel_op
SRC="$bbs_buttons/message_archive_top.gif"
BORDER="0">
<P>
</CENTER>
</FORM>
</BODY>
</HTML>
__ENDHTML__
```

CHAPTER 26

WebChat

OVERVIEW

WebChat is a useful CGI program that allows a number of people on the World Wide Web to talk to one another simultaneously. It differs from a BBS (bulletin board system), in which the messages are typically read hours or days after they are posted. The ability to chat on the Web can be a quick way to hold a "virtual meeting." Figure 26.1 shows an example of what WebChat looks like.

Although both WebChat and WebBBS store messages for other people to read, there is a major difference in how the user sees and posts messages. The BBS emphasizes long-term storage of messages, including statistical data such as the date and time the message is posted. The BBS also encourages users to branch out into different topics in "threads" of replies.

On the other hand, WebChat emphasizes the quick posting of small messages much like a conversation among a group of people. Dialogue is designed to flow swiftly in small, easily digested chunks. Additionally, because the topic is being discussed by everyone at the same time, there is little room for different people discussing many different things in the same chat session. Thus, there is no reason to keep track of different threads of conversation.

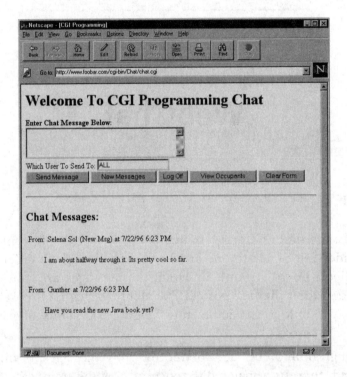

Figure 26.1 An example dialogue in WebChat.

Because people are discussing things simultaneously in real time, another feature of WebChat is the ability to refresh or display new messages as quickly as desired. This is done using the META HTML tag to force refreshes within a certain time frame.

WebChat includes many features designed to facilitate this kind of dialogue. In WebChat, users can refresh messages using a button that is displayed in plain view. In addition, if the user is using a browser such as Netscape, that supports the META REFRESH HTML tag, the user can choose to have the chat messages refresh or redisplay themselves automatically at a user-defined interval.

Messages are displayed in chronological order of posting from most recent to oldest so that users can quickly look through a list of statements. In addition, users can specify whether to see only new messages each time they refresh the screen or to include a user-defined number of previous messages. Viewing several of the previous posts along with new ones tends to provide the user with greater continuity.

By default, messages are posted to everyone, and the user's information is embedded as part of a posted message. This arrangement facilitates quick posting. By default, posted messages are seen by everyone. However, the user has a choice of entering a different username to specify whom the message should go to; the message is then entered as a private message from one person to another. This is option analogous to someone whispering a comment to someone else in the middle of a larger meeting.

Additionally, Netscape-style frames are supported; messages are refreshed in one frame while the user types messages in another frame. This feature allows a user to set a relatively high refresh rate for seeing new messages, while leaving the message submission form intact while the user is typing a message. Figure 26.2 shows an example of WebChat with frames.

WebChat also has configurable options such as the automatic announcement of a user's entry into the chat area, allowing people to keep track of who is currently in the system. Also, when a person leaves, he or she is encouraged to announce the departure by pressing the **Log Off** button. Nothing is more disturbing than to find out the person you were chatting with has left the room!

In addition, WebChat can be customized to remove old messages by age and by number of messages. For example, if WebChat is used for real-time conversations, it is generally not useful to keep the conversation messages for more than an hour. Additionally, you may want to make sure that not more than 10 or 20 messages stay around at any given point, because messages older than the first 10 may be irrelevant to the current course of conversation. On the other hand, on other chat areas, you may want to keep the messages around for a long time to keep a full transcript of the discussion or meeting.

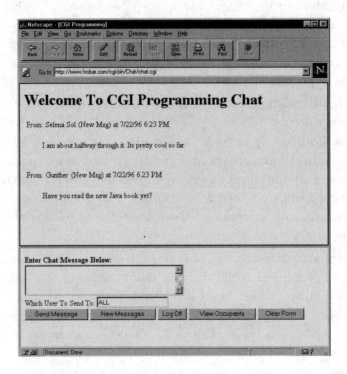

Figure 26.2 WebChat with frames on.

INSTALLATION AND USAGE

The chat files on the accompanying CD-ROM will install into a directory called **Chat**. The files and subdirectories associated with this application along with their required permissions are shown in Figure 26.3.

Chat is the root directory. It must be readable and executable by the Web server. In addition to the application files, the **Chat_open**, **Chat_CGI**, and **Sessions** subdirectories are located here. Because **CGI-LIB.PL** is the only non–application-specific library that is used, it is stored in the main **Chat** directory along with the application.

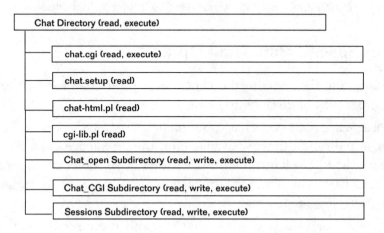

Figure 26.3 *Chat Script Directory Structure And Permissions.*

chat.cgi is the main CGI script that performs all the chat room functions, including displaying and posting new chat messages. This file must be readable and executable.

chat.setup is the setup file for the **chat.cgi** script. This file must be readable.

chat-html.pl contains Perl code that has various routines to output HTML related to the chat script. This file must be readable.

The **Sessions** subdirectory is used by the chat script to store the files related to each user's session after he or she first logs on to the chat room. This directory must be readable, writable, and executable.

The **Chat_open** subdirectory is used by **chat.cgi** to store messages for the Open Forum chat room. This is one of the chat rooms set up in the default **chat.setup** file. This directory must be readable, writable, and executable.

The **Chat_CGI** subdirectory is used by **chat.cgi** to store messages for the CGI talk chat room just as **Chat_open** does for the Open Forum . This directory must be readable, writable, and executable.

> In addition to the chat messages, the various chat room directories also store "who" files that contain information about who is currently in each chat room. The chat script generates and deletes these files automatically, so you do not need to bother with maintaining them.

N O T E

Server-Specific Setup and Options

The **chat.setup** file contains the configuration variables for **chat.cgi**. The following is a list of these setup items.

@chat_rooms is a list of chat room names. These names are descriptive names of the rooms that are available on the interactive chat. For example, if you had one chat room for discussing open topics and another for discussing CGI programming, this variable would be set to ("Open Chat Room", "CGI Programming Chat Room").

@chat_directories is an array that contains the directory names that match the list of rooms in @chat_rooms. Each of these directories stores only the chat messages related to its own corresponding room in the @chat_rooms array.

@chat_variable is a list of form variable names related to each chat room. Whenever **chat.cgi** is called after the initial logon, **chat.cgi** must have the variable chat_room sent to it. This variable should be equal to the name in the @chat_variable array. Each element of this array corresponds to each chat room listed in the @chat_rooms array. Because the values here are variable names, you should use lowercase text, underscores instead of spaces, and no special characters.

$chat_script is the **chat.cgi** script name. Most systems keep this variable set to "chat.cgi," but some systems rename the script. For example, some Windows NT Web servers require the script name to be changed to a **.bat** extension. The $chat_script variable is used by **chat.cgi** to make references to itself from a URL.

$no_html is set to on to filter HTML out of a user's messages. It is a good idea to prevent users from posting HTML within their messages, because they can inadvertently do nasty things such as leave off a closure tag (such as </H1> if they are including a header), extending the rogue tag to all the other messages. Figure 26.4 shows an example of how messages with HTML tags look after they are filtered.

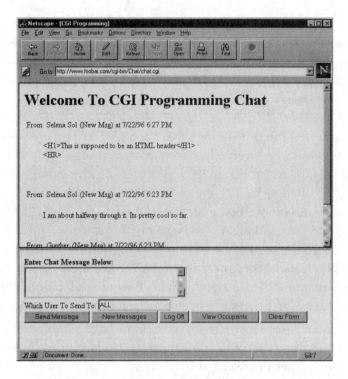

Figure 26.4 *WebChat with HTML filtering activated.*

$no_html_images is set to on if you want to prevent people from referencing images in their messages. Setting $no_html to on also filters out image-related HTML tags, so setting this variable to on is for administrators who want to continue to allow HTML posting but not images. In other words, $no_html filters all HTML tags, including image tags, so $no_html_images need not be set if you have already configured $no_html to be on.

$chat_session_dir is the location of the directory where the session files are stored for chat users. When users log into the chat area, a session file is created so that they do not have to keep respecifying their information.

$chat_session_length is the time in days that session files stay active before being deleted. This value can be a fraction. For example, a value of .25 would delete sessions every quarter day (six hours).

NOTE

Because Perl is actually processing the setup file, you can use a formula instead of a standard fractional value. A formula can be easier to read and maintain. For example, "1/24" (1 divided by 24) is a one-hour time frame. "1/24/12" (1 divided by 24 divided by 12) is a five-minute time frame.

$chat_who_length is the time in days that the who files stay active. Who files show who is active in a given chat room at a given time. This value can be fractional. Ideally, it should be very short. Using the value "1/24/12" (1 divided by 24 divided by 12) means that the who files stay around for about five minutes before being removed. A user can always "leave" a chat room by going to another WWW page on the Internet, and this act of leaving is not guaranteed to be sent to the chat script. If the who files are deleted often enough, they provide a relatively accurate way of determining who is currently in the system. Who files are refreshed whenever a user refreshes the chat messages or submits a message to the chat room.

$chat_announce_entry is on if you want a message to automatically post when someone enters a room. This message usually announces to everyone in the room that the user has logged on.

$prune_how_many_days is the number of days after which a chat message is considered too old to leave on the system. These messages are deleted. If this variable is set to zero, the chat messages will not be removed on the basis of age. This number may be fractional. For example, setting it to ".25" will delete messages older than six hours.

$prune_how_many_sequences is the maximum number of messages you want to leave on the system before the oldest ones are deleted. For example, if you specify this number to be 10, then only 10 messages will be allowed per chat room. In this case, after the 11th message is posted, message number 1 is deleted. Setting this value to zero means that you do not want any messages deleted on the basis of a maximum number of messages to keep on the system.

NOTE For a real-time chat system, it is recommended that you set up the system to keep few messages around. For one thing, in a real-time conversation, after about five or 10 minutes, people have probably moved on to another topic. Also, the chat script operates more efficiently if it does not have to process so many messages in the chat directory.

The following is an example of all the setup variables in the **chat.setup** file.

```
@chat_rooms = ("CGI Programming", "Open Forum");
@chat_room_directories = ("Chat_CGI", "Chat_Open");
@chat_room_variable = ("cgi", "open");

$chat_script = "chat.cgi";

$no_html = "off";
$no_html_images = "off";

$chat_session_dir = "Sessions";
$chat_session_length = 1;
$chat_who_length = 1/24/12;
$chat_announce_entry = "off";

$prune_how_many_days =          .25;
$prune_how_many_sequences =     10;
```

USING OTHER SETUP FILES

The chat script has the ability to reference another setup file in case the default **chat.setup** file does not meet the needs of every chat room. For example, although **chat.setup** accommodates multiple chat rooms, you may want to assign a different automatic removal of messages policy for each one. In the Open Chat Room, you may want to delete messages older than five minutes, but in the CGI programming chat room, you may not want to delete any messages.

You can do this by using another setup file that is loaded with the same variables defined in **chat.setup**. **chat.setup** is always loaded by the **chat.cgi** script. However, if you send the setup variable on the URL link to the script as a Url-encoded variable, **chat.cgi** will read a setup file on the basis of that variable. For example, if you specified the call to **chat.cgi** as

```
http://www.foobar.com/cgi-bin/Chat/chat.cgi?setup=test
```

the **test.setup** file would be loaded by the chat script after the **chat.setup** file is loaded.

chat.setup is always necessary. This means that if you choose to override **chat.setup** using the setup form variable, you need specify only the variables you want changed in the new setup file instead of all the variables originally residing in **chat.setup**.

NOTE

MODIFYING THE HTML

The HTML used by the chat script is stored in the **chat-html.pl** file. This Perl script outputs the various HTML forms for viewing and posting chat messages. To modify the cosmetics of the chat script, you need only edit this file. The structure of this script is discussed in more detail in the "Design Discussion" section.

Because the chat script allows the user to choose frames versus a nonframes view of the chat script, the Perl code that generates the HTML for printing to the user's Web browser can seem a bit complex. If you plan to edit the HTML for the chat script, you should study the "Design Discussion" of **chat-html.pl**. Also, as usual, you should make a backup of any files you are planning to edit so that you can go back to the original if anything becomes messed up after something is changed.

NOTE

Running the Script

To use **chat.cgi**, you simply call it by itself. A sample URL for this script, if it is installed in the **Chat** subdirectory underneath the **cgi-bin** directory, follows. The chat program automatically prints an HTML form asking the user to log on to a chat room. An example of this form is displayed in Figure 26.5. However, if you are using a setup file other than **chat.setup**, you need to specify this in the URL that you use to run the chat script. An example of this alternative setup file was previously discussed.

```
http://www.foobar.com/cgi-bin/Chat/chat.cgi
```

Figure 26.5 *Example of chat room logon.*

CHAT ENTRANCE FORM VARIABLES

In the chat room logon screen shown in Figure 26.5, there are several form variables that the user is asked to fill out. These variables affect how the rest of the chat session is processed.

Username is the alias that the user will be referred to in the chat room. This field must be entered.

Email address is the E-mail address of the user. This is optional. If the user chooses to fill in this variable, a MAILTO hypertext reference tag will be displayed whenever the user's name is shown in the chat room.

Home page is the URL of the home page of the user. This field is also optional. If the user chooses to give the home page URL, a hypertext reference will be displayed whenever the user's name is shown in the chat room.

How many old messages to display determines how many old messages are displayed along with the new messages whenever the chat messages are loaded. Generally, an overlap of about 10 old messages is good for maintaining the continuity of a conversation. If you see only new messages and if they refer to a topic discussed previously, it is harder for most people to visualize how the conversation is flowing. Seeing a couple of the old messages serves as a reminder. This is especially true in chat rooms where many topics might be discussed at once.

Refresh rate is the number of seconds before the browser automatically reloads the script to display the new messages. This field is useful only for browsers that support the META refresh tag. Setting this field to zero disables automatic refreshing of messages.

If the check box for using frames is turned on, Netscape-style frames will be used to display messages in one frame while the submission form for a post is displayed in another frame. An example of frames was shown in Figure 26.2.

The **chat room** variable allows the user to select the chat room to enter.

DESIGN DISCUSSION

The chat application performs all its functions inside **chat.cgi**. These operations include the listing of messages in a chat room as well as the creation of those messages. Depending on the value of incoming form variables, **chat.cgi** determines which procedure to perform. A basic flow-chart of the Web chat features is shown in Figure 26.6.

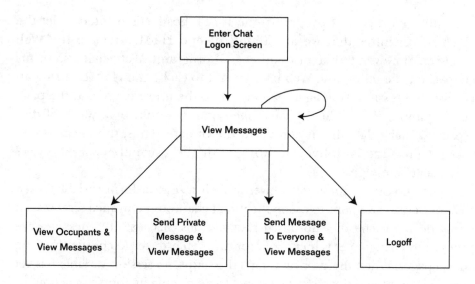

Figure 26.6 *Basic flow chart for the Web chat.*

Chat.cgi

The first line of the following code sets up the location of the supporting files to the program. By default, $lib is set to the current directory. Then the **cgi-lib.pl** library (for form parsing routines), the setup file for the script, and the Perl library containing the HTML code for the chat script are loaded.

```
$lib = ".";
require "$lib/cgi-lib.pl";
require "./chat.setup";
require "./chat-html.pl";
```

The incoming form variables are read to the %in associative array using the ReadParse subroutine.

```
&ReadParse;
```

As with the other CGI programs, the HTTP header is printed to let the Web server know that we are about to send HTML data to the Web browser. However, unlike most other CGI programs, Web Chat also prints a special code telling the Web browser not to cache the HTML during an active chat session. During a real-time chat, the user may reload the page every minute to look at the latest messages. It would be a waste of disk space to cache data that is constantly out of date. Thus, the `"Pragma: no-cache"` message is delivered along with the normal `"Content-type: text/html"` message.

The "no-cache" message is given only if a session form variable is set. This is because we want to cache the initial chat room entrance screen even if we do not cache the individual chat sessions. Because the messages are constantly changing, it is inefficient for the Web browser to constantly cache those pages. When the user first starts the script, no session variable has yet been set, and the script can use this fact to determine its course of action.

```
print "Content-type: text/html\n";

if ($in{'session'} ne "") {
    print "Pragma: no-cache\n\n";
} else {
    print "\n";
}
```

The form variables are read to regular Perl variables for easier processing later. `$chat_username` is the username of the user who is chatting. `$chat_email` is the E-mail address of the user. `$chat_http` is the URL that the user is associated with.

```
$chat_username = $in{'chat_username'};
$chat_email = $in{'chat_email'};
$chat_http = $in{'chat_http'};
```

`$refresh_rate` is the number of seconds before the browser automatically reloads the chat script to display the new messages.

```
$refresh_rate = $in{'refresh_rate'};
```

$how_many_old is a user-defined variable that determines how many old messages should be displayed along with the new messages.

```
$how_many_old = $in{'how_many_old'};
```

$frames is set to on if the user has chosen to use Netscape-style frames for interacting with other users in the chat room. With frames, the chat room is divided into two windows: one frame for viewing the messages and another frame for submitting new posts.

```
$frames = $in{'frames'};
```

If frames are currently being used, the script must figure out which frame it is currently being called from. If it is being called from the frame that displays messages, the $fmsgs variable is set to on. If the script is being called from the frame where messages are submitted, the $fsubmit variable is set to on. We need these variables in order to determine later whether the script should output the message list or the message submission form.

```
$fmsgs = $in{'fmsgs'};
$fsubmit = $in{'fsubmit'};
```

Figure 26.7 shows how **chat.cgi** is called when frames are activated. Figure 26.2 shows an example of the frames' output. When frames are activated, an HTML page that sets up the frames is printed by **chat.cgi**. This main frame HTML code sets up a top frame that contains messages and a bottom frame that contains the message submission form. As indicated previously, **chat.cgi** outputs the main frame HTML when the form variable frame is on. Then **chat.cgi** is called once for each of the two frames. When the form variable fmsgs is set to on, **chat.cgi** outputs the messages frame; when the form variable fsubmit is set to on, **chat.cgi** outputs the message submission frame.

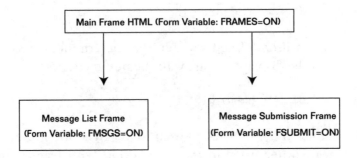

Figure 26.7 Structure of frames in chat.cgi.

$user_last_read stores the last read message relative to each user in the chat room. Because we want only new messages to be shown to the user (plus maybe a few old ones for continuity in the conversation), we keep track of the user's last read message number. The messages are created using ascending sequence numbers, so only numbers greater than the $user_last_read variable will be displayed. By default, $user_last_read is set to zero by the script. $user_last_read will be used later in the script when messages are being processed.

```
$user_last_read = 0;
```

$chat_room is set to the current chat room variable name. $setup is set to an alternative chat room setup filename. After this, if the alternative setup file is defined, it is also loaded by the chat script.

```
$chat_room = $in{'chat_room'};
$setup = $in{'setup'};

if ($setup ne "") {
    require "$setup.setup";
}
```

The chat script name is placed in the $chat_script variable. If this variable is not defined, it becomes "chat.cgi" by default. This variable should be defined in the **chat.setup** file if you are planning to change the name of the script. Generally, the only reason you would want to change the name is if your Web server does not support the **.cgi** extension. Some Windows NT Web servers fall into this category.

```
if ($chat_script eq "") {
    $chat_script = "chat.cgi";
}
```

$enter_chat is set to the value of the **Enter Chat Room** button on the initial login HTML form. This value will be used later by **chat.cgi** to see whether the user has just entered the chat room and must be set up by the script.

```
$enter_chat = $in{'enter_chat'};
```

The following routine sets up variables from incoming form data as the result of a button being pressed on the Submit Chat Message form. $refresh_chat, $submit_message, $logoff, and $occupants are set to the value of their corresponding button labels if they were pressed. Only one of these variables will have a value associated with it, because only the pressed button has its value transferred as an incoming form value. This fact will be used later by **chat.cgi** to determine which operation to perform.

```
$refresh_chat = $in{'refresh_chat'};
$submit_message = $in{'submit_message'};
$logoff = $in{'logoff'};
$occupants = $in{'occupants'};
```

If a message is currently being submitted, the values of $chat_to_user and $chat_message are set by the incoming form variables. $chat_to_user defines the user to whom a chat message is directed. $chat_message is the chat message itself.

```
$chat_to_user = $in{'chat_to_user'};
$chat_message = $in{'chat_message'};
```

$session is set to the current session number. When users log in to a chat room, they are assigned a session number that **chat.cgi** uses to track their user information as well as their last read message number.

```
$session = $in{'session'};
```

By default, $new\_session$ is set to no. This variable will be used later by the script to determine whether certain files still need to be set up for the newly logged in user.

```
$new_session = "no";
```

If the session has not yet been defined, then one of two things happens. If the user has seen the chat room logon screen, a session is created and the script continues processing. If the user has not yet seen the chat room logon screen, this HTML form is printed.

To see whether the user has been to the logon screen, the script checks the $chat\_username$ variable. Remember that the $chat\_username$ variable corresponds to the incoming username form variable. If this variable is not set, it is assumed that the user either has not entered all the information on the chat logon screen or has not been there yet. The script checks the $enter\_chat$ variable. Again, recall that $enter\_chat$ is set to a value if the **Enter Chat Room** button was pressed on the logon form. Thus, if $enter\_chat$ has a value but $chat\_username$ has none, the script prints the chat room logon screen using the PrintChatEntrance subroutine. It also prints an error message asking to the user to enter a username. Otherwise, the logon screen for the chat is simply displayed to the user.

```
if ($session eq "") {
    if ($chat_username eq "") {
        if ($enter_chat eq "") {
            &PrintChatEntrance($setup,"");
        } else {
            &PrintChatEntrance($setup,
            "Hey! You did not " .
            "enter a username.");
        }
    exit;
    }
```

A new session ID is created if no session ID is currently defined for the user and if the user already has a username. First, the $new\_session$ variable is toggled to yes. Then the new session ID is created and assigned to $session using the MakeSessionFile subroutine. This subroutine places all the logon information in a file for future reference by the chat script.

Notice in the following code that the last parameter is a zero. This value is the last read message number for the user. In other words, the user's session is initialized so that all the messages in the chat room are currently "new."

```
    $new_session = "yes";
    $session =
     &MakeSessionFile($chat_username, $chat_email,
        $chat_http, $refresh_rate,
        $how_many_old, "0");
}
```

Although we assigned the chat room name to the $chat_room variable, the script still must obtain the descriptive name of the chat room as well as the directory containing the chat messages. It uses the GetChatRoomInfo subroutine.

```
 ($chat_room_name, $chat_room_dir) =
  &GetChatRoomInfo($chat_room);
```

GetSessionInfo is called to retrieve information about the user currently being served by the chat script. Frame information ($fsubmit and $frames) is also submitted to GetSessionInfo because it normally updates the user's last read message count. However, if the chat script is currently outputting the submit message frame ($fsubmit) or outputting the main HTML frame document ($frames), then we do not update the user's last read message count.

A frame not related to message output may send a call to the script. If such a call updates the user's last message count, then another call—such as a call to the script where the messages are displayed in a different frame—will not display new messages. That's because the user's last read count has already been adjusted by the first frame. To avoid this problem, we send information to GetSessionInfo that specifies whether the script will output information to the user.

```
($user_name, $user_email, $user_http,
$refresh_rate, $how_many_old,
$user_last_read, $high_message) =
        &GetSessionInfo($session, $fsubmit, $frames);
```

If $new_session is yes and if $chat_announce_entry has been set to on in **chat.setup**, then variables are set up to generate an automatic chat message informing everyone of the user's chat room entrance. Figure 26.8 shows an example of an automatic logon message.

```
if ($chat_announce_entry eq "on" &&
    $new_session eq "yes") {
    $submit_message = "on";
    $chat_to_user = "ALL";
    $chat_message = "Automatic Message: $user_name
                    Joined Chat Room";
}
```

Figure 26.8 *Automatic logon message.*

702

If the logoff button was pressed, an automatic message is generated letting everyone know that the user has left the chat room. We use the same method that we used to generate the automatic chat entrance message. Figure 26.9 shows an example of the automatic logoff message.

```
if ($logoff ne "") {
    $submit_message = "on";
    $chat_to_user = "ALL";
    $chat_message = "Automatic Message: $user_name
                    Logged Off";
}
```

Figure 26.9 *Example of automatic message for logoff.*

NOTE

You cannot really log off in a connectionless environment. However, the logoff button exists to help make it clear who is in the chat room. It works if everyone follows the etiquette of pressing the logoff button before moving to another Web page on the Internet.

703

The following routine reformats the date and time parts of the `localtime(time)` command into a `$current_date_time` variable. This variable will be used later to associate a nicely formatted date and time with each posted message.

```
 ($min, $hour, $day, $mon, $year) =
     (localtime(time))[1,2,3,4,5];
$mon++;
if (length($min) < 2) {
    $min = "0" . $min;
}
$ampm = "AM";
$ampm = "PM" if ($hour > 11);
$hour = $hour - 12 if ($hour > 12);
$current_date_time =
    "$mon/$day/$year $hour:$min $ampm";
```

SUBMIT CHAT MESSAGE

The next part of the main script processes the submission of a chat message. If the `$submit_message` button was pressed, the submission process begins.

```
if ($submit_message ne "") {
```

The next `if` statement checks to see whether `$chat_to_user` is addressed to no one (blank), `"all"`, or `"everyone"` without regard to case. If the statement is true, `$chat_to_user` is set to `"ALL"`. `"ALL"` is used to define the message as being posted to everyone in the chat room. If an explicit user name is given, then only the addressee to and the user who posted the original message can see the post.

```
    if ($chat_to_user eq "" ||
        $chat_to_user =~ /^all$/i ||
        $chat_to_user =~ /everyone/i) {
        $chat_to_user  = "ALL";
    }
```

First, we obtain the highest message number. Each time a post is made, the message number is incremented by 1. This arrangement keeps the message filenames unique and also gives us a way of to check whether a user has seen a message. If the user's last read number is less than a given message number, the script knows that the user has not yet read that message.

```
$high_number = &GetHighMessageNumber;
$high_number++;
```

The message number is formatted, using `sprintf`, into an integer with six characters. If the length of the number is less than six spaces, the leading spaces are converted to zeros using the `tr` function.

```
$high_number = sprintf("%6d",$high_number);
$high_number =~ tr/ /0/;
```

N O T E `sprintf` **is used to format variables in various ways. In the chat script,** `"%6d"` **tells** `sprintf` **to format the** `$high_number` **variable as a decimal integer (**d**) with a length of six (**6**).**

Next, the routine creates the new message file and writes all the fields to it. These fields include the username, E-mail address, URL link, the user the message is addressed to (usually ALL), the current date and time, and, of course, the chat message.

```
open(MSGFILE, ">$chat_room_dir/$high_number.msg");
print MSGFILE "$user_name\n";
print MSGFILE "$user_email\n";
print MSGFILE "$user_http\n";
print MSGFILE "$chat_to_user\n";
print MSGFILE "$current_date_time\n";
print MSGFILE "$chat_message\n";
close(MSGFILE);
```

Whenever messages are posted, the script also calls `PruneOldMessages` to delete any messages that are old.

```
&PruneOldMessages($chat_room_dir);
```

Because a new message has been posted, the user's last read field in the session file must be increased to accommodate the new message. We do this by calling `GetSessionInfo` all over again. However, we do not want to lose track of the last read message from the last time this script was called by the user. Thus, `$old_last_read` is used to mark the `$user_last_read` message. Then, after `GetSessionInfo` is called, `$user_last_read` is set back to the old value.

```
    $old_last_read = $user_last_read;
    ($user_name, $user_email, $user_http,
     $refresh_rate, $how_many_old,
     $user_last_read, $high_message) =
       &GetSessionInfo($session, $fsubmit, $frames);
    $user_last_read = $old_last_read;
}
```

READ THE CURRENT OCCUPANTS LIST

When the occupants list is displayed to the user, it is displayed as part of
the general $chat_buffer, which contains all the messages to display.
Before the script starts filling $chat_buffer, it is cleared. Figure 26.10
shows an example of the final occupants list on a user's Web browser.

```
$chat_buffer = "";
```

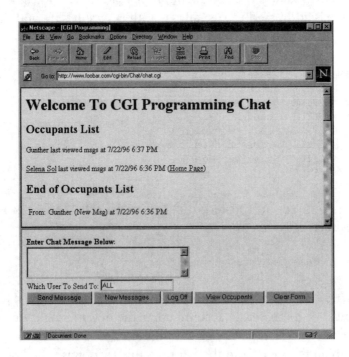

Figure 26.10 *Example of the WebChat occupants list.*

If $occupants has a value, then the **View Occupants** button was clicked by the user. This action starts the collection of the list of occupants into a form that can be displayed via HTML.

```
if ($occupants ne "") {
```

The chat room directory is opened, and all the files ending in **who** are read to the @files array using grep to filter the results of the readdir command.

```
opendir(CHATDIR, "$chat_room_dir");
@files = grep(/who$/,readdir(CHATDIR));
closedir(CHATDIR);
```

The occupants list header is appended to $chat_buffer, which contains the HTML output for the messages to be displayed. Then, if there are who files in the @files array, each file is checked using a foreach loop.

```
$chat_buffer .= "<H2>Occupants List</H2><P>";
if (@files > 0) {
 foreach $whofile (@files) {
```

Each who file is opened, and a single line is read to the $wholine variable. Because the fields in $wholine are pipe-delimited, the split command is used to separate the fields into elements of the @whofields array.

```
open (WHOFILE,"<$chat_room_dir/$whofile");
$wholine = <WHOFILE>;
@whofields = split(/\|/,$wholine);
close(WHOFILE);
```

A sample who file looks like the following:

```
Gunther|gb@foobar.com|www.foobar.com|7/2/96 5:17 PM
```

Different HTML code is generated based on whether all the @whofields have values. For example, if an E-mail address exists for the user ($whofields[1]) then a hypertext reference is generated with a "MAILTO" tag. Otherwise, the plain username is printed as HTML.

```
        if ($whofields[1] ne "") {
         $chat_buffer .= qq!<A HREF=MAILTO:! .
            qq!$whofields[1]>!;
        }
        $chat_buffer .= $whofields[0];
        if ($whofields[1] ne "") {
         $chat_buffer .= "</A>";
        }
```

$whofields[3] contains the last date and time that the person viewed messages. Remember, the who file is regenerated every time messages are viewed or submitted.

```
        $chat_buffer .= " last viewed msgs at ";
        $chat_buffer .= $whofields[3];
```

$whofields[2] contains the URL link for the user. If the user has given that information, then HTML code is generated to show a hypertext link to that URL.

```
        if ($whofields[2] ne "") {
         $chat_buffer .=
            qq! (<A HREF="$whofields[2]">! .
                qq!Home Page</A>)!;
        }
```

The occupants list portion of the $chat_buffer HTML code is ended with a paragraph break (<P>).

```
        $chat_buffer .= "<P>";
    }
```

If there were no occupants to be found (no who files found), then $chat_buffer is merely set to "No Occupants Found."

```
    } else {
     $chat_buffer .= "No Occupants Found";
    } # End of no occupants
```

Finally, `$chat_buffer` is ended with a footer stating that the end of the occupants list has been reached.

```
    $chat_buffer .=
      "<P><H2>End of Occupants List</H2><P>";
} # End of occupants processing
```

PROCESS CHAT MESSAGES

The next part of the chat script processes the chat messages for display to the user. Here, there is one thing to take into consideration: frames. If frames are activated, the chat program should display messages only if it has been called upon to read messages (`$fmsgs` is `on`). If the main frame HTML document is being output (`$frames` is `on`) or if the message submit frame is being output (`$fsubmit`), the script will not enter the part of the script that processes messages.

```
if ($fmsgs eq "on" ||
    ($frames ne  "on" &&
     $fsubmit ne "on")) {
```

PROCESS WHO FILES

Before the messages are collected, a new who file is generated indicating that the user has read new messages. First, the old who file is deleted using `unlink`. Then the who file is re-created and the user information is printed to it: `$user_name`, `$user_email`, `$user_http`, and `$current_date_time`.

```
$whofile = "$chat_room_dir/$session.who";
unlink($whofile);
open(WHOFILE, ">$whofile");
print WHOFILE "$user_name|$user_email|$user_http";
print WHOFILE "|$current_date_time\n";
close (WHOFILE);
```

NOTE The code deletes the file instead of writing over it, to ensure that the who file is assigned a different file creation time. A subroutine discussed later removes old who files on the basis of creation time. Because this script is meant to run on multiple operating system platforms other than UNIX, the file is deleted and re-created to ensure consistency on as many platforms as possible.

The `RemoveOldWhoFiles` subroutine is called to delete who files for users that have not read messages within the `$chat_who_length` period of time. `$chat_who_length` is a global variable that is specified in **chat.setup**.

```
&RemoveOldWhoFiles;
```

READ CHAT MESSAGES

To read the chat messages, the script can be configured to restrict the number of messages that are seen. Generally, users do not want to see all the old messages over and over again, so the chat script keeps track of the last read message of the user. When it is created, each message is assigned a unique sequence number in ascending order. Whenever a user reads all the messages in the chat room directory, the current highest message number is set to the user's last read message number. Then, the next time the script is called to view messages, the "last read" message number can be compared against the message numbers in the directory. If the message number is lower than the last read number, we know that the message is old.

The `$msg_to_read` variable is set up to reflect the preceding algorithm except that 1 is added to it. Later, when the message numbers are compared, we will use the greater than or equal to (>=) 0 operator to compare the current message numbers to the last read message number stored in `$msg_to_read`.

```
$msg_to_read = $user_last_read + 1;
```

Next, `$how_many_old` is subtracted from `$msg_to_read`. As a result, some old messages are displayed with the new ones. Remember that in the chat room logon screen, the user chooses how many old messages to display with new ones.

```
$msg_to_read -= $how_many_old;
```

If there are fewer messages in the directory than $how_many_old messages, $msg_to_read could become a negative number or zero and the chat script would spend extra work trying to read files that do not exist. Thus, the next piece of code converts $msg_to_read into a positive value.

```
if ($msg_to_read < 1) {
    $msg_to_read = 1;
}
```

The next if statement checks quickly to see whether $msg_to_read is greater than the current $high_message number. If $msg_to_read is greater than $high_message, we do not need to bother iterating through all the files in the directory, because nothing would be displayed.

```
if ($high_message >= $msg_to_read) {
```

Now we begin reading the messages within the for loop started here.

```
for ($x = $high_message; $x >= $msg_to_read; $x-){
```

The sprintf command is used to format the current message number, $x, to an integer with a length of 6. Because $x is usually fewer than six characters long, sprintf pads it with leading spaces. Immediately afterward, the tr command is used to convert all the leading spaces to zeros. Thus, sprintf converts a number such as "5" to "   5", and the tr command converts "   5" to "000005." This is done because the messages are stored in the chat room directory as six-digit numbers with leading zeros.

```
$x = sprintf("%6d",$x);
$x =~ tr/ /0/;
```

The message is checked for existence using the -e operator. If it exists, it is opened. If the opening of any message fails, the program exits with an error message printed to the user's Web browser.

```
if (-e "$chat_room_dir/$x.msg") {
    open(MSG,"$chat_room_dir/$x.msg") ||
        &CgiDie("Could not open $x.msg");
```

If the file is opened successfully, the message is processed. Each line of the message corresponds to a field of information. The format of a message appears below:

```
[USERNAME OF USER WHO POSTED MESSAGE]
[EMAIL OF USER WHO POSTED MESSAGE]
[URL LINK TO USER WHO POSTED MESSAGE]
[USERNAME OF USER MESSAGE IS ADDRESS TO (USUALLY ALL)]
[MESSAGE DATE AND TIME]
[MESSAGE BODY]
```

All the preceding fields (except the message body) are read to the following variables: $msg_from_user, $msg_email, $msg_http, $msg_to_user, and $msg_date_time. The <MSG> command is a Perl convention that takes any file handle surrounded by brackets (<>) and returns the next line in the file. In addition, any fields that the user has entered are processed using the HtmlFilter function to remove HTML codes if you have disallowed them in **chat.setup**.

```
$msg_from_user = <MSG>;
$msg_from_user = &HtmlFilter($msg_from_user);
$msg_email = <MSG>;
$msg_email = &HtmlFilter($msg_email);
$msg_http = <MSG>;
$msg_http = &HtmlFilter($msg_http);
$msg_to_user = <MSG>;
$msg_to_user = &HtmlFilter($msg_to_user);
$msg_date_time = <MSG>;
```

The last character of all the variables is chopped, because a superfluous newline character is always appended to the end of a line read from a file.

```
chop($msg_from_user);
chop($msg_email);
chop($msg_http);
chop($msg_to_user);
chop($msg_date_time);
```

Messages are displayed to a user only if the addressee is "ALL," if the addressee matches the current username, and if the poster username matches the current username.

```
if ($msg_to_user eq "ALL" ||
    $msg_to_user =~ /^$user_name$/i ||
    $msg_from_user =~ /^$user_name$/i) {
```

The information about the message is then converted to HTML code to be displayed to the user. This code is placed in the $chat_buffer variable, just as the occupants list HTML code was placed there previously.

Each message header is formatted as an HTML table. The first field set up in the table is the "From:" field.

```
$chat_buffer .= "<TABLE>\n";
$chat_buffer .= "<TR><TD>";
$chat_buffer .= "From:</TD><TD>";
```

If there is an E-mail address associated with the user who posted the message, a hypertext reference to the user's address is placed in $chat_buffer. Otherwise, $msg_from_user is placed in $chat_buffer.

```
if ($msg_email ne "") {
  $chat_buffer .= qq!<A HREF=MAILTO:! .
                  qq!$msg_email>!;
}
$chat_buffer .= $msg_from_user;
if ($msg_email ne "") {
  $chat_buffer .= "</A>";
}
```

If $msg_http is defined, the user's URL link will be added as a hypertext reference in $chat_buffer.

```
if ($msg_http ne "") {
  $chat_buffer .= qq! (<A HREF="$msg_http">! .
                  qq!Home Page</A>)!;
}
```

Periodically, the $chat_buffer fields are delimited with the standard <TR>, </TR>, <TD>, and </TD> HTML tags.

```
$chat_buffer .= "</TD>\n";
$chat_buffer .= "\n<TD>";
```

If the current message number ($x) is greater than $user_last_read, then a New Msg tag is appended to the information header.

```
if ($x > $user_last_read) {
    $chat_buffer .= " (New Msg) "
}
```

The date and time of the message are added to $chat_buffer.

```
$chat_buffer .= " at $msg_date_time</TD>";
```

If the message was generated for a particular user, a tag is generated for the information header that lets the user know that this is a private message to him or her or that it is a private message that the user posted to someone else.

```
$chat_buffer .= "</TR>\n";
if ($msg_to_user =~ /^$user_name$/i ||
    ($msg_from_user =~ /^$user_name$/i &&
     $msg_to_user ne "ALL")) {
$chat_buffer .= "<TR><TD>";
$chat_buffer .= "Private Msg To:" .
                "</TD><TD>$msg_to_user</TD>" .
                "</TR>\n";
}
```

The table is closed using the </TABLE> HTML tag, and then the body of the message is read from the file inside <BLOCKQUOTE> HTML tags. Each line is filtered using the HtmlFilter subroutine. In addition, each line is printed with a <BR> tag to show a line break.

```
$chat_buffer .= "</TABLE>\n";
$chat_buffer .= "<BLOCKQUOTE>\n";
while(<MSG>) {
    $_ = &HtmlFilter($_);
    $chat_buffer .= "$_<BR>";
    }
```

When the message body is finished, the file is closed and the program loops back to process another file unless the current message number ($x) has reached $high_message_number.

```
            close(MSG);
            $chat_buffer .= "\n";
        }
        $chat_buffer .= "</BLOCKQUOTE>\n";
        } # End of IF msg is to all or just us
    }
}
# End of IF we are not in the submit msg frame
#    or simply printing the main frameset
#    document
}
```

PROCESS LOGOFF

If the logoff button was pressed, the who file is deleted immediately using unlink. The user will no longer show up on the occupants list.

```
if ($logoff ne "") {
    $whofile = "$chat_room_dir/$session.who";
    unlink($whofile);
}
```

Because the Web is connectionless, it is possible to stay online after you "log off." The ability to "log off" is presented as a means to allow a group of people who follow chat room etiquette to gain an accurate picture of who is in the chat room. It is not a security measure.

NOTE

PRINT THE CHAT SCREEN

The final part of the main **chat.cgi** program is the printing of the chat page. The logic contained in the PrintChatScreen subroutine is complex, because it must account for both frames and nonframes printing of the chat messages and submit message form. An example of a new message in the chat message frame appears in Figure 26.11.

```
&PrintChatScreen($chat_buffer, $refresh_rate,
                 $session, $chat_room, $setup,
                 $frames, $fmsgs, $fsubmit);
```

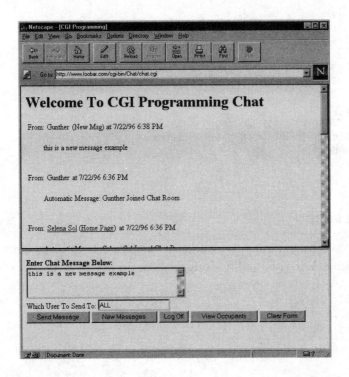

Figure 26.11 *Example of a new message appearing in the chat message frame.*

THE GETSESSIONINFO SUBROUTINE

The GetSessionInfo subroutine in the chat script retrieves information about the user's current session. This includes the username, E-mail address, URL link, refresh rate, use of frames, and last read message number. The routine starts by accepting the current session number and data about whether we are currently using frames ($frames) and, if so, whether we are refreshing the submit message frame ($fsubmit).

```
sub GetSessionInfo {
local($session, $fsubmit,$frames) = @_;
```

$session_file, $temp, @fields, @f, $high_number, and $high_message are declared local to the subroutine.

```
local($session_file);
local($temp,@fields, @f);
local($high_number, $high_message);
```

`$session_file` appends a **.dat** extension to the session ID. This is the name of the session file. Then the session file is opened in the **$chat_session_dir** directory.

```
$session_file = "$session.dat";

open (SESSIONFILE, "$chat_session_dir/$session_file");
```

The session file is read using a `while` loop. The session file should consist of one line of fields that are pipe-delimited. (The fields are separated by the pipe (|) symbol.) Here is an example session file:

```
Gunther|gb@foobar.com|http://foobar.com/|0|10|000067
```

The fields in the preceding session file are the username, E-mail address, URL, automatic refresh rate (in seconds), number of messages to display, and last read message number.

```
while (<SESSIONFILE>) {
$temp = $_;
}
```

A `chop` is added so that the last field does not have a hanging newline at the end. (A file read typically reads the whole line including the newline character that separates lines in a file.) The fields are separated into the `@fields` array. Finally, the session file is closed.

```
chop($temp);
@fields = split(/\|/, $temp);
close (SESSIONFILE);
```

`$high_message` is set to the highest message number in the current chat room. This message number is used to overwrite the last read message for the user. In other words, now that the user's last read message number has been read to @fields from the session file, we update it with the highest message number so that the next time the script runs, only the latest messages will be displayed to the user.

```
$high_message = &GetHighMessageNumber;
```

@f stores the contents of @fields as a temporary holder for the old session values. Then the last field in the @fields array is set equal to $high_message. This last field corresponds to the user's last read message number.

```
@f = @fields;
@fields[@fields - 1] = $high_message;
```

NOTE @fields - 1 **returns a number representing the number of the last element of the** @fields **array.** @fields **returns the total number of elements in the array, but because arrays start counting at zero instead of 1, we subtract 1 from** @fields **to get a reference to the last element of the** @fields **array. This technique is used throughout the chapter.**

If frames are not on and if we are not printing the submit portion of a frame, the session file is updated with the new high message number. We open the session file and write the new @fields values to it.

```
if ($fsubmit ne "on" &&
    $frames ne "on") {
    open (SESSIONFILE,
      ">$chat_session_dir/$session_file");
    print SESSIONFILE join ("\|", @fields);
    print SESSIONFILE "\n";
    close (SESSIONFILE);
}
```

Finally, the original session values in @f are returned, along with the current high message number. This message number is returned because the script must know up to what sequence number to display new messages.

```
(@f, $high_message);

} # End of GetSessionInfo
```

Because the user's last read message number is set to $high_message, **there is a chance that more messages might be posted to the chat room while this script is processing the messages to display. Although** $high_message **is actually out of date with regard to the true high message number, it is important to see that the user's last read message is in sync with the** $high_message **number of messages that have been displayed to the user.**

N O T E

GetHighMessageNumber Subroutine

The GetHighMessageNumber routine reads the current chat room directory and returns the highest message number found. It uses $last_file and @files as locally declared variables to do this processing.

```
sub GetHighMessageNumber {
local($last_file, @files);
```

First, $chat_room_dir is opened and all the files are read. The grep command is used to filter in only files that have **msg** in the filename. In addition, the messages are sorted.

```
opendir(CHATDIR, "$chat_room_dir");
@files = sort(grep(/msg/, readdir(CHATDIR)));
closedir(CHATDIR);
```

If the number of files in the array is greater than zero, the highest message number in the array is placed in $last_file. If there are no files with **msg** in the chat room directory, $last_file is set to zero. Note that the filenames are all six digits long and use leading zeros to pad the number.

```
if (@files > 0) {
    $last_file = $files[@files - 1];
} else {
    $last_file = "0000000";
}
```

The substr command is used to return the first six characters of the filename. Because the filenames contain six-digit numbers, this arrangement effectively returns just the numeric portion of the message filename.

```
substr($last_file,0,6);

} # End of GetHighMessageNumber
```

THE MAKESESSIONFILE SUBROUTINE

The `MakeSessionFile` routine creates the session file that stores the current user information. `GetSessionInfo` later uses this session file to retrieve information about the currently logged on user every time the current session ID is sent to the routine. This routine starts by accepting a list of fields that make up the user information and then returns the newly acquired session ID that is associated with the session file.

```
sub MakeSessionFile {
local(@fields) = @_;
local($session, $session_file);
```

The first thing `MakeSessionFile` does is to call a routine (`RemoveOldSessions`) to remove old session files that are no longer being used. Then a new session ID is generated by generating a random number.

The random number is first seeded in the `srand` function by taking the value of the process ID and current time variable and combining them with the `or` operator (|). This random number, the time, and the process ID are converted to a long hexadecimal number that serves as the new session ID. A hexadecimal number is made up of digits that cover the numbers 0 through 9 and the letters A through F instead of the digits found in the base 10 system, 0 through 9. The session filename consists of the session ID plus a **.dat** extension.

```
&RemoveOldSessions;

srand($$|time);
$session = int(rand(60000));
$session = unpack("H*", pack("Nnn", time, $$, $session));

$session_file = "$session.dat";
```

Next, the session file is opened for creation in the directory specified by the `$chat_session_dir` variable, which has been set in **chat.setup**. The user information fields are joined by the pipe symbol and are written to the file as a single line. Finally, the file is closed and the newly created session code is returned from the subroutine.

```
open (SESSIONFILE, ">$chat_session_dir/$session_file");
print SESSIONFILE join ("\|", @fields);
print SESSIONFILE "\n";

close (SESSIONFILE);

$session;
} # End of MakeSessionFile
```

THE REMOVEOLDSESSIONS SUBROUTINE

The RemoveOldSessions procedure goes into the **$chat_session_dir** directory and removes all files that are older than $chat_session_length. These variables are set up in **chat.setup**. The @files array is used to contain all the filenames in the current directory. $file is a temporary variable used to hold the filename of the current file that the program is checking for age.

The directory is opened using the opendir command, and the files in the directory are read to an array using the readdir command. The output from readdir is passed to Perl's internal grep function to make sure that the special filenames "." and ".." escape the removal process.

```
sub RemoveOldSessions
{
local(@files, $file);

opendir(SESSIONDIR, "$chat_session_dir");
@files = grep(!/^\.\.?$/,readdir(SESSIONDIR));
closedir(SESSIONDIR);
```

The age of each file is then checked using the -M (modification date) operator. This operator returns the age of the file in days. If this age is greater than $chat_session_length, the unlink function is called to delete the file.

```
foreach $file (@files)
    {
```

```
# If it is older than session_length, delete it
        if (-M "$chat_session_dir/$file" >
            $chat_session_length)
                {
                unlink("$chat_session_dir/$file");
                }
        }
} # End of RemoveOldSessions
```

THE REMOVEOLDWHOFILES SUBROUTINE

RemoveOldWhoFiles takes who files in the current chat directory and checks to see whether they are old enough to expire. If they are, they are deleted. @files and $file are declared as local variables that are used throughout the routine processing.

```
sub RemoveOldWhoFiles
{
local(@files, $file);
```

The chat room directory is opened for reading by using the value stored in $chat_room_dir, a global variable that corresponds to the current chat room directory.

```
opendir(CHATDIR, "$chat_room_dir");
```

The filenames are read into the @files array, and the grep function is used to restrict these filenames to those that end in **who**.

```
@files = grep(/who$/,readdir(CHATDIR));
closedir(CHATDIR);
```

The body of the routine goes through each filename in the @files array.

```
foreach $file (@files)
        {
```

If the file in the **$chat_room_dir** directory is older than $chat_who_length, the file is deleted using the unlink command. When all the files have been checked, the subroutine exits.

```
        if (-M "$chat_room_dir/$file" >
            $chat_who_length)
                {
                unlink("$chat_room_dir/$file");
                }
        }
} # End of RemoveOldWhoFiles
```

THE GETCHATROOMINFO SUBROUTINE

GetChatRoomInfo takes the chat room variable name ($chat_room) and
returns the full descriptive name of the chat room as well as the directory
where the chat room messages are stored.

```
sub GetChatRoomInfo {
   local($chat_room) = @_;
```

$chat_room_name, $chat_room_dir, $x, $chat_room_number, and $error are
defined as local variables that will be used later in the subroutine.

```
   local($chat_room_name, $chat_room_dir, $x);
   local($chat_room_number, $error);
```

Initially, $chat_room_number is set to –1. At the end of the routine, the
script will know that the name was not found in the list of chat room
names if $chat_room_number is still –1. $chat_room_number will be set to the
number of the element in the @chat_room_variable array in which the
name of the chat room is defined if it exists.

```
$chat_room_number = -1;
```

The body of the GetChatRoomInfo routine uses a for loop to step through
each element in the @chat_room_variable array.

```
for ($x = 1; $x <= @chat_room_variable; $x++)
        {
```

If the current element is equal to the contents of $chat_room, then
$chat_room_number is set to the number of the current element in the
array and the for loop exits when it encounters the last command.

```
    if ($chat_room_variable[$x - 1] eq $chat_room)
            {
            $chat_room_number = $x - 1;
            last;
            }
    } # End of FOR chat_room_variables
```

Now that the array has been processed, $chat_room_number should no longer be –1. If it is not –1, then $chat_room_name and $chat_room_dir are assigned their respective values based on the corresponding elements in the @chat_rooms and @chat_room_directories arrays.

```
if ($chat_room_number > -1) {
    $chat_room_name = $chat_rooms[$chat_room_number];
    $chat_room_dir = $chat_room_directories[$chat_room_number];
```

If $chat_room_number is still –1, then $chat_room_name and $chat_room_dir are cleared. To generate a better error message, $chat_room is set to "None Given" if $chat_room is an empty string. $error is set to a message telling the user that the $chat_room was not available Then PrintChatError sends the error message to the user, and the program exits with the die command.

```
} else {
    $chat_room_name="";
    $chat_room_dir = "";
    $chat_room = "None Given" if ($chat_room eq "");
    $error =
        "<strong>Chat Room: '$chat_room' Not
        Found</strong>";
    &PrintChatError($error);
    die;
}
```

If the routine successfully found that chat room information, it returns it as an array of two elements: $chat_room_name and $chat_room_dir.

```
($chat_room_name, $chat_room_dir);

} # end of GetChatRoomInfo
```

The PruneOldMessages Subroutine

The `PruneOldMessages` subroutine is responsible for removing old messages in a chat room directory.

```
sub PruneOldMessages {
```

`$chat_room_dir` is the only parameter that is sent to `PruneOldMessages`. It is declared local to `PruneOldMessages`. However, the global variables `$prune_how_many_days` and `$prune_how_many_sequences` affect how this routine deletes messages. These variables are defined in the setup file. `$x`, `@files`, and `$prunefile` are declared as local variables that will be used at various points during this subroutine.

```
    local($chat_room_dir) = @_;
    local($x, @files);
    local($prunefile);
```

The first major part of the routine reads all the filenames in the supplied chat room directory. The routine opens the directory and reads every filename that has a **msg** extension. These message filenames are sorted into the `@files` array.

```
opendir(CHATDIR, "$chat_room_dir");
    @files = sort(grep(/msg/, readdir(CHATDIR)));
    closedir(CHATDIR);
```

The routine then goes through each of the files in the `@files` array.

```
    for ($x = @files; $x >= 1; $x-) {
```

`$prunefile` is set to the full path and filename of the file that is currently being checked for age. The `-M` parameter is used to check the last modification date in days. If it is greater than `$prune_how_many_days` and if `$prune_how_many_days` is greater than zero, the file is deleted and the name is removed from the `@files` array.

```
$prunefile = "$chat_room_dir/$files[$x - 1]";
# First we check the age in days
if ((-M "$prunefile" > $prune_how_many_days) &&
    ($prune_how_many_days > 0)) {
    unlink("$prunefile");
    &RemoveElement(*files, $x - 1);
    next;
}
```

$x is the current number of the element that we are processing in the @files array. If $x is less than or equal to the total number of elements in the array minus the maximum number of sequences to keep around ($prune_how_many_sequences) and $prune_how-many_sequences is not zero, then the file is deleted and the corresponding element is removed from the @files array.

```
    if (
        ($x <= (@files - $prune_how_many_sequences))
        && ($prune_how_many_sequences != 0)) {
        unlink("$prunefile");
        &RemoveElement(*files, $x - 1);
        next;
    }
    } # End of for all files
} # End of PruneOldMessages
```

THE REMOVEELEMENT SUBROUTINE

The RemoveElement subroutine is simple. It takes a reference to an array and the number of the element to delete from the array and uses Perl's splice function to remove the element. Finally, the routine returns the resulting array.

```
sub RemoveElement
{
local(*file_list, $number) = @_;

if ($number > @file_list)
    {
    die "Number was higher than " .
        "number of elements in file list";
    }
```

```
splice(@file_list,$number,1);
@file_list;
} # End of RemoveElement
```

THE HTMLFILTER SUBROUTINE

HtmlFilter is a function that takes a string and strips out all the HTML code in it depending on how the global variables $no_html_images and $no_html have been set.

```
sub HtmlFilter
{
```

$filter is a local variable that is assigned the string of characters that may contain HTML code to be filtered out.

```
local($filter) = @_;
```

If $no_html_images is on, then all HTML tags that contain "IMG SRC" have the brackets (<>) transformed into "&LT" and "&GT" tags, respectively. The HTML tags "&LT" and "&GT" are used to print "less than" and "greater than" symbols in the place of the brackets for the HTML tags.

```
if ($no_html_images eq "on")
{
    $filter =~ s/<(IMG\s*SRC.*)>/&LT;$1&GT;/ig;
} # End of parsing out no images
```

If $no_html is on, all HTML tags have their brackets (<>) transformed into "&LT" and "&GT."

```
if ($no_html eq "on")
{
    $filter =~ s/<([^>]+)>/\&LT;$1&GT;/ig;
} # End of No html
```

Finally, the subroutine returns the filtered text.

```
$filter;

} # End of HTML Filter
```

Chat-html.pl

Chat-html.pl contains the procedures that print the various HTML screens for **chat.cgi**. If you wish to modify the user interface or look-and-feel of the program, you will most likely find the target routine in this file.

THE PRINTCHATENTRANCE SUBROUTINE

`PrintChatEntrance` prints the original HTML form that logs the user into a chat room. It takes two parameters: `$setup` and `$chat_error`. If an error occurs in processing the user's logon information, the nature of the error is placed in `$chat_error`, and `PrintChatEntrance` is called again to make the user enter the correct information. `$setup` is passed so that the HTML form can pass a hidden input field with the alternative setup file-name.

```
sub PrintChatEntrance {
local($setup,$chat_error) = @_;
```

`$chat_room_options` is declared as a local variable. It contains the list of descriptive names for all the chat rooms the user can enter.

```
local ($chat_room_options);
```

`$setup` is set to nothing if it is already set to the default setup file prefix, "chat."

```
$setup = "" if ($setup eq "chat");
```

`$chat_room_options` is built up as a string of all the HTML <OPTION> tags that go along with each chat room name.

```
$chat_room_options = "";
```

```
for (0..@chat_rooms - 1) {
$chat_room_options .=
  "<OPTION VALUE=$chat_room_variable[$_]>" .
  "$chat_rooms[$_]\n";
}

if ($chat_room_options eq "") {
    $chat_room_options =
        "<OPTION>Chat Room Not Set Up\n";
}
```

Finally, the main HTML form is printed using the HERE DOCUMEN" method. The $setup and $chat_room_options variables are included in the output. The output of this HTML code is shown back in Figure 26.5.

```
print <<__END_OF_ENTRANCE__;
<HTML>
<HEAD>
<TITLE>Chat Page</TITLE>
</HEAD>
<BODY>
<H1>Welcome To The Chat Page</H1>
<H2>$chat_error</H2>
<FORM METHOD=POST ACTION=chat.cgi>
<INPUT TYPE=HIDDEN NAME=setup VALUE=$setup>
<HR>
<STRONG>Enter Information Below:</STRONG><p>


<TABLE BORDER=1>
<TR>
<TD ALIGHT=RIGHT>User Name:</TD>
<TD><INPUT NAME=chat_username></TD>
</TR>
<TR>
<TD ALIGHT=RIGHT>Your Email Address(*):</TD>
<TD><INPUT NAME=chat_email></TD>
</TR>
<TR>
<TD ALIGHT=RIGHT>Your Home Page (*):</TD>
<TD><INPUT NAME=chat_http></TD>
</TR>
<TR>
<TD ALIGHT=RIGHT>How Many Old Messages To Display:</TD>
<TD><INPUT NAME=how_many_old VALUE="10"></TD>
</TR>
```

```
<TR>
<TD ALIGHT=RIGHT>Automatic Refresh Rate (Seconds):</TD>
<TD><INPUT NAME=refresh_rate VALUE="0"></TD>
</TR>
<TR>
<TD ALIGHT=RIGHT>Use Frames?:</TD>
<TD><INPUT TYPE=checkbox NAME=frames></TD>
</TR>
<TR>
<TD ALIGHT=RIGHT>Chat Room</TD>
<TD><SELECT NAME=chat_room>
$chat_room_options
</SELECT>
</TD>
</TR>
</TABLE>
<P>
<INPUT TYPE=SUBMIT NAME=enter_chat
VALUE="Enter The Chat Room">


<P>
<STRONG>Special Notes:</STRONG><P>
(*) Indicates Optional Information<P>
Choose <STRONG>how many old messages</STRONG> to display if you want
to display some older messages along with the new ones whenever you
refresh the chat message list.
<P>
Additionally, if you use Netscape 2.0 or another browser that supports
the HTML <STRONG>Refresh</STRONG> tag, then you can state the number
of seconds you want to pass before the chat message list is automati-
cally refreshed for you. This lets you display new messages automati-
cally.
<P>
If you are using Netscape 2.0 or another browser that supports
<STRONG>Frames</STRONG>, it is highly suggested that you turn frames
ON. This allows the messages to be displayed in one frame, while you
submit your own chat messages in another one on the same screen.


  <HR>
</FORM>
</BODY>
</HTML>
__END_OF_ENTRANCE__
} # end of PrintChatEntrance
```

The PrintChatScreen Subroutine

The `PrintChatScreen` routine is the heart of the chat program's HTML output. All the chat messages and message submission forms are printed in this subroutine. In addition, the routine also detects whether the user has chosen to use frames rather than one Web browser screen to display the messages and submission form.

`PrintChatScreen` accepts a variety of parameters. `$chat_buffer` contains the HTML code for the messages the user will see along with an occupants list if the user requested it. `$refresh_rate` is set if the user has chosen to use the META refresh tag to make the HTML page reload after a predetermined number of seconds. `$session` is the current session ID that **chat.cgi** uses to keep track of the user from screen to screen. `$chat_room` is the current chat room name. `$setup` is the alternative setup file name for **chat.cgi**.

`$frames`, `$fmsgs`, and `$fsubmit` are all related to processing frames. If `$frames` is on, `PrintChatScreen` is printing with frames. If `$fmsgs` is on, the script is currently printing the messages frame. If `$fsubmit` is on, the script is printing the frame with the message submission form. If neither `$fsubmit` nor `$fmsgs` is on and if `$frames` is on, the main frame HTML document that points to a message and a submission form frame is printed. `$frames` should be on only if the main frame HTML document is being sent to the user's Web browser.

```
sub PrintChatScreen {
local($chat_buffer,
    $refresh_rate, $session,
    $chat_room, $setup,
    $frames, $fmsgs, $fsubmit) = @_;
```

Several other variables are declared local to the subroutine. `$chat_message_header` will contain HTML code that will serve as a header for the chat messages if they are currently being printed. `$chat_refresh` will contain the HTML META refresh tag if `$refresh_rate` has been set to a value greater than zero. `$more_url` and `$more_hidden` will be used to keep tabs on form variables, such as the name of the alternative setup file and the session ID, that must be passed from chat screen to chat screen.

```
local($chat_message_header, $more_url,
      $more_hidden, $chat_refresh);
```

If $setup is the prefix "chat" for the default setup file, **chat.setup**, the value of $setup is cleared. There is no need to pass unnecessary information about the default setup file from screen to screen.

```
$setup = "" if ($setup eq "chat");
```

As mentioned previously, $more_url and $more_hidden contain extra fields of information that is passed from chat screen to chat screen. $more_hidden formats these fields as hidden input fields on the HTML forms. $more_url is used to extend the URL that is used to call the **chat.cgi** script using the META refresh tag so that the URL includes the variables listed in $more_hidden.

```
$more_url = "";
$more_hidden = "";
if ($setup ne "") {
    $more_url = "&setup=$setup";
    $more_hidden = "<INPUT TYPE=HIDDEN NAME=setup " .
                   "VALUE=$setup>";
}
$more_url = "session=$session" .
                "&chat_room=$chat_room" .
            $more_url;
```

If $refresh_rate is a positive number, a META tag is generated to make the Web browser automatically reload the page after $refresh_rate seconds. The URL that is called has $more_url added to it so that certain variables, such as the session ID, are passed from script to script and hence from screen to screen.

```
if ($refresh_rate > 0) {
    $chat_refresh =
      qq!<META HTTP-EQUIV="Refresh" ! .
      qq!CONTENT="$refresh_rate; ! .
```

```
        qq!URL=chat.cgi?$more_url!;
```

In addition to `$more_url`, if `$frames` is currently on and if the messages frame is printing, then the META refresh tag must have `"$fmsgs=on"` added to the list of variables being sent.

```
    if ($frames ne "on" && $fmsgs eq "on") {
        $chat_refresh .= "&fmsgs=on";
    }
    $chat_refresh .= qq!">!;
} else {
    $chat_refresh = "";
}
```

The Perl qq **command is used in several places here to change the default string delimiter from double quotes (") to an exclamation point (!). This technique is explained in more detail in Appendix A.**

NOTE

If `$fsubmit` is on and if the main `$frames` HTML document is not being printed, then `$chat_refresh` is cleared.

```
if ($frames ne "on" && $fsubmit eq "on") {
    $chat_refresh = "";
}
```

If `$frames` is on, the main HTML frame document is printed to the user's Web browser using the HERE DOCUMENT method. This document sets up the two frames and points to the **chat.cgi** script for printing the messages in one frame (`fmsgs=on`) and the submission form in another one (`fsubmit=on`).

```
if ($frames eq "on") {
    print <<__END_OF_MAIN_FRAME__;
<HTML>
<HEAD>
<TITLE>$chat_room_name</TITLE>
</HEAD>
<FRAMESET ROWS="*,210">
   <FRAME NAME="_fmsgs" SRC=chat.cgi?fmsgs=on&$more_url>
```

```
   <FRAME NAME="_fsubmit" SRC=chat.cgi?fsubmit=on&$more_url>
</FRAMESET>
</HTML>
__END_OF_MAIN_FRAME__
}
```

If the main frame document is not being printed, then the standard
HTML header is output using the "here document" method.

```
if ($frames ne "on") {
print <<__END_OF_HTML_HEADER__;
<HTML>
$chat_refresh
<HEAD>
<TITLE>$chat_room_name</TITLE>
</HEAD>
<BODY>
__END_OF_HTML_HEADER__
}
```

If $fsubmit is on, the message submission frame is being printed. This
means that the <FORM> tag should target the "_fmsgs" (message list) frame
whenever information is submitted from the message submission form to
the chat script. The target is set to the messages frame instead of the message submission frame; when a new message is submitted or another button, such as **View Occupants**, is pressed, we want the messages frame—
and not the message submission frame—to be updated with the new messages.

```
if ($fsubmit eq "on") {
$form_header = <<__END_FORM_HDR__;
<FORM METHOD=POST ACTION=chat.cgi TARGET="_fmsgs">
__END_FORM_HDR__
```

If the submission frame is not being printed, a normal form header is
derived that has no specific frame target.

```
} else {
$form_header = <<__END_FORM_HDR__;
<FORM METHOD=POST ACTION=chat.cgi>
__END_FORM_HDR__
}
```

Additionally, if the submission frame is being printed, the form header must include a hidden tag telling the script that it must refresh the messages frame (fmsgs=on).

```
if ($fsubmit eq "on") {
    $form_header .= qq!<INPUT TYPE=HIDDEN NAME=fmsgs! .
                    qq! VALUE=on>!;
}
```

If the messages frame is being printed, no form header should be generated.

```
if ($fmsgs eq "on") {
    $form_header = "";
}
```

By default, there is no chat message header. But if we are printing the message frame, we want a small header to print, so the $chat_message_header variable has a header assigned to it.

```
$chat_message_header = "";
if ($fmsgs ne "on") {
    $chat_message_header = "<H2>Chat Messages:</H2>";
}
```

If the message frame is being printed or if frames are not activated, a general chat screen header is printed using the HERE DOCUMENT method.

```
if (($frames ne "on" &&
     $fsubmit ne "on") ||
    $fmsgs eq "on") {
    print <<__END_OF_CHAT_HEADER__;
<H1>Welcome To $chat_room_name Chat</H1>
__END_OF_CHAT_HEADER__
}
```

If the message submission frame is being printed or if frames are not activated, then the submission form is printed to the user's Web browser.

```
if ($fsubmit eq "on" ||
       ($frames ne "on" && $fmsgs ne "on")) {
    print <<__END_OF_CHAT_SUBMIT__;
```

```
$form_header

<INPUT TYPE=HIDDEN NAME=session VALUE=$session>
<INPUT TYPE=HIDDEN NAME=chat_room VALUE=$chat_room>
$more_hidden
<STRONG>Enter Chat Message Below:</STRONG>
<BR>
<TEXTAREA NAME=chat_message
ROWS=3 COLS=40 WRAP=physical></TEXTAREA>
<BR>
Which User To Send To:
<INPUT TYPE=TEXT NAME=chat_to_user
VALUE="ALL">
<BR>
<INPUT TYPE=SUBMIT NAME=submit_message
VALUE="Send Message">
<INPUT TYPE=SUBMIT NAME=refresh_chat
VALUE="New Messages">
<INPUT TYPE=SUBMIT NAME=logoff
VALUE="Log Off">
<INPUT TYPE=SUBMIT NAME=occupants
VALUE="View Occupants">
<INPUT TYPE=RESET
VALUE="Clear Form">
</FORM>
__END_OF_CHAT_SUBMIT__
```

An extra HTML <HR> tag is printed to separate the submission form from the message list if frames are not used and if the submission form has just been output to the user's Web browser.

```
if ($fsubmit ne "on") {
    print "<HR>\n";
}
}
```

If the messages frame is being output or the frames feature is not being used, then the chat messages are printed ($chat_buffer) along with the chat message list header ($chat_message_header).

```
if (($frames ne "on" &&
     $fsubmit ne "on") ||
     $fmsgs eq "on") {
```

```
    print <<__END_OF_CHAT_MSGS__;
$chat_message_header
$chat_buffer
__END_OF_CHAT_MSGS__
```

Just as with the submission form, an extra <HR> is printed at the end of the message list if the frames feature is not being used.

```
if ($fmsgs ne "on") {
    print "<HR>\n";
}
}
```

Finally, the chat footer is printed and the subroutine ends.

```
    if ($frames ne "on") {
      print <<__END_OF_CHAT_FOOTER__;
</BODY>
</HTML>
__END_OF_CHAT_FOOTER__
    }
} # end of PrintChatScreen
```

THE PRINTCHATERROR SUBROUTINE

PrintChatError prints any errors that have occurred in the **chat.cgi** program. It accepts only an $error parameter. The routine uses the contents of $error to store the nature of the error message. Figure 26.12 shows an example of an error occurring in the chat script.

```
sub PrintChatError {
local($error) = @_;

print <<__END_OF_ERROR__;
<HTML><HEAD>
<TITLE>Problem In Chat Occurred</TITLE>
</HEAD>
<BODY>
<h1>Problem In Chat Occurred</h1>
<HR>
<blockquote>
$error
```

```
</blockquote>
<HR>
</BODY></HTML>
__END_OF_ERROR__
} # End of PrintChatError
```

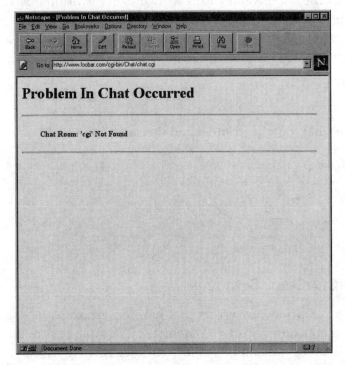

Figure 26.12 Sample output for the PrintChatError subroutine.

APPENDIX A

CGI Programming Techniques in Perl

OVERVIEW

Perl (Practical Extraction and Report Language) is not a CGI-specific programming language. In fact, it is a powerful language with many applications far beyond the needs of CGI. Thus, as a CGI programmer, your mastery of Perl need only extend initially to a small subset of the Perl universe.

In this appendix, we will try to identify the most commonly appearing Perl functions used with the CGI applications in this book to give the beginner a quick and dirty, but by no means all-inclusive, introduction to Perl. If you are a beginner to Perl as well as to CGI, this appendix should give you the very basic foundation which you will need in order to understand the scripts in this book. However, intermediate and advanced readers should only "selectively" browse this appendix as needed. Most of the information here should already be familiar to you.

If you would like more than a cheat-sheet, we strongly recommend that you go out and buy *Learning Perl* by Randall Schwartz and *Programming Perl* by Randall Schwartz and Larry Wall which are published by O' Reilly and Associates, Inc. Both of these books outline Perl completely and, as such, are invaluable resources for the CGI programmer.

In the meantime, let this appendix be your guide.

DISCUSSION

Sending text to the Web browser

Every CGI application must output information. For example, both the HTTP header and the HTML code necessary to generate whatever graphical user interface (GUI) the client will be using to navigate must be sent to the Web browser.

USING THE PRINT FUNCTION

The most basic method for sending text to the Web browser is the "print" function in Perl. The print function uses the following syntax:

```
print "[string to print]";
```

By default, the print function outputs data to standard output "<STD-OUT>" which in the case of a CGI application, is the Web browser. Thus, whatever you tell Perl to print will be sent to the Web browser to be displayed.

For example, the following line sends the phrase, "Hello Universe" to the Web browser:

```
print "Hello Universe";
```

Of course, in order to comply with HTTP protocol, you must first send the HTTP header when communicating with a browser using the following syntax:

print "Content-type: text/html\n\n";

However, print does have some limitations. For example, the print function is limited in its ability to handle Perl special characters within an output string. For example, suppose we want to print the HTML code:

```
<A HREF = "mailto:selena@foobar.com">selena@foobar.com</A>
```

You might extrapolate from the syntax above, that you would use the following Perl code to display the hyperlink:

```
print "<A HREF = "mailto:selena@foobar.com">selena@foobar.com</A>";
```

Unfortunately, this would yield a syntax error. Additionally, because this is a very common line of HTML, it is a common source of Perl CGI customization errors. The problem lies in the incorporation of the at sign (@) and double-quote (") characters within the code.

As it so happens, these characters are "special" Perl characters. In other words, they each have special meaning to Perl and, when displaying them, you must take precautions so that Perl understands what you are asking for. For example, consider the double quote marks in the "mailto" hyperlink. How would Perl know that the double quote marks in the "mailto" hyperlink are supposed to be part of the string to be printed and not actually the end of the string to be printed? Recall that we use the double quote marks to delineate the beginning and the ending of a text string to be printed. Similarly, the at sign (@) is used by Perl to name list arrays.

Many other "special" characters exist and are discussed in other Perl references.

One solution to this problem is to escape the Perl special characters with a backslash (\). The backslash character tells Perl that whatever character follows should be considered a part of the string and not a special character. Thus, the correct syntax for the mailto hyperlink would be

```
print "<A HREF =
\"mailto:selena\@foobar.com\">selena\@foobar.com</A>";
```

USING "HERE DOCUMENTS"

Unfortunately, much of what your CGI applications will be sending to the Web browser will include the double-quote mark. It becomes tedious, especially for long blocks of HTML code, to make print statements for every line of HTML and to escape every occurrence of a double-quote with a backslash. Consider the following table definition:

```
print "<TABLE BORDER = \"1\" CELLPADDING = \"2\"
       CELLSPACING = \"2\">";
print "<TR>";
print "<TD ALIGN = \"center\">Email</TD>";
print "<TD ALIGN = \"center\">
   <A HREF = \"mailto:selena\@foobar.com\">
   selena\@foobar.com</A></TD>";
print "</TR>";
print "</TABLE>";
```

If any one of those backslashes are missing, the whole script breaks down. And this is a very small block of code!

One solution to the sending of large blocks of HTML code which incorporate the double-quote is to use the "here document" method of printing. The "here document" method tells Perl to print everything within a certain block of code within a set of boundaries. The "here document" uses the generic format:

```
print <<[TEXT_BOUNDARY_MARKER];
[Text to be printed]
[TEXT_BOUNDARY_MARKER]
```

For example, this code will print out the basic HTML header:

```
print <<end_of_html_header;
<HTML>
<HEAD>
<TITLE>My Title</TITLE>
</HEAD>
<BODY>
end_of_html_header
```

In short, the "here document" method of printing tells the Perl interpreter to print out everything it sees (print <<) from the print line until it finds the text boundary marker specified in the print line (end_of_html_header). The text boundary marker can be anything you like of course, but it is useful to make the flag descriptive.

Further, the ending flag must be "exactly" the same as the flag definition. Thus, the following code will fail because the final flag is not indented correctly:

```
print <<"  end_of_header";
  <HTML><HEAD><TITLE>$title</TITLE></HEAD><BODY>
  end_of_header
```

The final "end_of_header" tag should have been indented four spaces, but it was only indented two.

 Though the "here document" method of printing does avoid having to escape backslashes within the block to print, the at sign (@) and other special Perl characters still need escaping.

N O T E

USING QQ

"qq" is another Perl trick which helps a programmer solve the double-quote problem by allowing her to change the double-quote delimiter in a print statement.

Normally, as we said, double-quotes (") are used to delimit the characters in a print statement. However, by replacing the first quote with two q's followed by another character, that final character becomes the new print statement delimiter. Thus, by using "qq!", we tell Perl to use the bang (!) character to delimit the string instead of the double quotes.

743

For example, without using qq, a print statement that outputs, 'She said, "hi"'. would be written as

```
print "She said, \"hi\".";
```

But with the qq making bang (!) the new delimiter, the same statement can be written as

```
print qq!She said, "hi"!;
```

Why would we do this? Readability. If the print statement was surrounded with the normal double-quotes, then every double-quote would have to be escaped with a backslash whenever it was used within a string. The backslashes clutter the readability of the string. Thus, we choose a different character to delimit the string in the print statement so that we do not have to escape the double-quotes with backslashes.

USING THE PRINTF AND SPRINTF FUNCTIONS

The Perl printf function is much like the printf function in C and awk in that it takes a string to be formatted and a list of format arguments, applies the formatting to the string, and then typically prints the formatted string to standard output, which in our case, is the Web browser.

The printf syntax uses a double quoted string which includes special format markers followed by a comma-delimited list of arguments to be applied to those markers. The format markers are typically in the form of a percent sign followed by a control character.

For example, the generic format of printf might look like the following code:

```
printf ("[some text] %[format] [other text]", [argument to be
formatted]);
```

In usage, we might use the %s formatting argument specifying a string and the %d formatting argument specifying a digit using the following syntax:

```
$name = "Selena Sol";
$age = 27;
printf ("My name is %s and my age is %d.\n", $name, $age);
```

The code above would produce the following output in the Web browser window:

```
My name is Selena Sol and my age is 27.
```

In reality, the `printf` function is rarely used in Perl CGI since, unlike C which almost demands the use of `printf`, Perl has much easier ways of printing. However, the `printf` routines are essential for another, more useful (to CGI developers) function, `sprintf`.

Unlike `printf`, `sprintf` takes the formatted output and assigns it to a variable rather than outputting it to standard output (<STDOUT>), using the following generic syntax:

```
$variable_name = sprintf ("[some text] %[format] [other text]",
[string to be formatted]);
```

A good example of using `sprintf` comes from Chapter Seventeen, the HTML shopping cart script. In this script, we need to format subtotals and grand totals to two decimal places so that prices come out to numbers like "$99.00" or "$98.99" rather than "99" or "98.99876453782". Below is a snippet of code from that chapter which uses `sprintf` to format the price string to two decimal places.

```
$option_grand_total = sprintf ("%.2f\n",
$unformatted_option_grand_total);
```

In this example, the variable, `$unformatted_option_grand_total` is formatted using the "%.2f" argument which formats (%) the string to two decimal places (.2f).

There are a multitude of formatting arguments besides "%s", "%d" and "%f", however. Table A-1 lists several useful ones.

Table A.1 *printf and sprintf Formats*

FORMAT CHARACTER	DESCRIPTION
c	Character
s	String
d	Decimal Number
x	Hexadecimal Number
o	Octal Number
f	Floating Point Number

FORMATTING THE OUTPUT

Finally, we close this section with a note about formatting the outputs of your CGI applications so that your HTML is legible when "viewing the source." When reading an HTML document, a Web browser really does not care how the code is formatted. Since it ignores carriage return and linefeed characters anyway, a Web browser would be just as happy receiving one huge line of HTML code all strung together as it would receiving a neatly formatted and human-legible HTML document. However, human readers (especially you when debugging) need to have HTML code in a format which helps you read lines and quickly analyze the output generated by your scripts.

Thus, it is very useful when printing with Perl, to use the newline character "\n". This character will introduce a new line into your output much like a <BR> does in HTML so that the text sent out by your CGI application will be formatted for easy reading.

For example, the following HTML could be displayed in two ways. First, you could type:

```
print "<TABLE>";
print "<TR>";
print "<TD>First Name</TD>";
print "<TD>Selena</TD>";
```

```
print "</TR><TR>";
print "<TD>Last Name</TD>";
print "<TD>Sol</TD>";
print "</TR></TABLE>";
```

This might seem pretty legible as Perl code, but you would receive the following HTML source code, compressed into one line:

```
<TABLE><TR><TD>First Name</TD><TD>Selena</TD></TR><TR><TD>Last
Name</TD><TD>Sol</TD></TR></TABLE>
```

This code would be difficult to read, especially if an entire HTML page was formatted that way. On the other hand, you could use the following code:

```
print "<TABLE>\n";
print "<TR>\n";
print "<TD>First Name</TD>\n";
print "<TD>Selena</TD>\n";
print "</TR>\n<TR>\n";
print "<TD>Last Name</TD>\n";
print "<TD>Sol</TD>\n";
print "</TR>\n</TABLE>";
```

This time, when viewing the source, you would see the following HTML code neatly formatted:

```
<TABLE>
<TR>
<TD>First Name</TD>
<TD>Selena</TD>
</TR>
<TR>
<TD>Last Name</TD>
<TD>Sol</TD>
</TR>
</TABLE>
```

There are many other formatting constructs that can be included within a double-quote print or variable assignment, of course. Table A-2 outlines several important ones.

Table A.2 *Formatting Constructs*

Construct	Description
\n	Newline
\r	Return
\t	Tab
\b	Backspace
\v	Vertical Tab
\e	Escape
\\	Backslash
\"	Double Quote
\l	Make next character lowercase
\L	Lowercase every character until \E
\u	Uppercase the next character
\U	Uppercase every character until \E
\E	Terminate \L or \U

It is not essential for you to keep formatting in mind, but it will make debugging much easier if it involves investigating the HTML code. Conscientious formatting is also considered good style in general.

NOTE Another benefit of using the "here document" method is that since Perl prints out the text within the marker field exactly as you type it, you need not use the \n for newlines, because they are already incorporated.

Scalar variables, list arrays, and associative arrays

WHAT IS A SCALAR VARIABLE?

You can think of a variable as a "place holder" or a "name" that represents one or more values. The generic syntax for defining scalar variables (also known as variables for short) is as follows:

```
$variable_name = value;
```

Thus, for example, we might assign the value of twenty-seven to the scalar variable named "age" with the syntax:

```
$age = 27;
```

The dollar sign ($) is used to let Perl know that we are talking about a scalar variable. From then on, unless we change the value of $age, the script will translate it to twenty-seven.

So if we then say:

```
print "$age\n";
```

Perl will send the value "27" to standard output, which in our case, will be the Web browser.

If we are assigning a word or a series of words to a scalar variable rather than just a number, we must mark the boundary of the value with single or double quotes so that Perl will know "exactly" what should be assigned to the scalar variable.

We use single quotes to mark the boundary of a plain text string and we use double quotes to mark the boundary of a text string which can include scalar variables to be "interpolated". For example, we might have the following lines:

```
$age = 27;
$first_name = 'Selena';
$last_name = 'Sol';
$sentence = "$first_name $last_name is $age";
print "$sentence\n";
```

The routine would print the following line to standard output:

```
Selena Sol is 27
```

Notice that the scalar variable $sentence is assigned the actual values of $first_name and $last_name. This is because they were "interpolated" since we included them within double-quotes in the definition of $sentence.

There is no interpolation inside single quotes. Thus, if we had defined $sentence using single quotes as follows:

```
$sentence = '$first_name $last_name is $age';
```

Perl would print the following to standard output:

```
$first_name $last_name is $age
```

USING SCALAR VARIABLES

The benefit of substituting a scalar variable name for a value is that we can then manipulate its value. For example, you can "auto-increment" a scalar variable using the "++" operator:

```
$number = 1;
print "$number\n";
$number++;
print "$number\n";
```

Perl would send the following to standard output

```
1
2
```

You can also perform arithmetic such as:

```
$item_subtotal = $item_price * $quantity;
$shipping_price = 39.99 * $quantity;
$grand_total = $item_subtotal + $shipping_price;
```

Scalar variables are the meat and potatoes of CGI. After all, translating between the client and the Web server is essentially the formatting and the reformatting of variables. Be prepared to see them used a lot.

USING THE "." OPERATOR

Another cool Perl trick is the use of the "." operator which "appends" a value to an already existing scalar variable. Thus, the following code would print out "Selena Sol":

```
$name = "Selena" . " Sol";
print "$name";
```

An alternative shorthand for appending to scalar variables is using the ".=" operator. for example, the following code does the same thing as the code above.

```
$name = "Selena";
$name .= " Sol";
print "$name\n";
```

CROPPING SCALAR VARIABLES WITH THE CHOP FUNCTION

Sometimes, you do not want the entire value that has been assigned to a scalar variable. For example, it is often the case that the lines you retrieve from a data file will incorporate a newline character at the end of the line. In this book, data files often take advantage of the newline character as a "database row delimiter". That is, every line in a database file is a new database item. For example, here is a snippet from an address book data file:

```
Sol|Selena|sol@foobar.com|456-7890
Birznieks|Gunther|gunther@foobar.com|456-7899
```

When the script reads each line, it also reads in the newline information. Thus, the first line is actually represented as:

```
Sol|Selena|sol@foobar.com|456-7890\n
```

The final "\n" is a new line. Since we do not actually want the "\n" character included with the last database field, we use the chop function. The chop function chops off the very last character of a scalar variable using the syntax:

```
chop ($variable_name);
```

Thus, we would take off the final newline character as follows:

```
$database_row = "Sol|Selena|sol@foobar.com|456-7890\n";
chop ($database_row);
```

FINDING THE LENGTH OF A SCALAR VARIABLE WITH THE LENGTH FUNCTION

Finding the length of a scalar variable is incredibly easy using the length function. The syntax of length is as follows:

```
length ([$variable_name]);
```

Thus, if the scalar variable $name equals "Selena", then the scalar variable $length_of_name will be assigned the value of six in the following line:

```
$length_of_name = length ($name);
```

MANIPULATING SUBSTRINGS WITH THE SUBSTR FUNCTION

Sometimes, you want to work with just part of a string that has been assigned. In WebBBS, the script uses the "substr" technique to get the message id number portion from the entire message filename. The substr function follows the syntax:

```
$substring = substr([string you want to extract from],
        [beginning point of extraction],
        [length of the extracted value]);
```

For instance, to assign "Sol" to the scalar variable $last_name you would use the following code:

```
$name = "Selena Sol";
$last_name = substr ($name, 7, 3);
```

The substr function takes the scalar variable $name, and extracts three characters beginning with the seventh.

Warning: as in array indexing, the substr **function counts from zero, not from one. Thus, in the string "Gunther", the letter "t" is actually referenced as "3" not "4".**

NOTE

NOTE

The final number (length of extracted value) is not necessary when you want to grab everything "after" the beginning character. Thus, the following code will do just what the previous did since we are extracting the entire end of the variable $name: `$last_name = substr ($name, 7);`

SCALAR VARIABLE NAMING CONVENTIONS

Finally, you might notice that in these examples, we choose very descriptive names. Rather than saying for example:

```
$x = 27;
$y = "Selena Sol";
```

we say something like the following:

```
$age = 27;
$full_name = "Selena Sol";
```

Though it is not necessary that you make your scalar variable names descriptive (sometimes it can mean a lot more typing), we recommend that you do your best to choose names which will clearly communicate the function of the variable to you and to others a month or a year down the line.

List Arrays

WHAT IS A LIST ARRAY?

List arrays (also known simply as "arrays" for short) take the concept of scalar variables to the next level. Whereas scalar variables associate one value with one variable name, list arrays associate one array name with a "list" of values.

A list array is defined with the following syntax:

```
@array_name = ("element_1", "element_2"..."element_n");
```

For example, consider the following list array definition:

```
@available_colors = ("red", "green", "blue", "brown");
```

NOTE   As you might have guessed, the at sign (@) is used to communicate to Perl that a list array is being named much like the dollar sign ($) is used to denote a scalar variable name.

In this example, the list array `@available_colors` is filled with four color "elements" in the specific order: red, green, blue, brown. It is important to see that the colors are not simply dumped into the list array at random. Each list element is placed in the specific order in which the list array was defined. Thus list arrays are also considered to be "ordered."

USING A LIST ARRAY

The benefit of ordering the elements in a list array is that we can easily grab one value out of the list on demand. To do this, we use Perl's subscripting operator using the format:

```
$array_name[list_element_number]
```

When pulling an element out of a list array, we create a scalar variable with the same name as the array, prefixed with the usual dollar sign which denotes scalar variables.

For example, the first element of the array `@available_colors` is accessed as

```
$available_colors[0].
```

Notice that the first element is accessed with a zero. This is important. List arrays begin counting at zero, not one. Thus, `$available_colors[0]` is a variable place holder for the word "red". Likewise, `$available_colors[1]` equals "green" and `$available_colors[2]` equals "blue".

FIGURING OUT HOW MANY ELEMENT ARE IN AN ARRAY

Fortunately, Perl provides an easy way to determine how many elements are contained in an array. When used as a scalar, the list array name will be equal to the number of elements it contains. Thus, if the list array @available_colors contains the elements: red, green, blue and brown, then the following line would set $number_of_colors equal to four.

```
$number_of_colors = @available_colors;
```

NOTE Be careful when using this value in your logic. The number of elements in an array is a number counting from one. But when accessing an array, you must access starting from zero. Thus, the last element in the array @available_colors **is not** $available_colors [@available_colors] **but rather** $available_colors[@available_colors - 1].

ADDING ELEMENTS TO A LIST ARRAY

Likewise, you can add to or modify the values of an existing array by simply referencing the array by number. For example, to add an element to @available_colors, you might use the following line:

```
$available_colors[4] = "orange";
```

Thus, @available_colors would include the elements: red, green, blue, brown, and orange.

You can also use this method to overwrite an element in a list array. To change a value in @available_colors, you might use the syntax:

```
$available_colors[0] = "yellow";
```

Now, the elements of @available_colors would be: yellow, green, blue, brown, orange.

DELETING AND REPLACING LIST ELEMENTS WITH THE SPLICE FUNCTION

The splice function is used to remove or replace elements in an array and uses the following syntax:

```
splice ([array to modify], [offset], [length],
    [list of new elements]);
```

The array argument is the array to be manipulated. offset is the starting point where elements are to be removed. length is the number of elements from the offset number to be removed. The list argument consists of an ordered list of values to replace the removed elements with. Of course, if the list argument is null, the elements accessed will be removed rather than replaced.

Thus, for example, the following code will modify the @numbers list array to include the elements, ("1", "2", "three", "four", "5").

```
@numbers = ("1", "2", "3", "4", "5");
splice (@numbers, 2, 2, "three", "four");
```

A more common usage of splice is simply to remove list elements by not specifying a replacement list. For example, we might modify @numbers to include only the elements "1", "2" and "5" by using the following code:

```
splice (@numbers, 2, 2);
```

ADVANCED LIST ARRAY MANIPULATION WITH THE PUSH, POP, SHIFT, AND UNSHIFT FUNCTIONS

Of course, once we have created a list array, we can do much more than just access the elements. We can also manipulate the elements in many ways. Throughout this book, list arrays are most often manipulated using the operators push, pop, shift and unshift.

push is used to add a new element on the right hand side of a list array. Thus, the following code would create a list array of ("red", "green", "blue")

```
@colors = ("red", "green");
push (@colors, "blue");
```

In other words, the push operator, adds an element to the end of an existing list.

pop does the exact same thing as push, but in reverse. pop extracts the right side element of a list array using the following syntax:

```
$popped_variable_name = pop (@array_name);
```

Thus, we might pop out the value blue from @colors with the following syntax:

```
$last_color_in_list = pop (@colors);
```

Thus, the @colors array now contains only "red" and "green" and the variable $last_color_in_list is equal to "blue".

unshift does the exact same thing as push, but it performs the addition to the left side of the list array instead of to the right. Thus, we would create the list ("blue", "red", "green") with the following syntax:

```
@colors = ("red", "green");
unshift (@colors, "blue");
```

Similarly, shift works the same as pop, but to the left side of the list array. Thus, we reduce @colors to just "red" and "green" by shifting the first element "blue" with the following syntax:

```
$first_color_in_list = shift(@colors);
```

Thus, @colors again contains only "red" and "green" and $first_color_in_list equals blue.

Though push, pop, shift, and unshift are the most common list array manipulation functions used in this book, there are many others covered in more complete references. Table A.3 Summarizes some of the common array manipulating operators.

Table A.3 *Array Manipulation Operators*

Operator	Description
shift(@array)	Removes the first element in @array
unshift (@array, $element)	Adds $element to the beginning of @array
pop (@array)	Removes the last element of @array
push (@array, $element)	Adds $element to the end of @array
sort (@array)	Sorts the elements in @array
reverse(@array)	Reverses the order of the elements in @array
chop (@array)	chops off the last character of every element in @array
split (/delimiter/, string)	Creates an array by splitting a string
join (delimiter, @array)	Creates a scalar of every element in @array joined by the delimiter.

Associative Arrays

What is an Associative Array?

Associative arrays add the final degree of complexity allowing ordered lists to be associated with other values. Unlike list arrays, associative arrays have index values which are not numbers. You do not reference an associative array as $associative_array_name[0] as you did for the list array. Instead, associative arrays are indexed with arbitrary scalar variables. Consider the following associative array definition:

```
%CLIENT_ARRAY = ('full_name', 'Selena Sol',
        'phone', '213-456-7890',
         'age', '27');
```

In this example, we have defined the associative array %CLIENT_ARRAY to have three sets of associations.

NOTE the percent sign (%) denotes the associative array name just as the dollar sign ($) did for variables and the at sign (@) did for list arrays.

Thus, "full_name" is associated with "Selena Sol" as "age" is associated with "27." This association is discussed in terms of "keys" and "values." Each key is associated with one value. Thus, we say that the key "full_name" is associated with the value "Selena Sol."

ACCESSING AN ASSOCIATIVE ARRAY

If we want to extract a value from the associative array, we reference it with the following syntax:

```
$variable_equal_to_value = $ASSOCIATIVE_ARRAY_NAME{'[key]'};
```

Thus, to pull out the value of the "name" key from %CLIENT_ARRAY, we use the following syntax:

```
$full_name = $CLIENT_ARRAY{'full_name'}
```

The variable $full_name would then be equal to "Selena Sol". Think of it as using a "key" to unlock a "value".

NOTE When accessing an associative array using a scalar variable as a key, you should not surround the key with single quotes because the scalar variable will not be interpolated. For example, the following syntax generates the value for the age key

```
$key_name = "age";
$age = $CLIENT_ARRAY{$key_name};
```

Accessing an associative array is one of the most basic CGI functions and is at the heart of the ReadParse routine in **cgi-lib.pl** which creates an associative array from the incoming form data. By accessing this associative array (usually referred to in this book as `%in` or `%form_data`), your CGI script will be able to determine what it is that the client has asked of it since HTML form variables are formed in terms of administratively-defined NAMES and client-defined VALUES using syntax such as the following:

```
<INPUT TYPE = "text" NAME = "full_name" SIZE = "40">
```

The "key" of the associative array generated by `ReadParse` will be "full_name" and the "value" will be whatever the client typed into the text box.

USING THE KEYS AND VALUES FUNCTIONS

Perl also provides a convenient way to get a list of all the keys or of all the values in an associative array if you are interested in more than just one key/value pair. Keys and values are accessed with the keys and values functions using the following formats:

```
@associative_array_keys = keys (%ASSOCIATIVE_ARRAY_NAME);
```

and

```
@associative_array_values = values (%ASSOCIATIVE_ARRAY_NAME);
```

Thus, the keys and values list of the associative array %CLIENT_ARRAY defined above can be generated with the following syntax:

```
@client_array_keys = keys (%CLIENT_ARRAY);
@client_array_values = values (%CLIENT_ARRAY);
```

In this example `@client_array_keys` would look like ("full_name", "phone", "age") and `@client_array_values` would look like ("Selena Sol", "213-456-7890", "27").

ADDING TO AND DELETING FROM AN ASSOCIATIVE ARRAY

Like list arrays, associative arrays can be internally modified. The most common function, other than defining an associative array, is adding to it. Adding to an associative array simply involves telling Perl which key and value to add using the format:

```
$ARRAY_NAME{'key'} = "value";
```

or, using our example above:

```
$CLIENT_ARRAY{'favorite_candy'} = "Hershey's with Almonds";
```

%CLIENT_ARRAY now includes full_name, phone, age and favorite_candy along with their associated values.

Similarly, you can easily use the delete function to delete a key/value pair in an associative array. The delete function follows the syntax:

```
delete ($ASSOCIATIVE_ARRAY_NAME{'key'});
```

or for our %CLIENT_ARRAY example:

```
delete ($CLIENT_ARRAY{'age'});
```

Thus, %CLIENT_ARRAY would contain only full_name, phone, and favorite_candy.

Manipulating strings

Another important function provided by CGI is the manipulation of strings of data. Whether called upon to display or manipulate the contents of a data file, to reformat some text for Web-display, or simply to use in some logical routine or external program, Perl has a diverse array of string modification functions at its disposal.

EQUALITY OPERATORS

One of the most important string manipulation functions is that of matching or testing of equality. It is an important tool because you can use it as the basis of complex logical comparisons necessary for the intelligence demanded of a CGI application.

For example, most of the applications in this book use one of the most basic methods of pattern matching, the "ne" operator, as the basis of their decision making process using the following logic:

```
if (the user has hit a specific submit button)
 {
 execute a specific routine.
 }
```

Consider this code snippet:

```
if ($display_frontpage_submit_button ne "")
 {
 &display_frontpage;
 }
```

If you are confused about the usage of the "if" test, it is explained in greater detail in the "Control Structures" section later in this appendix.

N O T E

The "ne" operator asks if the value of the variable $display_front-page_submit_button is not equal to an empty string. This logic takes advantage of the fact that the HTTP protocol specifies that if a FORM submit button is pressed, its NAME is set equal to the VALUE specified in the HTML code. For example, the submit button may have been coded using the following HTML:

```
<INPUT TYPE = "submit"
     NAME = "display_frontpage_submit_button"
     VALUE = "Return to the Frontpage">
```

Thus, if the NAME in the associative array has a VALUE, the script knows that the client pushed the associated button. The script determines which routines it should execute by following the logic of these pattern matches.

Similarly, you can test for equality using the "eq" operator. An example of the "eq" operator in use is shown below:

```
if ($name eq "Selena")
 {
 print "Hi, Selena\n";
```

```
}
```

When comparing numbers instead of strings however, Perl uses a second set of operators. For example, to test for equality, you use the double equal (==) operator as follows:

```
if ($number == 11)
 {
 print "You typed in 11\n";
 }
```

Warning: Never use the single equal sign (=) for comparison. Perl interprets the equal sign in terms of assignment rather than comparison. Thus the line:

```
$number = 11;
```

actually assigns the value of eleven to $number rather than comparing $number to eleven.

There are many other types of comparison operators, but they are better researched in more comprehensive texts. However, we do include several important ones in Table A-5

Table A-5 Numeric and String Comparison Operators

NUMERIC OP.	STRING OP.	DESCRIPTION
==	eq	Equal
!=	ne	Not equal
<	lt	Less than
>	gt	Greater than
<=	le	Less than or equal to
>=	ge	Greater than or equal to

REGULAR EXPRESSIONS

Regular expressions are one of the most powerful, and hence, the most complicated tools for matching strings. You can think of a regular expression as a "pattern" which can be used to match against some string. Regular expressions are far more versatile than the simple "eq" and "ne" operators and include a wide variety of modifiers and tricks. Other books have detailed chapters focusing on the use of regular expressions, so we will only touch upon a few common uses of regular expressions found this book.

PATTERN MATCHING WITH //

Perl invokes a powerful tool for pattern matching which gives the program great flexibility in controlling matches. In Perl, a string is matched by placing it between two slashes as follows:

```
/[pattern_to_match]/
```

Thus, /eric/ matches for the string "eric". You may also match according to whole classes of characters using the square brackets ([]). The pattern match will then match against any of the characters in the class. For example, to match for any single even numbered digit, you could use the following match:

```
/[02468]/
```

For classes including an entire range of characters, you may use the dash (-) to represent the list. Thus, the following matches any single lower case letter in the alphabet:

```
/[a-z]/
```

Likewise, you may use the caret (^) character within the square brackets to match every character which is "not" in the class. The following matches any single character which is not a digit.

```
/[^0-9]/
```

MATCHING OPERATORS

Further, the "//" operator can be modified to include complex pattern matching routines. For example, the period (.) matching operator is used to stand for "any" character. Thus, "/eri./" would match any occurrences of "eric" as well as "erik".

Another commonly used matching operator is the asterisk (*). The asterisk matches zero or more occurrences of the character preceding it. Thus, "/e*ric/" matches occurrences of "eeeeeric" as well as "eric".

Table A-6 includes a list of useful matching operators.

Table A-6 Commonly Used Matching Operators

OPERATOR	DESCRIPTION
\n	Newline
\r	Carriage Return
\t	Tab
\D	Any non-digit (same as [^0-9])
\w	A Word Character (same as [0-9a-zA-Z_])
\W	A Non-word character
\s	Any whitespace character (\t, \n, \r, or \f)
\S	A non-whitespace character
*	Zero or more occurrences of the preceding character
+	One or more occurrences of the preceding character
.	Any character
?	Zero or one occurrences of the preceding character

ANCHORS

Regular expressions also take advantage of anchoring patterns which help match the string in relationship to the rest of the line. For example, the "\b" anchor is used to specify a word boundary. That is, "/\beric\b/" matches "eric", but it does not match "generic".

Similarly, the caret (^) anchor will match a string to the beginning of the line. Thus, "/^eric/" will match the following line

```
eric is my name
```

but it will not match

```
my name is eric
```

WARNING The caret (^) can be confusing since it is used as an anchor when included "outside" of the square brackets ([]) but is used as the "not" operator for a class when used "within".

Table A-7 summarizes a few of the most common anchors.

Table A-7 Common anchors

ANCHOR	DESCRIPTION
^	Matches the beginning of the string
$	Matches the end of the string
\b	Matches a word boundary (between \w and \W)
\B	Matches on non-word boundary

STRING MODIFIERS

Finally, pattern matching can be used to modify strings of text. One of the most common methods of modification is substitution. Substitution is performed using the format

```
s/[pattern_to_find]/[pattern_to_replace_with]/
```

Thus, for example, the line:

```
s/eric/selena/
```

would change the line

```
eric is my name
```

to

```
selena is my name
```

The substitution function is modified most commonly with the /i and the /g arguments. The /i argument specifies that matching should be done with case insensitivity and the /g specifies that the match should occur globally for the entire string of text rather than just for the first occurrence.

Thus, the line

```
s/eric/selena/gi
```

would change the line:

```
I am Eric, eric I am
```

to

```
I am selena, selena I am
```

without the /i, you would get

```
I am Eric, selena I am
```

and without /g but with the /i, you would get

```
I am selena, eric I am
```

There are many, many different kinds of matching operators, anchors, and string modifiers. If you want a more detailed explanation we recommend that you find a good reference source on Regular Expressions. Otherwise, the above discussion should explain how we use operators and anchors in this book.

THE =~ OPERATOR

Pattern matching can also be used to manipulate variables. In particular, the scripts in this book take advantage of the "=~" operator in conjunction with the substitution operator using the format

```
$variable_name =~ s/[string_to_remove]/[string_to_add]/gi;
```

For example, if we want to censor every occurrence of the word "Frack" from the client-defined input field "comment", we might use the line:

```
$form_data{'comments'} =~ s/frack/censored/gi;
```

USING THE SPLIT AND JOIN FUNCTIONS

Finally, regular expressions can be used to split a string into separate fields. To do so, we use the "split" function with the format:

```
@split_array = split (/[pattern_to_split_on]/, [string_to_split]);
```

For example, the applications in this book often use the split function to read the fields of database rows. Consider the following code snippet:

```
$database_row = "Selena Sol|213-456-7890|27";
@database_fields = split (/|/, $database_row);
```

Now @database_fields will include the elements "Selena Sol", "213-456-7890" and "27". Each of these fields can then be processed separately if need be.

The reverse operation is performed with the "join" function which uses the following format:

```
$joined_string = join ("[pattern_to_join_on]", [list_to_join]);
```

Thus, we might recreate the original database row using

```
$new_database_row = join ("\|", @database_fields);
```

NOTE

Notice that in the above line, the pipe (I) symbol must be escaped with a backslash (\) because the pipe is a special Perl character.

Control structures

Some of the most powerful tools of Perl programming are control structures. Control structures are used to create the basic logic which drives many of the routines used in CGI applications. These control structures use Boolean logic to imbue your script with the intelligence necessary to manage the diverse needs of the clients with the abilities and requirements of the server.

STATEMENT BLOCKS

All control structures are divided into the control statement (which we will explain below) and the statement block. The statement block is simply a group of commands that are executed together. This block is grouped by enclosing the commands within curly braces ({}). For example, the following is a simple statement block.

```
{
  statement one
  statement two
  statement three
}
```

Perl will execute each statement in a statement block from beginning to end as a group. When, how, or if the script will execute the commands however, is determined by the control statement.

USING THE IF, ELSIF, ELSE AND UNLESS CONTROL STATEMENTS

The most common control statement used throughout the scripts in this book is the "if" test. The if test checks to see if some expression is true, and if so, executes the routines in the statement block. Perl uses a simple binary comparison as a test of truth. If the result of some operation is true, the operation returns a one and the statement block is executed. If the result is false, it returns a zero, and the statement block is not executed. For example, consider the following code:

```
if ($name eq "Selena Sol")
 {
 print "Hello Selena.\n";
 }
```

In this example, Perl checks to see if the scalar variable $name has the value of "Selena Sol". If the patterns match, the matching operation will return true and the script will execute the print statement within the statement block. If Perl discovers that $name is not equal to "Selena Sol" however, the print will not be executed.

NOTE Be careful with your usage of "eq" versus "=". Within an "if" test, if you write $name = "Selena Sol", you will actually be **assigning** "Selena Sol" to the variable $name rather than **comparing** it to the value "Selena Sol". Since this action will be performed successfully, the if test will always test to true and the statement block will always be performed even if $name did not initially equal "Selena Sol".

The if test also provides for alternatives: the "else" and the "elsif" control statements. The elsif alternative adds a second check for truth and the else alternative defines a final course of action for every case of failed if or elsif tests. The following code snippet demonstrates the usage of if, elsif, and else.

```
if ($name eq "Selena Sol")
 {
 print "Hi, Selena.\n";
 }
elsif ($name eq "Gunther Birznieks")
 {
 print "Hi, Gunther\n";
 }
else
 {
 print "Who are you?\n";
 }
```

Obviously, the else need not perform a match since it is a catch-all control statement.

The "unless" control statement works like an inverse "if" control statement. Essentially it says, "execute some statement block unless some condition is true." The unless control statement is exemplified in the code below:

```
unless ($name eq "Selena")
 {
 print "You are NOT Selena!\n";
 }
```

FOREACH

Another very useful control statement is the `foreach` loop. The `foreach` loop iterates through some list and execute a statement block for each iteration. In this book, the `foreach` loop is most commonly used to iterate through a list array. For example, the following code snippet will print out the value of every element in the list array `@names`.

```
foreach $name (@names)
{
print "$name\n";
}
```

WHILE

The `while` loop also performs iteration and is used in this book primarily for reading lines in a file. The `while` loop can be used to read and print out every line of a file with the following syntax:

```
open ([FILE_HANDLE_NAME], "[filename]");
while (<[FILE_HANDLE_NAME]>)
 {
 print "$_";
 }
close ([FILE_HANDLE_NAME]);
```

The script would print out every line in the file "filename" because the "$_", the Perl "default" variable, represents "the current line" in this case.

The process of opening and closing files is covered in the "File Management" section later in this appendix.

N O T E

FOR LOOPS

The `for` loop is another excellent control statement tool. The basic syntax of a `for` loop follows:

```
for ([initial condition]; [test]; [incrementation])
 {
 [action to perform]
 }
```

The "initial condition" defines where the loop should begin. The "test" defines the logic of the loop by letting the script know the conditions which determine the scripts actions. The "incrementation" defines how the script should perform the loop. For example, we might produce a visible countdown with the following `for` loop:

```
for ($number = 10; $number >= 0; $number−)
 {
 print "$number\n";
 }
```

The script would initially assign "10" to the scalar variables $number. It would then test to see if $number was greater than or equal to zero. Since ten is greater than zero, the script would decrement $number by subtracting one from the value of $number.

To decrement, you use $variable_name−. **To increment, you use** $variable_name++.

N O T E

Executing the statement block, the script would then print out the number nine. Then, it would go back through the loop again and again, printing each decremented numbers until $number was less than zero. At that point, the test would fail and the `for` loop would exit.

Using logical operators (&& and ||)

Control statements can also be modified with a variety of logical operators which extend the breadth of the control statement truth test using the following syntax:

```
[control statement] (([first condition])
          [logical operator]
          ([second condition]))
{
[action to be performed]
}
```

For example, the "&&" operator can be translated to "and". In usage, it takes the format used in the following example:

```
if (($first_name eq "Selena") && ($last_name eq "Sol"))
{
print "Hello Selena Sol";
}
```

Translating the logic goes something like this: if the first name is Selena AND the last name is Sol, then print "Hello Selena Sol". Thus, if $first_name was equal to "Selena" but $last_name was equal to "Flintstone", the control statement would test as false and the statement block would not be executed.

Notice that we use parentheses to denote conditions. Perl evaluates each expression inside the parentheses independently and then evaluates the results for the entire group of conditions. If either returns false, the entire test returns false. The use of parentheses are used to determine precedence. With more complex comparisons, in which there are multiple logical operators, the parentheses help to determine the order of evaluation.

Similarly, you may wish to test using the double pipe (||) operator. This operator is used to denote an "or". Thus, the following code would execute the statement block if $first_name was Selena OR Gunther.

```
if (($first_name eq "Selena") || ($first_name eq "Gunther"))
{
```

```
print "Hello humble CGI book author!";
}
```

FORMATTING CONTROL STRUCTURES

As a final note, it should be said that different programmers have different styles of representing statement blocks. Most programmers prefer to include the first curly brace ({) on the same line as the control statement using the following syntax:

```
if ($number = 1) {
 print "The number is one";
 }
```

Others prefer to include the curly brace ({) on the second line indented with the rest of the statement block as used throughout this section. To a certain degree, this is simply a matter of style. Perl does not care how you write your code so long as it is syntactically correct. Some say that it is easier to read the code if the curly braces are on their own lines. Others, especially those using the text editor EMACS, say that it is more efficient to include the first curly brace on the same line as the control statement. The debate will go on forever since there is no right answer.

File Management

OPENING AND CLOSING FILES

One of the main resources that your server provides is a file management system. The scripts in this book, for example, use a multitude of supporting files in the server's file system such as temporary files, counter files, user files, data files, setup files, and libraries. Perl includes several excellent tools for working with these files.

First, Perl gives your scripts the ability to open files using the open function. The open function allows you to create a "filehandle" with which to manipulate a file. A filehandle is another name for a connection between the script and the server. Often, filehandles manage connections between the script and standard input, output, or error, however, in the case of open, any file can be read into a filehandle using the syntax:

```
open ([FILE_HANDLE_NAME], "[filename]");
```

For example, we might open a data file for reading using

```
open (DATA_FILE, "inventory.dat");
```

In this case, all of the lines of **inventory.dat** will be read into the filehandle "DATA_FILE" which Perl can then use within the program. However, you must also close a file once you are done with it. The syntax for closing a file is as follows:

```
close ([FILE_HANDLE_NAME]);
```

Finally, Perl gives you the ability to execute an error routine if there is a problem opening a file. The "or" logical operator is sometimes discussed in terms of a short circuit. For instance, the logic of the "or" operator is such that if the first expression evaluates to true, there is no need to evaluate the next. On the other hand, if the first expression evaluates to false, the second expression is executed. Thus, using the double pipe (||) operator, you can specify the default action to perform if an "open" fails. In CGI applications, the alternate action executed is usually something like the subroutine, CgiDie located in cgi-lib.pl. For example, the following routine would execute the CgiDie subroutine if there was a problem opening "address.dat".

```
open (ADDRESS_BOOK, "address.dat") || &CgiDie("Cannot open
address.dat");
```

Thus, if the script has a problem opening a needed file, the double pipe (||) operator provides a convenient and elegant way to quit the program and report the problem.

READING A FILE LINE BY LINE

An often used technique in this book for the manipulation of files is the reading of each line of a file. Perhaps we want to check each line for a keyword, or find every occurrence of some marker tag on a line and replace it with some other string. This process is done using a while loop as discussed previously. Consider this routine which will print out every line in a address file:

```
open (ADDRESSES, "address.dat") ||
    &CgiDie ("Cannot open address.dat");
while (<ADDRESSES>)
 {
 print "$_";
 }
close (ADDRESSES);
```

Thus, the script would print out every line in the file address.dat because "$_" is Perl's special name for "the current line" in this case.

You can also manipulate the "$_" variable in other ways such as applying pattern matching on it or adding it to an array.

N O T E

WRITING AND APPENDING TO FILES

You can do more than just read a file of course. You can also open a file-handle for writing with the greater than sign (>) using the syntax:

```
open ([FILE_HANDLE_NAME], ">[filename]");
```

or for appending using the double-greater-than symbol (>>) with the syntax:

```
open ([FILE_HANDLE_NAME], ">>[filename]");
```

The difference between appending and writing is that when you write to a file, you erase whatever was previously there whereas when you append to a file, you simply add the new information to the end of whatever text was already there.

If the file which Perl is asked to write or append to does not already exist, Perl will create the file for you.

N O T E

Typically, when writing to a file, you use the `print` function. However, instead of printing to standard output, you would specify the filename to print to. Consider the following example:

```
open (TEMP_FILE, ">temp.file") ||
   &CgiDie ("Cannot open temp.file");
print TEMP_FILE "hello there\n";
close (TEMP_FILE);
```

The file "temp.file" will now have the solitary line:

```
hello there
```

DELETING, RENAMING AND CHANGING THE PERMISSIONS OF FILES

Perl also provides you with all of the file management functions typically offered by your operating system. In our experience, the three most utilized functions in CGI scripts are `unlink`, `rename`, and `chmod`. `unlink` is Perl's function for deleting a file from the file system. The syntax is pretty straight forward.

```
unlink ("[filename]");
```

This line of Perl code will delete the file called filename provided that the script has permissions to delete the file.

Your Perl script can also rename a file using the rename function:

```
rename ("[old_filename]", "[new_filename]");
```

In this case, the file's name will be replaced with the new filename specified.

Finally, Perl gives you the ability to affect the permissions of files in the file system using the `chmod` function. The syntax is also fairly straight forward as follows:

```
chmod (0666, "filename");
```

In this case, "filename" will be made readable and writable by user, group and world.

FILE TESTS

Finally, Perl provides many methods for determining information about files on the file system using "File tests." For the purposes of this appendix, there are too many types of file tests to cover them all in depth. Further, they are covered extensively elsewhere. However, we will note the most frequent syntax of file tests used in this book which follow the form:

```
if ([filetest] [filename] && [other filetest] [filename])
 {
 do something
 }
```

Consider the following example which checks to see if a file exists (-e) and is writable (-w) by us, and if so deletes it:

```
if ((-e "temp.file") && (-w "temp.file"))
{
unlink ("temp.file");
}
```

Table A-8 lists several common file tests.

Table A-8 *Common File Tests*

TEST	DESCRIPTION
-r	File or directory is readable
-w	File or directory is writable
-x	File or directory is executable
-o	File or directory is owned by user
-e	File or directory exists
-z	File exists and has zero size
-s	File or directory exists and has non-zero size
-f	Entry is a plain file
-d	Entry is a directory
-T	File is text
-B	File is binary
-M	Modification age in days
-A	Access age in days

GETTING INFORMATION ABOUT A FILE WITH STAT

The stat function produces useful information about files that you can use in your file management functions. The stat function returns a thirteen-element array of file information using the syntax:

```
open ([FILE_HANDLE_NAME], "[filename]")||
    &CgiDie ("Can't open file");
($dev, $ino, $mode, $nlink, $uid, $gid, $rdev, $size,
    $atime, $mtime, $ctime, $blksize, $blocks) =
    stat([FILE_HANDLE_NAME]);
close ([FILE_HANDLE_NAME]);
```

Table A-9 Describes the elements returned by stat

Table A-9 *Stat Information*

VARIABLE	DESCRIPTION
$dev	The device that the file resides on
$ino	The inode for this file
$mode	The permissions for the file
$nlink	The number of hard links to the file
$uid	The numerical user ID for the file owner
$gid	The numerical group ID for the file owner
$rdev	The device type if the file is a device
$size	The size of the file in bytes
$atime	When the file was last accessed
$mtime	When the file was last modified
$ctime	the file status was last changed
$blksize	The optimal block size for i/o operations on the file system containing the file
$blocks	The number of clocks allocated to the file

For the most part, CGI scripts will need to take advantage only of $atime, $mtime, $ctime, $mode, and $size. $size and $mode are fairly straight forward in usage. However, the usage of the "time" variables is a bit subtle.

The time values returned by `stat` are formatted in terms of the number of non-leap seconds since January 1, 1970, UTC. Thus, the `stat` function might yield a result such as `$mtime` is equal to "838128443". Likewise, the time function returns the current time in the same format. Thus, the scalar variable `$current_time` is assigned the current time with the following syntax:

```
$current_time = time;
```

Once you have both the age of the file and the current time, you can use arithmetic to compare them for various operations such as the pruning of a Session Files directory after a certain amount of time.

For example, the following code snippet can be used to prune the file "289576893.dat" if it is older than an administratively-defined amount of time.

```
$seconds_to_save = 3600;
$age_of_file = $current_time - $mtime ;
if ($age_of_file > $seconds_to_save)
 {
 unlink ("289576893.dat");
 }
```

NOTE

If you are interested in what the actual day is, and not the number of seconds since 1970, you must use the localtime function to convert the value to a more human-recognizable form using the syntax:

($sec, $min, $hour, $mday, $mon, $year, $wday, $yday, $isdst) = localtime (time);

The following code gets the same information for an $mtime value extracted from stat:

($sec, $min, $hour, $mday, $mon, $year, $wday, $yday, $isdst) = localtime ($mtime);

OPENING, READING AND CLOSING DIRECTORIES

Just like files, Perl gives you the ability manage directories. Specifically, Perl allows you to open a directory as a directory handle, read in the current contents of the directory and then close it again.

To open a directory, you use the following syntax:

```
opendir ([FILE_HANDLE_NAME], "[directory_location]") || &CgiDie
("Can't open [directory_location]");
```

Thus, for example, you might open the directory "/usr/local/etc/www/" with the syntax:

```
opendir (WWW, "/usr/local/etc/www/") || &CgiDie ("Can't open www");
```

As you can see, like opening files, Perl allows the program to die elegantly in case there is a problem opening the directory. Also, as with file manipulation, you must close a directory after you are done with it using the syntax:

```
closedir ([FILE_HANDLE_NAME]);
```

For example, to close the directory opened above, you use the command:

```
closedir(WWW);
```

Once you have opened a directory, you can also read the contents of the directory with the `readdir` function. For example, the following code snippet assigns all of the filenames in the www directory to @filenames:

```
opendir (WWW, "/usr/local/etc/www/") ||
     &CgiDie ("Can't open www");
@filenames = readdir (WWW);
closedir (WWW);
```

NOTE **If you want to avoid including the "." (current directory) and ".." (root directory) files you can use the `grep` function to avoid including them in the `readdir` function using the syntax:**

@filenames = grep (!/^\.\.?$/, readdir (FILE_HANDLE_NAME);

APPENDIX B

The Future Of Perl & CGI Programming

OVERVIEW

Although Perl 5 has been available for quite a while now, not many CGI authors have taken advantage of Perl 5 specific features. There are several reasons for this. First of all, not all Internet Service Providers (ISPs) have upgraded to Perl 5. It is very frustrating to write a Perl /CGI program for the masses only to discover that a large number of people cannot use your program because they are still stuck using Perl 4. Second, there is not a great deal of information about Perl 5 released yet. The O'Reilly books on Perl discussed in Appendix A are the de facto standard reference guides for the language, yet as of this writing, they have not been updated to include information about Perl 5.

However, the future of Perl 5 looks bright. More and more ISPs are upgrading their Perl executables to version 5. And as time goes on, literature about Perl 5 will be released into the hands of willing and able programmers. In addition, Perl 5-specific libraries for handling CGI programming are out now. The most popular of these is Lincoln Stein's CGI.pm module. Because CGI.pm takes advantage of the new features in Perl 5, it is a much more powerful library than CGI-LIB.PL. This in itself will entice more and more CGI programmers over to Perl 5 and CGI.pm. While we will not go into the details of either Perl 5 or CGI.pm, a brief overview should impress upon you some of the advanced features that can be utilized when you decide to make the move to the next generation of Perl and CGI. CGI.PM is also included on the CD-ROM accompanying this book for your own use.

PERL 5

Perl 5 does not actually add a lot more features to Perl 4, but those that it does add are fairly significant. For example, the ability to do object-oriented programming in Perl 5 can change the way that entire Perl programs are written.

Object-Oriented Programming

Perl 5 now includes a number of features that support object-oriented programming (OOP). Basically, OOP allows you to encapsulate data and the functions that operate on that data. Encapsulating data in this way allows you to change the internal structure of an object without affecting the rest of the program. This can make programs more modular and efficient. In addition, rather than writing new objects each time you want to perform a new type of task, you can expand upon more generic objects by inheriting the capabilities of those objects.

Arbitrarily Nested Data Structures

In Perl 4, arrays only have one dimension. In other words, you can only store items as a single list in an array referenced by one index number. Perl 5 enables you to use nested data structures where arrays can reference other variables and other arrays. This allows you to form multidimensional arrays that can model the real-world more effectively. For example, the contents of a chess board or pixels on a computer screen are more easily modeled in terms of X and Y coordinates (2 dimensions). A two-dimensional array that takes two index numbers (X and Y coordinates) can easily represent these types of objects.

The following would be an example of a chess board array mapping numeric index coordinates to the equivalent algebraic notation (letter plus number coordinates) using Perl 5:

```
$chess =[['a1','a2','a3','a4','a5','a6','a7','a8'],
         ['b1','b2','b3','b4','b5','b6','b7','b8'],
         ['c1','c2','c3','c4','c5','c6','c7','c8'],
         ['d1','d2','d3','d4','d5','d6','d7','d8'],
         ['e1','e2','e3','e4','e5','e6','e7','e8'],
         ['f1','f2','f3','f4','f5','f6','f7','f8'],
         ['g1','g2','g3','g4','g5','g6','g7','g8'],
         ['h1','h2','h3','h4','h5','h6','h7','h8']];

print "$chess->[0][0]\n";
print "$chess->[1][2]\n";
print "$chess->[7][7]\n";
```

The above code would produce the following output:

```
a1
b3
h8
```

Regular Expression Enhancements

Perl 5 contains enhancements to the regular expression engine in Perl. There are a couple new pattern match operators for use within a regular expression as well as new arguments for use with the s (substitution) and m (match) Perl commands.

Grouping Paired Arguments

Perl 5 now allows you to substitute "=>" for the comma "," in a list. This allows you to write your code in such a way that associative array references are really obvious. For example, in Appendix A, we learned to create an associative array by making a list of pairs. An example of this appears below:

```
%program_authors =
    ("chat", "Gunther Birznieks",
     "shopping cart", "Selena Sol");
```

In Perl 5, you could also create the same array as:

```
%program_authors =
    ("chat" => "Gunther Birznieks",
     "shopping cart" => "Selena Sol");
```

Here it becomes much more obvious which elements are associated with which other elements in the associative array.

Dynamic Modules

Perl 5 allows modules to be loaded on an "as-needed" basis rather than always loading all the routines into memory with the require command like Perl 4 does. The require command in Perl basically loads and compiles the entire library at once which takes up extra time and resources. Using dynamically loaded modules that only load when needed can increase performance significantly if you use a lot of external modules/libraries and do not necessarily use all the routines within them.

Perl 4 To Perl 5 Migration Issues

Unfortunately, with the advanced features that Perl 5 offers, there are also some issues involved with making sure a program will run under Perl 5. Thankfully, the changes are really not that difficult to implement.

First, the at symbol (@) must be escaped inside a string in Perl 5. For example, if you have an assignment such as the following:

```
$myaddress = "gunther@foobar.com";
```

then this must be replaced with

```
$myaddress = "gunther\@foobar.com";
```

In addition, parenthesis must be used to place parameters for calls to subroutines. For example, in Perl 4, the following is acceptable:

```
open FILEHANDLE || &CgiDie("File Not Opened");
```

but in Perl 5, the "FILEHANDLE" argument must be encapsulated with parenthesis:

```
open (FILEHANDLE) || &CgiDie("File Not Opened");
```

In Perl 4, you could sometimes leave quotes off of strings. However, you should always use quotes (or at least some other character) to delimit strings in Perl 5 or you may risk the elements in the string being interpreted as function calls.

Finally, the package delimiter in Perl 5 has changed to double-colons (::) from the apostrophe (') that was used in Perl 4. However, this is not strictly enforced so, for now, it is not vital that you switch over to the new method, but keep in mind that this may not always be the case in the future.

Web Servers Pre-loading Perl (Windows NT)

Some Web Servers on Windows NT now have the capability of loading Perl 5 and running it permanently in memory. Normally, when a Perl CGI program is called from a Web server, Perl is loaded in memory, the script is executed, and Perl unloads in memory. The Web Servers that can keep Perl loaded in memory avoid the extra steps of always loading Perl and then unloading it. This can result in a significant performance increase for your server depending on how many Perl-based CGI programs run on it.

NOTE This is not necessarily a Perl 5 specific feature. Currently, only one implementation of Perl 5 on Windows NT supports this functionality. However, we are listing it as an enhancement if you are moving to the flavor of Perl 5 on Windows NT which supports the pre-loading of Perl.

CGI.PM

CGI.pm was written by Lincoln Stein as a Perl 5 module to perform CGI programming tasks. However, CGI.pm goes beyond the features of CGI-LIB.PL for Perl 4 discussed in Chapter Five since it takes advantage of the features in Perl 5.

Object-Oriented

When CGI.pm is used by a Perl 5 program, the "new" operator is used to construct a CGI object. When the "new" operator is called, Perl creates the CGI.pm object and automatically parses and reads in the form variable names that have been passed to the script. From then on, the object can be referred to in order to read the parameters or perform other CGI-related operations. For example, if $cgi was set up as the CGI object, we would use the following code to bring it to life:

```
use CGI;
$cgi = new CGI;
```

After these few lines, any reference to CGI routines can be made by using the $cgi object that has been created. For example, to get all the form variables that have been passed to your CGI script, simply use the following code:

```
@parameters = $cgi->param;
```

To get a specific form variable such as "email_address" use the following code:

```
$email = $cgi->param('email_address');
```

Values split automatically into arrays

Normally, you can access form variables inside the CGI object by using the param method. For example, to get the value of a "first_name" form variable from the `$cgi` object, you would use the following code:

```
$firstname = $cgi->param("first_name");
```

But what about multi-valued form variables such as multiple selection list boxes? In CGI-LIB.PL, we have to explicitly call the `SplitParam` function on the returned value in order to split the form variable's values into an array. With CGI.pm, all you have to do is reference the `param` method with an array and the elements will be automatically parsed out into this array without doing any extra work! For example, if I had selected the items "English", "French", and "German" among the languages that I know from a multi-select list box, then the following would break down this form variable value into its constituent elements.

```
@langs = $cgi->param("which_languages_do_you_know");
```

`@langs` would now contain "English," "French," and "German" as elements.

Environment Variables

The environment variables that are associated with CGI are already parsed and defined in the CGI object that CGI.pm creates. For example, to reference the server name, simply use `$cgi ->server_name()`. Each environment variable is referenced as a method in the $cgi object used above.

Migration From CGI-LIB.PL

Since there are many programs written to use CGI-LIB.PL, CGI.pm includes the capability of being compatible with most of CGI-LIB.PL's syntax. This is accomplished by using the following commands:

```
use CGI qw(:cgi-lib);
&ReadParse;
```

By using these commands, the form variables are read into the "%in" associative array just as they would be in CGI-LIB.PL. However, CGI.pm goes one step further. In addition to being able to use "%in", you can still use the functions of the CGI object itself to manipulate the form variables and these changes will be reflected automatically in the "%in" associative array.

Dynamic Form Creation

CGI.pm supports a variety of functions to automatically create various headers, footers, forms, input fields, and a lot of other commonly used HTML tags. You may recall from Chapter Ten that CGI-LIB.SOL was written to do a similar task. CGI.pm has more features and is integrated with the main library without needing to call another set of routines. For example, to create a text field with the $cgi object in CGI.pm, you would use the following code:

```
print $cgi->textfield(-name=>'first_name',
                      -value=>'Gunther');
```

Saving State

A powerful feature of CGI.pm is the integrated ability to maintain "state." Many chapters of this book rely on the scripts being able to recognize the different users who are currently using an application such as the BBS or Chat without having to ask for their user information over and over again. CGI.pm allows the current form variable values to be written to a file. This file can be reloaded at a later time in order to retrieve the previous state of the form.

Standard HTTP Headers

CGI.pm also provides functions for printing the standard HTTP CGI header ("Content-type: text/html\n\n") as well as many other headers. For example, CGI.pm can send a redirection signal to a user's Web browser to tell them to go to another site just like we discussed previously in Chapter Twenty-Four about the Advertising Tracker. In addition, CGI.PM can generate and retrieve Netscape cookie information.

CONCLUSION

Perl 5 and CGI.pm clearly have a lot to offer CGI programmers. It is just a matter of time before Internet Service Providers are pressured into upgrading their versions of Perl, and programmers start getting their hands on Perl 5 books. When these things happen, the advantages of using Perl 5 and CGI.pm will play a significant role in the future of CGI programming.

INDEX

Hundreds of subroutines have been described in this book, but only those appearing in the reusable libraries of routines (those with the extension .pl) have been indexed by name as main entries. For example, the CgiError subroutine that appears in the CGI-LIB.PL module has been indexed under "CgiError subroutine (CGI-LIB.PL)." Other subroutines have been indexed under the names of their respective applications, i.e. "WebBBS (Web-based bulletin board system), CreatePosting subroutine."

Special Characters

Index

A

-A access age file test, 778

Address Book application. *See* SQL Database Address Book

Address directory (SQL Database Address Book), 368, 369

address.xxx files (SQL Database Address Book), 370, 371–372

addr_maint.xxx files (SQL Database Address Book), 368–369

administrators. *See* intranets; Web site administrators

Adobe Acrobat, 48

Ad_track directory (Advertising Tracker), 586, 587

ad_track.xxx files (Advertising Tracker), 586, 587, 588, 589

advertisements on Web sites
tracking with Advertising Tracker, 585–586, 589
See also Random Banner Generator

Advertising Tracker
described, 585–586, 589
directory structure and files, 586–587
HTML document retrieval, 590
permissions, 586–587
running script, 588–589
sample, 588–589
server-specific setup, 587–588

algorithms, 52–53

alternative_image.list (Random Banner Generator), 567

anchors, 765–766

"and" logical operator (&&), 773

animation of text. *See* NPH (non-parsed header) scripts

applications. *See* databases; HTML file-based applications; libraries

archiving files, 17

arrays. *See* associative arrays; list arrays

ASCII files
as databases (flatfiles), 203
mismatches, 39–40
See also databases

associative arrays
accessing, 759–760
adding to, 761
delete function, 761
described, 758
grouping of paired, in Perl 5, 785–786

keys function, 760
printing with CGI-LIB.PL, 64
reading, parsing and splitting form variables with CGI-LIB.PL, 58–59, 62, 66–76
values function, 760

$atime variable returned by stat function, 779

.attach filename extension, 643

attachment files with BBS posts, 597

Attach subdirectory (WebBBS), 597, 598, 602

AuthEncryptWrap subroutine (AUTH-LIB-EXTRA.PL), 167–168

AUTH-EXTRA-HTML.PL
described, 129, 139
HTMLPrintNoSearchResults subroutine, 172
HTMLPrintRegisterFound-Duplicate subroutine, 175–176
HTMLPrintRegisterNoPassword subroutine, 176–177
HTMLPrintRegisterNoValid-Values subroutine, 177–178
HTMLPrintRegisterSuccess subroutine, 174–175
HTMLPrintSearchResults subroutine, 171–172
PrintLogonPage subroutine, 168–170
PrintRegisterPage subroutine, 172–174
PrintSearchPage subroutine, 170–171

AuthGetFileLock subroutine (AUTH-LIB-EXTRA.PL), 166–167

AUTH-LIB-EXTRA.PL
AuthEncryptWrap subroutine, 167–168
AuthGetFileLock subroutine, 166–167
AuthReleaseFileLock subroutine, 167
CgiLogon subroutine, 152–154
described, 129, 139, 143, 144, 147–148
MakeSessionFile subroutine, 154–155
PrintCurrentFormVars subroutine, 165–166
RegisterUser subroutine, 160–165
RemoveOldSessions subroutine, 155–156
SearchUsers subroutine, 156–160
VerifyUser subroutine, 148–152

AUTH-LIB-FAIL-HTML.PL, 129, 139, 146–147

AUTH-LIB.PL
calling with GetSessionInfo subroutine, 138–139, 144–146
described, 125–137, 143
directories used by, 128, 129, 142
E-mail specifications, 134–135, 136
field naming conventions, 136–137
group identification, 132
installing, 128
libraries, files and sample applications, 129
logon validity periods, 135

H

Index

S

ABOUT THE CD-ROM

Overview

The companion CD-ROM includes all the scripts discussed in this book ready to use for both UNIX and Windows NT Webservers. Since there are a variety of Web server environments in which the scripts can run, certain assumptions have been made related to how the scripts are distributed on the CD.

The UNIX directory contains all the scripts discussed in the book. For every chapter, there is a separate directory which contains the CGI scripts, data files, and their subdirectories. In addition, the scripts related to each chapter are also archived using the tar format.

The CGI applications which have a Windows NT equivalent are stored in their chapter subdirectories under the WINNT directory. Just like their UNIX equivalents on the CD, the full application is already laid out as separate files and subdirectories. In addition to this method of distribution, the applications are also archived in the zip format.

 The applications discussed in this book use long filenames. You will need to unzip the files using a program that recognizes long filenames such as WinZip95. Programs for dearchiving the applications on the CD can be found at http://www.shareware.com/.

N O T E

Finally, if your machine has a CD-ROM which does not recognize long filenames, short filename versions of all the zip and tar files are located within the DOS directory. Remember though that the files within these archives still use long filenames. The short filenames are provided in the DOS directory of the CD in order to allow you to at least copy the files off of the CD-ROM if your machine does not recognize long filenames. Then, you can transfer them later to the actual machine running your Web server which may not have CD-ROM access. The machine upon which the files are untarred or unzipped should support long filenames.

Further information on the CD-ROM can be found at:

```
http://www.eff.org/~erict/Scripts
```